readings in mass communication

readings in mass communication
concepts and issues in the mass media

third edition

michael c. emery
California State University,
Northridge

ted curtis smythe
California State University,
Fullerton

Wm. C. Brown Company Publishers
Dubuque, Iowa

Consulting Editor

Curtis D. MacDougall
Northwestern University

Copyright © 1972, 1974, 1977 by Wm. C. Brown Company Publishers

Library of Congress Catalog Card Number: 77—74675

ISBN 0—697—04148—4

Printed in the United States of America

Contents

Contents by Medium

Because our topical categories do not fit the course organization of some instructors, we have reorganized the articles into categories that reflect mass media orientations, such as broadcasting, newspapers, and the like. In a few cases, articles naturally fit into more than one category; we have placed some of those titles in appropriate categories when it has appeared reasonable to do so. Titles which appear in more than one category in this Table of Contents have been "flagged" by an asterisk after the name of the author. The Index is not included in this table.

PART THREE   Other Mass Media

PART FOUR   Regulating the Media

Preface

America's 200th birthday celebration included a serious scrutiny of the role being played in this nation by the mass communication industries. Media critics, journalism professors, politicians and concerned citizens filled magazines, books, radio and television talk shows and newsletters with enough media criticism to engage all but the most outspoken opponents of the largely commercial system of communication developed in the United States.

This third edition—the first was prepared in 1971 during the Pentagon Papers case and the second in 1973 in the midst of Watergate—attempts to capture representative samples of that Bicentennial period media analysis. A new section has been included here, dealing with "Obscenity, Violence and Drugs," because of the never-ending debates about sexually explicit words and pictures, violence on film and the influence of the media on youth. As part of this discussion we've included a selection about the lyrics of popular songs.

During the so-called post-Watergate period writers and broadcasters were preoccupied with examining the ethics employed in major institutions. We've added a discussion of news media ethics which should cause some thought about the role of news persons who hold others up to public exposure.

The book contains many other new pieces—there has been a torrent of new information about books, movies, magazines, minorities and women—but holds to balance between "conceptual" material and articles which describe the function of the particular medium of communication. Throughout all of this a number of suggestions are made for improvement of the systems which bring us news, entertainment and opinion. We look forward to the 1980s.

We have followed our regular format, "Changing Concepts of the Function and Role of the Mass Media," "Revolution in the Mass Media" and "Multiplying Media Debates." Again, in many cases we have presented new ideas with the understanding that the other side of a situation is part of what we call "conventional wisdom"—meaning that the argument is well known and could be further explained in the classroom. We assume the instructor will assign these articles to supplement basic lecture information given in perhaps an entirely different order than our table of contents. To assist the more curious, we have provided a brief bibliography after each article, a second Media Contents section and an Index to the basic terms and names.

Overall, we notice many of the problems discovered while preparing the first collection are still with us and may always be there. We are talking about the struggle of those attempting to gain access to "establishment" newspapers and broadcast stations, reporters trying to conceal their sources, persons outside the media crying for changes within the economic and social makeup of media institutions.

Above all, the one thing that never will change is the tough relationship between larger and more progressive news media outlets and the federal government. Spiro Agnew was gone, as was Richard Nixon. But media cynicism of the Watergate days was hard to remove and the deep dissatisfaction of the American public, principally with economic matters but also with foreign policy decisions and constant revelations of domestic spying and bugging, was reflected in the coverage. This in turn revealed the hatred held by powerful persons for the major news organizations and the fragility of the First Amendment in times of stress.

Just as before we sometimes were limited in the selection of articles by space considerations. Some pieces have been edited for timeliness and clarity but few substantial changes were necessary. We do not necessarily agree with the opinions expressed by an author, and in some cases we strongly disagree. But we feel these writers and critics deserve the attention of those learning about the media in our challenging times. In that spirit we take full responsibility for the selections and welcome suggestions for further improvement of the contents.

Michael Emery
Ted Curtis Smythe

Introductory Bibliography

Two standard bibliographic sources for every student of mass communications are those by Warren C. Price, compiler, *The Literature of Journalism* (1959) and by Price and Calder M. Pickett, compilers, *An Annotated Journalism Bibliography: 1958-1968* (1970), both published by the University of Minnesota Press. Dr. Pickett's contribution to *An Annotated Journalism Bibliography* was substantive following Dr. Price's death. These bibliographies offer basic, comprehensive annotations of most of the books dealing with American mass communications published through 1968. A student may start here and build upon this base by seeking information about contemporary books and articles from other sources.

For an up-to-date, thorough analysis of recent *books* in mass communications, a student should consult the following sources: the book review sections of *Journalism Quarterly* and *Journal of Broadcasting*. Eleanor Blum at the School of Communications, University of Illinois, publishes in mimeograph form, a list of books which college libraries receive. These are annotated. The list may be available in some schools and departments of journalism and communication. An excellent source for extensive annotation is Christopher H. Sterling's *Mass Media Booknotes* from Temple University. This mimeographed monthly lists on the front page the books reviewed in that issue. It is an outstanding source of information on and criticism of books in the mass communications field.

The standard bibliographic sources of *articles* in mass communications should be supplemented by searching the *Business Periodicals Index, International Index, Topicator* (which indexes only advertising, public relations and broadcasting publications). Here, too, the student should consult the back pages of *Journalism Quarterly, Columbia Journalism Review*, and *Journal of Marketing*. All three journals list and categorize current articles from journals of mass communications. Using these sources, a student quickly can find up-to-date sources on nearly any topic of mass communications that is receiving attention in the nation's periodicals. Many specialized indexes also are available. A few of these indexes or bibliographies appear in the appropriate lists which follow each article or topic in the book.

Most of the sources listed in the bibliographies in this edition are of books dealing with mass media subjects. There are, however, some subjects that have not yet been covered—or covered well—in a book. In those cases where the material is either of recent origin or has not been treated in a book, we have listed magazine articles. Many pertinent articles and books will be printed after this book has gone to press, and the listing of those that will be available to the student during the effective life of this book cannot, therefore, be complete. For this reason, we suggest that students establish a habit of regularly reading some of the following periodicals. Such a reading practice will help the student to keep abreast of media issues.

For a general overview of what is happening in mass communications, students should regularly consult *Columbia Journalism Review,* the top magazine in the field of media criticism, *Quill,* and *[More].* There are several journalism reviews available—some twenty have been established in the past eight years—but at least seven have ceased publication or have reduced their publishing schedule drastically as we go to press. A student should consult one of the journalism reviews appropriate to his community, state, or area, if one is available.

Excellent sources of industry statistics, news and media practices can be found in *Editor & Publisher*, a weekly newsmagazine for publishers; *Publishers' Auxiliary*, a publication for suburban and weekly newspaper publishers; *Broadcasting*, a weekly newsmagazine on radio, television and cable; *Variety*, a weekly tabloid dealing with news about broadcasting and film; *Advertising Age*, a weekly tabloid on the advertising industry.

In addition to these news publications, students should regularly read *The Bulletin* of the American Society of Newspaper Editors, a monthly magazine on issues as viewed by editors of the metropolitan press; *Grassroots Editor*, a bimonthly dealing with issues of press responsibility, law, and practice, primarily from the small newspaper point of view; *Nieman Reports*, a quarterly dealing largely with comment about topics of press practices and press freedom by former Nieman Fellows; *Quill*, a monthly dealing with issues of press freedom and news of broadcasting and newspapers; *Freedom of Information Center Reports* (FoI), a biweekly dealing with issues of freedom of information and surveys of current issues in mass media; *FoI Digest*, a bimonthly bulletin summarizing FoI news developments around the United States; *Public Relations Journal*, a monthly magazine dealing with comment about that field; *AV Guide—The Learning Media Magazine* and *Media & Methods*, both dealing with application of media to teaching; and *Film in Review*, a magazine issued by the National Board of Review of Motion Pictures.

There is another classification of publication with which students intent on mastery of the field should become acquainted. This classification includes the scholarly publications which give—usually—much greater depth and insight on media issues, past and present. These publications seldom are able to keep abreast of the issues in the field; when articles appear in these journals they are usually the result of comprehensive research conducted with the perspective of the passage of time. Included in this group are *Journalism Quarterly* and *Journal of Communication*, both of which encompass the entire field of mass media experience; *Journal of Broadcasting; Public Telecommunication Review; Index on Censorship*, which covers free press problems around the world; *Gazette* (in English), which deals primarily with European media subjects, often historical; *European Broadcasting Review*, Sec. B, which thoroughly covers the radio and television field in Europe from an administrative, program, and legal point of view; *Public Opinion Quarterly*, often useful for studies on the effects of mass media; *Film Quarterly*, which offers serious comment on the art of the film, and *Television Quarterly, Public Re-*

lations Quarterly and *Public Relations Review* carry thoughtful articles on their respective fields. *Journalism History*, a quarterly, deals with both print and broadcast topics.

In a category by itself is the outstanding *Handbook of Communication*, edited by Ithiel de Sola Pool, Wilbur Schramm, and others. It is a compilation of special articles prepared by a galaxy of scholars in communication. The authors give excellent, general summaries of their fields and include comprehensive bibliographies. The book is published by Rand McNally College Publishing Company, 1973.

Students who regularly sample these magazines and journals will find a wealth of current information and comment on the issues and trends in mass communications.

Changing Concepts of the Function and Role of the Mass Media

If the amount of comment about the mass media in American society is any measure of their power, persuasiveness and impact, then the mass media are very powerful indeed. For probably never in the history of the American experience have so many critics written and said so much about the mass media: newspapers, magazines, broadcasting, film, advertising and public relations. It probably is true that comment about the mass media, if considered as a *percentage* of the vast outpouring of those same media, is not all that large. When the *total* amount of comment is counted, however, we begin to see that whatever else Americans may be concerned about, they are greatly concerned about the roles, functions and performance of their mass media.

There exists, then, a large number of issues to be considered, and this section—indeed, the entire book—barely scratches the surface of those stimulating and abrasive media-social issues that both contribute to and reflect the tension and conflict in our society. Nevertheless, we feel that where we have succeeded in scratching the surface, we have dug deeply enough to mine nuggets of information, insight and inspiration. We sought to define areas of concern that were important to society and then sank shafts in order to bring to the light some of the more important points in those issues.

One area of current concern grows out of the social activitism of the late Sixties and early Seventies when there was a movement on behalf of the disen-franchised segments of our society—the racial, ethnic, religious and sexual minorities and the poor. One goal of this activism was to secure a voice in or access to the mass media; to the established agencies of mass communication in the U.S. In some cases, there was great success; in others the movement met a rebuff both by the agencies of communication and by the government, including the Supreme Court.

In *Miami Herald v. Tornillo*, 1974, mentioned in the readings to follow, the Supreme Court seemingly wiped out all efforts to re-define the First Amendment so as to create a requirement that newspapers, in particular, must open their pages to diverse voices, to political opponents, to whomever wishes to use those pages to express personal or group viewpoints. As our readings indicate, the access concept still lives; writers now are suggesting ways of getting around the Supreme Court's decision, largely because they feel the need still is there—they argue that in modern society, access to the mass media must be available to more groups than now receive access.

Others have sought to harness the press through methods that do not require a rewriting or a reinterpretation of the Constitution. News councils, national and local, have been implemented; journalism reviews by professional reporters have been published; and criticism by informed observers has been undertaken. These issues are covered in the readings that follow. Yet another type of "control" over the press has been exerted by the press itself in the form of ombudsmen, those staff members who represent the public in newspaper editorial and management decisions. See the bibliographical suggestions which follow Chapter 2 for sources of information about ombudsmen.

Two other issues affecting the function and role of the mass media are closely related. The first has to do with the on-going public concern over reporting practices, methods and content. The second grows out of the journalistic concern in protecting sources.

For decades people have been concerned about the kind and quality of American reporting, a concern shared by professionals as well. Various methods have been suggested as a means of escaping from straight-forward, objective reporting. Three approaches to reporting that have found support among many professionals have been interpretive reporting, backgrounding, and depth reporting. Whatever the methods were called (and all three denote different reporting concepts) they were efforts to get beyond the surface story in order to help the reader. In recent years a "new journalism" has arisen which was bound neither to objectivity nor to interpretation. Instead, it shared affinities with a literary school of writing. Other forms of journalism grew up around the new journalism, however, and our reading helps to sort out the differences among the several approaches.

Even while debate swirled around the new journalism, certain members of the press renewed an interest in investigative reporting—intensive and persistent reporting which seeks out criminal or anti-social activities in public and private places. Although this has been an important ingredient in American journalism since the 1880s, the practice of investigative journalism has varied from paper to paper, broadcast station to broadcast station, and historical period to historical period. We are in an upswing today. One manifestation of the trend toward more investigative reporting was the *Washington Post's* handling of the Watergate break-in and related cover-up activities. Perhaps even the consumer-type reporting practiced by some newspapers and broadcast stations is related to it. The readings deal with both.

One of the pressing problems in contemporary reporting is the protection of sources of information because this bears a close relationship to the types of reporting we have been discussing. Investigative reporting virtually requires anonymity of sources, or so reporters feel. The tenuous ties which have bound bench, bar and police, on one side, to the press, on the other, have been stretched to the breaking point largely because of the vigor with which investigative reporters have pursued their craft. As our readings indicate, the concern among all parties is very real; not all newsmen agree as to the proper way to attack or solve the problem.

Another element in the bench-press confrontation has been resurrected of late in the form of "gag laws", rules imposed by the courts upon the reporting of "prejudicial information" in pre-trial and trial situations. Despite much discussion and the development of "guidelines" during the past decade, the problem of judicial restraint of the press continues to exist, in fact it is growing worse. According to an editorial in the *Los Angeles Times*, which grew out of increasingly restrictive decisions by the judiciary, "We have reached a strange point in this country. The publicity generated not by the press but by the nature of monstrous crimes is used as an excuse by the courts to impose censorship on the public. Under the rationale used by the federal court in Atlanta [which ordered a new trial for the man who abducted the former editor of the *Atlanta Constitution*, Reg Murphy] all information about the Watergate conspiracy could have been suppressed once the Watergate burglars, the most petty actors in the sordid drama, were arrested and charged. The implications of this kind of judicial tyranny by the courts need to be thoroughly understood by the public.'' The Supreme Court acted in the summer of 1976 to reduce areas of ''judicial tyranny''—see Chapter 4.

1 Access to the Mass Media

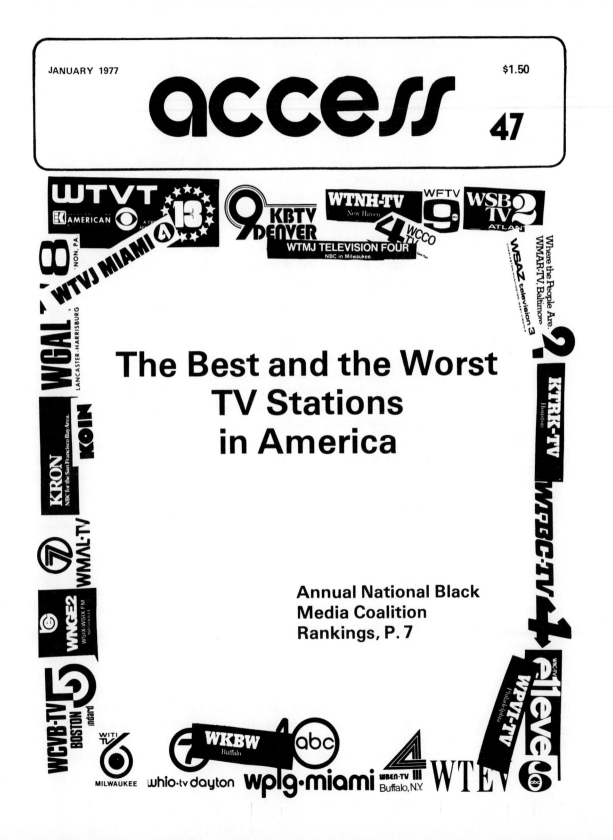

JANUARY 1977

$1.50

access

47

The Best and the Worst TV Stations in America

Annual National Black Media Coalition Rankings, P. 7

The Issue of Access

Who Will Take Care of the 'Damrons' of the World?
By Roy M. Fisher

The magnificent building that houses *The Miami Herald* stretches for more than a city block aside the shallow waters of Biscayne Bay. It rises at the land side of MacArthur Causeway, an architectural bulwark separating the work-a-day world of the Miami residents from the pleasureland of Miami Beach, on the yonder side of the bay.

The Herald building rivals the resort hotels in size and opulence. It is of brown brick, glass, and stone and is properly called *The Miami Herald* and *The Miami News* building, for it houses both newspapers. The first is the powerful flag paper of the nation's most vigorous newspaper group, founded in the thirties by Editor John S. Knight. The second is the once financially anemic *News*, a sort of kissing cousin of *The Herald*. *The News* is owned by the Cox newspaper chain, but depends upon *The Herald* for its business management, advertising sales, printing, and distribution. While this agreement came into being before Congress got around specifically to legalize joint operating arrangements, the result was consistent with the purposes of the Newspaper Preservation Act of 1970. Miami remains one of the decreasing number of cities to have more than one newspaper voice. Editorially, at least, the papers are competitive.

The Herald, nonetheless, dominates Miami and most of South Florida. And while Jack Knight, an unpretentious man, would not build his newspaper's plant in the style of a gothic cathedral—as did the late Col. Robert R. McCormick of *The Chicago Tribune*—*The Herald* building on Biscayne Bay obviously bespeaks more than simply, "This is a newspaper plant."

Its proportions are monumental. Dominating the west facade which overlooks the city is a gigantic portico mounted on eight granite columns, each four stories tall. Even the biggest Cadillac limousine appears underscaled alongside those massive columns. No one can drive up to the building of *The Miami Herald* without an awesome feeling that he is about to enter a Very Important Place; that if, indeed, this be the free press that defends the freedom of America, this freedom rests in very strong hands.

The visitor who pulled up under that portico at a few minutes before 11:30 a.m. on September 27, 1972, drove up not in a Cadillac limousine, but in a little black and white Pontiac Firebird. He was a short dapper fellow wearing modishly long hair and a sharply tailored suit. He glanced up at the towering portico, gestured with his head to his attorney who climbed out of the Firebird after him, and strode through the huge glass doorway. He passed around the escalator that angles up through the four-story lobby, and together the two men walked to an elevator used mainly by *Herald* employees. The visitor punched the fifth floor button that would

Roy M. Fisher is dean of the school of Journalism of the University of Missouri and is a former editor of the *Chicago Daily News.* Reprinted with the author's permission, this article appeared in *The Trial of the First Amendment,* a monograph published by the Freedom of Information Center, Columbia, Mo., 1975.

take him and his attorney to the offices of the editor of *The Miami Herald*, Don Shoemaker.

The visitor that morning was Pat Tornillo, Jr., whose name has since become an important part of our constitutional history: the case of *Tornillo v. The Miami Herald*. Pat is the peppery little labor boss of the 8,000 Dade County classroom teachers. His perennial battle for collective bargaining rights for teachers, which led to an illegal strike, had made Tornillo, over the years, a sort of minor public enemy in the eyes of Editor Shoemaker. Now Tornillo was running for the State Legislature, and *The Herald* had blasted him and his candidacy editorially. The primary election was only four days away.

Politicians in Miami routinely go to *The Herald* building before elections, hat in hand, to seek the newspaper's endorsement of their candidacy. For the more timid ones, the thought of advancing through that portico and up that elevator is enough to keep them awake at night.

Even Tornillo says he felt "that certain awe" on that morning as he rose to the fifth floor editorial rooms. "It wasn't as though I were a stranger there, myself," he said later, bragging a little "Why, I guess I'd been at *the Herald* building 50 or 60 times before. Once I even had lunch with Don Shoemaker, himself, in the executive dining room. Some of *The Herald* guys are my personal friends, after hours."

As Pat Tornillo and his attorney, Toby (for Tobias) Simon, reached the editorial offices they were met not by Shoemaker, who was busy, but by one of his editorial writers, Frederic Sherman. "Hi, Pat. What can we do for you?" Sherman called.

"I want you to print my reply to that editorial you clouted me with last week," Pat said. "Here's my reply: same number of words, same length. I'd like it on the same page, just as the law says."

As Tornillo recalls the conversation, Sherman looked at Tornillo in disbelief. "You gotta be kidding."

"No, I'm not kidding. I'm demanding my right under the law. Here Toby, read Fred the law."

Tornillo's attorney read a 60-year-old Florida statute that provides that any political candidate depicted unfavorably by a newspaper must be permitted a right to reply. A criminal statute, its violation could result in an editor's imprisonment and, a few months earlier, had been used to that end briefly in Daytona, Florida, against another editor.

"You're threatening us," Sherman said.

"No, we're not threatening, we're just telling you that we're going to court if you don't follow that law."

The Miami Herald took it as a threat, although some thought it was more grandstand politics by Tornillo, who needed publicity to fire up his faltering campaign. *The Herald* rejected Tornillo's reply.

Thus was laid the basis for *Tornillo v. The Miami Herald*, an exceptional challenge to the traditional interpretation of the First Amendment to the United States Constitution, which permits the American people to speak freely, worship as they please, and publish without legal inhibition. Before the *Tornillo* case was concluded the First Amendment, itself, would stand trial.

We will follow the fascinating path of this battle to the highest court in the land—and beyond into the legislative halls and American homes, where, ultimately, our freedoms are written. But first we should explore more fully the reasons why Editor Shoemaker, by refusing Tornillo's demand, triggered the case on its way.

The Miami Herald had long before established a reputation as a fair, honest, and independent reporter of news. It had opened its columns countless times to views in sharp conflict with those of the editor. It had, in fact, on many occasions published previous statements and letters from this same Pat Tornillo. James Dance, associate editor who sometimes marked Tornillo's letters for the typesetters, estimates that eight of every ten Tornillo contributions were published by *The Herald* without hesitation. "Why," said Dance, "Pat's publishing record in our paper was probably better than my own!" To which Tornillo replied, "I don't doubt that—and Jim is a better writer than I am, too."

This particular demand, however, coming as it did from an active candidate for public office, fell afoul of one of *The Herald*'s traditional policies: that during a political campaign *The Herald* would not permit candidates to preempt editorial space normally reserved for reader comments. The rationale of Editor Shoemaker was that during such times *The Herald* devotes many columns of space to reporting the candidates and their various campaigns. Thus satisfactory avenues are available to candidates without using the letters-to-the-editor columns.

But obviously, Shoemaker gave special consideration to this particular Tornillo request. Before making up his mind, he asked the advice of Dan Paul, *The Herald*'s attorney. Paul told him that the old right-of-reply statute was obviously invalid. And, furthermore Paul said he considered Tornillo's demand, in itself, a challenge to the intent of the First Amendment: that an editor make his editorial judgments without coercion.

So Shoemaker rejected the Tornillo demand, muttering that, "No one shoots his way into *The Miami Herald*." Tornillo, good as his word, beat it to the Circuit Court of Dade County, where he asked Judge Francis J. Christie to order *The Herald* to print his reply and to pay him damages. In an emergency hearing, Judge Christie held that the old statute was an unconstitutional restraint upon freedom of the press. On Tuesday, Tornillo was defeated at the polls, in spite of the endorsement by the "other" newspaper, the *Miami News*.

Undismayed, Tornillo appealed to the Florida Supreme Court, where, in a decision that surprised even Toby Simon, the court ruled 6 to 1 in favor of Tornillo. *The Herald* took the battle on to Washington, where Chief Justice Warren E. Burger led the Supreme Court of the United States in a unanimous decision supporting *The Miami Herald*.

On its way up the judicial escalator, *Tornillo v. The Miami Herald* picked up a lot of extra riders. Almost all of the major news organizations, including the National Association of Broadcasters, joined as friends of the court on behalf of *The Herald*. On the other hand, some politicians, including Senator John McClellan (D.-Ark.) and President Richard M. Nixon sided publicly with Tornillo's cause. A number of state legislatures prepared to enact right-of-reply laws similar to Florida's.

Then one morning in April, 1974, the Supreme Court called for oral arguments in *Tornillo v. The Miami Herald*, now, because *The Herald* had brought the appeal, renamed *The Miami Herald v. Tornillo*. After questioning of Dan Paul, *The Herald*'s Miami attorney, the court turned its eyes on Professor Jerome Barron, an outspoken civil liberties lawyer, a former dean of the Syracuse University School of Law, now a professor at George Washington University, and Tornillo's joint counsel, with Toby Simon.

Before we can understand the position in which Professor Barron found himself at that moment, we should know something of his own philosophical views of the First Amendment.

For some years, Barron had been among those who had deplored the increasing centralization of the mass media in the United States. Newspaper mergers, the growth of newspaper chain operations, and the common ownership of newspaper and broadcasting companies, he pointed out, gave a few corporations massive influence on the media. A combination of economic problems, tax law, and new technology had made this so.

As newspaper production costs increased and advertisers diverted more of their advertising dollars to broadcasting, many metropolitan newspapers fell on hard times. In city after city, competing newspapers merged, partly (as in Miami) or totally (as was more common). The result: another city with only one newspaper voice. In the 20 years between 1945 and 1965, the number of American cities having more than one metropolitan newspaper fell from 117 to 65. Today, newspaper monopoly exists in 19 of every 20 cities.

While the number of newspapers in metropolitan cities declined, the number of newspaper owners declined even more sharply as newspaper chain operations boomed. Tax laws offered tempting benefits to local publishers who would sell their properties to the big operators. Thus by 1973, two of every three newspaper copies printed in the United States each day were printed by chain owners.

The advent of television did little to preserve the declining diversity. Three networks that dominate television news deliver identical programs to all of their owned or affiliated stations. Furthermore, owners of television stations often are the same people who own radio stations or newspapers. More than half of the television stations and 80 percent of the radio stations, F.C.C. records show, are owned by companies that also own one or more other media outlets, either broadcast or print.

To preserve diversity of news and opinion amidst this increasing standardization, Barron had advanced the idea that each newspaper should be required by law to open its columns to stories and opinions adverse to its own. This, he said, would make each newspaper a true community forum, accessible to any person and any idea regardless of the views of the publisher. Barron contended that in fact this is what the Founding Fathers had in mind when they wrote the First Amendment. Picking up a phrase from a previous Supreme Court case, he said this right of access would encourage "open and robust debate on public issues." Thus Barron argued that it is no longer enough to guarantee press freedom just "to those who are rich enough or lucky enough to own a printing press." Every man should be assured access to the press. If so, surely the Florida statute of right-to-reply was consistent with that objective.

Now here he was in the highest court of the land, faced with the need to convince the justices that they should reinterpret one of our nation's basic documents. He had considered carefully the difficulty of this task before permitting himself to be persuaded by Tornillo and Simon to join them in the case. At worst, he had decided, he would be able to project his new doctrine to a large and sensitive audience. So as the court finished with its questions to Dan Paul and looked now at him, Professor Barron realized that his historic moment was at hand. He had been greatly encouraged by his unexpected victory at Tallahassee. He was bolstered also by what he had construed as being a growing disillusionment by the public in the mass media. Certainly he could count some benefit from the obvious anti-press attitude of members of the Nixon administration, whose appointees now dominated the thinking of the Court. But Professor Barron's hopes were quickly dashed.

In a series of rapid-fire questions by the justices, he began to sense the existence of a seemingly unlikely alignment of court conservatives and court liberals—both hostile to his thesis. Conservatives Rehnquist, Blackmun and Chief Justice Burger, and a liberal, Marshall, began to chip away at Barron's stated philosophy of the First Amendment freedom.

Rehnquist, President Nixon's last appointee, fired an early question at the professor. To Barron's contention that the First Amendment was operating only to guarantee freedom to the owners of the media—not to the public—Rehnquist wanted to know whether he was suggesting that the First Amendment intended that one man could commandeer another man's printing press for his own use. Rehnquist's was a traditional, conservative question based upon a simple statement of property right. (It's my ball; I can play with it as I like.)

Then Chief Justice Burger took a whack: "What if Tornillo announced that on next Friday night he was going to hold a public meeting and take care of *The Miami Herald*, and *The Miami Herald* informed him that it wanted one of its editors present to answer Tornillo from the platform at that meeting. Would the newspaper have that right?"

Professor Barron replied that that statute wouldn't apply to that situation.

Then Marshall, the liberal, took the floor: "The Florida statute covers only candidates for public office, is that right?"

Barron: "I guess so; it only covers candidates."

The Justice: "Then we must presume that the press can attack to destruction in Florida anyone excepting a candidate, is that right?" To which a puzzled Jerome Barron replied, "Sadly, that's true."

"So," said Marshall, "anyone could silence the press by simply becoming a candidate!"

Justice Brennan took a small part in the dialogue, Stewart was seen to nod in agreement from time to time, and Powell and Douglas kept their own counsel. But any doubt about which way the wind was blowing must have vanished when Rehnquist added this rhetorical question:

"Mr. Barron, isn't the First Amendment there for only one reason, this is to protect the people from the government? The government is the entity that the First Amendment is there to protect you from. It wasn't intended to protect one citizen from the speech of another citizen, was it, Mr. Barron?"

Barron gamely battled for his thesis, but, even before his final argument was completed, one justice walked out of the room. And Barron, himself, gave up his argument with five minutes still available on the clock. He still held hope that he might have won over a majority of the court, but it was an idle hope.

It was no surprise to most people when the opinion came down, three months later. By a vote of nine to zero, the United States court overturned a one-to-six finding of the Florida court: the Florida right-to-reply statute was an unconstitutional infringement upon the First Amendment.

Chief Justice Burger wrote the court's opinion himself. While there was little doubt as to his destination, the chief justice explored a number of paths. Obviously, the concentration of the press in so few hands bothered him, as well as Professor Barron. The chief justice said:

"The result of these vast changes has been to place in a few hands the power to inform the American people and shape public opinion. . . .The abuses of bias and manipulative reportage are, likewise, said to be the result of the vast accumulations of unreviewable power in the modern media empires. In effect, it is claimed, the public has lost any ability to respond or to contribute in a meaningful way to the debate on issues. . . .

"The obvious solution . . .would be to have additional newspapers. But the same economic factors which have caused the disappearance of vast numbers of metropolitan newspapers have made entry into the marketplace of ideas . . .almost impossible."

Thus Justice Burger tended to support Professor Barron's description of the problem, but not his proposed solution. He saw no difference between a law that would force an editor to publish a given story and a law that would prohibit the editor from publishing a given story. He stated very simply that, "The clear implication has been that any such compulsion to publish . . .is unconstitutional."

Elaborating further, Justice Burger wrote:

"The choice of material to go into a newspaper . . .and treatment of public issues and public officials—whether fair or unfair—constitutes the exercise of editorial control and judgment. It has yet to be demonstrated how governmental regulation of this crucial process can be exercised consistent with the First Amendment guarantee of a free press. . . ."

The court's opinion was a clear, if perhaps visceral and simplistic, enunciation of the traditional view of press freedom. It laid to rest the movement in other states for Florida-style access laws and shushed the clamor in Washington for a federal statute of similar intent. In that respect, we all owe a debt to Pat Tornillo for bringing his confrontation, and to Editor Don Shoemaker for defying a bad law and refusing to let Tornillo shoot his way into print.

The case confirmed the judgment of Malcolm Johnson, editor of the *Tallahassee Democrat*, who said, ''Motherhood is a noble concept, but under compulsion it is a product of rape and begets illegitimacy.''

While the Supreme Court of the United States snuffed out a grassroots movement for laws that would infringe upon a newspaper's editorial judgments, its opinion leaves untreated a certain social sickness that expressed itself at this particular time in the *Tornillo* case, but will break out again on another day in another state with an entirely different set of symptoms.

Many persons will agree that the American people suffer from a gnawing anxiety that the press—and the other communications media as well—have grown too big for their britches, that the economic concentration of media control has reduced the average citizen's access.

The public senses—even though it may not articulate its feelings well—that our civilization has, indeed, entered into a new age. That just as we passed through the stone age, the bronze age, the iron age, and the space age, we now stand on the threshold, and are about to enter, the ''communications age.'' . . . That the man who controls the world from this time on will not necessarily be the man who commands the biggest armies or holds the biggest bomb, but rather the man whose finger is closest to the mechanism that turns on the radio and television stations and controls the starting and the stopping of our newspaper presses . . . That wars will no longer be won or lost by the capture of a man's land or even his body, but by the capture of his mind . . . And that this will go to him who controls the media.

While we can hail the simple logic of the Burger opinion, we may get a more ominous view of the threat to press freedom today from the Florida decision, where six of seven justices held for Tornillo. Theirs was bad law, no doubt, but it may still have been good politics. And the Florida justices, who sit in their Neo-Greek whitewashed courthouse in Tallahassee, are, after all, politicians first and Supreme Court justices later. They must be elected in a partisan campaign, and they must keep their political fences mended if they are to be reelected after six years. They sit in the eye of a political hurricane and have learned to read the political skies with care.

When this writer interviewed the Florida justices in their chambers, he found they had accepted their federal rebuff calmly. They believe time is on their side, that if they have misread the law as it stands today, they have not misread the political realities which ultimately determine all laws. Furthermore, the justices had more immediate problems distracting them at the moment.

The Florida Supreme Court, which often has had occasion to defend its honor, was now virtually fighting for its life. Three of the seven justices faced possible impeachment, another's capacity to serve was impaired by alcoholism, and a fifth was being asked to justify the court's unusual intervention in a parole board matter on behalf of a robber who had good connections in the crime underworld. This sorry state of affairs had resulted from a number of challenges of the court's integrity and competency. The Judicial Qualifications Commission had recommended that two justices be removed for accepting improper help from a utilities lawyer in the preparation of a decision favorable to the utility (a court-appointed panel later settled for reprimands only). The commission similarly denounced a third justice for failing to exclude himself from a deliberation which involved lawyers with whom he was engaged in real estate transactions. Further undermining the court's credibility at the moment was the discovery of a notation written on a court document that indicated a strong personal bias against *The Miami Herald*, although the justice whose initials appear under the notation denied this was so.

This bad situation does not mean that the court is without any wisdom. To the contrary, this same court upheld the toughest open meetings law in the land, and was duly hailed by the press and public spirited groups for its position. The Florida meetings law, incidentally, guarantees the public (and the press) access to all meetings of public bodies, regardless of the subjects to be discussed. In Florida, two members of a local school board who happen to meet on a street corner cannot legally mention board business without first notifying the public of their intent.

The man who wrote the bold opinion upholding this open meetings law is Justice James C. Adkins, Jr., who claims with good reason that he has fought fiercely to protect the rights of the press.

"I have no animosity toward newspapers," he told us. "I wrote the first opinion construing our Sunshine Law. I believe in the right of the press to be present at every meeting so that we can have a real marketplace of ideas any time any public body meets."

A little later, however, Justice Adkins talked about some things that make him uneasy about the press today:

"Twenty-five years ago the editor of a newspaper was a leader in his community. He more or less formulated the ideas of that community. If you had a community project you went to him and you got the support of the newspaper, because he was so closely attuned to the problem. He was looked upon with a great deal of respect, and people usually followed the newspaper. Today, people look at the newspaper as being managed by someone outside their own community. When these editors of outside chains come into communities—especially smaller communities—they are accepted socially, you understand, but insofar as their thoughts and views are concerned, the public doesn't have the confidence in them that they had in those days when the editor was more accepted as one of them. As a result I think the newspapers have lost a great deal of their community influence."

So when Justice Adkins explains how he feels about newspapers, he says, in effect, that they have become sort of outside intruders, not really as "attuned" or as much a part of the "in" communities as before. Now, there is no law requiring that an editor be "attuned" to a community, and Justice Adkins did not use such a reason for casting his vote against *The Miami Herald*. As he explained later, Justice Adkins sided with Tornillo on the grounds that Tornillo was a candidate running for public office. It has long been established that the government can regulate free speech as part of the election process. For example, the justice pointed out, the government can prevent anyone from making a campaign speech or handing out handbills within 100 feet of the polls. This is a restriction on free speech and free press, but it is legal. So, why can't the government also require certain standards of fairness elsewhere during a campaign? What's the magic about 100 feet? he asks.

One can wonder, after talking with the Florida justices, how much of their legal thinking had been influenced by their personal opinion that the press has grown away from the people it serves. This wonderment becomes even stronger when one learns that the Florida court became greatly preoccupied during its hearing of the *Tornillo* case with another case, legally quite disassociated. This unreported chapter leads one to believe that the Florida court—essentially Populist in spirit—decided as it did partly because it had the fortune, or misfortune, to have sitting with it on the *Tornillo* case a substitute, Justice J. S. Rawls, who was summoned from the state appellate bench to take the place of a Supreme Court judge who was unable to be present for this case. In the opinion of some persons most familiar with the Tornillo case, including Tornillo's lawyer Toby Simon, Justice Rawls swung the court to his view.

Imagine if you can the scene in that Florida Supreme Court Building that day when the *Tornillo* case was called up on the docket. The seven judges—six elected judges of the Supreme Court and one six-foot, 235-pound substitute called up from his lower court bench—were seated in their leather chairs behind one long bench. Before them sat labor boss Tornillo, his lawyers, and those who represented the powerful interests of the Knight Newspapers and *The Miami Herald*, plus friends of the court, associated by counsel, and a few spectators.

Dan Paul, *The Herald*'s attorney, was stating the opening arguments on behalf of *The Herald* when he was interrupted by an unfamiliar voice from the far end of the bench:

"Mr. Paul, what is *The Herald* doing about the Damrons of this world?"

Mr. Paul, perhaps not hearing the remark, continued, but was interrupted again. "The Damrons, what about the rights of the Damrons of this world?"

The voice this time was identified as that of Justice Rawls, the substitute judge. While Paul searched for an answer, Toby Simon sat bewildered. Then Simon jotted down a note on a scrap of paper, and handed it to the bailiff. The bailiff slowly walked to the end of the bench, proceeded behind six other justices to Rawls' chair. He handed Judge Rawls the note. Rawls scribbled an answer, and the bailiff proceeded slowly back to Simon's table. He opened the answer and showed it to Barron, who now recognized the citation: *"Leonard Damron, appellant, v. the Ocala Star-Banner."* From that point on, in the opinion of some informed lawyers, the Florida court may have been talking about Tornillo that day, but was thinking more about Leonard Damron. It became preoccupied by what it considered to be a judicial injustice to Damron, who in 1966 was mayor of the Florida town of Crystal River, population 1,423.

Leonard Damron was running for the office of county assessor when, two weeks before the election, a story about a federal perjury charge against his brother,

James, appeared in the regional newspaper, the *Ocala Star-Banner*. Because of a
"mental aberration," the rewriteman who transcribed the story from the court
reporter mistakenly substituted the mayor's name for that of his brother, James. The
story appeared under a three-column headline on page one. Although the *Star-Banner* printed two corrections prior to the election, the mayor lost and blamed the
Star-Banner for his defeat.

The mayor sued for libel. He won by directed verdict in the trial court, which
awarded him $22,000 in damages. The *Star-Banner* immediately appealed to the
Florida District Court of Appeals. There, as fate would have it, sat Justice J. S.
Rawls, now the substitute judge in *Tornillo*.

The Rawls court upheld a finding of libel against the *Star-Banner* assessing
compensatory damages for its gross negligence in reporting. The *Star-Banner* appealed to the U.S. Supreme Court, which overturned Justice Rawls' court with a
curt citation of *New York Times v. Sullivan*. As you know, *New York Times v.
Sullivan* made libel against a political figure dependent upon proven malice. In
effect, the U.S. Supreme Court spanked Justice Rawls on the presumption that he
should have read the Sullivan case more carefully.

Justice Rawls had been smarting ever since. In *Tornillo*, he was to get his
retribution. And hence his question, "What are you doing for the Damrons of this
world?" the innocent people who are wronged by careless or negligent or hurried, or
just simply wrong reporting. If the editor of the *Star-Banner* had run over Damron
in a street because of careless driving, he would have been liable. What's the
difference if the instrument of negligence is a printing press instead, Justice Rawls
wanted to know.

If a public figure is to remain immune from libel, the Florida Supreme Court
reasoned, is not a legal right of reply at least an acceptable alternative? So it upheld
the 1913 Florida law, which, incidently, had been introduced by a legislator who
was, himself, a newspaperman, and signed into law by a Florida governor, who was
himself a newspaper publisher.

By such ironies history is made.

Justice Rawls and his one-time associates on the Florida Supreme Court are
not at all persuaded that the Supreme Court spoke the final wisdom in the *Tornillo*
case.

Justice Joseph A. Boyd makes that clear. Boyd (the "Herald's man," according to another justice) is the "one" in the Florida Court's six to one decision. He
alone, of all the court, voted against Tornillo, holding that, indeed, the Florida
1913 statute infringed upon the First Amendment.

"The whole bill of rights I consider a sacred document," Justice Boyd said
when we talked with him. "But under the law it is no more sacred than any other
part of our constitution. I remember what happened to the 18th Amendment, that
was extremely popular among some people when it was adopted. But the 21st
Amendment cancelled the 18th Amendment because the people finally decided that
there was not a proper respect being shown for the 18th Amendment.

"That can happen to the First Amendment, too, whenever the people feel that
there is not a proper respect being shown to it. So in a way, it doesn't matter too

much what I said—or what even the Supreme Court of the U.S. said in *Tornillo*. It's the attitude of the people of the United States that finally counts.

"My very firm hope is that the *Tornillo v. The Miami Herald* will be construed by the media as a greater opportunity for them to write what needs to be written. But to do so in such a way that they will not alienate a number of Americans."

Which brings us to the concluding chapter of our narrative.

What lies ahead? If Justice Boyd's fears are well founded—that the American people are, indeed, capable of repealing the First Amendment—how much *time* do we have, in what *form* will our new restrictions likely appear, and what steps can we take to forestall such a tragic and decisive action in the history of freedom?

Perhaps we have less time than we think.

Clay T. Whitehead, former head of the White House Office of Telecommunications Policy, has observed that even now, "the courts are building precedents that will lead to do-goodism regulation of the print media." He predicts that the First Amendment will be re-interpreted to apply some sort of so-called "fairness doctrine" to newspapers, similar to that already imposed on the broadcasting industry.

If this should come to pass, the courts would embrace the basic philosophy propounded by Professor Barron. In the *Tornillo* case, such a doctrine would no doubt have required Editor Shoemaker to print Pat Tornillo's reply, regardless of the editor's judgment as to its accuracy or its worth. Chief Justice Burger's opinion would collapse.

Richard M. Schmidt, Jr., general counsel to the American Society of Newspaper Editors, believes that the present Supreme Court has already reined back on press freedom.

On the same day the court returned its findings in *Tornillo*, it also handed down a decision in the case of *Gertz v. Robert Welch, Inc.* The two opinions were connected in no way but a happenstance of the calendar, but they spoke to the same general issue. And they took essentially opposite sides. Whereas the court ruled clearly *for* editorial freedom in *Tornillo*, it ruled *against* editorial freedom in *Gertz*.

The decision in *Gertz*, a case brought by Chicago attorney Elmer Gertz against a John Birch Society publication, reinterpreted the laws of libel in such a way as to make it easier for private citizens to establish proof of a newspaper's wrong-doing. By further revising the libel laws, the court seriously inhibits newspaper behavior in the future.

Thus we see emerging two thrusts that would seek to counter the growing power of the media. One would modify the First Amendment to permit the courts, or some other agency, to enforce standards of performance, presumably those considered by that agency to be in the public interest. This would be a simple extension of the regulatory philosophy already controlling broadcasting. It is the kind of action Whitehead has in mind when he predicts that the courts will reinterpret the First Amendment to include some sort of "fairness doctrine" for the press. This is what Justice Boyd warns against, and it is perhaps what Professor Barron believes would make newspapers the kind of "public forums" he envisions.

Of the two thrusts against media power, this has been the most frequently discussed and, upon examination, appears as the most radical departure from our First Amendment concept of a free and independent press. Such a move, in effect, says the Founding Fathers were wrong when they made government powerless to preempt the editor's decisions. To paraphrase Malcolm Johnson, we would have legalized editorial rape, so long as the rapist carried the imprimatur of government.

The second thrust against growing media power would work within the First Amendment, seeking to dismantle the financial concentration of the media and thus to restore local ownership and control. This would mean busting up the group operations, eliminating cross-ownerships, and restricting the role of the conglomerates. Its wrecking tools would be the anti-trust laws—from which newspapers are now given special exemptions—and tax reforms that would remove the present enticement for independents to sell to group owners. The first legislation to bring such a dismantling was introduced to Congress in 1970 by Senator Thomas J. McIntyre (D-N.H.). It was short-lived, but would have prohibited any newspaper and television cross-ownership in the same market. It also would have restricted the number of daily newspapers owned by any group to five.

Opponents of this approach point out that dismantling of big business flies in the face of economic winds. The very essence of capitalism is the use of capital to increase capital. That's how the big publishing and big broadcasting companies grew to what they are today. To attempt to reverse this trend is to attempt an unnatural economic act. Is it possible, or even desirable? If it could be done, what would be the fate of the independent companies so created? Would they survive as economic units against the ever-increasing need for larger capital to meet increased production and creative costs? Or would these independents ultimately become economic wards of the government, thereby ending the concept of freedom embodied in the First Amendment?

Chief Justice Burger's tortuous opinion agonized about the state of the media today. But within the confines of existing law and the First Amendment, the Chief Justice had no better alternative to suggest. In this regard, his opinion perhaps reflects a cautious wisdom which is likely to be overlooked.

If we are seriously to consider reshaping our media, we have little enough time in which to judge their merit against likely alternatives. For all their faults, America's corporate press and broadcast media contribute in many ways to the strength of our society. They provide American people with the most complete and balanced news report available anywhere. They report government more thoroughly and monitor it more effectively. The media serve their respective publics, more solicitous of public concerns and more knowing of public habits than any other mass communication system in the world.

The fact that our media are run as business enterprises—and not as instruments of political action—shapes their basic character. Typically of business enterprises, they are beholden ultimately to their customers. Unlike the press and broadcast systems of most of the world—and of earlier times—the American media do not answer to any political party or candidate.

As corporate journalism supplants personal and party journalism, the publisher himself becomes not so much the entrepreneur as the manager appointed by a board of directors, which is answerable, in turn, to the stockholders. Ultimately, the corporate communications enterprise flourishes to the extent that it retains the respect of the public and is able to satisfy the needs of its customers. The rise of the professional manager in the publisher's office coincides with the rise of the professional editor in the newsroom. Each exists to serve the customer.

With all the faults described by Chief Justice Burger and Justice Adkins, such a system embodies powerful safeguards for our society. A whole new editorial ethic has developed to support this new professionalism. So all pervasive is this ethic that it is a rare publisher who would buck its code to bias a news report even for his own or his corporate interests. To make such an attempt would trigger a newsroom explosion and a public outcry. Thus the corporate media possess controls inherent in their nature. Such controls lie beyond the reach of anyone who would bend them to his personal ambition, governments included. That is good.

Surely Editor Shoemaker would agree with that, and so also would Justice Rawls and his colleagues of the Florida Supreme Court, and Chief Justice Burger, and Professor Barron—and even Pat Tornillo.

Bibliography

Consult the bibliography which follows the Jacklin essay for books and articles on access to the press. Students should familiarize themselves with the entire publication from which the Fisher piece has been reprinted. See *The Trial of the First Amendment,* Freedom of Information Center monograph, 1975 and the article by Paul A. Freund, "The Legal Framework of the Tornillo Case." Opinions of the U.S. Supreme Court and of the Florida Supreme Court are reprinted in the monograph.

A New Fairness Doctrine: Access to the Media

By Phil Jacklin

Phil Jacklin is chairman of the Committee for Open Media of the Santa Clara Valley (Calif.) chapter of the American Civil Liberties Union. He teaches philosophy at San Jose State University. Reprinted with permission from the May/-June 1975 issue of *The Center Magazine,* a publication of the Center for the Study of Democratic Institutions, Santa Barbara, California.

Government regulation of broadcasting is under attack. This is nothing new. Like all industries, the broadcast industry resists regulation. Unfortunately, only the industry point of view is heard and good people are persuaded by it. Thus, in the May, 1973, issue of *Civil Liberties*, Nat Hentoff argues against the Federal Communication Commission's fairness doctrine. He understands the fairness doctrine in the conventional way as the obligation imposed on broadcasters to balance their presentation of controversial issues. More generally, the broadcaster faces an obligation to present programming in the public interest; this general obligation is particularized by the fairness doctrine which requires the broadcaster to balance discussion of controversial issues *and* to cover and present issues of public importance.

The standard argument against regulation of broadcast programming goes as follows:

There is an asymmetry in the regulation of radio and television on the one hand and the print media on the other. We have government regulation of radio and television under the fairness doctrine; but the First Amendment is understood to prohibit government regulation of newspapers under any comparable fairness doctrine.

There is no longer a justification for this asymmetry. The rationale of the fairness doctrine (and of all regulation of broadcast content) is the scarcity of usable broadcast frequencies. But there are now far fewer daily newspapers than there are radio and television stations (1,749 to 7,458). Few cities (five per cent) have competitive daily newspapers, but most are served by several television stations and plenty of radio.

Therefore, in order to be consistent, we should defend freedom of the electric press and oppose the fairness doctrine.

Hentoff does not affirm this conclusion. He offers it for discussion. As he says, it is "new ground" for him. His argument is all too familiar to those who read *Broadcasting* magazine and follow industry attempts to expropriate the First Amendment. On the strength of it, Senator William Proxmire has recently filed a bill to end regulation of broadcast programming.

The two premises of the above argument are correct. There is an asymmetry and there is no basis for it. Still, the conclusion of the argument is a *non sequitur*. We need not achieve consistency by changing broadcast law and giving up the fairness doctrine. We can also achieve it by extending the fairness doctrine from broadcasting to the print media. We can do this using the media-scarcity rationale as in broadcasting. If daily newspapers are more scarce than broadcast frequencies, it does not follow that frequencies are not scarce. There is scarcity when demand exceeds supply; in the media case there is scarcity when more people want access to the public than can have it.

We have a choice. Should we extend the fairness doctrine to newspapers which have no competitors and risk further government involvement? Or should we adopt the same laissez-faire policy for broadcasting that is traditional in the print media? I submit that there is a third and better alternative. If we believe in an open society and political equality, if we want to avoid the domination of mass communications by a few big corporations, then we must regulate any preponderant message-source in any medium. But, there is available to us a regulatory strategy which is fundamentally different from that involved in the fairness doctrine as presently understood and is wholly consistent with the First Amendment. We can choose to regulate access rather than content, to insure fairness about who is heard rather than fairness in what is said.

When, if ever, is there a need (justification or rationale) for government regulation of media? If there is media scarcity, does that justify regulation? Is there a way to regulate media without abridging freedom of the press? Answers to these questions are suggested by a model well known to political economy. Consider the following principles—all applicable to the problems of media law:

That a free (unregulated) and competitive marketplace is preferable to a government-regulated or planned economy.

That when there exists an economic monopoly or a concentration of economic power, the government must regulate that power to prevent abuses and protect the public interest. As Adam Smith explained, laissez-faire or the absence of regulation is desirable only in a condition of natural competition. When merchants must compete for their customers, the competition insures that people will be well served. But when economic power is monopolized or concentrated in a few hands, then competition ends and the government must protect the public interest. This takes us to a third and less familiar principle.

That, in the absence of natural competition, it is better to regulate so as to guarantee a competitive marketplace by limiting the extent to which power can be concentrated (e.g., to establish antitrust laws) than to attempt to regulate the behavior of monopoly powers (e.g., by setting production quotas and standards of quality, and administering prices and wages).

I take the traditional view that democracy absolutely requires the kind of communications generated in a competitive marketplace of ideas.

The problem is that in a society of millions dependent on the technology of mass communications, most messages that reach any substantial number of people are transmitted by means of a very limited number of media. In general, the scarcity of access to substantial audiences exists, not because there is a physical scarcity of communication channels, but for economic and sociological reasons. There is no shortage of "channels" in the print media, no shortage of presses or paper; but most dailies enjoy absolute monopolies. And, although there are weekly papers and periodicals, the publisher of the daily newspaper controls eighty per cent of all print communications on local and state issues.

In most big cities, there are at the present time fifteen to twenty usable television frequencies (VHF and UHF)—the same number as will be provided in a standard cable system. But the three network-associated stations control the programming viewed by eighty-five per cent of the total television audience. (Cable television and future technology will not solve our problem.)

Each of the channels with a substantial audience—print or broadcast—is wholly controlled by a single large message-source. Thus, in a typical city, control of mass communications is concentrated in the hands of a single daily newspaper and three television stations, with the addition in some places of an all-news radio station. The power of a message-source is a function both of the number of messages produced (as counted roughly by measuring the space and time they fill) and of the number of people actually reached by those messages.

It is at this point that the battle is joined by the newspaper and broadcasting industries, which argue thus: "Suppose, as is claimed, that media regulation *is* necessary when a concentration of the power to communicate reduces competition in a marketplace of ideas. There is indeed a limited number of important communicators, but there has been no showing at all that these communicators have abused their powers or refrained from a competition of ideas. The press is doing its job. Our Watergate experience proves that the system works. It is unnecessary and foolish to run the risk of government regulation of communications.''

What, then, is the performance of the media? What, if anything, is left out? National media coverage is issue-oriented and admirable in that way. But ''Presidential television'' and dominance of the media generally led us in the late nineteen-sixties to the brink of disaster and over. Denied regular television exposure, neither congressional leaders nor the opposition party could check Presidential power. The Chief Executive dominates national attention. He is the only one with enough continuity of access to exercise national leadership. On state issues, and especially on local issues, there is virtually no one with the access appropriate to leadership except perhaps the press itself.

What ideas are left out? Ask those moved by a conception of the public interest, those who would seek access to their brothers and sisters in the media marketplace of ideas, Ask elected officials, consumer advocates, reformers, ecologists, socialists, the would-be vocal poor, church people, feminists, *et al*.

On both the national and local levels, the restraints on the competition of ideas are most apparent in the absence of day-to-day political competition. Political competition is the competition of leaders and their programs for public support as expressed in the formation of public opinion. No one except the President has long-term visibility or the concomitant ability to engage in the long-term communications essential to leadership.

Why? Part of the answer lies in the fact that the most powerful media are commercial and business-oriented. There is competition, but it is a competition for the advertiser's dollar and not a competition of ideas. We ignore this because we have been taught to identify the media with the press and to understand the press on the old model of precommercial, crusading journalism. In the good old days, the newspaper publisher wrote and edited his own stories and even ran the press himself. He was a political activist, a Sentinel, an Observer vigilant in behalf of his subscribers, an Advocate with the courage to set himself and his paper against the powerful few. Things have changed. The publisher's source of revenues has shifted from subscribers to advertisers and this has changed the newspaper business in two ways. Advertisers are more interested in circulation than in editorial policy. As a result, in almost every city the largest daily has slowly achieved a monopoly position, not because of the superiority of its editorial policy but because it is the first choice of advertisers. Second, the shift of revenues has changed editorial policy. It has shifted the editor's attention from the problems of the many to the ambitions of a few. As a monopoly message-source on local issues, the paper becomes, in a technical sense, propaganda. On one hand there is the propaganda of boosterism and Chamber of Commerce public relations (e.g., in San Jose, a new sports arena before new schools, airport expansion before noise abatement). On the other hand, with respect to the problems of ordinary people, and especially the poor, there is silence, the propaganda of the *status quo*. Most big city dailies do not by themselves sustain a marketplace of ideas on local issues.

What, then, is added by the multiplicity of broadcasters? Broadcasters are typically large corporations, not crusading journalists, not people at all. Corporate broadcasters program so as to generate the largest possible audiences. Then they rent these audiences to advertisers at the rate of four dollars per thousand per minute. The lawyers and public-relations men who represent them try to identify the electronic medium with the electronic press. But does the corporation have a First Amendment right to program exclusively for profit? (The fairness doctrine prohibits it.) In fact, only about five per cent of the electronic medium is occupied with the traditional journalistic function—news, documentaries, and public affairs—the rest is electronic theater. Audience-profit maximization leaves very little place for authentic journalism. Television journalists go unprotected while the First Amendment is interpreted as the right of the broadcasting corporation to edit in order to maximize profits, and even to make the local news a form of entertainment, to make of the news itself just another format for stories of sex and violence. What these corporations seek is not freedom for journalism but freedom from journalism. (They have succeeded very well. In point of fact, the F.C.C.'s fairness obligation to cover issues has been enforced in only one case.)

There is nothing wrong with an electronic circus as long as the medium also delivers the kind of communications required for democracy. We owe very much to the journalism of the last five years. Still, even the best journalism is no substitute for free speech. There is a profound reason why this is so. Journalists are supposed to be objective and non-partisan. They themselves are not supposed to participate in the competition of ideas, or to lead people to action. The press sustains a competition of ideas only to the extent that it provides access to spokesmen who are not themselves journalists.

The question then arises: How can a journalist decide in a disinterested way what issues and spokesmen to present? There is no solution to this problem. Indeed, the question is unintelligible. Message-choice, like all choice, presupposes the chooser's interests and needs. Journalists usually avoid the problem by reporting new events relative to something that is already in the news. But in a mass society, the news is identical with what is reported; and what has not been reported is not yet news.

How, then, can the journalist decide what *new* issues and spokesmen should gain access to the public? He can decide only because he does have values and interests; hopefully only by making a judgment about what people want and need to know. Authentic journalism is public-interest journalism. But when businessmen-publishers and corporations do the hiring and the firing, there is no guarantee that we will have authentic journalism. Spiro Agnew's concern was not misplaced: "A small group of men decide what forty to fifty million Americans will learn of the day's events. . . . We would never trust such power in the hands of an elected government; it is time we questioned it in the hands of a small and unelected elite."

There is another consideration here which is decisive all by itself. Even if there were a competition of ideas between five or ten powerful sources that would not be good enough for democracy. As society is democratic to the extent that all its citizens have an equal opportunity to influence the decision-making process. Clearly, communication is essential to this process—just as essential as voting itself. (Imagine a society of one thousand in which everyone votes, and all are free to say what they please, but only five people have the technology and power to reach *all* the others. Each of the other 995, except at overwhelming expense, can communicate only with a small circle of friends. Suppose the "five" are wealthy businessmen.)

The media must be regulated, not only to insure a competition of ideas, but so that all citizens have an equal opportunity to influence and shape this competition. "Fine, but is democracy possible in a society of two hundred million people?" Representative democracy is possible. As voters, we are represented in city hall, at the state capitol, and in the Congress by people who, to some extent at least, vote on our behalf and answer to us. These people are supported at public expense and use public facilities. All right, we need to establish parallel institutions which give us representation in public debate, i.e., representation in the media market place.

There are many possibilities. Our elected representatives and their ballot opponents and/or prospective opponents—leaders all—might be provided free media time and space on a regular basis. But we should not limit representation in the media marketplace to elected officials and party leaders. There are other ways in which spokesmen representative of whole groups can be identified. Formally organized nonprofit groups like the Sierra Club and the Methodist Church can select spokesmen, and membership rolls will demonstrate that these spokesmen are representatives. Small, informally organized groups of the type characteristic of much citizen activity could achieve short-term access by demonstrating by petition that a substantial number of people supported their efforts (as in the access-by-petition procedure in Holland). A plan for a system of representative access recognizing these four kinds of access has been drawn up by the Committee for Open Media. The details establish the feasibility of the general proposal. The F.C.C. could establish some such system of access in broadcasting under its present authority, or Congress could do it. But what about the monopolistic daily newspapers?

It is useful to imagine what a new Communications Act would be like if we sought to develop a new strategy for media regulation oriented to regulation of access. We could regulate monopolistic or dominant message-sources in order to protect a competition of ideas in which all have some opportunity to participate or be represented. We could create a system of representative access of the sort sketched above or, alternatively, a new Communications Act might have the four following provisions:

The One-tenth Concentration Rule

Any dominant message-source (one which controls over one-tenth of the messages reaching any population of over one hundred thousand) in any medium—be it print or broadcast—shall recognize an affirmative obligation to provide access to the public.

The Tithe in the Public Interest

Each dominant message-source shall make available ten per cent of all message capacity (time and/or space) for citizen access. Message capacity shall be defined in terms of time and space and also audience-availability to that time and space. Since in broadcasting there is a fundamental difference between the function of full-length programs and spot messages, ten per cent of each would be made available. (Perhaps there should also be a tithe or tax of ten per cent on all profits to pay for production of citizen messages.)

The Allocation of Access by Lot

Access to time and space shall be allocated by lot among registered citizens. Every registered voter is, in virtue of this act, a registered communicator.

The Access-Contribution Mechanism

It shall be permissible for individuals to make access-contributions to designated representative persons or groups. It will be permissible for the citizen to designate a representative person or group to use his or her access spot. Individual organizations will be permitted and encouraged to solicit contributions of access time and space.

The access-contribution mechanism makes possible effective grass-roots support for various organizations at low cost (in time and money) and may lead to individual identification with the groups supported. It is a communications institution which generates community and community organization.

Access designations will, in effect, be votes—expressions of concerns and priorities—with respect to what is communicated. Everyone will participate in message-selection. Communication will reflect the needs, values, and priorities of all citizens.

The great advantage of the access approach is that it provides a strategy for media regulation which is in the spirit of the First Amendment and wholly consistent with it. The decisive difference between the regulatory strategy of the old law and the proposed new law is the distinction between the regulation of message content and the regulation of access. Or, to put the difference another way, it is the difference between the prohibition of certain message-content and the prohibition of monopolization of access by any message-source or group of sources.

The First Amendment prohibits government censorship; it prohibits laws regulating message content. But regulation of access does not entail regulation of content. Whatever source gains access is free to express any message whatever in the sole discretion of that source. While it is arguable that total denial of access is a form of censorship, surely it is not censorship to tell someone who talks all the time to stop talking for a bit so that others may speak. In contrast, the present law requires a regulation of content (broadcast programming). It requires ''government censorship'' in order to protect ''the public interest'' and especially to prevent an imbalance of programming that is not ''fair'' to some points of view. The tension between the Communications Act of 1934 and the First Amendment generates a choice between finding a way to regulate program content which does not risk government control of mass communications, and not regulating broadcast programming out of respect for the First Amendment. Given the preferences and power of the broadcast industry, the government has usually opted for no regulation. The fairness doctrine is rarely enforced. Unfortunately laissez-faire—*de jure* or *de facto*—is morally unacceptable in any context in which power is concentrated.

This returns us to the three principles of political economy and the general theory of regulation. Consider the third principle once more: that, in the absence of natural competition, it is better to limit the size and power of large entities, so as to protect competition, than it is to regulate the behavior of these powers. Thus, it is better for the government to use antitrust laws to force, say, Standard Oil to divest than for the government to mandate production quotas, set product standards, and administer prices. Surely, in such a sensitive field as communication, it is better to regulate access than to rely on government paternalism in the regulation of message-content. As always, free speech in a marketplace of ideas is our best hope.

Bibliography

Much of the material discussed by Jacklin also is included in David M. Hunsaker, *The Print Media and Equal Time*, Freedom of Information Center, Opinion Report No. 0016 (April 1975), but Hunsaker proposes a ''Model Right of Access Statute'' which would give political candidates for office access to the press. Arguments supporting the broader issue of access to the print media have been covered thoroughly in Jerome A. Barron, *Freedom of the Press for Whom? The Rise of Access to Mass Media*, Indiana University Press, 1973. This book was published before the Supreme Court's decision in *Miami Herald v. Tornillo, 1974*. The book still is useful for background. It should be supplemented by Benno C. Schmidt, Jr., *Freedom of the Press Versus Public Access*, Praeger Special Studies Edition, 1975. See also the bibliographies that appear in the bi-monthly *FoI Digest*, published by the Freedom of Information Center at the University of Missouri. These bibliographies include articles on mass media legal issues which have appeared in general periodicals as well as in the legal journals. An excellent article summarizing many of the issues covered in this section of the book is Ben H. Bagdikian, ''First Amendment Revisionism,'' *Columbia Journalism Review* (May/June 1974), pp. 39-46.

One of the reasons there is such concern for access to the media is that the newspapers and newspaper/ broadcast ownerships constitute a monopoly situation in many cities in the U.S. An excellent place to start research on this related topic is Bryce Rucker, *The First Freedom*, Southern Illinois University Press, 1968. For more up-to-date information, consult Stephen Barnett, ''Merger, Monopoly and a Free Press,'' *The Nation* (January 15, 1973), pp. 76-86, and ''Congress, FCC Consider Newspaper Control of Local TV,'' *Congressional Quarterly* (March 16, 1974). Two Rand Corporation publications dealing with the cross-ownership, monopoly issue are Walter S. Baer, *et al., Concentration of Mass Media Ownership: Assessing the State of Current Knowledge,* Rand Report (September 1974), and *Newspaper-Television Station Cross-Ownership: Options for Federal Action,* Rand Report (September 1974), also by Baer and others. For a scathing rebuttal to both of these reports, see the abstract on ''Harmful Effects of Cross-Ownership'' in *Telecommunications Policy Research, Report on the 1975 Conference Proceedings,* edited by Bruce M. Owen and published by Aspen Institute Program on Communications and Society, 1975.

Print Media

Rights of Access and Reply

By Clifton Daniel

Clifton Daniel, associate editor of the *New York Times,* was a member of a six-man panel before the Section on Individual Rights and Responsibilities, 1969 American Bar Association Convention. The text was reprinted in the December 1969 *Seminar Quarterly* and is used with Mr. Daniel's permission.

Mr. Daniel's comments are directed toward proposals which were being advanced (in 1969) by Professor Jerome Barron and others regarding access to the press by minorities and politicians. Daniel's arguments stand today in rebuttal to Jacklin's article.

So far as I am concerned, we can begin with a stipulation. I am perfectly prepared to concede that there is a problem of access to the press in this country. However, the dimensions of the problem have been greatly exaggerated, and the proposed legal remedies are either improper or impractical.

My contention is that the remedies should be left largely to the press itself and to the reading public, and that adequate remedies are available.

About the dimensions of the problem: I suppose there *are* some publishers and editors who capriciously and arbitrarily refuse to print material with which they disagree. But I don't know them.

In an adjudication made two years ago, the British Press Council, which is the official British forum for complaints against the press, had this to say: "We are finding more and more that even quite large localities cannot support more than one newspaper. We are satisfied, however, that most editors of such newspapers are now accepting it as a duty to see, as far as possible, that events and views of interest to all shades of opinion are impartially reported while reserving the editorial right to come down on one side or the other."

Exactly the same thing could be said—and truthfully said—about the press in this country. More than thirty years ago, Eugene Meyer, who had quarreled with the New Deal, resigned from the Federal Reserve Board, and bought *The Washington Post*, set out deliberately to find a New Deal columnist for his newspaper. He thought his readers were entitled to get the New Deal point of view as well as his own.

Hundreds of American publishers and editors take the same attitude today. They go out of their way to find columnists and commentators who are opposed to their own editorial policies.

New ideas are not being suppressed. On the contrary, a hurricane of dissent is blowing through the world. It is shaking the foundations of all our institutions. Can anyone here doubt the truth of that statement?

When and where has it ever before been possible for a man like the Rev. Ralph D. Abernathy to reach an audience of millions by simply painting a few signs, assembling 150 poor people, and appearing before the television cameras at the gates of Cape Kennedy?

The great guru of the right of access, Prof. Jerome Barron of the George Washington Law School . . .speaks of insuring "access to the mass media for unorthodox ideas."

I thought until I got into this argument that the main complaint against the press was that we were giving too much access to the unorthodox—hippies, draft-card burners, student rioters, black militants, and the people who make dirty movies and write dirty books. At least, that's the message I get from the mail that comes across my desk.

In spite of the mail, I still concede that there is a problem of access to the press. But its dimensions are not great and the solutions proposed are not practical.

Advocates of the right of access blandly ignore the problems and techniques of editing a newspaper. Prof. Barron speaks of the press as having "an obligation to provide space on a non-discriminatory basis for representative groups in the community."

Note the key words: Space. Non-discriminatory. Representative groups.

First: Space! How much space?

The New York Times received 37,719 letters to the editor in 1968. At least 85 to 90 per cent of these letters, in the words of our slogan, were "fit to print." However, we were able to accommodate only six per cent. If we had printed them all—all 18 million words of them—they would have filled up at least 135 complete weekday issues of *The New York Times*. Yet, every letter-writer probably felt that he had some right of access to our columns.

Some letter-writers and readers have been aggressively trying to enforce that presumed right. For many months the adherents of an artistic movement called Aesthetic Realism have been petitioning and picketing *The New York Times*, demanding reviews for books and paintings produced by members of the movement. Criticism, incidentally, would be meaningless if critics were required to give space to artistic endeavors they consider unworthy of it.

Art galleries in New York plead for reviews. They contend that it is impossible to succeed in business without a critical notice in *The Times*. That is probably true. But no one, surely, is entitled to a free ad in the newspapers. No artist has a *right* to a clientele. He has to earn his audience by the forcefulness of his art, the persuasiveness of his talent. How much more cogently does this apply to political ideas!

Non-discriminatory! Discrimination is the very essence of the editing process. You must discriminate or drown.

Every day of the year *The New York Times* receives an average of a million and a quarter to a million and a half words of news material. At best, we can print only a tenth of it. A highly skilled, high-speed process of selection is involved—a massive act of discrimination, if you like—discrimination between the relevant and the irrelevant, the important and the unimportant.

When I was preparing these remarks, I suggested to my secretary that she buy a bushel basket, and fill it with press releases, petitions, pamphlets, telegrams, letters and manuscripts. I wanted to empty the basket here on this platform just to show you how many scoundrels, scroungers and screwballs, in addition to respectable citizens and worthy causes, are seeking access to the columns of our newspaper.

Actually, 168 bushels of wastepaper, most of it rejected news, are collected and thrown away every day in the editorial departments of *The New York Times*. Do you imagine that the courts have the time to sort it all out? Do they have the time and, indeed, do they have the wisdom? Even if judges do have the time to do my job as well as their own, I think Ben Bagdikian, the leading critic of the American press, is right when he says that "judges make bad newspaper editors."

Representative groups! What constitutes a representative group? Who is to decide? I would say that representative groups already have access to the press. It's the unrepresentative ones we have to worry about.

I am not prepared to argue that it's easy for anybody with a cause or a grievance to get space in the newspapers. Indeed, it isn't easy. In my opinion, it shouldn't be. When you begin editing by statute or court order, your newspaper will no longer be a newspaper. It will be "little more than a bulletin board," as Mr. Jencks has said, [Richard W. Jencks, [then] President, Columbia Broadcasting system Broadcast Group] "—a bulletin board for the expression of hateful or immature views."

Nowhere in the literature on access to the press do I find any conspicuous mention of the hate groups. Does this newfangled interpretation of freedom of the press mean that an editor would be obliged to give space to ideas that are hateful to him? Must he give space to advertisements that are offensive to his particular readers? Must a Jewish editor be forced to publish anti-Semitism? Must a Negro editor give space to the Ku Klux Klan?

Prof. Barron, it seems to me, looks at these problems in a very simplistic way, and defines them in parochial terms. All but the most localized media have national connections of some sort: They broadcast network television programs. They buy syndicated columnists. They subscribe to the services of the great national news agencies. An idea that originates in New York is, within a matter of minutes, reverberating in California.

In determining who is to have access to the press, who would decide how widely an idea should be disseminated? Must it be broadcast in prime time on the national networks? Must it be distributed by the Associated Press and United Press to all their clients? And must all the clients be required to publish or broadcast it? Just asking these questions shows how impractical it is to enforce access to the press by law or judicial fiat.

It is impractical in another sense. In contested cases, it might take a year or more to gain access to the press for a given idea or item of news. And if there is anything deader than yesterday's news, it's news a year old.

Not only is it impractical to edit newspapers by statute and judicial interpretation, but it would, in my view, be improper—that is to say, unconstitutional.

My position on that point is a very simple one: Freedom of the press, as defined by the First Amendment, means freedom of the press. It doesn't mean freedom *if*, or freedom *but*. It means freedom *period*. Prof. Barron's proposition, however exhaustively elaborated, cannot disguise the fact that it involves regulation of the press—freedom *but*.

I cannot guess what the makers of our Constitution would have said about television, but I have a pretty good idea of what they meant by freedom of the printed word, and they certainly did not mean that it should be controlled, regulated, restricted or dictated by government officials, legislators or judges. Indeed, the makers of the Constitution meant exactly the opposite—that officialdom, constituted authority, should keep its hands off the press, that it should not tell newspapers what to print or what not to print.

To repeat: My proposition does not mean that there is no need for greater access to the press. It simply means that legislators and judges should not be—indeed cannot be—the ones to decide how much access there should be. Editors should decide, under the pressure of public and official opinion, constantly and conscientiously exercised.

There are effective devices that the newspapers and their readers could employ. Mr Bagdikian mentions some of them in the *Columbia Journalism Review*:

1. Start a new journalistic form: an occasional full page of ideas from the most thoughtful experts on specific public problems.
2. Devote a full page a day to letter-to-the-editor.
3. Appoint a fulltime ombudsman on the paper or broadcasting station to track down complaints about the organization's judgment and performance.
4. Organize a local press council of community representatives to sit down every month with the publisher.

Press councils have already been tried in several small cities. They work well. A press council for New York City—or perhaps a media council, taking in broadcasters as well as newspapers and magazines—is under consideration by the Twentieth Century Fund. In September, 1969 the Board of Directors of the American Society of Newspaper Editors went to London to make a study of the British Press Council. [See Chapter 2 for a report on the National News Council as it now exists in the United States.]

There are also other ways, as Mr. Bagdikian says, "of keeping the press a relevant institution close to the lives of its constituents."

One way is hiring reporters from minority groups, as the newspapers are now doing. Not only is opportunity given to the minorities, but also they bring into the city room the special attitudes of their communities.

In New York the communities themselves, with outside help, are bringing their problems to the attention of the press. Community representatives have been meeting with newspaper editors and broadcasting executives under the auspices of the Urban Reporting Project. A news service is being organized by the Project to provide continuous reporting from the neglected neighborhoods to the communications media.

In one of the neighborhoods—Harlem—a new community newspaper, the *Manhattan Tribune*, has been established to train Negro and Puerto Rican journalists.

I am aware that not everybody with a cause can afford a newspaper to promote it. It is not as difficult, however, to launch a new newspaper as some people would have you believe.

In 1896 a small-town publisher, Adolph S. Ochs, came to New York from Chattanooga, Tenn., borrowed $75,000, bought the moribund *New York Times*, and converted it into an enterprise that is now worth $400 million on the American Stock Exchange.

They say nobody will ever be able to do that again. But I wonder.

Fourteen years ago, Norman Mailer, the novelist, and Edwin Fancher put up $5,000 apiece to start an offbeat, neighborhood weekly in Greenwich Village. Altogether, only $70,000—less than Adolph Ochs needed to gain control of *The New York Times*—had to be invested in the *Village Voice* before it turned a profit. Its circulation is now more than 127,000—greater than the circulation of 95 per cent of United States dailies. Its annual profit is considerably more than the capital that was required to launch it.

From the beginning, the *Village Voice* has been a forum for those unorthodox opinions that are said to be seeking access to the press.

It was the *Village Voice* that blazed the trail for the underground press. While you may think that the underground press is scatological and scurrilous, its existence is nevertheless welcome proof that our press is indeed free, and that the First Amendment does not have to be reinterpreted, rewritten or wrenched out of context to give expression to unorthodox ideas.

I had not intended in these remarks to discuss the right of reply. But I think I should respond to Commissioner Cox, [FCC Commissioner Kenneth A. Cox] who says that Congress could constitutionally apply equal time and right-of-reply obligations to newspapers.

I don't agree with him. The First Amendment very plainly says—it couldn't be plainer—that Congress shall make *no law*—*no* law—abridging freedom of the press.

However, the right of reply does not provide as much of a problem for newspapers as enforced access to the press. Indeed, the right of reply is widely recognized and accepted. In practice, most newspapers recognize a prior-to-publication right of reply when dealing with controversial matters.

On *The New York Times*, we have a standing rule that anyone who is accused or criticized in a controversial or adversary situation should be given an opportunity to comment before publication. The rule is sometimes overlooked in the haste of going to press. It is often not possible to obtain comment from all interested parties, but the principle is there and the effort is required. More importantly, the same is true of the news agencies which serve practically every daily paper and broadcasting station in the United States.

The right of reply after publication is also widely accepted. However, I would caution against creating an absolute right of reply or trying to enshrine such a right in law. Newspapers, it seems to me, *must* have the right to refuse to publish a reply, provided they are willing to accept the consequences of doing so—a suit for damages, for example.

Bibliography

Clifton Daniel's argument that the First Amendment protects the print media against access efforts was reaffirmed in *Miami Herald v. Tornillo, 1974*. Several law articles have been written on this case. A good, general survey is found in Note, "Reaffirming the Freedom of the Press: Another Look at *Miami Herald Publishing Co. v. Tornillo*," *Michigan Law Review* (November 1974), pp. 186-214. Daniel's point that newspapers already are opening their pages to non-staff members is treated in David Shaw, "Newspapers Offer Forum to Outsiders," *Los Angeles Times* (October 13, 1975).,pp.I-1 ff. The Shaw study deals with the Op-Ed pages (pages opposite the editorial page) of metropolitan newspapers, treating in depth the *New York Times* and the *Los Angeles Times*. It is reprinted in this volume in Chapter 6.

What Can We Do About Television?

Electronic Media

By Nicholas Johnson

Television is more than just another great public resource—like air and water—ruined by private greed and public inattention. It is the greatest communications mechanism ever designed and operated by man. It pumps into the human brain an unending stream of information, opinion, moral values, and esthetic taste. It cannot be a neutral influence. Every minute of television programing—commercials, entertainment, news—teaches us something.

Most Americans tell pollsters that television constitutes their principal source of information. Many of our senior citizens are tied to their television sets for intellectual stimulation. And children now spend more time learning from television than from church and school combined. By the time they enter first grade they will have received more hours of instruction from television networks than they will later receive from college professors while earning a bachelor's degree. Whether they like it or not, the television networks are playing the roles of teacher, preacher, parent, public official, doctor, psychiatrist, family counselor, and friend for tens of millions of Americans each day of their lives.

TV programing can be creative, educational, uplifting, and refreshing without being tedious. But the current television product that drains away lifetimes of leisure energy is none of these. It leaves its addicts waterlogged. Only rarely does it contribute anything meaningful to their lives. No wonder so many Americans express to me a deep-seated hostility toward television. Too many realize, perhaps unconsciously but certainly with utter disgust, that television is itself a drug, constantly offering the allure of a satisfying fulfillment for otherwise empty and meaningless lives that it seldom, if ever, delivers.

Well, what do we do about it? Here are a few suggestions:

STEP ONE: *Turn on*. I don't mean rush to your sets and turn the on-knob. What I do mean is that we had all better "turn on" to television—wake up to the fact that it is no longer intellectually smart to ignore it. Everything we do, or are, or worry about is affected by television. How and when issues are resolved in this country— the Indochina War, air pollution, race relations—depend as much as anything else on how (and whether) they're treated by the television networks in "entertainment" as well as news and public affairs programing.

Nicholas Johnson, former FCC Commissioner, is the author of *How to Talk Back to Your Television Set*. This article appeared in *Saturday Review,* July 11, 1970, and is reprinted with the permissions of Mr. Johnson and of *Saturday Review,* copyright 1970. Mr. Johnson now is publisher of *access,* bi-weekly magazine of the National Citizens Committee for Broadcasting, located in Washington, D.C.

Dr. S. I. Hayakawa has said that man is no more conscious of communication than a fish would be conscious of the waters of the sea. The analogy is apt. A tidal wave of television programing has covered our land during the past twenty years. The vast majority of Americans have begun to breathe through gills. Yet, we have scarcely noticed the change, let alone wondered what it is doing to us. A few examples may start us thinking.

The entire medical profession, as well as the federal government, had little impact upon cigarette consumption in this country until a single young man, John Banzhaf, convinced the Federal Communications Commission that its Fairness Doctrine required TV and radio stations to broadcast $100-million worth of "anti-smoking commercials." Cigarette consumption has now declined for one of the few times in history.

What the American people think about government and politics in general—as well as a favorite candidate in particular—is almost exclusively influenced by television. The candidates and their advertising agencies, which invest 75 per cent or more of their campaign funds in broadcast time, believe this: to the tune of $58-million in 1968.

There's been a lot of talk recently about malnutrition in America. Yet, people could let their television sets run for twenty-four hours a day and never discover that diets of starch and soda pop can be fatal.

If people lack rudimentary information about jobs, community services for the poor, alcoholism, and so forth, it is because occasional tidbits of information of this kind in soap operas, game shows, commercials, and primetime series are either inaccurate or missing.

In short, whatever your job or interests may be, the odds are very good that you could multiply your effectiveness tremendously by "turning on" to the impact of television on your activities and on our society as a whole—an impact that exceeds that of any other existing institution.

STEP TWO: *Tune in.* There are people all over the country with something vitally important to say: the people who knew "cyclamates" were dangerous decades ago, the people who warned us against the Vietnam War in the early Sixties, the people who sounded the alarm against industrial pollution when the word "smog" hadn't been invented. Why didn't we hear their warnings over the broadcast media?

In part it is the media's fault, the product of "corporate censorship." But in large part it's the fault of the very people with something to say who never stopped to consider how they might best say it. They simply haven't "tuned in" to television.

Obviously, I'm not suggesting you run out and buy up the nearest network. What I am suggesting is that we stop thinking that television programing somehow materializes out of thin air, or that it's manufactured by hidden forces or anonymous men. It is not. There is a new generation coming along that is substantially less frightened by a 16mm camera than by a pencil. You may be a part of it. Even those of us who are not, however, had better tune in to television ourselves.

Here is an example of someone who *did.* The summer of 1969, CBS aired an hour-long show on Japan, assisted in large part by former Ambassador Edwin Reischauer. No one, including Ambassador Reischauer and CBS, would claim the show perfectly packaged all that Americans want or need to know about our 100 million neighbors across the Pacific. But many who watched felt it was one of the finest bits of educational entertainment about Japan ever offered to the American people by a commercial network.

Ambassador Reischauer has spent his lifetime studying Japan, yet his was not an easy assignment. An hour is not very long for a man who is used to writing books and teaching forty-five-hour semester courses, and there were those who wanted to turn the show into an hour-long geisha party. He could have refused to do the show at all, or walked away from the project when it seemed to be getting out of control. But he didn't. And as a result, the nation, the CBS network, and Mr. Reischauer all benefited. (And the show was honored by an Emmy award.)

There are other Ed Reischauers in this country: men who don't know much about "television," but who know more than anyone else about a subject that is important and potentially entertaining. If these men can team their knowledge with the professional television talent of others (and a network's financial commitment), they can make a television program happen. Not only ought they to accept such assignments when asked, I would urge them to come forward and volunteer their assistance to the networks and their local station managers or to the local cable television system. Of course, these offers won't always, or even often, be accepted—for many reasons. But sooner or later the dialogue has to begin.

There are many ways you can contribute to a television program without knowing anything about lighting or electronics. Broadcasters in many large communities (especially those with universities) are cashing in on local expertise for quick background when an important news story breaks, occasional on-camera interviews, suggestions for news items or entire shows, participation as panel members or even hosts, writers for programs, citizen advisory committees, and so forth. Everyone benefits. The broadcaster puts out higher-quality programing, the community builds greater citizen involvement and identification, and the television audience profits.

Whoever you are, whatever you're doing, ask yourself this simple question: What do I know or what do I have to know or might find interesting? If you're a Department of Health, Education and Welfare official charged with communicating vital information about malnutrition to the poor, you might be better off putting your information into the plot-line of a daytime television soap opera than spending a lifetime writing pamphlets. If you're a law enforcement officer, you might do better by talking to the writers and producers of *Dragnet, I Spy,* or *Mission: Impossible* than by making slide presentations.

STEP THREE: *Drop out.* The next step is to throw away most of what you've learned about communication. Don't make the mistake of writing "TV essays"— sitting in front of a camera reading, or saying, what might otherwise have been expressed in print. "Talking heads" make for poor television communication, as educational and commercial television professionals are discovering. Intellectuals and other thinking creative people first have to "drop out" of the traditional modes of communicating thoughts, and learn to swim through the new medium of television.

Marshall McLuhan has made much of this clear. If the print medium is linear, television is not. McLuhan's message is as simple as one in a Chinese fortune cookie: "One picture worth thousand words"—particularly when the picture is in color and motion, is accompanied by sound (words and music), and is not tied to an orderly time sequence.

Mason Williams, multitalented onetime writer for the Smothers Brothers, is one of the few to see this new dimension in communication. He describes one of his techniques as "verbal snapshots"—short bursts of thought, or poetry, or sound that penetrate the mind in an instant, then linger. Here are some that happen to be about television itself: "I am qualified to criticize television because I have two eyes and a mind, which is one more eye and one more mind than television has." "Television doesn't have a job; it just goofs off all day." "Television is doing to your mind what industry is doing to the land. Some people already think like New York City looks." No one "snapshot" gives the whole picture. But read in rapid succession, they leave a vivid and highly distinctive after-image.

Others have dropped out of the older communications techniques and have adapted to the new media. Those students who are seen on television—sitting in, protesting, assembling—are developing a new medium of communication: the demonstration. Denied traditional access to the network news shows and panel discussions, students in this country now communicate with the American people via loud, "news-worthy," media-attractive aggregations of sound and color and people. Demonstrations are happenings, and the news media—like moths to a flame—run to cover them. Yippie Abbie Hoffman sees this clearer than most.

> So what the hell are we doing, you ask? We are dynamiting brain cells. We are putting people through changes. . . . We are theater in the streets: total and committed. We aim to involve people and use. . . . any weapon (prop) we can find. All is relevant, only "the play's the thing." . . . The media is the message. Use it! No fund raising, no full-page ads in *The New York Times*, no press releases. Just do your thing; the press eats it up. Media is free. *Make news*.

Dr. Martin Luther King told us very much the same thing. "Lacking sufficient access to television, publications, and broad forums, Negroes have had to write their most persuasive essays with the blunt pen of marching ranks."

Mason Williams, Abbie Hoffman, Dr. Martin Luther King, and many others have set the stage for the new communicators, the new media experts. All dropped out of the traditional communications bag of speeches, round-table discussions, panels, symposia, and filmed essays. And they reached the people.

STEP FOUR: *Make the legal scene.* Shakspeare's Henry VI threatened: "The first thing we do, let's kill all the lawyers." Good advice in the fifteenth century perhaps. But bad advice today. We need lawyers. And they can help you improve television.

Examples are legion. The United Church of Christ successfully fought *two* legal appeals to the United States Court of Appeals for the District of Columbia, one establishing the right of local citizens groups to participate in FCC proceedings, and one revoking the license of WLBT-TV in Jackson, Mississippi, for systematic segregationist practices. In Media, Pennsylvania, nineteen local organizations hired a Washington lawyer to protest radio station WXUR's alleged policy of broadcasting primarily right-wing political programing. In Los Angeles, a group of local businessmen challenged the license of KHJ-TV, and the FCC's hearing examiner awarded them the channel. [Editor's Note: The challenge was rebuffed by the Commission.] There are dozens of other examples of the imaginative use of rusty old legal remedies to improve the contribution of television to our national life.

For all their drawbacks, lawyers understand what I call "the law of effective reform"; that is, to get reform from legal institutions (Congress, courts, agencies), one must assert, first, the factual basis for the grievance; second, the specific legal principle involved (Constitutional provision, statute, regulation, judicial or agency decision); and third, the precise remedy sought (legislation, fine, license revocation). Turn on a lawyer, and you'll turn on an awful lot of legal energy, talent, and skill. You will be astonished at just how much legal power you actually have over a seemingly intractable Establishment.

STEP FIVE: *Try do-it-yourself justice*. Find out what you can do without a lawyer. You ought to know, for example, that every three years *all* the radio and television station licenses come up for renewal in your state. You ought to know when that date is. It is an "election day" of sorts, and you have a right and obligation to "vote." Not surprisingly, many individuals have never even been told there's an election. [Editor's Note: The renewal schedule is given on page 37]

Learn something about the grand design of communications in this country. For example, no one "owns" a radio or television station in the sense that you can own a home or the corner drugstore. It's more like leasing public land to graze sheep, or obtaining a contract to build a stretch of highway for the state. Congress has provided that the airwaves are public property. The user must be licensed, and, in the case of commercial broadcasters, that license term is for three years. There is no "right" to have the license renewed. It is renewed only if past performance, and promises of future performance, are found by the FCC to serve "the public interest." In making this finding, the views of local individuals and groups are, of course, given great weight. In extreme cases, license revocation or license renewal contest proceedings may be instituted by local groups.

You should understand the basic policy underlying the Communications Act of 1934, which set up the FCC and gave it its regulatory powers. "Spectrum space" (radio and television frequencies) in this country is limited. It must be shared by taxicabs, police cars, the Defense Department, and other business users. In many ways it would be more efficient to have a small number of extremely high-powered stations blanket the country, leaving the remaining spectrum space for other users. But Congress felt in 1934 that it was essential for the new technology of radio to serve needs, tastes, and interests at the local level—to provide community identification, cohesion, and outlets for local talent and expression. For this reason, roughly 95 per cent of the most valuable spectrum space has been handed out to some 7,500 radio and television stations in communities throughout the country. Unfortunately, the theory is not working. Most programing consists of nationally distributed records, movies, newswire copy, commercials, and network shows. Most stations broadcast very little in the way of locally oriented community service. It's up to you to make them change.

You have only to exercise your imagination to improve the programing service of your local station. Student groups, civic luncheon clubs, unions, PTAs, the League of Women Voters, and so forth are in an ideal position to accomplish change. They can contact national organizations, write for literature, and generally inform themselves of their broadcasting rights. Members can monitor what is now broadcast and draw up statements of programing standards, indicating what they would like to see with as much specificity as possible. They can set up Citizens Television Advisory Councils to issue reports on broadcasters' performance. They can send delegations to visit with local managers and owners. They can, when negotiation fails, take whatever legal steps are necessary with the FCC. They can complain to sponsors, networks, and local television stations when they find commercials excessively loud or obnoxious. If you think this is dreamy, pie-in-the-sky thinking, look what local groups did in 1969.

Up for Renewal?

All licenses within a given state expire on the same date. Stations must file for license renewal with the FCC ninety days *prior* to the expiration date. Petitions to deny a station's license renewal application must be filed between ninety and thirty days prior to the expiration date. Forthcoming expiration dates* for stations located in the following states include:

- Iowa and Missouri: February 1, 1977; and 1980.
- Minnesota, North Dakota, South Dakota, Montana, and Colorado: April 1, 1977; and 1980.
- Kansas, Oklahoma, and Nebraska: June 1, 1977; and 1980.
- Texas: August 1, 1977; and 1980.
- Wyoming, Nevada, Arizona, Utah, New Mexico, and Idaho: October 1, 1977; and 1980.
- California: December 1, 1977; and 1980.
- Washington, Oregon, Alaska, Guam, and Hawaii: February 1, 1978; and 1981.
- Connecticut, Maine, Massachusetts, New Hampshire, Rhode Island, and Vermont: April 1, 1978; and 1981.
- New Jersey and New York: June 1, 1978; and 1981.
- Delaware and Pennsylvania: August 1, 1978; and 1981.
- Maryland, the District of Columbia, Virginia, and West Virginia: October 1, 1978; and 1981.
- North Carolina and South Carolina: December 1, 1978; and 1981.
- Florida, Puerto Rico, and the Virgin Islands: February 1, 1979; and 1982.
- Alabama and Georgia: April 1, 1979; and 1982.
- Arkansas, Louisiana, and Mississippi: June 1, 1979; and 1982.
- Tennessee, Kentucky, and Indiana: August 1, 1979; and 1982.
- Ohio and Michigan: October 1, 1979; and 1982.
- Illinois and Wisconsin: December 1, 1979; and 1982.

*Dates subject to change.

Texarkana was given national attention [in 1969] when a large magazine reported that the city's population of rats was virtually taking over the city. Of lesser notoriety, but perhaps of greater long-run significance, was an agreement hammered out between a citizens group and KTAL-TV, the local television station. In

January 1969, the Texarkana Junior Chamber of Commerce and twelve local unincorporated associations—with the assistance of the Office of Communications of the United Church of Christ—filed complaints with the FCC, and alleged that KTAL-TV had failed to survey the needs of its community, had systematically refused to serve the tastes, needs, and desires of Texarkana's 26 per cent Negro population, and had maintained no color origination equipment in its Texarkana studio (although it had such equipment in the wealthier community of Shreveport, Louisiana). But they didn't stop there. Armed with the threat of a license renewal hearing, they went directly to the station's management and hammered out *an agreement* in which the station promised it would make a number of reforms, or forfeit its license. Among other provisions, KTAL-TV promised to recruit and train a staff broadly representative of all minority groups in the community; employ a minimum of two full-time Negro reporters; set up a toll-free telephone line for news and public service announcements and inquiries; present discussion programs of controversial issues, including both black and white participants; publicize the rights of the poor to obtain needed services; regularly televise announcements of the public's rights and periodically consult with all substantial groups in the community regarding their programing tastes and needs.

The seeds of citizen participation sown in Texarkana have since come to fruition elsewhere. Just recently five citizens groups negotiated agreements with twenty-two stations in Atlanta, Georgia, and similar attempts have been made in Shreveport, Louisiana; Sandersville, Georgia; Mobile, Alabama; and Jackson, Mississippi.

In Washington, D.C., . . .a group of students under the supervision of the Institute for Policy Studies undertook a massive systematic review of the license applications of all television stations in the area of Washington, D.C., Virginia, West Virginia, and Maryland. They used a number of "performance charts" by which they evaluated and ranked the stations in amounts of news broadcast, news employees hired, commercials, public service announcements, and other factors. The result was a book that may become a working model for the comparative evaluation of television stations' performances.* Citizens groups all over the country can easily follow their example.

I have felt for some time that it would be useful to have detailed reviews and periodic reports about the implications of specific television commercials and entertainment shows by groups of professional psychiatrists, child psychologists, educators, doctors, ministers, social scientists, and so forth. They could pick a show in the evening—any show—and discuss its esthetic quality, its accuracy, and its potential national impact upon moral values, constructive opinion, mental health, and so forth. It would be especially exciting if this critical analysis could be shown on television. Such professional comment would be bound to have *some* impact upon the networks' performance. (The 1969 *Violence Commission Report* did.) It would be a high service indeed to our nation, with rewards as well for the professional groups and individuals involved—including the broadcasting industry. It is not without precedent. The BBC formerly aired a critique of evening shows following prime-time entertainment. It would be refreshing to have a television producer's sense of status and satisfaction depend more upon the enthusiasm of the

*(IPS, *Television Today: The End of Communication and the Death of Community,* $10 from the Institute for Policy Studies, 1540 New Hampshire Avenue, N.W., Washington, D.C.) Citizens groups all over the country can easily follow their example.

critics and audience than upon the number of cans of "feminine deodorant spray" he can sell.

These examples are only the beginning. Television could become our most exciting medium if the creative people in this country would use a fraction of their talent to figure out ways of improving it.

STEP SIX: *Get high (with a little help from your friends)*. Have you ever made a film, or produced a TV documentary, or written a radio script? That's a real high. But if you're like me, you'll need help—lots of it—from your friends. If you've got something to say, find someone who's expert in communication: high school or college filmmakers, drama students, off-time TV reporters, or local CATV outlets with program origination equipment. Bring the thinkers in the community together with the media creators. CBS did it with Ed Reischauer and its one-hour special on Japan. You can do it too. Get others interested in television.†

STEP SEVEN: *Expand your media mind*. Everyone can work for policies that increase the number of radio and television outlets, and provide individuals with access to existing outlets to express their talent or point of view. Those outlets are already numerous. There are now nearly ten times as many radio and television stations as there were thirty-five years ago. There are many more AM radio stations, including the "daytime only" stations. There is the new FM radio service. There is VHF television. And, since Congress passed the all-channel receiver law in 1962, UHF television (channels 14-83) has come alive. There are educational radio and television stations all over the country. There are "listener-supported" community radio stations (such as the Pacifica stations in New York, Los Angeles, Houston, and Berkeley). This increase in outlets has necessarily broadened the diversity of programing. However, since the system is virtually all "commercial" broadcasting, this diversity too often means simply that there are now five stations to play the "top forty" records in your city instead of two. In the past couple years, however, educational broadcasting has gained in strength with the Public Broadcasting Corporation (potentially America's answer to the BBC). Owners of groups of profitable television stations (such as Westinghouse and Metromedia) have begun syndicating more shows—some of which subsequently get picked up by the networks.

Cable television (CATV) offers a potentially unlimited number of channels. (The present over-the-air system is physically limited to from five to ten television stations even in the largest communities.) Twelve-channel cable systems are quite common, twenty-channel systems are being installed, and more channels will undoubtedly come in the future. Your telephone, for example, is a "100-million-channel receiver" in that it can call, or be called by, any one of 100 million other instruments in this country.

Cable television offers greater diversity among commercial television programs—at the moment, mostly movies, sports, and reruns—but it can also offer another advantage: public access. The FCC has indicated that cable systems should be encouraged and perhaps ultimately required to offer channels for lease to any person willing to pay the going rate. In the *Red Lion* case, the Supreme Court upheld the FCC's fairness doctrine and, noting the monopolistic position most broadcasters hold, suggested that "free speech" rights belong principally to the

† A free pamphlet, "Clearing the Air," has been published by Media Ithaca Department of Sociology, Cornell University, Ithaca, New York 14850. It explains how average citizens can obtain free air time over radio, television, and CATV.

audience and those who wish to use the station, not the station owner. This concept—which might raise administrative problems for single stations—is easily adaptable to cable television.

If someone wants to place a show on a single over-the-air broadcast station, some other (generally more profitable) program must be canceled. A cable system, by contrast, can theoretically carry an unlimited number of programs at the same time. We therefore have the opportunity to require cable systems to carry whatever programs are offered on a leased-channel basis (sustained either by advertising or by subscription fee). Time might even be made available free to organizations, young film-makers, and others who could not afford the leasing fee and do not advertise or profit from their programing. Now is the time to guarantee such rights for your community. City councils all across the nation are in the process of drafting the terms for cable television franchises. If your community is at present considering a cable television ordinance, it is your opportunity to work for free and common-carrier "citizens' access" to the cables that will one day connect your home with the rest of the world.

Television is here to stay. It's the single most significant force in our society. It is now long past time that the professional and intellectual community—indeed, anyone who reads magazines and cares where this country is going—turn on to television.

Bibliography

Consult Nicholas Johnson's *How to Talk Back to Your Television Set*. See also *Public Access/Public Interest*, Notebook No. 11 (Spring 1975), The Network Project. Following the publication of this notebook, The Network Project ceased to produce its Notebook series on electronic communication issues. These typescript publications have been useful attempts to inform people about major issues, including such problems as satellite communications, cable television, public television and other major electronic organizations or industries. For a list of publications and cassette tapes, write The Network Project, 101 Earl Hall, Columbia University, N.Y. 10027.

Broadcast Regulation by Contract: Some Observations on "Community Control" of Broadcasting
By Richard Jencks

Richard W. Jencks, now President, CBS Broadcast Group, delivered these remarks on "Broadcast Regulation by Private Contract: Some Observations on 'Community Control' of Broadcasting" at the 1971 Broadcasting Industry Symposium, Washington, D.C. This edited version is used with his permission.

As America enters the second year of the decade of the Seventies, its most characteristic protest movement is no longer the Civil Rights Movement—or the Peace Movement—or the revolt of youth.

Instead, it is that combination of causes which has been summarized by the awkward word "consumerism." . . .

The consumerism movement is in many ways typically American. It is reform-ist in its objectives, populist in its rhetoric, intensely pragmatic in its methods.

On issues ranging from the ecological impact of pesticides to the urgent need for automobile safety, and from thermal pollution to the SST, consumerism is persuading the public to demand of government that it reorder its priorities, and that it pay less attention to conventional notions of progress.

In all of these activities the aim of consumerism was to induce government action, whether by the executive branch, by the Congress, or by regulatory agencies.

In broadcasting, consumerism has stimulated regulatory action in a number of areas, of which one of the most notable was in connection with the broadcast advertising of cigarettes.

Consumerism is responsible for another development in the broadcast field in which its role is quite different—in which it seeks not so much to encourage regulatory action as to *substitute* for government regulation a novel kind of private regulation.

That development is a trend toward regulation of broadcasting through con-tracts entered into by broadcast licensees with private groups—contracts entered into in consideration of the settlement of license challenges. This form of regulation has been called the "community control" of broadcasting. It begins with the monitoring and surveillance of a broadcast station by the group. It ends with the group's use of the license renewal process in such a way as to achieve a greater or lesser degree of change in—and in some cases continuing supervision of—a broad-cast station's policies, personnel and programing. . . .

A strategy was developed in which a community group would, prior to the deadline for a station's renewal application, make demands for changes in a sta-tion's policies. If a station granted these demands they would be embodied in a contract and embodied, as well, in the station's renewal application. If a station refused to grant these demands the group would file a petition to deny renewal of the station's license. Such a petition, if alleging significant failures by the licensee to perform his obligations, can be expected to bring about a full-scale FCC hearing. As a result, there is obviously a powerful incentive in these situations, even for the best of stations, to try to avoid a lengthy, costly and burdensome hearing by attempting to reach an agreement with such a group. . . .

Probably the most fundamental demand made in recent license challenges is that a large percentage of the station's weekly schedule be programmed with mate-rial defined as "relevant" to the particular community group—usually an ethnic group—making the demand. . . . The demands I am referring to here go far beyond even what the most responsive broadcast stations have done in the way of local public service programming or what the FCC has expected of them. In one recent case it amounted to a demand that more than 40 percent of a station's total pro-gramming schedule must be programmed with material defined as "relevant" to the minority group. . . .

Philosophically, this kind of demand raises a basic question as to the purpose of a mass medium in a democratic society. Should the broadcast medium be used as a way of binding its audience together through programming which cuts across

The controversial "family hour" plan whereby shows depicting much sex and violence would be kept off the air until small children supposedly were in bed brought cries of censorship from television artists. But other critics said it was not stopping the flow of offensive materials. Others suggested that while the networks should be more responsible, each family was responsible for its own hours of watching television.

Television's Family Viewing Concept...
A <u>Big</u> Step Forward!

We believe in Freedom of Expression...
Freedom without responsibility
destroys itself.

Broadcasters are increasingly demonstrating their responsibility through their adoption of the Family Viewing concept of the NAB Code.

The family is the most important organization in our society. There is a crucial need for television programs that—
   —effectively communicate the moral standards and vital ideals so essential in a wholesome society.
   —help strengthen the family and the home.

WE ENDORSE THE NAB CODE **FAMILY VIEWING** CONCEPT AND SUPPORT ALL THOSE WHO ARE CONCERNED AND ACTIVE IN ITS IMPLEMENTATION.

> "Television is a gift from God....
> and God will hold those who utilize this
> divine instrument accountable to Him."
> —Philo T. Farnsworth
> Leading Inventor of Television

Bonneville
International
Corporation

The Bonneville Group

KIRO AM-TV Seattle, Washington	KSL AM-FM-TV Salt Lake City, Utah
KSEA-FM Seattle, Washington	KMBZ/KMBR Kansas City, Missouri
WRFM New York, New York	KBIG/KBRT Los Angeles/Avalon, Calif.
WCLR Skokie/Chicago, Illinois	Bonneville Broadcast Consultants, Tenafly, N.J.

racial and cultural lines? Or should it be used as a means of communicating separately with differentiated segments of its audience?. . . .

It seems possible that there is a strong thread of racial separatism in the demand for relevance. Like the demand of some black college students for segregated dormitories, it may be regarded in large part as a demand for segregated programming. . . .

Connected with the notion of relevance is the interesting idea that programming done as part of a requirement of ''relevance'' must be an accurate reflection of the ''life-style'' of the particular minority community.

The director of a national organization whose purpose is to encourage license challenges by local groups recently spelled out what he meant by the idea of the truthful portrayal of a life-style. On his arrival in Dayton, Ohio, to organize license challenges by local groups there *Variety* described his views as follows: ''If one third of Dayton's population is black, then one third of radio and TV programming should be beamed to the black community. And this should be produced, directed and presented by blacks.'' Referring to JULIA, the NBC situation comedy, he was then quoted by *Variety* as saying: ''How many black women really live like JULIA? I'd like to see her get pregnant—with no husband. That would be a real life situation.''

Now, I think that was meant seriously and it is worth taking seriously. . . .

Considerations like these go directly to the heart of what a mass medium is, and how it should be used. We live in an era in which the mass media have been dying off one by one. Theatrical motion pictures are no longer a mass medium and less and less a popular art form. They now reach relatively small and diverse social groups—not infrequently, I might add, with strong depictions of social realism. They no longer reach the population at large. Magazines, once our most potent mass medium, are almost extinct as such. There are plenty of magazines to be sure, but almost all serve narrow audiences. . . . Central city newspapers, as suburbanization continues, find their ability to reach megalopolitan areas steadily decreasing. . . .

Television can be said to be the only remaining mass medium which is capable of reaching most of the people most of the time. Is it important to preserve television as a mass medium? I think so. I think so particularly when I consider the racial problem in this country.

For the importance of television as a mass medium has not been in what has been communicated *to* minorities as such—or what has been communicated *between* minority group leaders and their followers—but in what has been communicated *about* minorities *to the general public*. . . .

Such communication occurs when programs are produced for dissemination to a mass audience for the purpose of *uniting* that audience in the knowledge of a problem, or in the exposure to an experience, not for the purpose of fragmenting that audience by aiming only at what is deemed ''relevant'' by leaders of a single minority group. . . .

I referred earlier to the excoriation by some black leaders of NBC's JULIA, the first situation comedy to star a black woman. The question may well be asked whether the shift for the better in white American attitudes about black people is not more likely to have been caused by programs like JULIA—and by the startling increase in the number of black faces on other television entertainment programs which began in the mid-60s—as it is to any other single cause.

No one should doubt that racial attitudes *have* changed, even though much remains to be done. A Gallup poll, published last May, asked white parents in the South whether they would object to sending their children to school where any Negroes were enrolled. In 1963, in answer to the same question, *six* out of every *ten* white parents in the South had told Gallup pollers that they would object to sending their children to schools where any Negroes were enrolled. In 1970, seven years later, according to Gallup, only *one* parent in *six* offered such an objection. Other recent public opinion polls show similar gains in white attitudes toward blacks.

These advances in the direction of an integrated society were made possible in part, I suggest, by a mass medium which, with all its faults, increasingly *depicted* an integrated society. . . . Americans who in their daily lives seldom or rarely deal on terms of social intimacy with black people have been seeing them on the television screen night after night for some years now. . . .

If audience fragmentation to meet the special requirements of minority groups would destroy television as a *local* mass medium it would, by the same token, of course, make impossible the continuance of network television as a *national* mass medium. Again, some might welcome this. Some think it might happen anyway. John Tebbel, writing recently in *The Saturday Review*, observed: "There is no reason to suppose that network television is immune to the forces that are gradually breaking up other national media." He does not, however, celebrate that possibility. "It is seldom realized," writes Tebbel, "how much network television binds the nation together . . . To fragment television coverage into local interests might better serve the communities, as the egalitarians fashionably argue, but it would hardly serve the national interest which in the end is everyone's interest."

I have discussed what seems to me to be the basic objective in community group demands upon the media—the fragmentation of programming to serve what are perceived as ethnically relevant interests.

The *means* used by the community groups may have an important impact on the nature of American broadcast regulation, and in particular upon the FCC. Commissioner Johnson often has provocative insights and this instance is no exception. He has praised the idea of regulation by community groups and has called upon his colleagues on the Commission to, in his words, "set a powerful precedent to encourage local public interest groups to fight as 'private attorney generals' in forcing stations to do what the FCC is unable or unwilling to do: improve licensee performance."

This puts the question quite precisely. *Should* private groups be encouraged to do what official law enforcement bodies are "unable or unwilling to do"? In particular, should they police a licensee by means of exploiting the power of that very regulatory agency which is said to be "unable or unwilling" to do so?

It would seem that to ask the question is to answer it. Despite the trend of vigilantism in the Old West, it is not a theory of law enforcement which has found many supporters in recent times.

In the first place, private enforcement is unequal. Although Commissioner Johnson may refer to the role of these groups as that of "private attorney generals," they do not act as a *public* attorney general has to act; the demands they make on a television or radio station are rarely if ever concerned with any constituents other than their own.

In the second place, private law enforcement is hard to control. Whenever law enforcement depends on the action of private groups, the question of private power is apt to become all too important. A medium which can be coerced by threat of license contest into making such concessions to black or Spanish-speaking groups can as readily be coerced by a coalition of white ethnic groups. More so, in fact, since in most American cities there is, and will continue to be for some time, a white majority. To expect a situation to exist for long in which tiny minority groups can coerce stations into providing special treatment, and not to expect the majority to seek the same power over the station, is to expect, in Jefferson's famous phrase, "what never was and never will be."

Clearly there is at the heart of this matter a broad question of public policy—namely, whether public control of licensee conduct should be supplemented by any form of private control. It is plain that the encouragement of "private attorney generals" will result to some degree in the evasion of the legal and constitutional restraints which have been placed upon the regulation of broadcasting in this country. . . .

For a weak broadcaster, if not a strong one, will doubtless be found agreeable to entering into a contract under which he will be required to do many things which the Commission itself either *cannot do, does not wish to do* or *has not yet decided to do.* . . .

All this might be questionable enough if community group leaders were clearly representative, under some democratically controlled process, of the individuals for whom they speak. However public spirited or *bona fide* their leadership, however, this is rarely the case. The groups making these challenges are loosely organized and tiny in membership. Not infrequently, the active members of a group seeking to contract with stations in a city of several million number scarcely more than a few dozen.

So far the effectiveness of community group strategy has rested upon the paradoxical willingness of the Commission to tacitly support these groups and their objectives. . . .Many of those who believe that the Commission is a "do-nothing" agency may not be concerned with where regulation by private contract is likely to lead. Others may feel that to weaken duly constituted regulatory authority by condoning such private action is, in the long run, to make the performance of broadcast stations subject to undue local community pressures. These pressures may not always be exerted in socially desirable ways.

Not long ago the Commission held that it was wrong for a broadcast licensee to settle claims made against it by a community group by the payment of a sum of money to the group even for the group's legal expenses. The Commission felt that this would open the way to possibility of abuse, to the detriment of the public interest. But nonmonetary considerations which flow from the station to a community group can be just as detrimental. Suppose, for example, a weak or unwise station were to give a community group special opportunities to influence the coverage of news. Is such a concession less damaging to the public interest than the payment of money?. . . . I mentioned early in this talk that the consumerism movement, at its best, is in many ways fully within the American tradition. . . .But it must be added that the movement is also typically American in its excesses. It is sometimes puritanical, usually self-righteous and often, in its concern with ends, careless about means.

The American system of broadcasting, while not perfect, has made real contributions to the public good and social unity. It has done this through the interaction of private licensees, in their role as trustees of the public interest, on the one hand, and the authority of government through an independent nonpartisan regulatory agency. Heretofore in this country when we have spoken about the community, we have generally meant the community as a whole, acting through democratic and representative processes.

I suggest that those who are interested in the quality of life in this country—as it pertains to the preservation of a vigorous and independent broadcast press—should wish to see that private community groups do not supplant the role either of the broadcaster or of the Commission.

Bibliography

Richard Jencks' complaint regarding challenges to station renewals expresses a view shared by many professional broadcasters. Since this is clearly a regulatory issue, publications that deal with license renewals are valuable. Don R. LeDuc, editor, ''Issues in Broadcast Regulation,'' *Broadcast Monographs*, No. 1 (1974) is an excellent source of information on this and related issues. Richard E. Wiley, chairman of the FCC, has expressed his views regarding challenges in a speech delivered to the Florida Association of Broadcasters. It has been reprinted in Ted C. Smythe and George A. Mastroianni, eds., *Issues in Broadcasting: Radio, Television, Cable*, Mayfield Publishing Company, 1975. Two solid books on regulation are Roger G. Noll, *et al.*, *Economic Aspects of Television Regulation*, Brookings Institute, 1973, and Erwin Krasnow and Lawrence Longley, *The Politics of Broadcast Regulation*, St. Martin's Press, 1972.

Cable Television   # Voices on The Cable: Can The Public Be Heard?

By Barry Head

If things keep going the way they are going now (and that's what things generally do), cable communication will soon be chalked up on the Big Board of our social stock exchange alongside all those other issues: poverty, crime, environment, war, urban decay, civil rights, transportation, and so on. When that happens we will have yet one more subject for experts to disagree about and for the rest of us to avoid on the ground that there's nothing we can do about it. At that point, we will doubtless sit around blaming inaccessible experts and shadowy corporations for the grotesque shape of our wired-up nation.

Then, perhaps in the pages of this very magazine, some irritating social historian will point out that cable communication was not a "problem" at all. It was, instead, an instrument of such enormous power that it held the promise of solutions to our *real* social problems. Worst of all, the decisions that finally rendered the instrument inaccessible, or ineffectual, or both, were not, in fact, made in unreachable boardrooms and distant corridors of government: they were made at the municipal level where franchises to wire up individual communities were handed out—by local, identifiable, flesh-and-blood decision-makers to whom each of us had access and whom each of us could have influenced.

As local cable systems begin to interconnect, they will form a kind of electronic railway system that will span the nation. There will be railheads and switching yards in thousands of communities, and from these will run dozens of feeder lines into virtually every home. What will be remarkable will not be the clarity of picture—which is all most people now associate with "being on the cable"—but the flexibility, the practically limitless capacity, and the viewer-response capability of this new communications configuration. Freed from the tyranny of one-way transmission over the airwaves' limited spectrum space, we will have a cornucopian abundance of wide, continuous, two-way frequencies that can handle all our communications needs—from an electronic impulse to instantaneous mail transmission to a printout of any book in the Library of Congress.

It will be tragic indeed if the only cargoes that move on these rails are thousands of reels of old film, thousands of tapes of game shows and situation comedies, thousands of exhortations to buy thousands of products, and thousands of hours of useless information. What is at stake is nothing less than a chance for us, collectively, to bring coordination to our disjointed society, and for each of us, individually, to become an identifiable, responsive, and significant member of that body. More specifically, cable communication could:

● give us new access to our decision-makers;

● provide a survival kit for the disadvantaged by bringing them essential information on employment, housing, health, nutrition, day care, and other assistance in providing for their needs;

● significantly raise the level of public education uniformly across the nation, ease overcrowded classrooms, offset the shortage of teachers by giving everyone electronic access to continuing education;

● provide the means to monitor and combat environmental deterioration;

● open new international perspectives on ourselves and others by clarifying our different aspirations while emphasizing the commonality of many of our problems;

● permit the population of our overcrowded cities to disperse, enable those who remain to form cohesive communities with easy and effective access to each other and to the central urban entity;

● enable minority interest groups to reach their members, each other, and the

Barry Head is director, Workshop on Public-Interest Communications, Education Development Center, Newton, Mass. He has been associate producer of "The Advocates" for PBS. Copyright 1973 by Minneapolis Star and Tribune Co., Inc. Reprinted from the March 1973 issue of *Harper's* Magazine by permission of the author.

rest of us, giving the "right of a minority to become a majority" a new practical validity;

- lessen the likelihood of violence born of the inability to communicate anxieties and grievances;
- bring new methods to bear on crime prevention and control;
- carry family-planning information beyond the reach of field workers to those who most need it;
- obviate unnecessary business trips by making two-way video communication, data transmission, and facsimile printout possible.

These are but a few of the more obvious changes that cable communication could make in our lives. (The details of how they may come about—together with the new problems cable may usher in—can be found in the sources mentioned at the end of this article.) But while there is consensus among communications experts that cable offers us a potent new problem-solving instrument, there is also agreement that the tool may never take realizable form. The chances of the experts being proved right increase enormously so long as an uninformed and largely uninterested public considers the question somebody else's business. The worst error is the assumption that the whole thing will one day be properly resolved in Washington.

But wait, you say, there are all those good men in Congress . . .No, there aren't. A well-informed official who deals with Congress over cable issues puts it this way: "There are perhaps ten men on the Hill who understand what cable communication is about—and that's being generous." Chances are the Congressmen *you* elected don't even know what CATV stands for.

. . .and there's the Federal Communications Commission . . .In fact, the FCC's vacillating attitude toward the growth of cable has been another clear indication (as if yet another were needed) that it does not and cannot speak for the public interest. One of the FCC's most serious problems is the complete lack of leadership from Congress. Unsurprisingly, the FCC has a history of mediation between competing industry and government interests rather than one of statesmanlike trusteeship of the public airwaves. In addition, the FCC may well be the most understaffed, underfinanced, and overpressured regulatory agency in Washington. It won't help you in Dubuque.

. . .and the Office of Telecommunications Policy . . .The OTP is the three-year-old communications arm of the Executive Office of the President. It runs on an annual budget of $2.6 million, and its functions, according to its controversial former director, Clay T. ("Tom") Whitehead, are as follows:

> First, the Director of the Office is the President's principal adviser on electronic communications policy. Second, the Office enables the Executive Branch to speak with a clearer voice on communications matters and to be a more responsible partner in policy discussions with Congress, the FCC, the industry and the public. Third, the Office formulates new policy and coordinates operations for the Federal Government's own very extensive use of electronic communications.

"We like to think that we are representing the public interest," says Brian Lamb, the thirty-one-year-old assistant to the director for Congressional and media relations, but clearly there is scant room for that role in the Office's job description.

Moreover, there is no identifiable "public" with which the Office might act as a "responsible partner."

   ...and the Cable Television Information Center...The newly established CTIC, a semiautonomous unit within the Urban Institute, stands quite apart from the regulators, the lawmakers, and the policymakers. Funded by $3 million from the Ford and Markle Foundations, the Washington-based Center is headed by a wunderkind named W. Bowman Cutter. Faulted by his adversaries for being short of field experience in cable communication, Cutter—and his youthful staff—is nonetheless highly knowledgeable about cable and its implications. "Cable communications," Cutter says, "present *the* critical test of whether or not we can manage our technology." The Center's charter is to "provide to government agencies and to the public the results of objective, nonpartisan analyses and studies and technical assistance about cable television. The Center will also attempt to assist state governments in their regulatory decisions regarding cable television; and provide, when needed, information regarding federal government policy toward cable."

   But though the Center will, according to Cutter, "make clear that its function is to serve the public interest," the individual citizen or citizen coalition will find it little help; it shuns advocacy. Its job is to provide the facts, just the facts, on request.

   ...and Publi-Cable, Inc. Springing bravely through the Washington mulch, Publi-Cable is a voice of *pure* advocacy with no organization, no office, no money, and, as of its recent first birthday, minimal influence. "We're an ad hoc group, a brush-fire operation," concedes Dr. Harold Wigren, director of Publi-Cable as well as educational telecommunications specialist for the National Education Association. "We're trying to alert as many communities as possible to the dangers and opportunities in the franchise decisions made by their local officials. But there aren't many of us and we've all got other jobs. We're spread pretty thin." Out of more than 150 individuals representing various groups concerned about cable, a core of sixty or so meets every month in Washington. They are a well-connected lot, and their influence, small though it may be, is well directed and quite out of proportion to their number. Such loose consortia, however, are always prey to internal dissension, suffer from financial anemia, lack long-range strategies, and have no way of ensuring the stability or rational behavior of local groups that may spring up in their wake. Publi-Cable is no exception; it certainly cannot be regarded as heralding sustained public attention to the future configuration of our wired-up nation.

   But isn't there a National Citizens Committee for Broadcasting? The NCCB, Thomas Hoving's once-bright hope for reforming broadcasting in this country, has imploded. All that remains in Washington is a tiny holding operation in a signless, unnumbered room in the back of the United Presbyterian Church's headquarters way out by American University. There are a paper board of trustees and a fitful newsletter. There is vague talk of resurgence.

   Who, then, will speak for you during the next several years as our new communications systems take shape? The simple truth is that there is no voice with a broad public constituency to address the all-important questions of uses and programming. (Critically short of manpower and resources, even the New York-based Office of Communications of the United Church of Christ—that redoubtable and astonishingly effective manifestation of the Church Militant—will reach few communities.) You will have to make yourself heard where you live, and the costs and benefits of local action vs. inaction are indicated by two examples.

• By the time that an Illinois state statute authorized municipalities to grant cable franchises in 1965, Peoria—in a sealed-bid process with no public hearings, no citizen involvement, and no outside consultation—had contracted an agreement with General Electric Cablevision that included no specific performance requirements. Six years later no cable had been laid. "In January 1971," says Peoria's corporation counsel, Paul Knapp, "we asked GE to renegotiate. Cable technology had changed a lot, and there were experiences in other cities to learn from. GE refused and insisted on sticking to the old contract. Because nothing had been done—no studies, nothing—we declared them in default in February and considered the contract invalidated. In April GE took us to court to challenge our action. In December the court decided in their favor, holding that because the city had failed to act affirmatively during the intervening years it had effectively waived its rights to invalidation. We appealed. The appellate court sustained the trial court's decision. I am now recommending we appeal to the Illinois Supreme Court."

The other side of the argument is presented by Boyd Goldsworthy, whose Peoria firm of Goldsworthy & Fifield is representing GE Cablevision. The trouble, says Goldsworthy, lay in FCC restrictions on importing programming from distant markets—in this case bringing, say, Chicago and St. Louis channels to Peoria cable subscribers. Precluded from offering this inducement to subscribers, GE Cablevision believed that building a Peoria system would be economically unfeasible—a contention with which Paul Knapp, naturally, disagrees. Who is in the right may be a murky question, but for the average Peorian the consequences of inattention are crystal clear: his city is involved in expensive and lengthy litigation; he has none of the benefits that cable could bring, and he may lack them for a long time to come.

• The experience in another heartland city, Oshkosh, Wisconsin, was dramatically different. There, the city manager, Gordon Jaeger, had already weathered a four-and-a-half-year franchise struggle as city manager of Normal, Illinois. Soon after taking the Oshkosh post, Jaeger recommended to his city council that they employ a consultant and draw up a model cable ordinance *before* they were faced with deciding among contenders. With the help of a veteran consultant, Robert A. Brooks of the Chesterfield, Missouri, firm of Telcom Engineering, Inc., a model was duly adopted. Bids were solicited and three subsequently received. The job of evaluating the competitors was turned over to a small but representative citizens committee, and the franchise was granted to the Cypress Communications Corporation of Los Angeles (now a part of Warner Communications), which, unlike the other two bidders, accepted a September 1973 deadline for commencement of service. What is Oshkosh getting? A thirty-six channel cable system in which two channels are reserved for municipal use and two for public access on a first-come first-served basis—in both instances an allocation twice the minimum FCC requirement.

But in addition Oshkosh is getting a separate, two-way, twelve-channel "loop" interconnecting the University of Wisconsin, all public and private schools, the Fox Valley Technical Institute, the library, and the museum. Robert Snyder, the coordinator of radio, TV, and film for the university and a member of the citizens committee, expects a major payoff to be in community-wide curriculum development and teacher training. "But although the loop will be primarily a closed circuit," Snyder explains, "programs on it can be fed into the regular cable system. Thus the possibilities for adult education in general are enormous." The greatest danger is that the loop will stand idle. To prevent this eventuality, Gordon Jaeger has appointed a twelve-member committee to plan now how it can best be put to use.

Few communities will be as fortunate as Oshkosh in having a knowledgeable city manager, concerned key citizens, and a progressive cable company with which to work. The operative question, then, is what can the rest of us realistically try to do? Influencing the FCC is an unlikely option. Within the FCC's bailiwick logically lie considerations of copyright, assurance of service to all sectors of the public, minimum technical standards and channel allocations, non-discriminatory access, and limits to concentration of ownership. Shaping even the broad outlines of these important areas, which is all the FCC will do, should provide ample grounds for combat, but only the most sophisticated citizens and citizen groups will have the ability to enter the fray at the national level.

State government is a good deal more accessible and must be forced to play a leadership role. Governor Patrick Lucey of Wisconsin impaneled a blue-ribbon citizens committee to hold hearings all over his state—a laudable initiative but one that also demonstrated the difficulty of arousing citizen interest without local groundwork by library associations, religious organizations, PTAs, and similar centers of social concern. (All such associations, at the national, regional, and local level, should place on their agendas the dual question: "What can cable mean to us and what can we do about it?"). Last May, Governor Nelson Rockefeller signed a bill to create a five-member commission that will regulate the growth of cable in New York. The commission will set franchising guidelines for local governments, regulate contract obligations between cable companies and their subscribers, set rates, and oversee the coordination of separate systems. Few states are taking any interest in cable, however, and while the layman may well hesitate to enter hassles over the details of state regulation, there is no excuse for tolerating a recklessly high level of ignorance and apathy on the part of state officials. We are all adequately equipped to ask the offices of our secretaries of state what attention is being paid to the growth of cable and to urge that a responsible commission be established or that other appropriate action be taken.

But the most important determinations of what we see on our local cable systems—how much of it and whether it is cumulatively a positive, negative, or irrelevant influence on our immediate community—will be made much closer to home in our town halls. Here, we can help shape the details of the franchise, applying our own perceptions, needs, and desires. Here, as individuals or in small coalitions, we can monitor the acquisitiveness of cable interests, the defensiveness of entrenched broadcasting interests, and the heedlessness of the officials empowered to act on our behalf.

Three actions are immediately appropriate for every citizen:

1. Call your corporation counsel (town attorney) and find out where your community's franchise stands. Has one been granted? On what terms? Is a grant pending? What is your town's franchising authority?

2. Inform yourself. Two important and comprehensible sources for basic information on cable communications are *On the Cable*, the report of the Sloan Commission on Cable Communications (McGraw-Hill, cloth, $7.95; paper, $2.95) and *Cable Television: A Guide for Citizen Action* by Monroe Price and John Wicklein (Pilgrim Press, $2.95). An excellent survey of the history, technology, and implications of cable is to be found in *The Wired Nation* by Ralph Lee Smith (Harper Colophon, $1.95). Ben Bagdikian's *The Information Machines* (Harper & Row, $8.95) is a useful survey of mass media—past, present, and future.

3. Join a citizens-concerned-about-cable group in your community. If there isn't one, start one or act as an individual. The *Guide for Citizen Action* mentioned above will help you; if, having read it, you still don't know how to proceed, get in touch with Publi-Cable, % The National Education Association, 1201 16th Street, N.W., Washington, D.C. 20036, phone: (202) 833-4120; or the Office of Communications, United Church of Christ, 287 Park Avenue South, New York, N.Y. 10010, phone: (212) 475-2121.

Finally, though each community will present a different mosaic of issues, interests, and alignments, at least three principles for citizens action should hold true in all cases:

1. Insist on widely publicized public hearings well before franchise decisions are to be made. A community needs ample time to identify all its options and to air all its viewpoints.

2. Avoid the simplistic ''good guys vs. bad guys'' trap. There are many legitimate interests competing in the cable controversy. Speedy cable penetration *is* in the public interest, and this means providing adequate economic incentive to offset the enormous capital investment needed to build a system. Although the huge multiple-system owners bear watching, they are *not* automatically the enemy; they may be the only entrepreneurs who can afford to extend cable's range of services. Wholesale destruction of existing broadcast structures is *not* in the public interest, and this means providing some economic safeguards. Successful pursuit of elusive public interest is more likely through statesmanlike compromise than through shrill consumerism.

3. Let nothing be given away for too long and without provisions for frequent periodic review. Nobody knows for sure what configurations of ownership and technology will serve what social and economic needs and produce what social and economic effects. Thus, while it may be necessary to grant a ten-year franchise in order to ensure incentive, development, and stability, such a franchise should

stipulate at least biennial amendment. This is necessarily a period of trial and error; make sure that what goes wrong today can be set right tomorrow.

These simple actions and basic rules of thumb are well within any citizen's capability and, if taken and followed, should have a profound effect on how our inexpert experts wire us together. The single clear question we all face is this: "Are the implications of cable serious enough to warrant my participation?" If our conclusion is no, it should be a no of decision rather than of oversight, and before arriving at that conclusion it would be well to ponder Fred Friendly's words in *Due to Circumstances Beyond Our Control:*

> The great malfeasances against the people of our country are more an indictment of the society that permitted them to happen than of the individual rogues who committed the frauds. In the case of television, it isn't a question of scoundrels or frauds; rather an indifferent society has given away more than it was ever entitled to, like an executor who permitted the trust in his care to be squandered.

Noting the imminence of revolutionary new technology, Friendly concluded:

> If indifference and naïveté caused us to give away our electronic inheritance when the industry was in its untested infancy, to do so again with the stakes so high would be little short of cultural suicide.

Cultural suicide is a dire eventuality indeed. But if things keep going the way they are going now (and that's what things generally do—unless each of us takes a hand in stopping them), it could just come to that.

Bibliography

The cable television field already has a vast "literature" dealing with the access issue. A scholarly work is Ithiel de Sola Pool, ed., *Talking Back: Citizen Feedback and Cable Technology*, MIT Press, 1973. An interesting report on the success of public access in New York City can be found in David Othmer, *The Wired Island, The First Two Years of Public Access in Cable Television in Manhattan*, Fund for the City of New York (September 1973). It should be supplemented by several works that are more current. The *Journal of Communication* (Summer 1975) carried three articles dealing specifically with the access problem on cable television: Alan Wurtzel, "Public-Access Cable TV: Programming," pp. 15-21; Rudy Bretz, "Public-Access Cable TV: Audiences," pp. 22-32, and Pamela Doty, "Public-Access Cable TV: Who Cares?" pp. 33-41. The conclusions are sometimes provocative.

2 Criticism of the Mass Media

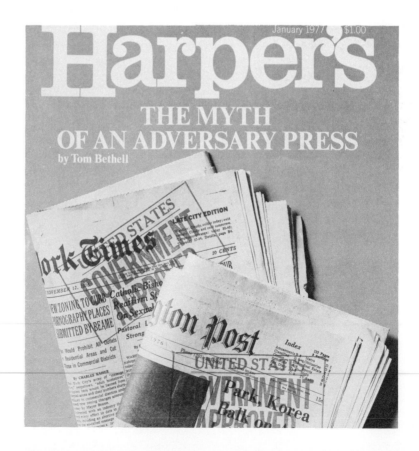

The Messenger's Motives

By John L. Hulteng

Through the Side Door . . ."*The American press is afflicted with the country club mind. It doesn't make much difference how much of a crusading Galahad a young publisher may be when he starts; by the time he begins to put his paper across he is taken up by the country club crowd, and when that happens he is lost. He joins the country club, for that is our American badge of success. And before he knows it, he sees his community from the perspective of the country club porch, and he edits his paper to please the men who gather with him in the country club locker room.*" —William Allen White

Not all of the situations that put journalists to the ethical test crop up in the reporter-source relationship, or arise out of conditions peculiar to the craft. Some may be the result of pressures that are applied subtly and indirectly from outside, or from within the news-gathering organization itself—usually from the direction of the offices of the publisher or the advertising director.

When William Allen White of the *Emporia* (Kans.) *Gazette* wrote his pessimistic prediction about the country club syndrome, some segments of the newspaper industry were in the big business category. Today *most* daily newspapers, television stations, mass circulation magazines, the broadcasting networks—both radio and television—and some individual radio properties are very definitely classifiable as big business.

Many of the major media properties are owned by industrial conglomerates with a wide range of other interests from banking to chemicals. And, increasingly, the ownership of the channels of communication is being concentrated into fewer and fewer hands as chains and groups grow and merge with each other.

These trends have a tendency to accentuate the kind of attitudinal alteration that White was talking about. Ownership may not only begin to reflect the values of the "country club crowd" but also those of true Big Business—the vast, interlocking corporate structures that sprawl across the nation, or the world.

Now it should be made very clear at this point that the concentration of ownership, or even conglomerate takeover, doesn't *invariably* or *inevitably* convert the media managers into "profits-first" types. Many present-day publishers and owners are thoroughly conscious of the social responsibility they must shoulder. Moreover, the growing professionalism of the men and women who staff the mass media constitutes a force that is resistant to the compromise of standards in accommodation to the interests of conglomerate or corporate ownership.

Yet, when these qualifications have been entered on the record, it is necessary to add that there does exist an array of evidence of various kinds to suggest that the basic ethic of the news media is being perverted in numerous ways—sometimes in obvious ways, sometimes in only half-visible ones—because of pressures that are generated by ownership or by the friends and associates of ownership.

When such pressures prevent the journalist from adhering to the professional standards he believes are binding, he can protest, resist, even resign—and many have done all three. But personal and family obligations, the difficulty of locating

John L. Hulteng is dean of the School of Journalism, University of Oregon, and a well known researcher and writer in the field of news and opinion communication. This excerpt is taken from his most recent book, *The Messenger's Motives: Ethical Problems of the News Media,* Prentice-Hall, 1976. Reprinted by permission of Prentice-Hall, Inc., copyright 1976.

another job, or a weary conviction that it wouldn't do any good in any event prevent others from putting their careers on the line in defense of journalistic ethics.

Without attempting to inventory all of the kinds of side-door pressures that can pose ethical challenges for journalists, let's look at a representative sampling of cases and comments in order to get a clear understanding of the nature and dimensions of the problem.

Where the Money Comes From

It is commonplace today to assert that large newspapers are relatively immune from direct advertiser pressure, and that this sort of thing now rarely occurs; this is a thesis expressed in most introductory mass media texts, and it is based on sound reasoning. After all . . .virtually all daily newspapers are in a semimonopoly situation; in very few communities does any true, head-to-head print competition between different ownerships survive. An advertiser theoretically shouldn't be able to bring off a squeeze play, since he needs the advertising medium represented by the daily newspaper more than the paper needs any single advertiser. Or so the thesis goes. And cases can be cited in which advertiser power plays were successfully resisted by individual papers. But there are other cases to be cited as well.

The *Wall Street Journal*, whose reporters periodically present some of the most penetrating analyses of newspaper practices to be found anywhere, documented an embarrassing instance involving the respected *Denver Post*.

A reporter for another paper somehow came into possession of an internal memo from one *Post* executive to another detailing an arrangement whereby the newspaper had agreed to run 1,820 column inches of free publicity about a new shopping center because the shopping center had bought and paid for 30 pages of advertising. Nor was this the only instance of such cozy *quid pro quo* arrangements; the *Post* had also promised a block of free space to another advertiser, and the news staff was complaining that there was no more to say about them "short of repetition," even though the promised quota of puffery was far from filled.

More often, of course, the pressure is not applied so openly or so brutally, and the puffery is at least partially veiled. According to the *Journal* writers, the *Dallas Times Herald* used to print each Monday from 2½ to 3 pages of what was described as commercial, business, and industrial news of Dallas. Actually, the news space assigned to a given company was carefully calculated to reflect the amount of advertising space the company had been buying in the paper.

And, as Carl E. Lindstrom, a former editor of the *Hartford* (Conn.) *Times* once wrote:

> Would there be travel pages if travel agencies and airlines didn't advertise? Would there be recipes in the paper if food advertisers didn't come in with a bang on Thursday afternoon and Friday morning? Would there be a stamp column or a dog column if there were no related revenue?

In the broadcast media the influence of advertisers on the content of entertainment programs has been pervasive and traditional. News departments on radio and television, by contrast, have attempted to shield themselves from similar pressures. They have not, however, in all cases been successful. Fred W. Friendly recounted in his book *Due to Circumstances Beyond Our Control* how pressures generated by advertisers affected the nature and content of news and documentary shows under his direction at CBS. The experience of newsmen at other networks has been similar.

As John C. Merrill and Ralph L. Lowenstein point out in an overview book of the media, the influence of advertisers on the content of broadcasting is not necessarily overt and direct:

> Sponsors do not act in a positive manner to deliberately censor programming material, as is commonly thought. Rather their influence on the total programming picture is *negative*. Their reluctance to sponsor a program that is either controversial or likely to attract a small audience assures that such programs will not be shown frequently.

Still, there are cases in which television advertisers have been known to bring a more direct pressure to bear to prevent, say, mention of a competitor on a sponsored news show.

And others have been successful in efforts to prevent a negative reference to their company or their product from getting attention on broadcast news programs. Robert Cirino recounts how representatives of Coca-Cola were given an opportunity to preview a documentary depicting the plight of migrant workers; Coca-Cola was one of the companies depicted as profiting from the work of migrants in Florida. When the company representatives had viewed the film, they asked the president of NBC to meet with them before the film was shown, in order to consider some cuts in the film that would have the effect of softening the impact on Coca-Cola. The meeting was held and some, at least, of the requested cuts were made before the documentary went on the air.

How Many Hats?

Another form of awkward internal pressure peculiar to the broadcasting news field is the prevalent practice of requiring announcers on news programs to serve also as voices for commercials.

Some of the top network anchormen refuse to switch hats, and because of their stature they can get away with it. But less prominent newsmen can find themselves in cowboy costumes (or dog's heads) to push a product or a program when they are not busy intoning the latest bulletins.

In a speech to radio news executives in 1970, Walter Cronkite spoke with feeling for his fellow newsmen:

> Reliability is a handmaiden to integrity and I fear that many of us are not as careful as we might be to keep our escutcheons unbesmirched. It is beyond me to understand how anyone can believe in, foster, support, or force a newsman to read commercials. This is blasphemy of the worst form. A newsman is nothing if not believable. And how can he be believed when he delivers a news item if in the next breath he lends his face, his voice and his name to extolling in words the public knows he never wrote a product or service that the public knows he probably never has tested? When a newsman delivers a commercial he puts his reputation for honesty in the hands of an advertising copy writer and a client whose veracity is sorely tried by the need to make a buck. It is difficult if not impossible for the individual newsman who wants to protect his family to stand up to a management that demands that he indulge in this infamously degrading and destructive practice.

On the small-market radio or TV station, Cronkite's depiction of the vulnerability of the newscaster who is asked to double as huckster certainly does apply. The trend to the "happy talk" format, with the chummy interchanges sliding almost imperceptibly from the news to the commercial messages, poses the problem in an even more insistent form for the newscaster.

Yet the growing importance of news on the electronic media, and the discovery through surveys that increasing numbers of Americans are dependent upon these media for most of the news that they receive in a given day, ought eventually to strengthen the hand of the newscaster and give him better leverage with which to insist that his role as reporter not be confused with the different job (certainly respectable enough in itself) of the salesman.

Some broadcast newsmen have adhered to Cronkite's philosophy and have refused to do the double-hat routine even though their stand has cost them lucrative opportunities.

When Frank McGee, co-host and news anchorman for NBC's morning "Today" show, died in April 1974, there followed a search for the right man to fill the prized post with its $350,000-a-year salary. The network finally narrowed down the list to eight, but then discovered that several of the best prospects balked at the requirement that they would have to read commercials as well as serve as host and newscaster. One of them, Garrick Utley, said: "I question whether a reporter does not lose his journalistic virginity by doing commercials. And can you recover that virginity later?"

Another, who had appeared to be the most promising of the finalists in the tryout sessions on the show, was Tom Brokaw, NBC's White House correspondent at the time. He said flatly: "I find doing commercials repulsive. If that is a job requirement, it would not be negotiable with me."

Both stuck to their principles and did not take over the McGee role, but the network did find someone who would. The stakes were high, since the "Today" show was drawing about five million viewers each morning and reportedly made $10,000,000 a year for the network. For Utley and Brokaw, however, and for many others who have had to face similar decisions with less momentous financial consequences, the ethical value involved was more important than the network's profit margin—*or* the impressive salary. [Editors' Note: Brokaw later became a co-host *without* doing commercials.]

By the Bushel

Not all of the pressures that impinge on the journalist from advertiser or outside corporate institutions come in the form of direct power plays or through the side door of management influence. Many of them arrive courtesy of Uncle Sam.

Every newspaper city desk, every electronic newsroom, is daily deluged with vast quantities of public relations releases of various kinds. Every corporation of any size, most goverment agencies, trade associations, even civic groups and educational institutions, employ skilled staffs to prepare "news" stories to be sent to the various media outlets—all of them designed to result, if possible, in the publication or broadcast of an item that will depict the sending agency in a favorable light before the public.

Much of this expensively prepared material goes directly into the wastebasket, but a very large amount of it gets into print or on to the air in some form. Press critic Ben H. Bagdikian has estimated that if one were to trace down the origins of all the news items in the columns of a daily newspaper of substantial size, it could be demonstrated that up to 60 percent of the material started out as some kind of release from the news source itself.

It is obvious, of course, that most of the material put out by a public relations officer on behalf of his company or organization is going to include an element of self-interest, sometimes blatant, sometimes subtle. But it is also true that much of that volume of paper that flows over the transom each day also contains kernels of news that the newspaper or broadcasting station might not otherwise come upon.

So the welter must be gone through, and the solid substance of news sifted out and fed into the media. If the job is done conscientiously, the self-serving spin put on the releases by the public relations authors will be removed, and the genuine news will remain. The careless, hurried, or cynical desk man will "railroad" the copy through without bothering to work it over—and as a result the reader, listener, or viewer is exposed to adulterated news.

The ethical editor suffers a particularly nasty twinge when the public relations copy coming over his desk has an invisible "must run" stamp on it because it in some fashion involves an organization or a cause in which the publisher is known to be intensely interested.

On one small-city daily, for example, all staff members knew that anything involving the Boy Scouts must get special handling, for this was one of the most sacred cows in the publisher's stable and *always* must have tender, loving care—and plenty of news space.

Perhaps no great harm is done if an organization such as the Boy Scouts gets the benefit of some extra puffery. But there are more insidious critters in the sacred cow corral.

Melvin Mencher, a Columbia University professor writing in *Nieman Reports*, notes:

> I know now why so many newspapers use acres of newsprint on year-end bank statements; their publishers serve on the boards of directors of the local banks. Perhaps these stories are newsworthy. After all, depositors do want to know the state of health of their banks. But I wonder how many newspapers whose publishers are bank directors will want to examine the mortgage loan policies of banks, which in many urban communities can accelerate the decline of a neighborhood by refusing to grant home improvement loans. This practice, called redlining, is well-known to real estate editors, but it's rarely made the subject of hard-digging journalism.

Let me note again that in at least part of the reams of news releases turned out by public relations officers there is legitimate, significant news to be found. Persons who work in the public relations field are typically highly skilled, often former journalists. They frequently make the point that their efforts save reporters and editors valuable time, both because they dig out hard-to-locate facts and because they do at least part of the job of packaging the information for processing by the news media. These are defensible arguments.

Yet the fact remains that what the public relations man or woman is paid for is to see to it that the best possible version of the news about his or her organization or company gets through the media pipelines. The job of the journalist, if he subscribes to the ethical guidelines of his business, is to report the news without bias, without favor to any organization or cause, exposing the face of reality fully rather than focusing only on the best profile.

There may be times when these two functions coincide. Much of the time they do not. And the flood of public relations material through which desk editors must regularly wade is a wearing test of their principles and their stamina.

Sometimes it would appear that their defenses have indeed been worn down, and the gates left open wide for the public relations people to pour through. One example was chronicled by *Columbia Journalism Review* after its editors had noted a sudden spate of stories and broadcasts by the New York media about the 75th anniversary of the birth of composer George Gershwin—hardly a day of national observance under ordinary circumstances. Among those that voiced tributes, almost in chorus: the *New York Times, Saturday Review/World, Newsweek, Vogue, New York,* NBC's "Today," and public television.

When the *CJR* editors looked into the matter they discovered that the outpouring had been orchestrated by the efforts of Alice Regensburg, staff member of a New York public relations agency, as a device for promoting the sale of a new $25 book about the composer. As Ms. Regensburg put it, "People are hungry for material and if you offer them good, well-planned ideas, they welcome them."

Journalists with a sense of respect for the integrity of their business will welcome legitimate news, yes. But they will firmly shut the gates on blatantly promotional copy, no matter how "good" and "well-planned."

Living-Color P.R.

In recent years public relations experts have discovered new dimensions to their field in the form of the radio or television news release.

Most public relations copy still goes out in the form of paper, handouts printed or mimeographed in handy triple-spaced format so that they can be sent to the composing room or the newscaster with a minimum of editing. But much of that handout material . . .goes into the round file unused. Public relations messages for broadcast, while much more expensive to produce, stand a far better chance of getting through to the ultimate target—the consuming public.

Radio and TV stations at the local level—TV stations in particular—need material to fill out their local news shows. It is expensive to send reporting and camera crews out to get local footage, and many kinds of local stories are unproductive in any case; they result only in "talkinghead" interviews with inarticulate city managers or school board members.

Then along comes a lively, colorful, beautifully produced short film about an interesting, topical subject. It's all free, and it can be used anytime. There's even a script with it so that the local announcer can "read over" the film footage to give the impression that the item was produced locally. Somewhere in the film there will be a message subtly promoting the interests of the organization supplying the film; but it usually won't be intrusive. It doesn't have to be. Just a fleeting glimpse of a recognizable product or a brand name in a favorable setting will be enough to justify the very considerable expense that has gone into producing the film.

And the beauty of it, from the standpoint of the public relations people, is that the film is very difficult—by design—for the local station to edit. Whereas the mimeographed handout can be edited so that the commercial overtones are removed, this is all but impossible with the public relations film.

As the features appear, with the local announcer's familiar tones reading the words-over, they all seem to be just parts of the regular news report—during which they typically are run, particularly by the small-market stations hard up for genuine local footage to keep the screen alive.

This living-color credibility has quite understandably caught the attention of a group that classifies as just about the most indefatigable public relations practitioners in any field—the politicians. And the results pose a new set of ethical headaches for the journalists.

Greening the Grassroots

For many years officeholders have been well aware of the advantages of the conventional press release. The oftener a senator or congressman can show up in the pages of the home-district newspapers, or on the newscasts of stations in the area, the better name familiarity there will be among the electorate next time polling day rolls around. Virtually all of the members of the Senate or the House have at least one former journalist on their staffs, and some have several. These aides crank out the press releases with a sure knowledge of style, deadlines, news values, and the names of the right news editors to target.

One Western senator was famous during his incumbency for an expensive but highly effective gambit—not a single working day went by in the offices of the major newspapers of his state that some editor in each of these offices didn't get either a personal letter, a telephone call, or a telegram from the senator. He could be pretty certain that when his press releases came around to these carefully cultivated editors they usually got special treatment.

In recent years, with the growing importance of the electronic media in campaigning, the politicians have turned to radio and television press releases, emulating corporate P.R. That is not to say, of course, that the old-fashioned printed press release has been abandoned. Literally tons of them still go out of legislators' offices in a steady stream. But the same factors that make the TV press release so useful to the corporate public relations men make it attractive to the congressmen.

One of the impressive sights of Washington—and one hardly ever seen by any but insiders—are the television studios maintained for members of the Senate and the House to use in filming "news" footage to be shipped home to key TV stations nestled in the vital grassroots.

These studios have all the most up-to-date equipment—color cameras, tape facilities, and duplicating devices for producing multiple copies of video film or tape. And, according to Ben H. Bagdikian, Washington correspondent for *Columbia Journalism Review*, the cost to a congressman or senator for producing a five-minute color video tape in 25 copies for home-district stations is about one-twentieth to one-tenth of the amount that would be charged by a commercial pro-production unit.

From these studios the films or tapes are shipped off weekly or monthly to the home front, there to be presented in some cases as "reports from our senator (or our congressman)," but in many other instances to be fitted into the regular news shows as though they were the genuine article.

To give these televised press releases as authentic a touch as possible, the legislators are able to select from several official looking "sets." As Bagdikian describes it:

> There is a choice of backgrounds for the representative. He can choose a scholarly-looking "library" background with legal-bound books. He can also appear in front of a blue curtain or a carefully contrived photograph of the Capitol as though seen through his office window. Unfortunately, this view of the Capitol is not seen from the office of any senator or representative, either in size or perspective, but it has appeared in thousands of TV shots, implying that the local politician occupies a high-status office overlooking the great dome.
>
> Another background is a special screen on which a slide or movie (provided by the member, not the studio) can be projected, either for a stable background or for action footage that dramatizes the subject the member wishes to discuss.
>
> The other basic set is the "office," with a big congressional desk, the standard black-leather high-backed chair behind it, a desk pen, perhaps the blue and red books, and the choice of backgrounds . . .
>
> There is one other scene, not exactly a full set. It is a paneled wall with two hooks on it from which may be hung the standard gold-plated nameplate of every standing committee of the House—Agriculture, Appropriations, Armed Services, so on; thus, the member may be photographed as though standing outside a committee room from which he has just emerged to share with his voters the inner secrets and wisdom. . . .
>
> Last year 352 of the 435 members of the House repaired to their studio, most of them every week.

It seems obvious that the home stations that integrate such living-color press releases into their regular news programs, without flagging them for what they really are, have failed the ethical litmus test. They also may be helping to magnify the advantages of incumbency to almost unbeatable proportions.

Any incumbent officeholder has an advantage over a challenger, whether the race is for the presidency or the state legislature. He is likely to be better known, more often legitimately in the news, and able to use the platform of his office to generate pseudo-news in the form of releases of various kinds that command at least some attention simply because they come from a current public official.

But the advantages accruing to a member of Congress who has learned how to make the most of his cut-rate private studios for the production of TV news releases far outclass anything previously known in politics, particularly as television assumes more and more significance in campaigning.

As one congressman told a committee on ethics of the New York Bar Association, "A challenger needs $25,000 just to get even with me."

The end result, as Bagdikian points out in his *Columbia Journalism Review* analysis, is that there tends to be less and less turnover in Congress as the firmly entrenched incumbents deluge the home folks with see-it-now evidence of their impressive labors at the Capitol. The struggling challengers have to be extremely well heeled, or extremely well known, before they start, in order to overcome the incumbents' built-in advantages. And so as Bagdikian writes:

> *Congressional Quarterly* tells us that in the 1870s more than half the members of each session of the House were newly elected, but that by 1900 only a third were first termers and that by 1970 the figure had dropped to 12 per cent. Of 330 incumbents running for re-election in 1972 (the other 135 having retired, died or given up in primaries), only ten incumbents—3 per cent—were defeated.
>
> Obviously, as these figures show, the renewal of the House on the basis of performance and changes in public desires is not working. One important reason is that the news media simply don't tell the folks back home what their member of Congress really does. Worse than that, most of the media are willing conduits for the highly selective information the member of Congress decides to feed the electorate.

As Bagdikian points out, the turnover rate for congressmen has been strikingly higher in districts where voters have access to newspapers or broadcasting stations with their own Washington bureaus. Reporters in such bureaus can keep tabs on what the State's representatives at Washington are really up to, and relay that information to the reader or viewer back home to weigh along with the press-release picture painted by the legislators and reproduced by complaisant local media. But few newspapers and even fewer broadcasting stations can afford full-time Washington bureaus, and the wire service, network, and news magazine bureaus cannot provide individual coverage of senators or congressmen except in very special circumstances; the big bureaus quite naturally concern themselves with the flow of the major news at Washington. The answer, according to Bagdikian, is more pooling of Washington coverage by papers or stations unable to afford their own bureaus, and above all more honesty in the handling of the various forms of press release material—print and broadcast—that come their way.

One Small, Sad Footnote

Before turning from the topic of side-door pressures and the ethical tests these ubiquitous forces impose on journalists in all media, let's note one final item that bears on the subjects that we have been discussing. It pretty much points its own moral, without any exposition of embellishment.

It is taken from the introductory comment to a searching analysis of the press of New England, undertaken in 1973 by newsmen and press observers in the area with financial support from a foundation.

The editor of the survey report, Loren Ghiglione, himself an editor, observed in the prefatory comments:

> If the editorial page is the newspaper's soul, then a large number of New England dailies are in danger of going to hell.
>
> At least one-third of the region's dailies occasionally—or almost daily—publish editorials purchased from one of a half-dozen services located outside the region.

These canned editorials are presented in the papers as though they were the home-written opinions of the local editors. And, as Ghiglione points out:

> The services produce editorials for hundreds of papers throughout the country. The pieces discuss nonlocal topics and rarely take a stand on anything more controversial than motherhood (pro) and heart disease (con).

And Melvin Mencher, a Columbia University professor who served as one of the evaluators in the New England newspaper survey, adds this:

> The Survey gives us a picture of newspapers that will not endorse candidates, will not take a position on controversial local issues, will not permit staffers to write columns. Our inheritors of the tradition of Elijah Lovejoy, William Allen White, and Joseph Pulitzer willingly preside over their own emasculation. But the loss of virility can be profitable. It does keep the newspaper from offending the partisans among its readers. The non-combative editorial page tells readers the newspaper has no axes to grind at a time of public suspicion of the press. . . .Publishers buy up syndicated columnists by the score to make a sufficient din to conceal their quavering voices.
>
> But is this journalism? Is the journalist, to use a phrase of Harvey Swados, "a publicly useful man" when he refuses to put himself on the line?

These comments on the use of "canned" editorials were made with respect to the small-city newspapers of New England, but the practice is by no means characteristic only of that region.

Papers short of manpower—and editors short of ethics—plug up their editorial columns with mislabeled factory-produced editorials or with "safe" columnists in many areas of the country. They represent exceptions rather than the rule, but even so they are too numerous for comfort.

Bibliography

Books dealing with some of the ethical problems in news and opinion include John Hulteng's *The Messenger's Motives: Ethical Problems of the News Media,* Prentice-Hall, 1976, from which this article was reprinted. See also Robert Cirino, *Don't Blame the People: How the News Media Use Bias, Distortion and Censorship to Manipulate Public Opinion,* Random House, 1971; Curtis D. MacDougall,*News Pictures Fit to Print . . .Or Are They?* Journalistic Service, 1971; Alfred Balk and James Boylan, editors, *Our Troubled Press: Ten Years of the Columbia Journalism Review,* Little, Brown and Company, 1971; Hillier Krieghbaum, *Pressures on the Press,* Thomas Y. Crowell, 1972; Laura Longley Babb, ed., *Of the press, by the press, for the press (And others, too),* The Washington Post, 1974, and Richard Pollak, ed., *Stop the Presses, I Want to Get Off! Tales of the news business from the pages of [more] magazine,* Random House, 1975. These books, which are listed in chronological order, contain large numbers of examples of ethical problems in American journalism, print and electronic.

Ethics and Journalism

By John C. Merrill

When we enter the area of journalistic ethics, we pass into a swampland of philosophical speculation where eerie mists of judgment hang low over a boggy terrain. In spite of the unsure footing and poor visibility, there is no reason not to make the journey. In fact, it is a journey well worth taking for it brings the matter of morality to the individual person; it forces the journalist, among others, to consider his basic principles, his values, his obligations to himself and to others. It forces him to decide for himself how he will live, how he will conduct his journalistic affairs, how he will think of himself and of others, how he will think, act and react to the people and issues surrounding him.

Ethics has to do with duty—duty to self and/or duty to others. It is primarily individual or personal even when it relates to obligations and duties to others. The quality of human life has to do with both solitude and sociability. We do right or wrong by ourselves in that part of our lives lived inwardly or introvertedly and also in that part of our lives where we are reacting and responding to other persons. This duality of individual and social morality is implicit in the very concept of ethics. The journalist, for example, is not simply writing for the consumption of others; he is writing as *self*-expression, and he puts himself and his very being into his journalism. What he communicates is in a very real way what he himself *is*. He pleases or displeases himself—not just those in his audience. What he does to live up to some standard within him not only affects the activities and beliefs of others, but in a very real way, the very essence of his own life.

A concern for ethics is important. The journalist who has this concern obviously cares about good or right actions; such a concern indicates an attitude which embraces both freedom and personal responsibility. It indicates also that the journalist desires to discover norms for action that will serve him as guiding principles or specific directives in achieving the kind of life which he thinks most meaningful and satisfying. Ethical concern is important also for it forces the journalist to commitment, to thoughtful decision among alternatives. It leads him to seek the *summum bonum*, the highest good in journalism, thereby heightening his authenticity as a person and journalist.

What characterizes most journalists today is a lack of commitment and consistency, a lack of a coherent life plan. Before any journalist chooses any particular ethics he must decide whether or not to be ethical: this is the first and most important choice facing him. However, it may well be, as Sartre and other Existentialists have believed, that "not to choose is already to have chosen"; that the "refusal to choose the ethical is inevitably a choice for the nonethical." There is a tendency today to identify as "ethics" any personal decision to act; anything I want

John C. Merrill is professor in the School of Journalism, University of Missouri. He is the author of several books in the field of mass media criticism and evaluation. His latest is *Ethics and the Press,* Hastings House, 1975, edited with Ralph D. Barney. This selection is reprinted with permission of Dr. Merrill and is taken from *The Imperative of Freedom,* Hastings House, 1974. This edited version also appears in *Ethics and the Press.*

to do, I do—therefore, it is ethical for me to do it. Hazel Barnes points out that this is exactly parallel to what has happened to "religion." She says that "an age which is willing to apply the term 'religion' to communism, aesthetic awe, devotion to one's fellow man, and allegiance to impartial demands of pure science has no difficulty in labeling any guiding motif or choice a personal ethics." If one accepts this position he is really saying that nobody is really nonreligious or nonethical; all meaning will have been drained from the concepts "religious" and "ethical" if nobody can be non-religious or non-ethical.

Ethics is that branch of philosophy that helps journalists determine what is right to do in their journalism; it is very much a normative science of conduct, with conduct considered primarily as self-determined, voluntary conduct. Ethics has to do with "self-legislation" and "self-enforcement"; although it is, of course, related to *law*, it is of a different nature. Although law quite often stems from the ethical values of a society at a certain time (i.e., law is often reflective of ethics), law is something that is socially determined and socially enforced. Ethics, on the other hand, is personally determined and personally enforced—or should be. Ethics should provide the journalist certain basic principles or standards by which he can judge actions to be right or wrong, good or bad, responsible or irresponsible.

It has always been difficult to discuss ethics; law is much easier, for what is legal is a matter of law. What is ethical transcends law, for many actions are legal, but not ethical. And there are no "ethical codebooks" to consult in order to settle ethical disputes. Ethics is primarily personal; law is primarily social. Even though the area of journalistic ethics is swampy and firm footing is difficult, as was mentioned earlier, there are solid spots which the person may use in his trek across the difficult landscape of life.

First of all, it is well to establish that ethics deals with *voluntary* actions. If a journalist has no control over his decisions or his actions, then there is no need to talk of ethics. What are voluntary actions? Those which a journalist could have done differently had he wished. Sometimes journalists, like others, try to excuse their wrong actions by saying that these actions were not personally chosen but *assigned* to them—or otherwise forced on them—by editors or other superiors. Such coercion may indeed occur in some situations (such as a dictatorial press system) where the consequences to the journalist going against an order may be dire. But for an American journalist not to be able to "will" his journalistic actions—at least at the present time—is unthinkable; if he says that he is not so able and that he "has to" do this—or—that, he is only exhibiting his ethical weakness and inauthenticity.

The journalist who is concerned with ethics—with the quality of his actions—is, of course, one who wishes to be virtuous. Just what a virtuous person, is, however, is somewhat circular and gets us back to the question: What is a moral or ethical person? However, the nature of virtue is not really so relative or vague if we have any respect for the great thinkers of history; there has been considerable commonality of meaning among philosophers generally, even though "virtue" has been conceptualized in terms containing considerable semantic noise.

The "Virtuous" Journalist

The virtuous journalist is one who has respect for, and tries to live by, the cardinal virtues which Plato discusses in *The Republic*. First is *wisdom*, which gives "direction" to the moral life and is the rational, intellectual base for any system of ethics. Wisdom is part natural and part acquired, combining knowledge and native abilities; it largely comes from maturing, from life experiences, from contemplation, reading, conversing and study. Second, there is *courage*, which keeps one constantly pursuing his goal, the goal which wisdom has helped him set for himself. Courage is needed to help the journalist resist the many temptations which would lead him away from the path which wisdom shows.

The third virtue is *temperance*, the virtue that demands reasonable moderation or a blending of the domination of reason with other tendencies of human nature. It is this virtue, giving harmony and proportion to moral life, which helps us avoid fanaticism in pursuit of any goal. And, last, there is *justice*, distinguished from the other cardinal virtues in that it refers more specifically to man's social relations. Justice involves considering a man's "deservingness"; each man must be considered, but this does not mean that each man has to be treated like every other—for example, justice would not require that every person elected to a city, state or national office receive equal attention on television or the same amount of space in a newspaper. Equal treatment simply does not satisfy deservingness—does not imply "just" coverage.

One sign of virtue in journalism may well be a deep loyalty to truth. At least the pursuit of truth by the journalist surely takes wisdom, courage, temperance and justice. John Whale, an editorial writer for the *Sunday Times* of London, contends that at the base of journalistic ethics is an allegiance to truth. It is the authenticity of the information contained in the story that is the journalist's chief ethical concern, according to Whale. What methods should a journalist use in trying to get at this "truth"? Whale answers: *Only those methods which the journalist would be willing to publish as part of the story*. This is one reason why Whale and many others (including me) are opposed to the passage of "shield laws." What is far more important than keeping a source's name secret, he maintains, is whether what he said is true. It is hard to verify truth if the source's name is hidden from the public. This allegiance to truth, not to some person (source) who reveals information, is what is important. Too often those who reveal information and elicit the journalist's promise not to identify them have motives other than a desire to let the truth come out. Virtue in journalism, believes Whale, has to do with getting as much truth as possible into the story—and, of course, the source of the information is *part* of the "truth" of the story.

The desire to search out and present the truth does, indeed, seem to be one of the moral foundations of libertarian journalism. Most journalists think of truth as they do of objectivity—as temporary, splintered and incomplete. Accuracy, fairness, balance, comprehensiveness are generally related to objectivity by the journalist—and, therefore, have to do with truth.

Naturally, the main problem with such truth is that it must be considered in context with editorial determinism. *What* truth—or what parts of what truth—will a journalistic medium choose to present? "All the news that's fit to print," replies *The New York Times*, proclaiming to all that certain matters (even if *truthful* or contributing to the truth) which are not considered "fit" will not be printed. Therefore, *The Times* is explicitly saying what all journalists believe and practice: truth is what journalists consider fit to call truth, just as news is what they decide is news—nothing more and nothing less.

Moral philosophers have at least given us a wide variety of alternative standards for determining virtuous actions. In general, these ethical standards boil down to two main ones: *teleological* theories and *deontological* theories. The first consider the moral rightness or wrongness of an action as the good that is produced. The second, on the other hand, hold that something other than (but sometimes, perhaps, in addition to) consequences determine which actions are morally right or good.

Teleological Theories

Teleologists look at the consequences of an act; they consider consequences and only consequences as determining the moral rightness or wrongness of actions. Teleologists differ among themselves only as to whose good it is that one ought to try to promote. Egoists, for example, hold that one should always do what will promote his own greatest good; this view was held by Epicurus, Hobbes, and Nietzsche, among others. Utilitarians—or ethical socialists—take the position that an act or rule of action is right or good if and only if it is, or probably is, conducive to the greatest possible balance of good over evil everywhere. Some utilitarians (e.g., Jeremy Bentham and J. S. Mill) have been hedonists in their view of good being connected with the greatest happiness (pleasure) to the greatest number.

Ethical egoism, one of the teleological theories, holds that it is the duty of the individual to seek his own good. This stance has a great deal to say for itself; for if we regard the moral end as perfection, it is likely that we can do very little to achieve the perfection of anybody other than ourselves. A man may influence to some degree the activities of others, but he can *control* only his own activities. This is somewhat related to Kant's "duty ethics" whereby man is urged to seek his own perfection by being obligated to a rationally accepted principle or maxim. Self-perfection is the goal of a moral life.

The universal or social ethics of utilitarianism, on the other hand, holds that every person should seek the good of his group, community, nation—or world—as a whole. It claims, in a way, to combine the true elements of egoism and altruism—as the good of the group or community will include, of course, the agent's own good. Its appeal is that it sets no narrow limits on the range of moral obligations. One form of utilitarianism, the extreme *altruistic* stance, emphasizes the seeking of good of other individuals with no regard for the agent's own good; this is the stance of self-sacrifice, with the emphasis being entirely on *others*.

The social (utilitarian) ethical theory enthrones others—the group, collective or society generally—and sees the good as that which benefits the life of the group or the society. This is usually the ethics of collective altruism, and has been expressed generally in terms of the utilitarian principle that good conduct is that which results in the greatest good to the greatest number. There are two practical problems with this theory: (1) the problem of determining what is really good for most people, and (2) the problem posed by equating "good" with majority opinion or action. The journalist, for instance, in deciding whether or not to present a story, has no sound way of knowing which action will result in the greatest good to the greatest number of people. He can only guess—and hope. The second problem above leads the journalist to a kind of "give them what they want" ethical stance, abdicating personal commitment (and personal reason) for the social determinism of "vote-morality."

Deontological Theories

These theories are quite different from the teleological ones just discussed for they hold that something other than consequences determine which actions are morally right. Some deontologists say the important thing is the motive of the agent; Kant, for example, contends that an action is justified if the intentions of the doer are good, regardless of the consequences that might ensue from the action. A deontologist believes that producing the greatest possible happiness to the greatest possible number has nothing (or may have nothing) to do with the morality of the action. He also believes that personal satisfaction or gain is irrelevant to ethical action. He sees an action being right or obligatory simply because of some fact about it or because of its own nature.

Probably the best example of a deontologist is Immanuel Kant, and his basic principle or rule—the Categorical Imperative—lies at the base of his ethical system: "Act only on that maxim which you can at the same time will to be a universal law." Kant is here offering this "imperative" as the necessary principle for determining what more specific and concrete ethical rules we should adopt to guide our behavior. He is saying, in effect, that a person is acting ethically only if he is—or would be—willing to have everyone act on his maxim. Or, said another way, a person is acting ethically if he would be willing to see his rule applied by everyone who is in a similar situation.

If we ask "Which actions are right" we are really asking for some way to identify right actions. Utilitarians (teleologists) would reply: Those which maximize utility or which do the greatest service for the greatest number, or something like that. Kant and other deontologists would claim that those actions are right which pass the test of some personal and rationally accepted imperative. For Kant, for example, virtue has nothing to do with pleasure or with any other "consequences."

If consequences and states such as happiness are not important in determining ethical actions, then what is relevant must be something to do with basic maxims or principles. For the deontologists what is important is the principle from which the action has been performed; and the test applied to the maxim must be something independent of consequence. The Categorical Imperative is not really a specific maxim from which one acts—rather it is a principle or general rule which will allow a journalist (or anyone else) to test all maxims from which he acts. It is a kind of "super-maxim" which serves to guide thinking about specific rules to be applied in specific cases. If a journalist accepts the Categorical Imperative, then it is unnecessary for him to carry around in his head (or on a printed Code or Creed) specific rules or guidelines to follow. These he formulates on the basis of his "super-maxim" as the various occasions arise. If these guidelines for each case pass the test of the Categorical Imperative, then his action based on that "super-maxim" is ethically sound, and the journalist may be considered virtuous.

Although Kant's philosophy has profoundly influenced Western thought, it is obvious that at least among modern intellectuals his strict and absolutist "duty ethics" has lost considerable appeal and force. A kind of relativism or situationism is in ascendency, an ethics which has a great appeal to those who like to think of themselves as "rational." This new situationism is a kind of synthesis emerging from the clash of ethical legalism, on one hand, and ethical antinomianism on the other. It will be discussed in the following section.

The Appeal of Relativism

The ethics of "law," of "duty" and "absolute obligation" is a little strong for most thinkers. So this *legalistic* stance in ethical thinking has been confronted by its opposite: what has been called *antinomianism*. The rebel against Kantianism and other legalistic ethics has accepted what might actually be considered by some as a "non-ethics"—a completely open kind of morality which is against any rules. The antinomian has, in effect, tossed out all basic principles, precepts, codes, standards and laws which might guide his conduct. Just as the legalist tends toward absolutist or universal ethics, the antinomian tends toward anarchy or nihilism in ethics. He is against standards; he thinks he needs no *a priori* guidelines, directions or moral rules. He is satisfied to "play it by ear," making ethical judgments and decisions intuitively, spontaneously, emotionally, and often irrationally. He is a kind of Existentialist—or very closely related—in that he has great faith that personal, existential instincts will give the ethical direction needed.

The antinomian in journalism is usually found in the free-wheeling ranks of rebellious journalism where an anti-Establishment stance is considered healthy. The antinomian journalist affronts mainstream journalism, making his ethical decisions as he goes—almost subconsciously—about his daily activities. His ethical (or nonethical) system might be called "whim ethics," and his confrontation with mainstream journalism is not very potent or successful because it is weakened considerably by a lack of rational force.

From the clash of these two ethical "extremes"—legalism and antinomianism—a kind of synthesis has developed which has a potent impact on ethical thinking. It is usually known as *situation ethics*. Although it is related to code or legalistic ethics more closely than it is to antinomian ethics in most of its characteristics, it does synthesize certain strains of both orientations. Like code ethics, it is basically rational, and like antinomian ethics it is relativistic and is not tied securely to absolute principles. Situation ethics begins with traditional legalistic ethics but is willing to deviate from these basic principles when rationality and the situation call for it.

The journalistic situationist may well be the one who believes that he should tell the truth *as a basic principle*, or that he should not generally distort his story, but who will, after due consideration of the situation in which he finds himself, conclude that it is all right to distort *this particular story*, or even to lie. Do the circumstances in this case warrant a departure from basic—generally held—moral guidelines: this is the rational question which always confronts the situationist. He is one, then, who takes special situations into consideration in making his ethical decisions; he is a relativist to be sure, but a rational relativist, one who *thinks* before breaking a basic ethical rule.

One who subscribes to what may be called "Machiavellian ethics" is one type of situationist. Maurice Cranston has pointed out that Machiavelli believed that persons (statesmen, at least) should not allow their relationships with other states always to be governed by the same ethical scruples that govern their dealings with private persons. His ethics, however, were really absolutist, says Cranston; he accepted one true morality, but he believed the ruler should sometimes disregard it. As Machiavelli says in *The Prince*, the ruler "should not depart from what is morally right if he can observe it, but should know how to adopt what is bad when he is obliged to." Machiavelli does not contend that the bad is anything other than bad; he only contends that bad things are to be done only sparingly—and then only in a concealed manner, if possible.

Journalists like to point out Machiavellianism in others (especially in government officials), but they themselves very often operate under this variant of situation ethics. They usually contend they believe in absolutes (such as giving their audiences all the pertinent facts or not changing or distorting quotes from a source), yet they depart from these principles when they think that "in this special case" it is reasonable to do so. They normally talk about their belief in "letting the people know" but they determine innumerable exceptions to this principle—times when they will not (because of the circumstances of the special situation) let the people know. And, of course, they are not very interested in letting the people know that they are not knowing.

The press is much more interested, of course, in pointing out Machiavellian situationism in government officials. This is natural and it is very healthy for the press to do this, for certainly our government is filled with myriads of Machiavellian functionaries busy justifying to themselves (and sometimes to others) their departure from basic moral principles. It is interesting to note how closely members of the Nixon Administration—especially some of his closest "advisors"—followed Machiavellian situationism in rationalizing the many unethical practices connected with the Watergate Affair which got world-wide airing in 1973. Not only did these officials seem to know that what they had done was wrong or unethical, but they felt that it would be best if they kept these things secret. Certainly they were not inclined to reveal them until the press and the Congress (and the courts) forced their disclosure.

Very little has been written about journalistic ethics beyond certain repetitious phrases appearing in ''codes'' and ''creeds'' designed largely for framing and hanging as wall trappings. Perhaps one reason for this is that most editors, publishers, news directors and other journalists simply write the whole subject of ethics off as ''relative,'' giving little or no importance to absolute or universal journalistic principles. A newspaper friend put it succinctly recently when he said that he looked at ethics as ''just the individual journalist's way of doing things.'' Certainly a free journalist has the right to consider ethics in this way, but such a relativistic concept relegates ethics to a kind of ''nothingness limbo'' where anything any journalist does can be considered ethical. Or, said another way, what one journalist does can be considered just as ethical as what any other journalist does.

If we throw out absolute theories of ethics (exemplified by Kant), then a discussion of morality becomes merely a discussion of preferences, arbitrary choices, detached judgments—none of which establishes obligation. The statement ''this was the right journalistic decision'' means no more than ''I liked this decision''—just as one might say ''I liked the view of the ocean.'' One form of relativism in ethics contends that a journalistic practice in Context A may be quite good—ethical—while if practiced in Context B it might be bad or unethical. In other words, it would be all right to submit to government censorship without objection in the Soviet Union but not all right to submit to government censorship in the United States. Or, taking this further, it would be all right to submit to censorship in the United States ''under certain conditions'' but wrong to do this under other conditions. Circumstances dictate the ethics; contexts determine ''rightness'' or ''wrongness,'' say the relativists.

Often I have heard, for instance, that in Mexico journalists often accept bribes to supplement their meagre incomes; I am also informed that many journalists also work for a newspaper part-time and for some politician as a sort of private ''press agent''—therefore having a conflict of interest. And, I am told, that this is all right in Mexico—maybe not in the United States—but quite ''acceptable'' (therefore ethical?) in Mexico where the conditions are different. The relativist's position here is: If it's good in a particular society, it's good, and if it's bad, it's bad—there is really no objective or universal principle. Also I hear from Soviet journalists that close party-government control of what goes into the press and over the air-waves is quite ''ethical'' in the Soviet Union; it is not only ''all right'' that this happens—it is actually the best situation, the most moral.

The situationist positions mentioned above can be considered a part of ''subjectivist'' ethics for what one does in a certain situation is determined *subjectively* by the individual at the time when an ethical decision is demanded. The temper of the times has thrust the subjectivist into a dominant moral position—at least from the point of being in the majority. And for many persons today if the majority believe something ethical, then it is ethical. These are the days of the subjectivist— the relativist and situationist. These are the days when it is considered unenlightened to make a value judgment, to take a stand, to feel a sense of ''duty'' or have a commitment. These are the days of the person who believes one opinion is as good as another and that one man's moral standards are as good as his neighbor's.

These are the days of the "we-are-probably-both-right" school of thinking, the days of the tolerant men—the "adapters"—who feel no impulse to speak out loudly and clearly on moral standards.

Although the relativistic position is indeed intriguing due to its aura of individualism . . .I must reject it. In fact, at the risk of making a value judgment, I will even say that it is not really an ethical position at all; rather it is a "non-ethics" or an "anti-ethics." When the matter of ethics is watered down to subjectivism, to situations or contexts, it loses all meaning as ethics. If every case is different, if every situation demands a different standard, if there are no absolutes in ethics, then we should scrap the whole subject of moral philosophy and simply be satisfied that each person run his life by his whims or "considerations" which may change from situation to situation. . . .

Bibliography

Books dealing specifically with John Merrill's topic include his own *The Imperative of Freedom*, Hastings House, Publishers, 1974, from which this was reprinted, and his edited volume, with Ralph D. Barney, *Ethics and the Press*, Hastings House, Publishers, 1975. See also Richard L. Johannesen, *Ethics in Human Communication*, C. E. Merrill, 1975; and Lee Thayer, ed., *Communication: Ethical and Moral Issues*, Gordon and Breach, 1973. An article by John M. Harrison, "Media, Men and Morality," *The Review of Politics* (April 1974), pp. 250-264, cites several examples of media performance that Harrison feels violate "a loosely defined set of standards of fairness, decency and honor in human relationships—not a monolithic dogma, but a generally accepted body of principles." (p. 256)

Journalism and Criticism:
The Case of an Undeveloped Profession

By James W. Carey

Means of Criticism: Standards

It is a truism, albeit a contentious one, that in the United States there is no tradition of sustained, systematic, and intellectually sound criticism of the press. The press is certainly one of our most important institutions but in serious attention it ranks slightly ahead of soccer and slightly behind baseball. The press is attacked and often vilified, but it is not subject to sustained critical analysis—not in public, and rarely within universities or the press itself.

The task of this paper is to demonstrate that a tradition of press criticism does not exist in the United States, that a critical tradition is indispensable to the operation of democratic institutions, and that journalism criticism, properly conceived, is the criticism of language. . . .

Let us begin from this simple observation, contained implicitly at least, in everything that has been previously said: democracy is not only a form of politics; it

James W. Carey is Professor of Journalism at the University of Iowa. He has written extensively in the field of mass media criticism. This article appeared first in *The Review of Politics* (April 1974) and has been edited rather severely because of space limitations. Students wishing to see the full development of Dr. Carey's arguments should turn to the original publication. Reprinted with permission of *The Review of Politics*.

is a form of community. As perhaps our greatest theorist on these matters John Dewey argued, democracy is a form of associated life, of conjoint communicated experience. But he also argued, in *The Public and Its Problems*, that today all individuals find their interests and concerns conditioned by large impersonal organizations and consequently the possibility of community as well as ethical fulfillment is seriously compromised. Dewey insisted upon communication and public debate as the instrument of realizing society as a process of association, as a community. This process of criticism, of debate, became in his thought the means by which human experience can be expanded and tied together not only in the domain of politics but in all the domains of our experience.

One of the domains of experience shared by members of modern society is that experience of the media of communication, the newspapers particularly. And this is a domain about which there is little debate of significance out in the brightly lit arena where the public lives.

Let us now assume that all areas of experience, all institutions of modern society, must be subjected to criticism. This criticism must be based upon precise observation, clear procedure, unemotional language, subject to the cooperative correction of others, and occurring in the public forum where all affected by the institution can at least observe and comment on the critical process. Moreover, it must clarify our experience of the institution and scrutinize the values upon which the institution is based. The only things sacred in this process are the rules and procedures by which it is done and the manners necessary to make this a continuing process.

If we assume that the newspaper press is the most general forum in which this process can operate, let us look at an omnibus newspaper like the *New York Times*. In its pages, particularly the Sunday edition, one finds information, analysis, criticism of every contemporary institution. It treats art, architecture, literature, education, politics, business, religion, finance, film, and so forth. We need not discuss how well it treats these several institutions it covers. The record is, of course, quite uneven. But that aside, the fact remains that one institution is curiously exempt from analysis and criticism—the press itself. The *Times* does, of course, deal with books and devotes a daily and Sunday column to television. Aside from the quality and relevance of this, the *Times* is virtually silent about the newspaper: itself in particular, the medium in general. A rise in the wholesale price of newsprint will be reported, but that, we all know, is merely to signal an impending rise in the price of the newspaper itself. The newspaper does not, perhaps it cannot, turn upon itself the factual scrutiny, the critical acumen, the descriptive language, that it regularly devotes to other institutions. And one of the things readers are curious about, one of the things that is an important fact of their experience, one of the things they must understand if they are to critically know anything, is something critical about the newspaper itself.

There are a number of responses to this argument that must be anticipated. The first argument heard from many editors, namely, that "we are criticized all the time, that criticism of the press is abundant," simply will not wash. The critical literature in all the fields about which newspapers report, from art through education, to government and science, is enormous and often of quite high quality. For every first-class work of journalistic criticism there are a hundred exemplary works of literary criticism. There is, simply, no important critical literature concerning journalism and while the newspaper fosters such literature in every other field, it does not foster it in its own domain.

It is often argued that criticism of the press is found in the newspaper because the press reports the statements of its critics and in turn press professionals respond. But this is wholly inadequate. First, it is altogether too sporadic and undisciplined. . . . Moreover, it is usually opinions undisciplined on both sides by fact or substantial analysis, a kind of shouting match that usually talks by the point in question.

In making such responses the press often violates every standard of journalism. Journalists generally agree that dispassionate language and analysis, where affect is tightly controlled and information is maximized, are the appropriate mode of reasoned public discourse. But any criticism of the press or threat is treated as a matter of high drama. It calls forth new versions of Armageddon and the most stereotyped, bloated language imaginable. Norman Isaacs in the *Columbia Journalism Review:*

> The date was June 29, 1972—and while the countdown to 1984 stood at eleven years and six months, one had to reflect that George Orwell was, after all, author, not infallible seer. The Supreme Court of the United States, by five to four vote, ruled that the power of a grand jury took precedence over the heretofore presumed protection of the first amendment.

The problem here is in Mr. Isaacs' facts and tone. How can something be right—the sly inclusion of presumed almost saves it—that has never been recognized in common, constitutional or legislative law? Moreover, the lead violates every standard of argument known to journalism. He is talking about an important problem, but he brings to it deceptive high church rhetoric. . . . Rarely does the press respond in the language [it] expects from others, and all too often banners of constitutional rights and the people's right to know are used to paper over real difficulties.

Let me anticipate two more responses to the argument that the press is perhaps the least criticized of our important institutions. Editors often point to attempts on the part of some newspapers to create columns about the press or to create a new role within the newspaper, that of ombudsman. I applaud both of these gestures, look upon them as promising, and wish to say nothing that would discourage them. . . . Neither of these practices is completely sufficient. . . . .[Both suffer] from the same ailment of being within the newspaper, internal to it rather than outside of it . . . While [they] enlarge the critical compass, [they do] not create a sufficiently diverse forum for the critical examination of the newspaper. . . . .

A final defense against criticism is usually expressed as the belief that the public does not, and probably cannot, understand newspapers, and that independent critics, because they are not journalists, are not qualified to criticize the press. This is argument by mystification. When a university president rejects criticism directed against him and his institution because journalists are not academics and cannot hope to understand the university, the press quite properly points out that every institution attempts to protect itself by hiding behind special mysteries of the craft,

THE SAN FRANCISCO

BAY
GUARDIA

3. THE LARGEST CIRCULATION ALTERNATIVE NEWSPAPER WEST OF THE HUDSON. MAY 3 THROUGH MAY 16, 1975. VOL. 9 NO. 14.

C.I.A. DIARY

EXCERPTS FROM THE CIA-SUPPRESSED BOOK:
THE INCREDIBLE STORY OF PHILIP AGEE, EX-DIRTY TRICKS
OPERATIVE IN LATIN AMERICA. PAGE 17

BOOK SUPPLEMENT: INSIDE THE FICTION COLLECTIVE, THE RISE OF
WEST COAST PUBLISHING, THE FALL OF STRAIGHT ARROW BOOKS

GOVER
BRO
HAS HE O
IN HIS FIR

CH
FLI
AVE UP

THE SENSITIVE
OF BUDDY HA Page 23

THE MEDIA MAGAZINE

OCTOBER 1976

MorE

January 17, 1977 / $1.00

ewsw

Local Programs Dec. 6-12

TV
GUIDE

25¢

DOES
AMERICA
WANT

FAMILY
VIEWING
TIME?

**RESULTS OF
TV GUIDE'S
NATIONWIDE POLL**

EW YO

THE DAILY
plash

PRESS

New Yorker cover drawing by Saxon; © 1972, The New Yorker Magazine, Inc.

mysteries decipherable only by the initiated and that the mystery behind the mystery is that there is no mystery at all. Newspapers defend themselves against outside criticism in the same terms they properly reject when offered by the institutions they cover. . . .

I sometimes feel, and I do not wish to be overly argumentative here, that the press has been corrupted by its own influence. Since World War II we have witnessed a decline in the independent influence of character-forming, culture-bearing agencies such as religion, the family, the ethnic group and neighborhood. The Commission on Freedom of the Press recognized this, perhaps even encouraged it, and argued that the press itself would have to become an authoritative source of values, would have to, along with the schools, enter the vacuum left by the decline of older agencies of culture and character. The press has happily stepped into this vacuum not only for the profit it brings but also for the influence it yields. Journalists, particularly those drawn in from the arts and the "new journalists," have also sensed the new avenue to power and fame through the press. But as the press has become more important, as it has become more professional, as it has become the spokesman for the community, it has also become more remote from community life. And whenever there is remoteness of an institution, a critical community grows to mediate between that institution and the community itself.

The emergence of a critical community should not be resisted by the press: it should be encouraged. . . . The criticism of the press in America, as sporadic, as inadequate, as ill-intended as it often is, is a tribute to the importance of the press in American life, an importance felt not only by government officials but by the community generally. The proper response is not a retreat behind slogans and defensive postures but the encouragement of an active and critical tradition and an important body of professional critics. . . .

But how does a newspaper connect with its community? The most generally accepted method of connection is through the roles of the representative and spectator. Here the newspaper is the eyes and ears of the audience; it goes where the reader cannot go, so that the newspaper is representing the audience at city hall because the audience as an assembled community, a public, cannot be present. It is in this vein that the newspaper takes itself to be representing the public, or more fashionably these days, the people. . . .

In fact, I think it is not a system of representation at all. The reporter at city hall less represents his audience than he represents his profession in both its commercial and literary aspects. . . . The newspaper becomes effectively responsible to itself: to its own professional standards and to its own commercial needs. In the process it loses contact with its audience [which], like the spectator at the construction of a new building grotesquely marring a community, [is] asked to bow to the standards of the professionals constructing the building when those standards are not even explained let alone defended.

A second and more desirable method of connection is through criticism; that is, through the creation of an ongoing process of judgment that sets standards for the production, distribution and consumption of journalism, and in which the community participates in significant ways. There are, at the moment, three modes of criticism: two of them are inadequate and it is to the third that I wish to pay major attention.

The first form of criticism is what we might call criticism by standards of public or social responsibility. This is the form of criticism that we have largely talked about up to this point. It involves the discussion of freedom, rights and objectivity. As a critical process it largely involves various government officials and members of the press who have, at this point, largely succeeded in talking by one another and the public. The weakness of this situation has led to the recommendation for national and local press councils to be the vehicle of assessment of social responsibility.

Are such institutions the answer? I think not. In the United States national press councils are likely to be presided over by blue-ribbon panels though run by a professional staff. That is, the blue-ribbon panel is selected so as to represent the community under the theory that the press itself does not and cannot adequately represent the public interest. This interest also cannot be represented by government. . . . The operation of these councils is likely to be invested in the hands of professional staffs and the blue-ribbon panel is likely to be remote from their everyday operation. . . . In the United States press councils are likely to become one more bureaucracy.

What about local press councils? Perhaps they will work, but I am not sanguine for the reasons announced above. The people who are expected to participate in the details and time-consuming work of such councils—participation absolutely necessary if they are not to become bureaucratized—are already riddled by over-participation. This crisis in participation has already defeated some of the best elements of the public and does not augur well for local councils.

A second critical tradition to connect the public with the media is that proposed by the social scientists and might be called scientistic criticism. Here the standards for judging the press are not abstract rights, or codes of press performances or press council evaluations of responsibility—all things on which social scientists are rather quiet—but standards derived from scientific studies of the impact of the media upon audiences. The prototype here is the national commissions on violence and pornography where the fitness, rightness, and suitability of the material are judged not by intrinsic merit or abstract rights but by the effect the material has on audience attitudes and behavior. This standard of criticism is simply wrongheaded. Its disastrous results already can be seen in the report of the Commission on Obscenity and Pornography, for the social scientific standards are in a general way destructive of culture. The questions permit no consideration of the quality, truth, or reasonableness of material, and it is obvious that any criticism of the press cannot merely test audience reactions—this would enshrine public opinion into an even more unbearable niche than it now occupies—but must work toward autonomous standards in which the audience participates but which does not allow the mere criterion of audience appetite to dictate the cultural terms of journalism.

A third tradition of criticism can be termed cultural criticism and defined, first of all, by what it excludes. Cultural criticism is not debate over abstract shibboleths such as the people's right to know, problems of access, protection of reporters'

sources or standards of press performance derived from abstract canons. As much
as these items may occasionally enter the critical tradition, they do not constitute
such a tradition in any significant measure. By cultural criticism I mean an ongoing
process of exchange, of debate between the press and its audience and, in particular,
those among the audience most qualified by reason of motive and capacity to enter
the critical arena. But what is the substance of this criticism, toward what is it
directed? Earlier on I argued that a democratic tradition of criticism required at least
three things: a set of procedures for indicating how we observe what we observe, a
language relatively neutral in terms of affect or emotional coloring, and a forum in
which an active response can be made to the procedures of observation and the
language of description. In addition I indicated certain habits of mind were necessary: a desire to take account of contrary findings, to correct errors and revise
postulates. These are the terms and manners of press criticism at the highest level of
development and also the form and character of criticism that are in the shortest
supply.

I am arguing that press criticism is essentially the criticism of language: it is a
vital response on the part of the public to the language the press uses to describe
events and to the events that accepted standards of journalistic language allow to be
described. It is fully analogous to literary criticism or criticism of any cultural
object: an assessment of the adequacy of the methods men use to observe the world,
the language they use to describe the world, and the kind of world that such methods
and language imply is in existence. It requires therefore close public attention to the
methods, procedures and techniques of journalistic investigation and the language
of journalistic reporting. Moreover, this scrutiny must occur before the same audience that every day consumes the end product of these procedures and language.
This is the basic critical act in journalism, or so I take it, but I take it also to be the
case that little criticism of this kind is in existence and that which is in existence—
found largely in the reviews—rarely reaches the public.

It is a remarkable fact that each year most of us read more words by a reporter
such as Homer Bigart of the *New York Times* than we do of Plato and yet today
2500 years after Plato wrote there is more critical work published on Plato every
year than there is on Bigart. In fact, there is nothing published on Bigart, here used
as an archetypal reporter, yet what he writes provides the critical diet for a major
segment of the national "elite" community. I myself have read more words by
James Reston than perhaps any other human, living or dead, yet I have never seen
this work "reviewed" or criticized except when a few pieces are collected in book
form and then the review is inevitably by a comrade in the press. It is an anomalous
fact that all of us consume more words by journalists than any other group and yet
our largest and perhaps most important literary diet is never given close critical
scrutiny in any systematic way. In universities we critically review the work of men
in every field, devoting thousands of hours to the perceptions, methods and style of
obscure 18th-century Romantic poets, yet never consider that journalists, who daily
inform our lives, require, for their good and ours, at least the same critical attention.
In journalism schools, preoccupied as they are with teaching the givens of the craft
plus the academic asides in press history and law, critical attention is rarely given to

journalistic procedure or writing or the major figures whose work exemplifies the strengths and limitations of journalism practice. Moreover, unlike other professions, journalists rarely gather to critically review one another's work, to expose its weaknesses, errors of commission and omission, and its failure to live up to professional let alone public standards. Let me make the judgment general: journalists, of all groups who expose their work to the public, are less critically examined by professional critics, the public or their colleagues. At journalistic gatherings professionals do not critique one another's work; they give one another awards.

Why should this be true? There are a number of reasons deriving from the nature of journalism but a fundamental reason is that journalism is rarely thought of as a literary act, parallel with the novel, the essay and the scientific report. However, journalism is, before it is a business, an institution or a set of rights, a body of literature. Like all literature journalism is a creative and imaginative work, a symbolic strategy; journalism sizes up situations, names their elements and names them in a way that contains an attitude toward them. Journalism provides what Kenneth Burke calls strategies for situations—"strategies for selecting enemies and allies, for socializing losses, for warding off evil eye, for purification, propitiation and desanctification, consolation, and vengeance, admonition and exhortation, implicit commands or instructions of one sort or another." Journalism provides audiences with models for action and feeling, with ways to size up situations. It shares these qualities with all literary acts and therefore like all literary acts must be kept under constant critical examination for the manner, method and purpose whereby it carries out these actions.

Journalism is not only literary art; it is industrial art. The inverted pyramid, the 5 W's lead, and associated techniques are as much a product of industrialization as tin cans. The methods, procedures and canons of journalism were developed not only to satisfy the demands of the profession but to meet the needs of industry to turn out a mass-produced commodity. These canons are enshrined in the profession as rules of news selection, judgment, and writing. Yet they are more than mere rules of communication. They are, like the methods of the novelists, determiners of what can be written and in what way. In this sense the techniques of journalism define what is considered to be real: what can be written about and how it can be understood. From the standpoint of the audience the techniques of journalism determine what the audience can think—the range of what is taken to be real on a given day. If something happens that cannot be packaged by the industrial formula, then, in a fundamental sense, it has not happened, it cannot be brought to the attention of the audience. If something happens that is only rendered in distorted fashion by the canons of journalism, then it is rendered in such distorted fashion, often without correction.

Now I am overstating the case to give a deliberate emphasis. We do not think of the conventions of journalistic investigation and reporting as stylistic strategies which not only report the world but bring a certain kind of world into existence. These canons, as I think I could demonstrate if space allowed, were derived from 19th century utilitarianism and today reflect a basically utilitarian-scientific-capitalistic orientation toward events. The conventions of journalism implicitly dissect events from a particular point of view. It is a point of view that emphasizes, as one would expect from utilitarianism, the role of personalities or actors in the creation of events and ties the definition of news to timeliness. What these conventions lack, to engage in a little criticism of my own, are precisely those elements of news which constitute the basic information on which popular rule rests: historical background and continuity, the motives and purposes of political actors, and the impact of technology, demographic change and other impersonal forces which contribute so much to the shape of contemporary events.

We must, in short, devote continuous critical attention to the methods and conventions of journalism for these methods and conventions order the world we live in into a comprehensible or baffling whole. Many of the conventions in which journalism is rooted—the inverted pryamid style, the obsessive reliance on the interview as a method of observation—are products of the 19th century and their contemporary existence implies a silent conspiracy between journalists and audiences to keep the doors of the house locked tight even though all the windows have blown out. What we lamely call the conventions of journalism were developed for another time and place. They were designed to report an orderly world of politics, international alignments, class structure and culture. Such conventions reflected and enhanced this order and fleshed out with incidental information an already settled mode of life. Human interest, entertainment, trivia, political events could be rendered in a straightforward 5 W's manner for they occurred within a setting of secure meanings and structures. Today the structure is not set and the meanings are not firm. Politics, culture, classes, generations, and international alignments are not at all orderly, yet we still filter them through conventional glasses which reduce them to type, which exorcise the realities of the world through conventional stylistics and conventional names. Indeed, this is what is meant by the now occasionally heard epithet that ''communications is a menace.''

Let me give three examples of the way in which journalism as a stylistic strategy renders a disservice to its audience. The examples are not new or unusual; in fact, they are well known. The first case is the reporting on Viet Nam. Allow me an extended quote from an essay I wrote in 1967:

> How does one render the reality that is Viet Nam in intelligible terms? The question is not merely rhetorical, for increasingly the ability of the American people to order and enhance their existence depends on their ability to know what really is going on. But we have this great arrogance about ''communications.'' We treat problems of understanding as exercises in message transmittal. So here we sit shrouded in plastic, film, magnetic tape, photographs and lines of type thinking that two minutes of film or four column inches of canned type adequately render what is happening in Viet Nam or for that matter anywhere else. In point of fact, the conventions of broadcast and newspaper journalism are just about completely inadequate to ''tell'' this story. I am not merely caviling about turning the war into an elaborate accounting exercise of hills, tonnage and dead (after all, that is the only measure of hope and progress one has in such a war). But why is this after all a war of accounting exercises? What are the political realities that underscore the day to day events? They are known—dimly of course—and can be found in the pages of more esoteric journals of opinion and in a half hour conversation

with a war correspondent when he is not talking through an inverted pyramid. But this is not a war that affects elites alone nor is it a time when we can all spend after hours with exhausted correspondents. What is sinful is that what is known about the war, and, what is the same thing, the stylistics that can render this knowledge rarely make their way to the television screen or the newspapers. There the conventions of the craft reduce what is a hurly-burly, disorganized, fluid, non-rectilinear war into something that is straight, balanced, and moving in rectilinear ways. The conventions not only report the war but they endow it, *pari passu*, with an order and logic—an order and logic which simply mask the underlying realities. Consequently, for opponents and advocates of the war, as well as those betwixt and between, the war haunts consciousness like a personal neurosis rather than a reality to be understood.

. . . Viet Nam might have been a story but it is not like one of those we read in our youth.

Second, American journalism is still absurdly tied to events and personalities. American journalists are, in general, at a loss for what to do on the days when there isn't any news breaking. We have not learned how to report to the underlife of the country, how to get at the subterranean and frequently glacial movements that provide the meaningful substructure which determines the eruption of events and the emergence of personalities that we now call news. We still do not know how to bring to life the significance of the invisible: a slow shift in Black migration patterns out of the South, the relation between grain sales to the Soviet Union and grain elevators failing in small Illinois towns, the significance of the reduction of the birthrate and the strains created by radically unequal age cohorts, the relatively rapid embourgeoisment of Blacks—all these "events" which, because they are not tied to personalities or timeliness, escape daily journalism yet constitute the crucial stories determining the American future.

A third example I draw from a colleague, Howard Ziff. The conventions of journalism have led to an increased distance between "the Press and the pace and detail of everyday life." The ordinary events of everyday lives—things which in their meaning and consequence are far from ordinary and insignificant for the audience—have no place in daily journalism. We lack the techniques of investigation and the methods of writing to tell what it feels like to be a Black, or a Pole, or a woman—or, God forbid, a journalist or professor today. This mainstream of overwhelming significant ordinary life—what a literary critic would call the "felt quality" of life—is a main connection between the newspaper and its audience, yet we do not know how to report it well. As a result the newspaper reports a world which increasingly does not connect with the life of its audience in the most fundamental sense that the audience experiences life.

The basic critical act in journalism is public scrutiny of the methods by which journalists define and get what we call news and the conventions by which they deliver it to the public. This criticism must not only be sustained and systematic, as with literary criticism, but it must also occur in the pages of the newspaper itself, in front of the audience that regularly consumes, uses or digests what is presented. Who should do it? In a certain sense, everyone. I have suggested that the newspaper itself must bring this critical community into existence. It must search out and find within its public those laymen that can and are interested in making a critical response to what they see and read daily. Hopefully such people will come from all strata of the public and represent its major segments. But such a community will not come into existence if the press passively awaits its appearance. The press must recognize that it has a stake in the creation of a critical community and then use its resources to foster it. For it is only through criticism that news and the newspaper can meet the standard set out for it by Robert Park: "The function of news is to orient man and society in an actual world. Insofar as it succeeds it tends to preserve the sanity of the individual and the permanence of society."

Bibliography

James Carey's article suggests the need for a type of media criticism that has not been practiced widely or well in the U.S. Two individuals stand out in their consistent pattern of media criticism, of a type suggested by Carey. One is Ben Bagdikian, national correspondent of *Columbia Journalism Review*. The other is Edward Jay Epstein. Both have written extensively, both books and articles. Bagdikian's *The Effete Conspiracy and Other Crimes by the Press*, Harper & Row, Publishers, 1972, reprints 15 of his articles and short reports. They are well worth reading. Epstein seems, in many ways, to be one of the more perceptive critics today. His range of analysis is exhibited in *Between Fact and Fiction: The Problem of Journalism*, Vintage Books, October 1975, which reprints many of his articles, most of which have appeared in *The New Yorker* and *Commentary*. His "Journalism and Truth," *Commentary* (April 1974), pp. 36-40, is a very careful analysis of the limitations of present methods of gathering and presenting news. It is reprinted as the lead article in *Between Fact and Fiction*. For a survey of media criticism, see Lee Brown, *The Reluctant Reformation: On Criticizing the Press in America*, David McKay Co., Inc., 1974. For a different approach to media criticism, see Loren Ghiglione, *Evaluating the Press: The New England Daily Newspaper Survey*, copyright 1973 by Ghiglione, and William Rivers, *et al.*, *A Region's Press*, University of California, Institute of Governmental Studies, 1971, which analyzes the newspapers of the San Francisco Bay region. Several writers discuss the role of educators in actively assessing media performance in Herbert Strentz, *et al.*, *The Critical Factor: Criticism of the News Media in Journalism Education*, Journalism Monograph No. 32, University of Minnesota School of Journalism, 1974. See especially the chapter "Criticism of the Media, With the Media," David L. Anderson and Loren Ghiglione. For an interesting, critical view of American journalistic practices under First Amendment protection, see Leopold Tyrmand, "The Media Shangri-La," *The American Scholar* (Winter 1975/76), pp. 752-775.

The role of journalism reviews is discussed briefly in Carey's article. For further information consult Marty Coren, "The Perils of Publishing Journalism Reviews," *Columbia Journalism Review* (November/December 1972), which was reprinted in the second edition of this book. Coren outlines the difficulties in producing journalism reviews; events occurring since the publication of our second edition bear out his pessimistic conclusions. The *Chicago Journalism Review*, one of the standard bearers in the field, folded in 1975; *The Unsatisfied Man* (Denver) collapsed in 1974. The loss of *CJR* was a particular blow because of the importance of Chicago as a media center. One of the trends in this field, aside from the tendency toward smaller numbers, is the movement toward journalism reviews produced by or in conjunction with departments of journalism. This has been particularly noticeable on the West Coast where the *Review of Southern California Journalism*, published by the campus chapter of the Society of Professional journalists, Sigma Delta Chi at California State University, Long Beach, started the trend. Unfortunately, it also died, in 1976. Following its inception, the department of journalism at San Francisco State University established *feed/back*, the School of Communications at the University of Washington established *NW Review*, and the Department of Journalism, University of Arizona, established *The Pretentious Idea*. The issues of "reporter power" and media ombudsmen have been deemphasized somewhat in recent years. Reporting on the national and world-wide condition of reporter power is Harry L. Connor, *Democracy in the Newsroom*, Freedom of Information Center, Report No. 328 (October 1974). For a brief discussion of the role of the ombudsman, see John Maxwell Hamilton, "Ombudsman for the Press," *The Nation* (March 16, 1974), pp. 335-338.

NNC Statement on Media Ethics

Press Councils

The following "Statement on General Ethics" was approved by the National News Council on December 10, 1974, at a meeting of the Council in Boston, Mass. Prepared by Norman E. Isaacs, Council Adviser, the statement was presented to the Council by the Council's Freedom of the Press Committee.

The issue of "full disclosure of association" by syndicated columnists has escalated strongly since the National News Council held that the National Conference of Editorial Writers was quite correct in objecting to Victor Lasky and the North American Newspaper Alliance not making clear to editors being serviced with the column that he had received a $20,000 fee from the Committee to Re-Elect the President.

Although no new formal complaints have as yet been filed, the National News Council has figured in editorial comment and in tart correspondence in three other cases.

Two of the episodes have focused on columns written by Tom Braden (Los Angeles Times Syndicate) and William Buckley (Washington Star-News Syndicate), both defending Vice President-designate Nelson Rockefeller in the matter of gifts, loans and other payments made by him, or in his behalf. The third has been a controversy prompted by a letter from the president of the National Conference of Editorial Writers to Publishers-Hall Syndicate over a trip made to the Peoples Republic of China by columnist Ann Landers as a delegate of the American Medical Association.

In a column defending Mr. Rockefeller's gifts, Mr. Braden failed to state that he had sought and received a $100,000 loan from the former New York Governor. Mr. Braden's friendship with Mr. Rockefeller was of long standing, the loan was repaid with interest and the record on the transaction is clear and clean.

The Des Moines Register & Tribune made the essential point that while the column appeared to be the viewpoint of a disinterested observer, it was "instead, the sentiments (of) a man who was himself a beneficiary of Rockefeller's generosity."

The issue was identical in the episode of Mr. Buckley's column, which devoted itself to commentary about the book written by Victor Lasky about Arthur Goldberg and financed by Laurance Rockefeller to assist his brother's campaign.

This statement and the two case studies which follow have been reprinted from official findings of the National News Council.

Mr. Buckley was not aware of all the nuances when he wrote his column, but certainly he was cognizant of the fact that the publisher of the book, Arlington House, is a subsidiary of Starr Broadcasting, Inc., of which he (Mr. Buckley) is chairman. In his column, however, Mr. Buckley saw fit only to describe Arlington House as a conservatively oriented publishing firm and that the editor "happens to be a good friend of mine."

After the matter had been publicized, Mr. Buckley acknowledged the point candidly and said in one of his regular columns that on any such future issues, he would notify editors of any possible conflicts.

The dispute surrounding Ms. Landers' trip to China was different in that it raised the issue of financing of a trip by an outside organization as well as whether ample disclosure had been made. Both Ms. Landers and the syndicate insist that the disclosure was clear. Some editorial writers hold that it was not. That the confusion exists at all indicates some lack of clarity. More important in this issue is the financing. Where do news organizations draw the line on journalists serving as delegates for outside organizations? It is obviously a matter deserving far more thought and consideration than American news organizations have seen fit to give it.

The year 1974 has been one of breakthrough in the long battle waged within journalism for higher ethical standards. The National News Council has played a vital part in this growing movement, if it is not indeed the fulcrum of the central drive for a more responsible journalism. Hence the Council cannot but approve the spirit which has brought a determined "patrolling of the precincts" by various national news organizations, including the American Society of Newspaper Editors, the Associated Press Managing Editors Association, the Society of Professional Journalists/Sigma Delta Chi, the National Conference of Editorial Writers, and those organizations representing photographers and business and food writers.

Many editors hold that the national syndicates have been remiss in not imposing and maintaining strong standards. The syndicates have a rational defense in that they are primarily service agencies selling and distributing the work of independent producers. However, the News Council is impelled to remind both the independent writers and artists and the syndicates that awkwardness for them is certain to grow unless there comes a general recognition that all communicators are under the obvious obligation to live under the same standards they demand of those who hold public office.

It is the Council's view that every journalist should either refrain from commenting upon matters in which he or she has a familial or financial interest or make those interests so clear there can be no misunderstanding.

Twenty-seven years ago, the Commission on Freedom of the Press issued its report on mass communication. In that report was this brief passage:

> "Freedom of the press can only continue as an accountable freedom. Its moral right will be conditioned on its acceptance of this accountability. Its legal right will stand unchallenged as its moral duty is performed."

The National News Council subscribes to that concept. It is the Council's considered view that American journalism faces the immediate responsibility of moving with all the means at its command to accept the principle of full accountability in ALL of its functions.

COMPLAINT NO. 46   (Filed September 7, 1974)   **Case Study I**
ACCURACY IN MEDIA
      against
JACK ANDERSON

Nature of Complaint: Accuracy in Media complained of Jack Anderson column (United Features Syndicate) published in *New York Post* on August 3, 1974, and in many other newspapers on or about that date.

      The column asserted that "students at the International Police Academy, a school run by the State Department to train foreign policemen, have developed some chilling views about torture tactics." In support of this statement it quoted from papers written by five students at the Academy—two from South Vietnam, one from Nepal, one from Colombia and one from Zaire. AIM asserted that the quotations were taken out of context, and misrepresented the attitudes of the students in question on the subject of torture. Mr. Anderson and his associate, Joseph C. Spear, denied this.

      Members of the Council staff visited Washington and examined the five papers in full and in detail. They found that the quotations by Anderson did in fact misrepresent the attitudes of the students toward torture as set forth in their papers. In addition, they found that all five papers were written in the years 1965-1967, a fact not mentioned in the Anderson column (which gave the impression that they were reasonably contemporary).

Response of News Organization: In a letter dated December 30, 1974, Mr. Anderson insisted that the statements in his column were supported by sources whose identity he could not reveal, and suggested that members of the Council staff "spend a couple of months talking to Amnesty International and the National Council of Churches," as well as with Sen. James Abourezk and unnamed members of his staff—all of whom, it was suggested, would support Anderson's charges.

Conclusion of the Council: If such support as was alleged by Mr. Anderson exists, it is up to him, not this Council, to develop and publish it. AIM's complaint alleged simply that the five quotations set forth and relied on in the original Anderson column misrepresented the views of the writers; and the complaint is quite correct.

      Nor can Mr. Anderson escape responsibility for the misrepresentations by pointing to the second sentence of his column, which stated, "After a lengthy investigation, we found no evidence that the academy actually advocates third-degree methods." In the first place, exculpating the academy itself does not excuse leaving a false implication with respect to the views of the five named students. In the second place, the sentence was simply inconsistent with the general thrust of the column, which Mr. Anderson's own syndicate titled "The Torture Graduates."

In the circumstances, we believe the complaint is justified.

Concurring, COONEY, DILLIARD, FULD, McKAY, OTWELL and RUSHER.

Dated: February 4, 1975

Note: Since adoption of the above conclusion, the Council has learned that the title to the article as prepared by Mr. Anderson's syndicate, was "U.S. Trained Foreign Cops Prefer To Stick To Torture." The title "The Torture Graduates" was placed on the column by the *New York Post*. The Council's conclusion is accordingly amended to reflect these facts. Approved by the full Council at its April 8, 1975 meeting.

Case Study II   **COMPLAINT NO. 47**   (Filed November 11, 1974)

HAYDON

against

NBC-TV

Nature of Complaint: John Haydon, former governor of American Samoa, complained that an NBC-TV "Weekend" program was inaccurate and "designed deliberately to malign the Samoan people, the administration of the territory, the Department of Interior."

The program was telecast on NBC-TV on October 19, 1974. The particular segment complained about was approximately twelve minutes in length. In his complaint, the complainant pointed out that the NBC crew spent several weeks in American Samoa filming material.

The complainant submitted his own lengthy analysis of the "Weekend" transcript, concluding with the statement:

> The film is viciously slanted and untrue. Its consistent and deliberate use of erroneous material makes it appear obvious that the producer and NBC came to American Samoa to make a film that would be controversial and would serve to give their new "Weekend" series a good kickoff. . . .

Response of News Organization: The Council held a public hearing on February 3, 1975, at which expert testimony was taken from Dr. Margaret Mead and Mr. M. G. Bales, a retired official with the Department of Interior's Office of Territorial affairs.

NBC News responded to the Council's inquiry and to the invitation to participate in the public hearing with the following statement:

> NBC will not have a representative at the hearing. As Mr. Richard Wald stated in his letter of November 14, 1974 to Mr. William B. Arthur, NBC News is interested in maintaining standards of fairness and objectivity; but NBC News does not believe that any purpose is served by debating comments such as those made by Mr. Haydon except before the Federal Communications Commission, to which NBC, as a licensee is accountable.
>
> NBC has cooperated with the Council in providing transcripts of the "Weekend" program involved in the Haydon complaint and in arranging for a viewing of a tape of the program.

In view of NBC's refusal to participate in the Council's investigation, the staff consulted with additional experts. These included:

John M. Flanigan, an educator in the school system of American Samoa for six and a half years.

Robert F. Williams, a television teacher in American Samoa who served also as Director of Education for a period during his stay of six years in American Samoa.

Lyle M. Nelson, an educator, presently Chairman of the Department of Communication at Stanford University, who has been associated with the Samoan educational system for almost ten years.

Judge Joseph W. Goss, an administrative judge who served in American Samoa with the High Court during the administration of Governor Haydon.

William Wohlfeld, who served as Special Assistant to Governor Haydon during his first year in American Samoa and who acquired particular familiarity with American Samoa while employed in the Department of Interior's Office of Territorial Affairs, the Department of State, the Bureau of the Budget, and various fiscal policy and management offices.

John R. Dial, who served as comptroller in American Samoa for two and one-half years, eight months under Governor Aspinall and the remainder under Governor Haydon.

Carl Mussen, who served as the Treasurer of American Samoa for six years, the first year under Governor Aspinall and the remainder under Governor Haydon.

Melvin Ember, Professor of Anthropology at Hunter College and Executive Officer of the Ph.D program in Anthropology at the Graduate School and University Center of the City University of New York.

Dan Klugherz, producer of the 1967 television documentary entitled "American Samoa: Paradise Lost?"

A. P. Lutale, the present Washington delegate-at-large from American Samoa.

In addition, the Council examined a study of instructional television in American Samoa by Wilbur Schramm of the Institute of Communication Research, Stanford University; reports of various hearings before the Subcommittee on Territorial and Insular Affairs of the House of Representatives; and newspaper articles which appeared in *The New York Times* and the *Los Angeles Times*.

Conclusion of the Council: The Council first viewed the television program complained of, then received the oral testimony of two witnesses: the distinguished and well-known anthropologist, Dr. Margaret Mead, and Mr. M. G. Bales, a government official who served in American Samoa under Governor Rex Lee, and thereafter in the Department of Interior until his retirement in 1973, visiting Samoa about twice a year. The staff also interviewed a number of other experts who offered additional views on various points. It is upon the Council's evaluation of this extensive record that this opinion is based.

In Mobil against ABC, the Council held that a television producer is not required, in producing a documentary, to meet the test of absolute fairness. Under the principles of free speech, the Council believes he is entitled to very considerable latitude in determining which facts he will stress and which he will play down or totally ignore. The result may not—indeed, probably will not—be altogether "fair," balanced or dispassionate, but the disadvantages of what is often described as robust journalism are surely preferable to any attempt—certainly by this Council—to suggest a standard that is probably unattainable in any case. We must, and do, have confidence that a free inter-play of biased views is likelier to produce effective guidance than a determined effort to compel adherence to a highly hypothetical "objectivity."

But while great latitude must be accorded to television producers in the case of any given documentary, that is not to say that there is not, or ought not to be, a limit to the degree of distortion and misrepresentation that a producer can indulge in. We believe that the NBC documentary on Samoa clearly exceeds that limit.

One of the most egregious single instances of misrepresentation in the documentary is its comparison of American Samoa with (formerly British) Western Samoa. The latter has ten times the area, and is capable (as American Samoa is not, and may never be) of sustaining itself economically. Political and economic solutions perfectly suited to Western Samoa are simply not applicable to American Samoa, according to expert after expert, and the documentary's clear implication to the contrary is seriously misleading.

But it is not the comparability (or otherwise) of Western Samoa, or any other single assertion in the documentary, that has led us to our conclusion. It is the over-all effect of a series of distortions and misrepresentations in the production, writing and editing, effectively contradicted by impressive witnesses in whom the Council has confidence.

We do not find or imply that Governor Haydon's administration of Samoa, or the entire American presence there, has been beneficial—or other-wise. There are clearly various opinions on both questions. Nor do we pass on Governor Haydon's charge that misrepresentations and distortions were delib-erate: that is unclear, and its determination is in any case, unnecessary. But we do find, on the basis of the detailed testimony of Dr. Mead and Mr. Bales, that the aforesaid distortions and misrepresentations go well beyond any that could be justified under the rubric of robust journalism, and to that extent we find the complaint warranted.

Concurring, COONEY, DILLIARD, FULD, GHIGLIONE, HEIGHT, IVINS, OTWELL, RENICK, RUSHER and STRAUS.

Abstentions: BRADY.
Dated: April 8, 1975

Bibliography

In the Public Interest, The National News Council, Inc., 1975, is a report by the NNC containing a summary of all of the Council's decisions from 1973-1975 as well as numerous special studies and reports. Appendix A lists all complaints and conclusions. See *A Free and Responsive Press: The Twentieth Century Fund Task Force Report for a National News Council*, 1972 for the rationale behind the establishment of the NNC. This report also contains studies of the Minnesota and Hawaii state news councils as well as a summary of local press councils in the U.S. A more complete report of local press council experiments in America can be found in William Rivers, *et al.*, *Backtalk: Press Councils in America*, Canfield, 1972. A recent account can be found in Robert Koenig, *Community Press Councils—II*, Freedom of Information Center, Report No. 331 (November 1974). While the news council or press council concept has met with general acceptance in the U.S. (in November 1975 the Society of Professional Journalists, Sigma Delta Chi passed a resolution supporting the concept of a National News Council without endorsing all of its specific procedures or the actions), many people, professionals and scholars, have argued against it. The *New York Times* has refused to cooperate in any way. The most articulate criticism has been that of Ralph L. Lowenstein of the School of Journalism, University of Missouri. Lowenstein, in two Opinion papers issued by the Freedom of Information Center, has attacked the council concept (in *The Case Against a Press Council*, 008 [December 1969]) and the council's performance (in *National News Council Appraised*, 0015 [December 1974]). For the council's rebuttal to his second report, see *NNC Appraises An Appraisal*, 0017 [May 1975]).

3 Relevance of Reporting Practices

The Lessons of Watergate

How *The Washington Post* Gave Nixon Hell—

Investigative Reporting: Is It Getting Too Sexy?—

New Journalism/Consumer Reporting

The New Journalism: How It Came To Be—

Is TV Ready for Consumer Reporting?—

How 'The Washington Post' Gave Nixon Hell

By Aaron Latham

The men Bob Woodward was after had worked burglar's hours, and if he was going to catch them he would have to work burglar's hours, too. Sometime after midnight, the reporter would leave the newsroom on the fifth floor of the *Washington Post* building and ride the elevator down to ground level. He would get in his car and drive through the empty Washington streets. The streets were deserted because the residents of the nation's capital were afraid of getting mugged. The Nixon Administration had promised to do something about crime in Washington, but it seemed simply to have added more crime of its own.

Woodward would arrive at a dark garage and park outside. He would go inside the echoing building, where he would walk down ramp after ramp, deeper and deeper into a subterranean world which seemed like a metaphor for the twisting, convoluted, shadowy plots he was uncovering.

Two stories beneath ground level, Woodward says, a man would appear out of the shadows. The reporter and his wary informant would huddle between empty cars and talk about political espionage. The stories which the reporter would later write would in a literal sense be Notes from the Underground.

Woodward would climb back up out of the ground and drive back to *The Post*, passing near the White House. He would find Carl Bernstein waiting in the newsroom, anxious to learn what he had found out. The two reporters had worked together on the Watergate story from the beginning. They were both young— Woodward 30, Bernstein 29—and neither had been in the newspaper business very long. And yet it was they against the entire White House propaganda ministry. What happened was as unlikely as if the Hardy Boys had begun snooping into a burglary and ended up shaking the President and the Presidency. They helped force Richard Nixon, who went on television twenty years ago to announce that he was not going to give up his dog Checkers, to go on television [one] week and say that he *was* going to give up Haldeman, Ehrlichman, Kleindienst and spaniel-like Dean.

But, best of all, Woodward and Bernstein forced a personal apology from the Administration and from White House press secretary Ron Ziegler, who had been accusing *The Post* of "shabby journalism" and "character assassination" since [October, 1972]. Such sublime vindication was not always forthcoming even for the Hardy Boys.

The White House is not the only institution that has been tormented by the two young reporters who are known around the newsroom as "the kids": *The New York Times* has been rocked by them, too. One night a few weeks ago, word was passed in *The Time's* New York newsroom to open for an extraordinary eight-column head.

Reporters asked, "What happened?"

One reporter guessed, "The first edition of *The Washington Post* just arrived at the Washington bureau."

He was right.

Aaron Latham, a former *Washington Post* reporter, restructured in the style of a traditional newspaper yarn the story of how the Watergate scandals made page one. His article is reprinted with the permission of *New York Magazine,* where it originally appeared May 14, 1973. © 1973 by NYM Corp.

Night after night, for months, reporters and editors at *The Times* have been able to do little but sit around waiting for *The Washington Post*.

At one time, *The New York Times* reportedly platooned the Watergate story with a troop of reporters; *The Washington Post's* combination of Woodward and Bernstein still beat them. *The Post's* young reporters not only embarrassed their rival, *The Times,* but they also defeated a whole system of journalism. *The Times* covers Washington with correspondents who see themselves not so much as reporters but as ambassadors. News sources are expected to seek an audience with them.

Just before the boil burst, *The Washington Post* had planned a party to thank everyone who worked on the Watergate story. But then the resignations started coming. *The Washington Post* called its party off. Executive Editor Benjamin Bradlee said that he did not want it to seem that *The Post* was dancing on any graves.

But in the *Washington Post* newsroom, the reporters and editors could not hide their elation. The Nixon Administration had called the paper every kind of name. And everyone at *The Post* had known that if the paper was wrong about the Watergate, then it meant that Richard Nixon was right about *The Washington Post* and American journalism. It was beginning, however, to look more and more as if *The Post* was not only right but conservative in its coverage of the scandal.

Katharine Graham, the publisher of *The Washington Post*, had come under especially heavy pressure and criticism. John Mitchell, the former Attorney General of the United States, had told a *Post* reporter, "Katie Graham is going to get her tit caught in a big fat wringer." It would seem, however, that Mitchell may have been the one who got caught where it hurts, and much of the rest of the Administration with him. The grand jury and the Ervin committee have turned into wringers through which the Nixon men must pass.

Ten months ago, another wringer—Woodward and Bernstein—had gone to work on the saboteurs in the Nixon Administration.

On June 17, 1972, Howard Simons, the managing editor of *The Washington Post*, got a call at about eight in the morning. It was a tip. Someone told him that there had been a break-in at the Democratic National Committee headquarters. Simons was especially intrigued by one detail: the burglars had been caught wearing surgical gloves.

Since it was a local crime story, Howard Simons called Metropolitan Editor Harry Rosenfeld at home and alerted him. Then Simons called Mrs. Graham and told her, "You will not believe what is going on."

Harry Rosenfeld called Barry Sussman, his District of Columbia editor. Sussman called two people: Alfred Lewis, one of his most experienced reporters, and Robert Woodward, one of his least experienced.

Bob Woodward graduated from Yale in 1965 and then went into the Navy for five years, working his last year in the Pentagon. He had planned to go to law school but he managed to get a job at *The Montgomery County* [Maryland] *Sentinel*. After six months or so, Woodward began calling Harry Rosenfeld at *The Post*

The Weather
Today—Partly cloudy, high in mid 80s, low mid to upper 60s. Chance of rain near zero today, 10 per cent tonight. Wednesday—Partly cloudy, high in 80s. Temp. range: Today, 84-67; Yesterday, 87-73. Details C3.

The Washington Post
Times Herald

FINAL

72 Pages—4 Sections

Amusements	B 7	Financial	D 8
Classified	C 5	Metro	C 1
Comics	B10	Obituaries	C 4
Crossword	B 4	Sports	D 1
Editorials	A20	Style	B 6
Fed. Diary	B11	TV-Radio	B 6

96th Year ···· No. 231   © 1973, The Washington Post Co.   **TUESDAY, JULY 24, 1973**   Phone 223-6000   Classified 223-6200 Circulation 223-6100   The Second Washington, Maryland and Virginia   10¢

President Refuses to Turn Over Tapes; Ervin Committee, Cox Issue Subpoenas

Baker: "Brink of a constitutional confrontation."

Cox: "To withhold ... is without legal foundation."

Ervin: "Greatest tragedy this country has ever suffered."

Photos by Joe Heiberger and Charles Del Vecchio—The Washington Post

Action Sets Stage For Court Battle On Powers Issue

By Carroll Kilpatrick
Washington Post Staff Writer

President Nixon set the stage yesterday for a major constitutional confrontation by refusing to turn over presidential tape recordings to either the Senate Watergate committee or to Special Prosecutor Archibald Cox.

Cox immediately served a subpoena for the tapes on presidential counsel J. Fred Buzhardt, who must respond in federal court by Thursday. The Senate Committee followed suit, serving two subpoenas on another presidential lawyer, Leonard Garment.

The committee chairman, Sen. Sam Ervin (D-N.C.), reacted to the President's decision with an emotional statement, saying:

"I deeply regret that this situation has arisen, because I think that the Watergate tragedy is the greatest tragedy this country has ever suffered. I used to think that the Civil War was our country's greatest tragedy, but I do remember that there were some redeeming features in the Civil War in that there was some spirit of sacrifice and heroism displayed on both sides. I see no redeeming features in Watergate."

The committee's vice chairman, Sen. Howard H. Baker (R-Tenn.), expressed disappointment at being "on the brink of a constitutional confrontation between the Congress and the White House" that sought by the subpoenas is "essential, if not vital, to the full, thorough inquiry mandated and required of this committee."

It seemed certain last night that the confrontation between the President and the investigators ultimately would have to be decided in the Supreme Court. How the court might rule on the central issues— executive privilege and the separation of governmental powers—is unknown.

The President made no concessions on those issues in a letter to Ervin yesterday. He would reply "at an appropriate time" to the issues raised by the Watergate affair and to charges concerning his own involvement, Mr. Nixon said in the letter. But "the special nature of tape recordings of private conversations is such that these principles of executive privilege apply with even greater force to tapes of private Presidential conversations than to Presidential papers," he declared.

The tapes in question were made secretly and involved alleged conversations between Mr. Nixon and various of his assistants on matters relating to the Watergate break-in and the subsequent efforts to cover up that crime.

The President said that contrary to the Ervin committee's assumptions, the "tapes would not finally settle the central issues before your committee. Before their existence became publicly known, I personally listened to a number of them.

"The tapes are entirely consistent with what I know to be the truth and what I have stated to be the truth. However, as in any verbatim recording of informal conversations, they contain comments that persons with different perspectives and motivations would inevitably interpret in different ways.

"Furthermore, there are inseparably interspersed in them a great many very frank and very private comments on a wide range of issues and individuals, wholly extraneous to the Committee's inquiry."

See PRESIDENT, A17, Col. 1

Haldeman Kept Close Check On Political Spies: Strachan

By Lawrence Meyer and Peter A. Jay
Washington Post Staff Writers

White House chief of staff H. R. (Bob) Haldeman kept in close touch with plans to gather political intelligence on potential Democratic presidential candidates, former Haldeman aide Gordon C. Strachan testified yesterday.

Haldeman held a series of meetings with Attorney General John N. Mitchell to discuss intelligence-gathering in 1971 and 1972, Strachan told the Senate select Watergate committee.

In April, 1972, Haldeman indicated with a check mark that he had read a memo item about the re-election committee's "sophisticated political intelligence operation," Strachan said. Other Senate testimony has established that this operation, designed and directed by G. Gordon Liddy, included plans to burglarize and bug the Democratic National Committee's Watergate headquarters.

Shortly after the Watergate break-in arrests on June 17, 1972, Strachan said Haldeman told him to make sure the White House files were "clean." Taking this statement as a directive, Strachan said, he destroyed the intelligence operation file, related documents and other materials that might be "politically embarrassing" if they became public.

In the course of his daylong testimony, Strachan also provided the committee with a fascinating picture of Haldeman's thorough-going efficiency as the man who presided over the operation of the White House staff.

"Mr. Haldeman had a well-deserved reputation as a very, very tough staff man," Strachan said, "and there were constant pressures to perform well, and I worked very hard."

Strachan told the committee that in April, 1972, Haldeman directed him to contact Watergate conspirator G. Gordon Liddy, then an official of the Committee for the Re-election of the President, and tell him to transfer whatever capability he had from (Sen. Edmund S.) Muskie to (Sen. George S.) McGovern with particular interest in discovering what the connection between McGovern and Sen. (Edward M.) Kennedy was."

According to testimony at the Watergate trial last January, it was in mid-April, 1972, that Tom Gregory, a

See HEARING, A19 Col. 1

Gordon Strachan: "John Dean would be telling the truth."

By Joe Heiberger—The Washington Post

Ervin Panel Felt Backed Into Corner

By Herbert H. Denton and Sanford J. Ungar
Washington Post Staff Writers

Most members of the Senate select Watergate committee indicated yesterday that President Nixon had backed them into a corner and forced them to issue subpoenas for tapes of his conversations and other White House documents and papers.

Only Sen. Howard H. Baker (R-Tenn.), according to accounts of an hour-long committee meeting, continued to urge some kind of amicable compromise to avoid a constitutional confrontation.

But Watergate committee Chairman Sam J. Ervin Jr. (D-N.C.) is reported to have posed what became the operative question at the beginning of the meeting: "The President has not done the court; let now what do we do?"

Later, Sen. Edward Gurney (R-Fla.), regarded by many as the strongest White House defender on the committee, explained the action to a reporter: "The President said he wasn't releasing the tapes. The subpoena was the next move."

In choosing to exercise its powers to serve a subpoena for the documents and tapes on the White House, Senate Watergate committee members did so with the clear knowledge that the action would in all probability lead to a protracted constitutional confrontation that would ultimately end up in the Supreme Court.

Symington Charges Pentagon Deception

By Michael Getler
Washington Post Staff Writer

Sen. Stuart Symington (D-Mo.), acting chairman of the Senate Armed Services Committee, yesterday accused the Nixon administration of obtaining millions of dollars from Congress under false pretenses to support the secret air war in Cambodia dur-

Prices Zoom On Chicken, Eggs, Pork

By Major C. Wells and Peter Milius
Washington Post Staff Writers

Washington area supermarkets sharply raised prices of chicken, pork and eggs yesterday—the first major increases since Wednesday when President Nixon lifted the price freeze on food other than beef.

Skyjackers Take Jet On Mideast Odyssey

From News Dispatches

DAMASCUS, July 24 (Tuesday)—The Japan Air Lines jumbo jet skyjacked in the name of the Palestinian cause was passed around the Arab world like a hot potato today and finally headed out into the Mediterranean toward the islands of Cyprus and Rhodes after three days on a runway in the Persian Gulf sheikhdom

The plane headed at first in the direction of Cyprus, but then told Cyprus airport authorities that it was heading for Rhodes.

There was speculation that, like other Arab countries, both leftist and conservative, Syria had made the plane unwelcome, despite its public expressions of support for the Palestinian cause.

Court Sets Resumption Of Subsidized Housing

By Paul Hodge
Washington Post Staff Writer

U.S. District Court Judge(s), acting in different Charles R. Richey yesterday ordered the Nixon administration to reinstate the federally subsidized housing programs it abruptly stopped slashing last January because administration officials said if they needed re-evaluation.

The action was announced

---

to ask if there were any openings. Rosenfeld said no. Woodward would call every three or four weeks. Rosenfeld always put him off. Then Rosenfeld went on vacation. He spent it at home painting his basement. One boiling afternoon, Rosenfeld was up on top of a ladder with paint all over him, mad at the world, when his wife yelled to him that he had a phone call. It was Woodward. Rosenfeld transferred his anger about the weather and the ladder and the paint to the young reporter and told him, more or less, don't call us, we'll call you.

When Rosenfeld angrily hung up the phone, his wife, Annie, said, "Isn't this just the kind of reporter you're always saying you want?"

Rosenfeld decided that she was right. In September of 1971, he hired Woodward, who by then had worked for *The Sentinel* for a year. Woodward went to work for Rosenfeld and began bothering other people with his insistent and persistent phone calls. His first day at *The Washington Post* he made close to a hundred calls looking for a story. He did investigative pieces on restaurant health violations, the drug traffic, and police corruption. Someone in the newsroom told Katharine Graham that Woodward was going to be the next managing editor of *The Post*. Mrs. Graham told her son, Donald (the heir apparent to the *Post* empire who has worked for the paper in every capacity from reporter to assistant production manager), but he disagreed about Woodward's future. He said that Woodward would not be the next M.E. because he would be dead first. He would work himself to death.

When Woodward went to work on the Watergate break-in, he had been with *The Washington Post* for only nine months. That first morning, Barry Sussman sent Al Lewis down to the Watergate. All of the other reporters from all of the other papers and television and radio stations waited downstairs for someone to come out and tell them what had happened. Al Lewis went upstairs to the Democratic National Committee headquarters. The police let him, perhaps because they had seen him around the police station for so many years that they thought he was a cop. Lewis called Sussman to report that two ceiling panels were out near the office of Democratic National Committee Chairman Lawrence O'Brien. Right away they suspected bugging.

Bob Woodward was dispatched to a hearing given the burglars caught inside the Watergate. He sat up in the very first row. The judge asked McCord what he did for a living. McCord said that he was a "security consultant." The judge asked for whom he had worked in the past. McCord whispered: "C.I.A." Woodward, sitting in the front row, overheard.

Meanwhile, Carl Bernstein was back at the office hovering around Sussman. Bernstein always had a nose for a good story and he was not shy about sticking that nose in whether it was wanted or not. He wangled an assignment writing a sidebar on who the suspects were. Bernstein's story included the information that Woodward had overheard: McCord had worked for the C.I.A.

Woodward and Bernstein, who were to work together on the story from then on, could hardly be more different. Other reporters call them "the odd couple." Woodward is a preppie Yalie; Bernstein dropped out of the University of Maryland after three years without a degree. Woodward is a neat, patrician WASP, the son of a Republican judge; Bernstein is Jewish, sloppy, and looks like a delivery boy. Bernstein started at *The Washington Evening Star* as a copyboy and came to *The Post* in 1966. He had been the protege of a former city editor until the editor walked into the District Building newsroom one afternoon and found Bernstein fast asleep on a couch. Since then he had had mostly sleepy assignments.

On the morning of June 18, *The Washington Post* carried the Watergate as the second lead of the paper. Their coverage included 83 inches of copy. *The New York Times* carried a thirteen-inch story on an inside page. The pattern for the next ten months had already been established.

Two days later, Eugene Bachinski, a *Post* police reporter, found the name E. Howard Hunt in two address books which had been in the possession of captured Watergate conspirators. In one book, someone had written 'W. H.'' beside Hunt's name; in the other, the name was followed by the notation ''W. House.'' It did not take Bachinski long to guess that the W. House might be the White House.

Bob Woodward telephoned Richard Nixon's residence to find out. A White House switchboard operator located Hunt's extension and rang it. No one answered. The operator then volunteered, ''There is one other place he might be—in Mr. [Charles] Colson's office.'' She dialed the number.

A secretary said, ''Mr. Hunt is not here now.''

The operator then suggested that Woodward try calling Robert R. Mullen & Co., a public-relations firm right across the street from the White House where Hunt moonlighted as a copywriter. Woodward tried Hunt there and got him. The reporter told the White House spy about the address books.

E. Howard Hunt said, ''Good God!'' Then he hung up and disappeared.

The Washington Post had established a tenuous link between the Watergate and the White House and the story was developing nicely, but then the vacations started coming. While reporters and editors went to the beach or painted their basements, the story seemed to sag and presumably the President's men sighed with some relief.

In July, Howard Simons went to Barry Sussman and told him that he did not think the paper was working hard enough on the Watergate story. Sussman decided to put Bernstein and Woodward on the story full time.

Woodward and Bernstein say that their first job was knocking down all of the misleading ''leaks'' that were coming out of the White House, seemingly designed to throw them off the trail. Most of the leaks had to do with what came to be called the ''Cuban connection.'' The White House leaked a story that the whole operation was organized by a right-wing Cuban exile group known as Ameritas. Ameritas turned out to be a real-estate firm.

(*The New York Times* wasted even more time on the ''Cuban connection'' than did *The Post*, and that was evidently one of the reasons they got so far behind that they could never catch up. They assigned their Cuban expert Tad Szulc to the story. He was the reporter who uncovered plans for the Bay of Pigs invasion before it happened—but *The Times* [had ''down played''] the story. The Watergate ''Cuban connection'' was to prove his own Bay of Pigs.)

Carl Bernstein wanted to go to Florida. The request gave Barry Sussman some pause because, as the editor says, ''Bernstein had spent more money covering the Virginia Legislature than Murrey Marder had spent on the peace talks in Paris.'' Sussman finally agreed to send Bernstein south, but he warned the reporter that if the expenses were too high, he would be off the story for good—the Republicans might throw money away but the Washington Post Co. did not. Since Bernstein was considered a spendthrift, Sussman did not tell his superiors that he had sent him to Florida until he was already gone.

Bernstein located a Florida prosecutor investigating several of the Watergate suspects who lived in the state. The reporter nagged the prosecutor endlessly, with no luck, while Woodward and Sussman waited nervously in New York for some kind of break in the story. Finally, the prosecutor, pestered to distraction by Bernstein, threw up his hands and said something like: "I have a murder I have to go out on. Here's the file."

Bernstein looked through the file and found a copy of a $25,000 check signed by Kenneth Dahlberg. He called Sussman at about 9 p.m. on the evening of July 31. No one had ever heard of Kenneth Dahlberg. Racing against deadline, Sussman and Woodward immediately searched the *Washington Post* morgue for old newspaper stories about anyone with that name. They found a five-year-old yellowing picture of a Kenneth Dahlberg posing with Hubert Humphrey.

By checking directories, they managed to locate two Kenneth Dahlbergs, one in Florida and one in Minnesota. They suspected that the Florida Dahlberg was the one they wanted, but he did not answer his phone, so they tried the Minnesota Dahlberg.

Bob Woodward's first question to the Kenneth Dahlberg who answered the telephone in suburban Minneapolis was: "Mr. Dahlberg, I was trying to reach you at your home in Florida. What is that, a winter home?"

Kenneth Dahlberg said, "Yes."

Fortunately for Woodward, he happened to call Dahlberg on a day when he was particularly upset and off guard. Dahlberg's neighbor was the Minneapolis socialite who had just been kidnapped in a celebrated ransom case. (She would later be found handcuffed to a tree in the wilderness.) Woodward and Dahlberg talked about the kidnapping and then they talked about what interested the reporter: the mysterious check.

Dahlberg said that it was a campaign contribution that he had personally handed to Maurice Stans, former Secretary of Commerce and Nixon's chief fundraiser. For the first time, *The Post* had evidence that the Watergate conspirators had been paid with money contributed to the Nixon re-election campaign.

When Woodward told Sussman what he had found out, the editor said, "We have never had a story like this." (*The New York Times* reportedly had had the Dahlberg check for over a week but had not known what to make of it.)

The Washington Post's Dahlberg-check story triggered an audit by the General Accounting Office which located a safe in Maurice Stans's office from which hundreds of thousands of dollars were doled out secretly for clandestine operations. The secret fund was reported by Philip S. Hughes of the G.A.O., who immediately became a hero to *Post* reporters.

Woodward and Bernstein settled down to weeks of gumshoeing. They got a G.A.O. report that listed all of the employees of the Committee for the Re-election of the President (C.R.P.). The list also gave vague titles, home addresses, and salaries. Rather than attempting to reach these people in their official capacity

during working hours, they went out in the evenings and knocked on doors. They were usually turned away, but occasionally someone would invite them in "for a few minutes" and they would end up staying until midnight. They began to look to see who had resigned from the re-election committee and knocked on their doors. Most of the people to whom they talked only knew a piece of the story, but slowly they were able to put together the pieces.

Their first important sources were Republicans who worked inside C.R.P. ("Creep," as reporters call it) but were upset about what was happening. Finally Woodward and Bernstein got hold of a "Creep" telephone directory. Since so little of the story was on paper, they were delighted to have something that they could really study, even if it was only a phone book. They poured over it as though it were a Rosetta Stone or a Kremlin Letter. (Bernstein says, "C.R.P. was set up like the K.G.B.") They were able to work out who shared offices and who shared secretaries. Slowly they branched out from C.R.P. and developed sources in the Justice Department and the White House itself.

They found one source right inside the *Washington Post* newsroom. Marilyn Berger, an attractive *Post* reporter whose beat is foreign affairs, happened to talk to Ken Clawson, who had been a reporter at *The Post* but had quit to take a job as deputy director of White House communications. Ms. Berger will not say what the circumstances of the conversation were, but while they talked, Clawson bragged to her that he had written the famous "Canuck" letter to *The Manchester Union Leader*. The letter charged that Senator Edmund Muskie condoned calling Americans of French-Canadian descent "Canucks."

Marilyn Berger did not know what to make of Clawson's admission and decided to wait until David Broder returned from covering the campaign trail and ask him what he thought. When he did return, Broder listened to Ms. Berger and then told her that "the boys" on the metropolitan desk were working on a story into which her information might fit. As it turned out, Woodward and Bernstein had already traced the letter to the White House.

At about the same time, someone mentioned to Woodward and Bernstein casually that a friend of his had been approached by someone trying to enlist political spies and saboteurs. The reporters contacted the source's friend and discovered that the recruiter's name was Donald H. Segretti. They also learned that F.B.I. reports estimated that there were at least 50 undercover Nixon spies and saboteurs who were attempting to disrupt the Democratic campaign.

On October 8, a Sunday, Woodward and Bernstein, under the direction of Sussman, went to work writing what was to be their seminal story. Executive Editor Ben Bradlee had already laid down the rule that the paper would not print anything about the Watergate or political espionage that could not be confirmed through two or more sources. They checked and double-checked facts. Sussman and the two reporters worked until two o'clock in the morning so that they would have a finished story to show their bosses on Monday morning.

The next day, Bernstein, Woodward and Sussman were virtually put on trial. Harry Rosenfeld, Howard Simons, and finally, Ben Bradlee each cross-examined them. When they were satisfied with the story, Bradlee called Mrs. Graham and told her what the paper planned to publish. He was not actually asking permission to print the story, but he knew and she knew that she could stop it. She didn't. Nor did she ask to read it before it went into the paper.

The next morning, October 10, Mrs. Graham, Richard Nixon, and other readers of *The Washington Post* read a lead story which began: "F.B.I. agents have established that the Watergate bugging incident stemmed from a massive campaign of political spying and sabotage conducted on behalf of President Nixon's re-election and directed by officials of the White House and the Committee for the Re-election of the President."

The Post followed its October 10 story with later reports that Dwight Chapin, the President's appointments secretary, was Donald Segretti's White House contact; that Herbert Kalmbach, the President's personal attorney, was authorized to approve payments out of the secret political espionage fund; that H. R. Haldeman, the President's White House chief of staff, was also authorized to approve such payments. In the last story, *The Post* made its one acknowledged mistake: the paper said Haldeman had been accused of approving secret payments in testimony before the grand jury. *The Post* still stands behind its story that Haldeman was authorized to approve these payments but concedes that there was no such testimony before the grand jury.

The Nixon Administration treated *The Washington Post* as though it were the one guilty of a felony. Administration sources accused *The Post* of "guilt-by-association," "hypocrisy," and of being George McGovern's "partners-in-mud-slinging."

Some evidence suggests that the Nixon Administration may have decided to put the stock of the Washington Post Co. through a wringer. On December 29, that stock had reached an all-time high, $38. Since then it has fallen drastically to $23½. While Nixon has been losing credibility, the Post Co. stockholders have been losing money. The fall in the price could be traced in part at least to challenges to the renewal of the licenses of the Post Co.'s two television stations in Florida. The challenges have reportedly been led or planned by a former counsel of C.R.P., a Nixon fund-raiser, and a man who made his house available to Agnew during the Republican Convention. Even if the company successfully rebuffs the challenges, the cost of defending itself in hearings which could go on for years could be half a million dollars.

Mrs. Graham will not attribute the license challenges directly to the White House, but she does say, "I've lived with White House anger before [Lyndon Johnson's] but I've never seen anything that achieved this kind of fury and heat." She says she never considered putting a brake on *The Post's* Watergate coverage, but she does concede, "There was a private point with me when I got a congealed feeling that there was a High Noon situation developing, that this really was for keeps, that this was the toughest thing you had ever faced, by far tougher than publishing the Pentagon Papers. We asked ourselves if there was some enormous Kafka plot, if we were being led down a road to discredit the paper. The reputation of *The Post* was totally at stake."

It was about two years ago that *The New York Times* broke the Pentagon Papers story. *The Washington Post* picked up the story but attributed it to *The Times* from one end of the article to the other. Ben Bradlee says, "There was blood on every paragraph."

Now things have changed. Bradlee says, "In the Pentagon Papers case, we were second, a strong second, but second. In the Watergate story, we were first and we were way first. And we were alone."

This time *The New York Times* is the one that has been beaten and it has not always been a graceful loser. For example, when *The Post* printed its October 10 story about widespread political sabotage carried on by the Republicans, *The Times* picked up the story but wrote it in such a way that *The Washington Post's* name did not appear until the article had jumped inside the paper.

Managing Editor Howard Simons says of *The Times*, "It is awfully hard for the Yankees to swallow the fact that the Senators are just better."

The Post's coverage of the Republicans' political sabotage story is in many ways a much more impressive reporting job than *The Times's* coverage of the Pentagon Papers because there is no "Ellsberg" figure in the Watergate story to simply dump all of the relevant documents in their laps. In fact, other than an occasional internal directory, there have been very few documents at all.

One of the few "scoops" *The Times* has gotten reportedly came in a phone call from Mitchell to William Safire, a former White House special assistant whom the paper had hired to write a column. Safire passed along the message that Mitchell admitted to sitting in on meetings where bugging was discussed although the former Attorney General claimed that he had been against it. Safire reportedly bypassed Managing Editor Abe Rosenthal and called R.W. Apple Jr. in the paper's Washington bureau. After an internal squabble, *The Times* ran the story with no by-line. *The Times's* answer to Woodward and Bernstein had turned out to be a former Nixon press agent. (*The Times's* coverage has dramatically improved, however, since it put Seymour Hersh on the case.)

Carl Bernstein and Bob Woodward recently went to the White House press corps' awards dinner to pick up first prize. The President sometimes hands out the awards, but this year he was late arriving at the ceremonies. The prizes were given out before he got there.

Woodward and Bernstein, who are, after all, city reporters, and who have never risen very high on the Washington dinner party circuit, did not know many people at the banquet. Reporters who knew the ropes escorted them around the hall, introducing them to various dignitaries. Woodward and Bernstein found themselves being introduced to two of their sources, men they had talked to on the telephone but had never met. Absolute lack of recognition was feigned on both sides.

A few days later, Woodward went up to the White House to check on something. While he was there, he was introduced to a high government official. He pretended not to know the man. But again the official was one of Woodward's sources.

Since the scandal has broken in earnest, Woodward and Bernstein have developed more and more White House sources. Almost everyone, it seems, wants to open a line of communication with them, to plant his version of what has been going on, to try to find out how much the young reporters know. Woodward says, "We've just about been invited to the prayer breakfasts."

The reporters' White House sources may soon shrink, however, if they have not shrunk already. Bernstein says, "Some of our people may be in the slam."

I was in *The Washington Post* cafeteria having lunch with two *Post* reporters. One of them said that working in the same newsroom with Bernstein and Woodward was "like living next door to Fabian." A color television was turned on and it played daytime soap operas. Suddenly CBS interrupted its regular programming to broadcast a special news bulletin. Patrick Gray had just resigned as acting director of the F.B.I. Then CBS returned to its regular programming—*As the World Turns, The Guiding Light*, or whatever it was. One soap opera had been interrupted to bring the nation a chapter of an even better soap opera. Not only was it important,

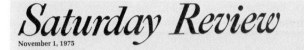

Saturday Review

75¢

November 1, 1975

Watergating on Main Street

What Is Happening to
Ethical Standards in

- GOVERNMENT

- LAW

- BUSINESS

- ACCOUNTING

Top of the Week   **Newsweek**

Putting Watergate Behind Us . . .

The so-called post-Watergate period included a flurry of pieces dealing with the effects of the scandals on American society and the role of the media in helping to bring all of this into the open.

scandalous, faithshaking—it was also entertaining. Richard Nixon had become the Clifford Irving of 1973.

We left the cafeteria and went upstairs to the fifth-floor newsroom. Reporters and editors were gathered in front of long strips of A.P. and U.P.I. wirecopy which had been hung on the walls. They could hardly believe it: the Gray resignation, the Ellsberg caper. *The Washington Post* had plugged away almost alone when every story required a dozen nocturnal visits and now, suddenly, the scandal was rising like the Mississippi, flooding the whole Administration. They were swimming in stories. Vic Gold, Agnew's former press secretary, wandered about talking to reporters; suddenly news was walking in off the street through the front door.

The Watergate flood may not have crested yet. . . .

The Watergate story crested, August 9, 1974.

THE WHITE HOUSE

WASHINGTON

August 9, 1974

Dear Mr. Secretary:

I hereby resign the Office of President of the United States.

Sincerely,

Richard Nixon

The Honorable Henry A. Kissinger
The Secretary of State
Washington, D.C. 20520

Bibliography

A spate of books have been published on the Watergate period (a term applied inappropriately to a large number of incidents involving people in the Nixon Administration executive staff as well as the Committee to Re-elect the President). The best book available is Carl Bernstein and Bob Woodward, *All the President's Men*, Simon & Schuster, 1974, which not only is quite readable it offers food for thought regarding methods of gathering information and the ethics of investigative reporting. This was followed by their book *The Final Days*, 1976. See also the special section on "Watergate and the Press" in *Columbia Journalism Review* (November/December 1973.) For a discussion of the Nixon administration's attack on the press, including White House memoranda as sources, consult William E. Porter, *Assault on the Media: The Nixon Years*, The University of Michigan Press, 1975, and Thomas Whiteside, "Annals of Television: Shaking the Tree," *The New Yorker* (March 17, 1975), pp. 41-48 ff. For a jaundiced view of the contribution of Bernstein and Woodward to the discovery of information about the Watergate-related activities, see Edward Jay Epstein, "Did the Press Uncover Watergate?" *Between Fact and Fiction*, Vintage Books, 1975. For a detailed analysis of the Nixon years, see *Nightmare*, by J. Anthony Lucas, The Viking Press, 1976.

Investigative Reporting: Is It Getting Too Sexy?

By Timothy Ingram

"I think it's going to get incredible," says Melvin Mencher of the Columbia School of Journalism, who was teaching seminars on investigative reporting when it was still considered a grubby trade. "Every little paper in the country and every reporter on a beat is going to want a scalp." As journalism schools, including his own, bulge with would-be Woodwards and Bernsteins, and reporters on every paper in the country try to nail a prominent hide to the wall, "investigative reporting" has become the profession's most popular—and most worrisome—gimmick.

"Ninety percent of these smaller newspapers have no tradition of this kind of digging, no editors with experience in it," Mencher says. "A lot of poor devils in public office are going to catch hell for simple mistakes. When the movie comes out, I guess it's going to get worse."

"The movie," of course, is the Robert Redford All-Star version of the Watergate case; the apprehension is that it may exaggerate the set of double standards under which many people publicly denounce political dirty tricks while glamorizing the dirty tricks of journalists who pressure middle-aged bookkeepers for information or filch private telephone or credit records. [Ed. Note: It didn't.]

According to Ben Bagdikian, a former *Washington Post* national editor and ombudsman, this trenchcoat psychology could easily lead to frivolous exposes and shoddy reportorial practices. The added pressure to unearth the "big stories," Bagdikian says, will make it almost impossible for reporters to resist pursuing the "easy fish," the scandal stories where information is obtained by dubious means.

Timothy Ingram is a contributing editor of *The Washington Monthly*. Reprinted with permission from *The Washington Monthly* (April 1975). Copyright by The Washington Monthly Co., 1028 Connecticut Ave., N.W., Washington, D.C. 20036.

"Editors want to look like investigative editors—but on the cheap," explains Bagdikian. "They tell a good reporter to come up with a story in two days. . . .It usually results in stories based on half-information and bad sources."

Even the tabloids are boasting of their tough muckraking approach. The *National Star*, "America's Lively Family Newspaper," recently headlined "Two New Shocks in the Kennedy Saga" under the credit, "by Star Investigating Team." The transition from kidnappings and mutilated babies to the political inside story has been made.

No newspaper has calculated the promotional value of "investigation" more closely than the Detroit *Free Press*, whose day-to-day coverage is mediocre but which pulls out all the stops on 10 or 12 investigative stories each year. The stories are designed to win Pulitzers, and often do. Even when they do not, they give the *Free Press* a national reputation out of all proportion to its daily performance.

Clearly, we are in the midst of an investigative craze—a craze that has obvious potential for good, even as it presents a less obvious danger of harm to both the profession of journalism and the public at large. It is with these dangers that this article is concerned. We see five that concern us the most.

Seducing the Source

The first hazard of investigative reporting concerns the actual means used to collect the facts. There are many methods of investigation, some of which are clearly improper. Others, however, are well within the commonly accepted rules of this rough game. A journalist may pretend, for example, to know all about X in order to seduce his subject into confirming his information; this confirmation, in turn, may reveal bits about fact Y, the checking of which may lead for the first time to Z. Generally the reporter approaches his source indirectly: "We have enough to run with now, but in the interests of accuracy I'd like your version of what happened." A variant is to convince the source that you have heard an incredibly shocking tale about him but are uncertain whether to print it. In his anguish, he is bound to spill his side of the story.

Sometimes these calls will be timed to catch people off guard: phoning the subject at home in the evening after he has a chance to unwind from the day, and perhaps is loosened by a sip of Scotch; or at 6 a.m. in hopes of catching him half-asleep.

Perhaps the most accomplished telephone technician is Seymour Hersh, now of *The New York Times*, who unearthed the My Lai massacre, and since has been generally regarded as the best investigative reporter in the country. Hersh's technique is to wear down reluctant sources through tenacious pursuit by phone—often badgering, terrorizing, insulting. "I don't know of anyone other than Don Rickles who can be as disgustingly insulting, yet have the right touch for getting someone to respond," says a former colleague. Hersh makes one phone call after another, trading on fine bits of information, and then milking more with sarcastic bursts of "Ah-h, come *awwn*." Those who have experienced the Hersh treatment are usually either amazed by it, or appalled. "What's with this guy?" one subject

The great
grain scandal:
you can't tell
the wheat
from the shaft

Casualties at home:
The wives of

Aggressive reporting forced the exposure of such events as the "grain scandal" but later some media critics worried that Watergate-style reporting was leading to excesses, including invasion of privacy.

said afterwards. "I tell him honestly I don't know anything, and he's yelling and screaming at me and going into tantrums."

James Angleton, who resigned from the CIA last December the day after a Hersh story charged him with being the overseer of a "massive, illegal" domestic intelligence operation against antiwar activists, had one term for Hersh: "son-of-a-bitch." Angleton said Hersh had awakened him one morning at seven to interrogate him about a story in that day's *Washington Post*. Angleton told a *Post* reporter, "I find Hersh's prose offensive to the ear. And his speech...I won't go into how I find that."

Free Enterprise

Angleton, not unexpectedly, considers such calls improper. It should be remembered, though, that the subjects of Hersh's aggressive, often vulgar, approach are public servants. While they do have a right to privacy and a good night's sleep, they must be prepared to answer questions about their official conduct, even when the questions come in unorthodox forms. And, when dealing with a man like Hersh, the officials have fair warning that he represents the *Times* and is looking for information he can publish. At the opposite extreme is the reporter who hides his connection with a newspaper, and obtains a story under false pretenses. The distinction—between the Seymour Hersh who announces he is a reporter and the journalist who masquerades as a cop, a waiter, or whatever, in order to trick his source—is significant, although the ethical guidelines are not always easily drawn.

Al Lewis, *The Washington Post's* veteran police reporter, for example, was the only newsman inside the Democratic headquarters at the Watergate on the morning the five burglars were arrested. Wearing white socks and looking very much the cop, Lewis simply accompanied the acting police chief past the 50 reporters and cameramen cordoned off from the Watergate complex by the police. Once inside, Lewis took off his jacket, sat down at a desk, and occasionally pecked at a typewriter. He looked for all the world as if he was supposed to be working there. With a phone at his desk, he was able to provide the *Post* with a description of the office floor plan, details about the surgical gloves and lock-picks and jimmies used, and the name of the security guard who foiled the break-in. Lewis sees nothing deceitful in his actions—all he was doing was remaining anonymous. He never *told* anyone he was a policeman, and presumably had anyone asked, he would have disclosed his true identity.

A similar case occurred in the spring of 1969, when Richard Helms, then-director of the CIA, was scheduled to speak at a dinner meeting of the Business Council, an organization of some 150 top businessmen at the Homestead in Hot Springs, Virginia.

Helms' speech was officially off-the-record and closed to the press; moreover, Helms would not be briefing the press on his remarks afterwards. This caused some grumbling among the reporters at hand, but individually they began to make their own arrangements to have friends in the audience fill them in later. As followers of last summer's impeachment hearings have learned, such second-hand accounts are not always the most accurate.

Jim Srodes, then with UPI, was in Hot Springs for his honeymoon. When he learned about the speech he went into the hall outside the dining room and twisted doorknobs until he found himself in the hotel kitchen. Helms' voice was booming through the room; a loudspeaker had been set up so that waiters would know when the speech was over and they could go in and clear off the tables. Srodes simply stood there and started taking notes.

Was this ethical? Most reporters would agree his actions showed more enterprise than deceit. The speech, as it happened, was a diatribe about the horrors of communism. Helms made a number of policy assertions which would normally be considered beyond his purview, referring to the "morally bankrupt Kremlin leaders" and the futility of disarmament talks. Russia and its satellites, in Helms' terms were "the bear and its pack of wolves."

Once he had the story, however, Srodes' troubles had only begun. UPI refused to use it. When Srodes called in his exclusive, he says, the UPI night editor told him the story would hurt UPI's world-wide relations with the CIA and its ability to get other stories. The story finally ran, Srodes is convinced, only because a *Washington Post* reporter to whom he told his tale that night had the *Post* make a client request to UPI for the story—the gun-to-the-head for the wire services, where a client paper in effect says we know you have the story and we want it.

At a certain point, however, the reporter crosses the line that separates enterprise from deceit. Harry Rosenfeld, then the *Washington Post*'s metropolitan editor, says that shortly after Howard Hunt became a suspect in the Watergate break-in, Rosenfeld could have obtained Hunt's telephone records through imperson-ation. The usual method of doing so is to call the phone company's business office and, posing as the person being investigated, claim that you don't recall making certain long-distance calls charged to you. You then request the business office to double-check the numbers and dates of the calls and report them back to you. (A similar pose is used with credit companies to ''re-confirm'' a loan, or with airlines to check a passenger's flight travel.) Rosenfeld says that *Post* executive editor Ben Bradlee vetoed the subterfuge.

Not all journalists are so moral. There was Harry Romanoff of the now-defunct *Chicago American*, a police reporter who, without leaving his desk, would assume a dozen different disguises in his pursuit of a hot lead. Harry's colleagues referred to him as ''the Heifetz of the telephone.'' He would work a phone 12 hours a day, masquerading as sheriff, governor, sympathetic stranger, or whatever character fit the occasion. After the 1966 mass murder of eight Chicago student nurses, he managed to get the gory details of the deaths from a policeman after introducing himself as the Cook County coroner, and to interview the mother of the suspect, Richard Speck, by pretending to be her son's attorney.

Few reporters use trickery as freely as Romanoff, but many have been tempted. What is wrong with this practice is not just its dishonesty—although that is no insignificant point. As James Polk of *The Washington Star*, who won a Pulitzer last year for his reporting on campaign spending, puts it: ''The ethical question is clear. If reporters are dedicated to openness in government and openness in subjects they cover, then they can't use covert methods themselves.''

There is, moreover, a practical problem—false premises can result in false information. A reporter conceals his identity in order to hear things the source would not intentionally tell the press. But he may also hear things the source would not tell the press because they are untrue: the source may be lying to impress a stranger; the information may be wrong, or couched in terms that are misunderstood; the person may be careless in what he says because he doesn't think he is speaking for the record.

The ethical rationale for misrepresentation, then, is that an individual has a right to keep his thoughts private and to know whom he's talking to. The practical rationale is that the reporter may get stuck with bad information.

The *Star*'s Polk explains: ''I think it's more effective to identify myself as a reporter for a Washington paper because, frankly, it carries a little more clout. Most persons you start asking questions of want to explain what they do, and why. They're leery of really getting a rap in the press and think if they turn the reporter off by being uncooperative they've got more chance of getting rapped—which is possibly true. So, if, instead of asking them to *defend* what they've done, you ask their help in *explaining* what they know about something so you can sort it out in your own mind—why, then you get results.''

Private Sins

If the first hazard of investigative reporting lies in the way the facts are collected, the second is in their use: is a reporter justified in publishing damaging material about people or institutions, even if the facts are true? In the aftermath of the Wilbur Mills [and Wayne Hays] episodes, we seem certain to be treated to a "new candor" in the coverage of public officials. This would be fine if it meant a less deferential treatment of their public activities. But the apparent effect has been open season for comment on the *private* lives of public figures. Whatever sins against the Republic John Mitchell may finally be called to account for, it is hard to imagine how the public interest is served by seeing the pilfered records of his checking account, which *New York* magazine published last year to prove that he had been short-changing Martha in their divorce proceedings. This is what we're calling "investigative reporting" these days, and such examples show that, when deciding whether to publish or remain silent, reporters and editors are not asking the most basic question: *Is it significant?* The same press which has a duty to fearlessly publish information about the performance of public officials also has a duty not to needlessly defame them.

The distinction doesn't seem clear to many reporters. On a recent television talk show, a respected political writer said, "I dread the first time I spend a day with a politician and find out he's a fag. It'll hurt me, but I'll write it." If the politician's sexual taste affected the way he performed his job—*if*, like Hadrian, he abused public office for the satisfaction of private desire—then, it seems to me, the story should be written.

Raking Muck

A third abuse in investigative reporting is when reporters start working with the institutions of public power they're covering, so that, in effect, they help create stories they will later report.

To give a classic Washington illustration, reporters who cover congressional hearings often chafe with frustration when listening to mushy questioning which leaves major gaps in testimony or whole areas of inquiry unexplored. Although officially they are only observers, some reporters will feed questions and leads to the committee. During the Senate Watergate proceedings, reporters phoned committee staffers after hours with tips or to swap information; some actually sent notes to the senators' table. More traditional reporters, wary of the appearance of collusion, would list the unanswered questions from the day's proceeding in their stories, thereby sending their message to the committee.

The reporters were not asking the committee for special favors; they were acting as any outside citizen might, to provide information. This kind of cooperation between reporters and public officials is not wrong, but there is another that has far more frightening implications. It is best illustrated by an investigation that took place in upstate New York four years ago.

Ray Hill is a hard-drinking Canadian, a bulldog of a reporter. He looks like a cross between TV's "Cannon" and Brendan Behan. His approach is that of prosecutor. He credits his investigations into suburban corruption with 23 convictions and one acquittal. Once his targets have been sent up the river, he takes pride in ensuring they remain there and are not paroled early through political dealings.

In the summer of 1970 the *Buffalo Evening News* assigned Ray Hill and Dan Perry to the city of Lakawanna, just south of Buffalo, with instructions to "shake the trees and see what falls." Perry, then 25, had been a leader in a young-turk revolt in the city room, and assignment to Lakawanna was a convenient way to direct his fire outside of town. Also, for the conservative Buffalo paper, writing about Lakawanna was like writing about California: it was politically safe.

Lakawanna, with its giant steel mills and rust-covered rooftops, is a polyglot community of working class Irish, Poles, Italians, blacks, and Arabs. The town is a muckraker's utopia, where palms are crossed and pockets filled at every political level. Finding corruption, says Hill, is "like tracking a bleeding elephant through fresh-fallen snow."

Within a year, as a result of articles by Hill and Perry a special grand jury had indicted nine members and officers of the Lakawanna school board; six were finally convicted. They were found guilty of accepting bribes, approving phony vouchers for non-existent school equipment, and shaking down local contractors. The series won a first place from the New York Publishers Association and was a finalist in the Associated Press Managing Editors awards.

Hill and Perry's first stories were based on solid evidence, such as the canceled checks and vouchers showing that the school board had kept a dead man on the payroll for four years and had paid out $2,645 for a tractor that was never supplied. They were followed by articles about mismanagement, bidding irregularities, thefts, and skimmings.

But like *The Washington Post*'s coverage of Watergate, after the grand jury was empaneled to look into the charges generated by the paper, the direction and momentum of the reporting changed. In an attempt to keep the momentum going, the reporters kept grinding out pieces, just to show that the story was still alive. Often they resorted to artificial exposés by the most dubious techniques.

The following tactics evolved:

Feeding the Mills. Hill fed recalcitrant sources straight to the District Attorney's investigators. "We would tell them, 'Interview X. He won't speak to us; but he'll be able to tell you this and this. We know because we have two others in our backpocket who can verify it. If he tells you something else, he's lying to you.' That's how we fortified our investigation all along."

Laundering Rumors. "We'd pick up a rumor," says Perry, "such as a Mafia-owned construction company having received a special contract with the board. Then we'd call the D.A., give him the tip, and ask, 'Are you going to look into it?' He'd say, 'Yes,' so we'd run a story the next day, 'Grand jury investigating charges that....' We used the D.A. and the grand jury as a springboard to get our stories printed."

Quid Pro Quo. Hill would turn information over to the D.A. only in return for other information. "Do you want to play ball with me? I want to know what information you're presenting to the grand jury—and I don't want the opposition paper to know." Hill would plea-bargain with a source in return for turning over evidence on higher-ups. His activities went further than bargaining for information. He eventually negotiated legal immunity with the prosecutor for a key source. For example, Hill and Perry located a local contractor who told them he had been approached in a contract bidding shakedown, but he was hesitant to be more specific. "When we talked to the guy," Hill explains, "we told him, 'We can't get you immunity for murder, but if you want immunity for this specific testimony, we won't mention your name in the story and we will go to the D.A. for you.' " Hill then persuaded the prosecutor to guarantee the man's immunity in return for testifying before the grand jury. Then he ran the contractor's story.

"What happens frequently," says James Doyle, the press aide for the Watergate Special Prosecutor's office, "is that reporters call up and say, 'Listen, I want to tell you such-and-such; and the next day you read 'The Watergate special prosecution force *is aware of*. . . .' Okay. He tricked me. But if that guy calls back, I tell him, 'Hey, shove it buddy; I know your number, and I don't even want to talk to you.' "

New York Times reporter David Burnham had interviewed Frank Serpico and Inspector Paul Delise in February 1970 and had written Serpico's story of corruption within the New York City police. According to Peter Maas's biography of Serpico, by late April the story had not appeared. Then Burnham met Mayor Lindsay's press secretary at a cocktail party and let slip that the *Times* had a story involving police corruption in the works, and that it was dynamite. Two days later—to blunt the expected *Times* story, Mayor Lindsay announced that a committee was being formed to look into allegations of police corruption. The *Times* editors at last had an obvious, undeniable hook for the story and Serpico's charges were headlined the next day: "Graft Paid to Police Here Said to Run into Millions."

If the *Times'* editors were confident in the story, there was no reason at all for them to have waited for the newspeg—nor should they wait on similar investigative stories. If its editors are satisfied that the story is strong, the paper should be willing to put its own name behind the story instead of waiting to quote the grand jury. On the other hand, if the case is *not* complete, then the grand jury newspeg is a fraud—and, unfortunately, a most common form of fraud. It reflects again the ineradicable journalistic belief that "responsibility" consists of diligent quoting of official sources. Real "responsibility" means putting the paper's imprimatur on the line as a guarantee that the stories it publishes are accurate—and that the paper will take the consequences if they are not.

Paying the Piper

The fourth abuse of investigative reporting is the boldest of all—"buying" information. The great danger of buying is that journalists may end up staging the news they have paid for. In the mid-sixties CBS is said to have bid more than $30,000 for exclusive film rights to a planned "rebel army" invasion of Haiti. The network apparently had second thoughts when it realized that instead of buying coverage of an invasion it might be subsidizing one.

Gossip, when checked out, plays an important role in all phases of news, not just investigative reporting. Some publications, of course, feature nothing but gossip.

Most reporters say they would hesitate to pay for news, and would consider the purchased information tainted. In eight years of listening to newsmen at American Press Institute seminars, the API's Malcom Mallette says that "only a few have ever related situations where they've paid. There's more chance of error, that they'll get caught with inaccurate information." Informants who talk to the press may have many ulterior motives: revenge, ego, ambition to destroy an opponent, public conscience, liking the reporter—but no motive is so suspect as the mercenary one.

One of the most controversial of these arrangements was *Life*'s purchase in 1959 of the astronauts' "personal stories." Aside from the question of whether government employees should be allowed to profit from recounting publicly-financed experiences, there was a more basic objection. Since *Life* had a vested interest in the success of NASA's space program, the magazine would not be likely to encourage dogged and objective reporting and analysis of the space effort.

Life's purchase of the astronauts' stories had a more profound effect, which helped shape the public reaction to its later investigative efforts, such as the story of Supreme Court Justice Abe Fortas. It was openly speculated that *Life* had kept several Justice Department employees on the payroll to get the information.

Denny Walsh, who joined *Life*'s investigative unit very shortly after its inception in 1967, insists that money was never passed to informants. "The Fortas story," says Walsh, "it was a disgruntled bureaucrat, a guy who saw something happening he didn't like. Simple as that." But Walsh also says that because of *Life*'s reputation of paying for the astronaut story and other "exclusives," every potential informant wanted a hand-out. "Not government people, but others approaching us every day in every way—letter, telephone, in person—with stories and a request for compensation." Walsh swears, "I'll never work anyplace else where every guy crossing the threshold holds his hand out. That was the case with *Life*, in spades."

Because of its many pitfalls, the purchase of information—even more than the other investigative tactics—should be a last resort, the journalistic equivalent of an act of war. As one illustration of the circumstances that *might* justify it, consider this case:

Jack Nelson, the Washington bureau chief of the *Los Angeles Times*, once paid a Mississippi detective $1,000 for police files on two local informants. The story Nelson broke was a complicated one: it involved the FBI, which had paid two Klu Klux Klansmen to set a trap for two other Klansmen, so that this latter pair could be caught in the act of bombing a home. While the Klansmen were attempting to place a bomb in the garage of a prominent Jewish businessman, the police attacked with guns ablaze, killing one of the Klansmen outright and wounding the other. There was evidence that the police never intended to take either Klansman alive. In his story, Nelson questioned an arrangement in which the FBI, in effect, hired murderers and *agents provocateurs*.

The detective had told Nelson about the incident and what the police files contained, and suggested that Nelson give him "credit" for the documents. Nelson says, "I think I could've gotten it for $250." But it was a hell of a story, Nelson says, and the man risked his skin to get the files. "I don't regret paying, not a bit." Nelson says he did not feel uncomfortable because he was not buying the man's word which might be altered or influenced by the money; rather, the detective was leading Nelson to documents which Nelson could independently verify with the FBI and other sources. Nelson viewed it as a finder's fee.

The Other Side of the Coin

The responsibility we advocate on the part of the investigative press should be accompanied by a burden of responsibility on the part of those whom it investigates and who take it to court. A recent $5-million suit against the worthy but impecunious *Texas Observer* is a reminder of the potential disaster a libel suit represents for all but the richest publishers. Even if the *Observer* wins the suit, the legal fees could easily drive it into bankruptcy. This is a publisher's worst nightmare—that a well-heeled and determined plaintiff will destroy him even when he is telling the truth, simply by appealing to court after court until the publisher runs out of money. This moment will come sooner than later for many of the more interesting and provocative periodicals for whom fiscal fragility is a chronic condition.

A solution would be for our federal and state legislatures to enact a statute providing that a plaintiff pay the defendant's legal fees in any case where the plaintiff is found not to have had a reasonable ground for asserting that he had been defamed. Or, in a reform that would strike fear into the hearts of litigants who are frivolous or vindictive at the same time that it would embolden those who are in the right, the law could provide that in every case all legal costs would be paid by the loser.

Many laymen think this is the way it is for now. It is not. Only in a tiny minority of cases are the winning side's fees paid by the losers.

Malicious Intent

The fifth and by far the greatest danger in investigative reporting is lack of fidelity to the facts. Developments in the law of libel during the 1960s tended to give some reporters the feeling that they could get away with less than the truth. The Supreme Court said in the famous case of *New York Times v. Sullivan*, "The constitutional guarantees require, we think, a federal rule that prohibits a public official from recovering damages for a defamatory statement relating to his official conduct unless he proves that the statement was made with 'actual malice' —that is, with knowledge it was false or with reckless disregard of whether it was false or not."

When reporters think they can safely go to the borderline of recklessness, there is a danger some will cross the line. A recent case illustrates that danger:

James Sprouse was the state Democratic candidate for governor of West Virginia in 1968, running a tight race against then-Congressman Arch Moore, now the governor. Ten days before the November balloting, the Charleston *Daily Mail* unveiled its explosive headlines: "Pendleton Realty Bonanza by Jim Sprouse Disclosed; Cleanup of Nearly $500,000 In View." A second set of banners appeared the next day, reporting on a news conference called by Moore: "Moore Asks Federal Probe Into Sprouse's Pendleton Land Grab; Dummy Firm Seen Proving Corruption." An accompanying editorial, comparing Sprouse's candidacy to "asking the horses to clean their own barn,'' asked: ''More of the Shabby Same or Some Cleansing Change.''

Arch Moore was quoted as saying that the ''land grab'' was achieved with a ''dummy corporation set up in the dark of night.'' The stories implied that Sprouse and his real estate partners had relied on inside information that the U.S. Forest Service would purchase most of the recently acquired property for a recreation area, and balloon the value of Sprouse's remaining sector. One fact was repeated four times in the articles—that the land company had been set up one month before plans for the federal recreation project were announced.

The story had been brought to the *Daily Mail*'s political writer, Robert Mellace, by Arch Moore's campaign manager and press aide, and Mellace said he relied on their investigative talents. Before the story was published, a copy was delivered to Moore's campaign aides, who distributed it to all daily and weekly papers for simultaneous publication throughout the state.

The reporter never interviewed Sprouse or any of the owners, or the real estate agent handling the deal. Instead, accompanied by the Moore PR man, Mellace went to see the property, and placed an appraisal value of $1,000 an acre on an estimated 400 acres remaining in the plot. He arrived at that figure by asking a local motel owner his estimate, as well as a stranger he met in a grocery store while buying a Coke. A land staff officer at the Forest Service who had surveyed and appraised the Sprouse property reportedly showed Mellace land charts indicating that there were less than 100 acres in the parcel, worth no more than $50,000 total; but this was not included in Mellace's story.

Mellace acknowledged in court that the sale was completely legitimate. Mellace said there was never any concealment of the public records listing Sprouse as the land company's president, and admitted he had found nothing to indicate Sprouse and his partners had any inside tip about the Forest Service's plans. As for the $500,000 ''bonanza,'' the remaining property later sold for $34,000, with Sprouse's share less than $14,000.

Sprouse lost the election by less than 10,000 votes. A jury awarded Sprouse $750,000. The State Supreme Court upheld the verdict but reduced the amount to $250,000.

[With a *Daily Mail* appeal], it is possible that the Supreme Court [would] find that Mellace's behavior did not meet the *Sullivan* test of recklessness. It is also possible that the Supreme Court will revise the test by making it negligence instead of recklessness. In other words, the test would become: Did the reporter exercise the care of a reasonably prudent man in carrying out the investigation that produced the story and did he have reasonable grounds for the allegations in his story, even if the allegations turn out to be untrue and defamatory? Whether the courts move towards this test or not—in the view of many libel lawyers, it, rather than recklessness, has been the test most consistently implied by the concepts of ''abuse of privilege'' and ''actual malice''—it certainly should be the minimum test that each reporter and his editors bring to the decision of whether to publish a possibly defamatory story.

Rules of Thumb

I believe there are two rules of thumb which reporters should employ in developing a story. The first is the rule of full disclosure. If the contents of a closed-door speech are so significant that a reporter must disguise himself to gain entry, or if a secret report involves such a crucial issue that the reporter is willing to steal a copy, then he and the paper should be willing to disclose the means by which they obtained it. Then the public will have the necessary data to decide for itself whether the reporter's calculation of ends and means was correct.

The second rule of thumb is the natural companion of the first: the reporter must be willing to accept responsibility for his actions. Careless defamation should be recognized throughout the world of journalism as a firing offense. Too many reporters now think of themselves as virtuous Davids who can do no wrong bringing down overbearing Goliaths. They could turn the coming wave of investigative reporting into a nightmare.

Bibliography

Timothy Ingram's article expresses a concern about the quality of contemporary investigative journalism, a concern shared by many others in the profession. See the special section in *The Bulletin of the American Society of Newspaper Editors* (September 1975), Stephen Hartgen, "There's More Here Than Meets a Dragon's Eye," *The Quill* (April 1975), pp. 12-15 and an earlier article by Rudy Maxa, "Dealing in Sweet Secrets: News Leaks as a Way of Doing Business," *The Quill* (September 1974), pp. 18-21. Two excellent articles dealing with the methods and results of investigative reporting are Seymour M. Hersh, "The Story Everyone Ignored," *Columbia Journalism Review* (Winter 1969-70), pp. 55-58, which discusses the exposure and publicizing of the My Lai atrocities, and Barry Lando, "The Herbert Affair," *The Atlantic* (May 1973), pp. 73-81, which discusses Lando's efforts as Washington producer of CBS' *Sixty Minutes* to unravel Col. Anthony Herbert's charges of military war crimes in Vietnam. Read together they reveal a temptation which confronts all journalists, print or electronic; that is, the tendency to accept stories at face value if they fit the reporter's preconceptions.

The New Journalism: How it Came To Be

By Everette E. Dennis

New Journalism/ Consumer Reporting

It was a time when old values were breaking down; new knowledge exploded all around us; people worried about drugs, hippies, and war. We talked of violence, urban disorder, turmoil. New terms like polarization, credibility gap and counterculture crept into the language. It was during *this* time, somewhere between 1960 and 1970, that the term "new journalism" also began to appear in the popular press. Almost as rapidly as the term became a descriptive link in the vernacular, it was used and misused in so many contexts that its meaning was obscured. First

Everette E. Dennis is on the faculty of the School of Journalism and Mass Communication, University of Minnesota. He is co-author with William L. Rivers of *Other Voices: The New Journalism in America,* 1974, co-editor of *New Strategies for Public Affairs Reporting,* 1976, and editor of *The Magic Writing Machine,* 1971, from which this selection was taken. Permission to reprint was granted by the School of Journalism, University of Oregon.

accepted and used by its practitioners, the term found its way into older, more established publications by the mid-Sixties. *Time* called former newsman-turned author Tom Wolfe "the *wunderkind* of the new journalism," while *Editor & Publisher* described Nicholas von Hoffman of the *Washington Post* as an "exponent of the new journalism." And there were others: Lillian Ross, Jimmy Breslin, Norman Mailer, Truman Capote, Gay Talese, and Pete Hamill, all were designated "new journalists" by one medium or another. At the same time a number of different forms of communication, from nonfiction novels to the underground press, were being labeled "new journalism."

By 1970 few terms had wider currency and less uniformity of meaning than new journalism. Yet one wonders whether this curious mix of people, philosophies, forms and publications has any common purpose or meaning. To some the term had a narrow connotation, referring simply to a new form of nonfiction that was using fiction methods. Other critics were just as certain that new journalism was an emerging form of advocacy in newspapers and magazines which previously had urged a kind of clinical objectivity in reporting the news. Soon anything slightly at variance with the most traditional practices of the conventional media was cast into the new journalism category.

While the debate over definition droned on, it began to obscure any real meaning the term "new journalism" ever had. The scope and application of new journalism was not the only point of contention, though. Some critics looked peevishly at the jumble of writers, styles, and publications and suggested that "there is really nothing very new about the new journalism."

And it was true. One could trace every form and application of the new journalism to an antecedent somewhere, sometime, The underground press, for example, was said to be a twentieth century recurrence of the political pamphleteering of the colonial period. "And isn't the alternative press simply muckraking in new dress?" And on it went.

Although much of the criticism of new journalism has concentrated, unproductively I believe, on whether or not it is new, no attempt will be made here to resolve this question. Perhaps we should think of the new journalism as we do the New Deal or the New Frontier. No one argues that using these terms means one believes there was never before a deal or a frontier. So it is with the new journalism.

What began as a descriptive term for a kind of nonfiction magazine article has been mentioned previously. As one who is viewing these journalistic developments I know that a number of dissimilar forms are called "new journalism." This is the reality of the situation. I will not argue with this commonly used and loosely-constructed definition of new journalism, but will look instead at its various forms, outlets, content and practitioners. Much of what is regarded as new journalism can be judged only by the most personal of standards. It is, after all, a creative endeavor of people seeking alternatives to the tedium of conventional media.

Carl Sandberg used to say every generation wants to assert its uniqueness by crying out, "We are the greatest city, the greatest nation, nothing like us ever was." If this is so, one might conclude that every generation will have its own "new journalism" or at least that it will regard its journalistic products as new.

Creative journalists have always tried to improve upon existing practices in writing and gathering news. The history of journalism chronicles their efforts. But even when one accepts the notion of each generation having its own new journalism, the decade of the Sixties still stands out as an unusually productive and innovative period.

Magazines and newspapers, having felt the harsh competitive challenge of the electronic media, realized that the public no longer relied upon them for much entertainment in the form of short stories and longer fiction. As the public demanded something new, the *new nonfiction*, an attempt to enliven the traditional magazine article with descriptive detail and life-like dialog, emerged.

Newsmen who tired of the corporate bigness of metropolitan dailies and their unwillingness to challenge establishment institutions, founded their own papers. We will, they said, offer an *alternative* to traditional journalism, the chain papers and their plastic personnel.

Other newsmen, who stayed with the conventional papers, were arguing against the notions of balanced news, objectivity, and stodgy use of traditional sources of news. They sought and were granted opportunities for open *advocacy* in the news columns.

The alienated young constructed a counter-culture which would reject most of the underlying assumptions of traditional society. Needing communciations media that were equally alienated from the straight world, they created the *underground* press which was, as one writer said, "like a tidal wave of sperm rushing into a nunnery."

Still other journalists found the impressionistic newsgathering methods of the media to be crude and unreliable measures. They would apply the scientific method and the tools of survey research to journalism, thus seeking a *precision* before unknown in media practice.

Any look back at the Sixties and the swirl of journalistic activity has the appearance of a confused collage of verbal and visual combatants, seeking change in the *status quo* but not knowing quite what or where in all that was happening; a concern for form, for style often seemed to supersede content. John Corry, who worked with the *New York Times* and *Harper's* during this period, offers this recollection:

It happened sometime in the early 1960's and although no one can say exactly when, it may have begun in that magic moment when Robert Frost, who always looked marvelous, with silver hair, and deep, deep lines in his face, read a poem at the inauguration of John F. Kennedy, and then went on to tell him afterwards that he ought to be more Irish than Harvard, which was something that sounded a lot better than it actually was. Hardly a man today remembers the poem, which was indifferent, anyway, but nearly everyone remembers Frost, or at least the sight of him at the lectern, which was perhaps the first sign that from then on it would not matter so much what you said, but how you said it.

With similar emphasis on form, Tom Wolfe recalls his first encounter with the new journalism: "The first time I realized there was something new going on in journalism was one day in 1962 when I pick up a copy of *Esquire* and read an article by Gay Talese entitled 'Joe Louis at Fifty.' "* Wolfe continues, " 'Joe Louis at Fifty' wasn't like a magazine article at all. It was like a short story. It began with a scene, an intimate confrontation between Louis and his third wife:

'Hi, sweetheart!' Joe Louis called to his wife, spotting her waiting for him at the Los Angeles airport.

*Wolfe's memory betrayed him. The correct citation is Gay Talese, "Joe Louis—The King as a Middle-Aged Man," *Esquire,* June, 1962. Ed.

> She smiled, walked toward him, and was about to stretch up on her toes and kiss him—but suddenly stopped.
> 'Joe,' she snapped, 'where's your tie?'
> 'Aw, sweetie,' Joe Louis said, shrugging. 'I stayed out all night in New York and didn't have time.'
> 'All night!' she cut in. 'When you're out here with me all you do is sleep, sleep, sleep.'
> 'Sweetie,' Joe Louis said with a tired grin, 'I'm an ole man.'
> 'Yes,' she agreed, 'but when you go to New York you try to be young again.''

Says Wolfe, ''The story went on like that, scene after scene, building up a picture of an ex-sports hero now fifty years old.''

Talese, who gained little recognition until the late Sixties, in the introduction to *Fame and Obscurity* cautions those who deceptively regard the new journalism as fiction:

> ''It is, or should be, as reliable as the most reliable reportage although it seeks a larger truth than is possible through the mere compilation of verifiable facts, the use of direct quotations, and adherence to the rigid organizational style of the older form.''

To Talese the new journalism ''allows, demands in fact, a more imaginative approach to reporting, and it permits the writer to inject himself into the narrative if he wishes, as many writers do, or to assume the role of detached observer, as other writers do, including myself.''

In the search for a definition of new journalism, Tom Wolfe explains ''it is the use by people writing nonfiction of techniques which heretofore had been thought of as confined to the novel or the short story, to create in one form both the kind of objective reality of journalism and the subjective reality that people have always gone to the novel for.'' Dwight MacDonald, one of Wolfe's severest critics, disagrees, calling the new journalism ''parajournalism,'' which he says, ''seems to be journalism—the collection and dissemination of current news—but the appearance is deceptive. It is a bastard form having it both ways, exploiting the factual authority of journalism and the atmospheric license of fiction. Entertainment rather than information is the aim of its producers, and the hope of its consumers.''

Dan Wakefield finds middle ground suggesting that writers like Wolfe and Truman Capote have ''catapulted the reportorial kind of writing to a level of social interest suitable for cocktail party conversation and little-review comment. . . .'' He continues:

> Such reporting is ''imaginative'' not because the author has distorted the facts, but because he has presented them in a full instead of a naked manner, brought sight, sounds and feel surrounding those facts, and connected them by comparison with other facts of history, society and literature in an artistic manner that does not diminish, but gives greater depth and dimension to the facts.

Each of the other forms of new journalism mentioned previously (alternative, advocacy, underground and precision) have also sparked vigorous criticism, related both to their content and their form. If there is one consistent theme in all the criticism, it is probably the McLuhanistic ''form supersedes content.'' The real innovative contribution of the new journalism has been stylistic. This theme will be expanded later as we examine examples of new journalism.

The theory of causality is of little use in chronicling the development of new journalism. Most of the innovations in form and approach have occurred simultaneously. Some were related to each other; some were not. The new journalism is an apparent trend in American journalism which involves a new form of expression, new writers and media, or an alteration in the patterns of traditional media. It has been suggested that this trend can be traced to the early 1960's and is related to (a) sociocultural change during the last decade, (b) a desire by writers and editors to find an alternative to conventional journalism, and (c) technological innovations such as electronic media, computer hardware and offset lithography.

Rarely has any decade in American history seen such drastic upheaval. Beyond the immediate surface events—rioting, student unrest, assassinations, and war—lies a pervasive youthful alienation from traditional society and the beginnings of a radical rejection of science and technology. Calls for a new humanism were heard. Young people, rejecting the materialistic good life, sought new meaning through introspection, drugs, and religion. The decade witnessed the beginnings of what some would call a counter culture: "a culture so radically disaffiliated from the mainstream assumptions of our society that it scarcely looks to many as a culture at all, but takes on the alarming appearance of a barbaric intrusion."

The new journalism, especially the new nonfiction and the writing of underground editors, seemed to respond to youthful needs. The practitioners of reportage attempted to bring all of the senses to bear in their journalistic product—with special attention to visual imagery. Thus Norman Mailer gave us sight, sound, and inner thoughts as he sloshed through great public events, and issues. It is probably too early to determine how much the social upheaval and its resulting influence on the young affected the organizational and perceptual base that the new journalists would use. Writers like Jimmy Breslin and Studs Terkel would go to the periphery of an event, calling on a spectator instead of a participant to summarize the action. Tom Wolfe thought the automobile and the motorcycle were better organizing principles than war or race relations. Ken Kesey, the central figure in Wolfe's *The Electric Kool-Aid Acid Test*, introduces the reader to the Age of Acid, while a small town in western Kansas is a vehicle with which Truman Capote orchestrates a nonfiction novel about violent crime and its effects.

Journalism would also be influenced by television. Technological change in communications has always meant new functions for existing media. With television bringing electronic entertainment into our homes, we had less need for the *Saturday Evening Post's* short stories. The ratio of fiction to nonfiction in magazines would change as would the nature of the package of the newspaper. The days when newspapers serialized books blended into the distant past. Even the traditional comic strip seems at times to be threatened. Television changed the programming habits of radio, just as it changed magazines and newspapers.

The technological innovation of greatest importance to the new journalism was probably offset printing. It suddenly became possible to produce a newspaper cheaply, without having to invest in typesetting equipment or presses. The rapid reproduction of photo-offset meant that a single printer could produce dozens of small newspapers and that the alternative or underground paper could be produced rapidly at limited cost. Offset also allowed for the inclusion of freehand art work without expensive engravings, thus permitting efforts of psychedelic artists to merge with the underground journalists.

Although "new journalism" is used most often to describe a style of nonfiction writing, the definition has been further expanded to include alternative journalism and advocacy journalism. Although the reiteration of these terms may be following the fads, they do provide some shades of meaning which contribute to an

A Schematic Look at the New Journalism

Form	Medium	Content	Practitioners
The new non-fiction also called reportage and parajournalism	Newspaper columns Books Magazine articles	Social trends Celebrity pieces The "little people" Public events	Tom Wolfe, Jimmy Breslin, Gay Talese, Norman Mailer, Truman Capote, others.
Alternative journalism also called "modern muckraking"	Alternative news-papers New magazines	Exposes of wrong-doing in estab-lishment organiza-tions, attacks on bigness of institu-tions	Editor and writers for *San Francisco Bay Guardian, Cervi's Journal, Maine Times, Village Voice.*
Advocacy journalism	Newspaper columns Point-of-view papers Magazines	Social change Politics Public issues	*Jack Newfield, Pete Hamill, Nicholas von Hoff-man, others.*
Underground journalism	Underground papers in urban areas, at univer-sities, high schools, military bases	Radical politics Psychedelic art The drug culture Social services Protest	Editors and writers for LA, New York and Washington *Free Presses, Berkeley Barb, East Village Other,* many others.
Precision journalism	Newspapers Magazines	Survey research and reporting of social indicators, public concerns	Editors and writers the Knight News-papers, other newspapers, news magazines.

understanding of the richly expansive scope of new journalism. These descriptive categories are offered more as a tool for analysis than a definitive up-to-the-minute classification of the rapidly proliferating output of the new journalists. Through an examination of a few of these new journalistic developments it is hoped that there will be fuller appreciation and awareness of what may be an important trend in the evolution of the mass media.

Reportage

In the early 1960's it occurred to Truman Capote, who already had a reputation as a writer of fiction, that "reportage is the great unexplored art form." While it was a metier used by very few good writers or craftsmen, Capote reasoned that it would have "a double effect fiction does not have—the fact of it being true, every word of it true, would add a double contribution of strength and impact." Some years after Lillian Ross used a nonfiction reportage form in the *New Yorker*, Capote and other writers had experimented with reportage in magazine articles. *Picture* (1952), a nonfiction novel by Miss Ross, had been hailed as a literary innovation. "It is," one critic said, "the first piece of factual reporting to be written in the form of a novel. Miss Ross' story contains all the raw materials of dramatic fiction: the Hollywood milieu, the great director, the producer, the studio production chief and the performers." Another of the new nonfiction reportage innovators was Gay Talese, whose articles in *Esquire* "adapted the more dramatic and immediate technique of the short story to the magazine article," according to Tom Wolfe. Wolfe says it was Talese's "Joe Louis at Fifty" that first awakened him to the creative potential of reportage.

Some of the best early examples of the new nonfiction, in addition to the writing of Miss Ross and Talese, are articles by Wolfe collected in an anthology with an unlikely title: *The Kandy-Kolored Tangerine Flake Streamline Baby* (1965). Wolfe, like Talese, used scenes, extended dialog, and point of view. A few years later Wolfe described this period of his life as a time when he broke out of the totem format of newspapers. He had worked as a reporter for the *Washington Post* and *New York Herald Tribune* but later found magazines and books a better outlet for his creative energies. Another new journalist, Jimmy Breslin, was able to practice the new journalism in a daily newspaper column. Breslin, whom Wolfe calls "a brawling Irishman who seemed to come from out of nowhere," is a former sportswriter who began using a reportage style in a column he wrote for the *New York Herald Tribune*. Breslin breathed life into an amazing assortment of characters like Fat Thomas (an overweight bookie) and Marvin the Torch (an arsonist with a sense of professionalism). Breslin met many of his characters in bars and demonstrated conclusively that the "little people of the street" (and some not so little) could say eloquent things about their lives and the state of the world. More important, Breslin brought the expectations and intuitions of these people to his readers in vivid, almost poetic style. In doing so, he as much as anyone else added the nonauthority as a source of information to the concept of new journalism.

Truman Capote tried the experimental reportage form on two articles in the *New Yorker* (one on the ''Porgy and Bess'' tour of Russia and the other on Marlon Brando) before writing his powerful *In Cold Blood* (1966). As Capote describes it: ''I realized that perhaps a crime, after all, would be the ideal subject for a massive job of reportage I wanted to do. I would have a wide range of characters, and more importantly, it would be timeless.'' It took Capote nearly seven years to finish the book which he himself described as ''a new art form.''

Contributing yet another variation on the new nonfiction theme during the 1960's was Norman Mailer, who like Capote, had already established himself as an important fiction writer. To new journalism reportage Mailer contributed a first-person autobiographical approach. In *Armies of the Night* (1968), an account of a peace march on the Pentagon, Mailer ingeniously got inside his own head and presented the reader with a vivid description of his own perceptions and thoughts, contrasting them with his actions. This was a variation on the approach Talese had used earlier in describing the thoughts of persons featured in his articles and books. He called this description of one's inner secrets ''interior monolog.''

Examples of nonfiction reportage, in addition to those previously mentioned are: Breslin's *The World of Jimmy Breslin* (1968), Miss Ross' *Reporting* (1964), Talese's *The Kingdom and the Power* (1969), and *Fame and Obscurity* (1970), Wolfe's *Electric Kool-Aid Acid Test* (1969), *The Pump House Gang* (1969), and *Radical Chic and Mau-mauing the Flak Catchers* (1970). Frequent examples of new nonfiction reportage appear in *Esquire, New York* and other magazines.

Alternative Journalism

While Tom Wolfe would like to keep the new journalism pure and free from moralism, political apologies and romantic essays, increasingly the term ''new journalism'' has been broadened to include the alternative journalists. Most alternative journalists began their careers with a conventional newspaper or magazine but became disillusioned because the metropolitan paper often got too big to be responsive to the individual. Certain industries or politicians become sacred cows, the paper gets comfortable and is spoiled by economic success. At least this was the view of one of the most vigorous of alternative journalists, the late Eugene Cervi of Denver. In describing *Cervi's Rocky Mountain Journal*, he said,

> We are what a newspaper is supposed to be: controversial, disagreeable, disruptive, unpleasant, unfriendly to concentrated power and suspicious of privately-owned utilities that use the power with which I endow them to beat me over the head politically.

Alternative journalism is a return to personal journalism where the editor and/or a small staff act as a watchdog on conventional media, keeping them honest by covering stories they would not have touched. The alternative journalists are in the reform tradition. They do not advocate the elimination of traditional social, political, or economic institutions. In their view the institutions are all right, but those who run them need closer scrutiny.

Little has been written about the contribution of the alternative journalists who have established newspapers, newsletters, and magazines which attempt to provide an alternative to conventional media. "The traditional media simply are not covering the news," says Bruce Brugmann, editor of San Francisco's crusading *Bay Guardian*. Brugmann, a former reporter for the *Milwaukee Journal*, asserts that the kind of material produced by his monthly tabloid is "good, solid investigatory journalism." The *Bay Guardian* has been a gadfly for San Francisco, attacking power companies, railroads, and other establishment interests. One crusade of long standing is a probe with continuity of the communications empire of the *San Francisco Chronicle*, which Brugmann calls "Superchron." The *Bay Guardian* is a lively tabloid with bold, striking headlines and illustrative drawings which are actually editorial cartoons. *Cervi's Journal*, for years a scrapping one-man operation, is being continued by the late founder's daughter. Cervi, sometimes called the La Guardia of the Rockies, was a volatile, shrill, and colorful man who, while providing news of record to Denver's business community (mortgages, bankruptcies, etc.), fearlessly attacked public and private wrongdoing. *Cervi's Journal* has taken on the police, local government, business, and other interests. Unlike the *Bay Guardian*, which has been in financial trouble almost since its founding, *Cervi's Journal* seems to have found a formula for financial success.

Other publications operating in an alternative-muckraking style are *The Texas Observer* in Austin, *I.F. Stone's Bi-Weekly* in Washington, D.C., [Stone retired and closed his publication] Roldo Bartimole's *Point of View* in Cleveland, and the *Village Voice* in New York City. All of these publications (including the *Village Voice*, which began as an early underground paper in 1955), are read by a middle and upper-middle class audience, although all espouse a decidedly left-of-center position on social and political issues. Brugmann and several of his fellow alternative editors agree that their function is to make the establishment press more responsible. While conveying a sense of faith in the system, the alternative press has little tolerance for abuse or misuse of power.

Also a part of alternative journalism are a little band of iconoclastic trade publications—the journalism reviews. Shortly after the Democratic National Convention of 1968 when newsmen and students were beaten by police in the streets of Chicago, a number of working journalists organized the abrasive *Chicago Journalism Review*, which confines most of its barbs to the performance of the news media in Chicago. Occasionally, other stories are featured, but usually because one of the Chicago dailies or television stations refused to run the story first. The journalism reviews are perhaps the most credible instrument of a growing inclination toward media criticism. The writers and editors of the reviews continue as practicing reporters for traditional media, at times almost daring their bosses to fire them for revealing confidences and telling stories out of school. Other press criticism organs include *The Last Post* in Montreal, the *St. Louis Journalism Review*, and *The Unsatisfied Man: A Review of Colorado Journalism*, published in Denver. [See bibliographical notes to James Carey's article in Chapter 2.]

A talk with the editors of the various alternative press outlets makes one wonder whether they wouldn't secretly like to put themselves out of business. As

Brugmann puts it: "In Milwaukee, a *Bay Gurardian* type of publication could never make it because the Milwaukee *Journal* does an adequate job of investigative reporting." Perhaps if the San Francisco media had such a record, the *Bay Guardian* would cease to exist.

Advocacy Journalism

The alternative journalist sees himself as an investigative reporter, sifting through each story, reaching an independent conclusion. He does not openly profess a particular point of view, but claims a more neutral ground. The advocacy journalist, on the other hand, writes with an unabashed commitment to a particular viewpoint. He may be a New Left enthusiast, a professed radical, conservative, Women's libber or Jesus freak. The advocacy journalist defines his bias and casts his analysis of the news in that context. Advocacy journalists, usually though not always, suggest a remedy for the social ill they are exposing. This is rarely the case with the alternative journalist who does not see the development of action programs as his function.

Clayton Kirkpatrick of the *Chicago Tribune* says advocacy journalism is really "the new propaganda." He contines, "Appreciation of the power of information to persuade and convince has been blighted by preoccupation and is a primary influence in the activist movement that started in Europe and is now spreading to the United States. It threatens . . .a revolution in the newsroom." John Corry, writing in *Harper's* says, "the most important thing in advocacy journalism is neither how well you write or how well you report, but what your position in life is . . ." Corry sees advocacy journalists as persons who are not concerned about what they say, but how they say it. The advocacy journalists "write mostly about themselves, although sometimes they write about each other, and about how they all feel about things," Corry says.

Advocacy journalism is simply a reporter expressing his personal view in a story. "Let's face it," says Jack Newfield of the *Village Voice*, "the old journalism was blind to an important part of the truth . . .it had a built-in bias in its presentation: Tom Hayden *alleges*, while John Mitchell *announces*." In the old journalism, Newfield continues, "authority always came first. The burden of proof was always on minorities; individuals never get the emphasis that authorities get." Central to advocacy journalism is involvement. Writers like Newfield, who is an avowed New Leftist, are participants in the events they witness and write about. They debunk traditional journalism's concern about objectivity. "The Five W's, Who Needs Them!", declares an article by Nicholas von Hoffman of the *Washington Post*. Von Hoffman, a community organizer for Saul Alinsky's Industrial Areas Foundation in Chicago before joining the *Chicago Daily News*, has established a reputation as an advocacy journalist who shoots from the hip and calls shots as he sees them, according to *Newsweek*. His coverage of the celebrated 1970 Chicago conspiracy trial likened the courtroom and its participants to a theatrical production. Von Hoffman produces a thrice-weekly column, "Poster," which is syndicated by the *Washington Post-Los Angeles Times* News Service. In his search for advocacy outlets, Von Hoffman has written several books: *Mississippi Notebook* (1964), *The Multiversity* (1966), *We Are The People Our Parents Warned Us Against* (1968), and a collection of his newspaper columns, *Left at the Post* (1970).

Jack Newfield, who writes regularly in *New York* as well as in the *Village Voice*, has produced *A Prophetic Minority* (1966), and *Robert Kennedy: A Memoir* (1969), said to be the most passionate and penetrating account of the late Senator's life. Another of the advocacy journalists is Pete Hamill of the *New York Post*. Hamill, who seems at times to wear his heart on his sleeve, writes about politics, community problems, and social issues for the *Post* and a variety of magazines ranging from *Life* to *Ladies Home Journal*. He also writes regularly for *New York* where his concern for the unique problems of urban crowding show through in articles like "Brooklyn: A Sane Alternative."

Publications such as *Ramparts* and *Scanlan's* are examples of advocacy journalism. The *Village Voice* seems to fit into both the alternative and advocacy categories as do a number of other publications. Many of the social movements of the recent past and present needed organs of communication to promote their causes. Thus Young Americans For Freedom established what is regarded as a new right publication, *Right-On*. Jesus freaks have a publication with the same name. The Women's Liberation movement has spawned a number of newspapers and magazines. Ecology buffs also have their own publications as do the Black Panthers and other groups too numerous to mention.

The Underground Press

While the literature about underground journalism is growing rapidly—even in such staid publications as *Fortune*—a clarifying definition is rarely offered. Underground journalism has its phycho-social underpinnings in the urban/university counter-culture communities of the 1960's. The underground newspaper is a communications medium for young people who are seeking alternative life styles. Often these persons feel alienated from the message of conventional media. The *Los Angeles Free Press* is regarded as the first underground. Editor Arthur Kunkin explains, "the underground press is do-it-yourself journalism. The basis for the new journalism is a new audience. People are not getting the information they desired from the existing media. The LA *Free Press* is aimed at the young, Blacks, Mexicans and intellectuals." Kunkin says his paper is open to "anyone who can write in a comprehensible manner." He believes the underground press serves as a "mass opposition party." He urges his contributors to "write with passion, show the reader your style, your prejudice." [Kunkin no longer edits the *Free Press*.]

Some critics, however, are not as generous in their descriptions of underground journalism. Dave Sanford, writing in *New Republic* said:

There is nothing very underground about the underground press. The newspapers are hawked on street corners, sent to subscribers without incident through the U.S. mails, carefully culled and adored by the mass media. About three dozen of them belong to the Underground Press Syndicate, which is something like the AP on a small scale; through this network they spread the word about what is new in disruptive protest, drugs, sex. Their obsessive interest in things that the ''straights'' are embarrassed or offended by is perhaps what makes them underground. They are a place to find what is unfit to print in the *New York Times*.

Early examples of the underground press were the *East Village Other*, published in Manhattan's East Village, not far from that latter-day Bohemian, the *Village Voice*, the *Chicago Seed, Berkeley Barb, Washington Free Press*, and others. The undergrounds are almost always printed by offset. This ''takes the printing out of the hands of the technicians,'' says editor Kunkin, a former tool and die maker. The undergrounds use a blend of type and free hand art work throughout. They are a kind of collage for the artist-intellectual, some editors believe. The content of the undergrounds ranges from political and artistic concerns (especially an establishment v. the oppressed theme), sexual freedom, drugs, and social services. Much of their external content (that not written by the staff and contributors) comes from the Underground Press Syndicate and Liberation News Service.

In addition to the larger and better known undergrounds, there are underground papers in almost every sizable university community in the country. Most large cities have a number of undergrounds serving hippies and heads in the counterculture community. Newer additions to the underground are the high school undergrounds and the underground newspapers published on and adjacent to military bases, both in the U.S. and abroad. Some critics foresee the end of the underground press, but the larger undergrounds are now lucrative properties. This, of course, raises another question about how long a paper can stay underground. Can a paper like the *Los Angeles Free Press* with a circulation of 90,000 stay underground? When does an underground paper become a conventional paper? These are among the many unresolved questions about the underground press. The undergrounds have been called the most exciting reading in America. Even David Sanford reluctantly agrees: ''at least they try—by saying what can't be said or isn't being said by the staid daily press, by staying on the cutting edge of 'In' for an audience with the shortest of attention spans.''

Precision Journalism

Perhaps the persons least likely to be classified as new journalists are the precision journalists, yet they may be more a part of the future than any of their colleagues in the new journalism ranks. Richard Scammon and Ben Wattenberg, authors of *The Real Majority*, a 1970 analysis of the American electorate, declare: ''we are really the new journalists.'' They are concerned with an analysis of people that is as precise as possible. Or, at least as precise as the social survey research method allows. These men try to interpret social indicators and trends in prose that will attract the reader and are doing something quite new in journalism.

A leading practitioner of precision journalism is Philip Meyer, a Washington editor for the Knight Newspapers. Meyer, who has written a book which calls for application of behavioral science methodology in the practice of journalism, conducted a much-praised study of Detroit Negroes after the 1967 riot. Meyer and his survey team interviewed hundreds of citizens of Detroit to probe the reasons behind the disorder. His study, *Return to 12th Street*, was one of the few examples of race relations reporting praised by the Kerner Commission. Meyer is a prolific writer with recent articles in publications ranging from *Public Opinion Quarterly* to *Esquire*. Whenever possible he uses the methods of survey research, combined with depth interviews to analyze a political or social situation. For example, early in 1970 a series of articles about the Berkeley rebels of 1964 appeared in the *Miami Herald* and other Knight newspapers. An editor's note explained the precisionist's approach:

> What happens to college radicals when they leave the campus? The whole current movement of young activists who want to change American society began just five years ago at the University of California's Berkeley campus. In a landmark survey, Knight newspapers reporters Philip Meyer and Richard Maidenberg located more than 400 of the original Berkeley rebels, and 230 of them completed detailed questionnaires. Of the respondents, 13 were selected for in-depth interviews. The results based on a computer analysis of the responses, are provided in a series beginning with this article.

Says Meyer, "When we cover an election story in Ohio we can have all the usual description—autumn leaves, gentle winds—but in addition we can offer the reader a pretty accurate profile of what his neighbors are thinking." The precision journalists combine the computer with vivid description. Meyer and his colleagues at the Knight Newspapers are also planning field experiments in which they will use the methods of experimental psychology to test public issue hypotheses in local communities. Of the future Meyer says, "We may never see a medical writer who can tie an artery, but a social science writer who can draw a probability sample is not unheard of."

"I like to think," Ben Wattenberg says, "that we are the new journalism—journalism which is not subjective but which is becoming more objective than ever before. We've got the tools now—census, polls, election results—that give us precision, that tell us so much about people. Yet, at precisely the time when these tools become so exact, the damn New Journalists have become so introspective that they're staring at their navels. The difficulty is that when you put tables in you bore people. Yet when I was in the White House, [he worked for L.B.J.] knowing what was going on, reading the new journalists was like reading fairy tales. They wrote political impressionism."

There are an increasing number of precision journalists—some of them are writers and editors who are integrating social science research into stories for news magazines and other mass circulation periodicals. They are, at present, the unsung heroes of the new journalism. Yet, their work is so boldly futuristic that they cannot long remain in the background. The work of precision journalists differs from the traditional coverage of the Gallup or Harris polls in the amount of information offered and the mode of presentation. The precision journalists extract data, add effective prose and attempt to interpret trends and conditions of concern to people.

How It Came To Be

The various forms of new journalism—new nonfiction, alternative, advocacy, reform, underground and precision—all grew up in the 1960's. The reasons for these developments are not easily ascertained in the short run. However, there were coincidental factors—a break away from traditional news format and style; bright, energetic journalists on the scene; established literary figures who wanted to experiment with reportage; urgent social issues and the advancement of technology. But it was more than all this. There was a mood and a spirit which offered a conducive milieu for new journalism.

In the late Fifties and early Sixties those on the management side of the American press were worried. Enrollments in schools of journalism were not increasing at the same rate as other area of study in colleges and universitites. This was only one manifestation of the tired, staid image of the American press. One editor on the speaking circuit in those days used the title, "You Wonder Where The Glamour Went," trading on a toothpaste advertising slogan in an address rebutting the notion that American journalism had lost its glamour. Such a defensive posture says something about the journalism of the day. It was true that youthful enthusiasm for journalism had waned considerably since the time when foreign and war correspondents had assignments any young person would have coveted. The glamour and excitement simply were not there. Journalism was increasingly being viewed as stodgy by many young people. Economic pressures had reduced the number of newspapers in the country. One-newspaper towns, without the lusty competition of another day, were becoming commonplace. Journalism—both print and broadcast—had taken on a corporate image. Personalities of days past gave way to teams of little gray men, and it was a foregone conclusion that starting your own paper was next to impossible. This image may not have represented the reality of the situation, but it was the dismal picture in the minds of college students at the dawn of the Sixties.

To many bright, young writers the form of journalistic writing itself seemed to constrict creativity. The inverted pyramid, which places elements of a news story in a descending order of importance, and the shopworn "five w's and the h" seemed to impose a rigid cast over the substantive issues and events of the day. Many writers, especially those like Wolfe and Breslin, found the traditional approach to journalism impersonal and dehumanizing, at a time when there was little debate in the trade journals about the concept of objectivity, an ideal to which every right-thinking journalist adhered.

The new journalists' assault on objectivity is displaced, press critic Herbert Brucker believes:

> . . .critics of objective news are not as much against objectivity as they make out. What they denounce as objectivity is not objectivity so much as an incrustation of habits and rules of news writing, inherited from the past, that confine the reporter within rigid limits. Within those limits the surface facts of an event may be reported objectively enough. But that part of the iceberg not immediately visible is ruled out, even though to include it might reveal what happened in a more accurate—indeed more objective—perspective.

It is probably too early to assess all of the elements of the Sixties that set the stage for the development of the new journalism. Yet, one might cite as factors the verve and vitality of the early days of the Kennedy Administration, the ascendency of the civil rights movement, the evolution of a counter-culture, the drug scene, the war in Southeast Asia, student unrest, riots, and urban disorder. The media were affected by these events.

Historian Theodore Roszak speaks of the uniqueness of the Sixties in *The Making of a Counter Culture*:

> It strikes me as obvious beyond dispute that the interests of our college-age and adolescent young in the psychology of alienation, oriental mysticism, psychedelic drugs, and communitarian experiments comprise a cultural constellation that radically diverges from values and assumptions that have been in the mainstream of our society at least since the Scientific Revolution of the seventeenth century.

Reporters who covered the turbulence of the Sixties were wont to maintain traditional objectivity or balance, and few claimed to have the necessary detachment. At the same time the dissent abroad in the land pervaded the newsrooms so that by 1969 even reporters for the *Wall Street Journal*, the very center of establishment journalism, would participate in an anti-war march. Today, the traditional news format is under fire. Subjective decision-making at all stages of the reportorial process is evident. As one reporter put it: "Subjective decisions confront reporters and editors at the stage of assignment, data collection, evaluation, writing, and editing." "Who," the reporter asks, "decides what events to cover, which ones to neglect? When does the reporter know he has gathered enough information? What if there are fifteen sides to a story—instead of the two usually acknowledged by the theory of objectivity? Finally, writing and editing are purely subjective acts."

Certainly the turmoil over objectivity has touched conventional media and enhanced the climate for the new journalism. The critics, however, had justifiable concern about some of the practices of new journalists. The work of writers like Breslin involves a good deal of literary license. Some new journalists are simply not as concerned with accuracy and attribution as are their more conservative colleagues. Some say the new journalism is simply undisciplined, opinionated writing. But it is difficult to determine whether the new journalism threatens any semblance of fairness the media has developed in the four decades since the era of jazz journalism, when sensationalism and embellishment were in full force. Many who criticize the new journalism are simply not ready for the diversity now available in the marketplace. Even a writer like Jack Newfield, perhaps the most strident advocacy journalist in America, says many of the new approaches including his own must serve as part of a total continuum of information which would include many of the traditional approaches to news gathering and dissemination.

As others have pointed out, most of the new journalists developed their style after learning the more conventional newspaper style. They are breaking the rules, but they know why. Even the most forceful advocates of the new journalism praise the organizing principles of the old journalism, in much the same way that Hemingway hailed the style book of the *Kansas City Star*. They part ways on matters of substance and content, but in the early organizing stages, nothing, they say, is better discipline. The inverted pyramid and the fetish for objectivity may have been too rigid, but these methods do offer something in terms of succinct treatment and synthesis of complex, inter-related facts. Perhaps the ideas and actions of the Seventies are too complex for such simplistic treatment.

The new journalism offers rich detail and what Tom Wolfe calls "saturation reporting." The new journalism in all its forms is a more sophisticated kind of writing aimed at a more highly educated populace than that which gave life and readers to the old journalism. The new journalism is in its earliest stages of development. It has not yet arrived. It is not yet—and may never be—the dominant force in American journalism. Perhaps, like minority parties in American politics, it may suggest opportunities for innovation and thoughtful change. The media will do well to listen to the sounds of the new journalism and the resultant response of the new audience. It may be the stuff that the future is made of.

Bibliography

The new journalism of which Everette E. Dennis has been writing is covered well in his own edited book, *The Magic Writing Machine*, School of Journalism, University of Oregon, 1971, and his co-edited work with William Rivers, *Other Voices: The New Journalism in America*, Canfield, 1974. See also Tom Wolfe and E. W. Johnson, eds., *The New Journalism*, Harper & Row, 1973, and Robert J. Glessing, *The Underground Press in America*, Indiana University Press, 1970. The "precision journalism" mentioned by Dennis receives a full treatment in Philip Meyer, *Precision Journalism: A Reporter's Introduction to Social Science Methods*, Indiana University Press, 1973. Meyer is one of the leading practitioners of social science research techniques in reporting. For an interesting historical background to the new journalism, see the special issue of *Journalism History* (Summer 1974) which contained several articles "Tracing the Roots of the New Journalism." A recent review of what has happened to the underground press, particularly in Boston, is Dan Wakefield, "Up From Underground," *The New York Times Magazine* (Feb. 15, 1976), pp. 14-17+.

Is TV Ready for Consumer Reporting?

By Liz Roman Gallese

Liz Roman Gallese is a staff reporter with *The Wall Street Journal*. This article appeared in the newspaper October 20, 1975 and is reprinted with permission of *The Wall Street Journal,* copyright 1975, Dow Jones & Company, Inc. All rights reserved.

Gillette was "incensed." There was Sharon King knocking its product in front of the several million viewers of the WBZ-TV nightly news.

Miss King had spent the previous two days walking back and forth tracing a thin, shaky line on a 25-foot piece of wrapping paper, first with Gillette's Flair felt-tipped pen and then with its five major competitors. Her conclusion, as she told viewers on her three-minute consumer spot, was that the Bic felt-tipped pen costs less per mile of writing than the Flair.

Gillette was particularly annoyed because it has a battery of $8,000 machines running eight hours a day doing exactly the same test. And, says the company, its machines show Flair is "the superior product."

It didn't help Gillette executives' blood pressure that earlier Miss King had knocked the company's Earth Born shampoo, which is promoted for its low alkalinity. Miss King had taken the product to four competitors and three hairdressers and all said, she reported on WBZ, that low alkalinity isn't "critically relevant" to washing hair "cleaner, shinier and bouncier," as the Gillette ads proclaim.

Companies just don't like that sort of thing. "We're upset to have some diddly consumer person get on the tube to five million people and blow our integrity to bits," huffs a man with one offended company. But viewers think it's just great. And at 31 Sharon King has become a star (in Boston, at least) among a new breed of television personality: the "warts-and-all" consumer reporter.

"I'm Evening Up the Score"

She gets lots of fan mail, has her own assistant, and WBZ has just given her her own one-hour daily talk show for women (the new show probably has resulted in the doubling of her $20,000-a-year salary.) Companies, she says, "just don't tell you the whole truth" in their advertising. "So I'm evening up the score and giving them a dose of their own medicine."

Consumer reporting in a medium not particularly noted for fierce independence from advertisers' influence isn't a particularly easy route to fame. Most television consumer reporters stop short of biting the hands that feed their stations. "They are held back by a station's dependency on advertising revenue," says Carol Tucker Foreman, the executive director of the Consumer Federation of America.

About 50 other local television stations now have consumer reporters, up from only five in 1970. But only a handful are allowed to be as open as Miss King. More often than not the sort of financial pressure that a company can exert becomes too great.

WCBS-TV in New York, for example, has killed its consumer affairs beat apparently because two companies have filed libel suits for a total of $26 million. In one case, CBS, which owns the station, is being sued by a computer training school because former consumer reporter John Strossel reported that the school's graduates have trouble finding jobs. In the other case, an apartment referral agency is suing because Mr. Stossel said most of the places on the agency's $35 list of apartments for rent were identical to those found in newspapers and that most were already rented.

"Antagonistic" Advertisers

Other stations are equally nervous. In Denver, David Minshall, a reporter for KOA-TV, charges he was pulled off the consumer beat because his stories were too hard-hitting for advertisers (the station, however, says he was removed for "journalistic" reasons). And in Oklahoma City, Byron Harris resigned as consumer reporter for KWTV because the station agreed to sit on an adverse report on local auto dealers until after a local trade-association meeting. (The station says it agreed to do this because the dealers had become ''antagonistic'' to the station over earlier stories.)

Not that WBZ, which is an NBC affiliate and is owned by Westinghouse Broadcasting, doesn't approach the knocking of advertisers with some trepidation. When the station hired Miss King away from her publicity job at the Massachusetts Consumer Protection Agency 3½ years ago, any script mentioning products by name first had to be approved by a lawyer and the news director. She has far more leeway now, but even so the station refuses to name companies that have either complained to the station or have withdrawn their advertising.

On one occasion a large soft-drink company pulled its ads off WBZ for a month after Miss King had read a list of ''10 terrible foods'' compiled by the Center for Science and the Public Interest, a Washington, D.C. consumer group. The list included sugar, Procter & Gamble's Pringles potato chips, Wonder bread, bacon, Gerber baby food and Coca-Cola.

"No Sacred Cows"

However, the station supported Miss King. ''We tell companies who complain that there aren't any sacred cows around here,'' declares Sy Yanoff, the station's general manager.

Not that all of Miss King's three-minute spots on the 6 p.m. news are that hard-hitting. On occasion she'll sit there telling the folks in a rather nasal monotone how to do such things as read the fine print on ''cents-off'' food coupons (some say that with her healthy good-looks she should be back home in Grand Forks, N.D., doing the morning farm report).

Some of her reporting is puffy enought to be worthy of Sue Ann Nivens on the Mary Tyler Moore Show. Recently, for instance, she devoted a full report to Tetley's new ''unsinkable'' tea bag and concluded that it brews tea more evenly than conventional tea bags. Other times she will give shopping tips, such as where to buy the fattest tunafish sandwich for the money in Boston or how to save a quarter by making your own Italian salad dressing.

But other times she will produce an imaginative report that will both help consumers avoid pitfalls and keep companies on their toes. For one report she lined up 14 different brands of ice cream under the hot TV studio lights and pointed out that they contained 25% to 50% air and so many additives that several of them wouldn't melt. Another time she sliced cucumbers on several razor-sharp dishwasher spray arms.

Miss King's habit of broadcasting consumer groups' findings (such as the ''10 terrible foods'') particularly enrages corporate advertising, marketing and public-relations people. ''You're trying to ruin the good name of Burger King,'' a lawyer for the fast-food chain, owned by Pillsbury, once blurted out to her assistant. The lawyer was angry because Miss King planned to quote from a Consumer Reports magazine story that called the "typical meal" at Burger King nutritionally inferior to the "typical meal" at McDonald's. (Despite the lawyer's wrath, Miss King went ahead and used the item.)

Another favorite tactic is to try to reproduce the product demonstrations often seen in TV commercials. She once rounded up six hungry dogs and turned them loose in front of the camera on plates of dog food. But unlike the dogs on the Alpo dog food commercial she was trying to recreate, only two of the dogs chose the Alpo. Two ate a competing brand and two refused to eat anything.

More recently she hauled a camera crew to a local diner to try to reproduce the Bounty paper-towel strength test. But unlike Rosie, the waitress in the commercial, Miss King found that none of the brands of paper towels she tested, including Bounty, would hold a full cup of coffee without tearing. She did find, though, that Bounty and another would stay together if held in a certain way.

Proctor & Gamble, Bounty's maker, wasn't amused. A spokesman says the company doesn't expect others to be able to reproduce its demonstrations although it does "in fact have a basis' for its claims.

Shortly afterwards, Miss King asked Procter & Gamble for help in recreating its Pampers disposable diapers commercial, which purports to prove that a special protective liner "keeps baby drier" than cloth diapers. But the company declined to help. Its policy now, it says, is to refrain from giving so many details about demonstrations "as to burden the average person."

On-screen testing of products is necessary because with Miss King's limited budget she can't afford to pay for laboratory testing (for example, she spends only $50 to $75 a week for products and props). It could be that her methods are better understood by most consumers than scientific data are. She once tested 10 brands of maple walnut ice cream for walnut content, based on cartons bought in a supermarket. She found the fewest walnuts in the ice cream made by Brigham's, a division of Jewel Cos. The company explained that the amount of walnuts in each box works out to a set average, which was actually more than found in her carton. Miss King replied, "Consumers don't care about your average. They care about their individual box."

This type of reporting has given Miss King a large audience in the Boston area. This was quickly discovered by Zayre discount stores last year when she called 10 Zayre stores on the third day of a sale and found they were out of four of the 10 sale items she was looking for. "It was absolutely devastating." says Stanley Berkovitz, a Zayre executive. "Some people very possibly haven't come back to Zayre to this day."

Some companies "are absolutely panicky about the kind of power they think I have," says Miss King. There's certainly a healthy respect. Once Leroy Raffel, chairman of the Arby's fast-food chain flew to Boston from Youngstown, Ohio, to try to stop her from using a report by a consumer group that Arby's used "additives" in its roast beef sandwiches. Miss King listened to Mr. Raffel and did indeed avoid the word "additives" in her report. Instead she said that Arby's used "saltwater and sodium tripolyphosphate" to hold sliced chunks of beef together.

About 25% of her ideas are suggested by viewers, many of whom have come to view her as an ombudsman for their own personal consumer troubles. She says she recently helped straighten out a viewer's quarrel with Bloomingdale's department store over damaged furniture. And Gretchen Grezina of Cambridge, Mass., says Miss King's intervention resulted in a refund on a rented U-Haul truck after three dealers had refused to give her the advertised cut price.

Miss King says her viewers are mostly "like the people I grew up with in North Dakota, the people who watch game shows and soap operas." It was in Grand Forks that she had her first introduction to consumerism in the local chapter of the Future Homemakers of America.

Then she traveled East to attend Wheaton College in Norton, Mass., from which she graduated Phi Beta Kappa in 1966. After college she held a variety of jobs, including a two-year stint as a publicist for the Massachusetts attorney general and publicity manager for Harvard University Press.

These days she spends a lot of time in the supermarket looking for ideas for her report. She certainly isn't buying for herself since the refrigerator in her one-bedroom apartment in Cambridge is bare but for orange juice and English muffins.

Most of the time Miss King eats out. When she does eat at home, she says, her tastes run to fast food and packaged convenience foods. But, she asserts, "I know what I'm doing when I buy all that stuff."

Bibliography

Consumer reporting, whether on television or in the newspapers, sometimes creates problems for reporters and editors with their superiors, the station managers and publishers. Two examples from the electronic media can be found in Melinda Nix, "Memoirs of a Consumer Reporter," *The Washingtonian* (May 1975), where Ms. Nix tells of her consumer reporting job at WMAL-TV in Washington, D.C., and Bob Ruggles, "Blowup at Channel 9: Consumer Coverage Clashes with Ad Dollars." *The Quill* (May 1974), pp. 29-34, which details a specific incident of alleged advertiser pressure. Arthur Levine, "Better Than Deep Throat," *The Washington Monthly* (April 1975), pp. 45-51, discusses the use of "Action Line" columns in newspapers by culling excellent examples from some of the best columns across the country. Levine argues that these columns, in addition to meeting specific subscriber needs and interests, also serve as excellent sources for investigative reporting. *Media & Consumer* was published as a journal devoted to the consumer world and to press reporting of that world. See the special issue "The Journalist as Consumer Critic" (September 1973).

Two horses at far center of picture (not visible in photo) are stranded by high water of Carroll Creek, which closed Rosemont avenue at U.S. 15

The Frederick (Md.) News and Post 10/12/76

Louisiana Governor Defends His Wife, Gift From Korean

The Milwaukee Journal 10/26/76

Dead Expected To Rise

The Macon (Ga.) News 8/11/76

Former Rep. Gray said last night: "Nobody's investigating me. Nobody's called me. I never had anything to do with selecting an architect. How can you investigate somebody for something he's never done? I've never received a nickel or any kind of favor from anybody associated with the building industry or an architectural firm in my 20 years in Congress."
Former Rep. Gray could not be reached for comment.

The Washington Post 11/11/76

James E. Kuechle, director of the home, said the number of bedsore cases is increasing, and is now about 60 a month, because "we don't have enough sides."

Buffalo Evening News 10/19/76

Men who dive for sea urchins spend up to eight hours a day under water. But the pay is good: often more than $1,000 a week, sometimes even more.

The New York Times 11/9/76

Jobless Ranks Thin Out Slightly In September

Sentinel Star (Orlando, Fla.) 10/9/76

Nationwide Heroine Crackdown Includes Arrest of Three Here

Gainesville (Fla.) Sun 10/8/76

He defined pneumonia as an inflammation of the lungs resulting in severe cases of a life-threatening national immunization program.

Atlanta Constitution 8/4/76

If Kline's plan is to die, the legislature must act

The Philadelphia Inquirer 11/25/76

It contains the richest array of gadgetry ever put in a Rolls, including color TV, a video cassette player, refrigerator, bar, ladies, vanity table, gaming table complete with money, telephone (with a driver's extension) and a rear seat that reclines to form a double bed.

The Philadelphia Inquirer 11/10/76

Drunk gets nine months in violin case

The Lethbridge Herald 10/30/76

Up the road at Goody's, an ice cream parlor and short-order establishment, poor Mr. Goody, who is actually Ben Saul, considered the $3,000 worth of ice cream commencing to melt in his freezers and then went on serving free food to the evacuees from the beach until the fool ran out.

The New York Times 10/2/76

Carter Applauds 'Tone and Spirit' Of Mayors' Body

(N.Y.) Daily News 11/10/76

The New York Times/Oct. 2, 1976

La Paz area was hard hit by storm

President Says He'll Veto Grain Bill With Teeth

The NFO Reporter (Corning, Iowa)

British pound begins rise on European money markets

Houston Chronicle 10/27/76, Chronicle News Service

British pound continues its slide on European markets

Houston Chronicle 10/27/76, UPI

4 Legal Restraints on News

Protection for Sources of News

The Federal Shield Law We Need—

Shield Law for Newsmen: Safeguard or Trap?—

Access to News—

Big-Time Pressures, Small-Town Press—

Free Press/Fair Trial

Court Control of "News" after *Nebraska*

The Federal Shield Law We Need

By Fred P. Graham
and Jack C. Landau

[In June, 1971], the U.S. Supreme Court ruled that the First Amendment does not grant newsmen a privilege to withhold from grand juries either confidential information obtained during legitimate newsgathering activities or the source of that information. In addition to this specific 5 to 4 holding in the *Caldwell-Pappas-Branzburg* cases, Justice Byron R. White implied even broader limitations against the press by repeatedly stating, in one form or another, that reporters have no more rights than ''all other citizens'':

> We see no reason to hold that these reporters, any more than other citizens, should be excused from furnishing information that may help the grand jury in arriving at its initial determinations. . . . Newsmen have no constitutional right of access to the scenes of crimes or disaster when the general public is excluded, and they may be prohibited from attending or publishing information about trials if such restrictions are necessary to assure a defendant a fair trial before an impartial tribunal.

What is important about these statements is that the issue of press access to public disasters or public trials was extraneous to the *Caldwell* case; and in fact the statements appear to be erroneous as a matter of public record.

1. A great many ''other citizens'' have privileges not to testify before grand juries. There are more than 300,000 attorneys who may, in all federal and state courts, invoke the attorney-privilege to protect confidential information from clients which might solve a case of heinous murder or treason; about 300,000 physicians who may withhold confidential information about crimes under certain conditions in federal and state courts; and several hundred thousand clergymen who have a recognized privilege, in one form or another, in federal and state courts to protect confidential information obtained from penitents. (The priest-penitant issue, however, is somewhat murky because there has never been a Supreme Court case in that area.)

2. So far as we know, newsmen may not be prohibited from attending public trials. In fact, the only Supreme Court cases on the subject state that newsmen must be admitted and that they may not be held in contempt of court for publishing public trial events.

3. It has never been decided that a representative of the public—in the person of the news media—is not guaranteed some access to public disaster areas. It is true that public officials would have a strong argument against admitting 1 million persons to a disaster area in New York City. But the current concept is that the public ''has a right to know'' and that, while the number of visitors may be restricted, to guarantee a flow of information the public is entitled to be represented by a reasonable number of journalists.

The point here is that Justice White felt so strongly about the *Caldwell* case that he interpreted issues against the news media which were not even litigated and made statements of constitutional policy which, consciously or unconsciously, appear to misrepresent existing constitutional law to the detriment of the media. It is therefore imperative for journalists to realize that, while they must continue activity

Fred P. Graham is a
Washington correspondent
for CBS News. Jack C. Landau is a Supreme Court
reporter for Newhouse
Newspapers. Both men are
members of the steering
committee of the Reporters
Committee for Freedom of
the Press. Reprinted from
*Columbia Journalism
Review,* March-April 1972.

in the courts—meeting every censorship challenge head-on—they must seek a redress of their grievances at the legislative level—an invitation, no matter how gracelessly offered, by Justice White in *Caldwell*:

> Congress has freedom to determine whether a statutory newsman's privilege is necessary and desirable and to fashion standards and rules as narrow or as broad as deemed necessary to address the evil discerned and equally important to refashion those rules as experience . . . may dictate.

Congressmen responded by introducing twenty-eight bills granting various types of newsmen's privileges in the last session and twenty-four bills within the first fortnight of the new session. Hearings were held on some of these bills last fall by a Subcommittee of the House Judiciary Committee chaired by Rep. Robert W. Kastenmeier of Wisconsin. Both Rep. Kastenmeier and Sen. Sam Ervin of North Carolina, who chairs the Constitutional Rights Subcommittee of the Senate Judiciary Committee, [continued holding hearings. The discussion goes on].

The Kastenmeier hearings were perhaps more educating for the press than for Congress. The news media displayed a disturbing lack of unity (with various organizations supporting different bills); a disheartening public exhibition of intramedia rivalry between a book author representative who accused TV of producing "warmed-over" documentaries, and a broadcasters' representative who declared, "I see the authors didn't mention Clifford Irving" (both comments were edited out of the formally published committee hearings); and a failure to present convincing factual evidence of the necessity for new legislation.

In an effort to consolidate the media position, Davis Taylor, publisher of the Boston *Globe* and chairman of the American Newspaper Publishers Assn., invited major media-oriented organizations to participate in an Ad Hoc Drafting Committee to prepare a bill which could be used as a model. The committee included representatives of the ANPA, the American Society of Newspaper Editors, the Newspaper Guild, the National Assn. of Broadcasters, the Society of Professional Journalists, the American Civil Liberties Union, the Reporters Committee for Freedom of the Press, the New York *Times*, *Newsweek*, ABC, CBS, and NBC. The ANPA has endorsed the whole bill; many other groups support only various portions of the bill or have not yet taken a formal position. The operative language of the bill is:

> Section 2: No person shall be required to disclose in any federal or state proceeding either
>
> 1. the source of any published or unpublished information obtained in the gathering, receiving or processing of information for any medium of communication to the public, or
>
> 2. any unpublished information obtained or prepared in gathering, receiving, or processing of information for any medium of communication to the public.

Because there are so many bills and they vary so widely, the following discussion will only briefly note particular bills—mainly the ANPA absolute privilege bill introduced in this session and the Joint Media Committee qualified privilege bill, and the Ervin bill (both of which were introduced in the last session). The Ervin bill is the most restrictive of those that appear to have some chance of widespread support.

Problem One: Which members of the "press" should qualify for a federal "shield law" privilege which at least protects the source and content of "confidential" information? (Underground newsmen? Freelance news writers? Lecturers? Researchers? Book authors?)

Pending suggestions: The narrowest commonly used definition is contained in several state shield laws which grant only protection to "newspaper, radio, or television . . . personnel." All of the pending Congressional legislation is considerably more expansive, ranging from bills which protect "persons directly engaged in the gathering of news" to the broadest possible definition of "any person who gathers information for dissemination to the public." This would appear to include even dramatists and novelists.

Comment: This threshold question—of who should receive shield law protection—poses most disturbing moral, political, and legal problems which could easily fragment the media.

Those who argue for the broadest definition—describing researchers and would-be authors as members of the press—present a strong historical and constitutional case that the First Amendment was written against a background, not of multinational communications and great news empires, but of individual letter writers, Committees of Correspondence, and citizen pamphleteers. Justice White, in the *Caldwell* opinion, emphasized the historical validity of a broad definition for members of the press by noting that the "liberty of the press is the right of the lonely pamphleteer who uses carbon paper or a mimeograph machine." The Authors League, in its testimony, stressed that many major political scandals of recent years have been unearthed by individual authors working alone, rather than by investigative reporters for major newspapers, magazines, or TV networks. In effect then, a broad definition—including authors, researchers, and freelances unconnected to any established news organizations—would, in many ways, make the newsman's privilege virtually coordinate with the freedom of the speech protection of the First Amendment and would mean, in practical terms, that any person interested in public affairs could probably claim shield law protection.

Those who argue for a narrower definition favor limiting the privilege to persons connected with recognized news organizations. They argue that the author-researcher definition is so broad as to create the privilege for virtually any person interested in public events. Such a broad definition might invite many fraudulent claims of privilege, perhaps even "sham" newspapers established by members of the Mafia (as Justice White hinted); would alienate Congress and the Courts; and would give opponents of a shield law their most powerful political argument against creating any privilege at all. Furthermore, they argue that while the legendary individual author from time to time does engage in muckraking on a grand scale in the most hallowed traditions of Lincoln Steffens, the great majority of investigative reporting is conducted by employees of established news organizations. It is they who are going to jail and it is they who need the coverage more than any other identifiable group.

Suggested solution: While politics and pragmatism would dictate limiting the privilege to news organization employees, morality and history dictate that the greatest possible number of journalists be covered without attempts to include all purveyors of information and opinion. Therefore we suggest that the bill grant the privilege to "recognized members of the press" and permit the courts to decide who should and should not qualify. The bill should specifically state that the privilege covers the underground and minority press (the true heirs of the eighteenth century pamphleteers), the student press, and at least previously published "legitimate" freelance nonfiction writers.

Case examples: The Justice Department has claimed recently that Thomas L. Miller, a writer for the Liberation News Service and other underground publications, is not a "news reporter" and should not be accorded any of the protections under the Justice Department Subpoena Guidelines for members of the press. The District Attorney for Los Angeles County has claimed that William Farr should not qualify for the newsman's privilege in California because at the time he was asked to disclose his confidential sources he was not regularly employed by any news organization. He obtained the information sought while he was a reporter for the Los Angeles *Herald-Examiner* but then left its employ.

Problem Two: Which proceedings should be covered by a shield law (grand juries, criminal trials, civil trials, legislative investigations, executive agencies)?

Pending suggestions: These range from the narrow coverage in the Ervin bill, which would grant the privilege only before federal grand juries and criminal trials, to the broadest coverage, which would protect a news reporter before any executive, legislative, or judicial body.

Comment: There is general agreement among the press as to which goverment proceedings should be covered—all of them. If a newsman is protected only from testifying at a criminal trial, his testimony can still be coerced by a legislative body or by an executive agency which has the contempt power, such as state crime investigating commissions. Furthermore, it seems unfair to deny to a criminal defendant confidential information which might help to acquit him but at the same time give the information to a state legislative committee which may have no better purpose than to further some ambitious Congressman's stepladder toward the governorship.

Suggested solution: While politics and pragmatism would dictate limiting the executive, and legislative proceedings.

Case examples: While the current subpoena problem originated with federal grand juries (Earl Caldwell), and with state grand juries (Paul Pappas and Paul Branzburg), the infection is spreading. Joseph Weiler of the Memphis *Commercial Appeal* and Joseph Pennington of radio station WREC were called before a state legislative investigating commission. Dean Jensen, Stuart Wilk, and Miss Gene Cunningham of the Milwaukee *Sentinel* and Alfred Balk of the *Columbia Journalism Review* (in a case involving an article in the *Saturday Evening Post*) were asked to disclose confidential sources during civil hearings before federal district courts. William Farr resisted a [Superior Court] judge's personal investigation into violations of his Manson trial publicity order. Three St. Louis area reporters appeared before a State Ethics Committee which appears to be some kind of executive committee authorized by the state legislature to investigate state judges. Brit Hume of the Jack Anderson column and Denny Walsh of *Life* resisted libel case subpoenas. [In late 1976, four reporters and editors of the *Fresno* (Calif.) *Bee* spent 14 days in jail for defending their source of information.]

Problem Three: What types of information should be protected?

a. Confidential sources of published information (e.g., Earl Caldwell was asked to disclose the confidential source of material published in the New York *Times*. William Farr was asked the confidential source of a Manson trial confession published in the Los Angeles *Herald-Examiner*)?

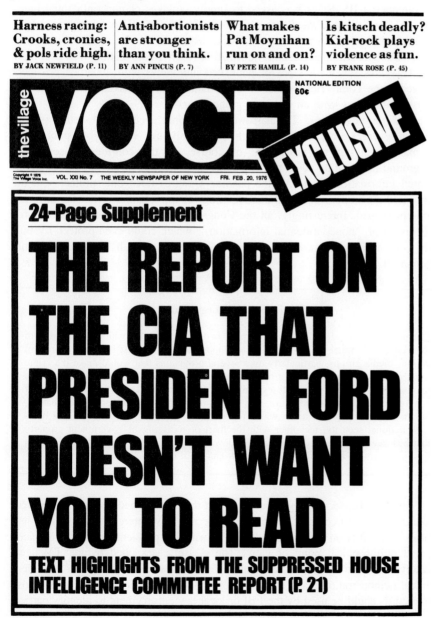

| Harness racing: Crooks, cronies, & pols ride high. BY JACK NEWFIELD (P. 11) | Anti-abortionists are stronger than you think. BY ANN PINCUS (P. 7) | What makes Pat Moynihan run on and on? BY PETE HAMILL (P. 14) | Is kitsch deadly? Kid-rock plays violence as fun. BY FRANK ROSE (P. 45) |

the village VOICE EXCLUSIVE

NATIONAL EDITION
60¢

Copyright © 1976 The Village Voice Inc.   VOL. XXI No. 7   THE WEEKLY NEWSPAPER OF NEW YORK   FRI. FEB. 20, 1976

24-Page Supplement

THE REPORT ON THE CIA THAT PRESIDENT FORD DOESN'T WANT YOU TO READ

TEXT HIGHLIGHTS FROM THE SUPPRESSED HOUSE INTELLIGENCE COMMITTEE REPORT (P. 21)

In a complicated case, CBS News correspondent Dan Schorr was forced to leave his job after he leaked a congressional report on the CIA to the *Village Voice* and was threatened with contempt by Congress when he refused to reveal his source. CBS, Schorr and Congress emerged tarnished after months of bitter arguments about the ethics used by all parties.

b. Confidential sources of unpublished information (e.g., TV news reporter Paul Pappas was asked what occurred inside Black Panther headquarters; CBS News was asked the identity of the person in New York who supplied a Black Panther contact in Algiers in connection with a *60 Minutes* story on Eldridge Cleaver)?

c. Unpublished nonconfidential information (e.g., Peter Bridge was asked further details of his nonconfidential interview with a Newark Housing Commission member; CBS News was asked to supply outtakes of nonconfidential interviews in *The Selling of the Pentagon*; the St. Louis *Post-Dispatch* was asked for unpublished photos of a public antiwar demonstration)?

d. Published nonconfidential information (e.g., Radio station WBAI in New York City was asked for tapes of published interviews with unnamed prisoners involved in the Tombs riot; WDEF-TV in Chattanooga was asked for the tapes of a published interview with an unnamed grand juror)?

Pending suggestions: The narrowest commonly accepted protection is contained in several state shield laws which protect only the "source" of "published" information, giving no protection, of course, to the confidential source of background information never published and no protection to the unpublished confidential information itself. All the pending Congressional bills protect both the *source* and the *content* of "confidential" information whether or not the information is published. Interestingly, all the Congressional bills also protect the source and content of "nonconfidential information," which could even protect TV outtakes or a reporter's notes of a Presidential speech ("nonconfidential information").

"Official Secrets" Legislation

Congress has introduced during the past two sessions bills which would reform the Federal Criminal Code—called S.1. Opposition to the latest bill has come from various media groups, particularly over several provisions that would make it a crime to publish certain information or to gather it in certain ways. While this particular law may not pass during the current legislative session, it most likely will be a subject of congressional inquiry in the future. The bill, as outlined at the time of our publication, has two broad categories under which reporters might commit illegal acts. One deals with national security; the other with the theft or receiving of government property that has been stolen. Students should follow closely the progress of the debates on this or on similar bills which might be introduced in future sessions.

While the broadcasters generally support the printed media's desire to protect "confidential" sources and information, the real TV interest in the shield law debates will center on the nonconfidential information problem, from both a practical and philosophical point of view. The classic cases cited by the TV news executives concern the difficulties of television cameramen covering riots, dissident political demonstrations, and student disorders—"nonconfidential" events whose film records could be used by the FBI or local law enforcement to identify partici-

"...COPY BOY...!"

pants for criminal prosecution. TV executives and, to a lesser extent, news camera-men recite incidents of stonings by demonstrators, breaking of cameras, and destruc-tion of equipment because demonstrators believed that journalists were collecting evidence for the police. The TV news executives argue that their news operations are not an "investigative arm of the Government" and that their cameramen must be able to represent to hostile demonstrators and to the general public that the only film the FBI will see is the film that is actually shown on the tube. But this raises a logical dilemma: Is a film outtake of a public demonstration to be given the same protection from subpoena as a "confidential" source in the Watergate bugging scandal?

Television also has a practical financial objection to permitting its film to be subpoenaed. It is expensive and time-consuming to run through reel after reel of film, an objection similar to that of newspapers whose morgues have been subpoenaed.

Suggested solutions: It is our suggestion that the shield law privilege might be bifurcated like the attorney-client privilege: There could be an "absolute" privilege to refuse to disclose the source or content of confidential information; there could be a "qualified" privilege to refuse to disclose nonconfidential information—such as outtakes of a public demonstrations. The outtakes would be available only if the Government demonstrates an "overriding and compelling need."

This two-level absolute-qualified privilege would be similar to the privileges available to attorneys. Attorneys may refuse to disclose the content of confidential communications from their clients and in some cases even the identity of their clients. However, attorneys have only a limited privilege to refuse to turn over nonconfidential "work product" evidence—such as an interview with a witness to a crime who is now unavailable. There are three advantages to offering to a news reporter or cameraman the absolute-qualified privileges held by attorneys.

First: The press is not asking Congress to create a novel or unique concept by establishing a specially privileged class of citizens. In facts the press is merely saying that confidentiality is as important for the performance of newsgathering as it is for the performance of legal representation; and to deny the press a privilege which Congress has granted to an attorney would be saying that the right of the public, via the press to learn about the Bobby Baker or Watergate scandals is to be accorded less protection than the right of a member of the public, via his lawyer, to be represented in a land transaction or a patent case.

Second: The attorney-client relationship is so well established that a whole new body of law would not have to be developed for the multitude of unanswered questions which naturally arise with establishment of a new and untested right. (How is the privilege asserted? Who has the burden of proving it is properly invoked? etc.)

Third: As of July, there will be in effect new federal rules of evidence which grant new federal confidentiality privileges to the attorney for his client, to the policeman for his informer, to the priest for his penitent, and to the psychiatrist for his patient. With regard to timing, it might be advisable for the press to obtain its privileges in connection with the new federal rules.

Problem Four: Should there by any specific exceptions to the privilege to refuse to reveal confidential and nonconfidential information or sources? (Libel suits? Eyewitness to a murder? Information about a conspiracy to commit treason?)

Pending suggestions: The Congressional bills vary. The Joint Media Committee qualified privilege bill would permit confidential and nonconfidential information to be obtained if "there is a compelling and overriding national interest." The Ervin bill would not protect information which "tend[s] to prove or disprove the commission of a crime." The CBS bill would permit the confidential information to be disclosed "to avoid a substantial injustice." The Pearson bill would force disclosure of confidential information to prevent a "threat to human life." The ANPA absolute privilege bill permits no exceptions.

Comment: Most of the bills would not have protected Earl Caldwell because the grand jury in the *Caldwell* case was allegedly investigating a threat by Eldridge Cleaver to assassinate the President. Once the Congress suggests that newsmen may protect confidential information except for national security or libel or felonies or to prevent injustices, the media will end up with a bill which is full of procedural loopholes, moral dichotomies, and legal inconsistencies.

Furthermore, judges have proved ingenious in discovering ambiguities in statutes in order to force reporters to testify in situations that would boggle the nonlegal mind. Paul Branzburg was ordered to name his source of a drug abuse story despite a state law protecting reporters' sources! The Kentucky courts ruled that he saw the sources making hashish and thus they became "criminals" and not news sources. A California law protects reporters' sources, but a Los Angeles judge waited until William Farr temporarily became an ex-newsman and then ordered him to talk; the California legislature promptly passed a new law protecting former newsmen. The moral is that shield laws should be as broad and tight as words will permit, or judges will find ways to evade the intent of the statutes.

Critics of the unqualified privilege often fall back on a stable of horribles ("what if a kidnaper had your child and a reporter knew where"?) to argue for leeway to compel testimony in extreme situations. But some states have had unqualified laws for years and no such incident has ever occurred. Either a reporter believes that it is his duty to talk or he feels so strongly against disclosing the information that no judge or turnkey could break his silence.

Of all the qualified bills, the Joint Media Committee bill is closest to the absolutist approach. Its exception for the "national interest" would place a heavy burden on the Government or a private litigant—a burden that would appear to be satisfied in those rare situations similar to the Pentagon Papers litigation.

The conceptual difficulties of attempting to cover all confidential and nonconfidential information under the same broad legal standards have persuaded us that the privilege perhaps could be tailored to the major problems of confidential and nonconfidential information rather than attempting to make a series of subjective evaluations for certain types of crimes or proceedings. Libel presents an unusual situation; in other testamentary confidentiality situations such as the attorney-client privilege, if the client refuses to waive the privilege then he is subject to an automatic default judgment as the penalty for invoking the right.

Suggested solutions: Attorneys, clergymen, and psychiatrists cannot be forced to violate the confidences of their clients, penitents, and patients, even upon a showing of an investigation into espionage or murder. In fact, how many attorneys know that their own clients or other persons are guilty of heinous crimes but are protected by the attorney-client privilege? It seems grotesque to accuse a news person of being an unpatriotic citizen because he has a privilege to refuse to disclose confidential information of a serious crime, when attorneys (50 percent of the Congress are lawyers), physicians, and clergymen are considered upstanding citizens if they invoke their privileges to refuse to divulge the same criminal information to a grand jury or a trial. Therefore it is suggested that any exemptions for confidential information be drawn as narrowly as possible and that there be a heavy burden of proof for forced disclosure of nonconfidential information.

Problem Five: Should the shield bill apply only to newsmen involved in federal legislative, executive, and judicial proceedings? Or should the bill cover newsmen involved in attempts by state government agencies to obtain confidential sources and information?

Pending solutions: All of the Congressional bills apply to federal proceedings. The ANPA bill would cover both federal and state proceedings.

Comment: No single issue divided the ANPA Ad Hoc Drafting Committee more than the question of federal-state coverage. While lawyers all agree that Congress can cover federal proceedings there is serious disagreement—both on constitutional and political grounds—as to whether the press should aggressively push for state protection in the federal bill.

If statistics were the only issue, then the media would all agree that Congress should cover state proceedings because the subpoena problem is much more serious now in the states and counties than in federal jurisdictions. Ever since Atty. Gen. John N. Mitchell promulgated his Justice Department Subpoena Guidelines in July, 1970, the Justice Department, which had issued a large number of subpoenas to the press in the prior eighteen months, has issued only thirteen subpoenas. The celebrated cases today are mostly state cases: William Farr, Peter Bridge, Harry Thornton, David Lightman, James Mitchell, Joseph Weiler, Joseph Pennington.

Furthermore, there are only eighteen state shield laws in effect and they offer varying degrees of coverage. A federal-state law would fill the void in the remaining thirty-two states, thus eliminating the necessity of new legislation in these states and of corrective legislation in most of the existing states whose laws offer less protection than the ANPA bill. A subcommittee of the Conference of Commissioners on Uniform State Law is now working on a model reporters' privilege law. But even if the commissioners eventually approve a model statute, it might be years before any substantial number of state legislatures adopt it.

Then there is the potential legal impact of the *Farr* decision in the California courts. They held that the state legislature has no power under the state constitution to pass a shield law which invades the inherent constitutional power of the state courts to protect their own integrity by forcing news reporters to disclose confidential information. What this means potentially is that California and perhaps other states must pass a state constitutional amendment—rather than a shield law—to give complete protection to news reporters involved in many types of contempt proceedings.

There are, however, serious constitutional and political problems with a federal-state shield law. Constitutionally, the ANPA bill attempts to give Congress two different methods to intervene in state court and legislative proceedings. First: It notes that news is in commerce and therefore the ANPA bill uses Congress's power to control "interstate commerce." Second: It notes that, under the Fourteenth Amendment, Congress has the power to pass legislation protecting rights guaranteed in the First Amendment. While Congress has used its power to protect federally guaranteed rights by passing the Civil Rights Acts of 1965 and 1968, Congress has never attempted to pass legislation implementing the Bill of Rights.

Suggested solution: The federal government is only one of fifty-one jurisdictions. In fact, when one remembers that the Farr-Bridge-Thornton cases were processed in the county courts, there are the federal government; fifty states; and some 3,000 county court jurisdictions. Under the Justice Department guidelines, there is a lessening danger from the federal government. Therefore, we consider it absolutely essential that, despite the political difficulties of this position, the shield law protect every news reporter in the nation—not just those who, by happenstance, are involved in federal proceedings.

Assuming that the media can agree on which bill they want, can the press persuade Congress to pass the legislation? Three years ago, the newspaper publishers succeeded in obtaining passage of the Newspaper Preservation Act with its exemption from the antitrust laws, over the public opposition of the then antitrust chief, Richard McLaren. Two years ago, the broadcasters, within forty-eight hours, were able to muster enough support to protect CBS president Frank Stanton from being held in contempt of Congress, over the objections of Rep. Harley Staggers, who was attempting to obtain nonconfidential outtakes of *The Selling of the Pentagon*. The conclusion is quite simple: What the media owners want from Congress, the media owners get from Congress. The only question that remains is whether the First Amendment is of as much concern to the media owners as was exemption from the antitrust laws.

Bibliography

The Graham and Landau article is one of the more comprehensive treatments of the concept of the need for a shield law. David Gordon, *Newsman's Privilege and the Law*, Freedom of Information Foundation, Series No. 4 (August 1974) is a useful treatment of the subject. It can be up-dated, even as the Graham and Landau article can be up-dated, by referring to the continuing series of Freedom of Information reports published by The Society of Professional Journalists, Sigma Delta Chi. The *1976 Report of the Advancement of Freedom of Information Commitee* of the SPJ/SDX summarizes current developments and includes a useful state-by-state compilation of cases related to freedom of information and shield laws. There also is a chapter on the electronic media. A useful bibliography is Lisa Epstein, *Newsman's Privilege: An Annotated Bibliography 1967-1973*, Law Library, California State Library, 1973. This 19-page booklet contains over 100 annotations, primarily from legal journals. In addition, The Reporters Committee, suite 1112, 1750 Penn Ave.. NW. Wash.. D.C.. 20006, distributes its bimonthly *Press Censorship Newsletter* (a thick booklet detailing all relevant First Amendment and FOI cases).

A related issue, and one where there is increasing tension between the press and the judiciary is that of Free Press and Fair Trial. An excellent basic work is Donald M. Gillmor, *Free Press and Free Trial*, Public Affairs Press, 1966. Marlan Nelson has compiled a 576-item—*Free Press-Fair Trial: An Annotated Bibliography*, Utah State University Department of Journalism, 1971, which includes citations through 1969. More current publications include Deby K. Samuels, *Judges and Trial News Challenges*, Freedom of Information Center, Report No. 317 (December 1973) and the several articles in *Nieman Reports* (Winter 1974). The *Nieman Reports'* articles deal with the problems that have arisen between the mass media an the law over trials, secrecy of grand jury information, and use of stolen documents. This entire issue is well worth consulting for deeply disturbing insights into the problems. See also Benno C. Schmidt, Jr. "A New Wave of Gag Orders," *Columbia Journalism Review* (November/December 1975), pp. 33-34.

Another area of increasing concern is the still ill-defined concept of "privacy." A good summary will be found in E. Jeremy Hutton, *The Constitutional Right of Privacy: Supreme Court Decisions and Congressional Action in Brief*, Library of Congress, Congressional Research Service, 1974. *The Privacy Act of 1974*, Freedom of Information Center, Report No. 342 (September 1975) was written by James T. O'Reilly. He outlines the provisions of the act and suggests that it will have a major impact on both the government's gathering of information and its dissemination of that information, including dissemination to the press.

Shield Law For Newsmen: Safeguard Or A Trap?

By John S. Knight

John S. Knight was editorial chairman, Knight Newspapers, Inc., at the time of writing this editorial. He won a Pulitzer Prize for editorial writing in 1968. This editorial was published in March, 1973, and is reprinted with the permission of the author.

Can a reporter be compelled by government to reveal the identity of confidential sources of information or the content of unpublished information?

Most newspaper editors and the television networks say "No," since Article I of the Bill of Rights specifically states: "Congress shall make no law . . .abridging the freedom . . .of speech, or of the press."

Yet the Supreme Court decided last June by a 5-4 vote in the Caldwell case that the sources of a reporter's information are not and cannot be held confidential.

The Caldwell decision has given rise to any number of state and local judicial actions which have held reporters in contempt of court for refusing to disclose confidential information to grand juries. Several newsmen have been jailed, and the subpoena process is currently being applied against the *Washington Post* in the Watergate case.

Members of the Fourth Estate, well aware of the Nixon administration's hostility toward the press, are pressing Congress to enact a shield law which will protect the reporter's position of confidentiality. Some 18 state legislatures have already passed laws which provide some form of protection. Similar bills have been before the Congress since 1929, but as Sen. Sam J. Ervin Jr. says, "To write legislation balancing the two great public interests of a free press and the seeking of justice is no easy task."

Sen. Ervin, an authority on constitutional law who has been attempting to draft legislation to protect the free flow of information, finds it a bothersome assignment indeed.

On the one hand, Ervin declaims, "there is society's interest in being informed—in learning of crime, corruption or mismanagement. On the other, we have the pursuit of truth in the courtroom. It is the duty of every man to give testimony. The Sixth Amendment specifically gives a criminal defendant the right to confront the witness against him, and to have compulsory process for obtaining witnesses in his favor."

Yet we find in a separate concurring opinion by Supreme Court Justice Lewis Powell a statement that the court may not in the future turn deaf ears upon newsmen if the government can be shown to have harassed the newsmen, or has otherwise not acted in good faith in the conduct of its investigation or inquiry.

But Justice Byron R. White, writing for the majority, stated: "Until now, the only testimonial privilege for unofficial witnesses that is rooted in the federal Constitution is the Fifth Amendment privilege against compelled self-incrimination. We are asked to create another by interpreting the First Amendment to grant newsmen a testimonial privilege that other citizens do not enjoy. This we decline to do.''

The net effect of the court's decision in the Caldwell case was to leave it to the Congress to determine the desirability and the necessity for statutory protection for newsmen. And that is where we are now.

For one, I confess to some ambivalence on this question. Can Sen. Ervin draft a law which, as he says, ''will accommodate both the interest of society in law enforcement, and the interest of society in preserving a free flow of information to the public?''

Or, will the enactment of any law—qualified or unqualified— invite Congress to tamper with the law as it serves its pleasure in the future? Vermont Royster of the *Wall Street Journal* sees ''booby-traps'' in this procedure, since ''for what one Congress can give, another can take away, and once it is conceded that Congress can legislate about the press, no man can know where it might end.''

The mood of the press is quite understandable. For here we have the Nixon administration's palace guard—a grim and humorless lot—in a posture of open hostility to the press and attempting to hinder the free flow in information with every device available to them.

We also have the courts, ''traditionally unhappy'' as Sen. Ervin says, ''about evidentiary privileges which limit judicial access to information, and by and large refusing to recognize a common-law right of reporters not to identify sources or to disclose confidential information.''

So the key question remains: Will the press and the public interest best be served by a congressional shield law holding confidentiality to be inviolate—a law which as Royster points out could be changed and diluted by a future Congress?

Or had we better stick with the First Amendment, under which a free press has survived for nearly 200 years without any law to make newsmen a class apart? Why not stand with the courageous history of the press, and continue to wage battle against all attempts at censorship by the courts and intimidation by a hostile administration?

Sen. Ervin now thinks he has devised a third-draft bill which ''strikes a reasonable balance between necessary, if at times, competing objectives.'' Yet what Congress gives, Congress can take away. Neither the senator nor the proponents of any protective law for journalists address themselves to this crucial point.

The more I study this question, the more I am persuaded that, since the First Amendment has nurtured the freest press of any nation, reporters, editors and publishers should not petition Congress but rather continue to contest all erosions of press or public freedom and be prepared to defend their convictions at any cost.

Our precious freedoms of speech and publication are guaranteed by the Bill of Rights which has served us well throughout our history. Freedom is not something that can be assured by transitory legislation, worthy as the intent may be.

When Congress is involved, there lies the risk—as Royster has said—that it might start legislating about the freedom of the press even in the guise of protecting it. This could be a dangerous precedent.

I readily concede that what I have written above represents a modification of what I had previously believed, and that it is open to challenge from my journalistic colleagues who hold a contrary view.

Before the press potentates pursue too enthusiastically the case for a shield law, they would be well advised to ask themselves whether the remedy they propose will ultimately sustain or destroy press freedom.

Access to News   Big-Time Pressures, Small-Town Press

By Robert Boyle

Pottstown, Pa.—The bee stings in Washington and the pain is felt in Pottstown, too. The Government clamps Les Whitten, Jack Anderson's aide, in jail for eight hours, and the clanking jail door is heard round the world. Pottstown Council holds a secret meeting, and when it's uncovered, the news about it is confined to Pottstown. Censorship, government controls and secrecy aren't limited to people like Anderson. The small-town newsman is also feeling the sting.

Certainly, officials in Washington aren't telling officials in Pottstown not to cooperate with the press. But when the Government hides things from the national press, and when Government officials make snide remarks against the press, small-town politicians feel that they, too, should follow the leader and they institute roadblocks to limit freedom.

The label a politician or an official wears doesn't matter. Pottstown is a swing community in a solid Republican county. But both Democrats and Republicans alike have started attacking the press.

Small-town police departments suddenly are setting themselves up as censors. They become "unavailable" when the press calls them. Justices of the peace are starting to determine what cases to give to the press and what cases to hold back.

One Pottstown justice of the peace tried to stop a *Mercury* reporter from using a pencil and notebook at a hearing because they were "recording devices." Use of a recording device is banned in justices of the peace courts. It took a ruling from the county solicitor before the reporter could use his pencil and notebook again.

School boards have been using the "executive sessions" ploy more and more. The public and press are barred from executive sessions. Board members decide at these sessions what course of action to follow, and then simply approve the action at a regular meeting.

Robert J. Boyle is editor of the Pottstown (Pa.) *Mercury*. This column appeared on the Op-Ed page of the *New York Times,* March 24, 1973. Copyright 1973 by the New York Times Company. Reprinted by permission.

The simple news story, too, is getting more difficult to come by. Recently there was a small fire in the Army officers' club of Valley Forge General Hospital. Damage amounted to $750. The *Mercury* tried to get an item on the fire and the story would have amounted to a paragraph or two.

But the Army refused to give any information until the "news release cleared the channels."

In Pottstown, a community of 28,000 some 35 miles from Philadelphia, the council meetings always have been open and above board. But late last year, council held a secret meeeting. It wasn't advertised, the press wasn't alerted, and those who attended were told to keep it secret. The action taken at the meeting affected the entire community.

The council voted, in secret, to get rid of the police chief, Dick Tracy. As God is my judge, that's his name. A group from council, including the Mayor, was selected to secretly tell the chief to look elsewhere for a job. He was told it would be in his best interest to keep the decision secret.

"Keep your mouth shut and we'll make it seem as if it is your choice to leave," he was told. "Open it and it'll make it rougher for you to get another job."

He kept his mouth shut.

But one of the participants of the secret meeting discussed it at a local bar. He was overheard and the newspaper, *The Mercury*, was tipped.

Chief Tracy was confronted with the story and confirmed that he was told to leave. He eventually did. He wasn't a bad cop. With a name like that he couldn't be. But he was ousted because he refused to play small-town politics. He refused to fix parking tickets, he refused to let old-time politicians run the department and he was strict. He got the axe because he wouldn't play ball.

The Mercury headlined the story of the secret meeting. And the community was disturbed for several weeks. Later *The Mercury* investigated and revealed conflict-of-interest possibilities on some council proposals.

In nearby Collegeville, a community of 5,000, the newspaper there, *The Independent*, was creating a stir in a nine-part exposé on the Pennsylvania state prison at Graterford. *The Independent* doesn't make much of a splash statewide but ripples from it reached the state capital at Harrisburg. The word went out that no one from the state prison was to talk to *The Independent* publisher, John Stewart. Because he uncovered and published some sordid facts about Graterford he was put on the "no comment" list.

If you multiply the troubles *The Mercury* and *The Independent* are having in their small areas by the number of smaller papers across the country then you must recognize the press is being hamstrung nationally and on all levels.

Remarks by the Vice-President and the President may be targeted at papers such as *The Washington Star*.

But they are also hurting the smaller papers. By design or not, those officials in Washington who are anti-Anderson, anti-*The Times,* anti-*The Post,* are also anti-*The Mercury* and *The Independent*. They're antipress. Antifreedom.

Court Control of "News" After *Nebraska*

By Ted Curtis Smythe

The long-simmering controversy between proponents of the First and Sixth Amendments to the Constitution came to a boil during 1975 when judges in Lincoln County, Nebraska imposed restrictive orders (''gag'' orders in newspaper parlance) on what the press could report about a brutal murder that had occurred in the community of Sutherland. The unanimous 9-0 Supreme Court decision affirming press rights created press freedom history.

While the issues decided by the Court are of primary interest and importance to us, it is necessary first to provide a little background to the case.

Six members of the Henry Kellie family were murdered in their home on the night of Oct. 18, 1975. Police issued a description of the suspect, 29-year-old Erwin Charles Simants, a neighbor of the Kellies. Simants was arrested and arraigned the next morning.

County Judge Ronald Ruff held a preliminary hearing to determine whether there was cause to hold Simants for trial (this hearing performs the same function as a grand jury in some states). At that hearing he restricted the press from reporting testimony given in the hearing and required that the Nebraska bar-press voluntary guidelines be mandatory.

Lawyers for Nebraska news media appealed to Judge Hugh Stuart of the district court to set aside the restaining order. Although Judge Stuart had earlier counseled Judge Ruff not to impose such an order, he now terminated Judge Ruff's order and imposed his own. His order was more selective than was Judge Ruff's order but it still restricted the press from reporting Simant's confession, the results of the pathologist's report (which had revealed the sexual basis for the assault as well as necrophilia), the identity of the victims who had been sexually assaulted, and the description of those crimes. He also required that the voluntary bar-press guidelines be mandatory. He then prohibited the Nebraska press from reporting the details of the ''gag'' order itself.

This order was appealed to the Nebraska Supreme Court. Because the Court delayed in acting on the appeal, the appellants sought help from Justice Harry Blackmun of the U.S. Supreme Court. Under a provision which permits a single Supreme Court Justice to intervene when he feels legal remedies have been exhausted at the local level and that an emergency exists (Justice Blackmun argued, ''delay itself is a final decision'' in these cases) he set aside certain provisions of the order, although ''he declined 'at least on application for a stay and at this distance, [to] impose a prohibition upon the Nebraska courts from placing any restrictions at all upon what the media may report prior to trial.'' '

The Nebraska Supreme Court finally issued its *per curiam* opinion [that is, it reflects the opinion of the whole court and is not identified with one justice] on Dec.

Ted Curtis Smythe is co-editor of this volume, and *Issues in Broadcasting,* Mayfield Publishing, 1975 and Professor of Communications, California State University, Fullerton.

2, 1975. It modified the District Court's order in an effort to balance the defendant's right to a fair trial against the Nebraska media's ''interest in reporting pretrial events.'' The order ''prohibited reporting of only three matters: (a) the existence and nature of any confessions or admissions made by the defendant to law enforcement officers, (b) any confessions or admissions made to any third parties, except members of the press, and (c) other facts 'strongly implicative' of the accused.''

The U.S. Supreme Court granted *certiorari* (a review of the case) in order to address the important issues raised in the District Court's order and the modification of it by the Nebraska Supreme Court. By the time the U.S. Supreme Court acted to decide the issue, Simants was convicted of murder and sentenced to death. His appeal was pending when the U.S. Supreme Court issued its decision.

The Court endorsed the rights of the press to report pretrial matters without restriction by the judiciary. Chief Justice Warren Burger, writing the opinion, was joined by four other justices, two of whom wrote concurring opinions. Justice William Brennan wrote a separate concurring opinion in which he was joined by two other justices, Justice Paul Stevens also wrote a brief concurring opinion.

In his opinion, Chief Justice Burger reviewed the historical conflict between the First and Sixth Amendments and recounted numerous Court decisions that had dealt specifically with the issue. He reaffirmed previous Court solutions to the problem—solutions that do not require prior restraint of the press.

He concluded that not only were there other avenues open to the trial judge but, given the circumstances, ''it is far from clear that [even] prior restraint on publication would have protected Simants' rights.''

What were those other ''avenues''? One would be to change the site of the trial (change of venue) to someplace ''less exposed to the intense publicity'' in the county. (One reason the judge had not done so is that Nebraska law permits a change only to adjacent counties and those counties had been exposed to the same pretrial publicity. The Supreme Court held that Nebraska law had to give way in this case—that fair trial was Constitutionally more important.)

Other avenues suggested by Justice Burger would be to postpone ''the trial to allow public attention to subside;'' to use ''searching questions of prospective jurors,'' and to use ''emphatic and clear instructions on the sworn duty of each juror to decide the issues only on evidence presented in open court.'' The Chief Justice even suggested sequestering the jury after it was chosen as a partial remedy because insulating the jurors ''enhances the likelihood of dissipating the impact of pretrial publicity and of emphasizing the elements of the jurors' oaths.''

The suggestion was made in passing that the ''trial courts in appropriate cases [could] limit what the contending lawyers, the police and witnesses may say to anyone.'' While the Chief Justice did not deal with this issue, Justice Brennan in his concurring opinion suggested that this was a viable alternative to prior restraint of the press. He wrote: ''As officers of the Court, court personnel and attorneys have a fiduciary responsibility not to engage in public debate that will redound to the detriment of the accused or that will obstruct the fair administration of justice. It is very doubtful that the court would not have the power to control release of information by these individuals in appropriate cases. . . .''

Does this mean that Chief Justice Burger and the entire Court support the press-promoted concept that prior restraint can never be imposed in Free Press/Fair Trial cases?

No.

Several times in his opinion, the Chief Justice argued against a blanket statement on prior restraint. He wrote that since the ''authors of the Bill of Rights did not undertake to assign priorities as between First Amendment and Sixth Amendment rights . . .it is not for us to rewrite the Constitution by undertaking what they declined.''

He concluded by reaffirming ''that the guarantees of freedom of expression are not an absolute prohibition [to prior restraint] under all circumstances, but the barriers to prior restraint remain high and the presumption against its use continues intact.''

The concurring opinions issued by other justices of the Court tended to go further, suggesting there may not be any situation in respect to Free Press/Fair Trial conflicts where prior restraint would be acceptable. Justice Brennan staked out such a position: '' . . .the press may be arrogant, tyrannical, abusive, and sensationalist, just as it may be incisive, probing, and informative. But at least in the context of prior restraints on publication, the decision of what, when and how to publish is for editors, not judges.'' Justices Potter Stewart and Thurgood Marshall concurred with him. Justices Byron White and Paul Stevens also indicated they were leaning in that direction.

The use of ''gag'' rules would now appear to be unconstitutional under all but extraordinary circumstances, and even then only after the trial judge had used other means of relief before restraining publication.

Since the press now has greater freedom than ever before in reporting criminal trials, another problem is raised—what is the proper ethical response of the news media?

Chief Justice Burger hinted at this problem when he wrote that ''it is not asking too much to suggest that those who exercise First Amendment rights in newspapers or broadcasting enterprises direct some effort to protect the rights of an accused to a fair trial by unbiased jurors.'' Many editors and reporters have made such efforts by seeking to accommodate ''on a voluntary basis, the correlative constitutional rights of free speech and free press with the right of an accused to a fair trial.'' The Nebraska Bar-Press Guidelines from which this quotation is taken was the result of such an accommodation.

Further voluntary efforts between bar and press should be accelerated in an attempt to accommodate both of these fundamental rights in American society.

Revolution in the Mass Media

Whether changes in the mass media are a reflection of social change or of technological change is an oft-debated subject in academic circles. Certainly we can choose a middle position and suggest that some changes are the result of new social mores and/or values while others appear to be the result of new technology. The decline in movie theater attendance and in the number of films produced during the Sixties, for example, is best explained as a result of the widespread dissemination of television, which was a relatively new technology. On the other hand, many changes in the content or themes of the movies during the same period are perhaps reflections of our changing social mores which permitted—indeed encouraged—the new content. A case can also be made for the interaction of technological and social change. Our selections in this section of the book tend to reflect one or the other of these views, usually without trying to establish a cause and effect relationship.

It is easily demonstrated that the established or commercial mass media are adapting to the new technology in many ways, just as they are adapting to social pressures from minority groups as well as from women. Change has taken place; improvement has been made, and those who historically have been excluded from the media have been heard. There still are obvious needs for further improvement but on balance what has occurred has been encouraging.

The auxiliaries to the mass media—advertising and public relations—also have been influenced by changes in society. Our selections describe just a few of the areas where further change is needed and/or can be expected. Two of the issues grow out of our increasing concern about truthfulness (or the lack of it) in advertising and from the need expressed in the public relations industry to improve its practices and, as a result, its image.

Finally, in this section we confront the problem of American mass media and their affect on international and national communication. Great resistance to American media and programming has arisen in some areas of the world in recent years. Canada is only one example of a country trying to protect its own communications industry by restricting the movement of American mass media in that country through tax laws and other regulations. If mass communication is important to a nation's well being, we should expect more reaction on the part of other nations in the years ahead.

Students who wish to explore these and other issues more fully should use the bibliographies which accompany each article. No collection of readings can include all issues or even all important articles; research in the bibliographies is absolutely necessary for a comprehensive view of the issues that confront the mass media and society in America during a period of rapid technological, social and international change.

5 New Technology

Publishing's Quiet Revolution—

Toward Totally Electronic TV News—

Journalism Educators and the Growing Tragedy of Journalism Employment—

Publishing's Quiet Revolution

By Ben H. Bagdikian

A funny thing happened two days in a row in New York.

I was talking to Paul Eberhart, thirty-seven-year-old associate editor for United Press International, at his desk on the twelfth floor of the Daily News Building in Manhattan when he said: "In the old days . . ." He stopped, his face went blank, and then he grinned sheepishly. He was talking about "the old days"—[Spring, 1972].

The next day I was talking to Louis Boccardi, executive editor of the Associated Press, eleven blocks away, on the fourth floor of the AP Building at Rockefeller Plaza. In the middle of a flow of intense conversation he said: "In the old days . . ." Then he, too, stopped, put his hand to his head, and broke into a grin. He was talking about April, 1971.

There was a time in the American newspaper business—and about every other place except Japan—when "in the old days" meant 1453, the year before Johann Gutenberg got disputed credit for inventing movable type. Things stayed pretty much the same until development of Mergenthaler's Linotype machine in 1886, and since then we have had about the same kind of machines run by paper tape.

But without most working journalists knowing it, the fine old fifteenth-century factories they work in are finally starting the terrifying leap from typewriter and lead pot to cathode ray tube and computer. To the naked eye, it isn't particularly visible in most newsrooms. But the underlying changes have begun. It seems safe to predict that in five years most newsrooms will look and sound substantially different. In some places there may no longer be a composing room.

The chief reason for the change is the refinement of communication technology and the delayed perception of the news business that, like any other major industry, it must design its own systems rather than wait for suppliers to make radical changes. The required hardware for the revolution not only has been adapted finally to news operations but its price is plummeting. Cathode ray tubes (CRTs), the TV-like screens with keyboards connected to computers, cost $80,000 in 1969 but now are in the $5,000-to-$18,000 range. Optical scanners—computers that read carefully typed copy—cost $90,000 three years ago and now come in $60,000 models. Computer time which cost $200,000 in 1955 now costs $1. Ten years ago 1 per cent of American dailies used computers; now at least 60 per cent do, though most are still unconnected to their newsrooms.

One of the most automated newsrooms of any major paper is at the Detroit *News*, which has forty-eight CRTs and a dozen more on the way. Most *News* reporters no longer use typewriters. From 30 to 40 percent of all copy there—the AP and UPI main wires, AP state wire, and AP and UPI sports wires, plus most staff-originated stories—is handled electronically without conventional typing or editing with paper and pencil.

Wire service material arrives on regular teletype lines at conventional speeds—about sixty words a minute—but, instead of actuating a teletype printer,

Ben H. Bagdikian conducted a study of the impact of technology on the American mass media for RAND Corporation; much of it was published in his book *The Information Machines: Their Impact on Men and the Media.* Today he is national correspondent for *Columbia Journalism Review.* Reprinted from *Columbia Journalism Review,* May-June 1973. Copyright © 1973 by Ben H. Bagdikian. Reprinted by permission of The Sterling Lord Agency, Inc.

the unique set of electrical impulses that represents each key struck in the originating machine goes directly into the *News'* computer. There it activates a letter or numerical character stored in the computer memory.

For locally originated stories, a *News* reporter—or one of the majority who have decided to use the new machines—sits down at the console keyboard of a CRT, the Hendrix 5700, which has a screen that shows eighteen lines of copy in 22-point type. The reporter hits a key called SLUG and his screen shows two blank lines to be filled. The first two characters he types instruct the computer where to send his completed story (LO for local SP for sports), the next four characters are the first four letters of his last name, and the next six characters whatever he chooses as the slug for his story. He types the edition the story is scheduled for, the date, and then writes his story.

As he types, the letters appear on his screen. If he wishes to delete or add to a line he has typed, he uses a set of command keys to move a cursor—a bright oblong of light—over the place he wishes to alter, types in the change, and the screen shows these and automatically makes room for the additions or closes up for deletions. He can move the story up to make more room, or roll it down to look at an earlier typed portion. If it is an urgent story he can send it to the proper desk in "takes" by pressing a MORE key. If he writes the story as one unit he looks it over to his satisfaction, then pushes a key marked END which sends it into the computer.

At a major desk of the *News*—say, the city desk—the editor can type LO for local copy, then press DIRECTORY, and this instructs the computer to display on the editor's screen a list of all the stories placed in the computer for his desk's use. He can call up any story on the list by pressing the NEXT key, then read the whole story on his screen, edit it, and type GE to send the story to the news editor. The news editor reviews the story, evaluates for length, column width, and body type, and makes notes on where it will go in the paper with size and style of headline (at this point, still written on paper). Then, by typing CE, he sends the story to the copy editor, who gives it a final perusal and a headline. When he is finished, typing GN sends it to a slotman, who gets a hard copy printout on a 200-line-a-minute impact imprinter. His hitting a key marked COMP ROOM tells the machines to send the story to the computer that automatically produces paper tape at about 1,000 words a minute; the paper tape then is fed into a linecaster that sets at the conventional fourteen lines a minute.

This procedure permits complete processing of a story ten minutes before the lockup deadline for a page. It also allows some of the copy for the early home-delivered editions of the *News*, an afternoon paper, to carry a deadline of 11 or 11:30 a.m. instead of the former 8 a.m. And this is just the start of a comprehensive system to be used when a new plant is completed in Sterling Heights, twenty-two miles north of Detroit. The plant will contain all the composing room and press facilities for the main editions of the paper (circ. 700,000), leaving in the downtown headquarters only news, advertising, and executive offices. In addition to hot type, the new plant will use photocomposition cold type handled by computers, with type set at 170 lines a minute. The communications link to the downtown offices will be a one-way "conditioned" (somewhat improved) telephone line costing $200 a month.

While the Detroit *News* has gone as far as any major paper in converting its newsroom to electronics, the most complete transformation from the traditional Linus blanket of reporters (the typewriter) and of editors (paper and pencil) has already been completed in those unlikely places, the Associated Press and United Press International.

The wires would seem unlikely to change, first, because they are creatures of (for UPI) their clients or (for AP) members. Most newspaper client-members are interested in paying as little as possible for their news, want little disturbance in their standard procedures, are themselves geared to the Gutenberg-Mergenthaler tradition in their factories, and distrust electronics. And broadcast stations—the majority of client-members—want simple, short items and assurance that the end of the world will not be announced without thirty minutes' notice.

The wire services internally have been the headquarters of the "green eyeshade school" of American journalism, with home-office bureaucracies populated by a disproportionate number of Old-Boy associates—a large number of them senior workers, since the New York headquarters was the top of the hierachy. It also has been at wire service headquarters where one saw something bordering on genius in the way experienced editors handled paper, for into their newsroom, through ninety or more teletype receivers, came miles of paper every day.

"In the old days" referred to by Eberhart and Boccardi copyboys would tear off each story as it came in and distribute copies to the appropriate desks. These were stories filed by correspondents and bureaus all over the world, stories to be weeded, edited down, combined, rewritten, and then transmitted to clients according to which specialized service he paid for and what interests he was, in the judgment of the editor, likely to have. (UPI New York, for example, handles 3 million words a day, counting both incoming and outgoing—the outgoing being about 80 per cent of what came in.) The editor scanned the story, decided on its priority (or on the appropriateness of the priority indicated by the originating bureau), and put it on the stack of other such stories on his desk, remembering what stories he already had in the pile (updates and corrections came in continually), and rearranging the pile to change priorities as new stories arrived by the minute. When the editor finished editing the story on top of the pile, or a rewrite he had ordered, and marked it for transmission, he handed it to a telegrapher (teletype operator) by his side who then punched out the story on paper tape. This, on completion, was fed into the teletype transmitted to clients of that particular wire.

The wire service newsrooms looked like badly managed paper recycling plants, with endless rolls of teletype paper snaking around machines, and desks piled high. The banks of clattering teletype machines sounded like the shuttle room of a Woonsocket textile mill. There were always stories of oldtimers who, after retirement, couldn't sleep without the customary seven and one-half hours of the noise.

It's gone, practically all gone, at UPI, and it's gone at AP regional news headquarters and is on the way out in Rockefeller Plaza. At UPI the only sound is a soft squirting noise from about sixty Extel printers typing abstracts of stories being stored in the computers downstairs; the sound is inaudible from three feet away

The miracles of electronic editing, computerized delivery systems and other innovations have eliminated much of the extra toil common to publishing, but reporters like Helen Thomas, United Press International's White House correspondent (on the opposite page), will always be there, ready to send important news around the world in minutes, and even seconds in the event of a "flash."

Press association staffers have the prime responsibility for keeping up with President Carter's public statements and appearances, and transmitting that news quickly and accurately to thousands of newspapers and broadcast stations. The interpretation and analysis can come later.

```
▼
▼
QUEUE aa ...... TIME IS 05:22▼
▼
ITEMS IN PROCESS▼                    °
▼
aa180 court... o. 0383 05:26▼
▼
ITEMS ON QUEUE▼
▼
aa181 europe-. o. 0418 05:34▼
aa177 opec.... o. 0290 05:40▼
aa213 talks-.. o. 0300 05:46▼
aa201 bufalino o. 0306 05:52▼
aa165 interest o. 0225 05:56▼
aa199 cuba.... om 0273 06:01▼
aa200 abortion o. 0243 06:06▼
aa204 tomcat.. o. 0363 06:13▼
aa207 freedom. o. 0139 06:16▼
aa208 Marchi.. o. 0181 06:20▼
aa210 defense. o. 0471 06:29▼
aa214 ervin... o. 0281 06:35▼
aa215 rescue.. o. 0221 06:39▼
aa221 boycott. o. 0531 06:49▼
aa225 turkey-. ■. 0299 06:55▼
```

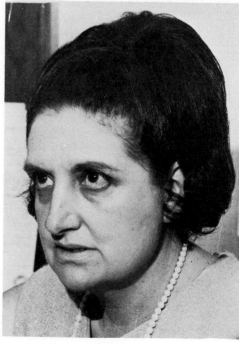

because the sixty-word-a-minute machines imprint by delicate letter—and number-shaped perforation of paper whose interior is purple, producing purple letters. Only occasionally is there the noise of a typewriter or the nostalgic sound of two remaining teletypes.

What has replaced the traditional machines of the trade are TV-like consoles with noiseless keyboards which enable editors or rewrite people to process stories in the same modern way they are handled at the Detroit *News*. What a client gets now is not very different from before—not different enough to impress many newsrooms that something basic has happened back at headquarters. He gets cleaner copy—from 50 to 90 per cent fewer typos and other errors because the editor, not a teletype operator, is the last handler of the story; this saves the newspaper client money, since many stories arrive on teletypesetter tape that is fed directly into composing room machinery. The client also gets more copy in the same time (even the best teletype operators must pause to sneeze or read illegible editing marks, or must feed tape they have just punched into a teletype sender). The computer maintains a queue of stories and sends them electronically and continuously without pauses. UPI figures it sends about 30 per cent more copy per day because of this.

The ultimate significance for newspapers, however, is not fewer typos or more news-per-hour, but the availability of the wire services' prodigious output in digital form in computers—in electronic impulses that can be transmitted at extremely high speeds when clients decide to get machines to receive them that way. These same digital impulses that carry news stories can, if publishers standardize and move toward twentieth century production techniques, practically eliminate the major part of their newspaper factories—the composing room, stereotyping, photocomposition setups for offset, and conventional plate-making. In seven years, says Ronald White of Gannett, one of the more knowledgeable experts in the field, it will be possible for electronic impulses from wire service headquarters, plus others that will represent local copy, to be used to etch printing plates directly without any intervening processes.

The AP and UPI systems, while both using electronic "typewriters" and computers, are organized on different systems. UPI has one headquarters for all its copy. Its three RCA Spectra 70/45 computers on the eleventh floor contain all UPI national news and practically all its international news. Instead of the ninety teletype receivers and thirty senders that used to fill the New York newsroom, there are now thirty-four VDT's—Video Display Terminals, the phrase used for the TV-like screen with keyboard connected to a computer. UPI uses the Harris-Intertype 1100. Five machines in the UPI Washington bureau and three in Chicago handle the system's national broadcast wire.

UPI bureaus and correspondents still file as they always did, by teletype, but now their stories go into computers. At the same time a conventional copy is made on a teletype receiver, and an abstract of the story—most of the first paragraph—is sent instantly by the computer to an Extel printer next to each editor that the originating bureau thinks will be interested. Some still find it easier to catch up by scanning the regular teletype report. But others use the Extel abstracts and then ask the computer to display on their screen all the slugs of stories stored in the past twenty-four hours.

Each slug on the screened list has a unique code number, the number of words, and its priority (''O'' for ordinary, ''B'' for Bulletin, ''U'' for urgent, ''M'' for message, etc.). If an item interests the editor, he types out the code for the story and almost instantly it appears on his screen. If it is longer than the twenty-five lines the screen holds, he pushes a button that moves the story up, showing the rest of it. His chief editing tool is the cursor—on this screen, a white oblong.

(There is a substantial Spanish-language service. For this the editor-translator calls up the English-language story on his screen and types out the Spanish translation paragraph by paragraph, the Spanish appearing on the screen just below the English paragraph. When the translator is satisfied, he pushes a button, the English paragraph disappears, and he goes on to the next paragraph.)

UPI is centralized, even for inter-bureau messages. ''In the old days'' if Atlanta wanted to send a message to San Francisco, it waited for a chance to break into the wire with the regular news. Now it sends it to the New York computer, which routes it directly to San Francisco without the Atlanta operator having to wait for a chance to get on the wire.

The UPI's three computers are specialized. One handles all the regular news wires, one stock listings, and the third does ''batch processing'' and serves as a backup. Each can handle the job of any of the other two if there is a breakdown. If there is a disaster—a blackout in New York City, or all three computers die simultaneously for a long period—UPI says it can decentralize and allow regional bureaus to handle the news on their regular teletype line network. Obviously, it would be a time-consuming switchover. Four times in the first year's operation, there have been computer breakdowns of an hour or two, all during the early months.

(UPI is considering regionalizing its automated operation sometime in the future, making state and regional news available in local computers, which would assist New York in the event headquarters has a blackout. Also planned are backup generators to supply electricity if any area loses public power.)

Associated Press has chosen a different strategy. It has created ten regional headquarters it calls ''hubs'' (including Boston, Philadelphia, Dallas, Kansas City, Atlanta, Los Angeles, Seattle, and Denver). These hubs do for their surrounding states what the UPI New York office does for the world. Each of the thirty-eight bureaus and seventy-five smaller offices used to be independent originating points for AP news, waiting to break into regional or main wires to put items into the system, and each state (except for the more sparsely populated) controlled its own selection and distribution. Each such former operation had its own teletype operators, except for the individual correspondent offices, where the reporter punched out his own stories.

All the AP hubs now have their own computers, fed both by CRT-keyboards from their regional offices and by datafax, the facsimile machine that transmits a page of copy in four minutes on a special telephone line. With the hub system, the outlying offices no longer need to monitor all the AP wires or wait for a break to insert their stories—or hire teletype operators. At the hub, an editor simply hands a teletype operator any copy that arrives in paper form and the operator types it into the hub's computer with the usual instructions for priorities.

AP headquarters in New York still looks and sounds pretty much like the conventional wire service newsroom—lots of teletypes, lots of typewriters, some Extels, but still the endless ribbons of teletype copy. It is a smaller operation than UPI's (about twenty-five electronic machines and a small computer) because only the main national news wires go out from Manhattan; most news operations are decentralized. AP selected different equipment, the Hendrix CRT and computer. Each CRT is less expensive—$14,000 each—than UPI's Harris, which in the UPI-altered model costs $18,000, and both types do essentially the same thing. But the AP machine has a black background with white letters; its cursor is a constantly flashing oblong; and the keyboard is more intimidating—less differentiation between regular alphabetic and numerical keys and command keys, and some keys with triple functions.

The wire services have been the first to convert to electronics because the technology of cathode ray tubes connected to computers has been the most highly developed in communications, and the wire services are purely in communications— the collecting and transmission of news. They could convert because the biggest human and technological problem in newspaper modernization—the production of printed papers—isn't their responsibility.

There, was, of course, the problem of human adjustment and relations with unions. Yet, to the astonishment of everyone involved, there was no massive resistance to the new machines. AP introduced its machines in the Columbia, S.C., bureau, which employs four people, three of them AP veterans. The results were so positive that Wes Gallagher, chief of AP, said he didn't believe the reports his subordinates gave him. "I was coming back from the South and I drove to Columbia to see for myself," he says. "It was true. Everyone liked and accepted the new system, including the older men."

At UPI, a set of machines was put in a room where the staff could "play" with them (and make mistakes) privately. Eberhart says that within four hours most men could run the machines and within two weeks feel comfortable with them. AP, whose machines are less simple looking, report slightly longer adaptation time.

William Laffler, who has been with UPI twenty-eight years and now is a general news editor, says, "I was skeptical at first but I found things easier. The screen is always clear and even. Before, when reporters did rewrite, some had clean copy, some had dirty copy; some had black ribbons, and some had faded ones; and when you read all day it's annoying. Also, I can see what I've got in one glance."

Laffler pushed a button and instantly on his screen twenty-three stories were listed. He pushed the code number beside one slugged FLU and instantly there was a story from Atlanta, by Charles S. Taylor, that looked like typewritten copy except it was on the screen, without the instability of normal TV pictures because the screens are finer and are synchronized so that no "jumping" occurs. Laffler saw a style error—a surplus hyphen—and pushed the delete button. And he thought that FLU should go above a story marked CARS, whose first paragraph he could see on his Extel; within seconds he had made that change.

Wire service executives appeared so euphoric about acceptance of the new machines that it seemed wise to check with representatives of the Wire Service

Guild. Norman Welton, administrator of the Guild (1,400 members in AP, 950 in UPI, 80 per cent of them newspeople), confirmed it: "Last spring we were in negotiations and an older member from UPI came to me and said, 'We'll go on strike before we'll let them move in those machines.' Two months after they put in the machines I went through the UPI shop and here was this same guy boasting to a visitor how he could do things with the machine better than he could with paper and pencil."

The Guild does have some problems, rectified in practice but not yet in contracts. Some members are concerned that newsmen will be judged on their technical proficiency with the machines rather than their editorial and reportorial judgment. They do not want editorial people to be given other persons' work to keyboard—to them, tantamount to having to retype another reporter's story. The Guild also is concerned about possible radiation effects from cathode ray tubes, and about eyestrain. However, a UPI-commissioned study by the University of Florida Radiology Department found that editors receive less radiation than is normal from TV sets; another study by the Ophthalmology Department of the Yale Medical School found no eyestrain problem. Welton says he wants contracts to affirm present practices, plus further study of eyestrain and radiation.

For all this, there is a paradox in the rapid electronic systems inside AP, UPI, and a few newsrooms like that of the Detroit *News*: While internal work is handled at electronic speeds, the national news transmission network is still basically a voice-grade telephone or telegraph line with the ancient capacity of teletype machines—officially, sixty words a minute but actually, with pauses and garbles, an average of forty-five. No matter how fast AP or UPI put together their news reports with the new gadgetry, with few exceptions it chugs out of their computers at forty-five words per minute. Some customers—about forty for UPI and 200 for AP—lease (for approximately $180 a month) Dataspeed machines which will receive 1,050 words a minute and produce hard copy, punched paper type, or computer signals at the same rate. Other available machines receive at 2,100 to 3,000 or more words a minute—but they are not in significant use.

As of now, few of AP's or UPI's customers feel compelled to lease or buy high-speed receiving equipment because their composing rooms can't handle material much faster than their old teletypes receive it. A few organizations have started to convert, however. Booth Newspapers, Inc. has its headquarters in Ann Arbor for the eight Michigan papers in its group (Ann Arbor *News*, Bay City *Times*, Flint *Journal*, Grand Rapids *Press*, Jackson *Citizen Patriot*, Kalamazoo *Gazette*, Muskegon *Chronicle*, and Saginaw *News*). Booth's Ann Arbor computer receives three AP and three UPI lines. As each item goes into the central computer, a teletype copy is fed to each member paper. An editor at each decides which story he wants to use and, through a keyboard, puts in a call to the Ann Arbor computer, typing out the date, index code for the desired story, and the size and style of type and column-width in which he wants the story set. Almost at once he receives the story at 300 words a minute in the form of punched tape already coded for the proper typesetting. Then the tape is fed manually into a linecasting machine.

Savings for Booth so far total about $50,000 a year in line charges, plus the wages ($120,000) of at least eight compositors no longer needed. Within five years Booth hopes to compose whole pages on its CRTs. The page then could be in electronic signal form which could make a printing plate directly, either by computer-instructed laser beam or production of an offset plate. Or there could be plateless printing with some magnetic, electrostatic process that draws dry ink spray onto magnetized moving newsprint.

Booth is switching totally to cold type, which permits electronic photocomposition, the ideal mate to computerized copy. To do this quickly, the chain did what most publishers avoid—rapid writeoff of existing hot metal equipment that is heavy, durable, and operable for years to come. This writeoff, for $1,250,000, has reduced dividends by 31 cents a share but promises mammoth production savings.

Gannett acquired one of the most accomplished technologists in the field by hiring Ronald White away from a less progressive Scripps-Howard organization, and the chain now is trying alternative systems in two plants before automating its fifty-three papers. Knight Newspapers expects all its plants to be completely converted to photocomposition—and thus totally open to use of electronics—by 1975. All fourteen Lee papers are expected to be converted by the end of this year, using a variety of electronic devices, including some from Japan. The New York *Times* has been negotiating with the International Typographical Union for fundamental changes in production—which accounts for 42 per cent of its expenses. The ITU has accepted in principle the need for modernization, and seems chiefly concerned with guarantees of lifetime pay for displaced workers plus ITU jurisdiction over new integrated systems.

The basic union problem is not simply displacement of individual workers; new devices usually aren't adopted until they save so much money they permit owners to pay displaced workers until death, retirement, or voluntary moves to other jobs. The basic problem is that truly radical change in newspaper production combines many traditional steps into one operation. This entirely eliminates some unions—sterotypers and engravers aren't needed in offset plants—and in others raises the issue of which union controls a machine that combines the work previously done by two or more different classes of employees.

The CRT connected to computer, for example, allows the reporter or editor to write and edit the story, automatically line it up for transmission (if at a wire service) or (if at a newspaper) cut tape or drive a photocomposition machine. Is this an editing or a composing function? In a unionized paper, do the keyboard and computer command buttons belong to the Newspaper Guild or the International Typographical Union?

At UPI the issue went to arbitration, producing a decision that the CRT-computer is an editing machine. Therefore the Wire Service guild has jurisdiction, and teletype operators are being phased out. At the Detroit *News* the issue remains unresolved. The paper has no Guild representation but does have the ITU, whose contract gives it control over preparation of all tapes for driving linecasting or photocomposition machines. Management and the ITU held talks for months while the *News* experimented with its new system. [In October 1972], while talks were still inconclusive, the *News* put the new system into operation. The paper offered to go to arbitration and the ITU agreed-meanwhile obtaining an injunction against the new process pending completion of arbitration. The injunction since has been lifted, and at this writing arbitration was continuing.

One of the most important decisions in the field was the so called Kagel Award in San Francisco (named for Sam Kagel, chairman of the local board of arbitration for the San Francisco Newspaper Printing Co.—joint production venture of the *Chronicle* and *Examiner*—and Bay Area Typographical Union No. 21). Almost everyone has a different interpretation of the decision, some calling it a "victory" for the union and some a "victory" for management. One reason for the ambiguity is that much of the decision concerns optical scanners, for which copy is typed with special clarity on electric typewriters, then read by computer and converted either to tape or more direct composition, eventually including possible whole-page makeup. Some systems, like those at AP, UPI, and some newspapers, do not use scanners.

The Kagel Award permits all "scanner-ready" copy to be processed directly by automatic machines no matter who produces it—presumably including reporters, editors, or members of other departments. "However," it specifies, "no typing pool will be created or used to prepare such copy." So unless reporters and editors become precision typists—which the Newspaper Guild wants to avoid in order to retain emphasis on journalistic skills—ITU members will do any retyping for computer-scanning.

The Kagel Award also provides, "If wire service copy is received in a form directly entering the computer, composing room employees will operate the CRT Terminals to make all alterations indicated by the editorial departments on the 'hard' copy." The agreement further specifies that the ITU will do all updating of texts and news, all corrections and alterations, and—perhaps the most significant phrase in the agreement—"original keystroking to be used for typesetting." This seems to mean that editors may not operate the CRT keyboards to edit or rewrite stories which can be sent directly to computers for automatic tape-punching or photocomposition. Either editors will continue to work with traditional paper and pencil, and hand copy to an ITU member to retype, or, less likely, employ an ITU member at the keyboard in the newsroom to receive verbal instructions from editors.

The outcome of these battles—just beginning at most newspapers—will determine who has maximum control over the editing process and how much money owners can realize from innovations. (Even with duplicated typing of copy, the new machines will make possible vastly greater profits—reducing some production costs 50 per cent.) But the stake of journalist and public is not in which unions emerge ascendant nor in the added profits of an industry which already records the third-highest profit of all American manufacturing industries. What matters is the impact on the quality of the product. Will news organizations, already fabulously profitable, shift production savings to the heart of the business—news and editorial?

The dream of all journalists and conscientious owners has been to free the American newspaper from being mostly a factory. That liberation has now begun. The result can be a continuing relatively meager expenditure on the editorial product, with small offices downtown transmitting editorial material to an automated printing plant. Or it can be the realization of the dream that most of a paper's energy will go into covering its community and region, that leaders of news organizations will no longer be executives rewarded for their commercial and mechanical management efficiency but men and women who are essentially recorders and analysts of social and political events—directors of enterprises whose place in society under the First Amendment has more to do with ideas than with producing pieces of lead.

Bibliography

Ben Bagdikian's survey of technology as applied to wire services and the metropolitan newspapers should be supplemented by his book *The Information Machines: Their Impact on Men and the Media*, Harper & Row, 1971. The information about the technology itself can be regularly up-dated by reading *Newspaper Production, Inland Printer,* and *Graphic Arts Monthly*. These three magazines, particularly the first, offer frequent articles on technical developments in the printing field. See especially P. L. Andersson, "Industry Update: On Video Terminals and Computer Storage Systems," *Newspaper Production* (February 1975), pp. 28-33, which contains a useful chart depicting characteristics of the various devices discussed in the article. Paul J. Hartsuch, "Electronics in the Newsroom," *Graphic Arts Monthly* (November 1974), describes the *Davenport Times-Democrat* (Iowa) operation.

Toward Totally Electronic TV News
By Robert Mulholland

Robert E. Mulholland is vice president, NBC News in New York City. Reprinted from *The Quill* (November 1973), published by the Society of Professional Journalists, Sigma Delta Chi, with permission of the publisher. Copyright 1974 by *The Quill*.

If you watch a television news program tonight, the odds are you'll see a report you couldn't have seen [in 1972].

Then, you would have seen that report tomorrow. Or maybe the day after tomorrow.

In simplest terms, that's what the new technology means to the television news viewer—more news now, not later.

Satellites, computers, microminiaturization, solid state components—all these fancy space-age terms now mean something to electronic journalism and journalists.

And more important, they mean something to the 90 million Americans who watch television news each day.

Satellite transmission of foreign news is now commonplace. What that means to a viewer is same-day coverage of an event in Europe or Japan.

Just 10 years ago, satellites were not available full-time. They could be available as little as 13 minutes a day.

Now, fixed position satellites over the Atlantic, Pacific and Indian oceans, plus nearly 90 earth stations for sending up pictures and sound, make it possible to transmit news to the United States from every continent, 24 hours a day.

However, most of what is transmitted by satellite for television news is film. And before you understand what the new technology means and where it can take electronic journalism, you must understand the difference between film and videotape.

When the Allende government was overthrown in Chile, the junta sealed borders and closed airports. Reporters couldn't get into Chile. Film couldn't be flown out.

A Santiago television station had covered all the fighting. Via satellite, from a ground station in Santiago, Chile, American television viewers saw their first report of what was happening.

But it was a film report. Film cameramen had covered the fighting. Then, after processing and editing, the film was satellited to the United States for broadcast on the network news programs.

Yes, new technology—the satellite—got the report here faster. Otherwise, the film would have been flown to New York, showing up possibly days after the actual event.

But now, there is a faster way. The networks are experimenting with it. And what the satellite has done for foreign coverage, even though it is film coverage, the new technology in hand-held electronic cameras will do for domestic coverage.

NBC News calls its camera the PCP-90. . . .CBS has dubbed its camera the Minicam.

The names are not important. What is important is that these new cameras are in the process of changing the way news is covered in this country.

First, these cameras do not use film. They record their pictures on magnetic tape. Just like home tape recorders. This means no processing time is needed. And that means news can be covered later in the day and still broadcast on the evening news programs.

Second, these cameras can be used to cover news ''live.'' By either hooking into a telephone company line, or using a portable transmitter, a major story can be put on the air as it is happening as a bulletin or special report.

The new technology has made these cameras possible. Ten years ago, the lightest electronic color camera available at NBC weighed over 200 pounds. Now, electronic color cameras are on the market weighing as little as 30 pounds. And two companies, RCA and Fairchild, have announced development of a six-ounce television camera. Right now, though, it is black-and-white.

The lightweight electronic cameras were originally developed by the networks for use at the political conventions. Then, they became part of most sports coverage.

But, in both cases, they were used ''live,'' cable connected. And they were used to cover a given event in a given location.

Then, the new technology came along with small, powerful batteries. And small portable videotape recorders. And the camera itself got smaller and lighter. As a result, the camera could be used to cover breaking news. And that's what is being done now.

In Washington, both NBC News and CBS use electronic cameras every day.

If you are a sophisticated viewer, you can tell what is film and what is electronic on the evening news programs. And when you see a correspondent or a major government official "electronic" on the news, the odds are that was a late story—too late to do on film.

In New York, Chicago and Los Angeles, some network-owned stations are now using the new cameras for their local news coverage. And as the price of the equipment drops, as it will, more stations throughout the country will be adding portable electronic cameras for news.

But all of this will soon pose a problem for the networks and the stations that start to go electronic. That problem is—how far do they go?

Do they go all-electronic? Do they go half and half? Or do they continue film as the basis for television news coverage, using electronic cameras only in special situations.

Each system requires a separate support system, and they are totally incompatible. The entire support system already exists for film. Networks and stations own their own processors. They have their newsfilm editing equipment. They are currently investing in new lightweight film cameras with solid-state sound systems.

To go totally electronic for news will require, for example, expanded videotape editing facilities. News producers complain videotape can't be edited as quickly as film.

Computer-controlled videotape editing systems exist. But they are expensive compared to newsfilm editing equipment. Yet, competition has a way of either forcing the price down, or making it seem not quite so important.

If the opposition network or station can do something you can't, because of a piece of new equipment, there's usually a fast way to get it—especially if you've been beaten on a story once or twice.

Incidentally, although the new excitement in television news is electronic cameras, the new technology is also at work on film and film cameras.

Film speeds are now faster than ever before. Color film processing is faster. Film cameras are lighter and more versatile. And all of this means more news, covered faster and better, for the viewer.

Our reporters, in Washington for example, can stay on their beat an extra hour in the afternoon if they know an electronic camera is hot in the hallway. Rather than bringing our White House correspondent back to our studio, he can step outside after a late briefing and do a report that can be taped on the spot, or fed directly back to the studio and into a news program live.

The new technology makes all of this possible. And it isn't over yet.

A friend of mine at NBC News whose job it is to keep abreast of the new developments that might help us cover news faster, predicts this for the future: The television reporter will wear a small hearing aid device, actually a microminiaturized satellite receiver, that will keep him in constant contact with his office.

He'll have a small electronic camera, about the size of today's home movie camera.

And he'll carry a small videotape recorder the size of today's small audio tape cassette recorders.

To get his story on the air, he'll open his briefcase, flip a switch, push a button on his recorder—and that's it.

His briefcase will contain a satellite transmission terminal. And that will allow him to get on the air from any location.

So, the new technology is here, at work every day helping us get news to the people of this country. What we didn't think would be possible 10 years ago, we do every night without thinking twice. And what we dream about now, we'll be doing in the future. Maybe next year.

Bibliography

Electronic news gathering (ENG) has received a great deal of attention in the professional journals recently. Consult *Broadcasting, Television/Radio Age* and *Broadcast Management/Engineering (BM/E)*, especially the last two. Special issues of *Broadcasting* will be worth consulting, but the last two publications will contain the most detailed discussions on a consistent basis. An example from *BM/E* is "Electronic News Gathering: It Is Off the Launching Pad, With Full Flight Ahead," *BM/E* (January 1975), pp. 34-41 ff., which provides short descriptions of programs and equipment at KMOX-TV (St. Louis), CITY (Toronto, Canada), WLAC-TV (Nashville), and CBS, NBC, and ABC operations in New York City. This is a very detailed compendium of articles on ENG. A useful bibliography for technical background is George Shiers, compiler, *Bibliography of the History of Electronics*, The Scarecrow Press, 1972.

Journalism Educators and the Growing Tragedy of Journalism Employment

By Joseph M. Webb

A tragedy is brewing in journalism—both print and broadcast! And we in journalism education are deeply implicated in it! Fortunately, we could become a major part of the solution to it, if we have the will and the courage.

To make clear the nature of the tragedy I see which could result in a media breakdown of immense proportions it is necessary to sketch several developments or trends and then pull them together. That is what I want to attempt to do in this monograph.

The first strand has to do with journalism enrollments and graduates. I don't know how accurate Prof. Paul Peterson's surveys are, but they do emphasize the growing enrollments of our journalism schools. His most recent survey shows that in 1974, 55,078 students were enrolled in journalism education across the country—an increase of 13.8 per cent over the previous year. The increase in 1973 was 15.9 per cent; in 1972, it was 13.6 per cent. Comparable growth figures may be compiled for graduates across the country in radio and television broadcasting.

Joseph M. Webb is on the faculty of the Department of Journalism, Southern Illinois University. Previous journalism experience included that of media critic for public radio (non-profit) KPFK, Los Angeles, where parts of this essay first were presented. Reprinted with permission of the author.

The second strand is more complex. It involves what I regard as a growing infatuation among many journalism educators with new forms of media technology now in use, in some form or other, in many broadcast and print news operations across the country. One major journalism school after another—from Ohio State to Kentucky to much smaller schools—is devoting a large chunk of its budget to installing these new machines on which students are to learn how to be media computer operators.

The academic euphoria, however, is nothing compared with that of the media owners themselves as any issue of *Editor and Publisher* makes clear; they are the ones who make big profits in the newspaper business, for example. They are literally revolutionizing their composing rooms and their newsrooms with the new technology; and they are doing it because of the substantially increased profits they stand to gain from it all.

But the new media technology—used for management profit—poses a crucial, if little understood, problem. It is a problem most vividly revealed by a fundamental dictum of Marxism: that technology always displaces labor! As Robert Heilbroner recently said: "to the extent that conventional economics accept the crucial Marxian assumption that technology tends to displace labor, they are driven to very 'Marxian' conclusions about the impending malfunction of the economy."

That is precisely what is happening throughout the establishment of media owners across the country! As newspaper and broadcast owners sink more and more capital into the new computerized machines, they are literally displacing hundreds upon hundreds of skilled media workers from their jobs! And we are only in the opening phases of this revolution in media technology!

To show you that the employment downtrend is already well-established in the media, one recent article in *Editor and Publisher* reported on a study of a typical seven day daily newspaper's profit and expense figures for 1973 and 1974. The trend is clear and well-established. Profits are increasing for the newspaper owners; some expenses are going up but—most importantly—the percentage of the owners' expense devoted to payroll is steadily going down. For that paper, the percentage of total expense devoted to payroll in 1973 was 48.7 per cent; it dropped to 45.8 per cent in 1974—and that despite the fact that those on the payroll received good pay increases! The cut in those employed on that paper was drastic in that one year! The message? The number of people needed to put a media product together are dropping substantially—because of new technology. Unemployment among skilled media people is climbing—and will get worse soon!

An occasional new publication does begin, of course; but the only way it can make it competitively is to use the new machinery to cut back labor costs. For example, *Inland Printer* magazine recently described the new daily newspaper in New York; the article said that "the new paper's ace-in-the-hole will be a payroll well beneath its competitors. 'We'll be able to put out a comparable product with 60 per cent of the production force,' John Keane, *The Press'* production manager, ger, said."

Everyone generally knows that the majority of those who have been displaced from media jobs in the past have been in the composing or press rooms. These workers are the ones who have, in the past, struck in order to preserve some semblance of their jobs. But, the transition from the use of hot type to cold type in newspaper production has drastically cut into the press and composition jobs available in all newspapers, large and small.

What is happening now is more startling. It is the introduction of machine and computer technology into the so-called "professional" levels of newspapers and broadcasting—into those areas which before felt themselves immune to replacement by machinery. Immune those professions certainly are not! Now it is the reporters and editors, the information and advertising people who are being phased down, who are now and who will in the future be fired and replaced by technology!

But let me be specific with another *Editor and Publisher* article. It is entitled "Computer Program Puts Ads In Paper In Minutes;" it is typical of many articles in this and other media trade journals like it.

The article begins, and I quote: "A computer program developed at MIT under an ANPA grant can place ads on newspaper pages in a fraction of the time it takes a human being to do them. And the program obeys to the letter instructions given to it about not 'burying' ads or not setting competitors' ads on the same or facing pages."

The article then describes one experiment with the *Boston Globe,* in which the computer first figured out that 44 pages would be required for a Tuesday edition. and its size, as well as special rules of the newspaper, before the machine began laying out pages.

"After all the information was read in, the computer first decided how many pages the paper would have that day. Editors could then preset certain ads before the computer took over. The machine then sorted out the tall, thin ads and laid them out first. Then it sorted out the large ads, and placed them next. The rest it stuck onto pages, subject to the rules it had been instructed to obey."

The article then describes one experiment with the *Boston Globe,* in which the computer first figured out that 44 pages would be required for a Tuesday edition. The human editors had also figured 44 pages would be required. "The computer then placed," the article says, "90 of 92 ads in the paper, saying the other two could not be placed without violating some rule of ad placement. The editors fit the remaining ads in by hand, with some minor rule-bending." The article then states—amazingly—that "It took the humans over three hours to do the real-life layout; the computer did it in 15 minutes."

Moreover, "in a similar experiment with one edition of the *Worcester Telegram,* the computer placed 89 of 95 of the ads given to it. The humans took four hours; the computer, 21 minutes."

Need more? The article continues: "In addition, the computer offered the editors a choice of layouts when a six-column ad came in after the newspapers deadline. Since a six-column ad represents a lot of revenue, the editors decided to expand the issue by two pages to accommodate it. The computer figured out a way to include all the ads in the same space, while still producing what the editors called an acceptable layout."

All of that means very simply that whereas in the past dozens of skilled individuals were needed to handle a newspaper's advertising design and layout functions every day—now, with a computer operation, only a couple of individuals are needed to run the computer—and make an occasional adjustment here and there. And the advertising staff of a newspaper can be cut by 50 or even 75 per cent!

The same—like it or not—is already true in the newsroom. The article I referred to says that the developers of the advertising layout computer program are now at work on a program to do news-story layouts. And there is no reason to think that they will not develop such a program very soon.

That will mean that whereas now, or in the past, it required a lot of skilled newsroom people—editors, layout specialists, headline writers, copy and slot people—to prepare the newscopy for printing, in the immediate future, with the computer in the newsroom, all of those functions can be filled by a few relatively unskilled people—again, a few who will program and run the computer and make an occasional adjustment. And then the news editorial staff can be chopped easily by 50 or 75 per cent!

Ironically, in the corner of the *Editor and Publisher* page on which this article appears is this short news note. Let me quote it: "Booth Newspapers, Inc., disclosed in its annual report to shareholders that increased efficiency resulting from improvements in photocomposition processes at its eight daily newspapers had cut the man hours per page composition rate by 50.5 per cent over the past three years.

"Booth is currently installing a total of 270 video display terminals (VDTs) at six of its newspapers to further speed and simplify the photocomposition processes at these publications."

VDT units are among the most widespread new forms of newsroom technology that are drastically cutting the number of people needed as both reporters and editors, to say nothing of the elimination of proofreaders and copy handlers. VDT units are, in short, computers that enable a reporter to bypass, practically, a typewriter; the reporter can set his own story into type, correct errors himself directly on the machine as he sees the type coming up on a monitor before him and have that type he is setting fed directly into the galley ready for computer make-up and paste-up.

A handful of individuals, in other words, are now able to do the work in the newsroom that, before, required the integrated labor of dozens of skilled workers! The unemployment among newsroom personnel is bound to skyrocket! And virtually every newsroom in the country is on the verge of converting their entire newsrooms to these machines. The *Los Angeles Times*, for example, is now in the midst of its transition. The wire services—AP, UPI and so forth—some time ago greatly reduced the number of people in their newsrooms by bringing in their VDTs.

But let's look at it from a slightly different angle, an angle that will let us see more clearly the way that news reporters themselves will be severely hit by this new technology.

Let's take an evening newspaper that must hit the streets at 5 p.m. Say the paper has four reporters; they have a deadline of 1 p.m. for their stories, because it takes four hours to prepare their stories for print. During those morning hours, each reporter can prepare one good story before that deadline, but those four stories are enough to fill the paper's newsslot. The rest of the day each reporter spends on longer term stuff, on filing and clipping chores or just generally looking busy. Then, the newspaper owner hauls in some new machines that can process story materials in drastically reduced time. Now, say, the deadline for the 5 p.m. edition is moved to 4 p.m., since it takes only an hour to process the stories for print. Now, however, each of those four reporters has sufficient time to prepare two good stories per day for that day's edition—a story in the morning and a story in the afternoon. But only four stories are really needed per day. The newspaper owner can, then, fire two of the reporters, and with the remaining two—presumably the best two—still have all the stories he needs for his daily edition. And since the owner can do that—he will! So the new technology means that the owner will have as good a newspaper as before—but with a substantial reduction in payroll expenses! He will have as good a paper as before, that is, with bigger profits for himself. Never mind that two of his previous four reporters are now out of work!

That is precisely the way that newsrooms across the country are being affected by the emerging forms of media technology.

I found recently a summary article on the 1975 annual convention of the national Newspaper Guild, a unionized group made up largely of newsroom employees; reporters, editors and so forth. The article began with these open statements: "The nation's economic recession and the rapid changeover to automated equipment were among prime concerns of the Newspaper Guild's 42nd annual convention in Denver [1975]. Responding to conditions that have led to increased layoffs of guild members and contract resistance frm newspaper publishers, guild delegates acted to beef up job security and wage bargaining power, increase benefits for striking and locked-out members and speed legal recognition for newly organized groups."

That's how hard the clash between new newspaper technology and the decline in employment is already hitting—and the Newspaper Guild is finding itself increasingly weak in combatting what it calls "no fault" dismissals of employees who are displaced by a new machine like the Video Display Terminal.

Moreover, a strong new call was made at the Guild's convention for the merger of the Newspaper Guild and the International Typographical Union—a move that union leaders hope will provide some additional strength in their battle against all of them being replaced by the new computerized machinery!

I have been talking primarily about newspapers thus far. Everything I have said, however, applies to broadcasting, with every bit as much force. Let me give you two examples of new technological developments in broadcasting that are—and will more so in the future—result in broadcast owners firing dozens upon dozens of skilled broadcast professionals and technicians.

First, new developments in tape recording, both audio and video, along with the computerizations of tape recording now make possible the programming of long stretches of broadcast time, virtually without the use of human hands or voices. For instance, in the past it took, say 10 people—engineers, announcers, programmers, etc.—to run a radio station for a 14 hour day; there were that many different and concurrent jobs that needed to be done. Now, it is possible—no, it is being done in many radio stations in this city—it is possible for no more than three or four people to run the radio station for that 14 hour day. This is because compact, but long-playing music and commercial tapes can be purchased by the station which can be operated almost the entire day by a computer. The computer must be programmed, of course, and someone must break in from time to time to give the station call letters—no, that too can be programmed by the computer. The point is that, with developments in computer taping—and syndication of those computer tapes—a radio station can operate with a fantastic profit—but requiring very few employees to keep the station functioning smoothly!

Here is part of one full-page advertisement from an issue of *Broadcasting* magazine: ''We'd like to claim that automation will make you number one. But we won't. That's because it can't work miracles by itself. But an automation revolution in radio is going on. Automated stations have proved to be more than just profitable. They're also very competitive in ARB and Pulse. Drake-Chenault's quality programming for automation is no exception. Our formats work. They're based on the proven 'more music controlled personality' concept. And that can be done more effectively automated than 'live' . . . And today we can provide you with a whole range of sounds: from Easy Listening/Middle of Road to Adult contemporary to Top 40 . . .''

It's a strong profit pitch for broadcast owners. Automated tape radio means better profits; and a major source of those increased profits for owners is that they can chop drastically the number of people needed to keep the radio station on the air. So the unemployment rate among those in radio broadcasting—both technicians and professionals—is rising drastically!

Everything I have said about audio computer tape technology, as it affects radio, is becoming increasingly true of video computer taping—and the effect will gradually become the same in television: more automated programming, fewer workers needed in television programming and production.

But I want to mention here a different technological innovation in television that is already being hailed by the owners of the industry, but which will, increasingly, result in fewer and fewer workers needed in television—particularly in television news and news production. It is what is being called the minicam television camera. The minicamera is simply a light-weight, portable television camera which can transmit by microwave; its effect will be incredible.

Let me try to outline, as clearly as I can, how it will effect employment in the television news business. Let's take, for simplification, an hour-long local television newscast. Say that now it takes—as it usually does—about four four-person news teams to fill that hour of local news each day. Each crew requires a reporter, a cameraperson, a soundperson and an editor back in the studio. These people are required because, up to now, these field crews have used 16mm film for the newscasts. Then the 16mm cameras and film are replaced with minicamera units, which are self-contained and can provide videotape or live pictures directly to the studio. Immediately, the size of the daily news crew can be cut to a reporter and a cameraperson; moreover, because video tape editing can be done on a companion computer, the reporter can now handle that. So, for starters, we have cut the number of people required for the hour-long local newscast in half—each crew has gone from four to two people. But we're not through yet. Since much less time and expense is required for the minicamera's videotape than for film, much more tape can be shot at much less expense and deadlines can be moved back—all of which means that now it is possible that three news crews can come up with as many video stories as four teams used to come up for the same newscast. So now, instead of needing a total of 16 people for our hour-long local newscast, we can put together the same newscast with 6 people! All because of the new camera and video editing technology. We could go farther with our illustration, but you see how it works!

This kind of argument usually prompts two kinds of responses from journalism educators. The first can, in my view, be dealt with fairly easily. The question is asked: what about those "good" media people, those who will save money with technology, but who will use that "extra" money to put more reporters on the street rather than just chucking it away as profit? Fair enough; except that it is not media people who run newspapers and broadcasting stations—they are run, purely and simply, by business people; and the "good" media people will have virtually no say in what happens to the money that is "saved" by bringing in machines and ditching workers.

Those "good" media people will react to these developments much the way that Edwin Baker, general manager of the *Eugene* (Ore.) *Register-Guard* did to its taking place at that paper. I quote an article again, in *Editor and Publisher:* "Baker is aware that automation will ultimately lead to a reduction in the number of personnel in certain departments. Although he is greatly concerned about a reduction in personnel, he realizes the necessity of the automation process towards the economic independence and financial strength of the newspaper industry." What he means, however, is not the "economic independence and financial strength of the newspaper industry:" but, rather, the preservation of the financial profits of those few fortunate enough to own the hardware and machinery of the newspaper business. Never mind, again, those insignificant workers in the newspaper industry who are being cut loose from the industry!

With that, in effect, we sum up the attitude of those "good" media people toward this coming employment tragedy in media!

The second response is more difficult. The assertion is made: OK, technology brought into one area means increased unemployment in that area, but new areas of employment subsequently open up. The question is then raised: isn't that happening in mass media?

The answer is in a sense, yes. But when we pursue this in journalism and broadcasting education, we run squarely into a dead-end that puts those of us in journalism education in an awkward position. The problem is difficult, and, admittedly, I must oversimplify it to make clear what I mean. What is happening in journalism education may, it should be said, stave off the final clash between media technology for private profit and media unemployment; but it cannot hold off that clash indefinitely.

If you ask most teachers in journalism and broadcasting schools what they are doing about this problem, they will most likely say they are channeling their students into those media areas in which technology is still not very prominent—and that major area is public relations. . . . The problem with this, however, is that these students are hired to do PR work for the owners of the media and those owners who depend on the media for their own profits. These students are hired, as it were, to try to convince the American workers that new technology is OK; that there is no problem with it; that unemployment in media and elsewhere is merely temporary; that the American capitalistic system will work all right if we just give it time. PR people, in a thousand ways, are hired to tell the unemployed and the under-employed that!

So we come full circle. Journalism and broadcasting schools tend to perpetuate the myth that more graduates and more technology for newspaper and broadcasting owners can exist side by side. And when it doesn't work like that, when media jobs are steadily and drastically eliminated by the new technology, we channel our students into PR kinds of jobs—where those owners who shut them out of media jobs pay them to tell the public that what is happening is OK; and pay them, in a sense, to tell the public that those who were shut out of media jobs altogether are just hollering ''sour grapes'' if they complain too loudly about the media, the technology or the capitalistic system.

There is the irony: that those who must, somehow, say the media and the system are OK are increasingly the very ones who are themselves the unwitting victims of the owners and their use of the marvelous new media technology!

Bibliography

Joseph Webb's article points out an area of concern about which most educators are not yet in agreement. The effects of electronics in the newsroom, especially their effects on printers and allied trades, are discussed in Bagdikian's article. Webb's thrust is somewhat unusual. His is one of the few articles dealing with this aspect of technological change. For the response of printers and allied trades to technological innovation, see A. H. Raskin, ''Bert Powers at War with Himself,'' *(More)* (May 1972), pp. 3-5, Philip Nobile, ''High Noon at the Washington Post,'' *New Times* (Nov. 14, 1975), pp. 18-19 ff., and Patrick Owens, ''Violence in the Morning,'' *(More)* (December 1975), p. 12 ff. The Nobile and Owens articles deal with the issues involved in the strike at the *Post*, issues which in part grow out of the effects of the new technology. See also the bibliography following ''The New Concerns About the Press.''

For a broader examination of the effects of the technological revolution, see Nathan Katzman, ''The Impact of Communications Technology: Promises and Prospects,'' *Journal of Communication* (Autumn 1974), pp. 47-58. A more extended treatment of the general issue of technological effects is *Information Technology: Some Critical Implications for Decision Makers*, The Conference Board, 1972. This report presents cogent expectations growing out of the merging of communication technology with computer technology. For a summary of its content, including an informative flow chart, see ''Information Technology and Its Implication,'' *The Futurist* (December 1972), pp. 244-249.

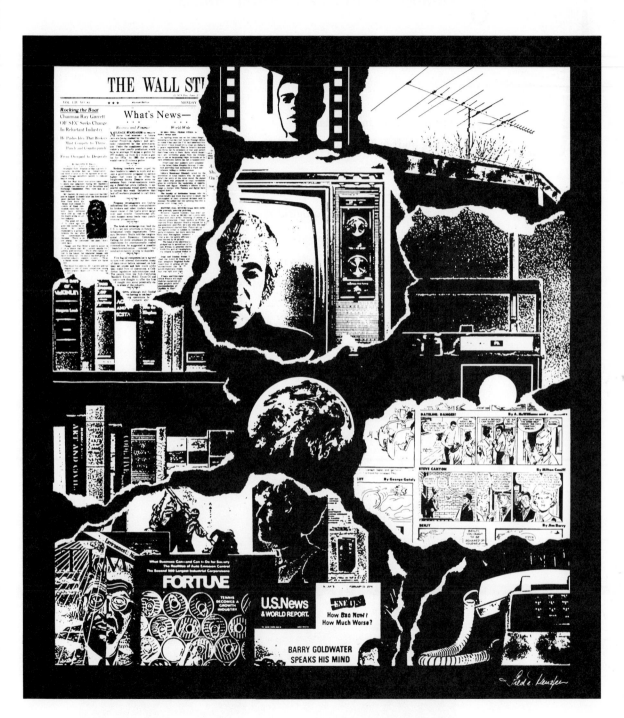

6 Change in the Traditional Media

The Intellectual In Videoland

By Douglass Cater

On a hot summer night in 1968 I was sitting in my Washington home, watching TV coverage of the disastrous Democratic convention in Chicago. Suddenly, all hell broke loose where the Wisconsin delegation was seated. TV cameras quickly zoomed in, of course, and reporters rushed to the area with walkie-talkies.

The whole nationwide TV audience thus knew in an instant what the uproar was all about. But Speaker Carl Albert, who was presiding over the convention, didn't have a clue, and he was the one who had to decide what to do about it. There, in microcosm, one saw how our leadership can be hustled by the formidable communications system of television.

No doubt about it, television is a looming presence in American life, even though most of us hardly know what to make of the medium. It arrived so swiftly and so totally: in January 1949 only 2.3 percent of American homes had the box with the cathode-ray tube. Five years later television had penetrated more than half of our homes. Today, 97 percent of them have one or more sets—a distribution roughly matching that of indoor plumbing. With American TV approaching its quarter-century anniversary as a household phenomenon, one might think we would by now have devoted serious attention to the effects of this medium on our culture, our society, our lives. Certainly, we might expect at this point to be trying to anticipate the consequences of the even more enveloping telecommunications environment that lies ahead. Yet, as the prescient Mr. Marconi predicted a long time ago, telecommunications has become part of the "almost unnoticed working equipment of civilization."

Why unnoticed? What has prevented thinking people from applying their critical faculties to this medium, which reaches greater masses than do all the other mass media combined (the number of sets in U.S. homes is nearly double the total daily circulation of newspapers)? Why haven't more of our talented scholars been attracted to the study of this new environment? Why do the media themselves devote so little attention to serious television analysis and criticism? Why have our foundations provided only very limited resources for the study of communications, which is as fundamental to society as education, health, and the physical environment?

I would suggest three reasons for these failures. In the first place, scientific evidence suggests that thinking people—at least those over 25—are left-brained in development. That is, they rely mainly on the left hemisphere, which controls sequential, analytical tasks based on the use of propositional thought. But TV, we are informed, appeals mainly to the *right* hemisphere of the brain, which controls appositional—that is, non-sequential, non-analytic—thought.

Scientists and theologians alike have pondered how the two halves of the brain relate—whether they ignore, inhibit, cooperate, or compete with each other, or simply take turns at the control center. Whole cultures seem to show a preference for one or the other mode of thought, and thinking people of the Western world up until now have plighted their troth with propositional thought. After five centuries of slowly acquired sophistication in distinguishing the truth from the trickery trans-

Douglass Cater is director of the Aspen Institute's Program on Communications and Society. Reprinted with permission from *Saturday Review* (May 31, 1975). Copyright *Saturday Review* 1975.

mitted by Mr. Gutenberg's invention, we now find ourselves having to master the nonlinear logic created by a steady bombardment of sights and sounds on our senses. The thinking person is therefore apt to be somewhat bewildered by the telly and to regard it in the same way that a backsliding prohibitionist regards hard liquor—as something to be indulged in with a sense of guilt.

According to *Television and the Public*, Robert T. Bower's analysis of viewing habits, the "educated viewer" has learned to live with ambivalence: although he may be scornful of commercial TV fare, "he watches the set (by his own admission) as much as others during the evening and weekend hours; . . .even when he had a clear choice between an information program and some standard entertainment fare, he was just as apt as others to choose the latter."

The peculiar structure of the American television industry is a second reason why the thinking person refuses to think seriously about the medium. The broadcast industry is based on a marketplace unlike any other in our private enterprise economy. Broadcasting offers its product "free" to the consumer and depends on advertising to supply, by the latest count, gross annual revenues of $4.5 billion. As a result, commercial TV's prime allegiance is to the merchant, not to the viewer. To attract the advertising dollar, the programmer seeks to capture the dominant portion of the viewers and to hold them unblinking for the longest period of time. Everything else is subordinated to this dogged pursuit of mankind in the mass. A program attracting many millions of viewers is deemed a failure and discarded if it happens to be scheduled opposite a program attracting even more millions.

Within this iron regime of dollars and ratings, a few ghettos of do-goodism exist. Network news and documentaries, as well as occasional dramas of exceptional quality, reveal an upward striving in television (some cynics dismiss this as tithing to the federal regulators). But these programs fare poorly in the competition for television's most precious commodity—time. A former network news chief has remarked of TV management, "They don't mind how much money and talent we devote to producing documentaries so long as we don't ask for prime-time evening hours to show them." Even the daylight hours have to be tightly rationed when the real-life marathon melodramas of Washington start competing with the soap operas of Hollywood.

Thinking people do not know how to cope with a system whose economic laws, they are led to believe, are immutable. Any suggestions they may have for the betterment of TV are characterized as naive, elitist, and offensive to the First Amendment. The proper posture is to sit back and be thankful when broadcast officialdom chooses to violate its own laws and reveal fleetingly what a fantastic instrument of communication television can be.

A third reason why thinking people have difficulty coming to grips with television is that they have yet to develop satisfactory ways to gauge the effects of this environmental phenomenon. Consider, as an example, the Surgeon General's inquiry into the effect of televised violence on the behavior of children. Conducted over a period of three years, at a cost of $1.8 million, and based on 23 separate laboratory and field studies, this probe was the most far-reaching to date into the social consequences of television. In its final report, the Surgeon General's committee could acknowledge only "preliminary and tentative" evidence of a casual relationship between TV violence and aggression in children.

As members of an industry dedicated to the proposition that 30-second commercials can change a viewer's buying behavior, producers would be foolish to ignore this warning about the not-so-subliminal effects of its program content. But these studies, mostly gauging immediate response to brief TV exposure, could not adequately measure the impact of the total phenomenon—the experience of the child who spends as many as six hours a day, year in and year out, before the set. This cumulative effect is what makes watching television different from reading books or going to the movies.

How to measure the longer-term, less flamboyant effects of the environment created by television? In 1938 E. B. White witnessed a TV demonstration and wrote, "A door closing, heard over the air, a face contorted, seen in a panel of light, these will emerge as the real and the true. And when we bang the door of our own cell or look into another's face, the impression will be of mere artifice."

Now, a third of a century later, comes Tony Schwartz to carry the speculation further in his book *The Responsive Chord*. Mr. Schwartz's insights have peculiar power, because he created the ill-famed political commercial for the 1964 campaign, which showed a child innocently picking daisy petals, one after another, as a countdown for a hydrogen bomb blast. Though there was no mention of the Presidential candidate at whom the message was aimed, the effect of the commercial was so unnerving that its sponsors withdrew it after a single showing. Schwartz appears to know whereof he theorizes.

Gutenberg man, he writes, lived by a communication system requiring the laborious coding of thought into words and then the equally laborious decoding by the receiver—similar to the loading, shipping, and unloading of a railway freight car. Electronic man dispenses with this by communicating experience without the need of symbolic transformations. What the viewer's brain gets is a mosaic of myriad dots of light and vibrations of sound that are stored and recalled at high speed. Amid this electronic bombardment, Schwartz speculates, a barrier has been crossed akin to the supersonic sound barrier—or, in his image, the 90-mile-an-hour barrier beyond which a motorcycle racer must turn *in to* rather than *out with* a skid: " . . .In communicating at electronic speed, we no longer direct information into an audience but try to evoke stored information out of it in a patterned way."

The function of the electronic communicator, according to Schwartz, "is to achieve a state of resonance with the person receiving visual and auditory stimuli." The Gutenberg communicator—for the past 500 years patiently transmitting experience line by line, usually left to right, down the printed page—is no longer relevant. TV man has become conditioned to a total communication environment, to constant stimuli which he shares with everyone else in society and to which he is conditioned to respond instantly. Schwartz believes that the totality and instantaneousness of television, more than its program content, contributes to violence in society.

His premises lead him to the shattering conclusion that "truth is a print ethic, not a standard for ethical behavior in electronic communication." We must now be concerned not with Gutenberg-based concepts of truth, but with the *effects* of electronic communication: "A whole new set of questions must be asked, and a whole new theory of communications must be formulated."

Without going all the way with Schwartz, we clearly need to examine the effects of TV more diligently. What, for example, is television doing to the institutions and forms and rituals of our democracy? Politicians are still struggling to learn the grammar of TV communication and to master its body English, which is so different from that of the stump speech. TV has markedly influenced the winnowing process by which some politicians are sorted out as prospects for higher office from those who are not. TV has contributed to the abbreviation of the political dialogue and even changed the ground rules by which candidates map their campaign itineraries.

TV has encouraged the now widespread illusion that by using the medium we can create a Greek marketplace of direct democracy. When citizens can see and hear what they believe to be the actuality, why should they rely on intermediating institutions to make the decisions for them? When political leaders can directly reach their constituents without the help of a political party, why should they not opt for "the people's" mandate rather than "the party's"? Recent Presidents and Presidential candidates have been notably affected by this line of reasoning. It exposes an ancient vulnerability of our Republic, in which too much political lip service is paid to the notion that public opinion should rule everything.

How can democracy be strengthened within the environment of televisoin? Why, in an age of abundant communication, has there been a continuing decline in voter participation? Prof. Michael Robinson, a political scientist, has cited surveys indicating that heavy TV viewers are more apt than light viewers to be turned off by politics. He speculates that the more dependent someone becomes on TV as his principal source of information, the more likely he is to feel that he cannot understand or affect the political process. TV, unlike newspapers, reaches many who are not interested in public affairs, and these "inadvertent" audiences, in Robinson's view, are frequently confused and alienated by what they see. Such a proposition runs directly counter to the usual reformist instinct to prescribe more programming to overcome voter apathy. Professor Robinson's speculations need to be probed more deeply.

What will be the future? George Orwell had a vision of a time—now less than a decade away—when the communications environment would be employed for the enslavement, rather than the enlightenment, of mankind. Orwell called his system "Big Brother." For the present, anyway, we can conceive of a less ominous communications future with MOTHER, which is the acronym for "Multiple Output Telecommunication Home End Resources."

What will be the technical characteristics of MOTHER? First, she will offer infinitely more channels—via microwave, satellite, cable, laser beam—than the present broadcast spectrum provides. There will also be greater capacity crammed within each channel—more information "bits" per gigahertz—so that one can simultaneously watch a program and receive a newspaper printout on the same channel.

A life-sized MOTHER, the images on her screens giving the illusion of three-dimensionality, will be able to *narrowcast* to neighborhoods or other focused constituencies. MOTHER will be "interactive," permitting us to talk back to our television set by means of a digital device on the console. Recording and replay equipment, which is already being marketed, will liberate us from the tyranny of the broadcast schedule, and computer hookup and stop-frame control will bring the Library of Congress and other Gutenberg treasures into our living room.

Finally, via the satellite, MOTHER will offer worldwide programming in what the communications experts artfully call "real time" (even if real time means that Muhammad Ali must fight at 4:00 A.M. in Zaire in order to suit the prime-time needs of New Yorkers). Although MOTHER will be able to beam broadcasts from the People's Republic of China directly to a household in the United States and vice versa, she may face political barriers.

Until recently, prophets foresaw that the cable and other technological advances would transform television from a wholesale to a retail enterprise, directly offering the consumer a genuine diversity of choice. The "television of abundance" would bring not just greater variety of programs but also new concepts of programming—continuing education, health delivery, community services. Television would become a participatory instrument of communication rather than a one-way flow.

Today, these visions are not so bright. Some critics now glumly predict that the new technology will suffer the fate of the supersonic transport. Others expect that the technology will be developed, but that it will serve strictly commercial, rather than social, purposes. Computer may be talking to computer by cable and satellite, but householders will still watch "I Love Lucy" on their TV sets.

My own expectation is that the next decade or two will radically alter America's communications. The important issue is whether the change will be for better or for worse. If it is to be for better, we must give more critical attention to TV than we have given in the past. Too much critical time has been wasted worrying about the worst of television. More attention should be paid to the best, not simply laudatory attention but a systematic examination of style and technique and message. Criticism should also extend its reach beyond the intellectual elite into elementary and secondary schools, where children can be stimulated to think about the medium that so dominates their waking hours. We must endeavor to raise the viewers' capacity to distinguish truth from sophistry or at least their awareness, in Tony Schwartz's vocabulary, of the "resonance" being evoked from them.

We should have more widespread analysis and debate on the potential for new media and for new forms within the media. Could an electronic box office for pay programming repeal the iron laws governing "free" commercial television? How do we move beyond the limits of present broadcasting toward broader social purposes for television? In an era when lifelong learning has become essential for the prevention of human obsolescence, television surely has a role to play. And television might regularly deliver some types of health service now that the doctor is seldom making house calls. Health and education are gargantuan national enterprises which cost upward of $200 billion annually. Yet only paltry sums are being invested for research and demonstration to develop TV's capacity to enrich and extend these vital fields of social service.

Finally, we must move beyond our preoccupation with the production and transmission processes in media communication. An equally important question is, What gets through? The editors of *Scientific American* report that man's visual system has more than a million channels, capable of transmitting instantly 10 million bits of information to the brain. Yet the brain has the capacity for receiving only 27 bits of information per second. These are the raw statistics of communication within the human anatomy. They lead Sir John Eccles, the Nobel Prize-winning physiologist, to believe that the most important frontier of brain research involves the study of inhibition—our capacity to censor stimuli in order to prevent overload. Sir John makes the comparison: "It's like sculpture. What you cut away from the block of stone produces the statue."

Our journalists, both on TV and in print, pledge fealty to the proposition that society thrives by the communication of great gobs of unvarnished truth. Our law courts make us swear to tell "the truth, the whole truth, and nothing but the truth." Yet we only dimly understand how, in an all-enveloping informational environment, man chisels his little statues of perceived reality. As we approach a time when communication threatens to fission like the atom, we need to delve more deeply into these mysteries.

Looking far ahead, Robert Jastrow, director of the Goddard Institute of Space Studies, foresees a fifth communications revolution even more radical than the previous four revolutions of speech, writing, printing, and radio. "In the long term," Jastrow predicts, "the new satellites will provide a nervous system for mankind, knitting the members of our species into a global society." He compares this breakthrough with that change in the history of life several billion years ago when multicellular animals evolved out of more primitive organisms.

Before such an awesome prospect, thinking people may feel overwhelmed. Or else, we can screw up our courage, ask the fundamental questions, and make the critical choices necessary for the shaping of our destiny.

Bibliography

Cater's reflections on television's potential includes many of the concerns that professionals and scholars have discussed for years. Three highly useful books that cover in one respect or another many of the points raised by Cater are Charles S. Steinberg, editor, *Broadcasting: The Critical Challenges*, Hastings House, 1974; Robert H. Stanley, editor, *The Broadcast Industry: An Examination of Major Issues*, Hastings House, 1975; and Ted C. Smythe and George A. Mastroianni, editors, *Issues in Broadcasting: Radio, Television and Cable*, Mayfield, 1975. Two general, contemporary examinations of television are Martin Mayer, *About Television*, Harper & Row, 1972 and Les Brown, *Television: The Business Behind the Box*, Harcourt Brace Jovanovich, 1971. A well thought out criticism of television is Harry J. Skornia, *Television and Society: An Inquest and Agenda for Improvement*, McGraw-Hill, 1965. The Skornia book is a decade old at the time of this writing, yet it still offers a worthwhile, comprehensive program for changing television in order to make it a more positive force in improving society. Of a much different order of analysis is Horace Newcomb, *TV: The Most Popular Art*, Anchor Books, 1974, which concentrates on prime time network programming, offering many examples of entertainment on television.

Strong Shift in TV's Role:
From Escape Toward Reality

Broadcasting

In the public mind American television has ceased to be primarily an entertainment center and has become a major force in journalism as well.

This change occurred in a decade when, paradoxically, viewers were losing some of their enthusiasm for television but nevertheless were watching it more—and enjoying it more—than when the decade began.

These are among many findings made public [in 1973] from 1970 research that duplicated—and thus permitted direct comparisons with—major elements of the 1960 surveys that formed the basis of the late Dr. Gary Steiner's landmark volume, "The People Look at Television" (*Broadcasting*, Feb. 18, 1963, et seq.).

Other major findings and conclusions from the 1970 study:

■ Viewers in 1970 found TV less "satisfying," "relaxing," "exciting," "important" and generally less "wonderful" than had those in 1960 (possibly, the report suggests, because some of the newness had worn off), but the change was not from "praise" to "condemnation"—more nearly it was "from summa to magna cum laude." (Table 2.)

■ Better-educated viewers in 1970, as in 1960, held TV in lower esteem than did other viewers, but they watched as much—and essentially the same things—as everybody else.

■ In 1970 as in 1960 viewers showed a high degree of acceptance of commercials. At most, viewer attitude has become only slightly more negative. "The average viewer still overwhelmingly accepts the frequent and long interruptions by commercials as 'a fair price to apy,' " (Table 4.)

■ Most adults in both surveys felt children are better off with television than they would be without it, but the percentage has increased from 70% to 76%. College-educated parents now give TV the heaviest vote on this score (81%, up from 68% 10 years earlier), and grade-school-educated parents the lowest (68%, down from 75%).

■ Educational benefits remain the biggest advantage adults see in television for chilren, but by a much bigger percentage in 1970 than in 1960 (80% versus 65%), and entertainment has replaced the baby-sitting function as the second greatest advantage. (Table 6).

■ "Seeing things they shouldn't" is still the top-rated disadvantage of TV for children in adults' minds, but there have been some changes since 1960 in what those things are. "Violence" is still number one, but sex, seminudity, vulgarity, smoking, drinking and drugs have increased as causes of concern. (Table 7).

■ Parents are "a bit stricter" than they were about controlling their children's viewing (43% say they have "definite rules" as against 41% in 1960). But better-

This *Broadcasting* magazine article is a condensation of Robert T. Bower's book *Television and the Public.* Dr. Bower has been director of the Bureau of Social Science Research in Washington, D.C. since 1950. Copyright 1973, Broadcasting Publications, Inc., publishers of *Broadcasting,* newsweekly of broadcasting and allied arts, *Broadcasting Yearbook,* and *Broadcasting Cable Sourcebook* (annual). Reprinted by permission.

See page 433 for a Summary of Broadcasting Industry Statistics.

Cloris Leachman
as 'Phyllis'

TIME

TV's Funny Girls

educated parents, the biggest group in approving of TV for children, are much more inclined to have rules (46%) than grade-school-educated parents (25%), who are most fearful about TV for children. In general, however, "there are about as many parents who look to the children for help in deciding what they (parents) are going to watch as there are parents who try to decide about their children's viewing."

The 1970 study was financed by a grant by CBS, which also underwrote the 1960 study, to the Bureau of Social Science Research, a Washington-based independent nonprofit organization. Based on a national probability sample, some 1,900 adults (aged 18 and over) were interviewed by the Roper Organization, New York, in late winter and early spring of 1970—exactly 10 years after interviewing was done in the 1960 study. In addition there was a separate special study in Minneapolis-St. Paul, where, in cooperation with the American Research Bureau, the researchers were able to measure what viewers said against what they actually watched, corresponding to a similar special study in New York as part of the 1960 work (see page 197).

The report is by Robert T. Bower, director of the Bureau of Social Science Research, who emphasizes in his preface that CBS had no control over any aspect of the study or report. It is being published as a 205-page book titled "Television and the Public" by CBS's Holt, Rinehart & Winston subsidiary, which will offer it later at $7.95 a copy, but for the present CBS is distributing it widely to editors, educators and other opinion leaders.

The report ranges over many areas covered in the 1960 study, but the rising role of television as a journalistic force in the public's perception of the medium represents one of the most striking changes of the decade.

It is demonstrated in many ways. In 1960, for example, television had been voted best mass medium in only one of four specified news categories: giving the clearest understanding of candidates and issues in national elections. But by 1970, Dr. Bower reports, "we find television surging ahead of newspapers as the news medium that 'gives the most complete news coverage', overtaking radio in bringing 'the latest news most quickly', edging out newspapers in 'presenting the fairest, most unbiased news' and increasing its lead" in the one area where it was ahead in 1960, national political coverage. (Table 5.)

Dr. Bower notes that these findings parallel the results of studies conducted—also by a Roper Organization—for the Television Information Office since 1959. (He also notes at another point that when an Apollo 13 moon-flight emergency occurred during interviewing in Minneapolis-St. Paul, where 52% had rated TV the fastest news medium, 58% got their first word of the emergency from radio, as against 40% from TV. However, he says, TV regained its position as predominant source of information in the remaining four days of the flight.)

As another evidence of the public's growing perception of TV's news role Dr. Bower recalls that viewers and critic in 1960 were talking primarily about entertainment and cultural values, but in 1970 had shifted their focus to news functions, objectivity, concentration of control and effects of news coverage on audience behavior. And even in the area of TV and children, he notes, much of the violence parents object to their children's seeing is violence that is reported in the news.

Table 1.

"Now, I would like to get your opinions about how radio, newspapers, television, and magazines compare. Generally speaking, which of these would you say. . .?"

In percentages

Which of the media:	Television 1960	1970	Magazines 1960	1970	Newspapers 1960	1970	Radio 1960	1970	None/NA 1960	1970
Is the most entertaining?	68	72	9	5	13	9	9	14	1	0
Gives the most complete news coverage?	19	41	3	4	59	39	18	14	1	2
Presents things most intelligently?	27	38	27	18	33	28	8	9	5	8
Is the most educational?	32	46	31	20	31	26	3	4	3	5
Brings you the latest news most quickly?	36	54	0	0	5	6	57	39	2	1
Does the most for the public?	34	48	3	2	44	28	11	13	8	10
Seems to be getting worse all the time?	24	41	17	18	10	14	14	5	35	22
Presents the fairest, most unbiased news?	29	33	9	9	31	23	22	19	9	16
Is the least important to you?	15	13	49	53	7	9	15	20	7	5
Creates the most interest in new things going on?	56	61	18	16	18	14	4	5	4	5
Does the least for the public?	13	10	47	50	5	7	12	13	23	20
Seems to be getting better all the time?	49	38	11	8	11	11	10	15	19	28
Gives you the clearest understanding of the candidates and issues in national elections?	42	59	10	8	36	21	5	3	7	9

1960 base: 100 percent = 2427
1970 base: 100 percent = 1900

Table 2.

"Here are some opposites. Please read each pair quickly and put a check some place between them, wherever you think it belongs, to describe television. Just your offhand impression."
Television is generally: Proportion of 1960-1970 samples choosing each of six scale positions.

	(1) 1960	1970	(2) 1960	1970	(3) 1960	1970	(4) 1960	1970	(5) 1960	1970	(6) 1960	1970	
Relaxing	43	33	21	23	19	27	9	11	3	4	4	3	Upsetting
Interesting	42	31	21	23	19	24	9	13	4	5	4	3	Uninteresting
For me	41	27	16	20	19	24	10	15	6	8	8	6	Not for me
Important	39	30	17	19	21	24	10	15	7	7	6	6	Unimportant
Informative	39	35	25	27	20	23	8	9	5	3	3	3	Not informative
Lots of fun	32	22	20	20	25	31	12	16	5	6	6	5	Not much fun
Exciting	30	19	18	17	29	35	13	17	5	7	4	6	Dull
Wonderful	28	19	16	15	33	36	16	22	4	6	3	3	Terrible
Imaginative	26	19	21	20	28	33	14	15	6	7	5	6	No imagination
In good taste	24	18	21	19	31	33	19	19	6	7	4	4	In bad taste
Generally excellent	22	15	19	18	32	36	18	21	5	6	4	4	Generally bad
Lots of variety	35	28	16	20	19	21	12	14	10	9	8	8	All the same
On everyone's mind	33	21	22	18	24	29	15	20	4	7	3	5	Nobody cares much
Getting better	25	16	19	15	24	23	16	21	8	11	9	15	Getting worse
Keeps changing	23	22	17	18	22	24	18	20	10	9	9	8	Stays the same
Serious	8	7	8	8	31	35	29	33	12	10	12	7	Playful
Too "highbrow"	4	3	3	4	29	28	42	43	11	12	9	11	Too "simple minded"

1960 Base: 100 percent = 2427
1970 Base: 100 percent = 1900
(Excluding NA's which vary from item to item)

Table 3.

Proportion of each group taking most extreme position on two scales.

	Superians Percent who check extreme positive positions				Vilifiers Percent who check extreme negative positions				Base: 100% =	
	"Wonderful"		"For me"		"Terrible"		"Not for me"			
	1960	1970	1960	1970	1960	1970	1960	1970	1960	1970
Sex:										
Male	27	17	40	24	3	4	7	7	1177	900
Female . . .	28	20	41	31	3	2	9	6	1246	982
Education:										
Grade school . .	44	33	54	43	3	3	9	7	627	367
High school . .	26	19	42	28	3	3	7	6	1214	1030
College . . .	12	7	20	15	3	2	11	8	516	490
Age:										
18-19	32	17	44	25	0	2	6	7	84	182
20-29	19	17	33	29	3	1	8	6	473	331
30-39	23	18	39	24	2	3	7	6	544	356
40-49	27	13	38	23	2	3	7	9	463	378
50-59	34	21	44	27	4	2	10	5	400	311
60+	36	24	50	33	4	5	10	6	440	419

He cites Vice-President Spiro Agnew's celebrated Nov. 13, 1969, attack on network news specifically. That was just three months before interviewing was done for the 1970 study—and still TV was voted the fairest and most unbiased medium.

The study looked for bias in a number of directions. In one, 53% of the conservatives, an equal percentage of liberals and a few more middle-of-the-roaders (56%) said they thought newscasters in general "give it straight," while 30% of the conservatives, 26% of the liberals and 25% of the middle-roaders thought newscasters tend to color the news. Republicans were more suspicious (32%) than Democrats (22%). In the total sample, viewers divided about equally as to whether the newscasters they individually watch most are liberal (14%) or conservative (13%); more consider them middle-roaders (36%) and even more can't tell (38%). But overwhelmingly they feel their favorite newscasters give the news straight (78%) rather than let their personal opinions color it (6%).

Dr. Bower offers this summary: "It appears that a sizable proportion (about one-fourth) of the public feels that television news is generally biased in its presentation. A much smaller group of hardcore critics think even their own favorite newscaster colors the news. But the vast majority of people either accept the objectivity of television newscasting in general or find a specific newscaster to watch who is felt to be objective in his reporting . . . If the public at large were the judge, the medium would probably be exonerated [of bias charges] or at worst be given a suspended sentence."

The study also undertook to learn which news medium people think puts most emphasis on "good things" and which puts most on "bad things"—and found that TV was voted number one on both counts. Dr. Bower suggest a possible explanation: "that for a large group of viewers television is simply so dominant a medium in

Table 4.

"Here are some statements about commercials. I'd like you to read each statement and mark whether you generally agree or disagree with each statement."

Percent who agree that:	1960 total	1970 total	1970 occupation of head of household White collar	Blue collar
Commercials are a fair price to pay for the entertainment you get .	75	70	69	71
Most commercials are too long	63	65	67	65
I find some commercials very helpful in keeping me informed	58	54	50	57
Some commercials are so good that they are more entertaining than the program	43	54	56	52
I would prefer TV without commercials	43	48	49	47
Commercials are generally in poor taste and very annoying	40	43	42	43
I frequently find myself welcoming a commercial break	36	35	31	38
I'd rather pay a small amount yearly to have TV without commercials	24	30	30	29
There are just too many commercials	(Not included in 1960)	70	71	70
Having special commercial breaks during a program is better than having the same number of commercials at the beginning and end . . .	(Not included in 1960)	39	35	42
Base: 100 percent = ...	(2427)	(1900)	(674)	(873)

Table 5.

"Now, I would like to get your opinions about how radio, newspapers, television and magazines compare. Generally speaking, which of these would you say. . ."

		Percent 1960	1970
"Gives the most complete news coverage?"	Television	19	41
	Magazines	3	4
	Newspapers	59	39
	Radio	18	14
	None or don't know . .	1	2
"Brings you the latest news most quickly?"	Television	36	54
	Magazines	0	0
	Newspapers	5	6
	Radio	57	39
	None or don't know . .	2	1
"Gives the fairest, most unbiased news?"	Television	29	33
	Magazines	9	9
	Newspapers	31	23
	Radio	22	19
	None or don't know . .	9	16
"Gives the clearest understanding of candidates and issues in national elections?"	Television	42	59
	Magazines	16	8
	Newspapers	36	21
	Radio	5	3
	None or don't know . .	1	9

1960 Base: 100 percent = 2427 (minus NA's which vary from item to item)
1970 Base: 100 percent = 1900 (minus NA's which vary from item to item)

bringing all the news, any sort of news, they see it as emphasizing all things—both the good and the bad—without any sense of contradiction. Yes, it emphasizes the good things; yes, it emphasizes the bad things; it emphasizes everything.''

The study found 57% rated TV's performance in presenting 1968 presidential election campaign issues and candidates as good (44%) or excellent (13%); 32% wanted more political programs in the 1972 campaign while 15% wanted fewer, and 43% said TV played a "fairly important" (30%) or "very important" (13%) part

Table 6.

"What do you think are some of the main advantages of television for children?"

*The advantages of TV for children by respondent's general attitude (pro or con) toward television for children ***

| Percent who mention: | 1960 | | | | | | 1970 | | | |
| | Parents | | Others | | 1960 Total | 1970 Total | Parents | | Others | |
	Pros	Cons	Pros	Cons			Pros	Cons	Pros	Cons
Education	74	49	72	45	65	80	85	69	85	62
Baby-sitting	34	21	31	13	28	16	17	13	18	9
Entertainment	21	15	23	8	19	22	27	20	21	17
Programs good generally	4	17	6	16	8	2	2	2	2	2
Stimulates socializing	2	—	1	—	1	2	3	—	2	2
Adult supervision necessary	4	2	10	4	6	2	2	1	2	1
Other, general	1	4	1	4	2	4	3	6	2	6
Base: 100% =	(858)	(292)	(781)	(419)	(2350)	(1592)	(589)	(159)	(607)	(237)

*Multiple response item: percentages do not necessarily add up to 100 percent.

Table 7.

"What do you think are some of the main disadvantages of television for children?"

*Disadvantages of television for children by parental status and general attitude (pro and con) toward television for children. ***

| Percent who mention: | 1960 | | | | | | 1970 | | | |
| | Parents | | Others | | 1960 Total | 1970 Total | Parents | | Others | |
	Pros	Cons	Pros	Cons			Pros	Cons	Pros	Cons
See things they shouldn't:	46	55	48	64	51	52	48	55	50	64
Violence, horror	26	32	28	40	30	30	27	32	30	35
Crime, gangsters	7	8	11	13	10	8	6	10	9	12
Sex, suggestiveness, vulgarity	4	7	4	6	5	11	10	12	11	13
Smoking, drinking, dope	2	2	2	3	2	5	4	5	6	7
Adult themes	2	3	1	3	2	9	6	11	10	12
Harmful or sinful products advertised	1	1	1	—	1	1	1	—	1	1
Wrong values or moral codes	3	5	2	5	3	8	8	11	8	9
Other, general	7	11	8	9	8	2	3	5	2	5
Keeps them from doing things they should	34	51	31	41	36	30	29	40	26	34
Programs bad, general	10	9	8	13	10	2	2	6	2	3
Other, program content	3	9	2	6	4	6	7	10	5	6
Physical harm	3	7	4	8	5	5	3	4	5	7
Advertising too effective	2	3	1	—	1	2	3	3	2	3
Other	2	3	1	3	2	5	6	5	5	3
Base: 100 percent =	(858)	(292)	(781)	(419)	(2350)	(1583)	(586)	(157)	(604)	(236)

*Multiple response item: percentages do not necessarily add up to 100 percent.

in helping them decide whom they wanted to win in 1968. He doesn't think that last finding should be construed to mean TV caused large numbers to bolt their parties but, rather, that it reflects "a sense of increased familiarity with the candidates and, most likely, a reinforcement of pre-existing tendencies."

At another point Dr. Bower says: "The indications are that television does not tend to favor one faction over another in such a way as to suggest a partisan political influence during a campaign, or even to discriminate among the social groups of which the population is composed. To an amazing degree, the perceived effects of television's political coverage are spread evenly among the public."

In summary, he says: "The high assessment of television in its journalistic role that has been shown in this chapter certainly represents a general public endorsement, all the more resounding since it occurs at a time when TV news is under attack.

"Clearly, this part of television's content has largely been exempted from the trend toward a lower public esteem for the medium as a whole. But the vote is by no means unanimous. TV news presentation is not free of the suspicion of bias that the American public accords to all the mass media; and while the improvements in the technology of rapid worldwide coverage of daily events may be roundly applauded, there are those who would prefer less emphasis on the unpleasant and disturbing national conflicts."

These presumably would be older viewers, for in another section the study found age to be the great differentiator of views about social strife such as riots, street protests, race problems and campus unrest. "The young applaud what the old condemn in what would seem to be expressions about the world at large, attributed to television only as the bearer of bad tidings," Dr. Bower observes.

Age also figured in one of the major changes found in viewing patterns in 1970. Ten years earlier, the heaviest viewing had been found among teenagers; in 1970, teenagers watched less than any of the other age groups. They also were the only age group that failed to watch more in 1970 than their counterparts did in 1960. In itself the decline was not considered large—from 26.25 median hours per week in 1960 to 25.33 in 1970—but in a broader context, Dr. Bower suggests, it could be huge.

The 1970 dip might be a transitory one, he says, with the teenagers increasing their viewing as they grow older, as viewers who were 28 or 29 in 1970 watched more than those 18 or 19 in 1960. "But," Dr. Bower cautions, "if it happens to be a way of life that will endure as the generation ages," the uptrend of TV viewing is threatened.

Among other changes found in 1970:

■ Where 1960 viewers preferred regular series to specials (49% to 32%), 1970's preferred specials (44%) to series (36%).

■ Despite a somewhat declining esteem for TV as a whole, viewers found more specific programs to applaud. On average, the proportion of all programs rated "extremely enjoyable" rose from 44% in 1960 to 50% in 1970. In addition, or perhaps as a factor in that increase, Dr. Bower reports that 70% of the viewers said they thought there were more "different kinds of programs" in 1970, giving them a broader range to choose from.

As for changes in television itself, reaction was overwhelmingly favorable (55% had only favorable things to say, as opposed to 16% who were solely unfavorable, with the rest neutral, balanced or in the no-answer category).

Generally they felt neutral about 10-year changes in sports programs and movies, were critical on such morality questions as sex, nudity and vulgarity (10%) and on violence (4%), which they often linked with news, and were favorable toward changes perceived in general entertainment (19%), technical advances such as color and increased numbers of stations (23%) and, most of all, changes in news and information (33%).

What They Said and What They Saw

The Bureau of Social Science Research's special study in Minneapolis-St. Paul, made in conjunction with its national study, confirmed again what many already knew: Viewers don't always watch what they say they want to see on television.

With the cooperation of the American Research Bureau, the researchers interviewed some Minnesotans who had previously kept ARB diaries, and then compared what they said with what they had watched. One conclusion: "The people who say they usually watch television to learn something do watch news and information programing more than others, but only a little bit more. Those who feel there is not enough 'food for thought' on television watch as many entertainment shows as the rest of the viewers. Those who want television stations to concentrate on information programs spend only slightly more time watching such programs than those who want the 'best entertainment', despite the fact that a great deal of informative fare is available in the Minneapolis-St. Paul area for those who could just switch the dial to another channel."

The researchers also rated respondents on a "culture scale" and examined their viewing in that context; the "high-culture" people, it turned out, "watched television somewhat less than those who scored lower; when they did watch, their viewing was distributed among program types in almost precisely the same way as the low-culture scorers, hardly a hair's breadth between them except in the news [higher viewing] and sports [lower] categories."

"Live coverage of national events, educational television, more channels, television by satellite and longer news programs are all viewed as changes for the better by 70% or more of the sample," Dr. Bower writes. "At the other end, talk shows, fewer westerns and live coverage of civil disruptions *are* approved by only about a third."

Noting that coverage of space shots and other national events ranked at the top of changes rated for the better, while coverage of riots and protests ranked at the bottom, Dr. Bower assumes that in these cases "people are responding to the message at least as much as to the medium, probably it is the space effort people like and the riots they dislike."

Dr. Bower also cautions that it should not be assumed that "the American television audience has changed in 10 years from a population of entertainment fans to a population of news hawks." Entertainment, he notes, still dominates TV fare and commands most of the viewer's time.

"But," he continues, "there is apparently a general shift in people's perception of what television is and what it means to them, and the new focus on the news and information content of television has undoubtedly altered people's views about various other aspects of the medium's role—from how it affects the 12-year-old to whether it is a benign or malevolent force in society.'' More than that, he concludes, ''the journalistic emphasis may have introduced important new criteria by which TV will be judged in the future.''

Bibliography

Dr. Bower's report, which is summarized here by *Broadcasting* magazine, should be supplemented first of all by turning to the full report, published as *Television and the Public*, Holt, Rinehart & Winston, 1973. For a comparative look at television of a decade earlier, see Gary A. Steiner, *The People Look at Television*, Alfred A. Knopf, 1963. Background readings on the development of the broadcast industry can be found in Sydney W. Head, *Broadcasting in America: A Survey of Television and Radio*, 3rd ed., Houghton-Mifflin, 1976; Giraud Chester, *et al.*, *Television and Radio*, 4th ed., Appleton-Century-Crofts, 1971; or Lawrence W. Lichty and Malachi C. Topping, *A Source Book on the History of Radio and Television*, Hastings House, 1975. The standard history of broadcasting in America is Erik Barnouw, *A History of Broadcasting in the United States*, Oxford University Press, 3 volumes, issued one each in 1966, 1968 and 1970.

The New Concerns About The Press
Fortune

Newspapers

These are the glory days of the American press. Never before has it exercised so much power so independently or found itself vested with such presitge and glamour. Journalism schools are flooded with applications. Carl Bernstein and Bob Woodward, the Washington *Post* reporters who dug into Watergate and helped bring down a government, are now being portrayed in a movie (Robert Redford plays Woodward and Dustin Hoffman plays Bernstein), and are well on the way to making $1 million apiece for telling the story of their story.

It's a far cry from the way things used to be. ''The lowest depth to which people can sink before God,'' wrote Sören Kierkegaard, the Danish philosopher, in a classic expression of the esteem in which newsmen were once held, ''is defined by the word 'journalist'. . .If I were a father and had a daughter who was seduced I should not despair over her; I would hope for her salvation. But if I had a son who became a journalist and continued to be one for five years, I would give him up.''

Despite their new prestige, there is an ominous sense among newsmen of a growing distance, if not outright antagonism, between the press and the larger society, and a corresponding sense of trouble shaping up. This unease is most often expressed as a fear that the First Amendment freedoms have been cut back—by

Reprinted from the April 1975 issue of *Fortune* magazine by special permission; copyright 1975 Time, Inc.

wiretaps and other Nixon Administration moves against the press, by "gag" orders and other court-imposed restrictions on the reporting of trials, and by the frequent subpoenas that force journalists to testify in legal proceedings.

At the end of a swing

In fact, this fear has little substance. Freedom of the press has not withered in recent years and in some respects has expanded. "The press is very likely freer than it ever has been," explains Robert L. Bartley, editorial-page editor of the *Wall Street Journal*. "The problem is that we're at the end of one pendulum swing, and we worry about how far it will go when it swings back the other way."

Bartley is right in worrying. The problem isn't that Americans are eager to repeal the First Amendment. It is rather that many Americans are increasingly hostile to the press itself—and that this hostility could lead to any number of disagreeable consequences, not least a restriction of journalistic freedom.

This hostility comes as a reaction against a near-revolutionary change that has been transforming American journalism during the past fifteen years or so. To some extent, what is involved in the change is a matter of structure and scale. Previously, American journalism and its audience had been extremely decentralized; among publications that focused on news, only *Time, Newsweek, U.S. News and World Report*, and the *Wall Street Journal* had significant national audiences. But during the 1960's some other sectors of the American press acquired a distinctly "national look."

Flying the news to Washington

In part, the new look simply reflected new conditions in the newspaper markets of New York and Washington, D.C. Since one is the communications capital of the U.S., and the other is the political capital, newspapers in both cities have always had some national influence and out-of-town readers. In the 1960's, it happened, the influence of the *New York Times* and the *Post* was considerably expanded by the collapse of a good deal of their own local competition. In addition, the *Times'* out-of-town circulation rose steeply; today, fully 25 percent of its daily circulation is outside the New York area—more than 200,000 copies a day in 1974. On the West Coast, the *Los Angeles Times* has also managed to expand its out-of-town influence, and it too has begun to look more "national." In a determined effort to further this view of itself, the paper has been flying copies to opinion leaders in Washington, D.C., every day.

Meanwhile, television news, too, was acquiring a more national perspective. In 1963, NBC and CBS expanded their nightly news programs from fifteen minutes to half an hour; they were followed by ABC in 1967. They began, quite consciously, both to run more national news and to seek out the national implications of the local stories they covered. And they got an increasingly national audience: the three networks' early evening news shows now have a combined audience of 50 million.

NATIONAL ENQUIRER

30¢

December 28, 1976   02-261   LARGEST CIRCULATION OF ANY PAPER IN AMERICA

How to Mend a Broken Friendship

PAGE 44

SIMPLE NEW BLOOD TEST DETECTS CANCER EARLY AND PINPOINTS LOCATION

PAGE 20

Claim Indians
Drew Pictures
Of UFOs 1,000
Years Ago

page 3

★ ★ ★

How to Argue
With Your Spouse
Without Wrecking
Your Marriage

page 35

★ ★ ★

The Incredible $$$
TV Networks
Pay for This
Year's Shows

page 30

★ ★ ★

What Jimmy
Carter's Clothes
Reveal About Him

page 14

★ ★ ★

How to Be
A Leader

page 47

'Kotter' Star John Travolta, 22, Madly in Love With 37-Year-Old

"This is the first time I have ever been in love," confesses 22-year-old John "Barbarino" Travolta — shown with actress Diana Hyland, 37, in Los Angeles. He says: "Her age doesn't matter to me and mine doesn't matter to her." Says Diana: "We clicked at our first meeting. We just love being with each other." (P. 29.)

The heavy consumption of publications like the *National Enquirer* and similar tabloids and magazines causes some to worry about what the public reads. However, since the days of the dime novel in the late 19th Century much of the public has opted for sensational reading. The same kind of discussion can be held concerning the "lowest common denominator" approach of many television shows.

Thus, from having had a local and a regional press, Americans suddenly found themselves with a national press as well. It is true that there are still plenty of healthy local newspapers; indeed, from a business point of view there are still many that are healthier than the *New York Times* (which was barely profitable in 1974). Still, the prestige and influence of many of the great regional papers, e.g., the *St. Louis Post-Dispatch,* the *Baltimore Sun,* and the *Louisville Courier-Journal,* have undergone something of a decline.

As this national press emerged, several of its members began to transform themselves in other ways. Previously, the media involved had been quite different from one another. The newspapers mostly reported facts about the day's events; the networks provided a bland headline service; the newsmagazines, in addition to summarizing the week's developments, offered interpretation and covered larger social and cultural trends. In principle, all this might have remained unchanged after the newspapers and networks acquired national audiences. In practice, the new national press was powerfully influenced by some new currents in American life.

Summary of Newspaper, Press Association Industries—1976

Every day except Sunday more than 60 million copies of newspapers are circulated throughout the United States. On Sundays the total drops to a mere 50 million. Figures released in 1976 showed there are 339 morning papers, 1,436 evening papers and 639 (many of them the same) on Sundays.

There is every indication that the newspaper business is a healthy one. For example, in 1975 more than $8 billion worth of advertising went into newspapers, while television attracted slightly more than $5 billion—this out of a total of about $28 billion spent on all mediums of communication.

The paper with the largest daily circulation is the *New York Daily News,* with a total of about 2 million. Following are the *Los Angeles Times* with 1 million and the *New York Times* with about 850,000. Others include the *Chicago Tribune* with 660,000, the *New York Post* with about 600,000 and the *Washington Post* with 520,000. The four regionally-printed editions of the *Wall Street Journal* total 1,370,000.

On Sundays, the *New York Daily News* prints almost 2,800,000 copies, the *New York Times* 1,400,000, the *Los Angeles Times* 1,400,000, and the *Chicago Tribune* 1,120,000.

However, only 36 newspapers command more than 250,000 circulation and many successful ones have circulations of 50,000 or less. In all, 1,500 have less than 50,000 circulation.

In addition to daily papers there were nearly 7,500 weekly papers in the nation with a total circulation of more than 35 million (many persons do read both a daily and a weekly).

Delivering the bulk of the news (an estimated 80%) to newspapers and broadcast stations are the men and women who work for the world's two largest press associations, United Press International and Associated Press.

The latest advances in communications technology are used—laser beams send photographs, video display terminals allow faster editing and distribution, computerized storage and retrieval systems help guarantee comprehensive coverage and satellites carry the stories around the world.

Not many of the daily newspapers can afford to have reporters in Washington, major U.S. cities and overseas. So they rely on the press associations (the "wire services") to bring them the news. The biggest U.S. dailies, however, use both their own stories and wire news.

While many print-oriented journalism students desire to be reporters or editors with a major newspaper or work in a press association bureau located in a large city (or maybe work for *Time* or *Newsweek*), it should be noted that most "big league" reporters and editors began their careers on one of the smaller or middlesized newspapers, or perhaps worked in a small press association bureau office. Importantly, many thousands of persons have stayed in those smaller settings, enjoying comfortable and satisfying careers.

The impact of intellectuals

A new generation of Americans—better educated, more interested in ideas, more concerned with political and social questions—gave many institutions a more "intellectual" character in the 1960's. The influence of this new generation on the press was dramatic. It had a special impact on the new national newspapers, which began developing new journalistic forms; furthermore, the national press as a whole seemed to have a new consciousness of American society and was conveying a new and more "serious" aganda to the American people.

To quite a few critics of the press, the change could be summarized as a great new wave of eastern Establishment liberalism. That definition of the case is somewhat simplistic. The national press is not consistently liberal; the *Wall Street Journal* is generally viewed as conservative, as is *U.S. News and World Report*; the New York *Times* is more liberal than the Los Angeles *Times* (or than *Time*). In the last presidential campaign the national press was at least as hard on McGovern as on Nixon. Still, the imputation of liberalism is not entirely unfair, and it is not entirely possible to separate the new ambitions of the national press from the politics it often reflected. But much of what the national press was up to was not political at all. It involved an effort to transcend the shortcomings of the traditional newspaper.

The trouble with "events"

The shortcomings of the traditional American newspaper were no secret fifteen years ago. They had been identified for some time, primarily by college-educated newsmen at the better papers, but also by serious critics who were not always working newspapermen themselves. They included Daniel Boorstin, Dwight MacDonald, Douglass Cater, and others, and their case was argued in a number of books (e.g., *BoOrstin's The Image*).

These critics deplored the low educational and intellectual levels of the average newspaper, but they were especially concerned with its rather limited conception of news. To some extent, they were proposing to move toward the more expansive conception that had been adopted by *Time* and, later, *Newsweek*.

The problem about conventional newspaper news, as they viewed the case, was that it was limited to daily events, which inevitably would be written about in haste, and thus unthoughtfully. Focusing exclusively on "events" also meant that long-term trends, such as the massive migration of southern blacks to the North during the 1950's, were systematically ignored. For the same reason, stable conditions—the situation of the poor, discrimination against minorities—were almost never written about because nothing "happened."

Moreover, said critics of the conventional newspaper, news stories dealt only with events that were recorded and announced by important organizations, be it the State Department or the New York Yankees. People in groups not represented by established institutions therefore didn't get fair "representation" in the traditional newspaper. By building the news story around an institution's announcement, the critics went on, traditional journalism tended to adopt the institution's language and bias. And this, in turn, made it possible for institutions to manipulate—and distort—the citizen's impression of the way things are.

Thoughtful newsmen were also bothered by the conventions of objectivity, which prevented a reporter from making it clear that any deceit had occurred, since interpretive or critical comment was ruled out. Senator Joseph McCarthy had exploited this to the hilt; many newsmen had seen through his demagogy, yet the conventions of their profession left them with little choice but to be the Senator's stenographers and mouthpieces.

Ultimately, the critics held, what was wrong with the traditional newspaper was that it had a narrow and distorted sense of reality. It imagined that uninspired persons, routinely turning out stories cast in stereotyped molds, were capable of giving an adequate picture of the world. It conceived life as a matter of day-to-day actions largely devoid of larger trends or ideas. It defined the world as an exclusive assemblage of institutions, and it depicted events from their point of view. The challenge confronting any serious journalism, the critics asserted, was to escape from all these constraints. Clearly, conventional newspapers had not even begun to do that.

The newsman became an expert

The newspapermen who accepted these criticisms had a number of proposals for change. In part, they wanted to do what newspapers had always done, but to do it better: to increase the resources of manpower, money, and space available for covering events; to raise the level of the newsman's education, talent, and seriousness; to cover more events; and to increase the flexibility of the news-story format. To this extent the critics' program was a simple matter of "more" and "better."

But some dissatisfied newsmen were seized by a much larger ambition, at once intellectual and political. They wanted to transcend the limits of daily journalism as such. They wanted to give a true picture of the world rather than merely to describe events as announced by responsible institutions, and they wanted to redress the unfairness, as it seemed to them, that was created by the newspaper's dependence on established organizations and indifference to the views of others. At this level their program involved a radical and qualitative change: the newspaper was to become more like the magazine and the book, and the newsman was to be transformed into a commentator and expert.

To some extent, then, the newspaper was to become more like the newsmagazines. As far back as the 1920's, *Time* had devised new forms in which to cast the news story, had redefined the news as something more than "events," had broadened the traditional range of coverage (to include even the press itself), and had served up the news with a good deal of interpretation and analysis.

It is not possible to put a precise date on the point at which the criticisms of conventional journalism were accepted by—and acted on by—the editorial executives of the new national newspapers. But during the 1960's, it seems clear, the ideas of the critics ceased to be viewed as heresy. Indeed, they rapidly became something akin to a new orthodoxy.

The new journalism led to the upgrading of staffs, and more coverage of public affairs and social problems. Journalism increasingly broke out of the old molds. There were more magazine-type articles in the national newspapers, which began to focus less on events and institutiions, more on ideas, trends, and miscellaneous non-institutional causes; e.g., the civil-rights and antiwar movements. There were also some changes in the rest of the national press. Articles in the newsmagazines became longer and more reflective. And television news too began to incorporate more documentary and interpretive material.

Although TV journalism still serves to some extent as a "headline service," it has in some ways become more like the newsmagazine and the new journalism in general. The networks rely heavily on the New York *Times* and Washington *Post* for ideas about what to cover. And there is often a striking parallel between filmed news stories—like, for instance, NBC's recent accounts of the world hunger problem—and the magazine-type interpretive and "feature" story. Thus, just as ideas, interpretation,and trends increasingly found their way into the daily newspaper, so did they make their way into the nightly news programs.

The result of all these developments was dramatic. The press—or, at least, a large chunk of it—was no longer the routine recorder of events and passive instrument of institutions. It had become much more influenced by ideas and more capable of communicating ideas.

Even more important, the national press conveyed a new concsiousness of the American condition. Reacting against the dominance of established institutions in traditional reporting, it became increasingly preoccupied with the non-Establishment and anti-Establishment worlds—with the poor, the aged, the blacks. Reacting against those previous "manipulations" by established institutions, it became preoccupied with the issue of credibility and was quick to expose any lack of it.

Carter envisions new U.S. spirit

weather

PARTLY CLOUDY .... **Page 15.**

index

digest

CITIZEN AGAIN — Iva Toguri D'Aquino, convicted as a "Tokyo Rose" who broadcast propaganda to U.S. troops during World War II, is again an American citizen, a privilege taken from her 27 years ago. President Ford pardoned the 60-year-old Chicago shopkeeper Wednesday. Mrs. D'Aquino thanked Ford for "his compassion and sense of fair play."

* * *

First it was frostbite in Brazil and now a fungus hits coffee crops in Nicaragua. .... **Page 15.**

Anti-government rioting in Egypt leaves more than 40 persons dead

WASHINGTON (UPI) — Jimmy Carter today intoned the solemn oath of the president and asked the American people to go forth with him into the nation's third century with "a new beginning ... a new dedication ... a new spirit."

In a simple ceremony almost as old as the Republic, the Georgia peanut farmer — echoing the populist theme that swept him to victory over an incumbent — acknowledged the awesome burdens he faces as the nation's 39th president.

"You have given me a great responsibility, to stay close to you, to be worthy of you, and to exemplify what you are," he said.

"Let us learn together and laugh together and work together and pray together — confident that in the end we will triumph together."

Carter, his right hand on a Bible given him a few months ago by his mother, "Miss Lillian," intoned the same 35-word oath of every president since Washington in 1789 — swearing to "preserve, protect and defend the Constitution of the United States."

The oath was administered by Chief Justice Warren Burger moments after Vice President Walter Mondale was sworn in by Speaker Thomas O'Neill. Four years ago, Carter as governor of Georgia and Mondale as senator from Minnesota stood on the same platform but out of the limelight as Richard Nixon and Spiro Agnew accepted second terms.

Carter's address broke no new ground. It was a philosophical speech, gentle in tone but firm in its commitment to human dignity and the American dream. He urged moderation in striving for that dream — lest the natural resources of a great nation be drained.

"More is not necessarily better," he declared.

He rattled no sabres, but said U.S. military strength must be "so sufficient that it need never be proven in combat."

He pledged that America will be "ever vigilant and never vulnerable, and we will fight our wars against poverty, ignorance and injustice — for those are the enemies against which our forces can be honorably marshalled."

Carter, as is his habit, awakened early. He watched the "sunrise services" at the Lincoln Memorial on television. The Rev. Martin Luther King Sr. and Carter's evangelist sister, Ruth, were among those leading the prayers for the new President.

Instead of the public ceremony, the Carter family attended a private church service. On returning from church, Carter and his wife arranged an hour of private time before walking from Blair House across Pennsylvania Avenue to join President and Mrs. Ford.

The 52-year-old Carter then rode with Ford in a black limousine up "The Avenue of Presidents" to the U.S. Capitol for the inauguration ceremony.

Yet to come before the rigorous day culminated at last in the White House were the 2½ hour parade back down Pennsylvania Avenue to the White House, and the seven gala parties expected to draw 60,000 celebrants.

A long, hard climb

Exactly two years ago today, Jimmy Carter began his campaign for the presidency.

He started with a speech in Baton Rouge, La., spoke in Texas and New Mexico and ended the trip in Sacramento, Calif.

Carter didn't get discouraged during that first year of campaigning, recalled press secretary Jody Powell Wednesday night, "because there wasn't much to get discouraged about."

One year ago Wednesday, Carter won the Iowa caucus, a victory that won him national attention and set him as the Democratic frontrunner for president.

Once he was "Jimmy Who?"
Now he is "Mr. President."

He pledged today that, under his leadership, the United States will move this year "a step toward our ultimate goal — the elimination of all nuclear weapons from this earth."

"We urge all other people to join us, for success can mean life instead of death."

Carter pledged the "perserverance and wisdom" of his nation "to limit the world's armaments to those necessary to each nation's own domestic safety."

He enumerated what he said were not his goals alone, but the "common hopes" of the nation he will lead into a third century.

And he said that if the goals were met, it would not be his triumph "but the affirmation of our nation's continuing moral strength and our belief in an undiminished, ever-expanding American dream."

Among the things for which he hoped his presidency would be remembered included:

— A "renewed search for humility, mercy and justice."

— "That we had torn down the barriers that separated those of different race and region and religion — and where there had been mistrust, built unity, with a respect for diversity."

— "Productive work" for everyone able to perform it.

— A strengthening of the American family — "the basis of our society."

— "Respect for the law, and equal treatment under the law, for the weak and the powerful, the rich and the poor."

— "And that we had enabled our people to be proud of their own government once again."

Carter noted that two centuries ago, America's birth was "a milestone in the long quest for freedom."

"But the bold and brilliant dream which excited the founders of our nation still awaits its consummation. I have no new dream to set forth today, but rather urge a fresh faith in the old dream.

"I believe America can be better."

He urged the nation to let its "recent mistakes bring a resurgent commitment to the basic principles of our nation, for we know that if we despise our own goverment we have no future."

He said Americans "have already found a high degree of personal liberty, and we are now struggling to enhance equality of opportunity," but he warned:

"Our commitment to human rights must be absolute ... The powerful must not persecute the weak, and human dignity must be enhanced."

Carter pledged that under his administration, the nation "will not behave in foreign plces so as to violate our rules and standards here at home, for we know that the trust which our nation earns is essential to its strength."

The new President noted that not only does America have a new spirit, but "the world itself is now dominated by a new spirit."

"The passion for freedom is on the rise," he said. "Tapping this new spirit, there can be no nobler nor more ambitious task for America to undertake on this day of a new beginning than to help shape a just and peaceful world that is truly humane."

Telegraph Herald

141st Year, No. 17 | 2 SECTIONS | 20 PAGES | DUBUQUE, IOWA, and EAST DUBUQUE, ILLINOIS | THURSDAY, JANUARY 20, 1977 | 20 cents

Los Angeles Times

LARGEST CIRCULATION IN THE WEST, 1,020,479 DAILY, 1,289,183 SUNDAY

VOL. XCVI | FIVE PARTS—PART ONE | 104 PAGES | FRIDAY MORNING, JANUARY 21, 1977 | CC † | Copyright © 1977 Los Angeles Times | DAILY 15c

Carter Calls for 'New Spirit of Unity and Trust'

TAKING THE OATH—Jimmy Carter, his wife Rosalynn at his side, is sworn in as the nation's 39th President by Chief Justice Warren E. Burger. Rear, Nevada Sen. Howard Cannon.
Times photo by Steve Fontanini

BREAKING TRADITION—The new President and the First Lady walking, hand-in-hand, the route from Capitol to White House.
AP Wirephoto

Sets a High Moral Tone in Inaugural

BY JACK NELSON
Times Washington Bureau Chief

WASHINGTON—Jimmy Carter of Georgia took the oath as the nation's 39th President Thursday and called in his inaugural address for "a new national spirit of unity and trust."

Carter, the first President of the nation's third century and the first President from the Deep South since 1848, returned time and again in the brief speech to the theme of a "new spirit."

"This inauguration ceremony," said the former Georgia governor, wearing a navy blue three-piece suit instead of the traditional morning coat, "marks a new beginning, a new dedication within our government, and a new spirit among us all. A President may sense and proclaim that new spirit, but only a people can provide it."

Then, to underscore his theme, Carter broke with tradition and shunned the presidential limousine, choosing instead to walk at the head of the inaugural parade for 1½ miles along Pennsylvania Ave. from the Capitol to the White House.

The new President's wife, Rosalynn, dressed in boots and a bright green coat, walked beside him as thousands of spectators cheered and applauded. Their 9-year-old daughter, Amy, walked part of the way and held up the long parade when she had to stop to tie a shoelace and to have her coat buttoned.

Carter set a high moral tone in his speech, calling not only for equality of justice at home but also for high standards in dealing with foreign countries.

He dealt mostly with the domestic scene, and then only philosophically and in general terms. But he was specific and emphatic on one foreign problem that is known to concern him deeply—the proliferation of nuclear weapons.

"The world is still engaged in a massive armaments race designed to ensure continuing equivalent strength among potential adversaries," he said. "We pledge perseverance and wisdom in our efforts to limit the world's armaments to those necessary for each nation's own domestic safety.

Carter text, other inauguration stories, pictures on Pages 16 to 22.

"We will move this year a step toward our ultimate goal—the elimination of all nuclear weapons from this earth."

The "step" Carter mentioned refers to strategic arms limitation talks with the Soviet Union. It apparently was included in the inaugural address as a reply to Soviet party leader Leonid I. Brezhnev.

Tuesday Brezhnev called on Carter to conclude quickly a simple agree-

ADS SELL URBAN LIFE

Cities Take Offensive to Lure Back Suburbanites

BY WILLIAM ENDICOTT
Times Staff Writer

SEATTLE—There was a 30-second commercial on a local television station the other night showing a traffic snarl on the Evergreen Point bridge across Lake Washington to Bellevue, a Seattle suburb.

For most of the 30 seconds viewers could see only the traffic jam and hear nothing but traffic noises—blaring horns, racing engines. Near the end, however, came a voice with a single line:

"If you lived in Seattle, you'd be home by now."

The commercial is one of six produced by the city of Seattle to promote the advantages of urban living and is illustrative of efforts by cities across the country to reverse the flight of middle-class families to the suburbs.

"Developing suburbs are largely able to control their images," said Paul Schell, director of the Seattle Community Development Department. "They're frequently tagged with titles reminiscent of English manors. Their advertising is encouraging and enticing.

[illegible] has accelerated in this decade.

Latest Census Bureau figures show that populations of 37 of the nation's 56 largest cities have fallen since 1970. Seattle, for instance, is down by 5.2% to its lowest population since 1950.

San Francisco is down 3.9%, Los Angeles 2.3%, New York 3.2%, St. Louis 10.2%, Boston 3.8%.

And most of those fleeing the cities are middle-and upper-class whites, taking with them their spending dollars and the tax base they represent, and leaving behind the poor, the aged and the minorities.

"All our studies show that while our population is stabilizing now," said Schell, "we're becoming a city of elderly, of young professionals with no children and of low-income families. We don't want to become a city of only the economic elite and the economic disadvantaged."

Consequently, Seattle and other cities are beginning to take the offensive. They are spreading the urban gospel in typically American fashion

LIFE-AND-DEATH DRAMA ON ICE AT JUNE LAKE

BY MICHAEL SEILER
Times Staff Writer

JUNE LAKE—By the clock, it all happened in just 10 minutes . . .

But clock-time can be deceptive, according to five members of an amateur hockey team who were resting Thursday and trying to explain exactly what happened to them in those 10 minutes Wednesday.

During that time, they had seen a Simi man and his wife fall through the ice of June Lake, fallen in themselves trying to reach the pair, and finally pulled the man to safety.

"Call it adrenalin," one said. "And fear . . ."

The five—a ski shop manager, a carpet installer, two ski patrolman

Please Turn to Page 3, Col. 1

Miss Yoshimura Found Guilty

Convicted on Weapon, Explosive Counts

From Times Wire Services

350,000 LINE PARADE ROUTE

Carter Takes It in Stride, Walks to White House

BY RICHARD T. COOPER
Times Staff Writer

WASHINGTON—It took the U.S. Army, two fire engines and a determined band of Georgia farmers to coax the giant helium-filled peanut balloon into the air for Jimmy Carter's inaugural parade Thursday. And Abe Lincoln took a pratfall on his roller skates just as he reached the main reviewing stand.

But the sun shone brightly. Washington's record cold snap eased and the new President followed the example of Andrew Jackson and walked all the way from Capitol Hill to the White House at the head of his own procession.

Daughter Amy skipped along beside Carter and his wife, Rosalynn, most of the way but, apparently mindful of the nursery rhyme warning "Step on a crack, break your mother's back," she prudently hopped over all the lines in the Pennsylvania Ave. crosswalks.

For the parade's 15,000 participants and the spectators who lined the 1½-mile route, Thursday's inaugural celebration seemed to be a down-home, good-time-was-had-by-all sort of day in which cold feet, another

the parade—including an Alaskan sled dog team whose managers had driven a 10-year-old truck virtually around the clock from Anchorage to get here on time. They had spent one night sleeping beside a North Dakota highway when the temperature plunged to 15 degrees below zero.

It was a damp and bone-chilling 28 degrees at noon when Carter and Vice President Mondale took their oaths of office on a specially constructed platform added every four years to the East Portico of the Capitol. The temperature nudged above the freezing mark before the parade had ended almost four hours later, however, and the cloudiness predicted by the weather bureau gave way to bright sunshine.

While Thursday was thus substantially warmer than the near-zero weather of preceding days, keeping warm still was the central preoccupation of most people.

Parents bundled children in old quilts and set them down on sheets of plastic or stacks of newspapers to ward off the cold. Ski masks, down parkas, fur hats and wool mufflers of

The *New York Times,* the nation's most prestigious newspaper, reports the advent of the Carter years, along with the largest paper in the west, the *Los Angeles Times,* and the midwestern giant, the *Chicago Tribune.* Typical of how the bulk of the nation's press covered this day was the display of the *Dubuque Telegraph-Herald.*

Here come the advocates

Some of the changes represented by the new journalism were unmistakable improvements over the traditional way of newspapering. Journalism took on a greater variety, provided more information, gave newsmen the flexibility to convey their best understanding of events. But the intellectual outlook conveyed by the new journalism also has created problems—for the press itself and, it would appear, for the American System.

One of the most serious of these is the problem of advocacy. "Nothing is excluded," said A. M. Rosenthal of the New York *Times* in 1966 in describing the kind of journalism he envisioned at that paper. But where there is freedom to break out of the traditional formulas and routines, there is also an opportunity to abuse the powers of journalism. A reporter can use a news story to push his own ideas so hard that the requirements of "fairness" are discarded.

The deliberate politicization of news has become an endemic problem, especially among young reporters. There were occasions, especially in the late 1960's, when young reporters were so outraged by the Vietnam war, or the state of race relations in the U.S., or the behavior of the police in Chicago, that they assumed a right to editorialize strenuously in their news stories. Editors have generally resisted such efforts in the name of objectivity—Rosenthal recalls of the 1968 Chicago Democratic Convention that "I stayed home and killed copy and added to my reputation as a son of a bitch"—but they aren't always successful.

The process implies some problems for the credibility of the press. Opinion polls reveal a more or less steady decline in public respect and trust accorded the news media (as well as all other institutions) since the early 1960's. Since there isn't any evidence that the press is less (or more) factually accurate than it used to be, the source of this credibility problem may be the newly controversial agenda and perspective being supplied by the national press.

Good spelling isn't enough

Partly because of this problem, and partly because of the expanding power of the national press (the power is increased by the supplementary wire services of the New York *Times* and Wasington *Post*—Los Angeles *Times*, which together have more than 750 newspapers as subscribers), the new journalism finds itself increasingly subject to overt political attack—with all the attendant dangers that inarticulate disaffection from the media will be transformed into a concerted movement to curb their freedom. "A lot of people in Congress and elsewhere think the press is so powerful that they can't ignore damaging coverage," says Alan Otten, national correspondent of the *Wall Street Journal*. "So they attack. The old idea was, 'You can say anything you want about me so long as you spell my name right.' It isn't anymore."

In the long run, the greatest danger to the national press is probably posed, not by public unhappiness with its political position, but by the intense feeling among executives, in business and government, about what they see as its systematic distrust of all established institutions. There is growing concern among these executives that the new journalism has made it hard for them to make their records and views known to the public on their own terms. As examples they point to the almost unremittingly hostile coverage received by the Pentagon and the oil industry in recent years.

The consequence, argue these executives, is that it has become increasingly difficult, if not impossible, to get the public's governmental and economic business done. "There's been a communications revolution," says Ian MacGregor, chairman of American Metal Climax. "As with all revolutions, someone is taken to the gallows. The victim of the communications revolution has been the political leader. He's no longer able to maintain a position of leadership; he's preempted by prior expressions of the media." Echoes Herbert Schmertz, a vice president of Mobil Oil, "There's too much accusatory journalism."

Thus despite the flaws of the traditional newspaper, many executives still prefer it to the new journalism. "The 'serious' papers today are crazy," exclaims one angry government executive. "The unserious ones are merely trivial."

The businessmen can't get through

Many thoughtful news executives are deeply concerned about the credibility problem that is being created by the press. "We're opening up the pages to elements of society never before covered,"says William Thomas, editor of the Los Angeles *Times*. "At the same time, we run the danger of closing out what used to be the Establishment voice. We don't listen enough to businessmen. The old Establishment voices aren't in the paper enough. Often we've put them in the same category that blacks occupied fifteen years ago."

The problem of credibility is by no meams the only one that has been created by the new journalism. Some of its larger ambitions simply seem unrealistic. It is a fallacy to suppose that daily journalism can transcend its dependence on institutions and its focus on events. A half century ago, in his *Public Opinion*, Walter Lippmann pondered the possibility that the press could do just that and convey "a true picture of life." He finally concluded, "It is not workable. And when you consider the nature of the news, it is not even thinkable."

Lippmann argued that the central transactions in a modern democracy are between its institutions, which do most of the actual work, and the publics that oversee and control them. The central role of the newspaper is to facilitate those transactions by simply reporting what happened—the one thing it can do with a precision and expertise all its own. But it can perform this function properly only when it leaves to responsible institutions the task of defining events.

Something will have to give

When newspapers try to usurp that function, they cease to be a window through which publics and institutions can look at each other, and start to act as a screen. That, said Lippmann, is why, "at its best, the press is a servant and guardian of institutions.'' When it relinquishes that role, he warned, it becomes a ''means by which a few exploit social disorganization to their own ends.''

Some aspects of the new journalism, then have put the System somewhat out of joint by making it more difficult for government, business, and other institutions to explain themselves to their publics. In the long run, it would seem, something will have to give: the effectiveness of government, the ability of public opinion to control it, the freedom of the press, or the character of the journalism it currently practices.

The ombudsmen will help

It is possible that the issue will be resolved in a moderate way. There is emerging within the national press corps a body of criticism of the new ''advocacy''; the views expressed by William Thomas are by no means eccentric. Some news organizations, in response, are increasing the variety of viewpoints expressed—in ''op ed'' pages, in letters-to-the-editor departments, in ''ombudsman'' columns—and admitting errors more readily, as may be seen in the increasing popularity of correction departments. And institutions, for their own part, are also adapting—by learning to deal with newsmen as something more than mere stenographers, for example, and by using paid advertisements as a means of getting their own views across.

The press had a lot of power in colonial America, and that power was very much on the minds of the Founding Fathers. In the years that led up to the Declaration of Independence, they had watched the journals of their day help transform thirteen colonies of obedient British subjects into a new nation of Americans determined to make a revolution. Yet despite this firsthand experience of the power of journalism to alter or destroy political systems, when it came to writing a constitution for the new nation they were agreed that freedom of the press should be one of the basic rights provided. Not only would a free press provide a check against tyranny, but it was integral to their entire vision of an open and informed society under a popular government.

But if the Founding Fathers believed in press freedom, they also insisted on press responsibility. To them press freedom was not an end in itself, but a means of securing certain higher values, particularly individual rights and the viability of popular government itself, While such concerns justify a large measure of freedom for the press, they also imply certain substantial obligations—to tell the truth, to observe standards of fair play, to make sure that responsible institutions are able to make their cases in public, and in other ways to accommodate journalism to the legitimate needs of the System. It is still a pretty good list.

Bibliography

Both the *Fortune* article and David Shaw's article, which follows this bibliography, show that profound changes have occurred in the American newspaper and its auxiliary organizations, particularly the wire services and press syndicates. For a statistical analysis of newspaper advertising, circulation and audience, see the special section on newspapers in *Advertising Age* (Nov. 17, 1975). This section is particularly valuable for its view of the economic health of newspapers. Three insightful articles dealing with the present and future state of newspapers have been written by Leo Bogart: "Urban Papers Under Pressure," *Columbia Journalism Review* (September/October 1974), pp. 36-43; "The Future of the Metropolitan Daily," *Journal of Communication* (Spring 1975), pp. 30-43; "How the Challenge of Television News Affects the Prosperity of Daily Newspapers," *Journalism Quarterly* (Autumn 1975), pp. 403-410. These articles are "must" reading. For a critical examination of the manner in which newspaper publishers have spent additional funds and news space available to them, see Ben H. Bagdikian, "Fat Newspapers and Slim Coverage," *Columbia Journalism Review* (September/October 1973), pp. 15-20. Ernest C. Hynds, *American Newspapers in the 1970s,* Hastings House, 1975, surveys the newspaper scene, reporting on the various kinds of newspapers generally being published, on problems of press freedom and on the leaders of the press. A study that gets behind the facade of newspapers is Chris Argyris, *Behind the Front Page: Organizational Self-Renewal in a Metropolitan Newspaper,* Jossey-Bass, 1974. This anonymous study (of the *New York Times*) is a little heavy for the general reader. It provides, nevertheless, an important glimpse at the process of managing a metropolitan newspaper. For a specific, critical examination of the *New York Times,* see Philip Nobile, "EXTRA! An Exclusive Report on How the New York Times Became Second Banana," *Esquire* (May 1975), pp. 85-99. Edwin Emery, *The Press and America: An Interpretive History of the Mass Media,* 3rd ed., Prentice-Hall, 1972 is the standard history in the field.

Information about the development of community or suburban newspapers can be found in Jeffrey A. Tannenbaum, "Suburban Newspapers Find News and Profits on Cities' Outskirts," *Wall Street Journal* (Nov. 14, 1972), pp. 1, 20; Lee Smith, "Softly Into the Suburbs," (*More*) (November 1972), p. 9 ff., which deals with the *New York Times'* development of regional editions, especially in New Jersey, and the competition this creates for suburban newspapers; Bruce M. Kennedy, *Community Journalism: A Way of Life,* Iowa State University Press, 1974, which is a practical book on producing a small weekly or semi-weekly newspaper. Jay Levin, "Extra. Extra! Read All About It," (*More*) (June 1973), p. 1 ff., explains with exhaustive and fascinating detail the stranglehold distributors have over newspapers and magazines. This article deals especially with the East Coast situation.

Newspapers Offer Forum
to Outsiders

By David Shaw

The *New York Times,* a journalistic institution almost as well known for its gravity as for its quality, has given prominent play in recent months to such uncharacteristic exercises in whimsey and frivolity as:

—A lawyer's account of why he enjoys eating at McDonald's.

—A purported exchange of letters between a 9-year-old boy and several famous politicians.

—The genealogy of Alfred E. Newman, the nonexistent character created by *Mad magazine.*

—Excerpts from a children's cookbook.

—Andy Warhol's explanation of why he began dyeing his hair gray before his 25th birthday.

All these stories ran on the *New York Times* op-ed page—literally, the page opposite the editorial page—sandwiched among stories written by U.S. senators, Pulitzer Prize-winning poets, foreign diplomats and university professors, as well as by housewives, construction workers, businessmen and people on welfare, unemployment and Social Security.

The opening of the op-ed page to this diversity of authorship—and, ineluctably, of subject matter, literary style and reader interest—is a relatively new phenomenon in American newspapers; until the last five years or so, Sunday book and music reviews and a few skimpy letters to the editor were about all that most newspapers published by writers other than their own reporters or syndicated columnists.

"We've finally realized there are a lot more things in this world than newspapers traditionally pay attention to," says Anthony Day, editor of the *Los Angeles Times* editorial pages. "For too long, our op-ed page presented a terribly narrow range of argument—all those boring columnists saying the same thing, day after day, week after week, year after year.

"Our op-ed page was too dull, abstract, official, impersonal and predictable."

The *Los Angeles Times*, more than most papers, did experiment from time to time with outside contributions, but the New York Times was the first major paper to make a total commitment to the regular daily publication of outside work.

The *New York Times* spends more money, devotes more space and has a larger staff for its op-ed page than does any other paper, and its op-ed page is generally regarded as the best in the country. But over the last few years, the *Los Angeles Times, Washington Post, Boston Globe* and *Chicago Tribune* have also opened their daily op-ed pages to a wide range of outside contributors—many of them previously unpublished amateurs—whose topics and viewpoints have ranged from the trivial to the heretical and from the scholarly to the scandalous.

Even poetry and essays, two literary forms heretofore all but ignored by the nation's major newspapers, now find an occasional home on the op-ed page in these papers. Other newspapers—the *Milwaukee Journal* and *Minneapolis Star* among them—have also, to varying and lesser degrees, opened their op-ed pages to outside contributors who may range from poets to plumbers.

In most newspapers, the evolution of the op-ed page has been accompanied by a substantial increase in the space devoted to letters to the editor—a confluence of events that is by no means coincidental.

Amid the sociopolitical upheavals of the 1960s and 1970s, many editors began to feel that their newspapers should provide a more thorough and diverse discussion of the increasingly complex and controversial issues of the day.

Even with the publication of a wide array of columnists, stretching all across the political and ideological spectrum, it was felt that there was a certain insular—if not downright incestuous—quality of most newspaper opinion pages.

"Syndicated columnists all tend to write about the same subject on the same day with the same Washington correspondent's point of view," says Philip Geyelin, editor of the *Washington Post* editorial page.

"We wanted to introduce some new voices on our op-ed page, people other than professional journalists, who might have some interesting things to say about what was happening in our society."

Many of these new voices have been experts, specialists, academicians, scientists. But, increasingly, the new voices have also included the common man—and woman—describing personal feelings about (or personal experiences with) a given issue or incident.

Newspaper editors realize that press coverage of the bitterly divisive issues of the past 15 years has left many readers skeptical of—and hostile toward—the media, and they hope to bridge this often-chasmic credibility gap by publishing more articles (and letters) from these readers.

Some editors see the development of the op-ed page as but one stage in a continuing evolution of the opinion pages.

"I think it presages a totally new attitude on the part of newspapers," says Gene Roberts, executive editor of the *Philadelphia Inquirer*. "In time, I think we'll become less institutionalized, more open, more accountable, especially on the editorial page itself.

"Instead of just unsigned editorials, speaking for the newspaper as an institution, we'll have signed editorials—by individual staff members and outsiders as well," Roberts says. "Then we can have genuine debates, maybe two editorials on different sides of the same issue."

Most newspapermen trace the origins of today's still-changing op-ed page to the *New York World* of the early 1920s. The *World's* op-ed page was essentially a cultural offering, but its inclusion of some political columns, along with movie and theater and book reviews, is generally thought to have been the first regular publication of a full page of commentary in a major American newspaper.

Over the decades that followed, other papers began to publish op-ed pages, most of them featuring syndicated columnists writing on primarily political issues. On Sundays, many major papers began to devote one entire section to a review and analysis of the week's news—with outside commentary often supplementing staff-written and syndicated material.

Through the 1960s, as the complexity and contentiousness of the day's events seemed to grow, newspapers began experimenting with occasional outside contributors in the daily paper as well, striving for what one editor calls "rapid expert analysis on developing stories."

At the *Los Angeles Times*, for example, such "expert analysis" was published about twice a week from July, 1967, to September, 1969, most of it under the bylines of such prominent academicians as Sidney Hook, Philip Kurland, Edward Teller, Bruno Bettelheim and Hans Morgenthau.

At about the same time, the *New York Times*—which published its own columnists on a regular schedule, but used no syndicated material—initiated serious discussions about developing an op-ed page.

Twelve newspapers had ceased publication in New York since 1900—five of them since 1949—and *Times* editors felt an increasing responsibility to provide their readers with a more diverse spectrum of opinion than their own generally liberal columnists then offered.

"We talked at length about an op-ed page once or twice a year for several years," says Harrison Salisbury, the *Times'* Pulitzer Prize-winning reporter who ultimately served as the first editor of the *Times* op-ed page.

"Jurisdictional disputes were what delayed the page," Salisbury says. Two editors each wanted control of it, and a third didn't want the page to exist at all.

Finally, on Sept. 21, 1970, in a decision that was as much a matter of corporate economics as civic responsibility, the *New York Times* introduced its op-ed page.

"We knew we had to do something to attract the readers of the old *Herald Tribune* (one of the last of the New York papers to fold)," Salisbury says.

"We'd also signed new union contracts that cost the paper a lot of money that spring. We had to raise advertising and subscription rates to offset this, and Punch Sulzberger (the publisher) decided it would be a good time to give the readers something extra for their extra money."

The *Times'* own columnists were moved from the editorial page to the op-ed page, to be complemented by two or three outside contributions a day.

The *Times* pays $150 per outside story—more an honorarium than an actual fee really, since most of the prominent people who write for the *Times* could command five or 10 times that amount from other publications.

Times editors hoped that the prestige of writing for the *New York Times* would compensate authors for their time—and that is exactly what has happened, despite some early consternation by Salisbury.

"We decided to have an ad on the page most days," Salisbury says. "One reason, obviously, was the money it would bring in. Another reason was that I thought it would help keep the page in touch with reality, prevent it from becoming an ivory tower.

"But, frankly, without the ad, I was afraid we wouldn't get enough stories to fill the whole page every day. I was haunted by the idea that I'd wake up one morning and have nothing to put on the page."

That apprehension, Salisbury now admits, was "incredible naivete on my part. We wound up getting 200 unsolicited manuscripts a week."

Almost from the day of its inception, the *New York Times* op-ed page has been something of a status cachet in many social, political and intellectual quarters. Prominent people from around the world have sought assignments from the op-ed page, and it has become, on most days, precisely the controversial and provocative "intellectual marketplace" Salisbury hoped for from the beginning.

In the second month of the page's existence, Salisbury published an open letter, written by a Southern physician to his college-bound son, urging the boy to avoid campus demonstrations. If the boy were to be killed in a campus protest, his father wrote, "Mother and I will grieve, but we will gladly buy a dinner for the National Guardsman who shot you."

More than 300 letters came in attacking the doctor.

A year later, a brief, four-paragraph excerpt reprinted from the British magazine *The New Statesman* brought the *Times* op-ed page an even greater avalanche of angry mail. In that article, author J. B. Priestley argued, tongue firmly in cheek, that most Britishers' preference for brown eggs over white eggs clearly demonstrated the superiority of British civilization to American civilization.

"We got so many letters of protest, I though we'd have to fight the Revolution all over," says one *Times* editor.

In January, 1974, Salisbury retired, and Charlotte Curtis, formerly editor of the paper's family/style section, assumed the editorship of the op-ed page.

Curtis had, she said, two basic objectives: "To get more ordinary people, rather than famous people, writing for the page, and to broaden and lighten the spread of the page."

Salisbury had relied too heavily, some critics felt, on big-name contributors who did not always have something important to say.

"A dull piece by a famous person is still a dull piece," says one editor.

Curtis made public her desire for pieces reflecting "the experiences and perceptions of people living ordinary lives away from the East Coast," and in response to her plea, unsolicited manuscripts received by the op-ed page have now increased to 300 a week.

Only a small fraction of those are good enough or original enough to be used, and Curtis estimates that 85%-90% of the published op-ed pieces are assigned by her or by one of her two full-time assistants.

The *New York Times* op-ed page, like those in other papers, also makes regular use of excerpts from noteworthy speeches and from articles printed in other, often technical or esoteric magazines, but Curtis' op-ed page is somewhat less issue-oriented than Salisbury's was—in part because of her personality and her commitment to modify the page, in part because of the quiescence of Vietnam, the campus, the ghetto and Watergate.

The *New York Times* op-ed page remains, however, the most cerebral of the nation's op-ed pages, containing not only some of the best writing published in any paper but also dealing regularly in pure, abstract ideas, independent of any current issue, as discussed by many of the most discerning intellectuals of our time.

Some critics think the page is too cerebral at times—"dull" and "turgid" are the words one editor applies. Others think it is too frivolous.

"The page was more vital, more provocative, under Salisbury," says Robert Healey, executive editor of the *Boston Globe*. "The page gives me a good surprise once in a while now, but it just isn't as consistently serious as it used to be."

Sometimes, the lightheartedness of the New York Times op-ed page is both contrived and counterproductive—as in April, when a well-reasoned, statistic-filled article on the federal government's "ferocious neglect" of rural America was published beneath the playful headline "Nix Pix of Stix as Hix."

More often, however, offbeat headlines and stories and large, stylized, often surrealistic illustrations on the op-ed page serve as an effective antidote to the stolid, somber quality of much of the *New York Times*. On May 31, for example, almost half the op-ed page was devoted to a story on flower-smuggling; the bold illustrations and eye-catching headline ("Flower Smuggler, Drop that Pistil!") probably lured several readers who might otherwise have neglected what proved to be a fascinating tale.

Curtis is aware of the criticism that her page is sometimes too frivolous, and she says John Oakes, editor of the editorial page, occasionally makes that charge himself. "He calls my softer pieces 'True Confessions' or 'Readers Digest' pieces," she says.

Nevertheless, the only story Curtis has published that she wishes, in retrospect, she had not published was a deadly serious attempt by a Southern conservative to equate the "persecution" of Richard Nixon with that of Jesus Christ.

"I think now that piece was tasteless," Curtis says.

Despite such lapses, most editors speak of the *New York Times* op-ed page with considerable envy and enthusiasm. They are far more critical of other op-ed pages—especially of the *Washington Post* op-ed page.

"I get the feeling the *Post* editors just dump in anything they have, then write a dull head (headline) for it," says Ed Hawley, editor of the *Chicago Tribune* op-ed page.

"I don't remember anything on the *Post* op-ed page ever attracting my attention," says another op-ed page editor. "That's pretty bad."

The *Post* began its op-ed page about the same time as the *New York Times*, although the *Post* really treats its facing editorial and op-ed pages as a single entity, sandwiching columns and outside contributions between editorials on the extreme left and letters on the extreme right.

Because Washington is the quintessential political town, the *Post* continues to run more political columns—syndicated and by *Post* staffers—than most papers. That leaves less room for op-ed page pieces than either the *New York Times* or *Los Angeles Times* run.

The *Post*, more often than not, publishes only one outside piece a day, and editors make an effort not to permit politicians to write that one piece too frequently.

"We feel they already have access to our news columns," says Philip Geyelin, editor of the *Post* editorial page.

Still, *Post* editors see politicians on the Washington cocktail party circuit, and op-ed page stories are frequently a byproduct of these casual meetings.

Geyelin recently met former Sen. William Fulbright at such a party, and when Fulbright began talking about a recent trip he'd taken to the Mideast, Geyelin asked him to write an op-ed page piece on the experience. Fulbright did so.

Although the *Post* op-ed material is often political, the paper has published an intriguing—if rarely compelling—variety of stories, including, in the past month:

—A Christian scholar's explanation of "the vitality of religion in a supposedly scientific age."

—An American motion picture director's comparison of British and American television, based on their respective coverage of the Wimbledon tennis tournament.

—A Washington attorney's account of a small, experimental college in Phoenix.

Other op-ed pages around the country have also produced an uncommon diversity of stories.

The *Chicago Tribune* op-ed page has been part of a continuing trend away from the singlemindedly conservative image the paper had for decades, and now, on any given day, the most interesting story in the paper may well appear on the op-ed page.

One recent piece argued that people in underdeveloped countries too often blame "demons and black magic," rather than international politics and economics, for overpopulation, food shortages and other problems of daily life.

Another piece, written by an Irish playwright, used the occasion of the death of an old Irish revolutionary leader, Eamon de Valera, to talk about de Valera's impact and philosophy.

The *Tribune*, which publishes outside contributions four or five times a week, also publishes a weekly "Speak Out" column by one of its readers and a twice-weekly column written by a local construction worker.

The *Boston Globe* publishes three or four outside pieces a week on its op-ed page, many of them designed to ventilate a local controversy.

The *Globe's* page was, in fact, born—and has continued to develop—in direct response to a series of conflicts in Boston: antiwar protests, a caucus of black elected officials, a feminist sit-in at the paper, anger in some white neighborhoods over the *Globe's* support of busing, complaints by local Arab leaders tha the *Globe* was pro-Israel.

Busing has dominated the *Boston* consciousness of late, and the *Globe* op-ed page has reflected that domination. One of the best pieces on that subject recently was written by a woman whose son was stabbed during last year's school unrest but who remains optimistic about the busing program.

Anne Wyman, editor of the *Globe* editorial pages, says she wishes she had more space available for outside contributions, "but we've got too damn many fixed columns."

Most editors have similar problems, and they're reluctant to run their syndicated columnists less frequently, for fear the columnists will take their columns to a competing paper instead.

"That's where you guys at the *L.A. Times* are lucky," says one editor. "You don't have any real competition in L.A. You don't have to run the columns three or four times a week, and there's really no place else for them to go if they don't like it."

The *Los Angeles Times* has, indeed, drastically reduced its use of syndicated columnists; few run more than once a week now, and most run far less often than that, thereby enabling the Times to publish two or three outside pieces a day on its op-ed page.

Most *L.A. Times* op-ed pages pieces are assigned by the op-ed staff, and only three or four of the 75 or so unsolicited pieces that come in every week are generally published. Whether assigned or unsolicited, outside contributors are generally paid $150 each, the same fee as the *New York Times* pays.

Although the *New York Times* and *Los Angeles Times* have made greater commitments than any other newspapers to the use of outside material on their op-ed pages, there are many differences between the two pages. Among these are:

—The *Los Angeles Times* permits its own staff writers to contribute to the op-ed page, and places no formal limit on the number of articles an outside writer may contribute. The *New York Times* prohibits its staffers from writing for the op-ed page, and limits outsiders to two pieces a year.

—The *Los Angeles Times* op-ed page appears five days a week, and is merged, in effect, with the "Opinion" section on Sunday; the same staff, for the most part, produces both "Opinion" and the op-ed pages. The *New York Times* op-ed page appears seven days a week, and is produced by a staff wholly independent from Sunday's "The Week in Review."

Unlike the *New York Times*, which runs one large ad on its op-ed page about four times a week, the *L.A. Times* prohibits advertising on its op-ed page.

"An ad would reduce the space available for stories, and it would be a commercial intrusion on one of the pages that, like the editorial page itself, should be free of that," says Anthony Day, editor of the *L.A. Times* editorial pages.

But the most substantive differences between the op-ed pages of the *New York Times* and the *Los Angeles Times* are in philosophy and content.

L. A. Times editors admit their page is less intellectual than the *New York Times'*, but they say that is deliberate.

"We have different papers and different audiences," says Peter Bunzel, editor of the *L. A. Times* op-ed page. "I think that for our readers, we have enough reportage on social issues on the news pages and enough pontification from the columnists.

I'd like the op-ed page to provide something that does not exist anywhere else in the paper. I'd especially like us to give our readers a clear feeling of what it's really like to live in Southern California in 1975.

"I want personal experience pieces, stories that tell how it feels to drive the freeway and to suffer a death in the family and to be out of work."

Thus, in one three-week period early this year, the *L. A. Times* published accounts of:

—What a patient's death meant to a switchboard operator in the hospital.

—What a Monrovia police officer remembered about his great-grandmother.

—A politician's bad experience with her doctor.

—A grocery clerk's encounters with customers who were angry about rising food prices.

On the broader social canvas, op-ed page pieces this year have also ranged from a Catholic educator's ruminations on Gov. Brown's seminary training to a discussion of the public policy implications of earthquake predictions to an excoriation of those who would misquote the Bible to condemn homosexuality.

The *L. A. Times* also likes contrapuntal dialogue on its op-ed page, often pairing articles representing divergent viewpoints on the same issue—feminism, welfare, the Mideast, rapid transit.

Some critics think the *L. A. Times* op-ed page still contains too narrow a range of opinion and too little trenchant social commentary.

Kenneth Reich, now a *Times* political reporter, served as *The Times'* first op-ed page editor in 1972, and he thinks the page is not sufficiently "abrasive or exciting."

"We seem to have a great reluctance around here to run pieces that represent truly new and different ideas," Reich says. "Our editors seem afraid that the paper will be perceived as lending credibility, if not actually support, to any far-out idea that's expressed on the page."

Reich asked to be relieved as op-ed page editor after only six months, largely because he felt he was often prevented from doing the job he was hired to do—that of bringing truly divergent ideas into the paper. Several articles he solicited for the op-ed page were killed for "political reasons," he says, and he found it "humiliating; I felt like a lackey when I had to tell some guy we couldn't run his piece, even though I personally thought it was a very fine, responsible piece."

Reich admits he was "never temperamentally suited to be an editor anyway, though," and he says his superiors probably "heaved a sign of relief when I quit."

Times editors scoff at Reich's charges that op-ed page stories were killed for political reasons and they agree he was ill-suited to the job (although they do think he got the op-ed page off to "a good start").

"The whole idea of the op-ed page is to bring in ideas we don't necessarily agree with," says Anthony Day. "We often reject pieces because they repeat something we've already said or because they're poorly written or inconsistently argued, but never for political reasons."

Because so many contributors to the op-ed page have never before written for a newspaper—or for any other publication—op-ed page editors frequently must work long hours helping them shape their stories.

"Authentication is also a big problem for us," says Peter Bunzel. "How can we be sure that a guy we never heard of before is writing a true story? That's especially difficult with personal experience pieces."

Bunzel has yet to run a piece he now wishes he had not run, but he does admit to "ex post facto reservations" about a short piece on poets and poetry by Rod McKuen that was published last month.

"Perhaps we dignified the author's simplistic notions about poetry and the role of poets by using it," Bunzel says.

In publishing the McKuen piece, *The Times* appended an editor's note that said, in part:

"In submitting this article at *The Times'* request, the author described himself as follows: 'Having sold more than 10 million books of poetry in hard cover in the past 10 years, Rod McKuen is considered not only the best-selling poet of all time, but the best-selling author writing in any medium in hard cover...'"

One letter-writer took *The Times* to task for this "immature treatment," and Bunzel himself admits, somewhat shamefacedly, that he used that editor's note because he rather enjoyed seeing McKuen "a celebrated fellow...sort of make a fool of himself in public."

The *New York Times* recently encountered far more embarrassment—through no apparent fault of its editors—with a frivolous op-ed page piece of its own.

The piece purported to be an exchange of letters between Martin Bear, a 9-year-old San Francisco boy visiting a relative in New York, and Sens. Edward Kennedy, Jacob Javits, Hubert Humphrey and James Buckley, as well as New York Congresswoman Bella Abzug and Mayor Abraham Beame (to whom Martin Bear sent a dime because "I heard that you need money").

In a typical exchange, Martin wrote to Humphrey:

"I saw you at our temple in New York. You were late and you never stopped talking. How come you talk so much?"

Humphrey's response, in part:

"One of the nicest things about being a United States senator is getting letters from young people like you. It's a great satisfaction to me to know that I have so many fine young friends..."

Martin's exchanges with the other politicians were equally charming and equally amusing, and all the politicians' letters were genuine.

But there is no such person as Martin Bear. He was a figment of the creative imagination of a young lawyer in a prominent Wall Street firm. The lawyer wrote the letters, then signed the "boy's" name.

Other Mass Media: Magazines, Books, Film, Cable Television and Music

Magazines: The Problem of Finding a Home for Ideas

By Carey McWilliams

The approaching end of another year is an appropriate time to draw back from the rush of events and assess where we stand. In doing so, I am struck by this inarguable fact: Rapid social and technological change, unchecked by criticism and traditional restraint, is impinging on the elusive process by which ideas are conceived, articulated, disseminated and, with luck, made part of the general culture.

This blockage in the flow of ideas should cause grave concern about the future course of our society, whose life blood is that flow.

Let me confess that I cannot offer a good working definition of an idea in the sense that I use the term. In my view, an opinion bears about the same relation to an idea that facts do to the truth or that information does to knowledge. Opinions are a dime a dozen.

If a person states that he or she is opposed to capital punishment, you can score one vote to that effect, and in a sense it is important to know how many people oppose or favor capital punishment. But however often or violently opinions are stated, they remain just that—opinions. An opinion is an opinion is an opinion; there is no life in it; it is neither very interesting nor important per se. It does not advance the dialogue. A stock response to most expressions of opinion is: "So what?" It is as though one person said: "I like tomatoes better than carrots" and the other said, "I like carrots better than tomatoes." There is not much you can do with an exchange of that kind.

But an idea is different. It has a life of its own. Ideas can lie dormant for years and then suddenly explode with surprising force. Ideas can travel great distances. They can leap over language barriers and penetrate alien cultures. Ideas have an inherent interest. They are often beautiful. There is a symmetry about them that

Carey McWilliams was for many years editor of *The Nation* magazine and has been a perceptive commentator on the journalistic field. Reprinted with permission of the author. This edited version appeared first in the *Los Angeles Times*.

opinions lack. And they are creative in the sense that they can combine with other ideas, or modify them, or lead to still more novel ideas. Ideas keep an intellectual tradition alive, viable, and relevant; they are the yeast of a culture.

Opinions, facts, and information are not to be scorned; they have their uses, indeed, they are indispensable. But ideas, truth, and knowledge are more important. It may seem far-fetched to say that they are more important today than ever before—for ideas, truth and knowledge have always been important—but there is more than a grain of sense in the suggestion. For today we live in an extraordinary time in which landmarks that long provided guidance have been obliterated before their replacements, if any, have been identified. Today we act at times as though we did not think either the past or the future were important.

If I cannot define an idea—and I can't—I can at least cite a few examples of what I mean. When Paul Valery wrote; "Do what you think, otherwise you will think what you do," he was expressing an idea. Herman Melville was voicing a variant of the same idea when he wrote: "In our hearts we mold the whole world's hereafter and in our hearts we fashion our own gods . . .we are precisely what we worship." When Charles de Gaulle cautioned that "one must not insult the future," he voiced an idea with many meanings and implications. When we encounter such statements we know that we are in the presence of ideas, not opinions, facts or information.

Just as I cannot define an idea, so I find the process by which ideas are conceived to be quite mysterious. One may struggle with a mass of data for a long time without being able to make any sense of it and then wake up, some morning, with an idea that illuminates, clarifies, and gives coherence to what was previously a chaos of unrelated facts and information.

If the process by which ideas are conceived remains elusive, something can be said about the conditions which further their expression. Ideas must struggle to be born. They must find expression so that they can be studied, distributed, criticized, assimilated, rejected or modified. Often a new idea emerges in a half-baked form; only later is it refined, restated and made properly presentable. The process takes time. It may not take nine months but there are few instant conceptions.

Ideas are not born on TV talk shows or panel discussions; they need to be stated in print, so that they can be preserved and passed, so to speak, from mind to mind, over wide intervals in time and great distances. They must be captured in print. Appropriate forms must exist in which they can find expression.

Because new ideas, in the nature of things, do not always or usually attract large audiences, a diversity of small circulation media is needed to insure their expression. The British and American experience would indicate that the intellectual magazines of limited circulation provide the best seed beds in which to plant and nurture ideas. Books, of course, are important, but the book is usually Step 2 in the process. In our time, social and technological change threatens to disrupt the always-precarious process by which ideas find expression. Consider, for example how the conveyor belt of ideas now functions.

Television is the main source of news for most people; for more than a majority it is their main reliance. The younger the viewer, the more confidence he

Popular general family
magazines like these
gave way to the
pressures of advertising
and specialized
publishing.

or she has in the reliability and objectivity of television news. The television world, as James Reston notes, is the world most people see and hear.

Ideas are not born on television but it can give them instant currency and a wide audience. But it has distinct limitations. Philip H. Abelson, editor of *Science,* says "The news media are not effective in presenting balanced news in depth, but are to a degree contributing to a malfunctioning of society. They have participated in creating and exacerbating a series of crises by overconcentrating their attention on particular topics. Typically, after a period of concentrated attention, the media suddenly drop one topic as they rush to indulge in overkill of the next one."

Television, by its dominance of news, forces most magazines of general interest—and to a degree, the press—to play the same game. Nowadays the news weeklies chase the same subject to such a degree that for many weeks of the year their covers are virtually identical.

To get at the reality of the conveyor-belt system as it functions today, we must bear in mind that the networks are to a degree parasitic to the printed media. The total of their budgets for news is a fraction of what newspapers and wire services and magazines spend in gathering news. Most of the TV expense has to do with transporting cumbersome equipment about, setting up portable ground stations, and the like. Yet despite this parasitic relation, the electronic media are constantly undermining the economic stability of the print media. (We would be more conscious of this state of affairs were it not for the fact that so many newspapers own TV stations.)

The electronic media use public airways while the print media must suffer the limitations of a monumentally inefficient and increasingly expensive postal service. As postal rates increase, the service deteriorates. I often wonder why we do not tax the networks for their use of public airways and use the proceeds to offset soaring postal rates; it would be a fair arrangement, the more so since the TV viewer does not pay for news on the tube except in the form of amortizing the cost of his set or the one-and-a-half-cent electricity charge for listening to a news broadcast. Meanwhile magazines and newspapers cannot raise subscription or newstand prices much more than they have been raised.

There is still a further weakness. Television concentrates exclusively on the present—its beat is today, not yesterday and not tomorrow. The result is to obliterate the past. Yet how can we evaluate the present if we cannot remember the past? How can we understand what happens on Cyprus without knowing some of its history or its social structure?

The electronic media are aware of the problem, but can do little about it. Television can do better with the future in the form of speculations and projections, but it seldom tries. So we are breeding, to the extent that we place more and more reliance on television, a new generation of Americans who know little of the immediate past, are obsessed with today, and discount the future.

The public is so mesmerized by television that it does not realize the extent to which small circulation magazines—those with circulations of less than 200,000—have long been the main seed bed for ideas of our culture. It is hardly possible to think of an important writer who did not first test and prove his talents in a small magazine. Even the best of ideas and the finest talent require a launching mechanism of some sort. On an average a dozen books a year come out of articles which have first appeared in *The Nation*.

Mass circulation magazines, by contrast, are not good vehicles for ideas whose time has yet to come. The small circulation magazines have discovered far more talent and spawned far more ideas than larger ones.

Today magazines, large and small, are caught in the turmoil and confusion of the times. A number of mass circulation magazines have failed or suspended publication: *Life, Look,* the *Woman's Home Companion* and the *Saturday Evening Post* (now reissued in a new format). These failures can be chalked up to the inroads television has made on advertising aimed at the mass market and, also, to the way in which magazines have sought to imitate television in their quest for ever-larger readerships. Some of them, *Life*, for one, finally tried to survive by cutting back their uneconomical circulation.

Most magazines, in fact, have severe problems today. Costs are steadily escalating. The newsstand situation is chaotic. As the volume of material delivered to newsstands steadily increases, the number of outlets declines. Some 60% of the total estimated $1.2 billion in annual magazines retail sales are now made through supermarkets and chain stores; the checkout counter is where the action is. You will not find quality magazines exhibited in super-markets.

When the magazine industry cites figures to prove that all is well with the print media, the figures include those of the new magazines. New magazines constantly come and go, exploiting fads of the moment and promoting new life-styles. Some of these new magazines are published to be looked at, not read; for example, the so-called ''skin'' magazines, the first of which was *Playboy*. One could have predicted that it would be followed by others of the same kind which would show more ''skin'' and different kinds of skin.

Indeed, this has happened, for a kind of cannibalism exists among mass circulation magazines; to succeed is to invite competition from a dozen imitators. Thus *Playboy* must now compete with *Penthouse, Playgirl* and *Venus* and the line keeps extending. Most of these magazines try to kid themselves and the rest of us by pretending that they are interested in issues and ideas when it is obvious that they are primarily interested in bodies. *Playboy* will run an occasional article by Arnold Toynbee...but it is hard to believe that its largely voyeur audience is interested in such fare.

To offset general mass-market advertising lost to television, magazines nowadays try to cater to special sections of the consumer market. If the special audience can be lured to subscribe, then the readership can in effect be sold to advertisers interested in the special market. Thus today we have magazines addressed exclusively to the interest of skiers, surfers, young working girls, antique car buffs and other special consumer groups. Some of these new magazines serve real needs and will survive for a time, but they have no relation to the problem of providing a home for ideas.

Perhaps the new technology will eventually help magazines; but to date it has presented them with new kinds of competition, including some that are difficult to counter.

In a society geared to mass media, mass markets and mass consumption, the quality magazines have a hard row to hoe and their survival cannot be taken for granted.

Yet the disappearance or decline of these magazines would have a much greater impact on the culture than might be imagined. Thus *Kenyon Review,* no longer published, with a circulation of 5,000, was an important magazine and published much interesting new writing.

So we come finally to the book, which has always provided ideas their best long-term readership and continuity of influence. But here, too, there are problems. Last year roughly 40,000 books were published and the industry grossed $3.2 billion. In 1880, 2,076 books were published. The figures indicate growth, no doubt of that; but what kind of growth?

Again, as with magazines, one must measure the impact of what happens when an industry begins to cater to a mass market, almost exclusively in terms of quick profits gained at the expense of intangible values. The gross figures seem splendid; but they do not tell the complete story.

Hardcover fiction has experienced a sharp decline in sales. Retail sales of books are up but library sales are down. Ten years ago the industry was 15% paperback; today it is 35% paperback. Nothing wrong with paperbacks, mind you; but the lure of the paperback market can have a demoralizing impact on manuscript selection.

The term ''super seller'' was invented for the hugely successful and profit-intensive books that have changed the editorial emphasis of the big publishing firms and made it increasingly difficult to publish otherwise meritorious—and otherwise profitable—books. Publishers stampede to a subject and engage in a kind of overkill with respect to it. Just as there was a kind of frenzy about books on black militancy, student unrest and the new feminism, so today there is an appalling backlog of books on Watergate, with more to come.

''What's happening in the book business is what happened on Broadway some years ago,'' comments William Ewald of Pocket Books. ''It's the hit attitude on the part of the public; they want the recognizable brand names.''

Publishers will pay fantastic advances—$200,000 or $1,000,000—for a book they have not seen but which they think may tap the mass market. The effect is to distort the finances of publishing and to stack the cards against the book which might have a modest sale over a long period of years. Publishers will gamble heavily on such quixotic items as Clifford Irving's non-book about Howard Hughes or an autobiography of Marilyn Monroe which may or may not have been ghosted by Ben Hecht. Oldline publishing houses are gobbled up by conglomerates or large enterprises.

In this whole process, many good editors, always in short supply, have dropped out of publishing. Writes John Simon, formerly an editor at Random House: ''To the extent that the editor and the writer are successful, it is because the book fits neatly into the established procedures of the company; books that would otherwise be successful, useful and perhaps even important are often now failures, because they are lost in the interstices of a corporate flow chart.''

To make matters worse, there are now only about 11,750 book stores, mostly in the large cities. The book club is one device, the chain bookstore another, to solve the distribution problem. In this instance, however, the solution is part of the problem. For the chain book stores are concentrated in the suburbs and are morbidly preoccupied with best-sellers. The atmosphere is as impersonal as in a bank or department store; the experienced book dealer, who once did so much to cultivate an interest in books, is long gone.

One also must be disturbed, if only slightly, by certain long range trends in the culture. Why is it it that we have a federally-funded, $12-million-a-year program on the ''Right to Know''? The inference seems to be that the influx of disadvantaged youngsters into the school system has resulted in a sharp decline in reading skills. But the evidence shows that these youngsters can be taught to read. And isn't the real problem that reading skills have declined generally? The prevalence of books with such titles as ''Getting People to Read'' provides an ironic footnote to our extraordinary achievements in collecting, sorting, and computerizing tons of information, subject to instant retrieval.

As one views what is happening to the traditional means by which ideas have been made available in the culture, it becomes clear that the library is a main line of defense against further erosion. Yet at a time when unprecedented demands are being made on libraries, government grants are declining.

In his fiscal year budget for 1975, former President Nixon applied the ax savagely to library services and facilities. At a time when publishers are bringing out 40,000 books a year, the San Francisco Library's book budget has been cut by 25%. I am told that in some libraries, due to staff shortages, it takes almost a year to catalogue a book and get it on the shelves, and yet still further cuts in clerical staffs are made.

All this is happening at a time when, as Jerome B. Wiesner, president of M.I.T., has pointed out, we are engaged in a battle to control information. Communication and information problems are inhibiting our ability to learn quickly enough about the effects of our collective decisions and our ability to respond to problems before they get out of hand. If we are not to drown in a sea of information, we need to strengthen libraries by increasing their funding in relation to the magnitude of the burdens we are imposing on them. But better correlation and integration of information and data will be of little help unless the culture of ideas is stimulated; in the end, ideas are sovereign.

So what concerns me is not any single problem but the general condition. Technology has made it possible to reach a new mass for news and opinion no less than products. But the drive to reach mass markets goes hand-in-hand with the obsession with quick profits.

As a result, the atmosphere of the fast buck permeates the society at all levels.

Recently radio station WCNC in New York announced that it would no longer play classical music; the revenues derived did not warrant it. William F. Buckley Jr., chairman of the board, made the announcement and went on to say: "I have no intention whatever of listening to it ever under the new format." One must applaud his intention but one more station playing classical music has now succumbed, not for lack of audience—almost $100,000 in special donations and pledges flowed in—but because a larger and hence more profitable audience wanted popular music.

What we confront is a crisis in values. Growth in a statistically measured GNP does not per se measure improvement in the conditions of human life. It does not measure moral or intellectual elements any more than the loss of clean air can be brought within the pricing system. Some values do not carry a price tag nor can they be computerized. What is best for the budget is not necessarily best for the values an institution is supposed to serve.

Henry James, perhaps anticipating the danger we now face once wrote: "It takes an endless amount of taste, by the same token, to make even a little tranquility." Not that tranquility is the goal, but some of it we must have, for without it human values—and the life of ideas—will be curtailed.

There is no specific remedy for this state of affairs. Rather, those who see the problem must join in reasserting the importance of ideas and insist that certain values be preserved—even to the detriment of cash-flow charts and growth tables. It is ideas, in the end, that give the society its character and direction, and we sacrifice them at incalculable peril.

Bibliography

The pressures under which magazines operate are very real, as Carey McWilliams demonstrates. Chris Welles has explained the market forces at work in the death of *Life* magazine in "Lessons from Life," *World* (Feb. 13, 1973). His "The Numbers Magazines Live By," *Columbia Journalism Review* (September/October 1975), pp. 22-27 delves into the conflict between *Time* magazine and W. R. Simmons & Associates Research over the accuracy of Simmons' audience studies. In the process he reveals just how important those "numbers" are to magazine publishers. Background books on the magazine industry include Robert E. Kenyon, editor, *Magazine Profiles*, Medill School of Journalism, Northwestern University, December 1974, a collection of reports categorized by types of magazines; Roland E. Wolseley, *The Changing Magazine*, Hastings House, 1973; James Playsted Wood, *Magazines in the United States*, 3rd ed., Ronald Press, 1971; Theodore Peterson, *Magazines in the Twentieth Century*, 2nd ed., University of Illinois Press, 1969. A useful bibliography is John H. Schact, compiler, *A Bibliography for the Study of Magazines*, Institute of Communications Research, University of Illinois, 1972. A slightly different problem is explicated in Dave Noland, "Flying Pussycats," (*More*) (November 1975), pp. 12-13. A former editor of *Air Progress*, Nolan brings special expertise and contacts to his discussion of the influence of advertisers, Beech in particular, on consumer aviation magazines. A review of news magazine journalism can be found in Edwin Diamond, "The Mid-Life Crisis of the Newsweeklies," *New York* (June 7, 1976), pp. 50-54+.

For Paperback Houses, There's No Business Like Show Tie-In Business

By Nancy Hardin

Not so long ago the publishing rights for a movie tie-in book could be picked up for the cash equivalent of a song. That is, if the buyer was persistent enough to make his way past the indifference of whoever was handling the sale—usually someone in the publicity department of a film company who felt he had better things to do than shuffle papers for a slow grand or two.

That was then. In the past few years it's become a whole different ballgame. Film and publishing people have finally become aware of how much each can offer the other. And in this era of belt-tightening, film companies no longer turn up their noses at the income they can derive from even a small override on a successful tie-in.

Tie-ins come in several forms, with two common denominators whenever possible: a cover featuring the movie art or star photos, and a publication date timed to coincide with the national release of the film. The traditional type of tie-in consists of merely repackaging the edition which has already come out in softcover—or even hard, with a success like "The Exorcist," for example—to include a tie-in cover and, occasionally, an insert of stills from the film. The other garden-variety type of tie-in consists of a novelization of the screenplay, again with a coordinated cover and stills from the film occasionally included. Least likely to turn up on mass market racks is a third type of movie tie-in, the screenplay itself,

Nancy Hardin is a former senior editor at Bantam Books and now is vice president and head of the literary department at Ziegler Associates in Los Angeles. She knows from experience both ends of the movie tie-in business. Reprinted from the Feb. 17, 1975 issue of *Publishers Weekly,* published by R.R. Bowker Company, a Xerox company. Copyright © 1975 by Xerox Corporation.

containing dialogue and scene settings from the film, minus the more esoteric camera directions but almost always including stills. Some screenwriters feel that their work should only be published in the form in which it was written; and if their names carry enough weight—a William Goldman, say, or a Robert Towne or a Michael Crichton—and the film in question seems assured of success, a publisher may agree to go with the screenplay even though most readers apparently find the form difficult to read, and sales orders can be cut by about two-thirds if even a highly successful film is published as a screenplay. Last, and least in number, since very few films are big enough to warrant such attention, are books written *about* a film—the making of it, its special effects, or whatever. Blockbusters like "Love Story," "The Godfather" and "The Great Gatsby" spawned such books; perhaps the most successful of the genre have been "The Making of 2001" and "William Peter Blatty on the Exorcist: From Novel to Film."

In the days when such deals didn't seem to count for much, an editor who had heard about a film that sounded promising would often have to scramble even to discover who owned the publication rights, much less where he could get hold of a copy of the script, or who was authorized to make a deal and draw up a contract. At best, there was a routine procedure. Someone from the merchandising or publicity department of the studio releasing the film in question would send around a blurry copy of the script, accompanied by what amounted to a form letter with information about the cast and a projected release date. After that, it was pretty much up to the editor to phone in a modest offer. As often as not, the editor in question had no particular expertise (beyond enjoying an occasional movie) in deciding which films to tie-in with; and even the big paperback houses had no one editor who was hired specifically to handle movie tie-ins, as nearly all of them have now (some even have a Los Angeles scout to boot).

Low Pay for Novelizers

Once the editor's offer was accepted, and the studio's lawyers, unused to the byways of publishing contracts, had laboriously been persuaded to return the contract more or less intact, the only further contributions expected from the film company's end were sporadic news of the anticipated release pattern of the film, and eventually—and often belatedly for publishing deadlines—a messenger bearing the film's logo, a few stills, and if you got lucky, a color transparency of the ad campaign. In those days, all the studio hoped to get out of the tie-in was the promotional value of having its film's title and ad campaign displayed in one more place before the public's eye. What went on behind that cover was left entirely to the publisher. This sounds like more of a creative blessing than it was, however, since everything was done so haphazardly on both sides. And the publisher's choice of writers was limited by the fact that the pay usually was a flat fee of between $1500 and $2500, and the novel frequently had to be written within a few weeks in order to be published in time to coincide with the release of the film and in order to make financial sense for the novelizer.

Actually, no matter how early the deal was made, changes in the script, revised release plans, belatedly organized ad campaigns and the like always seemed to wind up making the book a last-minute proposition. When I was handling the movie-tie-ins for Bantam Books I remember once feeling very smug about getting a novelization written and copy-edited months in advance, only to be told that there would be a slight change in casting: the lead would be black, not white. Since the novelizer had gone to some trouble to develop the character he'd originally been presented with, this meant considerable rewriting. Which, grumbling, he did. The film was subsequently made, with said black actor as the lead, and then previewed, whereupon it was discerned by the studio powers-that-be that the audiences were responding badly to the fact that the hero was killed in the end. Another ending was hastily filmed in which the hero was permitted to start a new life in another country. At that point I didn't have the heart—much less the time—to send the galleys to California, where the novelizer happened to live, for yet another rewrite, so that weekend I found myself substituting life for death on the last few pages of the proofs of our book. Small wonder that the book did not turn out to be a fiction masterpiece.

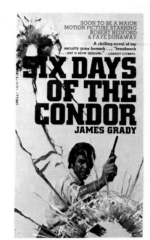

Then there are the times when the film is cancelled after the novelization has already been written. After a few such experiences, the tie-in editor finds himself in the awkward position of trying to explain to the film people that, yes, he wants to make a deal and get started on the book very early in the planning stages—but he'd rather not commit himself before the film becomes a sure thing. This is awkward because as everyone knows, a film is never a sure thing until the cameras start rolling, and sometimes not even then.

Even today, when agents and studios have become much more alert to the potential of tie-ins and prices have escalated in just the past year or so to the point where it's a safe rule of thumb to add at least one and sometimes two zeros to an advance, the publishers and the film people continue to complain about each other—and they're both right. However, new and mutually productive ways and means are being sought—and found—for them to work effectively in tandem.

It Started with "Love Story"

According to Robert Silverstein, a one-time editor at Dell and Bantam who also worked in the film business and now heads his own publishing company, Quicksilver, the change in attitude on everyone's part began with a writer who himself developed material bought for filming into a hugely successful novel, namely Erich Segal, with "Love Story." "Before then, although the screenwriters contractually had first crack at writing the novelization, they invariably turned it down because there wasn't enough money in it," Silverstein says. "But because of the success of this book, the higher figures that reprinters began paying for material in general, and the fact that the independent producers who were increasingly dominating the business wanted total control of the product from its inception to its release and to that end were retaining rights and approaching publishers directly,

tie-ins began to be regarded with new eyes.'' Around that time, Silverstein himself made a tie-in deal that remains the largest ever for a straight tie-in and he nabbed it right out from under both the studio in question and the publishers who were trying to buy it. As the editors dickered with various executives at United Artists for rights to the screenplay of ''Last Tango in Paris,'' he convinced UA's merchandising executive (who apparently unbeknownst to the other executives autonomously held the rights) that the book should come out as both a novel and a screenplay, and that he was the man to package the property. His deal made, he then held an auction, with a six-figure joint venture floor, and Dell emerged the winner by offering a guaranteed nonreturnable advance in excess of $250,000 against 50% of the publishing profits. At the time there was some flak about the low advance paid UA by Quicksilver, not to mention yelps of outrage from publishers who felt they'd been led down the garden path by the studio, but since UA wound up collecting about $250,000 on its share of the royalties from the publishing proceeds—100 times its original advance, according to Silverstein—and since the incident startled a lot of people on both sides of the fence into seeing potential that had been hitherto overlooked, everyone eventually came out ahead. Including Mr. Silverstein, who went on to package and sell ''Deep Throat'' to Dell in another successful arrangement.

A Failed Best Seller

''Tango'' and ''Throat'' were published in softcover tie-ins well after the films had been released, whereas ''Love Story'' appeared—at least to the eye of the public—in the traditional way, as a hardcover best seller first and then as a film with a softcover tie-in featuring a photo of Ali MacGraw and Ryan O'Neal on the cover. It had in fact been written as a screenplay first. This was novelizing at its most gloriously successful, particularly since the book and the film were hits independently and therefore neither could be accused of riding on the coattails of the other. Inevitably the approach has had its imitators. Some, such as Herman Raucher's "Summer of '42," succeeded fairly well; others, like Marc Norman's "Oklahoma Crude," and the recent "Harry and Tonto" by Josh Greenfeld and Paul Mazursky, didn't really make it. In their handling of "Oklahoma Crude," Columbia's Peter Guber and Rosilyn Heller consciously set out to try and repeat the success of "Love Story." It worked up to a point; publishing rights were sold to Dutton, Marc Norman wrote the novel, and Dutton sold the softcover rights to Popular Library for $190,000—roughly five and a half times what the prepublication sale of the softcover rights to "Love Story" had brought, incidentally, and certainly a whole lot more than a straight tie-in sale would have brought. But the attempt to create a best seller prior to and independent of the film failed, and since the film was not a box office hit, the tie-in didn't work either way.

In Los Angeles entertainment lawyer Tom Pollack's opinion, "Crude" was a definite setback to those who had thought "Love Story" would start a new era of partnership between the publishing industry and the motion picture industry. "Although there was a lot of talk about it, if you look at the best seller lists over the past couple of years, you see no indication of it. Softcover publishers are still benefitting a lot more from tie-ins than hardcover publishers," he says. But a few innovative behind-the-scenes deals were made during this period: Doubleday got involved in sponsoring the development of the screenplay for one of its books, "The Parallax View"; Bantam and Paramount cofinanced a book to be written by Fredric Morton on a subject suggested by Peter Bart, then vice-president in charge of production at Paramount, in a deal giving Paramount first crack at the film rights; and Universal initiated "The Bottom Line," a book about a business convention, with author Fletcher Knebel at Doubleday. For the most part, however, tie-ins were handled pretty much as usual, with only an occasional flurry of rumors that film studios were spending thousands of dollars buying up copies of books they owned at key bookstores to get them on best seller lists—rumors that have cropped up repeatedly over the years and are no doubt true in some cases.

Occasionally there was an attempt to market a novelization a la "Love Story"; in one case, a half-written novelization of the script for Robert Mitchum's upcoming film "Yacuza" was sent around to several hardcover editors but those who saw it passed on it, feeling it would have its best life in softcover. Their decision may have been colored by the fact that as novelizations enter the big time and are presented as hardcover entities unto themselves, they are suffering a certain degree of blacklash, at least from critics. In a recent pan of the hardcover novelization of "Harry and Tonto," *Los Angeles Times* book reviewer Digby Diehl said: "Book critics rarely ever deign to recognize the existence of a 'novelization,' much less go to the trouble of complaining about it." He went on to hypothesize "that neither Greenfeld nor Mazursky had the slightest interest in presenting this story as a book when they began working on the screenplay. The entire conception is cinematic. But somewhere, someone had the not very original idea that a lot of preproduction

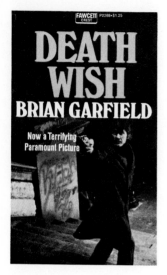

publicity could be drummed out of a novelization that would eventually help the movie." Another example of this attitude can be found in the *New York Times Book Review* critique of William Goldman's new novel "Marathon Man," which had been warmly received elsewhere. Taking tacit note of the fact that Goldman is a very well-known screenwriter, the reviewer goes beyond judging the book itself to describe his suspicion that "this is one of those cases where the screenplay is father to the novel. Part of the promotional package as it were."

Movie People Out East

From the looks of things, however, reviewers are going to be presented with more and more novels which have evolved from cooperative ventures between publishers and film companies. Movie people seem permanently ensconced at the Sherry-Netherland or the Park Lane, searching for "fresh material" or "first looks" and calling on publishers and agents. One of the first things Twentieth Century-Fox did, for example, with their recently appointed creative affairs executive Ronda Gōmez-Quiñones was to send her off to New York for a three-week round of mingling with the New York literary set. "It was," she says, "mainly to establish contacts." Which is just one indication of the weight being given to having open lines into the world of the written word.

Writers Keep the Rights

Peter Bart, after leaving Paramount to form Bart/Palevsky Productions, kept his lines open and bought, as one of his projects, an outline for a new novel, "Prometheus One," by the authors of "The Glass Inferno," Thomas Scortia and Frank Robinson. Believing that "the novelizing scheme is best used for developing material," Bart hired them to write a first-draft screenplay, with the understanding that they would then write the novel while another writer was brought in to polish the screenplay. The writer's polish was in turn sent to Scortia and Robinson for mulling over in terms of the novel. And the fact that it was Richard Parks at Curtis Brown who sold the outline of the proposed book to Peter Bart illustrates another change in the tie-in business: the increasing tendency of authors and their agents or producers to withhold publication rights from the studio and handle them themselves. According to William Grose, executive editor of Dell, "with only one exception ('Waldo Pepper' by William Goldman), we haven't done a tie-in where the studio controlled the rights for the past few years. On the bigger deals the writer is keeping the rights and writing the novelization himself or at least having a say in who does; either way, he's taking more of an interest, which is good." Grose also points out that since many talented writers are writing for films these days, publishers are looking to them as a good source for material for novels, period. "It could make a lot of sense to buy the novelization rights to just a treatment for a reasonable sum, say $7500, get a novelizer and pay him the same, and wind up with a good softcover original for $15,000 from something that might never see the light of day as a movie. In a sense, we are doing with paperback originals what television is doing with movies-of-the-week—marketing strong topical stories that can be encapsulated in a line or two.'' He, like other editors, is also buying novelization rights to films or movies-of-the-week well after they've been shown, to publish them not as tie-ins but simply as original paperbacks intended to stand on their own.

At Avon Judy Weber notes that ''one of the biggest changes in the past year or so is that there are more and more TV tie-ins and people are recognizing the importance of them.'' Even a one-shot television show with high ratings can sell large quantities of books. Ms. Weber cites ''Go Ask Alice,'' a preexisting book which had 308,000 copies in print in softcover when the television show first aired in January, 1973, six months after its publication and then spiralled to an additional 1,709,000 in the 10 months following it. She also mentioned the after-the-fact novelization of ''Sunshine,'' which came out, novelized by a distinguished writer, Norma Klein, with a first printing of 800,000 more than six months after the show was aired in November of 1973 and is now up to over 1,000,000 copies, a testament to the long-term sales effectiveness that a television special can have on a book tie-in. Bantam's ''The Autobiography of Miss Jane Pittman'' provides another case in point. Its first printing, in June of 1972, consisted of 160,000 copies; in January of 1973, when the Emmy-winning CBS television special was aired, there were still fewer than 200,000 copies out. But between January and November of 1974, 550,000 copies of the special tie-in edition were printed and shipped, 150,000 of them to coincide with the rerun aired on November 3.

Television has also boosted the book business in that bids from networks and TV producers have of late become competitive with those paid by film companies. And a new market is opening up for certain books that could not carry a feature film but work very well when adapted for television. Film director Ulu Grosbard points out that ''it used to be that if a book was dead for films it was just dead. Now, thanks to TV, that's not so.''

The tie-in boom is no surprise to Richard Fischoff at Warner Paperback Library. It is his view that people aren't essentially readers any more, that except for famous best-selling or category authors people don't buy by author, and that reading has become a time-killing activity rather than an avocation. This means that people who buy books are likely to be attracted by extra-literary factors such as eye-catching graphics, a photo of a star, a familiar logo—some recognition factor from a non-linear medium that makes the book stand out from the welter of other books on the stands. To Fischoff, tie-ins provide a way to get people back to enjoying reading. ''Also prices for tie-ins are going up,'' he adds, ''because of the competitive situation in the softcover industry. Whereas it used to be one or two houses bidding for a property, now half a dozen are going after the same thing. It's no longer a buyer's market. Agents, motion picture companies, publishers, writers, actors and producers—everyone seems to have realized there is pie now and they all want a piece of it.'' Or, as Patrick O'Connor, editor-in-chief of Popular Library, succinctly puts it, ''In the old days, they wanted us . . .desperately. And now, we want them . . .desperately.''

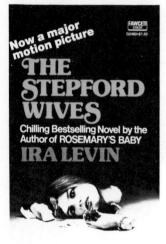

Killing the Golden Goose

In fact, some feel that the market may already be stretched to the breaking point. At Bantam, both editorial director Marc Jaffe and tie-in editor Wendy Broad feel that different criteria have to be used in judging tie-ins and potential best sellers. "We're gambling on the success of a film and that's quite different from gambling on a finished manuscript or an author whose work is proven in the marketplace," says Jaffe. Dell has come up with some pretty whopping advances lately, for "French Connection II" (a reputed $75,000 for a straight novelization), and a couple in which the advances will amount to over six figures if the novelizations come out in hardcover first, "Macho" by Richard Nash and "Ghost Boat" by George Simpson and Neal Burger. But although Grose states categorically that Dell is interested in publishing only the tie-ins they think will be really big, he warns that "if the advances and royalties continue to increase, it'll kill the goose that laid the golden egg. It now costs $25,000 to $45,000 for the tie-in that used to cost from $5000 to $10,000 and obviously not all tie-ins are going to be profitable at those prices."

Other houses take a cooler view of the inflationary spiral in the tie-in business. At New American Library, Robert Haynie says: "Rather than concentrating on novelizations, we've always given a lot of thought to what kind of movie a book will make; and we've been lucky in that books that we've bought reprint rights to have often subsequently become films." He sees no reason to change this approach. And Leona Nevler, publisher of the Fawcett Book Division, concurs: "You can strike it lucky but you can also have a lot of problems with tie-ins. We're primarily interested in books that can stand on their own as books."

Bypassing the Agents

Charles Bloch, Bantam's West Coast editorial representative, feels that a lot depends on whether agents continue to find it worthwhile to make the effort of dealing with publishing rights. Now that it's becoming big business worldwide— "The Sting," for example, has been translated into eight foreign languages—and now that so many factors can be involved (Does Paul Newman get cover approval? How exactly does the Writer's Guild stipulate that the screenwriter's credit should read on the cover? Who handles Charles MacArthur's estate when tying in with a remake of "The Front Page"? And so on . . .), this effort can be considerable. One studio, Universal, has decided to buck the trend to diversification and make dealing with publishers a full-time occupation for Stanley Newman, in a newly created position as vice-president and head of MCA Publishing. "Tie-ins are very complex to publish," he concedes. "But we think it's a big enough business and important enough so that we are pulling in all the rights and dealing [directly with publishers instead of dealing]through agents. Before, when the studios viewed tie-ins as strictly a merchandizing and licensing business and not a publishing operation, they just sat back and let the payments come in without trying to make it easier for anybody. The publishers did most of the work. Even the agents were not involved or interested. Then the agents started filling the gap that existed between film companies and publishers. However, what we are doing is offering a single point of communication for publishers with questions about any aspect of publishing or rights. In addition, we are actually creating books which would not otherwise have existed; when, for example, it's not possible to publish the screenplay or the novelization.'' Two cases in point: NAL's ''Earthquake, the Story of a Movie,'' which is essentially a rack-size variation of a theater program, and ''Airport '75,'' a souvenir 8 x 11-inch magazine published by Award Books with Universal and distributed by Select Magazines, with some copies being sold in the theaters.

Regarding remuneration for such cooperation, Newman feels that ''if we contribute to the success of the book, we want to participate in proportion to that success. On the other hand, if our product is not successful and the publisher therefore doesn't benefit, we don't want to be paid. We'll take the same risk as the publisher.'' What this amounts to is that in the case of a new tie-in edition of a previously published book—with a different title, perhaps, or a star's photo on the cover—Universal will not demand a flat fee for providing the tie-in art but will insist on a graduated royalty of, say, 1% on sales of from 100,000 to 250,000 copies, escalating beyond that up to 3%. Of course, he points out, there are exceptions, such as ''Jaws,'' out recently from Bantam and due in a tie-in edition in June, when the film is released. Where the book can obviously stand on its own, Universal is still willing to tie-in strictly for joint promotional purposes.

Like Fischoff, Newman commented on the importance of the instant recognition factor of a tie-in in selling books, especially in foreign countries. ''As the paperback business continues to develop in major non-English markets, tie-in books will be especially valuable. In fact, we are considering withholding world rights, taking less money originally and then selling off the rights country by country as we market our TV series or open our film in each country.''

Mel Bloom and Associates' Stuart Miller, a Los Angeles agent who handles a number of screenwriters, comments ruefully, ''I'm really surprised it took the studios so long to figure out that there is money to be made in tie-ins. Actually, they probably could make the most money by publishing the tie-ins themselves and then having them distributed by one of the big softcover houses, but the second best way is for them to control the rights and take a percentage. I don't like it, but I can't refute the logic of it. It's sound business on the part of the studio and there's nothing wrong in having a studio, which after all makes an enormous investment in a film, participate in the revenue that accrues from a novelization.'' He figures the other studios will more than likely follow Universal's lead very shortly. ''It would only take one picture that has a tie-in that really works, given that the studio has some significant piece of the profits, to pay for a tie-in operation like Universal's for a year or more, so they'd be foolish not to do it,'' he reasons.

Overestimating the Market?

However, he has a word of caution for the studios. ''Studio executives are tuned in to a whole other profit picture and because of their frame of reference and their eagerness to jump into the novelization game, they may be overestimating what the market will bear.'' He cites as an example a deal he himself just made for

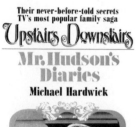

one of his screenwriters in which, over and above his fee for writing the screenplay, the writer—but only if the film is made—gets paid an advance in six figures against two-thirds of all publishing revenues, even though someone else will novelize the book. ''So if the advance is, say, $100,000, the studio has to make $150,000 from the publishing revenue just to break even and that's tough to do. With numbers like that, even a successful tie-in becomes risky.''

So far, the tie-in boom seems to be too new to have affected the Writer's Guild's rules and regulations governing publication rights. In fact, the West Coast branch seems virtually unaware of the situation, and close examination of the Guild's Theatrical and Television Film Basic Agreement, written in prose that is nearly impenetrable to the layman's eye, yields only confusion since the rules it contains bear no resemblance to how such deals are actually handled. As Stuart Miller says, ''The Writer's Guild has structured the rules dealing with the selling of a novelization so that not only do they not make any sense, but it would in fact become difficult to make a deal if you followed them.'' He conjectures that ''probably what happened is that somewhere along the line in some contract negotiation between the Writer's Guild and the Producer's Association, someone must have raised the issue of paperback novelizations and in those days the studio didn't care and the Guild clearly didn't understand the mechanics of it, so they just came up with a few guidelines to cover the writer as best they could and let it go at that.'' There have been no changes in these regulations to keep up with what's happening but it's safe to say that at some point—probably in 1976 during their next contract negotiations—there will have to be.

Tie-Ins for the Schools

Another area where success has not yet bred change is in the tie-ins marketed through the Scholastic and Xerox Education Publications (formerly A.E.P.) book clubs and magazines. According to Michael Hobson, publisher of Scholastic's book club division, ''We've been enormously successful with movie and TV tie-ins. They're probably our best-selling titles. The nicest situation for us is when there is a preexisting good book, like 'The Prime of Miss Jean Brodie,' that is made into a movie which enables us to really sell the book, although we've also done a good many novelizations, especially of Disney pictures, and a few screenplays, like our own edition of 'Cabaret,' which we bought from Random House and published with a movie tie-in cover. In other cases, we just buy copies of outside publishers' books to sell through our clubs.'' These club sales can climb to over a million copies (''The Love Bug'' and ''Sounder,'' for example). Strict editorial judgment is exercised as to suitability, for this audience and school use, of such books as ''The Godfather'' and ''The Exorcist'' has been considered beyond the pale. Although, according to Barbara McCall, managing editor of the paperback book club program at Xerox, ''we sometimes ask a publisher to make an abridgment excising offensive passages, as we did in the case of 'The Glass Inferno.'''

The Scholastic and Xerox magazines run either synopses or adapted and very condensed versions of scripts such as "Jeremy" and "Where the Lilies Bloom," the theory being that not only does this work as a good promotional device for the film but also that children with reading problems seem to like to read these simplified screenplays, so that teachers use them as teaching aids in classrooms. "Up until this year," says Katherine Robinson, editor of *Scope* at Scholastic, "we've had no trouble getting permission to use scripts and we've paid nothing. But now that is beginning to change—although when we were asked to pay, we refused." The only instances in which they are willing to pay to novelize a script is when it is a film that was released some time ago, such as "Cool Hand Luke," and therefore the book has no promotional value for the film.

Creative approaches are being taken to avenues of cooperative promotion these days on many levels. One film—an atypical one, admittedly—has two tie-ins, of sorts, namely, "The Towering Inferno." Just as Warner's and Fox solved the dilemma of having each paid huge sums for different books about the same kind of disaster—Richard Martin Stern's "The Tower" at McKay, and Scortia and Robinson's "The Glass Inferno" at Doubleday—by joining forces and coproducing a screenplay that combined the two narratives, so Warner Paperback Library and Pocket Books, the two softcover houses which bought rights to the books for sizable sums in each case, each have run cover copy lines indicating that the Irwin Allen film is based in part on their book.

Cover Art and Movie Ads

A less quirky example of intramural cooperation can be seen in the way Max Ehrlich's "The Reincarnation of Peter Proud" is being promoted by the company that made the film, Bing Crosby Productions. Arthur Manson, BCP's executive vice-president in charge of sales and marketing, has been involved from the minute the property was bought for filming, which was after it had been sold by Bantam to Bobbs-Merrill but before it was published. BCP helped design the hardcover book jacket so that it would coordinate with future movie art, put money into the hardcover advertising campaign, placed trade ads for the book in *Variety* and the *Hollywood Reporter* and designed a 30-second television commercial using a clip from the film to advertise the book in eight big cities. Prints of this commercial were also made available to theater exhibitors so that while the book was being launched the commercial was being shown on 500 screens all over the country, with a free book given to each exhibitor who ran it. In addition, Manson attended Bobbs-Merrill's sales conference, then followed up by writing an individual letter to about a thousand key accounts to tell them about the film and offer them a chance to see it free when it opens in their city. (He got a whopping 90% response to this offer, incidentally.) Further, every copy of the first edition of the hardcover contained a coupon which could be sent to Bobbs-Merrill in exchange for a free ticket to the film.

All of this adds up to a lot of cross-pollinating going on, and how fertile it will all prove remains to be seen. But right now; on almost any given day New York editors can be observed digging into the guacamole dip at the Polo Lounge in Beverly Hills, while jarringly tanned producers and creative heads of studios try to catch the waiter's eye at the King Cole Bar in New York as they all hotly pursue the same objective: developing and exploiting material from which they both can benefit.

Bibliography

The book industry is a specialized area which seldom receives the serious attention it deserves, outside of specialists in the field. As Nancy Hardin shows in her article, there is great affinity today between the producers of books and the producers of other popular culture media, such as the movies. One of the running debates occurring in the industry is the result of a series of articles by John P. Dessauer who suggests that book publishers should cut back in production in certain areas because there are just too many books being produced today. Dessauer, contributing editor of *Publishers Weekly*, published his conclusions in August, September and October of 1974. Three critical responses to Dessauer's thesis appear in *Publisher's Weekly* (Dec. 2, 1974), pp. 42-45, including Dessauer's rebuttal. These articles provide useful information to students interested in current practices in the book publishing field. *Publishers Weekly* should be read consistently in order to keep abreast of changes in the field.

On The Future of Movies

By Pauline Kael

Sometime during [1973], a number of the most devoted moviegoers stopped going to the movies. I say "a number" because I have no idea how many are actually involved, but I keep meeting people—typically, men in their late twenties and early thirties—who say, "You know, I just don't have the impulse to go to a movie anymore," or "There aren't any movies anymore, are there?" The interest in pictures has left these people almost overnight; they turned off as suddenly as they'd turned on, and, since they no longer care to go, they feel that there's nothing to see. It was no accident that the Americans walked off with most of the top awards at Cannes [in 1974]. Right now, American movies—not the big hits but many of the movies that Hollywood considers failures—are probably the best in the world. No country rivals us in the diversity of skilled, talented filmmakers, but there are few lines for the sorts of films that young audiences were queuing up for a couple of years ago. They talked fervently then about how they loved movies; now they feel there can't be anything good going on, even at the movies.

Pauline Kael is a film critic on *The New Yorker* and is author of numerous books of movie criticism. This article has been edited severely because of space considerations. It is edited from a larger article appearing in *The New Yorker* (Aug. 5, 1974). Students are advised to read the complete article. Reprinted with permission; copyright 1974 The New Yorker Magazine, Inc.

Whatever their individual qualities, such films as "Bonnie and Clyde," "The Graduate," "Easy Rider," "Five Easy Pieces," "Joe," "M*A*S*H," "Little Big Man," "Midnight Cowboy," and "They Shoot Horses, Don't They?" all helped to form the counterculture. The young, anti-draft, anti-Vietnam audiences that were "the film generation" might go to some of the same pictures that the older audience did, but not to those only. They were willing to give something fresh a chance, and they went to movies that weren't certified hits. They made modest—sometimes large—successes of pictures that had new, different perceptions. A movie like the tentative, fumbling ''Alice's Restaurant'' would probably be a flop now, because student audiences are no longer willing to look for feelings, to accept something suggestive and elliptical and go with the mood. Students accept the elliptical on records—the Joni Mitchell ''Court and Spark,'' say, and some of the more offbeat Carly Simon cuts—but not in movies. The subdued, fine-drawn ''McCabe & Mrs. Miller,'' which came out in 1971, managed to break even, but the soft-colored ''Thieves Like Us,'' the latest film by the same director, Robert Altman, has been seen by almost nobody. Those who might be expected to identify with Jeff Bridges in ''The Last American Hero'' are going to see Clint Eastwood in ''Magnum Force'' instead. They're going to the kind of slam-bang pictures that succeed with illiterate audiences in ''underdeveloped'' countries who are starved for entertainment. The almost voluptuously obsessive ''Mean Streets''—a film that one might have thought would be talked about endlessly—passed through college towns without causing a stir. The new generations of high-school and college students are going to movies that you can't talk about afterward—movies that are completely consumed in the theatre.

There is no way to estimate the full effect of Vietnam and Watergate on popular culture, but earlier films were predicated on an implied system of values which is gone now, except in the corrupt, vigilante form of a ''Dirty Harry'' or a ''Walking Tall.'' Almost all the current hits are jokes on the past, and especially on old films—a mixture of nostalgia and parody, laid on with a trowel. The pictures reach back in time, spoofing the past, jabbing at it. Nobody understands what contemporary heroes or heroines should be, or how they should relate to each other, and it's safer not to risk the boxoffice embarrassment of seriousness.

For many years, some of us alarmists have been saying things like ''Suppose people get used to constant visceral excitement—will they still respond to the work of artists?'' Maybe, owing partly to the national self-devaluation and partly to the stepped-up power of advertising, what we feared has come about. It's hardly surprising: how can people who have just been pummelled and deafened by ''The French Connection'' be expected to respond to a quiet picture? If , still groggy, they should stumble in to see George Segal in Irvin Kershner's ''Loving'' the next night, they'd think there was nothing going on in it, because it didn't tighten the screws on them. ''The Rules of the Game'' might seem like a hole in the screen. When ''The Getaway'' is double-billed with ''Mean Streets,'' it's no wonder that some people walk out on ''Mean Streets.'' Audiences like movies that do all the work for them—just as in the old days, and with an arm-twisting rubdown besides. College students don't appear to feel insulted (what's left to insult us?); they don't mind being banged over the head—the louder the better. They seem to enjoy seeing the performers whacked around, too; sloppy knockabout farce is the newest smash, and knockabout horror isn't far behind. People go for the obvious, the broad, the movies that don't ask them to feel anything. If a movie is a hit, that means practically guaranteed sensations—and sensations without feeling.

I often come out of a movie now feeling wiped out, desolate—and often it's a movie that the audience around me has reacted to noisily, as if it were having a high, great time—and I think I feel that way because of the nihilism in the atmosphere. It isn't intentional or philosophical nihilism; it's the kind one sometimes feels at a porn show—the way everyting is turned to dung, oneself included. A couple of years ago, I went with another film critic, a young man, to see a hard-core movie in the Broadway area, and there was a live stage show with it. A young black girl—she looked about seventeen but must have been older—did a strip and then danced naked. The theatre was small, and the girl's eyes, full of hatred, kept raking the customers' faces. I was the only other woman there, and each time her eyes came toward me, I had to look down; finally, I couldn't look up at all. The young critic and I sat in misery, unable to leave, since that would look like a put-down of her performance. We had to take the contempt with which she hid her sense of being degraded, and we shared in her degradation, too. Hits like "The Exorcist" give most of the audience just what it wants and expects, the way hard-core porn does. The hits have something in common: blatancy. They are films that *deliver*. They're debauches—their subject might almost be mindlessness and futurelessness. People in the audience want to laugh, and at pictures like "Enter the Dragon" and "Andy Warhol's Frankenstein" and "The Three Musketeers" and "Blazing Saddles" they're laughing at pandemonium and accepting it as the comic truth.

The counterculture films made corruption seem inevitable and hence something you learn to live with; the next step was seeing it as slapstick comedy and learning to enjoy it. For the fatalistic, case-hardened audience, absurdism has become the only acceptable point of view—a new complacency. In "The Three Musketeers," Richard Lester keeps his actors at a distance and scales the characters down to subnormal size; they're letching, carousing buffoons who don't care about anything but blood sport. The film isn't politically or socially abrasive; it's just "for fun." At showings of "Chinatown," the audience squeals with pleasure when Faye Dunaway reveals her incest. The success of "Chinatown"—with its beautifully structured script and draggy, overdeliberate direction—represents something dialectically new: nostalgia (for the thirties) openly turned to rot, and the *celebration* of rot. Robert Towne's script had ended with the detective (Jack Nicholson) realizing what horrors the Dunaway character had been through, and, after she killed her incestuous father, helping her daughter get to Mexico. But Roman Polanski seals the picture with his gargoyle grin; now evil runs rampant. The picture is compelling, but coldly, suffocatingly compelling. Polanski keeps so much of it in closeup that there's no air, no freedom to breathe; you don't care who is hurt, since everything is blighted. Life is a blood-red maze. Polanski may leave the story muddy and opaque, but he shoves the rot at you, and large numbers of people seem to find it juicy. Audiences now appear to accept as a view of themselves what in the movies of the past six or seven years counterculture audiences jeered at Americans for being—cynical materialists who cared for nothing but their own greed and lust. The nihilistic, coarse-grained movies are telling us that nothing matters to us, that we're all a bad joke.

It's becoming tough for a movie that isn't a big media-created event to find an audience, no matter how good it is. And if a movie has been turned into an event, it doesn't have to be good; an event—such as "Papillon"—draws an audience simply because it's an event. You don't expect Mount Rushmore to be a work of art, but if you're anywhere near it you have to go; "Papillon" is a movie Mount Rushmore, though it features only two heads. People no longer go to a picture just for itself, and ticket-buyers certainly aren't looking for the movie equivalent of "a good read." They want to be battered, to be knocked out—they want to get wrecked. They want what "everybody's talking about," and even if they don't like the picture—and some people didn't really care for "A Touch of Class," and some detested "The Three Musketeers," and many don't like "Blazing Saddles," either—they don't feel out of it. Increasingly, though, I've noticed that those who don't enjoy a big event-film feel out of it in another way. They wonder if there's something they're not getting—if the fault is theirs.

The public can't really be said to have rejected a film like "Payday," since the public never heard of it. If you don't know what a movie is and it plays at a theatre near you, you barely register it. "Payday" may not come at all; when the event strategy really works, as it has of late, the hits and the routine action films and horror films are all that get to most towns. And if a film turns up that hasn't had a big campaign, people assume it's a dog; you risk associating yourself with failure if you go to see Jon Voight in "Conrack" or Blythe Danner in the messed-up but still affecting "Lovin' Molly." When other values are rickety, the fact that something is selling gives it a primacy, and its detractors seem like spoilsports. The person who holds out against an event looks a loser: the minority is a fool. People are cynical about advertising, of course, but their cynicism is so all-inclusive now that they're indifferent, and so they're more susceptible to advertising than ever. If nothing matters anyway, why not just go where the crowd goes? That's a high in itself.

There are a few exceptions, but in general it can be said that the public no longer discovers movies, the public no longer makes a picture a hit. If the advertising for a movie doesn't build up an overwhelming desire to be part of the event, people just don't go. They don't listen to their own instincts, they don't listen to the critics—they listen to the advertising. Or, to put it more precisely, they do listen to their instincts, but their instincts are now controlled by advertising. It seeps through everything—talk shows, game shows, magazine and newspaper stories. Museums organize retrospectives of a movie director's work to coördinate with the opening of his latest film, and publish monographs paid for by the movie companies. College editors travel at a movie company's expense to see its big new film and to meet the director, and directors preview their new pictures at colleges. The public-relations event becomes part of the national consciousness. You don't hear anybody say, "I saw the most wonderful movie you never heard of;" when you hear people talking, it's about the same blasted movie that everybody's going to—the one that's flooding the media. Yet even the worst cynics still like to think that "word of mouth" makes hits. And the executives who set up the machinery of manipulation love to believe that the public—the public that's sitting stone-dead in front of its TV sets— spontaneously discovered their wonderful movie. If it's a winner, they say it's the people's choice. But, in the TV age, when people say they're going to see "Walking Tall" because they've "heard" it's terrific, that rarely means a friend has told them; it means they've picked up signals from the atmosphere. It means "Walking Tall" has been plugged so much that every cell in a person's body tells him he's got to see it. Nobody ever says that it was the advertising that made him vote for a particular candidate, yet there is considerable evidence that in recent decades the Presidential candidates who spent the most money always won. They were the people's choice. Advertising is a form of psychological warfare that in popular culture, as in politics, is becoming harder to fight with aboveboard weapons. It's becoming damned near invincible.

The ludicrous "Mame" or the limp, benumbed "The Great Gatsby" may not make as much money as the producing companies hoped for, but these pictures don't fail abjectly, either. They're hits. If Hollywood executives still believe in word of mouth, it's because the words come out of their own mouths.

The businessmen have always been in control of film production; now advertising puts them, finally, on top of public reaction as well. They can transcend the content and the quality of a film by advertising. The new blatancy represents the triumph—for the moment, at least—of the businessmen's taste and the businessmen's ethic. Traditionally, movies were thought linked to dreams and illusions, and to pleasures that went way beyond satisfaction. Now the big ones are stridently illusionless, for a public determined not to be taken in. Audiences have become "realists" in the manner of businessmen who congratulate themselves for being realists: they believe only in what gives immediate gratification. It's got to be right there—tangible, direct, basic, in their laps. The movie executives were shaken for a few years; they didn't understand what made a film a counterculture hit. They're happy to be back on firm ground with "The Sting." Harmless, inoffensive. Plenty of plot but no meanings. Not even any sex to worry about. . . . The company that has "The Sting" doesn't worry about a real sendoff for "The Sugarland Express": where are the big stars? The company with "The Exorcist" doesn't give much thought to a campaign for "Mean Streets": some of the executives don't find it "satisfying," so they're sure the public won't. The movie companies used to give all their pictures a chance, but now they'll put two or three million, or even five, into selling something they consider surefire, and a token—a pittance—into the others. And when an unpublicized picture fails they can always cover their tracks by blaming the director. "There was nothing we could do for it," the executives in charge of advertising always say, and once they have doomed a picture, who can prove them wrong?

If the company men don't like a picture, or are nervous about its chances, or just resent the director's wanting to do something he cares about (instead of taking the big assignments they believe in), they do minimal advertising, telling him, "Let's wait for the reviews," or "We'll see how the reviewers like it," and then, even if the reviews are great, they say, "But the picture isn't doing business. Why should we throw away money on it?" And if he mentions the reviews, they say, "Listen, the critics have never meant anything. You know that. Why waste money? If people don't want to go, you can't force them to buy tickets."

There's a natural war in Hollywood between the businessmen and the artists. It's based on drives that may go deeper than politics or religion: on the need for status, and warring dreams. The entrepreneur class in the arts is a relatively late social development; there were impresarios earlier, but it was roughly a hundred years ago, when the arts began to be commercialized for a large audience, that the mass-culture middleman was born. He functions as a book publisher, as a theatrical producer, as a concert manager, as a rock promoter, but the middleman in the movie world is probably more filled with hatred for the artists he traffics in than the middleman in any other area. The movie entrepreneur is even more of a self-made man than the others; he came out of nowhere. He has to raise—and risk—more money, and he stands to gain more. In a field with no traditions, he is more of a gambler and less of an aesthete than entrepreneurs in the other arts. . . .

The hatred of the moneyman for the ungovernable artist is based on a degradation that isn't far from that stripper's hatred of the audience—furious resentment of the privileged people who, as he sees it, have never had to stoop to do the things he has done. As in Mordecai Richler's exultant novel "The Apprenticeship of Duddy Kravitz" (which really enables one to understand what makes Sammy run), and the teeming, energetic Canadian film based on it, the entrepreneur is, typically, a man who has always been treated like dirt. And even after he's fought his way up, finagling like crazy every step of the way, a profligate director with the world at his feet may not only threaten that solvency but still treat him like dirt, as in Peter Viertel's thinly disguised account, in the novel "White Hunter, Black Heart," of the relations of John Huston and Sam Spiegel during the making of "The African Queen." There are few directors who feel such disdain, fewer still who would express it so nakedly, but the moneymen keep looking for signs of it: they tap phones, they turn employees into sneaks and spies—all to get proof of the disloyalty of those ingrate artists. It doesn't help if the artists like the tough bosses personally—if they prize the unconcealed wiliness or the manic, rude drive. In Richler's later novel "St. Urbain's Horseman," the now rich Duddy Kravitz appears as a minor character. When someone assures Duddy that his blond actress wife loves him, Duddy is exasperated: "What are you talking, she loves me? Who in the hell could love Duddy Kravitz?" Duddy's view of himself doesn't leave much of a basis for friendship, and any affection the artist may feel disintegrates as soon as the businessman uses his power to control the artist's work. The artist's crime is caring less for profits than for what he wants to do; the caring is an insult and a threat. The war of the businessmen against the artists is the war of the powerful against the powerless, based on the hatred of those who can't for those who can, and in return the hatred of those who can for those who won't let them.

The producers' complaint about the hothead director who puts up a fight to try something different is "He's self-destructive. He's irresponsible. You can't do business with him." And they make him suffer for it. The artists in Hollywood are objects of ridicule because they're trying to work as artists. When a gifted director is broke and needs to work, the producers stick him on a project that is compromised from the start, and then the picture is one more failure to be held against him. They frustrate him at every turn because he doesn't respect them, and he is humiliated by men he doesn't even respect. The producers feel secure with the directors and actors who don't have ideas of their own, who will take jobs because they need to work and don't really care what they do. Those are the ones the producers call "artists with discipline."

An actor or a director can become an "artist with discipline" when he has a huge box-office hit, and his reputation for discipline will soar if, like Paul Newman or Robert Redford, he has a string of hits. Actually, to the moneymen discipline means success plus a belief in success. Coppola isn't called disciplined, despite the success of "The Godfather," because he wants to work on his own projects (such as "The Conversation"), but George Roy Hill ("Butch Cassidy and the Sundance Kid," "Slaughterhouse Five," "The Sting") is disciplined, because he believes in big-name, big-star projects. Peter Yates ("Bullitt," "John and Mary") is considered a man you can do business with, despite a flop like "Murphy's War" and the far from successful "The Hot Rock" and "The Friends of Eddie Coyle;" his flops aren't held against him, because he believes in the same kind of projects that the moneymen do and he doesn't try to do anything *special* with those projects. His latest, "For Pete's Sake," probably won't bring in much of a bundle, but it's a model of Hollywood "disipline."

Peter Yates's lack of distinction, like the veteran Richard Fleischer's, is a proof of trustworthiness. The moneymen want a director who won't surprise them. They're scared of a man like Altman, because they just don't know what he'll do on a picture; they can't trust him to make it resemble the latest big hit. They want solid imitations, pictures that reek of money spent and money to come, pictures that look safe—like those Biblical epics that came rumbling off the assembly lines in the fifties. Twentieth Century-Fox and Warner Brothers . . .jointly produc[ed] a burning-skyscraper picture, "The Towering Inferno," with Steve McQueen, Paul Newman, William Holden, Jennifer Jones, Robert Wagner, Fred Astaire, Richard Chamberlain, and other assorted big names. It's Grand Hotel in flames at last. Universal, for starters, has signed up Anne Bancroft and George C. Scott for "The Hindenburg," described as "a multilayered drama with a gallery of international characters." In other words, Grand Hotel in flames in the sky. Every couple of years, the American movie public is said to crave something. Now it's calamity, and already the wave of apocalyptic movies—which aren't even here yet—is being analyzed in terms of our necrophilia. The studio heads are setting up disaster epics like kids reaching hand over hand up a baseball bat—all because of the success of "The Poseidon Adventure," which probably had about as much to do with a public interest in apocalypse as Agatha Christie's old "Ten Little Indians" had. I doubt whether there's a single one of the directors mounting these disaster specials— becoming commanders-in-chief in an idiot war—who wouldn't infinitely rather be working on something else. By the time the public is gorged with disasters and the epics begin to flop, the studio heads will have fastened on another get-rich-quick gimmick (pirate capers are said to be on the agenda), and the people who work for them will lose a few more years of what might have been their creative lives. The producers gamble on the public's wanting more of whatever is a hit, and since they *all* gamble on that, the public is always quickly surfeited, but the failures of the flaccid would-be hits never anger the producers the way the failures of the films that someone really fought for do. The producers want those films to fail; they often make them fail. A Sam Peckinpah film, an Altman film, a Kershner film—the executives get pleasure out of seeing those films fail. It's a *punishment* of the artist.

Since all the businessmen's energy goes into strategy and manipulation, they can outfox the artists damn near every time; that's really the business they're in. Their right of "final cut"—one of the great symbolic terms in moviemaking—gives them the chance to chop up the film of a director who has angered them by doing it his own way; they'll mutilate the picture trying to remove the complexities he battled to put in. They love to play God with other people's creations. Movie after movie is mangled, usually by executives' last-minute guesses about what the public wants. When they've finished, they frequently can't do anything with the pictures but throw them away. That's their final godlike act—an act easy for them to live with, because they always have the director to blame. To them, the artist is the outsider; he's not a member of the family, to be protected. A few years ago, when word was out in the industry that Brando didn't mean anything at the box office, the producer David Merrick fired him from a picture; I asked an executive connected with the production what Brando had done. "Nothing," he said. "Brando was working hard, and he was coöperative with everyone. But he suggested some ways to improve the script; they were good suggestions—the script was a mess. But legally that was interference, and Merrick could fire Brando and collect on the insurance" "But why?" I persisted. He shrugged at my ignorance. "What could make David Merrick bigger than firing Marlon Brando?" he said. . . .

A reviewer who pans a producer's picture is just one more person telling him he has no taste. When the reviewers praise movies that are allowed to die, the moneyman's brute instincts are confirmed, and the reviewers' impotence gives him joy. "Why must we sit back and allow the critics to determine if a film is acceptable as a consumer product?" Frank Yablans, the president of Paramount, [recently] asked. . . . He was speaking to some two hundred people who work in television, explaining to them that word of mouth, which can defeat downbeat reviews, will be Paramount's target. A reviewer speaks out once, or maybe twice. The advertisers are an invisible force pounding at the public day after day. Unfavorable reviews are almost never powerful enough to undo the saturation publicity. Besides, curiosity about an event like "The Exorcist" is a big factor; as the woman quoted in *Variety* said, "I want to see what everybody is throwing up about."

People often make analogies between the world of live theatre and the world of movies, and raise the question "Don't movie critics have too much power?" But in movies it's the businessmen who have the power. A reviewer's words can't be heard above the din unless they're amplified in the ads—which usually means reduced to a short, exclamatory quote and repeated incessantly. But that's only if the reviewer provided a quote for a picture that the company "has high hopes for;" if it's a picture that the company has lost interest in, there will be a few halfhearted ads, with apathetically selected quotes. Raves from even the dozen most influential papers and magazines can't make a success of "Mean Streets" if the company doesn't construct a campaign around those raves. The public indifference is a result of something that starts at the top of the movie company and filters down. Five years ago—even two years ago— a handful of reviewers could help persuade people to give a small or unheralded film a chance, but not now. The reviewers spoke to that audience which has lost the impulse to go to movies. The demise of ''the film generation'' means a sharp break with the past, since there won't be anything like that mass of youth—the Second World War babies reaching maturity—again. Because of its styles of hair and dress and manner, it was an identifiable generation; the members tuned in together for the last time at ''American Graffiti''—the pop-comics view of their own adolescence, before they became the counterculture. Now the links are mostly broken and they're the aging young, tuned out.

The younger audience—high-school and college students—grew up with the rating system. As kids, they couldn't escape to the movies, the way their parents did, and so movies weren't an important part of their lives (though television was). When *they* say they love movies, they mean the old movies that they're just discovering, and the new hits. Even the sub-teens want the events; they were born into sixties cynicism and saturation advertising. They've never known anything but the noise and the frantic atmosphere; they think it's a cop-out if a movie cuts away from mayhem and doesn't show them the gore. They loved ''Jesus Christ Superstar'' (a masochistic revel for eight-year-olds), and they're eager to be part of ''The Sting.'' and ''Blazing Saddles.'' They're saturated.

The students now who discover movies in college and want to get into film production have a different outlook from the young counterculture filmmakers of the sixties. They're not interested in getting into movie work in order to change movies; they just want to get into movie work. A young film student expressed anger to me about Elia Kazan, who had given a lecture at his university. Kazan had said that the studios wouldn't finance the subjects he was interested in, and offered him projects he couldn't face doing. The student, without a shade of sympathy for those caught in this basic Hollywood trap, said, ''How can we listen to him? We would do anything to break in, and he says he's turning down projects!'' Students have little interest in why a person refuses to direct the forty-sixth dope-heist picture or a romp about sprightly, beguiling swindlers; they don't care to hear some director say that he turned down ''The Exorcist.'' A hit makes a director a hero. A critic who speaks at a college now is almost certain to be asked such questions as ''How many times do you see a movie before writing your critique?'' and ''Do you take notes?'' The students are really asking, ''How do you do it? How did you get to be a film critic?'' They sometimes used to ask, ''What do you think of Academy Awards?''—a question that was a sure laugh-getter from an audience that anticipated a tart rejoinder. Now they ask, ''What [or who] do you think will win the Oscars this year?'' And they really want to know the answer. Celebrity and success are so big on campus that the Academy Awards are discussed as if they were a perfectly respectable academic issue.

Stardom is success made manifest, success in human form, and , naturally, the yes-sayers are, in general, the biggest stars. College students are impressed and contemptuous at the same time. Can one imagine any picture so reactionary or vile that it would diminish Clint Eastwood's standing at a university? Even a reputation for corruption—for being willing to do anything for money—increases a star's stature, and the money gained gives him power and standing that are admired in a way the no-sayer's intransigence isn't, especially if his intransigence puts him out of the scene. There is nothing a star can do now that would really disgrace him. "Celebrity" has destroyed the concept of disgrace: scandal creates celebrity, and public misbehavior enhances it. Maybe "The Sting" is such a whooping hit because it's really a celebration of celebrity and stardom; it's not about anything but the golden yes-yes images of Redford and Newman. It doesn't need sex; it's got the true modern sex appeal—success.

In Los Angeles this spring [1974], busloads of high-school students were brought in to listen to a Best-Sellers Panel composed of Helen Gurley Brown, Garson Kanin, Jacqueline Susann, and William Friedkin on the subject of how it feels to sell fifteen million books or to gross a hundred and twenty-five million dollars on a movie. From all accounts, there were no impolite questions, and no one made a rude noise when Kanin ("Tracy and Hepburn") said, "We have to recognize that the public is smarter than we are. As individuals, one by one, perhaps no. But when that thousand-headed monster sits out there in the auditorium or sits reading your book of fiction, suddenly that mass audience is what the late Moss Hart called 'an idiot genius.' " This conceit of the successful—their absolute conviction that the crap that is sold is magically superior to the work that didn't sell—is the basis for the entrepreneurs' self-righteousness. The public has nothing to gain from believing this (and everything to lose), and yet the public swallows it. . . .

There's no way for movies to be saved from premature senility unless the artists finally abandon the whole crooked system of Hollywood bookkeeping, with its kited budgets and trick percentages. Most directors are signed up for only one picture now, but after the deal is made the director gets the full de-luxe ritual: fancy hotels, first-class travel, expense money to maintain cool, silky blond groupies for travelling companions. The directors are like calves being fattened—all on the budget of the picture. The executives and their entourage of whores and underlings are also travelling and living it up on that same budget; that's how a picture that cost $1,200,000 comes in on the books at $3,000,000, and why the director who has a percentage of the profits doesn't get any.

It isn't impossible to raise money outside the industry to make a movie—the studios themselves finance some of their biggest pictures with tax-shelter money ("Gatsby," in part)—but even those who raise independent financing and make a picture cheaply ("Mean Streets" was brought in for $380,000, plus $200,000 in deferred costs, "Payday" for $767,000) are stuck for a way to distribute it and fall victim to the dream of a big Hollywood win. So they sell their pictures to "the majors" to exhibit, and watch helplessly as the films die or the swindled profits disappear. And they are beggars again. Brian De Palma's "Greetings" was made for $20,000, plus $23,000 in deferred costs in 1968; back in the fifties, Irvin Kershner made "Stakeout on Dope Street" for $30,000, plus $8,000 in deferred costs. If there had been an artists' co-op to distribute the films, the directors might have been able to use the profits to continue working, instead of pouring energy into planning films that they could never finance, and seeing the films they did make get sliced to ribbons.

If the directors started one distribution company, or even several (they could certainly get backing), they might have to spend time on business problems, but, with any luck, much less time on dealmaking sessions: those traumatic meetings at which the businessmen air their grievances while the artists anxiously vulgarize the projects they're submitting, hoping to make them sound commercial enough. If they have a book they want to film or if they try to get development money for a story idea, the lack of enthusiasm is deadly. One director says, "You look at them and you give up. And if, after a year or two years, they finally give you the go-ahead, then they cut you down to a twenty-five-day shooting schedule and *dare* you to make a picture." Right now, all but a handful of Hollywood directors spend most of their time preparing projects that they never get to shoot. They work on scripts with writers, piling up successions of drafts, and if they still can't please the producers and get a deal, the properties are finally abandoned or turned over [to other directors, who start the process all over] again, with new writers. One could outline a history of modern Hollywood by following the passage of one such project—the French novel "Choice Cuts," say, which more than a dozen of the best writers and close to a dozen of the best directors have worked on: script after script in insane succession, and the waltz still goes on, each person in turn thinking that he's got a deal and his version will be made. The directors spend their lives not in learning their craft and not in doing anything useful to them as human beings but in fighting a battle they keep losing. The business problems of controlling their own distribution should be minor compared to what they go through now—the abuse from the self-pitying bosses, the indignity, the paralysis. And if the directors had to think out how their movies should be presented to the public—what the basis for the advertising campaign should be—this mightn't be so bad for them. If they had to worry about what a movie was going to mean to people and why anybody should come to see it, they might be saved from too much folly. A fatal difference between the "high" arts and the popular, or mass-culture, arts has been that in one the artist's mistakes are his own, while in the other the mistakes are largely the businessmen's. The artist can grow making his own mistakes; he decries carrying out the businessmen's decisions—working on large, custom-made versions of the soulless entertainment on TV.

Privately, almost every one of the directors whose work I admire tells the same ugly, bitter story, yet they live in such fear of those spiteful, spying bosses that they don't dare even talk to each other. Hollywood is a small, ingrown community where people live in terror that "word will get back." They inhabit a paranoia-inducing company town, and within it they imagine the bosses to have more power in the outside world than they actually do. If such talents as Sam Peckinpah, Paul Mazursky, Martin Scorsese, Coppola, Kershner, Altman, De Palma, Woody Allen, Frederick Wiseman, Lamont Johnson, John Korty, Steven Spielberg, Michael Crichton and even some of the older directors, such as Kazan and Fred Zinnemann, joined together to distribute their own films, they'd be able to work on the projects they really want to work on, and they'd get most of the writers and performers and craftsmen they want, too. The main obstacles are not in the actual world. It's not impossible to buck the majors and to book movies into theatres, and it's not really hard to publicize movies; the media are almost obscenely eager for movie news, and the businessmen, who know only one way to advertise a film—by heavy bombardment—often kill interest in an unusual picture by halfheartedly trying to sell it as if it were the kind of routine action show they wanted it to be.

There's no way of knowing whether a new audience can be found; it's a matter of picking up the pieces, and it may be too late. But if the directors started talking to each other, they'd realize that they're all in the same rapidly sinking boat, and there'd be a chance for them to reach out and try to connect with a new audience. If they don't, they'll never test themselves as artists and they'll never know whether an audience could have been found for the work they want to do.

The artists have to break out of their own fearful, star-struck heads; the system that's destroying them is able to destroy them only as they believe in it and want to win within it—only as long as they're psychologically dependent on it. But the one kind of winning that is still possible in those terms is to be a winner like William Friedkin or George Roy Hill. The system works for those who don't have needs or aspirations that are in conflict with it; but for the others—and they're the ones who are making *movies*—the system doesn't work anymore, and it's not going to.

Bibliography

The film industry is a truly complex business ranging from the creative element, which borders upon classical art, to the most mundane business problem. The books reflect this diversity. It is suggested here that the serious student consult the following bibliographies for further study possibilities: John C. Gerlach and Lana Gerlach, compilers, *The Critical Index: A Bibliography of Articles on Film in English, 1947-1973*, Teachers College Press, Columbia University, 1974 and Richard Dyer MacCann and Edward S. Perry, compilers, *The New Film Index: A Bibliography of Magazine Articles in English, 1930-1970*, Dutton, 1975. Both books are excellent, comprehensive works that should be used in tandem—one book tends to supplement the other in several respects. For a reasonably current up-date of film books, consult the December issue of *Mass Media Booknotes* each year. *MMB* is issued monthly out of Temple University by Christopher H. Sterling, compiler. For an index of film reviews, consult Stephen E. Bowles, compiler, *Index to Critical Film Reviews 1930-1972* together with *Index to Critical Reviews of Books About Film*, Burt Franklin, 1974, two volumes.

The Cable Fable: Will It Come True?

By Anne W. Branscomb

Science fiction claims and "blue sky" promises oversold an industry and tied it up in red tape. A realistic assessment finds its future a matter of public concern.

The cable industry is slowly recovering from what can best be described as the TelePrompTer syndrome. This manifested itself in the crisis of September 1973, when two financial officers of the company blew the whistle at the Securities and Exchange Commission (SEC), precipitating the suspension of trading of Tele-

Anne W. Branscomb is a communications lawyer, now Vice President of Kalba Bowen Associates, Inc. This article was prepared with assistance from the Program on Information Technologies and Public Policy, Harvard University. It appeared in *Journal of Communication* (Winter 1975) and is reprinted with permission of the *Journal of Communication*.

Facts and figures cited in this article come from interviews with cable industry officials; from records of Federal Communications Commission proceedings and regulations and other legal sources; and from *Broadcasting, Cable News,* and other industry publications. Readers interested in detailed citations are asked to contact the author.

It may be indicative of TelePrompTer's financial and accounting difficulties that these figures are in substantial discrepancy with figures reported later in the year. After adjusting its accounting practices, the company announced that net income for 1972 was only 56 cents, and there was a net loss of 6 cents per share in 1973.

PrompTer stock on the New York stock exchange for several weeks. The rest of the industry waited in a state of suspended animation.

There were massive dismissals of personnel; all regional offices were closed; program production stopped; management was reorganized; and marketing efforts were reoriented toward increasing subscribers in existing systems rather than expanding services. Franchising operations, which had been brisk and successful, ceased. Personnel assigned to franchising turned to work on rate increases.

The time to make systems "operational" (a euphemism for profitable) had proved far longer than predicted. The projected earnings per share of TelePrompTer stock was 12 cents for 1973 compared with 79 cents per share in 1972. This news predictably precipitated much foreboding within and without the industry. Venture capital became apprehensive. The values of cable stocks dropped phenomenally. Although the entire stock market was unstable during 1973, the cable stocks were the greater losers. Market capitalization decreased from $1,110,129,000 in September of 1972 to $397,650,000 in September of 1973 for eight of the ten largest multiple system operators (MSO's) for whom such statistics are available.

Jack Kent Cooke, whose personal paper loss for his controlling interest in TelePrompTer was estimated at $43.4 million, took personal control of the company. TelePrompTer was not alone in its difficulties. The managements of several other companies were reorganized. Several mergers which had been attempted in order to amass enough equity to attract substantial funding for construction of new systems fell through, either because of antitrust action by the Justice Department or because the companies fell into disagreement about the fair exchange of stock during the plummeting of stock market values. American Television & Communications (ATC) and Cox, the fourth and sixth largest MSO's, who, if successful, would have become the Avis of the cable industry, abandoned their merger negotiations after the Justice Department took them to court.

Another Cox effort to merge with LVO Cable, Inc., came to naught, and Viacom International, Inc., with 260,000 subscribers, was unable to consummate a marriage with Communications Properties's 190,000 subscribers. Warner Communications Corporation backed away from the Birmingham, Alabama, franchise after TelePrompTer dropped out of the picture, and from the Dayton, Ohio, franchise, leaving minority group partners in both cities holding the bag. Time, Inc., divested itself of all cable interests except Sterling Manhattan, which nobody would buy because it had lost 15 million dollars over the previous two years.

Only a few months earlier, Fred Alger & Company, a brokerage firm, had run a full-page ad in the *New York Times*, saying: "The purpose of our new report, TelePrompTer, is to present the prospects on a leader in what may be the most promising road there is visible on the investment horizon—cable television."

On March 22, 1973, Bill Bresnan, then president of TelePrompTer, speaking to the San Francisco Society of Security Analysts in San Francisco, said:

> . . .rather than being light years away from the so-called cable revolution, the CATV industry in 1973 is standing on the threshold. Regardless of future regulatory posture, the CATV industry is destined to grow dramatically over the next several years . . .How

much it will grow is open to speculation. Most observers estimate that by 1980 at least one-half of U.S. households will be wired for cable. Specific estimates vary between 25 million and 45 million homes. A report prepared for the White House Office of Telecommunications Policy estimates the industry's potential total gross revenues for two-way services to reach 99 million by 1980, 3.8 billion by 1984 and upwards of 19 billion by 1989.

Only six months later, the cable industry was in serious trouble. What are the problems and what is the prognosis?

The cable industry was oversold to itself,
to the public, and to the investment community.

What started as a simple extension of antenna capacity to receive or improve television signals became the communications utility of the future, the umbilical cord through which every person would be plugged into the world. A communications revolution of two-way interactive cable, it was predicted, would bring the dawning of a new day of the individualized computer terminal through which all citizens would communicate with their peers, merchants, banks, elected representatives, libraries, investment counselors, and doctors, as well as receive a smorgasbord of specialized choices from the entertainment media.

Cable was a new toy to be teased, tested, and reflected upon. The promise of new markets captivated the investing public, and cable became a glitter stock of the early 1970s. Public officials latched onto the new industry as a means of increasing public resources—or at least of assuring substantial public use of the new channels of abundance. The dreamers dreamed of a great new electronic highway and a "wired nation" in which everyone could communicate with everyone—and a body of credible intellectuals predicted that 40-60 percent of the nation would be cabled by 1980. Responsible cable operators shook their heads in amazement, while their more apprehensive colleagues pocketed their profits and cable stocks soared ever higher. This was the era of "science fiction" which Ralph Baruch, president of Viacom, calls most damaging to the industry.

Clearly the acceptance of the dream by cable operators was not deliberately deceptive. The price of stock on the market is directly related to the ability to accumulate capital in order to expand. Most of the simple cable systems have been built; the expensive ones in suburbs and small towns, and the large capital expenses, are ahead of the industry. In order to amass the necessary capital there is a tremendous temptation to try to "talk a stock up" in the eyes of the investment community, in order to persuade the bankers that sufficient equity exists to borrow larger amounts of capital to construct new systems.

The financial difficulties which beset the cable
industry are real rather than contrived.

These difficulties are not temporary and very unlikely to decrease in severity. Partially they are the result of a general softness in the economy; partially a result of inflationary trends which have increased debt service, construction, and labor costs; partially the result of overselling the immediate potential of the industry to the investment community; and partially the result of rules restricting investment from a large number of potential investors. Very little is due to squandering of resources.

Investors are becoming more sophisticated about the risks inherent in cable investments, as costs have risen and return on capital investment has receded. Furthermore, the trend toward carrier status and possible rate-of-return regulation makes the pot at the end of the rainbow less reachable. Certainly cable operators consider the divorce of carriage from content a device to separate them from their just rewards after building the rainbows—and costs of construction keep climbing upward, rendering the completion of the system less likely with each passing year. The cost of constructing a strand mile of cable has increased from an average of $3,000 or $4,000 during the last decade to about $6,000 today for non-urban overhead installation. Putting the cable underground (as is more often required by franchising authorities and ecological mandates) can cost anywhere from $9,000 to $40,000 or $50,000 per strand mile in congested metropolitan areas.

Debt service has almost doubled in the last few years from 6 percent to more than 11 percent in 1973. Cable operators simply cannot afford to borrow money to build new systems unless they are in marginal television reception areas where the profitability and immediate return on investment is assured. Municipal or public ownership of some kind becomes more attractive both to the smaller communities (which are likely to be left in the interstitial spaces between successful cable operations) and to the larger cities, where the capital costs are high and the amortization of costs projected over too long a period for traditional venture capital to be attracted. The debt service on tax-free municipal bonds is approximately half the cost of conventional bank financing, so more and more cities will likely turn, as Baltimore has, to some mode of municipal financing. Cable companies are said to be attracted to partnerships which relieve them of the burden of arranging for construction capital but keep them in the role of lessee of the facilities or operator under some form of management contract.

The costs of wiring the nation are staggering: $1.2 trillion for a completely switched or dial-access system like the telephone or $123 billion for a traditional tree-branched system. Recent estimates, based upon 86 million families to be served in 1985 utilizing microwave interconnection, arrive at a more realistic figure of $82.5 billion, comparable with the current investment of $67 billion in telephone plant and annual construction commitments of $12.5 billion in the telephone system.

Two questions which do become apparent are: (1) whether or not it makes sense to duplicate transmission facilities at staggering costs when modification of the present nationwide system may achieve the desired results; and (2) how the cable industry, which represents a minuscule 1.8 percent of the $22 billion annual revenues of the communications industry, is expected to accomplish the communications revolution when the giants of the industry—telephone companies, television networks, and television stations—are prohibited from investing in the developing technology of cable.

The cable industry is primarily a "piggyback" operation which "has grown over the years by free loading."

Because the industry has developed as a transmitting rather than as a programming service, it has neither the will nor the creativity to produce new kinds of programming and services; nor is the subscriber base yet substantial enough to sustain much original programming designed for cable. The token commitment to program origination (which became legally binding upon TelePrompTer as a pre-condition for approval by the FCC of the merger with H and B American in August of 1970)—was the first promise to be broken in the financial crunch of 1973; practically the entire programming production capability was eliminated as an economy move. Cablecasters at the 1974 National Cable Television Association (NCTA) convention concluded that program origination was losing money and gaining few viewers.

Furthermore, the importation of distant signals to large metropolitan markets has been disappointing as a marketing attraction. The compromise which precipitated the 1972 FCC rules, with their incredibly complex formula for deciding who can import which signals, has not been the great boost to the development of cable in the cities which was anticipated. Penetration in the New York systems of Tele-PrompTer and Manhattan Cable remains stationary at less than 30 percent. Furthermore, the nonduplication and syndicated exclusivity rules are so stringent that a careful calculation of the permitted signals in the top 100 markets discloses that there are only 17 markets in which the importation will create attractive marketing potential. In the other markets, the cable system will be importing signals which will be largely blacked out because of existing program contracts in that market; the present attractions—largely sporting events not currently carried on the networks—would be exterminated by sports blackout legislation currently proposed in Congress.

Thus the industry is now relying upon pay cable as the way to salvation. However, despite all the protests to the contrary, there is no reassuring evidence emanating from the cable industry that it will provide a very different source of programming supply than the current broadcasters. Thus the primary advantage of pay cable may be merely the opportunity to pay for the same old movies but without the advertising interruptions—an advantage not to be ignored; but there is no evidence at the moment that the cable industry will produce the imaginative cable services promised by the cable dreamers.

On the other hand, the technology is rapidly being perfected to bring as many as 80 channels to all cable systems via satellite distribution at a modest cost. The predicted current capability, if all the earth reception facilities currently on the drawing boards were in place using existing microwave networks, is only about two million homes. [This projection was made for the NCTA Satellite Committee and is based on 50 ground stations reaching existing microwave networks. The cost is estimated at $3.5 million.] Nonetheless, the cable industry currently has installed coaxial cable in front of more than 12 million homes—the market which the Sloan Commission crudely estimated to be sufficient to support the revolutionary "blue sky" services which would constitute the communications revolution predicted. Thus it is particularly ironic that the crisis in financial capability has come at a time when technical capability is almost within grasp.

> *The dream was not dreamed by those upon whose labors*
> *the realization of the dream depended.*

The projection of potential for the cable industry came largely from the scientists and the social philosophers, not from the pole climbers and television salesmen who put the industry together. The cable industry is not populated by the AT&T's

the IBM's or the ITT's. It is populated by a large number of small-town operators predominantly in rural areas whose sole original purpose was to provide an antenna service to deliver existing television signals to customers unable to obtain an acceptable signal through their own devices. Many of these companies were and still are "mom and pop"–type operations, although the trend is toward amalgamation and the top 12 MSO's serve 50 percent of the cabled homes. Nevertheless, the largest of the MSO's was still operated in 1973 as a large family—which still had difficulty keeping track of its many branches and was yet unable to cope with modern administrative and accounting practices.

It is no quirk of fate that William Bresnan, interim president of TelePrompTer from 1972 to 1974, started his career in cable more than 20 years ago as a pole climber. A business school-trained executive like Amos Hostetter, vice president of Continental Cablevision, seventeenth largest MSO (with only 78,000 subscribers) is a notable exception in the industry. It is difficult for people whose main stock in trade is stringing coaxial cable from pole to pole to conceive of an information retrieval system.

The industry is certainly not unaware of its personnel problems, both administrative and technical. It may be that industry decision-makers are beginning to be more conscious of the management skills required for realizing the growth potential: two new MSO Presidents, Clifford Miner Kirtland, Jr., of Cox Broadcasting Corp., and Lawrence B. Hilford, of Viacom Enterprises, are Harvard MBA's. Russell Karp, the new president of TelePrompTer, is a graduate of the Yale Law School with financial and managerial experience in the entertainment industry.

The industry is regulated by a three-tiered system
which can only be described as excessive.

Ironically, the cable industry, which fought long and hard to avoid federal regulation as inhibiting the growth of the industry, now finds itself in the anomalous position of seeking federal preemption of regulatory authority in order to get the state and local authorities off its back.

The FCC has considerable doubts about its power to completely preempt cable regulation, although it has recently preempted regulation of leased and pay channels. However, the FCC cannot will away the cities' legitimate legal interest in cable strung over and under the city streets. There is, therefore, substantial doubt that federal preemption would completely exclude local authorities from the regulatory process or that such exclusion would be in the public interest. In the realm of truly local signal service, cable has the potential to provide an avenue of communication which the broadcasting industry has failed to provide and to develop the system of locally oriented program services which the Communications Act envisioned.

One weakness of the present FCC regulations is that they have come too early and with too much detail in the area of local preemption. Although the abuses of the franchising process are too well known to be reiterated, what is not so well known is the inhibitory influence of a standard rule in cutting off the more experimental modes of local ownership and/or regulation which might have developed without the heavy hand of the FCC.

Another weakness is that FCC rules were unfortunately written by regulators uninitiated in the mysteries of cable operations. Even the authors of the regulations often admit that they do not understand what a particular rule means. For example, rules which preceded the new cable rules have been continued without any rationale for their perpetuation. A cable system must provide non-duplication protection to a television station which its subscribers can receive with rabbit ears on a local television antenna. Certainly the system should not be required to provide non-duplication protection for television signals which it is required to carry. All ''significantly viewed signals'' which systems are required to carry should be treated equitably. The prior system of priorities of protection for Grade A contour signals against Grade B contour signals should be abandoned—but this is only one example of the complexity of the cable rules which defy the average cable system operator's ability to master and which force every system to have competent FCC counsel in order to decipher. It seems doubtful that the single system operator can survive without the economy of cost which can be realized by pooling systems and legal resources. The FCC has recently determined to review and simplify its cable rules by announcing some proposed changes, and the formation of a Cable Television Re-regulation Task Force may signify a more lenient future stance toward cable operations.

Another problem implicit in the present rules is that they have saddled a new technology with too much public responsibility in its infancy before it has had time to develop the economic base necessary to sustain such public commitments.

The reason the cable industry has been overloaded with public responsibilities is not difficult to discern. The early legislative debates on the Radio Act of 1927 and the Communications Act of 1934 are replete with promises of great public service responsibility of the then nascent radio industry. Each successive technology has been the repository of these hopes, and has failed them. In cable, public-service advocates feel they have finally found a medium that can deliver. The failure of the legislative architects to provide a workable framework for the use of radio for fruitful public debate led public-interest advocates to pursue the imposition of public responsibilities more diligently in the regulations governing cable.

From a financial standpoint, however well motivated the dedicated channels may have been, the promotion of their use and the commitment of financial support for program production must be undertaken with vigor if the new services are to fulfill their promise. Cable operators themselves are the least well equipped—psychologically or financially—to take responsibility for the development of these channels. The dreams of the wide-open, robust, and uninhibited public debate will not be realized by merely setting aside some channels. They will only be realized through the diligent cultivation of those channels by a public which wants to be heard.

State regulatory commissions are adding a third dimension to the regulatory scene which appears superfluous and oppressive. Few lawyers are proficient in the vagaries of state cable regulation, and an ailing cable industry which already must have both local and FCC legal capabilities can hardly be aided by another layer of regulatory forms and filings to meet.

The Massachusetts regulations defy the most diligent MSO to comply. In order to qualify its Massachusetts operations, TelePrompTer had five people work-ing several weeks attempting—not entirely successfully—to provide the informa-tion required to file for certification of its Worcester system (which serves less than 1 percent of TelePrompTer's total subscribers). This could not be considered cost-effective by any accounting method which allocated time proportionately to opera-tions involved, a system which TelePrompTer was manifestly not using. A prudent MSO would be well advised to pull out of Massachusetts unless it had very substan-tial investment and a highly profitable operation.

On the contrary, the New York Cable Commission looks upon itself as a promoter of cable development; to the extent that it pursues this goal diligently, it may, in fact, prove highly catalytic in helping to encourage intrastate interconnec-tions, providing legal and technical expertise which individual small operators cannot afford. However, New York is an ill-conceived geographic unit to encourage the kind of regional interconnection which would be optimum. The New York metropolitan area should logically coordinate its telecommunications planning and development with New Jersey and Connecticut, not with New York State. Virtually no states, in fact, with the possible exception of California, and Texas, Alaska, and Hawaii, contain within their boundaries the communications complexes which con-stitute the logical regulatory areas for regional amalgamation. If any regulatory entity is to be interposed between the local governing authority and the FCC, it should be regional—New England, Southwest, metropolitan authority.

However, the time is growing short for changing regulatory patterns. Three state cable commissions are already in existence (Massachusetts, Minnesota, and New York); seven states have some type of PUC-type regulation; eight states have regulatory legislation pending; four others have active study groups, and the remain-ing 28 are pregnant with possibilities. None of these is likely to be willing to relin-quish jurisdiction, once acquired, at the mere bidding of a federal regulatory agency. Judicial determination of the parameters of state and federal jurisdiction is likely to be time-consuming, costly, and inhibiting rather than stimulating to the growth of cable generally.

The draft bill of the Cable Communications Act of 1974 (drafted by the Office of Telecommunications Policy) is an effort to roll back the carpet toward a two-tiered regulatory framework, freeing cable operators of many of the more onerous requirements and severely limiting state or local interference with the free play of the marketplace.

The cable industry is beset with a cautious
investment community, an overzealous
triumvirate of government regulators, an honest
infusion of self-doubt, and a pessimistic public.

Clearly this is not a time for unbridled optimism about the future of cable *per se*. Neither is it a time for deep depression. There is no reason to believe that the "mom and pop" cable systems are in deep financial difficulties. Indeed, they seem to be plodding along doing what they've always done in the same old way. Even TelePrompTer claims to have weathered its financial crisis with blue skies ready to break overhead. The CATV industry will survive. The question is whether or not it will become the electronic highway of tomorrow.

Ironically, the Wired Nation is a reality. The technology is called the telephone, and it is not at all clear that the blue-sky visions of the cable enthusiasts cannot or should not be realized by the utilization or modernization of the existing plant, in which we already have invested $67 billion.

The home interactive computer terminal is a distant dream. This does not mean, as many doubters predict, that the hardware is the major problem and that cities should wait to franchise cable companies until home terminals are perfected. The problem is economic. What many people do not realize is that the capability to produce television sets existed for several decades before the television industry took off. The patents for an electronically produced facsimile newspaper were registered in 1935, but the facsimile newspaper has not yet found a place in our economy. Whether coaxial cable is the preferred material with which to wire the nation, and whether cable service is to become the ubiquitous communications utility of tomorrow, depends upon the conscious choice of policy and allocation of financial resources—both public and private.

Realization of the cable dream may depend upon the ability to reassess some established principles:

1. Cable should be encouraged to develop in partnership with and not as competitor to existing technologies—broadcasting and telephone companies. Much return capability can be provided by existing telephone lines, and experimentation with services using coaxial cable and the twisted pair technology should be encouraged.

The fibre optical communications system developed at Bell Labs provides the potential for greater transmission capacity even than coaxial cable. AT&T could provide, perhaps at less cost, the facilities about which we are dreaming: the completely wired, interconnected, two-way switched system.

AT&T is its own worst enemy, since its current financial investment in the Bell plant of $56 billion militates against a huge investment in fibre optics—and the regulatory climate portends a government unfriendly to a single communications giant providing all communications services, even on a common carrier basis. Apparently, the public lacks the capability to regulate Ma Bell. [The FCC has only one staff economist to cope with AT&T rate regulations. The cable industry was searching diligently during the summer of 1973 for an expert with sufficient knowledge of AT&T accounting practices to assist in negotiations with the telephone industry on the pole attachment rate increase.]

Nonetheless, a public decision must be made at some point: whether to continue discouraging the amalgamation of technological power through vigorous use of the antitrust laws or to regulate diversity of access and content in some more socially productive manner. The sooner policy-makers recognize the interrelatedness and interdependence of the various components of our communications sytem, the more workable and sensible the solutions to existing problems will become.

2. Prohibitions against cross-investment of one technology in another should be abandoned. Such prohibitions, which are the subject of extensive criticism, not only restrict the availability of investment capital, they align powerful political forces against the new technology which may effectively foreclose the potential for growth.

The broadcaster and the cablecaster should be natural allies—the broadcaster as the program producer and the cablecaster as the transmitting agency. The broadcaster is most logically the lessee of a cable channel and the cable operator the lessor who merely enhances the broadcaster's signal and increases his ability to reach viewers. But the rule requiring cable systems to originate programming (sustained by the courts and currently under reconsideration by the FCC) is ill advised, because it necessarily puts the cable operator into a competitive situation with broadcasters by forcing him to become a broadcaster too on his cable origination channel. This intensifies the ill will of the broadcaster.

The present animosity between broadcaster and cablecaster is more deeply rooted than the change of two rules could improve. Nonetheless, dropping the program origination requirement and the cross-ownership prohibition surely would be a step in the right direction, placing the two opposing factions into their more natural roles as program producer and program transmitter. However, the cross-ownership rule should be dropped now and not at the 50 percent penetration level proposed by the Office of Telecommunications Policy Report to the President on Cable, since the industry may never make the 50 percent level without the added impetus that cooperative investment would provide.

3. Ownership of the hardware should not result in control of the content. Control of the hardware is not necessarily an evil if control of the transmission is divorced from control of content. This is the major contribution to the cable debate of the OTP cable report. The Massachusetts Cable Commission has shown great insight in emphasizing this particular aspect of the cable development. The FCC, on the contrary, has been extremely unwise in the promulgation of rules which expand rather than restrict operator control of content. The cable operator is by nature a transmission expert, not a programmer, and it better befits his natural skills and inclination to remain in a role in which he feels comfortable.

4. Regulation, if it is to be effective, must be efficient and responsive. This means less state and national, and more regional and local regulation. Regulation of the hardware should be by a national standard, but regulation which affects people's political and sociological habits should be regulated by those units of government which have familiarity with the political and social consequences of regulation. Regulation at all levels should concentrate on the positive rather than the negative aspects of telecommunications development—on technical compatibility, quality of signal delivered, diversity of access to the maximum number of users. Above all, the regulatory apparatus should not be used as a device for inhibiting growth potential by competing technologies. Nor should we be afraid to look at alternatives to the current three tiers of regulation. It may very well be that all three are outmoded by the communications capabilities of the new technology. The optimum boundaries of the information utilities of the future may bear no logical relationship to the political boundaries of today.

5. If the public wants to participate in the message, then the public, or publics, whoever they may be, must be willing to pay the price in time, energy, and allocation of financial resources. This may take the form of a national investment in the hardware (either directly or in the form of matching funds to states of local governments) or of the insurance of loans used to construct systems. Whatever it means, it means money and lots of it, energy in great abundance, and persistence. A new telecommunications system can hardly succeed financially on a piecemeal basis, since the more imaginative uses require substantially full penetration—and the costs are staggering.

Either the existing telecommunications companies must be encouraged to incorporate the new technology or a substantial influx of funds from other sources—either public or private—must be stimulated. It is not unfair to conclude that Henry Ford would never have made it to the moon in his motorcar, and that the building of a nationwide, satellite, microwave, cable-connected system probably won't materialize in the foreseeable future without a conscious public decision to support the experimentation in software as well as a sizeable investment in the construction of the hardware.

Whether the cable fable becomes a reality depends largely upon the desires of public—not private—interests to make it so. It may be a serious public error to exhaust the resources of venture capital stringing the cable, leaving no resources for program development. A wiser public decision may be to install the cable with public funds, thus assuring equal access to all and amassing the market necessary to attract venture capital into the development of the software.

Bibliography

Cable television, as Barry Head's article in the first section of the book shows, has many legal, technical, social and educational issues. A readable background to the development and expectations of the industry is Ralph Lee Smith, *The Wired Nation: The Electronic Communications Highway*, Harper & Row, 1972. Two excellent books dealing with the regulatory problems of cable television are Martin H. Seiden, *Cable Television U.S.A.: An Analysis of Government Policy*, Praeger, 1972 and Don R. LeDuc, *Cable Television and the FCC: A Crisis in Media Control*, Temple University Press, 1973. An interesting position paper is *Broadcasting and Cable Television: Policies for Diversity and Change*, Committee for Economic Development, April 1975. Consult *Broadcasting* magazine for on-going information about cable's development.

The Bomp: Way of Life, Not a Sideshow
By Greil Marcus

Excerpted from "Who Put the Bomp" from *Rock and Roll Will Stand,* Beacon Press, 1969, copyright Greil Marcus, this is one of many pieces about music and community authored by Mr. Marcus, who has been an editor on the *Rolling Stone* and a contributor to *Creem;* he coauthored *Woodstock,* and edited *Rock and Roll Will Stand.*

The Beatles revolutionized rock 'n' roll by bringing it back to its sources and traditions. The new era, in America, began with a song, a joyous song, which had what one friend of mine calls the "takeover sound"—music that breaks from the radio and is impossible to resist. The first notes of *I Want To Hold Your Hand* were there, day after day. Everyone knew something different had happened. For months, every new Beatles song had part of that first record in it—that was just the way you had to hear it; that's what a new beginning, a sense of a new beginning means. All the rules were changing, as they'd changed in the fifties. Like the Beatles, groups had to write their own lyrics and music, and play their own instruments—they had to be as involved as possible. With the coming of the Rolling Stones, a new pattern was set: for the first time in the entertainment world, singers and musicians would appear, in photographs and on stage, in the clothes they wore every day. The music and the mystique were coming closer and closer to life as we lived it. For the new groups and for those of us who listened, rock 'n' roll became more a way of life than a sideshow. There was a hint that those stars up on stage might even be the same kind of people as the ones in the audience. Rock became more comfortable and more exciting at the same time.

Rock 'n' roll seeks to do something that earlier popular music had always denied—to establish and confirm, to heighten and deepen, to create and re-create the present moment. Rock, as a medium, knows that it is only up to a certain point that this can be done. To keep a moment of time alive it's necessary to make a song new every time it's performed, every time it's played, every time it's heard. When a song gets stale it only fills time, marks time, expends itself over two or three or ten minutes, but it doesn't *obliterate* time and allow you to move freely in the space that the music can give you. When a song is alive, the mind and the body respond—they race, merge with the music, find an idea or an emotion, and return. When a song is dead, the mind only waits for it to be over, hoping that something living will follow.

Judy Garland has sung *Over the Rainbow* some thousands of times; there's a man who keeps count. The tally is published in the newspapers occasionally, like the Gross National Product, which is really what it is: Judy Garland's GNP. You measure her progress that way. The same kind of mentality that demands this tune from Judy Garland, the same kind of mentality that makes her want to sing it, made a Santa Monica grandmother watch *The Sound of Music* over seven hundred times, once a day, at five o'clock. Listening to a rock song over and over, seeing *A Hard Day's Night* a dozen times, isn't the same—with that you participate when you must, stay away when you desire. The mind is free to remake the experience, but it isn't a prisoner. You don't demand the same songs from Bob Dylan every time he gives a concert—you understand that he's a human being, a changing person, and you try to translate his newness into your own.

This movement of the re-creation of the moment, with the constant changing of the dynamic, is mostly the result of the radio, the way it gives one music. When a song is new, and you like it, when it possesses that intangible grace that makes it part of you, you wait and hope all day that it will come out of the radio and into your ears. You listen, stop what you're doing, and participate. Finally, you'll get tired of it, ignoring the song when it comes on. Months or years later, when it returns as an oldie, the initial experience will be repeated, but with understanding, with a sense of how it all happened. You can't pretend that grace is there when it's not. When *Like A Rolling Stone* was released, I liked it, but I got tired of it pretty quickly. A few months later I put it on the phonograph and it jumped out and claimed me. I think it's the greatest rock 'n' roll record ever made—but I didn't decide that, I accepted it.

An incredible number of songs provide this sort of experience. Because of this, because of the way songs are heard, with an intensity that one provides for himself, they become part of one's mind, one's thought and subconscious, and they shape one's mental patterns. People sense this: there is a conscious effort by the members of the generation I'm talking about to preserve and heighten the experiences of rock 'n' roll, to intensify the connection between the individual and his music, between one's group of friends and the music they share. That effort takes the form of games and contests. These games reinforce the knowledge that this music is ours, that it doesn't and can't belong to anyone else. The kids who'll follow us will have a lot of it, but they can never really know the absolute beginnings of rock 'n' roll—that's our treasure. The generations that came before us are simply somewhere else. In a strange, protective way, people who are now in middle age aren't *allowed* to possess the music we have. When the Beatles were becoming acceptable, listenable for adults, with *Michelle* and *Yesterday*, the foursome responded with hard rock and experimental music, with sitars and tape machines and driving guitars. *Day Tripper* and *Strawberry Fields Forever* blasted the Beatles back home to students, kids, intellectuals, dropouts. The exclusiveness of rock 'n' roll is well-guarded. If the adults can take it, we'll probably reject it. In a way we want to share it, but in the end, it's better that we can't. If we're to be different, we'd best protect the sources of our differences, whenever they are re-created. That is what the Beatles did when they sang *I'm Down*, the toughest rock'n' roll since Little Richard—they returned to the beginnings, even as they stayed far ahead of everyone else.

And we preserve our possession with games. As small boys quiz each other on baseball statistics, young people today are constantly renewing each other's memories of rock 'n'roll. If you can't identify an old song by the first few bars, something's wrong. "Who did *Come Go With Me?*" "The Del-Vikings, 1957." That's a conversation between Yale and Harvard football players, caught on the field. Once, in an elevator on the Berkeley campus, a friend and I were singing "Who put the bomp in the bomp de-bomp de-bomp, who put the dang in the rama lamma ding dang, who was . . ." ". . .that man, I'd like to shake his hand . . ." joined in another passenger. "He made my baby fall in love with me!" sang a girl entering the elevator, completing the verse. Another friend of mine once made a list of all the Beatle songs released up to the time, about eight then, identifying the songs only by the first letter of each word in the title. He quizzed everyone on it. Two years later I asked him about the list—he remembered, and started the game all over again. Then there was the guy who, when about twelve, set up an incredible routine for responding to the current hits. He'd budget enough money to buy five records a week, and he'd buy the ones he dug the most. Then, when he got them home, having also picked up a copy of the most recent Top Forty survey, the ritual would begin: he'd draw elaborate tables, as he correlated his taste with that of the record-buying public, re-drawing the graphs each week as a song moved up or down the charts; and he had elaborate sets of figures establishing and revising the position of his all-time favorites on the same sort of scale. The next week would bring more new songs, adding to his mathematical history of his love for rock 'n' roll. And then there was the disk jockey on an FM rock show who played some records, and then announced: "You just heard *Since I Don't Have You* by the Skyliners, and *Ain't*

That Just Like Me by the Searchers, both of which formerly tied for the all-time record in repetitions of a final rock 'n' roll chorus, and *A Quick One While He's Away*, by the Who, a song that *destroyed* that record by going over *thirty*!'' In live performance, the Who have taken *A Quick One* past one hundred. Anyone who's seen them do it knows why that's important.

Rock 'n' roll has always had an awareness of its music as a special thing, reserved for a certain audience. There are dozens of songs *about* rock 'n' roll, a game within a game. There's *Roll Over Beethoven* and *Rock and Roll Music* by Chuck Berry, Little Richard's *All Around the World (Rock 'n' Roll Is All They Play)*, the magnificent *Do You Believe in Magic* by the Lovin' Spoonful, and the classic *It Will Stand* by the Showmen, released at a time when it looked like rock and roll might not:

> *They're always trying to ruin*
> *Forgive them, for they know not what they're doin'*
> *Cause rock and roll forever will stand . . .*

The vitality and determination of these songs, that consciousness of rock as a special thing, something to be cherished, has reached the listener, who might have come to it on his own anyway, and helped him into the greatest game of all, the use of lyrics and phrases, verbal, ''nonsense,'' and musical, as metaphors to describe and enclose situations, events, and ideas. ''Da do ron ron' to you too,'' wrote a reader in the letters column of a rock newspaper, responding to an offensive article on Phil Spector's Ronettes, and revealing at the same time the wealth of undefined and undefinable meaning possessed by that phrase David Suskind just couldn't understand.

This is a great game that never stops; and it's more than a game, it's a way of responding to life. Situations are ''set''; one puts himself down; reveals an irony; takes comfort in the knowledge that someone has been there before him. There is a feeling that if we could only hear enough, and remember all we hear, that the answers would be there on the thousands of rock 'n' roll records that have brought us to the present. It is the intensity of this game of metaphors that allows one to feel this way, to have this kind of innocent confidence. It's not that people haven't used metaphors before; ''metaphors,'' as opposed to ''explanations,'' have been drawn from all of literature and art for the same kind of reasons. What is different is that rock 'n' roll is a medium that is ever-present, thanks to the radio, and repetitive, thanks to Top Forty and oldies and record players, so that the habit of using metaphors in this way comes so naturally it is a characteristic of how the more articulate part of this generation thinks at any time and responds to any situation. The fact that rock 'n' roll is a body of myths private to this generation only heightens the fact.

People quote lines and phrases from songs to their elders, who can't possibly have any idea of what they're talking about; they quote them to friends, who do know. A line from Dylan can stop whatever action is in progress and return the group to the warmth of a mental community. Since the renaissance of rock 'n' roll, people are finding out that what they thought was their private fetish is the style of a generation. There is a shared body of myths, a common style of feeling and responding, a love of a music that allows one to feel the totality of an experience without missing the nuances and secrets—and as we become aware of our myths we deepen them and practice our own mythmaking. The metaphors drawn from these myths aren't just a matter of fitting the proper words to the proper situation, but of knowing the music is there, somehow, in the same place that the idea is, that somewhere the two have met, and that you have been allowed to see the connection. It is a way of thinking that allows one to give mood and emotion the force of fact, to believe one's instinctual reaction more than someone else's statistical analysis or logical argument.

The music is all around. There's a radio in every car, at least one in every apartment. They are on much of the time—maybe all day. There's a record player, more and more, as people become aware of their music, finding ''Oldies But Goodies'' and ''Greatest Hits'' albums on it, as it also plays today's music. A hit song, one you like, is heard at least a hundred times. For the month or so it's popular, it becomes part of the day's experience. If it's on a record you buy, you have control over that part of your experience, instead of receiving it as a surprise from the radio. But playing a favorite song on your own record player lacks the grateful thrill of hearing it cascade from the radio as a gift of smoky airwaves. Rock exists—something makes one want not to control it, but to accept and experience it as it comes. After a record has passed from the charts, it will come back, as an oldie, every once in a while. You only need the rarity of renewal. It's like the surprise of hearing the Beatles' *All You Need Is Love* for the first time, with all those old songs, some virtually legends, jumping and twisting in and out of the chorus: *Greensleeves, In the Mood*, and a line from *She Loves You* with just a hint of *Yesterday*.

The incessant, happy repetition of words and music that is provided when a song is a hit on the radio or a favorite on the record player makes the song part of one's mind. The musical patterns and lyrics become second nature, as they merge and separate. The fact and experience of repetition, a song half-heard, half-enjoyed, a quick turning up the sound when a favorite chord comes, then withdrawal—this makes a difference as to how one thinks or subconsciously reacts to a situation. Once a song becomes part of you it is accepted. Then you are more naturally inclined to take that song, or any song, as a metaphor, to ''name'' the place you're in, and leave it at that. A person who feels this wouldn't employ *For What It's Worth* by the Buffalo Springfield to help explain the Sunset Strip riots, as did two writers in the *New York Review of Books*; he'd just say, ''Listen to *For What It's Worth*—it's all there.'' The habit and facility of taking metaphors from music, taking music *as* metaphor, and even more importnat, using these metaphors in a simple and absolute way, is, I think, the result of the musical experiences I've tried to describe. The metaphor isn't even principally the ''meaning'' of the words to a song; more often it is that the music, or a phrase, or two words heard, jumping out as the rest are lost, seem to fit one's emotional perception of a situation, event, or idea. A pattern of notes or the way in which a few words happen to fit together hit a chord of memory and a perception takes place, a perception which structures and ''rationalizes'' itself into a metaphor, not on the basis of a ''logical'' relationship, but because of the power of music and song to reach into the patterns of memory and response. "If you could just listen to it, you'd know what I mean, completely. It's all there."

"It's all there" is an expression used so often in the making of a song or a musical experience into a metaphor it's as if some members of this generation had a secret language, with this phrase as the signal that an exclusive kind of discourse is about to begin. But no two people ever hear the same song in the same way, or connect the song with the same things. An organ movement in the "live" recording of Dylan's *Just Like Tom Thumb's Blues* is to me the terrifying presence of an evil serpent, swallowing the singer; to someone else, that part of the music slips by unheard, and the notes of the guitar become tears.

What this means is that a strange kind of communication must take place. In one sense, the communication is perfect—one person has complete trust in the other when he is told that a song holds all the truth of a moment or an experience. They both know it; they both accept the validity of the metaphor. Thus, on a non-verbal, non-visual level, they understand each other and the way in which they both think, and they share the knowledge that only certain people can understand them. They realize the privacy and the publicness of their communication. The repetition, over and over, of a two or three minute musical experience has given them an effortless metaphorical consciousness. One knows what the other is talking about. There is an identification, and a sharing. It is the language of people who comprehend instinctually and immediately. To know "where it's at" isn't rational, it's automatic. "You can't talk about it, you have to groove with it." Of course that can be valid. Two people may try to talk about it, perhaps; but they'll get closer to the truth by placing the experience in front of them, starting with a shared understanding of a common purpose and an unspoken language of intuition and emotion, ending with a respect for the experience as well as for each other. Thus the communication is perfect, among those lucky enough to be a part of it.

But on another level, communication is impossibly difficult and confused. One person will not hear what another has heard in a song. It is hard, and wrong, to force another to put specific meanings on music he can hear for himself. It will bring forth associations for him as well. They both know the truth is there; that is not in doubt. What's there? Who can tell? I know, you know—what else matters? What is vital is that the situation has been captured, robbed, made livable by understanding with a depth that is private and public, perfectly and impossibly communicable. Perfectly communicable in that there is mutual trust that the situation is *ours*, that we have each and together made it our own; it can't destroy us; it can only be relived and reexperienced with each hearing of our metaphor. Impossibly communicable in that we never know exactly what our friend *is* experiencing. But that can be accepted, when one can create or be given metaphors—imperfect knowledge that is perfect understanding, our kind of roots to joy and tragedy. In John Barth's *Giles Goat-Boy*, the various characters of the novel all go to the theatre, where the Barthian paraphrase of *Oedipus Rex* ("Taliped Decanus") is presented. All know that the drama has affected them profoundly, but none knows just how, for himself or for others. Yet all trust the play to give them the metaphors by which they will shape and interpret their lives, their actions, and the actions of the others. Each knows, by grace of the gift of art, that they will accept, instinctually and non-rationally, the validity of the others' pictures. All trust the play, as we trust our music. The Greeks perhaps lived with this kind of depth, within this pattern of myth. The same treasure the Greeks of the tragic era possessed is, in some prosaic way, ours again.

Out of the experience of growing up with rock 'n' roll, we have found out that rock has more to give us than we ever knew. With a joyful immediacy, it has taught us to participate with ourselves, and with each other. A repetitive history of songs and secrets has given us a memory patterned by games, within a consciousness of a shared experience exclusive to our generation. Fifteen years of a beat, and thousands of songs that had just enough humor in those words that are so hard to hear, have brought us a style of thought that allows ideas to create themselves out of feeling and emotion, a style of thought that accepts metaphors as myths. Those myths, when we find them, are strong enough to sustain belief and action, strong enough to allow us to fashion a sense of reality out of those things that are important to us. This is not an attempt to "justify" rock 'n' roll by linking it to something "bigger" than itself—we have nothing bigger than rock 'n' roll, and nothing more is needed to "justify" it than a good song.

The kind of thinking I've tried to describe, the manner of response, the consciousness and unconsciousness of metaphor, the subtle confidence of mystique that leads to the permanence of myth—such an intellectual mood, I think, will have a deep and lasting effect on the vision and the style of the "students" of this generation. They will, and already do, embrace an instinctual kind of knowledge. This is partly a reaction against a programmed, technological culture—but so is rock 'n' roll, a dynamic kaleidoscope of sound that constantly invents new contexts within which to celebrate its own exhilarating power to create a language of emotional communication, sending messages to the body as well as to the mind, reaching the soul in the end.

What rock 'n' roll has done to us won't leave us. Faced with the bleakness of social and political life in America, we will return again and again to rock 'n' roll, as a place of creativity and renewal, to return from it with a strange, media-enforced consciousness increasingly a part of our thinking and our emotions, two elements of life that we will less and less trouble to separate.

This is a kind of freedom we are learning about. Affecting our own perspectives—artistic, social, and political—it makes the tangible and the factual that much more reprehensible, that much more deadening. The intellectual leap, the habit of free association, the facility of making a single rock 'n' roll metaphor the defining idea for a situation or a time of one's life—that is the kind of thinking that makes sense. It is the factual made mystical, with a mythic consciousness given the force of fact, that is our translation of society's messages. It's the elusive situation or idea that fascinates, not the weight of proof or conclusion, and that fascination, captured by metaphor, will be, I think, our kind of knowledge, leading to our kind of vision.

The isolation that is already ours will be increased, of course; but that isolation, as politics and as art, is here now. If it isn't comfortable, there is at least a kind of fraternity to be discovered within its limits.

Bibliography.

Several books are available on the music industry. One that traces current as well as recent practices is R. Serge Denisoff, *Solid Gold: The Popular Record Industry*, Transactions Books, 1975. The role played by one of the leading innovators in the industry is found in Clive Davis and James Willwerth, *Clive: Inside the Record Business*, Morrow, 1974. Davis was head of Columbia Records from 1965 to 1973. Louis Kraar, "How Phil Walden Turns Rock Into Gold," *Fortune* (September 1975), pp. 106-111 ff., reveals the methods used by Capricorn Records in promoting unknown talent until it becomes successful. Two practical books on the industry are Walter E. Hurst and William Storm Hale, *The Record Industry Book: How to Make Money in the Record Industry*, Vol. I, and *The Music Industry Book: How to Make Money in the Music Industry*, Vol. II, both published by 7 Arts Press, 1971. Students will need to consult both volumes because of the organization of content. A study of the themes of the country music industry is reported in Ann Nietzke, "Country Music . . . Doin' Somebody Wrong," *Human Behavior* (November 1975), pp. 64-69. Her focus is on the woman's role in country music.

America's diversity—her people of all races, cultural differences, farms and cities—was focused on by all forms of the mass media during the Bicentenial. Here is an illustration of the spirit of that year-long ceremony and the potential of the American media.

7 Media for Minorities/Women

TV Usage Greater Among Non-Whites—

Have Blacks Really Made It in Hollywood?—

Black Journals Reflect Shift from Racialism —

Chicanos and the Media—

Women's Pages in the 1970's—

Ten Cogent Reasons Why TV News Fails Women—

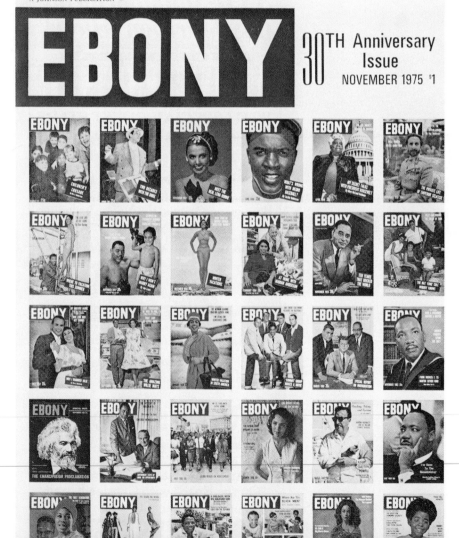

TV Usage Greater Among Non-Whites

Nielsen Newscast

Nielsen Television Index has distributed to clients "Television Viewing Among Whites and Non-Whites," a report providing broad benchmarks of comparative TV usage among non-white and white households nationally and among the persons in these households. The report, covering an eight-week period—during October-November, 1974, expands and updates a similar study covering January-February, 1973.

For white and non-white men, women and non-adults the recently released NTI report includes comparisons of: TV usage hour-by-hour and by major day parts, program audiences by major day parts and by selected program types.

Overall television usage in non-white households during October-November, 1974 averaged 52.1 hours per week, 16% more than in white households. The comparable mid-winter 1973 study showed almost the same differential—15% more TV usage among non-white households.

This report was prepared by Nielsen Television Index in a 1974 study. *The Nielsen Newscast,* 1975, from which this report is taken, is published by the Media Research Division of A.C. Nielsen Company. Reprinted with the permission of the A.C. Nielsen Company, Chicago, Illinois.

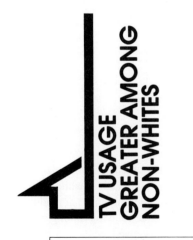

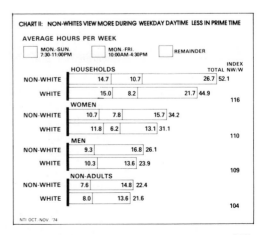

CHART I: NON-WHITE HOUSEHOLDS ARE LARGER AND YOUNGER

	WHITES	NON-WHITES	TOTAL (MM)	INDEX NW/W
TV HOUSEHOLDS	61.0	7.5 (11.0)	68.5	
PERSONS IN TV HOUSEHOLDS	174.4	24.5 (123)	198.9	
	PERSONS PER 100 TV HOUSEHOLDS	NW SHARE		
TOTAL PERSONS*	286	326		114
18-49	126	142		113
50+	61	76		80
WOMEN	106	111		105
MEN	92	96		96
NON-ADULTS*	84	123		146

——— NON-WHITE
- - - - - WHITE

*AGE 2+ YEARS   NIELSEN UNIVERSE EST'S 9/74

CHART II: NON-WHITES VIEW MORE DURING WEEKDAY DAYTIME LESS IN PRIME TIME

AVERAGE HOURS PER WEEK

	MON.-SUN. 7:30-11:00PM	MON.-FRI. 10:00AM-4:30PM	REMAINDER	INDEX TOTAL NW/W
HOUSEHOLDS				
NON-WHITE	14.7	10.7	26.7	52.1
WHITE	15.0	8.2	21.7	44.9
				116
WOMEN				
NON-WHITE	10.7	7.8	15.7	34.2
WHITE	11.8	6.2	13.1	31.1
				110
MEN				
NON-WHITE	9.3	16.8	26.1	
WHITE	10.3	13.6	23.9	
				109
NON-ADULTS				
NON-WHITE	7.6	14.8	22.4	
WHITE	8.0	13.6	21.6	
				104

NTI OCT.-NOV. '74

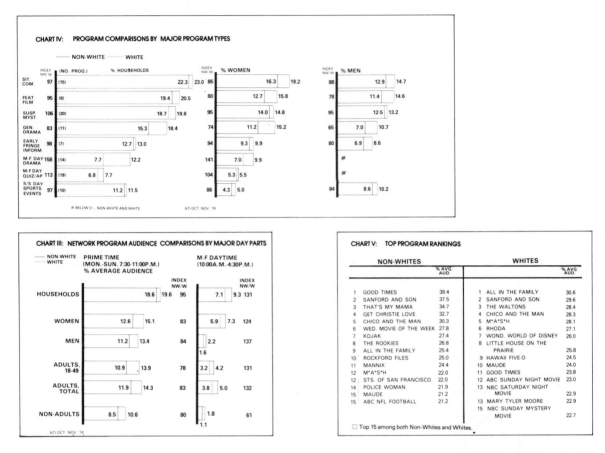

Non-white households make up approximately 11% of U.S. TV households and on the average have more persons, particularly non-adults, than white households. (Chart 1) Though non-white households have considerably more non-adults, greater overall household TV usage is due as much to more viewing among adults as to the greater number of non-adults. Non-whites outviewed whites on both a household basis and among persons during all times except the mid-evening hours. (Chart II) During prime time, on a household basis, the average network program rating for non-whites was only 5% lower than among white households. Persons ratings, however, were 16-22% lower among non-whites during prime time. (Chart III) During weekday daytime the average network program rated 24-37% higher among non-whites both on a household and adult persons basis. (Chart III)

By major program type, the greatest differences between white and non-white household audiences are seen in Weekday Drama (almost 60% higher-rated among non-whites) and Evening General Drama (a 20% edge among whites). In terms of audience levels among women and men, all five major evening program types averaged higher ratings among whites than among non-whites. (Chart IV)

The top four ranking programs among non-white households feature blacks and all are higher rated among non-whites than the top-ranking program among white households, "All in the Family," is among whites.

Six programs are in the "Top 15" both among non-whites and whites, on a household basis. (Chart V)

Bibliography

For an overview of Chicanos in the media, consult the bibliography at the end of the article by Félix Gutiérrez. This bibliography emphasizes the relationship between blacks and the electronic media.

For a general background on use of and access to the mass media in the U.S. consult the special issue of *Freedomways* (1974) devoted to the study of "The Black Image in the Mass Media." See especially the bibliography by Ernest Kaiser which lists books and magazine articles in five categories: general, television, radio, theater and film. Two recent studies on the image of blacks in television can be found in Churchill Robert, "The Presentation of Blacks in Television Network Newscasts," *Journalism Quarterly* (Spring 1975), pp. 50-55 and James L. Hinton, *et al.*, "Tokenism and Improving Imagery of Blacks in TV Drama and Comedy: 1973," *Journal of Broadcasting* (Fall 1974), pp. 423-432. See also Eugenia Collier, "A House of Twisted Mirrors: The Black Reflection in the Media," *Current History* (November 1974), pp. 228-231 ff. and Marilyn Diane Fife, "Black Image in American TV: The First Two Decades," *The Black Scholar* (November 1974), pp. 7-15.

Have Blacks Really Made It In Hollywood?

By Louie Robinson

At the near-deserted, cavernous MGM Studios in Culver City, Calif., the man with the power, Sidney Poitier, is making a motion picture, *Let's Do It Again*. It is his fourth directorial stint in a film in which he stars, and he is commander-in-chief of camera, cast and an almost all-black crew in a $2.6 million production for his own company, Verdun.

It is a much different situation than that which existed during the first half-century of American motion pictures when black men like Stepin' Fetchit, Mantan Moreland and Willie Best grinned and scratched their way through otherwise all-white films made by all-white people; when Hattie McDaniels and Louise Beavers and Butterfly McQueen knew that a call from a movie studio meant get out the maid's uniform again.

Louie Robinson wrote this article for *Ebony* magazine (June 1975). Reprinted with permission of Ebony Magazine, copyright 1975 by Johnson Publishing Company, Inc. *Ebony* is a *Life*-like black owned, published and edited magazine.

But many blacks who make their living in Hollywood today will tell you that if there had not been the clowns and maids then, there would be no flashy black dudes and dynamite chicks gracing the silver screen today. And now, for the first time in its glamorous history, Hollywood has what might be called a Black Film Colony—those who can live (although some choose not to) and work, with varying degrees of success, in the magic city of golden dreams.

Their names and faces are known throughout the U.S. and around the world: Diana Ross, Billy Dee Williams, Ossie Davis and Ruby Dee, Max Julien, Vonetta McGee, James Earl Jones, Paul Winfield, Cicely Tyson, Yaphet Kotto, Richard Roundtree, Fred Williamson, Ron O'Neal, Raymond St. Jaques, Calvin Lockhart, Lou Gossett, William Marshall, Brock Peters, Roscoe Lee Browne, Al Freeman Jr., Brenda Sykes, Pam Grier, Rosalind Cash, Jim Brown, Calvin Lockhart, Godfrey Cambridge, D'Urville Martin and others whose talent, power and beauty not only changed much of the nature of American films, but also helped stay the industry from financial ruin.

Black films, most of them made cheaply ($500,000 to $800,000) and grossing millions, became the new film genre of the '70s. Some excellent and some dreadful, they gave new status and opportunity to blacks, both on and off camera. Poitier, Gordon Parks Sr., Hugh Robertson, Ossie Davis, Melvin Van Peebles, Gordon Parks Jr. and Ivan Dixon assumed director status; playwright Lonne Elder III found his superb gifts in demand in Hollywood, and a variety of black craftsmen went to work.

Yet, the wizened maxim, "All that glitters is not gold," must have been coined for Hollywood. While Diana Ross and Billy Dee Williams film their new picture, *Mahogany*, amidst the splendor of Rome, and while St. Jacques roams the Beverly Hills in a Citroën-Maserati and Williamson luxuriates in his furry bachelor pad overlooking Sunset Boulevard, there are problems and pitfalls in the celluloid paradise. A few, notably Poitier and Williamson, make their own pictures and provide work for other blacks, but others still find jobs too scarce and the temporary fame of their name high on a movie marquee too fleeting. Some established black actors see themselves being passed over for lesser names whose services can be bought more cheaply. A male star whose name has proven a bell-ringer at the box office, may command salaries in excess of $100,000 or even $200,000 per picture, but an unknown actor works for $750 a week. A proven track record of professional talent may be worth as much as $2,000 to $5,000 a week, or, if only one week of work is involved, a fee of $10,000 to $15,000 for an actor.

Although many of the same figures apply to actresses, some of them are in unique circumstances: Diana Ross, coming into movies as a musical superstar much the same as Harry Belafonte or Sammy Davis Jr., is a highly-paid, instant success on the astounding success of her first role in the Oscar-nominated part of Billie Holiday in *Lady Sings the Blues*. Cicely Tyson, another Oscar nominee of the same year for her role in *Sounder*, makes less money and turns down much of what she could earn because of her insistence on quality scripts. (Miss Ross is picky too, but

JET

JAN. 27, 1977/75¢ A JOHNSON PUBLICATION

ROOTS OF BLACKS
SHOWN IN EIGHT
DAYS OF TV DRAMA

STARS IN 'ROOTS'
★ CICELY TYSON
★ JOHN AMOS
★ O.J. SIMPSON
★ BEN VEREEN
★ LESLIE UGGA...
★ RICHARD ROU...
★ LOU GOSSETT...
★ MAYA ANA AN...

lack Stars

...CATION

JANUARY 1977 $1.00

...DYSON
...YS GOD'S WILL

...VERS—
...CASE OF
...TALENT

...YEAR'S

...YS KNIGHT AND
...NKERSON MOVEMENT

Now

VOL. 1, NO. 1 $1
80223

Lola
Falana
"I'm the
first black
sex symbol"

NATALIE
COLE
Her meteoric
rise is 'huge
jar of candy'

Happiness hasn't
been easy for
James Earl Brown

IN THIS ISSUE
BEST
ACTRESS
AWARD
CONTEST
Win prizes—see pg. 5

with her money and the great resources of Motown Industries, Inc. behind her, she can afford to be.) There are still other actresses who have found the going rate for stardom to be a mere $10,000 to $20,000 a picture.

Those black actors and actresses who can demand and get such fees know another side of Hollywood where the dazzle and excitement give way to hustle and tenacity.

For Sidney Poitier, home is still the Bahamas, but he is now a recognizable force in Hollywood. Most other black actors say he is the most powerful among them. After years of stardom and salaries that sometimes approached a million dollars a picture, he now usually works for a percentage of the film, which is even better yet. But most of all, he is making films. *Let's Do It Again* represents the last of the three-picture deal between First Artists and his own Verdun Productions, a company in which he owns 100,000 shares of stock and is an officer, along with Paul Newman, Steve McQueen, Barbra Streisand and Dustin Hoffman. More importantly, his production firm has a new deal with Universal and the Mirsch Corporation to make some five films over the next five years at an estimated cost of $15 million.

Poitier sees the black film as being an integral part of the motion picture industry along with predominantly white-oriented films and believes that both will grow healthier in time. "What distresses me," he says, "is that there is not an appreciable number of black producers being developed."

Poitier is not wedded to the idea (as some are) that investment money for black films must come from black people. "Money is principally interested in multiplying itself, I don't care who owns it," he says. "If you put up two million and your return is six, everybody has made some money—the actor, the producer, the backer."

While Poitier says there is no real breakthrough in high earnings as far as the Black Film Colony is concerned, there are those who are making a good buck. "Stars like Jim Brown and Fred Williamson deserve every penny they get. Any actor who can turn in a profit on a film is worth his salary, whatever his salary may be." But he adds, "The only people who will get rich in this business are those who will make pictures and own them. There are a lot of talented people out here, but we all wait at home for the phone to ring. What we need is a cadre of initiators who husband a project through from idea to finished film. Money can be had. It's difficult; I don't mean to imply it isn't."

Diahann Carroll lives in an expensive house in an expensive part of town. She is an expensive girl. Her money is what might be called "old" money—she earned big salaries for a long time as a nightclub singer before she became the first black star of a television series, *Julia*. Her Benedict Canyon home has a stone fireplace, stained glass doors and a swimming pool. There are servants and a den with a well-stocked bar.

"I'm afraid the amount of money I've made in motion pictures in the last 15 years wouldn't afford the rent on this room," she says with a laugh as she looks around the dark, lush, wood-paneled den. "I'm very happy that I can eat by singing a song."

Miss Carroll was named one of the five best actresses of last year for the role she played in her sixth film, *Claudine*. "I want to get away from the Julia image," explains Diahann, remembering those elegant gowns and sugar-coated plots of TV. "What audiences see on that screen is what they believe you want to do. It never occurs to them that you have a problem getting roles. But how much clout do we blacks have?" Still, the screen is where she wants to work. "I want something that challenges me, so I can examine my skills," she says, with a feeling that *Claudine* was a major step in that direction. "I have come a long way on being half cute and working in nightclubs. I want something to challenge me to push myself as far as I can go emotionally."

Miss Carroll's private life is such that, she says, "I used to see almost everybody out here. Now, I see practically no one." She was married (to a Las Vegas businessman) and divorced in the span of a few months after a celebrated courtship with David Frost, and she notes that the moralistic eye of both press and public focuses more critically on the black actress than on the black actor. "Nobody seems to care what the man does," she says, "but they are quick to get on the woman's back for doing the same thing." Still, she feels that some of the more sensational aspects of Hollywood's well-scrutinized morality will be neither the black actor's or actresses' cup of tea. "We'll never be off the proving hook to that extent," she says.

At the top of a winding road in the North Hollywood hills is a rambling, rustic redwood house in need of paint and awaiting remodeling. It is the home of Max Julien and Vonetta McGee, who must be called—although Julien hates any sort of categorizing—a part of the new breed in the Hollywood Black Film Colony.

They live comfortably and casually with their cats and dogs (one of the latter, an Alaskan malamute, is named Bushrod from *Tomasine and Bushrod*—the recent film the couple made together, and although their union is without benediction of clergy, there is an air of permanency to the arrangement: They have planted 22 eucalyptus trees, propose to enlarge the house, and Vonetta speaks somewhat warmly of "when the children come."

Max, in blue jeans and a black wool turtleneck, and Vonetta in a grape tent dress, were warm and candid on a brilliant sunny California morning as they served wine and tea and talked of today's Hollywood and the black performer. Julien does not think the recent black vogue in films has slackened, "although it might be moving at the same pace." But, he adds, "Even when you saw all those black films in the theaters, it didn't mean all that many black people were working."

Julien's own unique gifts as actor, writer and producer cause him to look at both sides of the coin and examine the edges. "It's a terrible rat-race," he says of the movie job scene. "Larry Cook, who starred in *The Spook Who Sat by the Door*, is not working. Ron O'Neal, after the popularity of *Super Fly* and *Super Fly T.N.T.*, is not working." Still, he thinks "there are probably as many black films on the drawing boards as before, it's just that money is tight right now. We're on the lower part of the economic spectrum; the film world reflects society.''

Still, for the investor in a product with audience appeal, there is certainly money to be made. *Cleopatra Jones*, a film Julien wrote in Rome and which starred Tamara Dobson, grossed over $6 million in this country and is adding to that figure abroad. *The Mack*, in which Julien starred, has grossed $8 million, and *Tomasine and Bushrod*, which he wrote, co-produced and starred in, has grossed $2 million despite limited distribution. ''Distributors are clamoring for black films,'' he says.

Thoroughly aware of the controversy that black films have caused because of sociological content, Julien contends that ''Max Julien, Sidney Poitier and Melvin Van Peebles each has to be allowed to make his kind of films.'' Whether criticism of black films will change them qualitatively or simply reduce them in quantity is a moot question. ''The average agent, producer or director around Hollywood doesn't want any change,'' says Julien. ''But while black audiences don't listen to critics, white financiers and producers do listen to them.''

Julien believes that ''we have to continue to make black films that appeal to black audiences,'' and it is Miss McGee's contention. ''Black film,'' she says, '' is the most valuable art form in pictures since Andy Warhol and Campbell Soup cans because of the impact it made on the black community.'' Julien declares, ''I want to make films geared to black audiences, and if whites come to see them—good. That's where my head is—films that are pro-black but not necessarily anti-white.''

Twenty miles from the TV and motion picture production centers and just as far from the fashionable areas much of the Black Film Colony inhabits, lives one of its most active practitioners. His house in Pasadena is a relatively modest one, filled with African art and sculpture and he tends to hang out ''with truck drivers and stuff.'' Ivan Dixon, an actor turned director, has directed some 35 to 40 television shows, including segments of *Room 222*, *The Bill Cosby Show*, *The Waltons*, *Get Christy Love*, *Nichols*, *Apple's Way* and *The Sty of the Blind Pig* for the Public Broadcasting System. He has also directed two films, *Trouble Man* and *The Spook Who Sat by the Door*, a sparsely distributed film which Dixon says too many people thought ''a blueprint for revolutionary acts.''

Dixon feels ''there's a difference in the mediums and a difference in the prestige'' between working TV shows and features (as movies are referred to). ''I've been lucky enough to do both and survive.'' But, he says, ''Unless you're a really big director, nobody's out there looking for you. You have to go out and get jobs.'' In the craft unions, with which Dixon must deal as a director, he doesn't believe blacks ''represent anywhere near 10 percent of the industry. There are still some areas we haven't cracked yet.'' One of the problems Dixon sees, in addition to the entrenchment of ancient baronies in which the jobs were often hereditary, is that ''we don't know each other. There's no real exchange among those of us in the industry; so we don't know what each other is doing.'' Nevertheless, blacks now work as film editors, cameramen, electricians, makeup men and script girls.

Dixon thinks it may be time for a change in the content of black films, if not the quantity. "What we went through in 1972 and 1973 was like a cycle," he says. "Movies have always moved in cycles. We went through a cycle of black adventure-action films and now the box office has leveled off on those. It's not that black films won't make money. It's that there are a number of other types of black films. If somebody decides to make them and put them on the market, they will make a lot of dough and there will be a cycle of those. This is really an industry and not an art form."

An actress whom Ivan Dixon used in both *Trouble Man* and *Spook* is Paula Kelly, the sensational dancer who gained prominence as Shirley MacLaine's cohort in *Sweet Charity*. Paula has appeared in a total of eight films, among them the role of Leggy Peggy in *Uptown Saturday Night*. Although she has been in films since 1968, she lives today in economic uncertainty.

"Is there enough work around to sustain oneself as a black actress? No, there is not," she says, "The studios don't have enough material. A lot of actors and actresses have turned to writing in an attempt to create more roles. I'm lucky. I can keep myself going by doing a concert here and there, and going into TV and teaching. I don't depend on movies." The variety, says Paula, at least "keeps your energies going and you're creating." She is also getting into writing. One job difficulty she and others find is the approach producers take in seeking black actresses. "They have no gauge to discern our different talents and qualities," she says, "but they have that discerning quality about themselves. If they want an Ali McGraw type, they don't consider Dyan Cannon."

While the aura of Hollywood glamour persists as both illusion and reality, difficulties plague the black star. "You get batted back and forth, trying to find that little whirlwind that is yours," Paula explains. "It's exciting, but so much of it is based on whim and fantasy that it's hard to get your track record going because it's not based on anything concrete." Despite her film pursuits, Paula does not anticipate a day when true lightning might strike. "I'm not interested in being a really big star. I want to be in control of my life. I don't want to worry about the rent. I'm always working at something, If I'm not making a picture, I don't panic."

Fate's finger is never more fickle than in Hollywood, and so panic is the villain always waiting in the wings. One of the best ways to stave off panic is with a long-running TV series, one of the most secure jobs in town.

But what happens when that final episode is played? Denise Nicholas graced *Room 222* with warmth and beauty for five years. The series now finished, she is working in *Let's Do It Again*, her fourth film. "This is the first time I've ever free lanced in Hollywood," she explains. "I get very angry sometimes, and I get very sympathetic for other people in the business who go through this all the time. The business tends to treat actors and actresses very shabbily when you're not working. When you are, in something with a decent budget, then you get treated like royalty." The fact that black performers of different ages, types and physical characteristics are all summoned for a single role, says Denise, "speaks to that invisibility we have still."

She would like to confine most of her professional efforts to movies rather than television, but, she says, ''that's not about to happen. There's a good distance to travel yet.'' She writes songs as ''a hobby that I'm trying to develop into more than a hobby,'' and one of her works, *Can We Pretend*, is included in an album by her ex-husband, singer Bill Withers, titled ''Justments.''

Actress Rosalind Cash is soon planning to abandon her small, modern, efficiency apartment in Burbank for other quarters, but they will hardly be anything that would qualify in Hollywood as luxurious. She is simply tired of sleeping on a sofa. ''There are a lot of us who would like to assimilate all the glamour and fluff,'' she says, ''but the hard truth is, we're all out here trying to make a living.'' She has been acting for 18 years, much of that time spent with the Negro Ensemble Company in Harlem, where she worked for $75 to $90 a week (and held such jobs as keypunch operator, clerk, Kelly Girl, domestic, etc.). She remembers touring the South in a station wagon with no heater for the magnificnet sum of $25 a week. Rosalind has now made eight films, including *Shaft, Omega Man, Melinda* and *Cornbread, Earl and Me*. She retains a hard professional pride. ''My thing has always been to do qualitative work,'' she explains. ''I've been selective. I've turned down scripts—not a lot; I don't see too many—because *I* didn't want to be the one to do that.''

Rosalind knows full well the illusiveness of movie fame. ''My theatre and film record doesn't guarantee me a call,'' she declares. ''I have to get out and hustle like everybody else in this town. But you get the shot you deserve, I think. I try to keep a good mental attitude. I've had some good shots and I think I'll get better ones. I just feel it. It's an intuitive thing. But if I could never act again, my world would not fall apart.''

It is highly unlikely that Rosalind Cash will never make another picture; unquestionably black actors and actresses are here in abundance, to stay, whether they perform on the silver screen or the smaller cathode tube. (After all, TV stars Redd Foxx, Demond Wilson, Esther Rolle, John Amos, Teresa Graves, Georg Stanford Brown, Terry Carter, Theresa Merritt, Clifton Davis, Sherman Hemsley, Isabel Sanford and Mike Evans are all part of Hollywood, too.) They have paid their dues and gotten it all together. Black audiences are loyal and white audiences are receptive. Goodbye Rock Hudson and John Wayne; Tony King and Thalmus Rasulala, you're looking good.

Bibliography

Two very useful books dealing with blacks in film are Donald Bogle, *Toms, Coons, Mulattoes, Mammies and Bucks: An Interpretive History of Blacks in American Films*, Viking Press, 1973, and James P. Murray, *To Find an Image: Black Films from Uncle Tom to Super Fly*, Bobbs-Merrill, 1974. Ann Powers, compiler, *Blacks in American Movies: A Selected Bibliography*, Scarecrow Press, 1974 is a highly useful, annotated compilation of books, articles and indices.

Black Journals Reflect
Shift from Racialism

By J. K. Obatala

Its circulation was never more than 10,000, but the black magazine *Freedomways* was as much a part of the civil rights movement in America as denim shirts and picket signs. A left-of-center publication created in 1961, *Freedomways* was founded by, among others, the Marxist scholar W. E. B. DuBois and Loraine Hansberry, author of "Raisin In The Sun."

Now *Freedomways* is in trouble. Unless it raises more than $50,000 within a year, it probably will have to make drastic cutbacks. While the troubles of *Freedomways,* published in New York, do not necessarily reflect the fortunes of all black magazines, the fact that such an influencial magazine is having financial problems sheds light on some important changes in black thinking as well as on the relative position of blacks in American society.

As some blacks change their way of thinking and living, the magazine publishers who depend on them for a market must also change. Those magazines which once leaned toward black nationalism now take a more nonracial stance. Those which once saw their primary responsibility as "consciousness-raising" now find it necessary to deal more with day-to-day matters. Even the glamour magazines are becoming more serious, mainly because both black entertainers and their audiences are maturing socially.

That black magazines are having to become more pragmatic seems to be at least a part of the problem of *Freedomways*, which rose on the great wave of social unrest that swept the country in the 1960s. Abjuring advertising from major corporations, the editors got most of their money from contributions, subscriptions and an annual Freedomways Symposium held at Carnegie Hall.

Now, because of the current economic slump, the reduced moral outrage among wealthy white liberals and a declining black interest in social protest, the large contributions that once sustained *Freedomways* and similar black magazines are no longer rolling in.

This does not mean, however, that it is impossible to operate an ideological, issue-oriented magazine successfully. *Black Scholar*, of Sausalito, Calif. for example, seems to be one issue-oriented magazine that has solved this problem, although its shrewd marketing and management may have contributed to the magazine's current complications.

A direct outgrowth of the black studies movement, *Black Scholar* was founded in 1969 by Nathan Hare, who had been forced to resign the chairmanship of the Black Studies Department at San Francisco State College, and Robert Chrisman, one of Hare's faculty colleagues and a staunch political ally.

J.K. Obatala, a former professor of black history, also was a staff writer and editor with the *Los Angeles Times*. Copyright 1975, Los Angeles Times. Reprinted by permission.

Like the editors of *Freedomways*, Chrisman and Hare also shunned corporate ads. But *Black Scholar* relied less heavily than *Freedomways* on contributions of money from supporters—except for a few small grants from liberal foundations.

Instead, Chrisman and Hare viewed *Black Scholar's* constituency as a largely untapped source of creative talent. In addition to articles by leading black intellectuals, *Black Scholar* also published articles by militant and moderate writers who either were not established or could not find an outlet in the mainstream magazines—black or white.

But the very success of *Black Scholar's* marketing and publications strategy may have contributed to recent dissension in the editorial board.

When *Black Scholar* attempted to change its editorial views to coincide with those of the shifting freedom movement—from which it draws most of its readers and writers—the decision precipitated the resignation of publisher Nathan Hare. Hare complained that the magazine had been taken over by what he called "instant Marxists" and that black nationalists weren't getting enough exposure.

Whether there has been a "Marxist" takeover at *Black Scholar* remains to be seen. It is certain, however, that the black freedom movement has, for some time, been moving away from black nationalism.

Recently, this shift in black thinking has been most dramatically illustrated by the publicity surrounding the apparent conversion of several key Afro-American figures to Marxism-Leninism. Among those making the change are Ron Karenga, former chairman of US, and Amiri Baraka, a black poet and playwright previously known as Leroi Jones. Both men were militant black nationalists in the 1960s.

The *Black Scholar* controversy and the ideological turnabout of Baraka, Karenga and others, however, should not be taken to mean that the black community itself has embraced Marxism.

Even those activists, writers, scholars and intellectuals who have openly declared themselves "Marxist" will, for the most part avoid any white or black political party that in any way threatens the state. For most of them, "Marxism" is simply a way of getting out of the black nationalist movement without identifying themselves too closely with old-guard integrationists.

This turn away from racialism by certain Afro-American thinkers and activists is paralleled by a more serious and pragmatic outlook in some sectors of the black community.

Striking evidence of this trend is apparent in *Black Enterprise* and *Contact*, two New York-based magazines mainly concerned with economics and business.

Black Enterprise, the more important of the two, has a readership consisting largely of college and university students. Believing that business is the way for blacks to get ahead in modern American society, it stresses black achievement in business, management and related fields.

A New Orleans magazine, *Black Collegian*, also has a wide circulation among college and university students. "Consciousness-raising" formerly was a basic aspect of its editoiral policy, but *Black Collegian* now is primarily a service and career oriented publication because its editors realize that blacks have to earn a living to continue to have a "consciousness"—political or otherwise.

Some blacks have avoided the traditional issue of racial integration by stressing "Marxism," "black economics" and by generally acting and thinking more pragmatically while continuing to speak in racialist terms.

Encore, however, is one magazine which has faced the issue squarely. Published in New York, it is openly and assertively integrationist, though it does not mount the soap box. Rather, its perspective arises naturally out of its policy of publishing articles by authors of all ethnic groups and on a wide varity of subjects.

One of its recent biweekly editions included articles on Social Security, Zaire, and the Hirshhorn Museum in Washington, as well as a reprint on industry from the *New York Times*.

That *Encore's* growing circulation exceeds 250,000 shows the strength of the present intellectual trend among blacks and underscores the likelihood that it will continue.

One thing that helps make this possible is the increase in the number of blacks who have not only the desire but the ability to move or engage in social activities outside the black ghetto. It is these Afro-Americans who have enough contact with and interest in whites to want to read about them or know of what they have to say.

This phenomenon is often expressed in terms of the expansion of the black middle class. And it is true that the black middle income group has grown.

Yet a look at what has happened (and is still happening) to *Ebony* and other black magazines over the past few years indicates that the black middle class is not only growing, but also being transformed. It is receiving not just new people, but new kinds of people.

Dark-skinned Afro-Americans, for example, now have more effect on middle-class life than previously, when it seemed a more or less natural assumption that Afro-Americans with lighter complexion would predominate in social, political and cultural affairs.

This was clearly refelcted in the pages of magazines like *Ebony* and *Jet,* products of Johnson Publication in Chicago, which placed a high value on light skin. Today, the magazines have altered their policies largely because darker skinned Afro-Americans have become more important economically and more aggresive politically.

But color is not the only factor in the transformation of the black middle class. The current format and editorial policies of some black magazines also reflect the growing influence of artists, entertainers and athletes on black middle class culture.

Unlike the old days when most black celebrities had a lot of charisma but were of little economic or political importance to the Afro-American community, black stars such as Kareem Abdul-Jabbar, Whitman Mayo, Redd Foxx, Eartha Kitt and Harry Belafonte provide a model of affluence well worth imitating. Moreover, they often take political stands that affect all Afro-Americans. This new serious attitude of entertainers and artists has forced black magazines to abandon or at least alter the "gold Cadillac" approach that emphasized conspicuous consumption.

All of these trends in black magazines leave the unmistakable impression that things are changing, not only in black-white relations but in the Afro-American community itself. Just as the freedom movement changed its emphasis from integration to separatism in the 1960s, now another major ideological shift is in progress toward nonracialism, a social outlook which, broadly, views the problems of Afro-Americans as resulting from many factors besides the racial prejudices of whites.

In short, the changes at *Ebony, Black Scholar* and other magazines reflect a growing realization among Afro-Americans that blacks and other Americans are still faced with some complex and serious problems which are not likely to yield to simplistic solutions—no matter how strongly we believe they will.

Bibliography

A useful background book dealing with the black press is Roland E. Wolseley, *The Black Press, U.S.A.*, Iowa State University Press, 1971. This book includes both historical and contemporary treatment of the black press. Three studies printed by Mercer House include *The Black Press in America: A Guide*, 2nd ed., 1972, *The Black Press: A Bibliography* (which contains over 350 items), and *Perspectives of the Black Press, 1974*, edited by Henry G. LaBrie, III. The last book up-dates some of the information found in the other two and reprints articles on the role, growth and problems of the black press. A special issue of *Harvard Journal of Afro-American Affairs* was devoted to "The Black Press" in the spring of 1971. For an insightful viewpoint expressed by one of the more successful black columnists in the established white press, see Carl T. Rowan, *Just Between Us Blacks*, Random House, 1974.

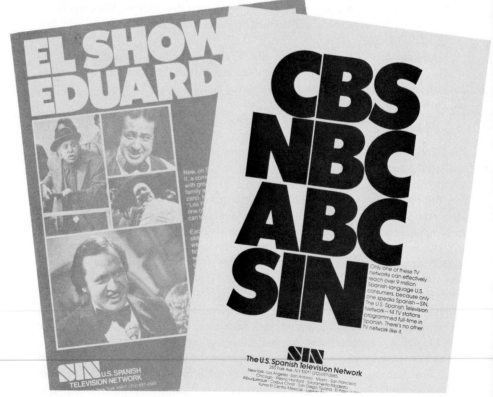

Chicanos And The Media

By Félix Gutiérrez

On a Spring day in 1972 a unique airplane hijacking took place in the skies between Albuquerque and Los Angeles. The skyjacker did not demand ransom money, ask to be flown to a foreign country, or even carry a loaded pistol.

The skyjacker, Ricardo Chávez Ortiz, only asked that the plane be flown to Los Angeles and that he be allowed to hold a press conference when it landed. The purpose of the press conference, held inside the captive airliner, was to expose the harsh life that his family and other Latinos had encountered in the United States. However, he added one critical stipulation: the press conference was to be open only to representatives of the Spanish-language communication media.

The act was a symbolic one that produced few direct benefits. Chávez Ortiz later received a stiff federal prison sentence for his act. And the press conference produced no substantive improvement in the living conditions of Latinos in the United States.

However, the skyjacking is important for several reasons. First, it was an act of self sacrifice that offered no possibility of personal gain and posed a direct threat to no one. Second, Chávez Ortiz used his exploit to talk with his own people and not the population others might consider more important: the Anglo mass audience. Thus, he was willing to sacrifice his life to use communication media to tell his people that they have the power to improve their individual and collective lives.

Chávez Ortiz placed his emphasis on two factors of Latino life in the United States. One is the reality of the subordinate and exploited status of Latinos in this country. The other is the potential power of communication media as a force for information and organization within the Latino community.

Latinos in the United States

Substantive gains in living conditions will not come easily for the estimated 16.9 million Latinos living in the United States. We have been a subjugated and colonized minority since the 1848 War with México added nearly half of the Mexican republic to the United States. Latinos who have come to the mainland United States in later migrations from México, Cuba, Puerto Rico and other Spanish-speaking areas have usually faced the same conditions.

Although we are often cast as a regional group confined to the Southwestern United States, Latinos are actually a national minority group (the nation's second largest) with substantial communities in the Midwest, Northeast and South. New York state accounts for 15 percent of the nation's Latino population and New York City has a higher concentration of Latinos (2 million) than any other city in the nation. Florida, Illinois, and New Jersey each have more Latino residents than either Arizona or Colorado.

Félix Gutiérrez is on the faculty of the Department of Journalism, California State University, Northridge. He has spoken and written extensively on this subject. This article was written especially for this edition.

Analyses of the 1970 census figures and other studies indicate that Latinos are a people for whom "equal opportunity" has had little meaning. These reports statistically verify that Latinos are generally undereducated, underemployed, underpaid and ill housed when compared with national averages.

Latinos can also be described as a hardworking people who take their family and community responsibilities seriously. However, many confront a system that was designed to work against them when they try to improve their lives. For instance, United States citizens speaking only Spanish weren't even allowed to vote in California until 1970. Spanish-language ballots and voter information weren't provided until 1975.

Communication media are among the many "systems" that Latinos must confront in working to improve their lives in the United States. Although media are not usually considered a "bread and butter" issue such as law enforcement, housing, health care, employment and education, the issues involving media have gained greater prominence among Latino activists in the 1970s.

This growing awareness of the importance of communication media has developed partly out of an understanding of the role played by media in shaping the collective consciousness of the public mind. It has also grown out of the need to develop communicators and communication media to serve Latino communities. Latino dealings with media systems have generally taken place on three levels. Each level represents a different media subsystem which Latinos must deal with. These three subsystems can be broadly designated as: (1) Anglo media, (2) Spanish-language media, and (3) alternative media.

Anglo Media

Anglo media can be described as English-language communication media directed at the mass audience of the United States. Under this group would fall most television stations, daily newspapers, magazines, and motion pictures. These media are identified by the fact that their primary audience is essentially non-Latino. Therefore, their role in relation to the Latino communities is essentially attempting to explain or portray Latinos to a predominantly Anglo audience.

The national press called Chicanos (Latinos of Mexican descent) the "invisible minority" and "the minority nobody knows" when it suddenly "discovered" Chicanos in the late 1960s. However, the invisibility and ignorance were more in the minds of the writers and editors than in the reality of the people they tried to write about. This is because consistent coverage of Chicanos and Latinos in the national media was virtually non-existent in the first six decades of the twentieth century. A survey of citations in the *Readers' Guide to Periodical Literature* from 1890 to 1970 reveals very few articles about Latino groups in the United States in the magazines indexed. The articles that were written often had a crisis or negative overtone. That is, they were written during periods when Mexican labor or immigration impacted national policy or when Latinos were involved in civil strife.

Local coverage apparently wasn't much better. One researcher noted that pictures of Chicana brides weren't even printed in El Paso newspapers until the 1950s;

this in a town that was over half Chicano. Speaking to a 1969 media conference in San Antonio, veteran *Los Angeles Times* reporter Rubén Salazar said "the Mexican-American beat in the past was nonexistent."

"Before the recent racial turmoil, Mexican Americans were something that vaguely were there but nothing which warranted comprehensive coverage—unless it concerned, in my opinion, such badly reported stories as the Pachuco race riots in Los Angeles in the early 1940s, or more recently, the Bracero program's effect on Mexican Americans," he explained. Salazar also predicted Anglo news media would not find the Chicano community easy to cover.

"The media, having ignored the Mexican Americans for so long, but now willing to report them, seem impatient about the complexities of the story," Salazar continued. "It's as if the media, having finally discovered the Mexican American, is not amused that under that serape and sombrero is a complex Chicano instead of a potential Gringo."

Salazar's analysis was based on his long experience as a reporter, war correspondent and bureau chief. It was also supported by the news media's bumbling efforts to "discover" the barrio during the late 1960s. Stories were often inaccurate and nearly always revealed more of the writers' own stereotypes than the characteristics of the people they tried to write about.

For instance, a *Time* magazine reporter riding through East Los Angeles in 1967 saw mostly "tawdry taco joints and rollicking cantinas," smelled "the reek of cheap wine (and)....the fumes of frying tortillas," and heard "the machine gun patter of slang Spanish." Such slanted reporting did little to promote intergroup understanding, but added the credibility of the news media to the prejudices of many in their audience.

One cause of such biased and inaccurate reporting was the lack of Chicano reporters and editors on Anglo publications. A 1971 survey of Texas daily newspapers revealed that Chicanos constituted only 3.2 percent of the editorial workers in the newspapers surveyed. Many of them were working in towns along the Mexican border where Chicanos are the majority.

Although many broadcasters and periodicals made overt attempts to hire Chicano reporters in the late 1960s and early 1970s, this priority on minority hiring apparently did not continue once vague quotas were met. When this writer inquired about a job opening at a Los Angeles television station, the assistant to the news director replied, "We did have an opening for a Mexican American, but we already hired one."

"The discrimination against Chicanos in media hiring prior to the 1960s has been replaced by the tokenism of the 1970s," said a Chicano reporter for a major metropolitan newspaper in 1975. He noted that most news organizations would hire at least one or two Chicano reporters, but no more. A 1975 national survey of minority employees supports his line of reasoning.

The Journalism Council, a group of journalism educators, surveyed the number of minority employees in mass media "image maker" job categories, primarily top level and professional positions. Earlier surveys had shown a slow but steady increase in minority representation, but a comparison of 1973 and 1974 figures revealed that minority employment had held steady at 4.9 percent. The percentage of minority "image makers" working in newspapers had actually declined in that period.

Although the decade between 1965 and 1975 witnessed an increased coverage of Chicano affairs and stepped up employment of Chicano reporters, this increased visibility has not necessarily resulted in an increased understanding of Chicano affairs by the Anglo community. Much of the news of the barrio is treated as "soft news" or feature stories with little impact beyond a "zoo appeal" that reveals the strange characteristics of people in the barrio.

When Chicano reporters meet, conversation will often turn to what they feel is discrimination on the job. Some report that editors will not allow them to pursue penetrating stories that probe the complexities of Chicano issues. Others have been told that the news media don't want "barrio specialists" and that they must be "reporters first and Chicanos second." Many editors apparently do not understand that the two designations are not mutually exclusive and that a qualified Chicano reporter can function equally well in several worlds.

One Los Angeles reporter complained when he was constantly assigned to cover the unveilings of wall murals in the barrio, but was not allowed to report on more substantive issues. His editor promptly took him off a wall mural assignment and sent him to cover the divorce of rock stars Sonny and Cher instead.

But inadequate and slanted reporting in the news media is only one side of the issues Chicanos have raised with Anglo media. In the news media the issue has revolved around invisibility. In the entertainment media the issue has concerned stereotyping.

Novelists, short story writers, movie makers and television producers have long delighted in portraying Chicanos and Mexicanos in stereotyped roles revolving around the Latin lover, the bandit, the faithful servant, the mustachioed overweight slob, the mamacita, and the woman with dark eyes, a low cut blouse and loose morals. These common stereotypes are nothing new. Neither is Chicano reaction against them.

In 1911 *La Crónica*, a Spanish-language newspaper in Laredo, Texas, waged a hard-fought campaign against stereotyping of Mexicanos and Native Americans in the cowboy movies then just emerging. The editor complained that Mexicanos and Native Americans were almost always cast as "villains and cowards" and argued that Mexicanos were the "most defamed in these sensational American films."

These negative stereotypes and other Latino caricatures have continued in movies and television during the 20th century. Even when Mexicanos and Chicanos are portrayed as lead characters the role has often been stereotyped or distorted. Thus, Spencer Tracy's part in "Tortilla Flat," Wallace Berry's portrayal of Pancho Villa, Marlon Brando's lead in "Viva Zapata," and Valerie Harper's role in "Freebie and the Bean" reveal more of the actors and actress' preconceptions than the character of the people they are trying to portray.

Latino actors and actresses found themselves similarly typecast in stereotyped roles when they sought work in Hollywood, although there has been some improvement since 1970. Ricardo Montalban, who signed with MGM in 1956, has written he was condemned to "the bondage of 'Latin-lover' roles" early in his career. Rita Moreno, who won an Oscar for her part in "West Side Story" in the early 1960s, didn't make another movie for seven years because she refused to play roles as the "Latin spitfire," the only type casting directors would offer her.

The coming of television in the 1950s added another weapon to the arsenal of the media barons. The most popular comedy show of the period, "I Love Lucy," regularly made fun of Desi Arnaz' supposed inability to speak unaccented English and his lapses into fast-paced Spanish when Lucille Ball made him angry. Reruns of the program were still prime time fare in many major metropolitan areas in the mid-1970s. Other early stereotyped characters included Frank, the Chicano gardener on "Father Knows Best;" Pepino, the farmhand on "The Real McCoys;" Sergeant Garcia, the bumbling soldier on "Zorro;" and most of the secondary characters in "The Flying Nun."

The adult westerns of the late 1950s and early 1960s ushered in a recycling of the Latino villains and loose women from earlier periods. And comedians, such as Bill Dana's "José Jimenez," continued to poke fun at the way Latinos were supposed to think, talk, and live. The situation on television became so bad that the Mexican consul in Los Angeles officially protested to the NBC network in 1966.

The civil disorders of the late 1960s awakened much of Hollywood to the harmful social and psychological effects of stereotyped portrayals of Blacks. But the benefits of this new awareness did not result in accurate or dignified portrayals of Latinos. In a widely circulated 1969 article a Chicano sociologist analyzed the racism behind portrayals of Latinos in advertising, including the corn chip stealing "Frito Bandito." In 1970 two Chicano media activists issued a "Brown Position Paper," that charged the electronic media had made the Chicano "The White Man's New Nigger."

"The greater openness of the media to the Black community spells a greater inaccessibility for the Chicano to the media," their report stated. "In providing access to the Black, the mass media believes itself to be free of prejudice or discrimination when, in effect, it is merely changing the emphasis from one group to another."

Latino media activist groups, such as the National Mexican American Anti-Defamation Committee, the National Chicano Media Council, Justicia, and Nosotros moved against advertising, television and motion pictures on a national scale in the early 1970s. Their efforts were only partially rewarded. Television and movies have increased the visibility of Chicano characters in the 1970s, but these roles are often stereotyped by social class. Thus, Chicanos portrayed as dignified, admirable characters are most often those with middle class credentials as teachers, police officers, social workers or other professional positions. Lower class Chicanos, particularly young people, are commonly portrayed as unable to deal with their own problems without assistance from Anglos, humorous characters, or members of the underworld.

Protests against media stereotyping has continued into the mid-1970s. In 1974 Chicano media groups reacted strongly to the NBC television series "Chico and the Man" and the Warner Brothers movie "Freebie and the Bean." The first episodes of "Chico and the Man" were so filled with racist "humor" that NBC agreed to edit subsequent programs and try to balance portrayals of Latinos. In 1975

Chicanos protested a stereotyped Mexican featured in an American Motors automobile commercial and the stream of Latino villains on network detective programs.

Latino media groups have also been active on the local level. Such organizations as San Antonio's Bilingual Bicultural Coalition for Mass Media, the Colorado Committee on Mass Media and the Spanish Speaking, and the California La Raza Media Coalition have launched license challenges, protests, and other actions against local media outlets. Such efforts resulted in agreements between broadcasters and citizens groups in San Antonio, El Paso, Fresno, Denver, Los Angeles and San Francisco.

By the mid-1970s Chicanos were no longer the ''invisible minority'' in the Anglo media. But it was not yet clear how long lasting or beneficial the increased media visibility would be. Much of the media's effort was apparently motivated by feelings of guilt over long standing injustices and spurred by mounting pressure from media activists. But guilt has its limits and pressure is effective only if it can be applied in increasingly sophisticated measures.

It is doubtful that Latinos will ever attain full and accurate coverage from the Anglo media. One reason is because Anglo media are primarily interested in attracting a non-Latino audience. Since there is a limit to the Anglo audience's appetite for Latino visibility, the Anglo media will most likely continue to treat Chicanos and Latinos as secondary characters.

Spanish-language Media

Although Latinos are a secondary audience for the Anglo media, they are the primary audience of the numerous Spanish-language media in the United States. Spanish-language media can be generally described as commercial media that direct their content toward the Spanish-speaking people in the United States, primarily Latinos.

Spanish-language media have a long history in what is now the Southwestern United States. The first regularly published newspaper in the region was *El Crepúsculo de la Libertad* (The Dawn of Liberty), founded in Taos in 1835, 13 years before the Yankee conquest of the territory. After the United States takeover of the Southwest some Anglo newspaper publishers began printing a few pages of news in Spanish. This was often done to win government printing subsidies for publishing laws and public notices in Spanish. Soon newspapers such as San Antonio's *El Bejareño*, Tucson's *El Fronterizo*, and Los Angeles' *El Clamor Público* began printing news entirely in Spanish.

These early Spanish-language newspapers regularly published jokes, short stories, poetry, and local commentary in addition to news coverage. News was generated out of local, national and international news sources, with editors freely borrowing items from each other's newspapers. During the 1890s Spanish-language newspapers in New México organized the Spanish American Associated Press to increase their viability as a force in the territory.

Since most early newspapers were dependent on a combination of government subsidies and advertising from Anglo merchants they cannot be described as solely an activist press. However, it is possible to note periods and issues in which they spoke on behalf of their people against the Anglo power structure. Many of their issues are similar to those being raised by Latino activists today.

For instance, in 1854 *El Bejareño* called for bilingual education for Chicano children. In the 1870s Los Angeles' *La Crónica* argued that Chicanos living in the "Barrio Latino" paid their fair share of city taxes, but didn't get an equal share of city services. In the 1880s *El Fronterizo* proposed a Chicano boycott of Tucson's Anglo merchants because some would not let Chicanos shop in their stores. In 1894 Santa Fe's *El Gato* printed an editorial on "The Capitalist and the Worker" that condemned local employers for extracting the labor of Chicano workers without paying decent wages.

A number of new Spanish-language newspapers were begun in the first two decades of the 20th century as civil strife in México and the promises of mine operators and growers brought a new wave of immigrants from México. Some of the newspapers, such as Ricardo Flores Magon's *Regeneración*, were organs for political movements in México. Others, such as San Antonio's *La Prensa*, were founded by former Mexican newspapermen who had moved to the United States.

A 1970 compilation identified 190 Spanish-language newspapers that were published in the five Southwestern states between 1848 and 1942. But daily newspapers and the foreign language press have both declined in numbers during the 20th century. By the mid-1970s there were only four Spanish-language dailies published in the United States.

Another reason for the decline of Spanish-language daily newspapers has been the growth of Spanish-language commercial broadcasting. Radio stations began broadcasting in Spanish in the 1920s, often at odd hours of the morning or evening when English-language listeners were scarce. After World War II more stations began programming Spanish on a full time basis and have since built Spanish-language programming into an important segment of the medium. A 1974 survey revealed 485 radio stations across the United States broadcasting Spanish programs, 55 of them on a full time basis.

However, the growth of Spanish-language radio has not necessarily benefited those in the audience. All full time stations are commercial operations, which means that they make money by cultivating their low income and language-dependent listeners as a consumer market for advertisers. A 1974 survey of the full time stations revealed that most Spanish-language stations are owned and managed by Anglos and that Spanish-surnamed personnel are employed mainly in jobs where knowledge of Spanish or visibility in the community are important. Thus, the flow of top employment opportunities and economic resources in Spanish-language radio is away from the Latino community to the Anglo community.

A newer entrant to the broadcasting field is Spanish-language television, which began on UHF channels in San Antonio and Los Angeles in the early 1960s. There are now full time stations in most Southwestern metropolitan areas, as well as

Chicago, New York, and Miami. An estimated 40 television stations air at least part of their programming in Spanish.

Most of these stations are dependent on shows produced in Latin American countries for their programming. These shows are produced for airing in Mexico, Argentina or some other country and then recycled to Latino audiences in the United States. The largest Spanish-language television network in the United States, Spanish International Network (SIN), is partly owned by the owner of Mexico's largest television system and serves as a syndication vehicle for the programs he produces in Mexico.

Latino communities also have a full complement of record stores, movie theaters, and newstands. But, like their broadcast counterparts, these media outlets are highly dependent on imports from Latin American countries. Just as Spanish-language broadcasters rely on records and programs from Latin America for their programming, barrio movie theaters generally show films produced across the border. Record stores are filled with tapes and records by artists from Latin America. Newstands offer primarily magazines and newspapers published in Latin America.

The Latino people in the United States are largely a secondary audience for much of the Spanish-language media directed toward them. The language is the same, but the socio-economic status of Latinos is different from Latin America (where we are the majority) to the United States (where we are a minority). Although some reinforcement of the identity with Latin America can have a positive effect, a near total dependence on such media content can redirect the audience's attention away from the immediate reality in the United States. The domination of media content also serves to block local Latino talent from media exposure, limits information on local issues, and works against the building of a Latino identity based on life in the United States.

One group that has realized the potential influence of Spanish-language media in the United States has been the national and local advertisers who ride on the television and radio airwaves to reach Latino consumers. In the early 1970s advertising publications were touting the "Spanish gold" that alert corporations could extract from the barrios. Attracted by what *Advertising Age* called a "$20 billion market" the advertisers began investing more of their money into cultivating Latino consumers.

The Spanish-language broadcasters were quick to sell themselves as the most effective way to penetrate and persuade the Latino market. Some even played on the low socio-economic status of their audience as a plus for advertisers. For instance, Spanish International Network told potential advertisers "Latins are brand buyers because, for many, advertised brands represent a status symbol!" The same network showed that Latinos must spend more of their household budgets for groceries and that advertisers using Spanish-language television have sharply increased their sales.

In highlighting the exploitation of their audience and allowing advertisers to prey on it, Spanish-language broadcasters become part of the system of exploitation. Their growth is dependent on their ability to attract a large Latino audience with low cost programming and deliver that audience to advertisers as a consumer market ripe for exploitation. Since most stations also have minimal budgets for news and public affairs programs, they also fail to equip the Latino people with the information necessary to make substantive improvements in their condition.

In addition to the extractive nature of the commercial media, the pattern of Anglo control and heavy dependence on Latin American program sources makes the relations between Latinos and Spanish-language analogous to people in Third World countries. In these nations the people are also targets of media controlled by outsiders and delivering programs produced in other countries. Thus, Chicanos share with other Third World people a basic contradiction in dealing with the media that considers them their main audience; the media are operated for the benefit of the dominating group and not the audience.

Chicano Alternative Media

The third media subsystem can be described as alternative media. This level of analysis includes media directed toward the Latino audience that is essentially non-commercial in nature. They differ from the Spanish-language commercial media in that their "profit" is measured in terms of dissemination of information and development of awareness in the audience, not in terms of money.

Chicano alternative media are most often operated as part of a community organization or a media collective, are staffed by community members who are often not media professionals, and provide information and analysis that is usually not presented in the established media. Their language, like the language of the people they are a part of, is usually a bilingual blend of Spanish and English, with frequent homegrown expressions in "barrio Spanish."

Chicano alternative media include movement periodicals, alternative radio programming, guerrilla teatros (theatrical groups), film makers, videotape producers, and book publishers. Such media can play a useful role in providing needed information and interpretation on issues of importance to Chicanos.

For instance, when a Los Angeles deputy sheriff killed journalist Rubén Salazar in 1970 *La Raza*, a local Chicano newspaper, furnished photographs of the events surrounding the shooting to local newspapers and the community. In the late 1960s El Teatro Campesino (The Farmworkers' Theater) toured the nation to raise awareness of the Chicano identity, the grape boycott, and other issues of importance to farmworkers. In the early 1970s Albuquerque's *El Grito del Norte* exposed mismanagement of a large foundation-funded project that was supposed to help low income rural residents, but actually produced few benefits for them. San Francisco's *El Tecolote* worked with community groups in the mid-1970s to persuade the Pacific Telephone and Telegraph Company to provide bilingual operator service for its many Spanish-speaking customers.

Chicano book publishers, such as Berkeley's Quinto Sol Publications and El Paso's Mictla Publications, produced several Chicano best sellers in the early 1970s. Commercial publishing houses often consider books by Chicano authors either too political or too limited in appeal to warrant publication. Thus, when Denver's Rudolfo "Corky" Gonzales wrote his epic poem "I Am Joaquin" in the mid-1960s he published it himself. The poem became instantly popular among Chicano activists, was later made into a film and subsequently reprinted by Bantam Books.

Chicano alternative newspapers, many of them based on college campuses, have made creative use of offset print technology in displaying stories, pictures, and graphics. Many feature full page pictures on the front page and elaborate borders. A 1975 listing of Chicano print media issues by Southwest Network, a Chicano media clearinghouse in Hayward, California, listed 87 Chicano periodicals actively published across the United States.

The Southwest Network directory also listed a number of Chicano alternative newspapers that had ceased publication over the previous years. One cause of the turnover in the Chicano press is lack of adequate financial backing and turnover in staff members. However, several publications have maintained continuous publication through the mid-1970s. One of these is *El Tecolote*, published in San Francisco's Mission District.

"We, of *El Tecolote*, see ourselves as an important political collective," reads a statement issued by the editorial staff. "*El Tecolote* is the major focus of our work. As writers we have a role to disseminate accurate information. We realize that the existing newspapers in the Mission, and the mass media in general, cannot be counted on to bring about any positive social, cultural and political awareness."

El Tecolote is operated collectively by the group, which is organized into subcommittees responsible for different aspects in operating the newspaper. The newspaper, which is circulated free, supports itself through limited advertising and contributions from supporters.

Other forms of Chicano alternative media include radio programs that mix community information and interviews with music, teatros that blend political messages into their acts, and filmmakers who treat subjects that commercial outlets usually shy away from.

As the 1970s evolved more and more Chicanos with media skills elected to work within the alternative media. Although such media must often deal with commercial sectors for necessary services, such as typesetting, printing, processing and mailing, they are not dominated by the economic motivation that usually governs such relationships. Thus, several Chicano publications have restrictions on who will be allowed to advertise on their pages and have turned down advertisers whose policies make them unwelcome.

The Chicano alternative media has also matured as it has grown. The Chicano Press Association (CPA) was an early attempt to build relationships between Chicano newspapers in the late 1960s. Later the Texas Institute for Educational Development (TIED) assisted Chicano media groups in starting alternative newspapers in small Texas cities. In Albuquerque the staff of *El Grito del Norte* reorganized to become the Chicano Communication Center, an alternative media support group dealing with different media. In Santa Rosa, California local Chicanos successfully organized a non-profit educational bilingual radio station in

1973. In Lansing, Michigan the staff of *El Renacimiento* has fought a long series of battles to increase recognition of Latinos as an important segment of that state's population.

There are limitations to the effectiveness of Chicano media. The lack of adequate financial resources has made many publications publish on indefinite schedules. Less politicized members of the Chicano community are often skeptical about the accuracy of such media, particularly those media which are heavy on rhetoric but light on factual content. Distribution continues to be a problem, since there are few reliable alternative dissemination networks. A high turnover in staff has also plagued some groups. But the freedom to use their skills to work directly with the community continues to draw young Chicanos into alternative media.

"You have more freedom when you write for alternative media," said Juan Gonzales, a former United Press International (UPI) reporter who helped start *El Tecolote* in 1970. "Because you are writing for your own people you are able to cover issues and topics that you know are relevant to our lives. Over the years the community has come to rely on us because we speak the truth. They know that if it wasn't for *El Tecolote* they wouldn't know all the news."

Conclusion

Each of the media subsystems offers opportunities and challenges for young Latinos interested in media careers. The Anglo media offer the opportunity to write about Latinos for the Anglo majority and, in the process, reach the many Latinos who use such media. The Spanish-language media offer the opportunity to communicate directly with the most exploited segment of the Latino community, those who speak little English. The alternative media offer the opportunity of greater freedom and responsibility, plus the chance to create media which relate directly to the needs of the people in the audience.

Skilled and committed Latino communicators are needed in all media subsystems. As one journalist told a campus audience in 1973, "The responsibility of the students is to train themselves to the best of their ability, work hard at developing their skills in practical situations, and enter the media at a level which will allow them to use their education and skills to develop uses of media which can serve the liberation of our people."

Bibliography

For a general introduction to the problems of minority media, see Sharon Murphy, *Other Voices: Black, Chicano and American Indian Press*, Pflaum/Standard, 1974, an attempt to draw together information by and about those who work in the minority media. For specific treatment of the Chicano press, see *El Grito* (Summer 1972), which contains an index of the first five years of the publication as well as a list of Spanish-language publications in Arizona, California, New Mexico and Texas, pp. 40-47, generally publications of the early period. *El Grito* (December 1973) contains a bibliography of articles on Chicano drama, prose and poetry with a highly useful list of Chicano/Raza newspapers and periodicals, 1965-1972. See also *Aztlán* (Fall 1971) for a supplementary serials listing. A description of a Spanish-language television program can be found in Wes Marshall, *et al.*, *FIESTA: Minority Television Pro-

gramming, University of Arizona Press, 1974, which is a report on the Spanish-language program *Fiesta,* which was produced for Mexican-Americans. The book also is a guide for those who would follow in this type of programming. Two studies bound together give unusual insight into media habits of Mexican-Americans. They are Nicholas Valenzuela, *Media Habits and Attitudes of Mexican-Americans,* and Frederick Williams, *et al., Prediction of Mexican-American Media Habits and Attitudes,* published by the Center for Communication Research, University of Texas, 1973.

Women's Pages In The 1970s

By Zena Beth Guenin

Ben Bagdikian's observation—"Most papers still look as though they are edited on the social assumptions of the 1940's and 1950's"—fits the women's pages of many newspapers. Commentators on contemporary society portray the American woman as an individual changing her outlook, life style and image of self, but the changing woman may be reading a paper that views her as a bucolically contented simpleton whose "most pressing questions are whether the decorations for the Beaver Lodge party should be white and gold or green and pink..."

Women's pages that operate on a stock formula of society, clubs, decorating, furniture, food, cooking, children and sewing represent an information failure obvious to their readers and often to the women who produce them. Within that limited field of coverage, such sections present shallow reporting—reflecting fashion in terms of the offerings of the newspaper's top advertisers, not discussing the high cost and poor quality of clothing; featuring cute layouts on a kindergarten party, not outlining the lack of day-care centers; and, in a surprisingly large number of dailies, reporting the total trivia of local women's clubs as if it were news.

Criticism of women's sections has been appearing in magazines, journals and reviews, and the current interest in this part of American newspapers is obviously linked to the liberation movement. In 1970, the late Maggie Savoy, then women's editor of the *Los Angeles Times,* explained the liberation movement to the nation's male editors. In her article in the American Society of Newspaper Editors' *Bulletin,* she suggested that because editors have "been reading the sports pages" (i.e., ignoring the women's pages), the change in interests of American women has gone unnoticed by editors.

Whether they're called Style, Family, Today, View or Women, the pages that could cover those facets of living that concern everyone—health, habitat, and, yes, happiness—are known both within the industry and to readers as the women's pages. If, as Nicholas von Hoffman, columnist for the Style section of the *Washington Post,* says, "people read the women's pages far more than the editorial pages," then why are the women's departments of many newspapers still consid-

Zena Beth Guenin has been women's editor and society editor of the Missoula (Mont.) *Missoulian* and home-living editor of the Albuquerque (N.M.) *Journal.* She is a member of the University of Iowa journalism staff. This article appeared in the *Montana Journalism Review,* 1973, which granted permission to reprint. Footnotes have been deleted. See also Ms. Guenin's "Women's Pages in American Newspapers: Missing Out on Contemporary Content," *Journalism Quarterly* (Spring 1975), pp. 66-69.

ered the backwater of the newsroom, scorned not just by management but often by the very women who work in women's news? Why do young women in journalism schools say, as I once said, they'll do anything to break into the newspaper business but "I'll be damned if I'll get stuck in 'soc,'" only to find they may be damned if they don't? The women's department may be the only one where they can get work, regardless of their credentials, training, experience or potential.

First-rate women's sections do exist and some were doing a top reporting job long before the theme of women's liberation was heard. And there have been women who strived for excellence despite indifference from management. "There have been islands of creativity all around—but the problem is that these did not turn out to be major theme sections, due of course to a lack of interest and awareness by people on the publisher-top editor level," Jean Taylor, women's editor of the *Los Angeles Times*, has said.

Critics within and outside women's departments often blame the editors and publishers for the condition of women's departments that use a marshmallow approach to stories closest to the genuine interests of readers. Management's tendency to ignore the women's page is partially responsible for its state of disrepair. "The afterthought of the managing editor" is how von Hoffman describes the women's page. Ms. Taylor says women's sections suffer from "lack of affection in high places. We are unloved. We are the pea under the publisher's pillow. When we come down the street on this side, the American Society of Newspaper Editors crosses to the other. . . ."

In the summary of a 1969 survey of women's and managing editors' opinions about women's pages, it was reported that "on some papers the old-fashioned women's pages are retained by the insistence of higher authority. . . ." Colleen Dishon, editor and president of Features and News, Chicago, and former women's editor of the *Chicago Daily News* and the *Milwaukee Sentinel,* lists "management's need to cling to the impossible ideal woman" and "top editors' needs to be accepted socially in their own communities" as reasons for the reluctance to change women's pages. One wonders just how many women's page editors, if given a chance to be publicly honest, could chronicle tales of stories written on the behest of not just the editor but more particularly a publisher—or, even more powerful in some cases, a publisher's wife.

Pressure from the top joins forces with pressure from another very viable power within a newspaper, the advertising department. Edwin Diamond, a former editor of *Newsweek*, realistically notes, in speaking about women's pages, that newspapers are a business and "the law of business is the law of commerce, which is maximized profits and minimized expenses—and if you do get good things, it's because there are a few media barons who operate on the principle of 'noblesse oblige.' "

Attitudes of some newspapermen toward women in journalism must be added to the list of pressures to oppose change. Those attitudes are enough to stoke the fires of the liberation movement for decades. "I have yet to encounter a woman as versatile as a man in the reporting business," an editor of the *St. Louis Post-*

Dispatch is quoted as saying, adding that it might be his own fault "for not experimenting more with women." Are women so oddly incompetent that their assignment to news stories must be an experiment? "Women just don't have the same flexibility in some areas," says James Hoge, editor of the *Chicago Sun-Times*. Such opinions are not relegated only to metro dailies with mass circulations. "As soon as this Vietnam war is over," grumbled the editor of a Montana daily, "I'm going to get all these goddamn women out of here." Logic cringes.

Credulity was stretched to its furthest limits by the "official, considered response" of the Associated Press Managing Editors to an article written by women journalists at the University of Iowa about the APME's *Guidelines*, which the young women considered to be "blatantly sexist." The reply, written by Edward M. Miller, *Guidelines'* editor and a retired editor of the *Portland Oregonian*, was enough to send any woman journalist off to the nearest bar. He said, "Generally speaking, women are either uncomfortable or unsuccessful in the executive role because of the difficulties they encounter in divorcing their personal feelings and ambitions from the job at hand. This leads to unhappy subordinates and inefficient production." Are men, "generally speaking," always cool and detached from their jobs? Innocent of having any personal feelings about their employers, their fellow workers, and their own tasks? And, honestly, should ambition be "divorced" from professional performance? Of course, the answer is no. The detached person goes robot-like through life and if newsmen and newswomen are anything, they certainly are not robots.

Miller says "women become excellent copy editors. They are patient, careful, cheerful and the repetitive nature of the work does not seem to bother them." But other editors do not share that view. Some, such as *Chicago Today's* copy desk chief, Cliff Bridwell, stage an absolute lockout against women. He reportedly "won't allow the female species to work on his desk, presumably because he had one once and didn't like the experience."

On the copy desk of an Albuquerque newspaper is a woman who edited a paper in the East and was bureau chief with a staff of three for another paper before moving to the Southwest, bringing her rich journalism experience with her. Last year, after several years on the rim, she was allowed to sit in the slot to prepare page schedules and cull wires for possible page-one stories—but she must get up when the slotman comes in. One day a week, she is "allowed" to "work the line," which means she goes to the backshop to direct the make-up of dummied pages. The irony of her situation is underscored by the fact that she fills her spare time by stringing for the *New York Times* and *Time* magazine, credentials that would qualify any man for an executive position. But the managing editor, after all, is a man—with a background of newspaper experience in Alamosa, Colo.

Despite a lockout on some desks and discrimination on others, some editors report they enthusiastically seek women for the copy desk. In the ASNE *Bulletin* in 1970, one editor said women "keep up with the men in speed, accuracy and interest—including creative approaches to handling news and in making judgments." Another commented, "We've been so pleased that we're considering expanding it [the use of women as copy editors] somewhat.'' Such enthusiasm is chillingly dampened when one realizes the sexist overtones—the suprise exhibited by men that women can do a good job.

Margot Sherman, senior vice-president and a director of the McCann-Erickson advertising agency, accurately describes the problems of many women in the media: ''Even the trained woman comes up against such stereotypes as 'Women are better at monotonous jobs. . . .' Probably what is being said is you can get better-type women than men at the same salary, and what is meant is that they are cheaper.''

City editors often have narrow attitudes about women, and those women who reach top reporting positions usually have had to be better than their male peers. Editors have been known to ignore stories about women and their political or social activism or encourage tips from the women's department, give the story to a male reporter and let the ''ladies'' be content with handouts. There are flocks of editors and reporters who view all women in the news business in that jocular, benevolent way that has helped inspire the contemporary use of the term ''male chauvinist.''

Discriminatory attitudes may be fertilized by fear that perhaps the gals aren't just kidding about equality. The result is a ''yuck-yuck'' attitude about the new movement toward full and equal rights for women. The prestigious *Los Angeles Times* and the even more monolithic Associated Press couldn't resist noting that the vote for the consitutional amendment to guarantee women's rights would be on ''leap year day''—noted by AP in the second graph of its story but headlined by the *Times*: ''Women's Rights Vote Due On Leap Year Day.'' One can hear the snickers.

Women's editors who want to change the content or the format of their sections need the support of management and that is a commodity desperately hard for some women's editors to acquire. Ms. Dishon notes that women often do not have ''the necessary clout with management'' to initiate change. Ms. Savoy challenged male editors in her 1970 article ''to take a bold peek at your women's sections. Do you duck the responsibility of helping your women's editor achieve excellence for her 51 per cent of your readership? Or do you just listen to one, two or a dozen irate society women and sigh, 'Don't rock the boat'?''

One reason newspapers isolate their women's staff by putting the department in a corner or down the hall from the photo lab may be the whole thing can be tidily isolated mentally too. It's easier for an editor to ignore the section and trust the competence of the women he has hired to keep quietly working within the pre-scribed format, catching their own errors, digging up story leads, fighting the layout battles with the printers, writing heads that fit—to do more, actually, than most city-side personnel and sometimes with less salary.

Is the accusation that women journalists receive less salary than their male counterparts a valid charge, or is it simply a tale of woe that managing editors are beginning to hear and skillfully ignore? A woman reporter at the *Washington Post* found that ''At least 27 papers where the American Newspaper Guild has contracts pay society or women's news reporters less than other reporters. The difference is as great as $60 per week.'' And since many non-Guild newspapers do not meet

Guild pay scales, it may well be that many women's editors receive slim paychecks in addition to their other problems.

Responsibility for the content of women's pages or for the status of women on newspapers cannot be placed solely with male editors and management. There are women's editors who have grown up in the stock society mold and couldn't break away from it any more than the traditionalist Edward M. Miller of *Guidelines* fame (or infamy) could be wrenched away from his convictions about "Our Friend on High," creating such markedly unchangeable differences between women and men that they carry right through to the keys of a typewriter and the end of a copy pencil.

The female traditionalists in the women's department (I like to think of them as the "white glove brigade") are those who are as engrossed in printing a full social calendar as the sports desk is in making sure all the box scores are run. Such women's editors are steadfast in their devotion to the local club-social circle to the detriment of the majority of their readers. They fit their pages to the interests of a special (and usually moneyed) few and provide a steady source of scrapbook filler for the clubs they slavishly chronicle. Or they are so involved typing all the wedding and engagement stories, they haven't time to be relevant even if they desired to be.

It may be true in some instances, as suggested by Ponchitta Pierce to a Penney-Missouri Awards audience, that a few women's editors "actually have little talent—either as editors or writers—but they have somehow landed the job. . . ."

No formula covers all attitudes of women in journalism just as there is no universal attitude among men. There are women like Joan Roesgen of the *Kingsport* (Tennessee) *Times-News* who says "women's editors are wallowing in relevance" because they are "having a hard time sorting out priorities." Roesgen says she's interested in getting her relevance in the general news columns rather than on the women's page. Such an attitude would inhibit rather than promote constructive change.

The basics of survival also might be one reason some women's sections don't change and don't challenge their readers. Unfortunate but true is the fact that though they are in the business of communication, most newspapers don't encourage internal feedback. Women on newspapers demonstrate the social-psychological theory that adherence to group norms is a function of the importance group membership holds for the individual. Although a women's editor may not be free or have the time and staff to produce the kind of journalism she would like to offer her readers, at least she is involved in the profession of newspapering and the importance that involvement holds for her may cause her to keep quiet, if maintenance of the status quo is what is expected by management.

Sadly enough, women often fulfill the "giddy gal" stereotype that some men expect. This bit of silliness came from an edition of *Editor & Publisher* under the headline "Oh deer—the gals edit quite a paper." The story, reprinted from the *Detroit News*, told how the male staffers of a small Michigan weekly left the paper to the women while the "boys" went hunting. The "all-girl" issue was "well received" with "all deadlines met," and the publisher said he was "not really surprised" because the women "on our staff are highly competent, very dedicated newspaper people." The women couldn't just do that highly competent job and let it speak for itself—they had to play the role of giggling girls by running "an eye-stopper of a picture layout on page one—leg shots of six members of the staff." If, as Jean Taylor says, the real point of women's liberation is to "get men to quit treating us as though we're a bad joke," then women will have to quit jumping at opportunities to parody themselves.

Although change in a newspaper, as in any social institution, may not come quickly enough for those who chafe under restricting, old-fashioned policies, attitudes toward women and the women's section are changing. Some fine-looking responsible journalistic efforts appear on women's pages in big and small newspapers around the nation. And some of the progress toward modern coverage of our rapid, mobile world has come from male publishers and editors. Noting readership surveys and predictably responsive to increased readership because it symbolizes an increase in advertising revenue, some publishers have initiated improvement in content and personnel in their women's departments. Occasionally there exist those gem-like editors who realize the women back in the corner have the same potential and training for reporting as the fellows in the city room.

Working too are strong-willed and intelligent women's editors, many with a background of city-wide experience, who approach their pages with a sense of professionalism and the goal of making their sections a relevant contribution to the newspaper.

The women's department offers a place for the "horizontal" story, for the feature, the probing effort—ignored and handled slip-shod city-side because of press of time or staff limitations. The boycott of women city-side on metro papers has, as noted in the *Chicago Journalism Review*, "caused one further development—some women now prefer writing women's page news to city assignments because it deals with areas of increasing concern. . . ." The liberation movement, beset, as all embryonic revolutions are, with strife and in-fighting among factions, would have gone begging had it not been for the straight coverage given it, even in some highly conservative women's sections.

Consumerism is one topic that newspapers have been forced to confront. It's a shameful truth that it took a nonjournalist to prod newspapers into a field they should have been covering. Nader is to consumerism what Steinem is to liberation. If it takes a national figure to move the press into areas where it long ago should have been involved, then we can only be grateful for those individuals. Editors would be wise to unleash the talents of their women's department on such stories because "the poorest solution to handling the new landslide of consumer-area stories is for the newsdesk to steal them. . . .It means women trained for years in food and shopping and housing and consumer fields are pushed aside."

The basic need—as many of us who have been involved in women's departments have realized for years—is for paper-wide communication and involvement, a fluid interdepartmental motion so ideas are exchanged and staff used on the stories that best suit their experience and interests. When something "new" comes into the field, editors have the hysterical tendency to seek someone "new" to handle the stories instead of reevaluating the talents of current writers. Women who could perform superbly in advocacy-reporting roles about nutrition, health, and merchandise quality control should not be overlooked and left to perform mechanically in the constricting fashion of the past. And the city-side reporter, when he spots and wants to do a feature removed from his routine, should not be thwarted because he thinks there's no place to take his idea or the story.

Critics of a new approach to women's news call it a "force fed" message of activism, but it doesn't have to be. I agree neither with the sneering comment about readers who are "merely performing the duties of a housewife" nor with the critic who says women's editors are "career-oriented" and "tend to forget the unliberated women . . .the masses of housewives . . .who are contemptuous and resentful of working wives . . ." There is rancor here where none should be. Having seen service, so to speak, in both roles, I can honestly say that each can be both devastating and challenging and that neither is more difficult or more rewarding than the other. A women's editor with professional integrity can achieve an understanding balance in coverage, avoiding that kind of destructive bitterness.

The liberation movement has inspired a break-out of suppressed attitudes on a national level and has given women the courage to express openly the frustrations they have silently endured. Gloria Steinem, so coyly covered by the ASNE *Bulletin* with both a "kitschy" with-kitten front-page photo and a beaming, full-page photo inside, may be causing the same newspaper editors who smiled as they read the *Bulletin* interview some headaches as their women's department editors take Steinem's cue and demand to be heard.

What, then, if women's liberation succeeds? Will there actually be room in newspapers of the future for the women's department? Ms Taylor of the *Los Angeles Times* says if the women's department were to disappear, "I could be a 'people' editor." Her point is well-taken. With audiences receiving more and more of their hard news coverage from television, there should be more newspaper emphasis on "life-style" stories and involvement with the actualities and frustrations of modern living.

As for content, papers seeking change in their women's sections will have to make some bold moves. I must agree with Nick Williams, retired editor of the *Los Angeles Times*, who says they are beautiful and beloved by those who know them but they should be banished. Gloria Steinem thinks space for bridal photos should be purchased just like advertising, and some papers have tried this procedure. She also suggests that if wedding photos are run, they should include the bridegroom. Having been exposed to small papers that use couple shots, I can't agree with this at all. Brides do have an aura of loveliness about them (or enough netting to disguise most of the flaws) but bridegrooms—well, it may be reverse chauvinism—but they generally look uncomfortably stupid. Papers might sell fewer extra issues over the counter if such frivolity were dropped, but it is difficult to imagine any real loss in advertising revenue or in canceled subscriptions. A monthly tabloid of brides is another technique newspapers could employ.

As for the club events—the metro papers handle only those enormously influential groups (such as the ones to which the publisher's wife belongs) or events of general interest—open-admission fund-raising parties, shows and so on, local priorities have to be set, but it seems logical to hold the same standards for women's club coverage as for men's service groups. Let's face it—women's pages often have an antiquated "women are doing something" approach. It has been firmly established that women can accomplish positive things in their communities—coverage of their activities should not be chained into a club meeting-flower show format.

One of the main reasons Sue Hovik, former women's editor of the *Minneapolis Star*, initiated a disposal of the women's pages in favor of wide-interest feature sections called Taste and Variety was to avoid the sexist treatment of club news. "If a club event or program is newsworthy, it should face the same criteria for publication—regardless of the sex of its members."

This change, from a section clearly labeled for women to one oriented to the problems and interests of living and entitled View or Style or some other "neuter" designation, is one route women's sections are taking. However, the "flag under which good stories appear" may be "incidental."

Critics and those involved in producing good sections stress content. Stylish appearance and a superficial nod to contemporary topics just won't reach the innovative goal. Diamond notes that "some [women's sections] are very impressive in the sense of big pictures, lots of white space, good heads and provocative stories. But it seems to me it's still some of the old Thunderbird wine in some new, French-labeled bottles. Is it really something new, or are we getting the same old segregated women's pages?"

Although the title may change with the direction, the need for a section involving women, both as writers and editors and as readers, is emphasized by most critics. At the A. J. Liebling Conference in New York in 1972, Ms. Steinem said she "has come back full circle in that I now feel the value of women's pages. They should cover all subjects, including men, from a point of view that is not being represented."

In an address to the 1972 Penney-Missouri Awards Conference, Molly Ivins, an editor of the *Texas Observer*, stridently advocated change but not abolition of women's sections. She suggested that the "cultural conditioning" that has produced the liberation-protested differences between men and women make women particularly able to communicate "because women have been forced to deal with people in the tightest pressure-cooker there is—the family." This "special ability to deal with people," she continued, can make women's pages "a forum, a center, a means of communication and discussion, a source of ideas and of perspective with warmth, with friendship, [with] kinship and with understanding."

And such sections, as a few already are, can be such a journalistic challenge to women (and to men) that no one who works on the women's page need feel the isolation of damnation—but rather the exhilaration of liberation.

Bibliography

Ms. Guenin's article should be read in conjunction with Ms. Pogrebin's, which follows. This listing includes books and articles useful in developing further insight into either issue. A general bibliography dealing with women in all of the mass media will be found in *Journalism History* (Winter 1974-1975), pp. 117-128. A bibliography related to the women's movement, but not entirely devoted to mass media sources or topics, is Helen Sheeler, compiler, *Womanhood Media: Current Resources About Women*, Scarecrow Press, 1972. A general view of how women who make their living in publishing and television view their jobs and their problems can be found in Ethel Strainchamps, ed., *Rooms With No View*, Harper & Row, 1974. The book was written by sixty-five women, many of whom felt it necessary to remain anonymous. Our article by Zena Beth Guenin can be supplemented by Ronnene Anderson, "Press Coverage of Women," *Montana Journalism Review* (1974), pp. 2-19 and Lindsy Van Gelder, "Women's Pages, You Can't Make News Out of a Silk Purse," *Ms* (November 1974), pp. 111-112 ff. A fascinating study of "Television and the Working Women" is reported in *Nielsen Newscast*, No. 3 (1975), which reports the number of hours women who work spend with television, as well as the types of programs they watch. If the working woman *is* home during the daytime and views the soap operas, she gets an unusual view of life, according to a study by Rose K. Goldsen, "Throwaway Husbands, Wives and Lovers," *Human Behavior* (December 1975), pp. 64-69.

Ten Cogent Reasons Why
TV News Fails Women

By Letty Cottin Pogrebin

How do the networks cover women's news? Not the fashion shows, but the vital issues that affect all women—and the men in their lives. News about sex discrimination in employment, credit and education. Legislation affecting divorce, housing, insurance and social security. News of gains in reproductive freedom, benefits for homemakers, protection against rape, prisoners' rights, child-care centers and health programs. Are news shows providing a window on *our* world?

To find out, I reviewed hours of video tape and transcripts of news segments and documentaries telecast during the first seven months of 1975.

I purposely began with an event that I knew first hand. March 8 was International Women's Day, the celebration that was to launch worldwide observance of U.N.-sponsored International Women's Year (IWY). In New York City, my daughters and I joined thousands marching down Fifth Avenue to a rally in Union Square. Surely it was newsworthy for Girl Scouts and household workers, lesbians and churchwomen, radical feminists and garden-variety Democrats and Republicans to join in solidarity to speak out on women's problems. If you couldn't be a witness, you deserved a full report.

But ABC's John Kelly uttered only four sentences, among them, "1000 women marched down Fifth Avenue behind an all-woman band." If ABC found the music the highlight, how can we trust them on a summit conference? On NBC, Tom Brokaw smirked about the demonstrator who "came dressed as a male chauvinist pig."

Only CBS wins a passsing grade. Newswoman Betty Ann Bowser saw "several thousand demonstrators," remarked on the "coalition of more than 50 women's organizations" and was alert to the day's emphasis on economic suffering.

Letty Cottin Pogrebin is a magazine editor and columnist, and author of the book *Getting Yours: How to Make the System Work for the Working Woman*. Reprinted by permission of the Julian Bach Literary Agency, Inc. Copyright © 1975 by Letty C. Pogrebin.

It's unusual for one network to deliver so much more than the others. Generally, CBS, NBC and ABC are guilty of similar sins, such as—

1. *They devote more time to either sports or weather than to news of 53 per cent of the population.*

2. *They report general interest stories—on poverty, education or unemployment—as if these things happen to men only.* "Experts" asked to comment on news are rarely women. In Detroit, CBS filmed men and women lined up for unemployment checks but all the interviews were with men.

3. *They distort or diminish women's stories for the sake of sensationalism.* The rape/murder aspects of Joan Little's case and the abortion details of Dr. Kenneth Edelin's trial were closely scrutinized, but the sexism/racism aspects of both cases weren't. One pregnant, unwed teacher banished from her Texas class gets national coverage but broader information on job rights for *all* pregnant workers doesn't.

4. *They undervalue events that would be given historic importance if men, not women, were the subjects.* Public hearings held by the Coalition of Labor Union Women (58 unions represented), and a press conference announcing the National Women's Agenda (endorsed by 90 women's groups), were ignored. Had American Legion, AFL-CIO, Americans for Democratic Action and National Football League united behind a common goal, the networks would have sent up flares.

5. *They make little effort during regularly scheduled news programs to deliver analyses of news events affecting women.* The Equal Rights Amendment, for example, is high drama: 34 states have ratified it; four more states are needed by 1979 to make it the 27th amendment to the U.S. Constitution. Between January and July there were dutiful three-line mentions when each of four states defeated the ERA but no comment on what the ERA would mean to women.

News specials and documentaries frequently offer interviews, discussion and commentary that illuminate viewer understanding. However, if you're not a TV addict but an on-the-run news-program watcher you could get a very shortened version of *AM America*'s series on breast cancer and rape; or excerpts from David Frost's abortion speak-out and from the Barbara Walters/Tom Snyder special on changing roles: or clips from CBS's *Magazine* segment on the woman who works in a coal mine to support two kids.

6. *They keep women in their "place" via subtle, sexist labeling.* Did we need to know that economist Alice Rivlin (director of the Congressional Budget Office), and lawyer Carla Hills (Secretary of Housing) are mothers? If personal facts *are* relevant, how come Secretary of Defense James Schlesinger isn't identified as a husband and father?

7. *They use a conspiratorial "us guys" tone to suggest that the target viewer is a man, and all news should be tested for its effect on men.* After announcing that Princeton's graduating-class valedictorian and salutatorian were women, NBC's Lew Wood whined: "If it's any comfort to traditionalists (or male chauvinists) the valedictorian at least is the *daughter* of a Princeton man." At CBS, Hughes Rudd sometimes hopes "the women around your house" aren't kicking up trouble like

those in news clips. After Margaret Thatcher's election as leader of Britain's Conservative Party, ABC's Hilary Brown quipped: "There's been no sign of panic yet among the men who will now have to follow her." Frankly, I'd trade all these "witticisms" for a few good quotes from the women themselves!

8. *They focus on women who are the "wife of," "daughter of," or otherwise male-identified.* Mrs. Anwar el-Sadat and Mrs. Yitzhak Rabin were the prime attractions of the IWY conference in Mexico City although they were only mouthing their husbands' words—while thousands of brave, unknown women were tackling universal problems.

9. *They seek conflict and ignore harmony.* In Mexico, news producers tracked the America vs. Third World split, rather than probe the international camaraderie. Two women arguing instantly attract cameras.

10. *They "lighten" the news with gratuitous jokes at women's expense.* The locker-room-humor award goes to Hughes Rudd (CBS) for his tasteless monologues—about Swedish women who throw herrings at lecherous men, a San Diego cabdriver who eavesdrops on "foulmouthed women," a go-go dancer who charged the state for her silicone injections. That's news?

Rather than squander air time and incense women, networks should hire more women producers and newscasters so they can do more of what they've occasionally shown they can do very well. Segments like Cassie Mackin's (NBC) report on lower salaries of women in Congress office jobs; or anything Ellie Riger does for ABC Sports; or Betty Rollin's (NBC) thoughtful profile on the woman police officer: or ABC's consistent coverage of health research and dangerous contraceptives. Why don't we blitz the networks with letters demanding more news coverage of substance and dignity? Tell them we're using the above 10 points as a checklist. Tell them the biggest news of all is that women make news, women watch news, and women *are* news.

8 The Persuasive Arts

Advertising

Soap Gets in Your Eyes—

When Advertising Talks to Everyone—

Public Relations

We Are Advocates!—

Public Relations Council: Alternative to Licensing?—

Polls/Television and Politics

Political Polling and Political Television—

ABC's "Wide World of Sports" and CBS's "60 Minutes." Only on United.

Time out, boss!

When you fly United Airlines, you're the boss. And we know even the boss deserves time out from business. So on most widebody flights, United shows you video entertainment like you'll find on no other airline.

Flying East, you can relive the most exciting moments in sports on ABC's "Wide World of Sports."

Coming back, it's "Sixty Minutes," the award-winning CBS news series that

probes behind the news to make its own headlines.

And you'll still find first-run feature films available on our other transcontinental and Hawaiian flights.

So next business trip, take time out in the friendly skies. Where you're the boss.

For reservations, call your Travel Agent, or United. Partners in Travel with Western International Hotels.

You're the boss.

Fly the friendly skies of United.
UNITED AIRLINES

Soap Gets in Your Eyes

Advertising

By Ron Rosenbaum

Eight years ago a 65-year-old adman with the improbable name Carroll Carroll had just retired from the J. Walter Thompson agency after 35 years in the ad business when Abel Green, editor of *Variety*, asked him what he planned to do with his future.

"Why don't you let me do reviews of TV commercials?" was Carroll Carroll's inspired suggestion.

"Try one," said Abel Green, a bit skeptically.

Carroll Carroll tried two. Abel Green liked them both. Carroll Carroll got his column. It's called "And Now A Word From . . .''; and it's the first and only regular review of TV commercials outside the advertising trade press.

I've always wondered why no one has followed in Carroll Carroll's footsteps. We live in a civilization that supports dozens of TV critics, scores of movie critics and hundreds of rock critics. Everyone knows that commercials are more complex and interesting than TV shows, more people see them than movies and they reveal far more about American culture than rock. Why then is Carroll Carroll alone in his important task?

Well, I've always had a minor ambition to review TV commercials, so this year I decided to see just what the work was like.

Maybe you think it would be easy street, reviewing TV commercials. Maybe you think there are plush screening rooms where the big national advertisers run preview showings of their fall campaigns for journalists. Maybe you think they provide you with transcripts and storyboards of each commercial for recollection in tranquillity. Maybe you think the leading frozen orange juice tastes more like fresh than Orange Plus.

Just look at the logistics of attempting even the most superficial review of the new season's commercials: Limiting oneself to just three hours of prime time and just three network outlets, that's still 9 hours a night, 63 hours a week, and—figuring 6 commercial minutes an hour, 2 spots a minute—it adds up to more than 750 commercial spots a week. Even though many of those 750 are repeated, so much calculation goes into the making of each second of a single 30-second spot that four or five attentive viewings are required before the craftier elements begin to become apparent. The job is overwhelming.

Most maddening is dragging one's way through hours and hours of pallid programming in search of a second glimpse of just one intriguing new commercial. Maybe someday someone will provide the commercial reviewers—and the commercial fan, for there are fans out there—with a kind of TV guide to commercial scheduling. Maybe someday all steel-belted radials will be made like Firestones.

But for now I'm condemned to sit in front of my set with a cassette recorder and a notebook trying to find ways to fill the time between the breaks. I'll admit I must have missed more than a few: The only way to make sure you've seen every ad

Ron Rosenbaum wrote this article for *New Times,* where it appeared in the fall of 1975. Copyright 1975 by New Times, Inc., reprinted by permission.

is to watch every minute of every show on TV, and the Geneva Convention has rules against things like that.

But I've seen enough and heard enough to pick up on some trends. After listening to 12 hours of pure commercials on tape, you begin to hear the spots talking to each other about certain common themes. In this first venture into commercial criticism, I'll forbear discussions of production, acting and directorial style and start by concentrating on the content of commercials that made their debut this season, specifically some strange new twists to some familiar old pitches.

Country Drug Taking   I knew a trend was in the making when Sominex sleeping tablets abandoned the mysterious ''Uncle Ned'' and other familial sleeping pill spokesmen. Now they've begun presenting cheery morning scenes in rural towns, complete with birds chirping on the soundtrack as several hearty, virtuous, hard-working plain ole country folk take time off from their country chores to confess that ''even here,'' despite long hours of honest work in the fresh country air, people ''occasionally'' have trouble falling asleep and rely on pills to knock them out for the night. The new Excedrin P.M. spot features a healthy, young country wife, emerging from her old-fashioned country house amidst country-morning sunlight and bird chirps, walking her horse along a grassy creek bed, awake to all the wonder in nature because she went to sleep with the help of Excedrin P.M. And the new spot for Enderin, the non-aspirin pain reliever, presents a couple returning from a walk along a magnificent stretch of shoreline, awestruck by the grandeur of the ocean and by the ability of *just one* Enderin tablet to take care of a troubling headache.

Now, needless to say, the point of these pastoral pill-pushing pitches is not to convince country folk to take more drugs: There aren't enough country folk around to make it profitable. The point is to convince potential pill takers in cities and suburbs that they needn't feel *guilty* about taking pills, that even saintly country folk do it, that pill taking is an integral part of the natural way of life.

The Revolt Against the Natural   It's really a counterrevolution. In the past three years, ''natural'' and ''country style'' themes have spread like the plague through the commercial industry—let just one brand in a competitive category of products show a cow, and the others would shoot their next spots on dairy farms standing knee-deep in manure.

There's still an element of McCarthyism in the attacks on products accused of being infiltrated with un-natural (as in un-American) ingredients. Spokesmen for products such as Wise potato chips and Dannon yogurt go through ''I have a little list'' speeches in which they read, in outraged accusatory tones, the names of artificial ingredients on their rivals' labels.

But this year the natural revolution seems finally to have peaked—if only because there are few products left that haven't already been naturalized (in addition to country sleeping pills, we now have Country Dinner dog food). And this season a number of commercials have begun to manifest clear-cut anti-natural, anti-country style themes. One impetus for this trend may be that certain New York admen are thoroughly sick of the hick schtick and are beginning to exact revenge on country folk for the years they've had to spend writing cute country style ad copy. How else explain the unbridled ridicule of the country fellow in the Bic lighter commercial:

An oafish hayseed offers to buy an attractive, urban-looking single woman a drink in a dimly lit bar. She lights her Bic lighter, illuminating his clownish, ill-fitting "country style" clothes and cretinous barnyard leer. One look and she laughs scornfully in his face: "A flick of my Bic and I can see you're a hick."

And how about the merriment Madison Avenue has at the expense of the gulled rubes in the Golden Griddle syrup commercial. The spot shows a cross section of country people from "the heart of maple country" tasting two syrups. Time after time they choose Golden Griddle, a non-natural blend, over their own pure, natural maple syrup. And just to rub in the triumph of food processing artifice over nature, the commercial doesn't bother to claim that Golden Griddle tastes *like* real maple; instead they take a deliberately aggressive stance: "Golden Griddle has the taste that *beat* real maple."

And Total—a processed, vitamin-sprayed cereal—takes savage delight in its triumph over "the leading natural cereals" in the vitamin percentage numbers derby. (Total claims a 100 percent RDA score versus 6 percent for the leading brand X granolas.) Sowing salt in the wounds of the defeated wheat, the Total spot takes an airborne shot of a field of wheat, and, lo, the defeat is carved in acre-sized numerals on the face of the field—graffiti in the grain.

The Original Skin Controversy   Things move fast in the ad world, and the counterrevolution against the natural revolution has given rise to a sophisticated third stage counter-counterrevolution. This year's Safeguard soap spot, for instance. A bit of background first. Some time ago Ivory soap jumped heavily on the Natural bandwagon and renamed itself Ivory "natural" soap, with spots featuring Ivory-natural people getting themselves clean and fresh without "harsh chemicals." This represented an assault on the whole premise of deodorant soaps, which had boasted for years about just how harsh their ingredients were on "odor-causing bacteria," those villainous microbes that turned natural sweat into problem perspiration. The Ivory commercials were clearly out to steal customers from the deodorant soaps.

More recently, deodorant soaps began to strike back. By far the boldest assault was last year's Lifebuoy commercial, which featured clean-cut people hopping up and down and crowing, "I smell clean." An admonitory slogan followed: "It's not enough to *be* clean. You have to *smell* clean."

This gets us into some very tricky metaphysical questions of existence and essence: If there were people walking around who *were* clean but didn't *smell* clean, what *did* they smell like? Neutral? Natural? Unclean? What is the smell of clean anyway? What is the smell of skin? Does skin in its natural state smell good or bad? Did odor-causing bacteria exist in prelapsarian Eden? Could Adam have used an antiperspirant or did the malignant microbes only begin their iniquitous work after the Fall?

If this isn't complicated enough, this year Safeguard has added a new twist to this debate on the nature of Original Skin.

The scene: a kissing booth at a country fair. Two women, one married, one unmarried, are inside the booth. A man buys a kiss from the married woman and exclaims so feverishly over her "naturally clean-smelling skin" that the woman's husband has to intervene.

"*Heavens!*
Buddy must have a girl!"

"What about me?" the unmarried woman in the kissing booth pipes up hopefully. "I use a deodorant soap."

Then the crusher. "*That's just it*," the kiss-buying guy tells her. "You *smell* like a deodorant soap."

Stunned by this heartbreaker, the rejected woman in the kissing booth is probably unaware of the finely honed distinctions that are implicit in the rebuff.

It's not enough to be clean. You have to smell clean, says Lifebuoy. But, argues Safeguard, there are different *kinds* of clean. Lavatory disinfectant smells clean, but it doesn't smell good. Safeguard skin smells "*naturally* clean," which means it is clean, it smells clean and it smells natural. And natural smells good. But you can't smell natural with a "natural soap." You need a deodorant soap that doesn't smell like a deodorant soap to smell natural these days. The Safeguard commercial takes us from complexity back to simplicity—of a sort.

The next move in the skin smell dialectic is hard to predict. Now that there are "natural-scented" deodorant soaps on the market, perhaps the ultimate step will be the introduction of "natural-scented" perfume for people scared of smelling like a deodorant soap, worried that their own natural smell isn't good enough and so confused they've decided to forgo the risks of bathing altogether in favor of a cover-up perfume.

New Fears   It's been a good year for New Fears. Complex new fears, such as Fear of Smelling Like a Deodorant Soap. Old-fashioned new fears, such as Fear of Foot Odor. (A commercial for a product called Johnson's Odor-Eaters depicts an embarrassed father's foot odor driving him and his family out of their house.)

But the most characteristic fear of the year so far is Fear of Surprise. *Don't let life take you by surprise*, warns Metropolitan Life Insurance. *The best surprise is no surprise*, chimes the new Holiday Inn commercials. "It's the *unexpected* bills that really hurt," warns the doom-tinged voice of the Quaker State Motor Oil announcer.

Holiday Inn, which once promoted the adventure and delight of travel in its commercials, now focuses on nerve-wracking perils—collapsing beds, canceled reservations, unfamiliar food and other unpleasant surprises—which await travelers if they don't play it safe and lock themselves up in the predictability and security of a Holiday Inn.

Auto products such as Quaker State and STP once promoted themselves as lubricants to a life of challenge and daring, even risk. STP was the "racer's edge." Now they all push fear of breakdowns, fear of "internal corrosion" and sell themselves as play-it-safe insurance. It's more than just economic fears; it's a whole new defensive posture toward life-style.

Fear of Women   The woman is wearing a clinging cocktail gown, she's caressing the shaft of a pool cue with one hand while the other hand rests casually on a pool table littered with balls.

"Some men are intimidated by women these days," she smiles smugly. "Maybe because we're free to do much more. But some men aren't intimidated at all. They enjoy our freedom. Those are the men I like . . .My men wear English Leather—or they wear nothing at all." Despite the infelicitous attempt at double entendre, the basic message is not sex but fear: The ad uses this caricature of a liberated woman to intimidate men into feeling they have to prove they're not intimidated by women.

And speaking of intimidation, the Wheaties commercial features a woman who beats the pants off her husband on the tennis court, then sits down at a courtside breakfast table and ridicules his slovenly eating habits while he cringes silently behind his newspaper. In a Jeep commercial a woman beats a man to the top of the hill in a king of the hill car race and laughs merrily at his humiliation.

The intimidated wretch is not just a new version of the old, stock henpecked husband. The women in these commercials beat men at their own games and mock them in defeat. One wonders if the real fear message built into all of these ads is that women's liberation inevitably means women's tyranny and male defeat.

Nathaniel Tweedy,
DRUGGIST,
At the GOLDEN-EAGLE in MARKET-STREET, near the COURT-HOUSE,
Has imported in the ANN and ELIZABETH, Capt. CHANCELLOR, from LONDON,
A large and univerſal Aſſort-ment of DRUGS and MEDICINES, which, as uſual, he will ſell on the *moſt* reaſonable *terms* : among which are,——

There is a new breed of reformist women's commercials, but most of them are either of the "I like housework and motherhood, but I know there are other things in life, so I'm particularly grateful for the fast-working enzyme action of this pre-soak because it allows me to get the family's wash clean more quickly so that I can be an independent woman in my spare time," or they're about slim, determined independent women who have glamorous jobs and drink diet colas.

A couple of commercials have recently surfaced that show men engaged in what is traditionally considered "woman's work." But the one liberated woman commercial that truly breaks new ground this season is the Italian Swiss Colony wine ad. Right off the bat the woman in the ad announces that she's separated from her husband and that it's been good for her. "When my husband and I first separated," she says, "I didn't know how to do anything or think I'd ever learn, but I tried and proved I could." She offers as prime proof of her new-found self-sufficiency the ability to choose a wine all by herself with confidence in her choice.

The fact that she's so smug about the superiority of her choice—something called Italian Swiss Colony Chenin Blanc—makes me suspect that her ex-husband had kept her on a diet of Boone's Farm Strawberry up until the separation. But Italian Swiss Colony deserves credit for the forthrightness of its pitch.

Shaving Narcissism   An odd little twist in this season's shaving commercials. The two big concepts in shaving spots always used to be "smooth" and "close." The words were used to describe the shave, not the face. Now suddenly it's "love" and "super" and "perfect." And those words are used to refer to the *face*, not the shave.

"C'mere superface," purrs the Noxzema shave cream girl, lather at the ready.

"You took your perfect face and gave it a perfect shave," exults the tuneful Trac II girl for Gillette.

"Send your face to Schick, let Schick love it," a girl singing group urges on behalf of that shaving company.

The visuals reflect this new preoccupation with the perfection and loveliness of men's faces. In shaving commercials of years gone by, once-grizzled men rubbed their newly shaven chins, women stroked their jaws. These days the archetypal post-shave shot shows a man gazing in his mirror, watching himself caress himself.

Is this a retreat from fearsome women into the self-sufficiency of infantile narcissism or adolescent autoeroticism? With such a perfect face and a perfect mirror image to love, who needs a third face to come between the two?

New and Improved   Few things are either this year. Retrenchment is all. Once the big rationale for advertising was its ability to educate consumers about valuable new products and improvements they would not know of otherwise. The only new product I noted was something called Egg Baskets, which seem to be pastry shells into which an egg can be cracked and baked if you are inclined to ruin your morning in that fashion.

And there's only one old-fashioned stop-the-presses announcement of a product improvement this year. "GREAT NEWS," says an excited voice. "New Ty-D-bol now has lemon fresh borax!"

Now this might seem anticlimactic to some, and the fact that it's the most exciting "new improvement" of the season may say something about the season. But you have to take into account that the Tidy Bowl announcement is delivered by a man in a glass-bottomed boat afloat in a toilet bowl, and that hasn't been done before.

The Official Cooking Oil of the U.S. Olympic Team   Something else to keep an eye on are the curious uses to which certain advertisers are putting the U.S. Olympic team. Consider the case of the perfect blower styler.

"Nothing demands perfection like athletic competition," begins a Sunbeam commercial over visuals of athletic competition and a blare of trumpets on the soundtrack. "Serious athletes expect it from themselves, expect it from the things around them." Perfection that is. So far so good.

Then, without transition, comes this portentous announcement: "The Sunbeam Professional Blower Styler. Selected for use by the United States Olympic team."

Wait a minute. Who selected it and how? Did the track and field coaches meet with the other team captains for a big blower styler try out? Or did Sunbeam send a truckload of blower stylers over to the Olympic Committee and get an official Olympic blower styler plug in return? Was there a cash contribution too? (The answer, according to a U.S. Olympic Committee spokesman, is that Sunbeam supplies blower stylers for the entire Olympic entourage and a $35,000 contribution, too.)

Then I noticed that Schlitz beer commercials feature the voice-over of a purported Olympic figure-skating hopeful as she describes the long, hard climb to Olympic glory. She never actually says she drinks Schlitz, but her "style" and "class" are attributes that the Schlitz announcer also imputes to his beer.

It seems to me that if the Olympic Committee is going to get into merchandising they ought to get into it in a much bigger way. Why not an Official Sleeping Pill of the U.S. Olympic team ("Yes, we athletes get real keyed up the night before a game . . ."). The Official Fish 'n Chips dinner of the U.S. Olympics. Perhaps even the Olympic torch bearer frying bread in Wesson Oil to prove that the oil doesn't soak through. The kind of thing you need for credibility.

Up-Front Post-Watergate Morality   First A&P led off the season confessing that it had let "Price" get ahead of "Pride," and then pardoned itself for that crime by pledging—it seemed—to raise prices. Now Parkay has leaped into the credibility contest with a totally original ploy. Perhaps remorse inspired Parkay, the shame of all those years when the talking Parkay margarine tub repeatedly and perjuriously told people who opened the refrigerator door that it was really butter.

None of that nonsense in this new commercial for liquid Parkay. The woman in the ad opens up by saying she works for the ad agency that peddles Parkay. She tells us she was skeptical about this liquid stuff when the Parkay people asked her to work on the pitch, but that she conscientiously tried a squeeze or two and found herself utterly knocked out by it. She raved about it so convincingly that the Parkay people asked her—a real advertising person—to be their TV spokesperson.

After all those years of trying to make the public think ads came from "real people" and not Madison Avenue, here's an ad exec to endorse the product. A brilliant turnabout. In a country where the President, the one man charged with the trust of the nation, turns out to be a liar and a cheat, why not promote the adman, traditionally considered most suspect and self-interested of all, as the only unimpeachable source of candor we can rely on?

Some people say the Golden Age of TV Commercials came to an end with the end of economic expansion and that thereafter nothing has approached the imagination, inventiveness, intelligence and cash expended on the finest of the late Sixties spots. And it's true that the TV commercial world this season is filled with signs of recession and regression: more dumb dishwasher demonstrations, contrived car comparisons, hideous "hidden camera" slices of life. But there's one genre that's entering a Golden Age all its own these days.

The inspirationals   You know the ones. Generally they have a large, vibrant chorus filling the background with a strong upbeat tune. Half-hymn, half-marching song, they are the national anthems of their products. On the screen energetic people of all races, colors and creeds do energetic things such as jogging, marching and eating fried chicken while singing their anthem, or getting ready to burst into song. The United Airlines commercial is about a group of strangers riding an airport limo bursting into the "Mother Country" anthem. In other ads whole towns filled with jolly oldsters, rollicking youngsters and peppy people of all ages explode into tuneful, muscular joy on the screen.

The Inspirationals are all so infectiously entertaining it's hard to choose among them. McDonald's "Good morning, America!" breakfast commercials never fail to wake some sparks of innocent morning joy in me no matter how tired and wasted I am. The Beauty Rest "Good Day" anthem is almost as good. Colonel Sanders' "Real Goodness" anthem, STP, 7-Up, even, I'm ashamed to say, Coke's "Look Up America"—they all get to me. Some of them get to me too much. The Sanka anthem, for instance. I spent two miserable weeks this fall trying to get the Sanka anthem to stop repeating endlessly in the back of my mind. The tune's okay, but the lyric somehow doesn't live up to the soaring tones of the choir-like chorus. One feels a bit silly walking around town with a choir chanting in one's head: "WE'RE THE THIRD LARGEST COFFEE IN AMERICA."

Whence comes the revivalistic outburst in TV commercials this year? Is it a depression-induced Happy Days Are Here Again/Gold Diggers of '33 trend designed to get depressed consumers happy enough to spend what little they have? Is it a bicentennial rebirth of Whitmanesque celebratory optimism? A secular Great Awakening (most of them are anthems of the morning)?

Or is it something more calculated, like the pepped-up Muzak fed to workers in big factories just before closing time? Is there something even darker behind all this upbeat hysteria, a sense of some more final Closing Time closing in on America?

Perhaps those darker notes are there, but no matter how suspicious I get about them the new Inspirationals never fail to work their happy-making magic on me. That's what makes them so impressive, even scary. Inspirational technology has grown so sophisticated and powerful that TV commercial makers are capable of making one feel happy, *naturally* happy, without any sense of being manipulated into feeling happy. Something like the feeling you get from the deodorant soap that gets you naturally clean without making you worry that you smell like a deodorant soap.

Bibliography

Ron Rosenbaum's subject of truth in advertising is explored in greater detail in Dr. Ivan L. Preston's scholarly *The Great American Blow-Up: Puffery in Advertising and Selling*, University of Wisconsin Press, 1975. Students should consult this work for background and insights into the problem of puffery in advertising. See also two articles that appeared in *Ramparts* (Summer 1974), Bruce Howard, "The Advertising Council: Selling Lies . . ." pp. 25-26 ff. and Henry Weinstein, " . . . And Selling Truth," pp. 64 ff.

A different advertising issue, but one that is very controversial today is the matter of advertising to children. See William H. Melody, *Children's Television: The Economics of Exploitation*, Yale University Press, 1973 and Charles Winick, *et al.*, *Children's Television Commercials: A Content Analysis*, Praeger, 1973. Articles dealing with the same subject are Marilyn Elias, "How to Win Friends and Influence Kids on Television," *Human Behavior* (April 1974), which describes advertising research designed to find the best way to persuade children; Joan Barthel, "Boston Mothers Against Kidvid," *The New York Times Magazine* (Jan. 5, 1975), pp. 14-15 ff., which describes the development of Action for Children's Television (ACT); William H. Melody and Wendy Ehrlich, "Children's TV Commercials: The Vanishing Policy Option," *Journal of Communication* (Autumn 1974), pp. 113-125, which describes and attacks the FCC's handling of ACT's proposals to remove commercials from children's television; and Shel Feldman and Abraham Wolf, "What's Wrong With Children's Commercials?" *Journal of Advertising Research* (February 1974), pp. 39-43, which summarizes and categorizes criticism against children's advertising.

Fairfax M. Cone told the story of his forty years in advertising in 1969 when he published *With All Its Faults* (Boston: Little, Brown). The final chapter is recommended for its estimate of how advertising can better serve the society in which it exists. This article on the future electronic age

When Advertising Talks to Everyone

By Fairfax Cone

When publicly contemplating the future of almost anything, there is nothing safer than to see in it all manner of drastic change, even to the point of disaster. Then, if trouble comes, the viewer with alarm can smugly regard the situation that he has predicted and be called a wise soothsayer. If, on the other hand, the prophet of crackup and break-down turns out to be wrong, no one is hurt, and he need only say that his timing was off or that vastly changed circumstances made the difference. I am going to take the long chance.

If we are indeed entering an era of news monopoly in terms of both national and world news, it seems more than likely that regional and local news services actually will be increased. The development of small-town and suburban community newspapers at a time when many big-city newspapers have ceased publication has been a phenomenon of the last two or three decades. Now, with local cable television coming to communities of all sizes, it can be predicted that this new emphasis on local news and interests will be intensified.

A recent broadcasting event in Newport Beach, California, illustrates this. The cable television station there invited thirty candidates for public offices ranging from the U.S. Senate to the local village council to tell their stories in terms of their own interests. All accepted with the result that hundreds of citizens of this small Southern California seaside community for the first time saw candidates in the light of their own problems.

In much the same way, I believe we are entering a time when much advertising also will become more local and more meaningful. Advertising aimed precisely at what might be termed need-groups promises a new and welcome relevancy.

When advertising tries to talk to everyone, the result is no different than it is when any other form of communication is aimed at the largest possible audience. The days of yellow journalism at the turn of the century are an example. The heyday of the great mass magazines in the 1950s is another. Neither could last, for audiences tire of unchanging fare, and either break up into separate interest groups or find new sources for their enlightenment and their entertainment. Both of these developments are occurring in broadcasting at this moment, and their effect on advertising will be profound.

One of the unhappy concomitants of today's television, with its enormous time and production costs for advertising, has been the unwillingness of many major advertisers to depart from commercial routines that have proved to be successful economically, no matter how wearisome they may be to millions of viewers. It is a demonstrable fact that one's reaction to almost any advertising message breaks down into two parts: the form in which the message is presented and the promise itself. The result is that the form may be, and often is, a subject of ridicule (e.g., the white tornado that blows through the kitchen or the eye-winking plumber who clears a clogged drain with nothing more than a sprinkling of powder that is available from your nearest friendly grocer), while the proposition that is made for the product involved is totally accepted.

If this sounds impossible, or even improbable, I can only explain it in terms of noises to which one becomes accustomed to the point of not hearing them at all, while a special sound of much lesser intensity comes through loud and clear. However, this is hardly an excuse for the foolishness that makes so many commercial minutes seem ugly and interminable.

The trouble lies in the lack of creative ability in the people in advertising agencies and production studios, and among the advertisers, who are caught be-

appeared first in *Saturday Review* (October 10, 1970). It is reprinted with permission of *Saturday Review*, copyright 1970.

tween two deadly dilemmas. One is to follow the leader with the implausible dramas of fun and games at the sink or in the bathroom or laundry; the other is to try anything at all that is different—for that reason alone. Of the two, it is questionable which is harder to take if one pays attention.

Both, however, may well be headed for the discard, for paying attention to the commercials is no longer a requirement of the television experience. In the beginning it was said, and it was probably true, that viewers gladly accepted the advertising as a reasonable price of admission to the shows they watched. But the audience has become more sophisticated. There has developed a little mechanism in the brain of almost everyone of us that can automatically shut off our attention to a point where only certain sounds come through: mostly product names and promises and pertinent details of unusual services.

To be sure, there are exceptions to the general low interest in commercial messages. Some are full of fun and the fun is to the point. Others, such as commercials for many food and household products, present demonstrations that help the homemaker with her relentless job. Still others substitute dramatic facts for throaty claims for automobile tires and batteries and insurance, etc.

The changes that one can foresee in advertising in the next few years, and that should make much of it more attractive and useful for everyone concerned, are becoming apparent in an about-face in advertising philosophy that will bring it into line with growing interest in the consumer as an object of concern and respect and not a faceless, nearly mindless purchasing unit. To say this another way, I believe the impersonality is going out of advertising much as I believe that it is going to be replaced in business for the very good reason that this works both ways: Customer loyalty simply cannot be maintained by an impersonal supplier, and business and advertising must, in the long run, depend on that loyalty. That they must also earn it is the reason for the inevitable changes.

The alternative is the complete breakdown of an imperfect system. The imperfection may be the result of growth and standardization, and the temporary subjugation of the individual during a period of great economic change and concentration of power. Whatever the reason, no one can doubt that as a nation we have arrived at a time when skepticism may be our most outstanding characteristic. Vietnam is only one reason for this. Rightly or wrongly, the maturing generation believes that we have been lied to and manipulated by business and government, and even in our educational and legal systems, and the young men and women who supply this generation with its conviction and strength see advertising as one of the worst sins of a venal establishment. Nor is this a question particularly of dishonesty or sharp practice. Unhappily, these evils are largely taken for granted. The overriding objection is to the mass appeal of advertising at a time when all the emphasis our young people can muster is on individuality. There is a thing called life-style that simply cannot be dictated by anyone—advertisers least of all.

This will unquestionably mean more special-interest publications, both magazines and community news organs (either printed or electronically reproduced), with special-interest advertising. Still, the biggest change will probably be in television and television advertising, where the messages for many products and services will be delivered almost as professional buyers' guides by a nationwide corps of competent local authorities who will evaluate and recommend products and services according to their own standards and experience. Products of only general interest (or those lacking interest at any given moment, such as analgesics) will continue to be advertised over the networks in national news and sports programs and the more popular comedy and variety and dramatic hours.

Despite considerable speculation to the contrary, it seems unlikely that either pay television or the cassette will mean the end of the big variety or dramatic programs or the ace news commentators as we have come to expect these from the networks. For one thing, entertainment that one must pay for must be a good deal better than entertainment that is free, and this may be hard to come by for more than a few hours in any week, for the costs will be considerable. Also, news cannot be canned; it must be contemporaneous. On the other hand, hundreds of independent cable television stations are going to compete, and successfully, I believe, with the run-of-mine programs by offering a conglomerate of special interest features for limited but extremely receptive audiences.

Cable television was introduced as a means of establishing or improving physical reception in remote areas, and this it has done very successfully. While no one knows precisely what its effect will be in metropolitan centers, where reception is satisfactory for the most part and where there is already a choice of channels and programs, the likelihood is that it will become not so much an extension of television as we now know it, but an essentially new medium.

It is not difficult to imagine the attraction of a station that performs service to the community by broadcasting purely local news and commentary and an almost unlimited number of programs of unique interest. The key factor, of course, is the freedom of the cable station operator from the demands for a large audience by any advertiser, for his audience is made up of paid subscribers. Such advertisers as there may be, and I expect there will be many, will be satisfied with any reasonable, and reasonably priced, audience whose special interest they share.

This, then, is where the greatest change in advertising is likely to take place. In recent years, most large advertisers increasingly have aimed their messages at the largest available audiences at the lowest possible cost per thousand. This led to the disastrous circulation races among the mass magazines, the strain of which caused the demise of half a dozen of them, and a gradual diminution in the number of daily newspapers. Neither could compete successfully with a medium that was wholly advertiser-supported and adored by advertiser and public alike. This was in television's long honeymoon stage. Today many an advertiser is beginning to wonder whether the large audiences are really worth the total expenditures involved, no matter how low the cost per thousand. The questions arise partly out of a desire to save money and so increase profits and partly out of a determination to talk only to one's most logical prospects. Clearly, such a change in advertising strategy should dictate a much more thoughful and much less blatant use of all advertising media.

It is safe to say that television is today the principal source of news as well as entertainment of the majority of American families. If this presaged a monopoly of either one by a monolithic television system, I would be fearful of the result. But I think the imminence of community cable television negates the possibility, in the very same way that it promises advertising that is less dictated and confined by formula.

It is necessary here to remember that all advertising is not alike either in its making or intention. Manufacturers' advertising, for the most part, announces innovations and product changes and improvements, and this advertising appears mostly in magazines and on television and radio. The advertising of retailers, which is concerned primarily with the values in those products in terms of style, size, price, etc., makes up the bulk of newspaper advertising, except for want ads.

The changes that I foresee will have little or no effect upon the division of advertising between the various media. It should stay much as it is, with only some diversion of special-interest advertising from the general magazines to the growing list of special-interest publications.

On the other hand, I believe that advertising may be greatly changed by still another factor. With two-way communication established between receivers and cable stations, whereby subscribers may dial requests for any information under the sun, which will be available by computer, it is unlikely that consumer reports will not be included. No service could be more natural or have greater effect upon advertising. For the reply to the subscriber's query and the advertising that floats freely through the air on the same subject must allow no disparity. Both must serve the recipient in his own best interest.

This is something that advertising has always promised to do. But the promise has not always been kept. In large measure, it may now be.

Bibliography

Changes in the advertising industry are reflected rather clearly in the leading journals in the field, including *Advertising Age* and *Madison Avenue*. Two excellent articles on the effects of radio and television upon the advertising world will be found in the special edition of *Advertising Age* (Nov. 21, 1973), entitled "The New World of Advertising." One of the results of the changes in advertising is the new role created for the advertising representative. See Rufus Crater, "Future Shock: It's Here Now for the Reps," *Broadcasting* (July 14, 1975), pp. 29-30 ff. This report contains tables on 1974 billings and a comparison of 1960 and 1974 TV and radio billings from New York and other markets. A report on advertising agencies appears in *Advertising Age* (Feb. 23, 1976). A related advertising issue grows out of comparative advertising—the naming of competing brands. Tom Bradshaw, "Comparative Ads: What's Their Status Now?" *Television/Radio Age* (April 29, 1974), pp. 29-32 ff. provides a good survey of the problem, mentions specific cases and describes the work of the review agencies that broadcast and advertising organizations have created.

Public Relations   We Are Advocates!

By Joseph P. McLaughlin

Joseph P. McLaughlin was president of the Beacon Agency, Inc., in Philadelphia, and an accredited member of PRSA. He is the author of a number of arti-

For several decades the goal of achieving for public relations the status of a profession, accepted as such by government, the academic community, business and opinion leaders, other professional societies and associations and laymen generally has been an elusive one.

There is not even agreement among public relations practitioners and public relations educators as to what needs to be done in order to raise what now is regarded essentially as an art or trade to professional status.

This despite the fact that public relations practitioners constantly use the term professional in talking loosely about other practitioners and their qualifications.

The passage of time, alone, will not bring this goal closer as optimists among us continue to hope. But much can be accomplished, we believe, if the practitioner can be persuaded to regard himself as what he truly is—*an advocate*—and to act in accordance with that self-image.

Among the more frequently mentioned ingredients that many in the field contend are essential to the "mix" that spells professionalism are (a) a code of ethics with procedures and machinery for disciplining those who violate its provisions (b) an agreed-upon "body of knowledge" which undergirds public relations theory and practice and (c) a system of examinations to determine the basic knowledge of those entering the public relations field coupled with certification of their qualifications and character by a panel of their peers. Some also believe that a system of governmental licensing should be added.

Largely through the efforts of the Public Relations Society of America and its various sections, particularly the Counselor's Section, two of these ingredients already are in being, though perhaps not fully developed. PRSA has a code of ethics binding on all of its almost 7000 members with provisions for enforcement and penalizing of transgressors. Through its Accreditation Program, PRSA also requires all who seek active membership to pass an examination and to satisfy a panel of already-accredited members as to their qualifications and character. The desirability of requiring government licensing of public relations practitioners is under study.

But the problem of what constitutes an accepted "body of knowledge" and how it is to be developed remains largely unresolved and may continue to defy solution for some time.

It is the purpose of this article to set forth the proposition that there is still another ingredient necessary for achievement of professional status—an attainable one—that is little talked about but is at least as important as the others mentioned and, in the opinion of the writer, may be a pre-requisite for solving the knotty problem of developing a body of knowledge concerning which there can be general agreement. That ingredient is independence.

It can be achieved only if the individual practitioner, and the societies and associations to which he belongs, can sharpen their perception of the public relations man's fundamental role in a society dominated by public opinion, which in turn is molded largely by the mass media of communication. This role is shaped by the fact—indisputable, the writer thinks—that public opinion can impose sanctions that are sometimes more severe than legal ones.

The PR man should be an advocate in the same sense that lawyers are advocates. It may be that he also should be granted legally the privilege of confidentiality insofar as conversations with clients [are] concerned, but that is a separate question.

We may speak of the PR man's role as an interpreter to his client or clients of society and events; an evaluator of the meaning and consequences of social and

cles in *Public Relations Quarterly,* in which this article appeared during the summer of 1972. Reprinted by permission of the *Quarterly.*

economic change; a prognosticator of future troubles; a prudent and imaginative preparer of programs designed to deal with problems before they descend in full force upon his employer; a transmission belt to carry the client's messages to various publics and to convey back to the client the reactions of those publics to his programs and activities. He undoubtedly, at various times, depending upon the scope of his responsibilities, is all of these. But primarily he is an advocate.

A fascinating chain of events that began in the fall of 1971 in Philadelphia, in which the writer was deeply involved, provided him an insight into the implications of the PR man's role as an advocate. Out of it grew a conviction as to how important recognizing this role is to the achievement of professional status.

Early in October of 1971, Philip Bucci, a highly-respected PR counselor with several decades of experience—an accredited member of PRSA and a member of its Counselor's Section—agreed to accept as a client a man who had been publicly described by the Pennsylvania State Crime Commission and other law enforcement officials as a leader in organized crime in Pennsylvania.

The man, Peter Maggio, owner of a South Philadelphia cheese plant, became the subject of controversy and newspaper headlines when he submitted what he thought was a routine request for a zoning change that would permit him to close a small street, unused by the public, so that he could expand his business. He asked the City Councilman representing the district in which the plant was located, William J. Cottrell, to introduce the necessary ordinance.

Cottrell did so, and the bill, after the usual hearing at which no opposition was voiced, was reported to the floor of the Council. District Attorney Arlen Specter then sent two assistant district attorneys to see Cottrell to inform him of the State Crime Commission characterization of Maggio and at the same time a story was leaked to the Philadelphia newspapers. Cottrell immediately backed away from the bill which was sent back to committee, presumably to die.

Mutual friends brought Maggio, who was smarting under the unfavorable publicity, and Bucci together. Maggio asked Bucci to help him. Before agreeing to do so, Bucci, in accord with his usual practice, researched the accusations to the best of his ability. He read all of the newspaper clippings and visited the South Philadelphia neighborhood to talk with district police officers, and Maggio's neighbors and customers.

He also read all of the available literature on the Mafia and the reports of the U.S. Senate (McClelland) Committee which had investigated organized crime.

He also wrote to the late J. Edgar Hoover, then Director of the Federal Bureau of Investigation, whom he knew and asked whether there was anything in FBI files to substantiate the accusation. Hoover sent him a letter stating that there was no derogatory information on Maggio in the files. Bucci's first impulse was to make this letter public, but, on mature consideration, he decided to give it instead to City Council President Paul D'Ortona. By this time he was convinced that Maggio was the victim of character assassination and that he was entitled to public relations help in having his name cleared and in obtaining the necessary Councilmanic approval for his expansion plans.

Before accepting Maggio as a client—and aware of the possibility of censure by the public and colleagues—he discussed the advisability of doing so with several public relations practitioners who also were close friends, including the writer. We finally advised him to accept and also pledged that, should he encounter adverse criticism, we would come to his defense.

Bucci's first action on behalf of Maggio was to set up an interview with the *Philadelphia Evening* and *Sunday Bulletin* which was published over several columns with photographs of Maggio and his wife, a talented amateur artist, in the editions of Sunday, September 12, 1971. In the interview, Mr. Maggio denied any connection whatsoever with the Mafia, and said he doubted the existence of such an organization. He said he was harrassed by governmental officials because he is the brother-in-law of Angelo Bruno, described by the FBI as a national leader of organized crime in the U.S. At the time Bucci was hired, Mr. Bruno was in prison in New Jersey following his refusal to answer questions at a hearing before a New Jersey commission investigating crime.

Two days later, the *Bulletin* carried a column-length story on page nine about Bucci and his representation of Maggio under the head "Maggio Hires PR Man For a New 'Image.' " It was factual and generally favorable to Bucci, detailing his representation of blue chip clients in the past, which included U.S. Senator Hugh Scott (R., Pa.), Superior Court Judge John B. Hannum (now a Federal Circuit Court Judge), the American Legion, Fraternal Order of Police, and sports personalities like heavyweight boxing champion Joe Frazier. The article also noted that among Bucci's references was one from Hoover, and one from former Pennsylvania Governor Raymond P. Shafer.

Meanwhile, armed with Hoover's letter, Council President D'Ortona wrote to Specter and demanded that he state publicly whether he had any evidence connecting Maggio with the Mafia. Specter wrote back a few days later stating that he had no such evidence.

The zoning bill then was revived in City Council and, at Cottrell's urging, passed unanimously. However, former Mayor James H. J. Tate did not sign it before leaving office. Cottrell was defeated for re-election to Council but his successor, Natale F. Carbello, re-introduced the bill. It was passed by Council and signed into law by Tate's successor Mayor Frank L. Rizzo.

The signing was a personal victory for Bucci. Without his courageous public relations advocacy—at considerable risk to his own image—in Maggio's behalf, City Hall observers say that the zoning change would have been dead and Maggio would have suffered not only financial loss, but also his reputation would have been irrevocably damaged. As evidence of the sanctions that can be inflicted by public opinion, the Maggio firm showed a loss in excess of $100,000 in 1971, the first such loss in 55 years of business. Because of the unfavorable publicity also, many of his customers had ceased doing business with him.

However, even before Maggio was cleared, Bucci and the writer agreed that a fundamental principle relating to the practice of public relations was involved, namely the right of a reputable public relations practitioner to represent any client without having attributed to him "the reputation, character or beliefs of the client." Even though Bucci believed, and publicly stated, that he was convinced that Maggio had no connection with the Mafia and had been maligned (as later developments were to demonstrate) we both agreed that the principle was important enough to have it endorsed by a professional public relations association made up of a jury of our peers.

We chose the Philadelphia Public Relations Association as the appropriate vehicle. This association, although it is unaffiliated with any state or national organization, is the largest group of public relations practitioners in the Philadelphia area (more than 225 members) and enjoys considerable prestige, particularly with the news media.

At the writer's request a meeting of the directors of the Philadelphia Public Relations Association was held at the Poor Richard Club on October 6, 1971 at which, after considerable, sometimes sharp discussion, the following statement was approved. It is reproduced here in full.

"A Public Relations practitioner, like an attorney, primarily is an advocate.

"An attorney seeks to represent his client in the most favorable light, consistent with the rules of evidence, his duty as an officer of the Court and the canons of ethics of the organized Bar in the various tribunals in the field of Jurisprudence. Through advice and consultation the lawyer endeavors also to help his client avoid situations which will involve him in litigation or criminal proceedings.

"A Public Relations practitioner seeks to represent his client in the most favorable light consistent with the facts and the ethical codes of professional Public Relations organizations, in the Court of Public Opinion.

"Except for the possible deprivation of his life or freedom, a client can be damaged as severely in the Court of Public Opinion as in a Court of Law.

"Many local and state bar associations have adopted resolutions which assert, in essence, that a lawyer may represent any client without having attributed to him the reputation, character and beliefs of the client. If, by virtue of such representation of an unpopular client, a lawyer incurs hostility, resentment or adverse criticism, the organized bar has committed itself to come to his defense.

"The Philadelphia Public Relations Association claims the same privilege for the Public Relations practitioner, operating in the Court of Public Opinion.

"It asserts that a Public Relations practitioner has the right to represent any client without having attributed to him the reputation, character or beliefs of the client.

"It asserts, also, the corollary right of any person who could benefit from such services, to representation by a competent Public Relations practitioner of good character and reputation."

The statement in its original version read "present his client in the most favorable light"—not "represent"—but got changed in the final, somewhat confusing, moments of this meeting.

The action formed the basis of a news article the following day in the *Philadelphia Inquirer*. The vote of the directors was 24-0 in favor of the statement. A small committee of the directors subsequently was appointed by Charles Ellis, president of the Philadelphia Public Relations Association, to draft a change in the association's by-laws to incorporate into that document the principle outlined in the statement. The directors, incidentally, also approved a resolution expressing their confidence in and admiration for Bucci.

Meanwhile, the writer wrote to Paul M. Werth, a Columbus, Ohio, public relations practitioner who at the time was chairman of the Counselor's section of PRSA, advising him both of the intention to have the matter considered by the Philadelphia Public Relations Association and of its subsequent unanimous approval of the statement. In reply, Mr. Werth described the situation as "very interesting" and said he would bring it to the attention of the Executive Committee of the Counselor's section. Copies of the letters of Mr. Werth and the newspaper clippings also were sent to Dr. Robert O. Carlson, president of the Public Relations Society of America.

What are the broad implications of this chain of events for the practice of public relations in the United States?

As far as the counselors are concerned, we think it is obvious that, if they are to be recognized as members of a profession, they must come out from behind the shadow of the client. They must not be considered merely a part of the client's retinue, lumped together with those who write speeches, arrange schedules, or merely carry valises. They must be "in charge" of the case, just as a lawyer, because of his superior training, knowledge and experience, is in charge of his client's case. To their credit, some counselors already operate in this manner.

Even those who are corporate or association or foundation public relations directors or staff members, we believe, must come to look upon themselves as advocates. They have the same problem as lawyers who serve as house counsel for corporations—who have a single client. But if they look upon themselves primarily as advocates, some of the doubts and confusions that have troubled them may be removed. For instance, many corporate PR men have been at a loss as to how to resolve the inner doubts and the conflict produced by charges of magazine writers that it is the job of public relations always to present the client in the most favorable possible light—to ignore the bad and publicize only the good and beneficial. In short, always to tell half truths instead of the whole truth. If the PR man frankly accepts his role as that of advocate, these doubts and conflicts largely will disappear. No one expects a lawyer to present, even to a jury deciding the question of freedom, or life itself, information damaging to his client. As an officer of the court, the lawyer is bound not to tell untruths or to deny the truth if it is brought out under questioning of opposing counsel. As a man of conscience, bound by the code of ethics of professional associations like the Public Relations Society of America, the corporate PR Director or staff member is bound not to tell untruths to the media or any of his client's publics and to answer truthfully the questions of the representatives of the media.

Our job as advocate is to present our client in the best possible light. It is an honorable role, and we should not feel defensive about it.

Bibliography

Joseph P. McLaughlin's article should be read along with Neil A. Lavick's article. Both writers reflect the difficulty of defining and establishing standards in the field of public relations. Two helpful bibliographies for this and related public relations issues are Robert L. Bishop, compiler, *Public Relations: A Comprehensive Bibliography: Articles and Books on Public Relations, Communication Theory, Public Opinion, and Propaganda, 1964-1972*, A. G. Leigh-James, 1974 and Scott M. Cutlip, compiler, *A Public Relations Bibliography*, 2nd ed., University of Wisconsin Press, 1965. The Bishop volume up-dates Cutlip's compilation. Also useful for students who wish to dig deeply is Raymond Simon, compiler, *Bibliography of Masters' Theses and Doctoral Dissertations Dealing with Public Relations Subjects 1960-1970*, Foundation for Public Relations Research and Education, with supplement for 1971-72 by Marie E. Mastin, undated.

Public Relations Council: An Alternative to Licensing?

By Neil A. Lavick

A new look at an old problem

The idea of licensing public relations practitioners is not new. It has occurred intermittently for at least a quarter of a century. Despite the longevity of interest in the topic, there is much disagreement over whether or not government regulation would be the most appropriate means of reducing criticisms made against the practice.

Several states—California, Arkansas, and Florida—have shown interest, albeit none seriously, in regulating public relations, and the Public Relations Society of America has drafted, but not endorsed, a model state statute providing for the mandatory certification of PR practitioners. PRSA members feel that the promotion of licensing by the Society would be premature and unwise at this time. The purpose of the model state statute, is, therefore, to show to PRSA members the elements which would be involved in such legislation.

Although government regulation of public relations could have far reaching impact, positive and negative, scant information about the licensing question has been reported in the press. The present purposes are to review contentions in the debate, to examine compromises, and to offer a new and perhaps more viable alternative.

Arguments by Proponents of Licensing

It would keep charlatans and incompetents out of the field. Ever since the nebulous beginning of public relations, its prestige and advancement have been hampered by individuals possessing little knowledge of the practice and little ethical comportment in their activities. As it is now, anyone, for any reason, with any background and training may proclaim himself a PR practitioner. Not only should the esteem and reputation of conscientious and capable practitioners be protected, but the public also must be safeguarded against unscrupulous opportunists who issue distorted and inaccurate information.

Government regulation of public relations is not new to the practice. Rules, regulations, and laws of the FTC, FCC, SEC, and others already impinge upon its

Neil A. Lavick is director of public relations, MoPaC International, Minneapolis. Reprinted with permission from *Public Relations Quarterly* (Spring 1975).

execution. And in recent years there has been a proliferation of regulations affecting public relations, especially financial public relations, which have had no unsettling or unduly restraining impact on the practice. Licensing would be merely another effort to protect consumers against unqualified practitioners.

PRSA's Accreditation program affects only a small percentage of practitioners, but it is a valuable foundation for a more pervasive licensing system. Of the 50,000 claiming to be PR practitioners, only 7,000 are members of PRSA and less than half of these are accredited. Nevertheless, PRSA Accreditation is useful and constitutes a sound basis from which to develop licensing requirements. Accreditation, in the form of licensing, could be strengthened and extended to include far more practitioners than are in PRSA.

Government regulation would bring the status of the PR vocation closer to that of a profession. Just as lawyers and physicians are licensed, so too must be PR practitioners in order to become professionals. The absence of a licensing system is one of the chief obstacles to being regarded as a profession.

Arguments by Opponents of Licensing

The above comprise some of the arguments in favor of licensing practitioners. There are also numerous counterarguments. Opponents contend with equal vigor that there should not be any licensing of public relations.

Although no reputable PR practitioner wants charlatans or incompetents in this line of work, licensing is not the solution. Looking at professions which already license their members, one finds that they too have charlatans and incompetents. Government regulation would not be a panacea against fakes or undisciplined and irresponsible individuals.

Protecting the public against unscrupulous practitioners who propagate distorted and inaccurate information is a laudable goal, but licensing would constitute a grave threat to constitutional freedoms of speech and of the press. If licensing were to deny to non-licensed persons their right to communicate messages and ideas related to public relations, this would probably violate their First Amendment freedoms. Furthermore, if the need for complete and accurate information were to justify licensing PR practitioners, the same philosophy could be extended to any segment of the public which disseminates information—newspapermen, radio announcers, TV commentators, and those in similar roles. (This potential causes many to strongly oppose licensing.)

Even though there are unscrupulous and incompetent practitioners, laws provide remedies for their transgressions. Laws of libel, fraud, misrepresentation, and so on apply to practitioners. If other activities should be restrained or controlled, then laws, not a licensing system, should be devised to cover those specific situations.

Every conscientious PR practitioner wants to be known as a professional and to work in an acknowledged profession, but these desires in and of themselves are not sufficient to warrant government regulation, nor would licensing alone render public relations a profession. If the latter were true, then members of any occupation, such as salesmen, secretaries, and custodians, could become professionals through a mere legislative act establishing a licensing procedure for them.

Considerations in Drafting Licensing Regulations

Beyond these pro and con arguments, there are fundamental legislative concerns. Although not insurmountable, they would create difficulties in drafting suitable legislation.

The intital problem would be to determine what or who should be licensed. If it were required of everyone calling himself a PR practitioner, then charlatans could simply use a synonym. If everyone engaging in specified PR activities were required to possess a license, would full and part-time employees need licenses? How about practitioners working full time for limited durations, as in political campaigns? It would probably be unconstitutional to compel everyone participating in public relations or some aspect of it to have a license in order to practice.

Another problem would be to ensure that being licensed would be meaningful and appealing to practitioners. If it were not, there would be no incentive for attaining it. This means that licensed practitioners would have to enjoy a special privilege, distinction, or benefit that non-licensed practitioners would not. At the same time requisites must not be too easy to attain, thereby allowing everyone to succeed, or too difficult, thereby deterring or precluding even capable practitioners from becoming licensed.

Should licensing be instituted by the federal or state governments? If it were done by the states, complications would develop over reciprocity. There is no guarantee that states would accept practitioners from outside their borders, especially if requirements for licenses differed among the states. Would practitioners be compelled to obtain a license and to pay a fee in each in which they seek to practice, even if only temporarily? The federal government, on the other hand, might be unwilling to enact regulatory legislation. And, before any licensing system is effected, there would have to be sufficient voter support.

Suggested Compromises

Many practitioners feel that public relations can and should be improved, but stop short of endorsing government regulation. Instead, they have proffered alternatives.

One suggestion is to license other, more clearly defined practices, such as publicity, and to defer public relations until its definition is less equivocal. However, this idea has obvious shortcomings. First, other vocations, such as publicity, are not defined more clearly than public relations. Second, criticisms against public relations would not be alleviated. And, third, this proposal shifts the debate to the publicity trade and only delays the inevitable dispute over whether or not to license public relations.

Another alternative is to educate members of the media, the public, and practitioners as to what constitutes proper and acceptable public relations and to have them act as policing agents. If they refuse to hire or employ individuals not meeting the standards, many of the current criticisms against public relations would disappear.

Unfortunately, such a campaign would probably be unsuccessful. Realistically, if institutions were not totally righteous in their operations, and there is no evidence that all are, some of them would likely employ practitioners with similar propensities. In addition, it is doubtful that institutions would want or be able to devote the time and energy necessary to ensure that this would be a workable plan.

A third suggestion seeks to circumvent the issue of mandatory licensing while recognizing qualified practitioners. This proposal would establish a voluntary certification program, like that in the accounting field. The primary drawback would be that journalists and others may view even this proposal as the government's creeping incursion towards regulation of the press. Moreover, this would not prevent untrained and incompetent practitioners from engaging in public relations.

Some practitioners advocate that there should be laws regulating specific PR functions but applicable to everyone, much the same as some FTC, FCC, and SEC laws control certain activities commonly undertaken by PR personnel, but at the same time regulate everyone engaging in those activities.

Although this suggestion has appealing features, it also has weaknesses. First, such a measure would operate in a piecemeal fashion, each activity would have to be legislated individually. Second, there would be problems drafting acceptable laws, some of which may be impossible to achieve because they abridge constitutional freedoms. And, third, the legal system itself generally makes difficult for the average person the redress of grievances, in terms of both expense and complicated, time-consuming procedures.

Undoubtedly there are strengths and weaknesses in every plan. However, any viable proposal will have to assure that constitutional rights will be safeguarded, the number of incompetents will be reduced, high professional standards will be met, the public will be protected against unscrupulous PR opportunists, and the status of the practice will be brought closer to that of a profession.

The most difficult requirement to meet will, of course, be the first mentioned; government regulation would resolve all the problems except this, the most important. But, perhaps there is a proposal which could satisfy all of the above, including safeguarding constitutional rights.

Public Relations Council

An alternative which might have the effect of silencing or at least reducing criticisms of the proposals discussed above and, yet, achieve the same goals would be to establish a public relations council, not unlike press councils which are known to many nations.

The council's purposes would include maintaining the character of the public relations practice in accordance with the highest professional and commercial standards, keeping under review developments likely to lead to abrogations of those standards, considering complaints about the conduct of PR practitioners and that of organizations relating to their public relations, and dealing with complaints in a systematic, orderly manner.

A group of concerned citizens and practitioners or a public interest group could draw up a constitution and select members to sit on the initial council. For example, fifteen individuals, with nine representing various segments of the public and six representing the PR practice, could comprise the council. Although officers would be chosen by the council, naming a non-practitioner as chairman would be advisable. Councils would be established locally, statewide, regionally or nationally. Financial support could come from educational institutions, professional groups, foundations, or others having no direct interest in its operations.

Tenure, rules of conduct, and other operating procedures would be delineated in its constitution. Either the constitution or the council would define all necessary and relevant terms, such as "public relations," "complainant," and "grievance." The council would also be responsible for publicizing its existence, functions, and procedures for bringing action.

A grievance committee would screen complaints, which would have to be in writing. Before handling a case, the committee would explain to the parties the standards, codes, and responsibilities of public relations and of practitioners and allow the parties to endeavor to resolve the issue themselves. This would tend to reduce the number of cases arising out of misunderstanding, ill-founded complaints, and those involving minor grievances.

If no accord were reached, the grievance committee would investigate and hear the case. The committee would have no legal power to subpoena evidence or witnesses, but all necessary evidence, practitioners as well as their employers, and the complainant would be expected to be present during the proceedings.

Although the hearings would be informal, the rights of due process would be observed closely. In this regard, parties would be able to cross examine witnesses and legal counsel would be available to both sides. After hearing the evidence, the committee would render a decision. Appeals could be made to the council, which would review the case and make a final determination. No investigation, hearing, or decision would be made in a case being adjudicated by a court.

Neither the grievance committee nor the council would have punitive or enforcement powers, other than those of admonition, moral suasion, and public opinion. All decisions of the committee and council would be presented to the media for dissemination to the general public.

Analyses of the Public Relations Council

This proposal would seem to offer a number of advantages over others. First, there would be no threat to constitutional freedoms; licensing and certification would be avoided. Voluntary compliance with no government regulation would be the norm.

Second, incompetents would be winnowed from the practice in the wake of unfavorable publicity. Employers would not be likely to hire or to retain incompetent practitioners or those bringing business unfavorable press coverage. This would be true especially of those who repeatedly disregard the professional standards. The council should also occasionally laud outstanding PR work and thereby preclude criticisms that the council's function is only to denigrate the practice.

Third, the council would devise and maintain high professional and commercial standards. It would probably be easier and more effective for an organization of this type to maintain standards in the public relations practice than too intricate laws, cumbersome legal processes, or the limited reach of PRSA. At the very least, the PR council would be an efficacious complement to existing institutions.

Fourth, such a council would provide the public with a convenient and inexpensive means of seeking redress of their PR grievances, something presently lacking. Most people do not know the procedures for taking complaints to court or have the necessary money for it. Moreover, most are unfamiliar with PRSA's judicial structure. Even if they were not, many practitioners do not belong to the Society and are not bound by its rules, procedures, or enforcement measures. A PR council, on the other hand, would furnish the public with an independent and convenient forum for airing complaints.

Fifth, by having the council devise and maintain high professional and commercial standards, public relations would come closer to attaining the status of a profession. Admittedly, a public relations council would not automatically transform public relations into a profession, but neither would government regulation in the form of licensing. However, a PR council would symbolize that a concerted effort is being made or upgrade the quality of practitioners' work, thus tending to heighten the public's regard and respect for the practice.

There are other advantages too. Because councils would not be constituted by law, there would be no problems of drafting suitable legislation, of garnering voter support, or of seeking workable reciprocity between jurisdictions.

Shortcomings

However, while this proposal has many strengths, it also has shortcomings. One of its chief virtues, voluntary compliance, is also one of its potential weaknesses. The success of the plan, from beginning to end, would be contingent upon voluntary compliance. If a party were to refuse to furnish evidence or to appear before a proceeding, there would be little the council could do. If a party were to refuse to abide by a council decision, there would be little the council could do. If the media for whatever reason were not to publicize adjudicated cases, there would be little the council could do. If the public were not interested in the cases, there would be little the council could do.

But, it is unlikely that all these situations would occur. The parties, aware of possible negative publicity resulting from noncompliance, would probably comply in most cases, in terms of both producing evidence and abiding by decisions. The media would probably print or broadcast the adjudicated cases because of their newsworthiness. Moreover, if there were more than one medium available to the council, the chances of promulgating the results would be even greater. Public interest in the council's activities would undoubtedly fluctuate, and it might be better if there were not constantly high interest in the proceedings. The important thing is that the council would provide a needed service to citizens wanting to voice complaints against the public relations practice and having no other forum in which to do so.

Another problem might concern the public relations-policy making overlap. Ideally, public relations practitioners are involved in policy formulation. But how does the council adjudicate a PR effort which is inextricably bound to policy decisions concerning management of a business? Would the council investigate, hear, and decide cases involving company policies? Would it determine what company policies should be? How far would the council delve into a business's operations? Precisely where would the line be drawn between the public relations function and other business matters?

Obviously, such cases would have to be dealt with in light of their situations and the council would have to proceed slowly and deliberately. But these kinds of problems would not prevent the council from handling them or from fulfilling its intended role. These potential difficulties only emphasize the importance of sound groundwork in establishing the council and in defining its role and jurisdiction.

Conclusion

In conclusion, there are compelling reasons both for and against government regulation of public relations. Some practitioners feel that it is inevitable, others feel that it is evitable, and most probably fall somewhere in between.

The one contention that is probably agreed upon, however, is that the practice needs improvement. Unfortunately, the best means for doing it is disputed. Suggestions for licensing PR practitioners and compromises to government regulation have been presented, but none has been widely accepted or tried. Another suggestion, a public relations council, is certainly a viable alternative or perhaps a complement to other remedies, and it could even be instituted locally on an experimental basis. If not, and if some measure for improving the practice is not undertaken from within, the debate over licensing may come to an end. The government will regulate a practice which cannot or will not regulate itself.

Bibliography

Several sources of information on this issue have been suggested by the author in preparing his article. They are Edward L. Bernays, "Should Public Relations Counsel be Licensed?" *Printers' Ink* (Dec. 25, 1953), pp. 50, 52–54, an early proposal along this line; Donald B. McCammond, *et al., Draft of a Model State Statute for the Licensing of PR Practitioners,* PRSA, New York (February 20, 1973), and Frank Wylie, "A Common Code of Ethics," *Public Relations Journal* (February 1974), pp. 14-15. Consult the magazines in the field for more recent developments in this area of public relations concern.

Polls/Television and Politics

Political Polling and Political Television

By Marion R. Just

Marion R. Just is research associate, Center for International Studies, Massachusetts Institute of Technology. Reprinted with permission from *Current History* (August 1974), © 1974 Current History, Inc.

The most prominent additions to American political campaigns in the twentieth century are public opinion polls and television. These new tools perform functions once served by campaign trains, seat of-the-pants reporters, political pundits, and Fireside Chats. Political campaigns have become less cozy and more quantitative than ever before. Apparently, a candidate who does not worry about his "ratings" is not a candidate at all.

Students of politics as well as politicians have been concerned with the effects of polling and television on the democratic process. Nor is this concern uniquely American. Both Germany and France now outlaw the reporting of poll results until after general elections; while Great Britain strictly limits and subsidizes political television broadcasts.

The question at issue is whether the use of opinion polling and television interfers with the choices which voters would otherwise make. A related question is whether the use of polls and television political campaigns prescribe the type of candidate who may successfully bid for public office.

While opinion is divided on these issues, those on both sides of the question appear to have their democratic *bona fides* on the table. Those who argue in favor of television campaigning point to the fact that the medium has already captured the leisure hours, if not the minds, of the American people. According to the Harris poll in September, 1973, 65 percent of Americans depend on television for information about politics. The airwaves have brought thousands of armchair politicians close to the center stage. More Americans than ever before have the opportunity (via television) to observe and evaluate the candidates and the issues. All of these are surely democratic effects.

Those who decry television, however, fear that viewers respond only to politicians who meet the medium's criteria: good looks, poise, and a "cool" personality. Furthermore, the time constraints on television are said to discourage reasoned political dialogue. One wonders, further, if the vicarious experience of participation through television may tend to depress actual political participation.

To introduce the morass of media problems, we turn to a relatively circumspect question, namely, election-night reporting. Many congressmen have registered their apprehension that televised election forecasts enhance early voting trends. Given the time difference between the East and West coasts, for example, televised coverage that begins after the polls close in New York reaches California three hours before polls close there.

The effects of the time lag have been hypothesized as follows:

(1) Voters for the underdog will give up and stay home.

(2) Voters for the underdog will be spurred on to voting.

(3) Voters for the leading candidate will not bother to go to the polls.

(4) Half-hearted voters for the leading contender will leap onto the victory bandwagon.

Obviously, the psychology of voting suffers from too many plausible hypotheses. In a study of California voting, Harold Mendelsohn and Irving Crespi found that election-night programs had only a negligible influence on the 1964 presidential election. With regard to 1968, they point out that when the election is too close to call the television effect is wiped out. In conclusion, the researchers expressed a pious hope that "bandwagon" and "underdog" effects are small and tend to cancel each other out.

The election-night question is only at issue, of course, at the national level. Most local television coverage begins after the polls close. There is reason, however, to enforce the same good taste in national elections. Surely New York television viewers can go to sleep a little later on election night, resting comfortably in the knowledge that their choices did not influence the voters in California. Since 1968, several bills have been introduced in Congress to ensure that televised election-night coverage does not unduly influence voters.

The charge of undue influence redounds against all poll predictions, not just on television, but in magazines and newspapers as well. The concern is heightened in the case of televised election coverage because of its broad impact. But if polling has a direct influence on voters, then, logically, publication (broadcasting) of poll results should be restrained throughout political campaigns and not just on election day. Direct polling effects are *least likely* to be important on election day, when the majority of citizens have already decided if they will vote, and for whom.

In order to assess whether polls directly affect voting, it would be necessary to isolate poll effects from other voting influences. Studies have shown that over-all poll results have a negligible effect on voters' preferences. Voters respond strongly to "long-term" predispositions such as party and group loyalties, and to "short-term" influences, such as issues and candidates. These long-and short-term effects leave only a minority of voters undecided as a campaign progresses. The "late deciders" are often those who have conflicting group loyalties. Polls probably have little effect on voters who face conflicts in their group loyalties. It has been shown that a key element in voting perferences is the reference group, that is, an identification group to whose views an individual tends to conform. For example, college students tend to conform in their opinions to a reference group of other college students. Studies have also shown that people "project" their views onto their reference group. Students, for example, are likely to believe that other college students hold the same opinions that they do. Even if the weight of national sentiment is against them, individuals may be reassured by perceiving consonant views within their own group. Selective perception further limits the impact of polls. People tend to recall only those poll results that confirm their own opinions and expectations and to forget those that do not.

Joseph Klapper concluded from a review of the literature that there was "no absolutely conclusive evidence that . . .the publication of poll results *does or does not* affect the subsequent votes." In the only study that was controlled with regard to both reference group and projective effects, the author found a shift in opinion when poll results *for the reference group* differed from prior expectations. Based on this study, [Harold] Mendelsohn and [Irving] Crespi infer that: "Only if one were exposed to a poll report concerning one's own reference groups, and if that report conflicted appreciably with impressions one had garnered from other sources, would there by any likelihood that one's own preference would be affected to any degree." Therefore, these authors find the direct poll effect "trivial."

While that conclusion may have been valid in 1968, it is more questionable today. Reporting of opinion polls has become increasingly sophisticated. Many more journalists now describe the nature and limitations of polls. But this increasing sophistication and the increasing media appetite for polls have led precisely in the direction to be feared. Gallup and other newspaper polls are now reported by region, race, religion, education, and age group. Today, the public has convincing evidence with regard to the opinions of its particular reference groups. To the extent that people bring their opinions into line with these reference groups, direct poll effects should increase. The size of effects in the aggregate, however, will depend upon the extent to which people make prior assessments about their reference groups. For example, if most blacks assume that their ethnic group supports a local Democratic candidate, and a local poll shows that blacks do support that candidate, then the net effect of the poll (i.e., the number of changed opinions) will be negligible. Opinions do not change if projections are accurate, and the charge of undue influence is only valid if opinions do change.

Projective "inaccuracy" probably varies from issue to issue. It is more likely to occur to voters who are "cross pressured," i.e., who hold conflicting group loyalties and opinions. It is widely believed that in the presidential race of 1972, for example, many voters were cross pressured by their Democratic and labor loyalties. Congressional elections in 1974 will also cross pressure many voters. For example, Republican partisans must contend with Watergate and impeachment, while Jews must weigh the Republican policy toward Israel against old Democratic loyalties. Reference-cued polls can show the cross-pressured voter that he is not alone in his dilemma. When a Republican waverer finds a poll showing that 40 percent of Republicans favor impeachment, for example, it may resolve his own conflict. Polls may not create opinions, but they may reinforce weakly held views or sow doubts among strong opinions.

Of course, while cross pressure increases vulnerability to poll results, it also depresses turnout at the polls. Conflicted voters make up their minds later in the campaign and are less likely to go to the polls at all. Since there is little hard evidence as yet concerning the reference-poll effect, it cannot be weighed against the no-vote effect. In 1972, for example, non-voting was particularly marked among the working class. Were these non-voters Democrats who did not like George McGovern, or were they McGovern supporters who knew a lost cause when they saw one?

While the impact of reference-cued polls is still in question, there is general agreement that polls significantly influence candidates, activists, and contributors. In the last presidential election the trailing candidate was bombarded with questions about his poor standing in the polls. McGovern's political director, Frank Mankiewicz, complained: "You don't...say 'Now tell us why he's not getting blue collar votes,' because if you keep on promoting that...he won't get blue collar votes." *Washington Post* political pollster Jim Hart countered that candidates are no worse off today than they were 30 years ago: "In 1936 and '40, there was probably an equal amount of 'What are you going to do now that the Teamsters have endorsed your opposition?' And so forth, which I simply see as generically the same sort of question, about how come you're not doing so well with this or that identifiable sector. Polling just makes it easier to specify a lot more groups that you're not doing well with."

Annoying the candidate may only amount to minor interference in the campaing process. A more serious problem concerns the demoralizing effect of polls on supporters and campaign finances. Mankiewicz, for example, believed the polls to have had a "devastating" effect on contributions to the McGovern campaign. He found the polls "very damaging to morale, too, in terms of volunteer workers, manning headquarters, getting people out into the street canvassing. They turned people off very early."

It may be argued that the polls save time and money for would-be supporters of the weaker candidate. The *net* effect of published polls, however, appears to be in the direction of spending. While there may be no bandwagon effect among voters, there certainly is a "bandwagon" for financial contributors. As the trailing candidate loses money, the leading contender gains it. If the last presidential election is any guide, the winning candidate can count on more money than he can spend. In the past, political contributions have been something of a gamble. With the current accuracy of public opinion polls, contributors can locate a sure win and gain a piece of the political action. Campaign finance reform would restrain the "polling-contribution" circuit, at least by limiting the size of such contributions.

Publication of polls throughout election campaigns probably widens the disparity between candidates' effectiveness. The harder it is for the loser to get money and supporters, the less effective his campaign is likely to be. And conversely, for the winning candidate. As campaigns draw to a close, however, political contests generally narrow. Other campaign forces come into play: old loyalties are activated; waverers are brought back to the fold; and political interest is awakened among the apathetic. The polls' widening effects between candidates and the campaigns' narrowing effects among voters may tend to cancel each other out. Public financing of elections would certainly help minimize the problem.

The effect of polls on contributions and supporters is more serious with respect to primary contests than with respect to election campaigns. The primary contests are the gatekeepers of American politics. Polls and media interference in this process can actually eliminate a political contender altogether.

In 1968, George Romney withdrew from the Republican presidential preference primary in New Hampshire largely because of his declining strength in opinion polls. Romney's early start in the presidential race was also attributable to polls which showed him to be the strongest opponent of President Lyndon Johnson. Thus, Romney's abortive campaign depended on private polls and not on actual voter intervention.

An egregious example of media interference in the primary process took place in the Democratic race in New Hampshire in 1972. The victim of this event was Edmund Muskie. The villains of the piece were the media interpretations of primary results. Muskie campaigned hard in the primary, laboring under the vicious opposition of Manchester's conservative press. He came away with 47 percent of the votes cast and a winning plurality. George McGovern polled 30 percent. The media reports were: "Muskie wins but loses, while McGovern loses, but wins." This bizarre turn of events drew the following comments from the dean of academic pollsters, Warren Miller:

> You have to avoid inadvertently creating news. In 1972, Muskie was supposed to get 50 [percent] and the fact that he didn't get 50 percent became news. Well, it may have been that he was really exceedingly lucky to get the 47 percent he got. One of the

functions of newspapers is to create expectations, and if you end up inadvertently creating totally unreasonable expectations, when the unreasonableness then gets exposed, it's treated as news rather than simply as a mistake of some time ago that has now been rectified.

It is interesting to conjecture where the "magic 50 percent" came from. One line of deduction leads to the group of reporters attached to a candidate. In the lulls of campaigning, these colleagues trade information and ideas. In a small group, ideas may be continually reinforced, perhaps making fact out of speculation. [Ed. Note: the same phenomenon was discussed during the 1976 primary and general elections.] Fifty percent is a nice round number. Absolutely speaking, 47 percent is very close to it. The impact of this media interpretation was dramatic. Muskie never recovered from the ignominy of the "defeat" he suffered in New Hampshire. The loser, George McGovern, stumped on to capture the convention and went on to a resounding defeat in the general election.

While this story illustrates the worse possible result of the polling-primary-media nexus, more favorable results are possible. In particular, the polling technique of matching opposition candidates can be extremely helpful to the nominating process. One of the weaknesses of primaries is that in most states only loyal partisans may participate. Tests of party loyalty vary from state to state (registration, declaration, and so on), but the effect of these regulations is to make only a portion of the electorate eligible to participate. Nor are these eligible voters representative of the voting population. They tend to be drawn from the more active and more partisan sector of each party.

The turnout for primary elections at the state and local levels is notoriously weak. In view of the peculiarity of the primary voting population, it is particularly helpful for party leaders to put the primaries in a more general context. Opinion surveys can show the extent to which primary outcomes reflect the preferences of the general voting population. It is especially important to gauge the intentions of independents, most of whom do not vote in primary elections. Candidate matching surveys can further temper the primary results. As the Republican nomination of 1964 and the Democratic nomination of 1972 both demonstrated, it is possible for a candidate to make a strong showing in partisan primaries and go down to ringing defeat in a general election. On the one hand, the primary defines the candidate's appeal to partisans. Generally, a candidate who cannot generate support among the party regulars will have a more difficult time campaigning. On the other hand, consultation of matched candidate surveys defines which candidates will serve the party's interest in the general elections. Party backers may have a difficult task when the polls and the primaries conflict.

The role of the media in the process is a delicate one. Both the primary results and matched preference polls must be fairly interpreted. If indeed the media has a legitimate role to play in the creation of expectations (as Warren Miller suggests), then those expectations should be wrought of some real evidence. A canvass of party leaders can be a source of "establishment" expectations for the primary candidates. Opinion polls are another solid data source for expected results. "Magic" (and probably all round numbers) should be eschewed.

In suggesting this particular role for media interpretation, we do not propose that news media increase the emphasis on polling. To the contrary. The media already stress the sporting aspect of elections. *Washington Post* reporter David Broder commented (probably typically): "It is a contest, like any other contest, people want to know who's ahead and who's behind. If you have ways of measuring that, that's legitimate information for the readers to have and that's legitimate news."

In Paul Weaver's analysis of presumed media bias in the 1968 presidential elections, he found that the agent of bias was not the predisposition of reporters, but their racing instinct. As a candidate fell behind in the polls, numerous stories chronicled his reactions to the bad news. The result was a preponderance of "negative" stories for the trailing candidate. In 1968, Hubert Humphrey received the negative preponderance. But late in the campaign, as the gap narrowed and the pace of campaign forecasts quickened, Richard Nixon felt the poll-media sting. The final result was a preponderance of "negative" Nixon stories in network broadcasts. Weaver believes that such bias could be overcome if the media avoided the "horse race" approach in reportage.

The people deserve to know who stands for what, rather than just who's ahead of whom. With the polls now married to journalism, the constructive side of this union should be explored. It is time for journalists to feed into the polls and not just the other way around. Political reporters are in an excellent position to generate interesting survey topics. With newspapers and magazines now funding the pollsters, the public should receive a more profound understanding of the issues and the candidates.

In reflecting on the impact of polls and television, we should bear in mind that both these tools are in their political infancy. Dire warnings also accompanied the advent of radio in politics. Until now, however, a certain equanimity has prevailed among social scientists who investigate campaign techniques. Voting research has shown that party and group loyalties have been the most important influences on the modestly informed electorate. Party identification has generally been stable throughout an individual's voting career. From time to time, an unusual candidate (such as Eisenhower) or an important issue (such as war) has produced short-term voting changes. The "swing" voters, who voted only occasionally, were predominantly uninformed as well as unreliable.

There is reason to believe, however, that this picture of American politics no longer reflects the character of the electorate. First of all, the New Deal Democratic coalition of ethnic groups and the working class is in danger of collapse. More Americans than ever before now style themselves "independent" of party. While some of the independents are of the old style, uninterested in politics, others are very opposite—vitally interested, highly educated, and politically sophisticated. The fact that many of these independents are young people may signal the beginning of a new phase in American politics. It may be that without the ballast of party loyalty, political campaigns may be much more important than they have been in the past. If that is the case, then the media and the polls will bear an even greater burden or responsibility.

[Editors' Note: Ms. Just's article was written before Congress passed amendments to the Federal Campaign Act of 1974, amendments that had the effect of establishing a Federal Election Commission (FEC) to "enforce campaign spending and disclosure laws" and to limit the amount of money candidates could spend on campaigns. Among other things, the campaign spending limitation was challenged in the courts. Late in January 1976 the U.S. Supreme Court repealed sections of the law which had required candidates for the House and Senate to limit expenditures on campaigns. Other provisions provided for unlimited spending by individual citizens and permitted presidential candidates and their immediate families to spend as much of their own money as they wished.

Whether the act and the new commission it created will have positive results for American democracy will be determined in part during the 1976 campaign. In any case, the importance of polling and of the mass media will not be decreased. At a Political Communications Seminar held in Washington in October 1975, as reported in *Advertising Age*, Walter De Vries, a consultant on polling and mass media with DeVries & Associates, North Carolina, said "Voters used to get their information from political parties, but now it's from the mass media. The law comes at a time when we need more money, not less." It would appear that the candidates will lean even more heavily on public relations techniques and on polling and that they will attempt to get more "bang for their buck" from whatever advertising they do in the mass media. Students should be vitally concerned about the effects growing out of this law and its amendments.]

Bibliography

The use of the mass media and of polling techniques in political campaigns long has been a concern in the United States. The advent of television and far more sophisticated polling techniques have exacerbated the problem. An excellent bibliography of books and articles dealing with this subject is Lynda Lee Kaid, *et al.*, *Political Campaign Communication: A Bibliography and Guide to the Literature*, The Scarecrow Press, 1974. The literature in this field is extensive. Students can find useful information in the following books, which are listed in chronological order of publication: Gene Wyckoff, *The Image Candidates: American Politics in the Age of Television*, Macmillan, 1968; Joe McGinnis, *The Selling of the President, 1968*, Trident Press, 1969; Kurt Lang and Gladys Engel Lang, *Politics and Television*, Quadrangle, 1968; Edward W. Chester, *Radio, Television and American Politics*, Sheed & Ward, 1969; Harold Mendelsohn and Irving Crespi, *Polls, TV and the New Politics*, Chandler, 1970; Sig Mickelson, *The Electric Mirror: Politics in the Age of Television*, Dodd, Mead, 1972; Robert E. Gilbert, *Television and Presidential Politics*, Christopher Publishing, 1972; Newton N. Minow, *et al.*, *Presidential Television*, Basic Books, 1973, and Kevin P. Phillips, *Mediacracy: American Parties and Politics in the Communications Age*, Doubleday, 1975, Thomas E. Patterson and Robert D. McClure, *The Unseeing Eye*, G. P. Putnam's Sons, 1976. Of particular interest to the student interested in the use of polls during campaigns is Ray E. Hiebert, *et al.*, *eds.*, *The Political Image Merchants: Strategies for the Seventies*, Acropolis Books, 1975, the result of a conference held for political campaign managers, journalists and social scientists. This up-date version of an earlier edition has useful, if uneven, contributions on the how and why of campaigns in the 1970s. See also *Political Broadcast Catechism*, Eighth Edition, National Association of Broadcasters, March 1976, for questions and answers on broadcaster responsibilities for political broadcasts.

9 International Communications

Multinational Media—

The Electronic Invaders—

Multinational Media

By William H. Read

As the Canadian Parliament reconvened (in January, 1975), a strange and perplexing, although not unique, immigration case confronted Prime Minister Trudeau's Cabinet. A very prominent American's offspring, who went North a few decades back and won fame and fortune, faced deportation. The ministers were pressed to decide whether to have their parliamentary majority yank this popular and successful American's visa. His foes, a vocal band of nationalists, had waged a bitter campaign, while millions of friends remained loyal although somewhat placid.

Who was this controversial American? Well, it happens to be son-of-*Time*, or, as the news magazine calls itself above the 49th parallel, *Time Canada*. And its "visa" has been a special tax law, vital to its extraordinary success as evidenced by 3 million Canadian readers.

This is not a unique case, for *Time Canada* is but one of many wares which America's mass media mercantilists have pedaled abroad so successfully that they, like multinational corporations, are significant and controversial transnational forces.

Not only are images of the United States presented around the world by globetrotting American magazines, news agencies, movies, and TV shows, but foreigners rely also on these media to be windows on third countries. What a Berliner knows about political developments in Japan may well come to him via a U.S. news agency; thus Germany's window on the world is partly through New York, headquarters of the Associated Press and United Press International. Indeed, foreigners even rely on U.S. media to mirror their own societies. The family of nations, particularly non-Communist members, have been bonded in recent times by a "made-in-America" mass media central nervous system.

Consider, for example, that besides the global reach of the giant American news agencies (AP and UPI), *The New York Times* news service is transmitted daily to 136 of the world's major newspapers, and *The Washington Post-Los Angeles Times* joint news service is purchased by about 60 other foreign newspapers. This means that in Hong Kong, for instance, it is possible to read China'watching stories written there by *New York Times* correspondents whose copy, after being edited in New York, is cabled back to *The South China Morning Post* and *The Hong Kong Standard*.

Or consider that American television companies earned $130 million in 1973 from foreign sales of programs (mainly entertainment shows). Who abroad watched "All in the Family" and "Gunsmoke"? It's easier to say who didn't: Chinese, Mongolians, North Koreans, North Vietnamese, and Albanians. One of the major TV programming distributors with a six-language catalogue boasts, "our audience is everywhere," by which is meant it sells in more than 100 countries doing business from offices in Tonorto, Sao Paulo, Zug (Switzerland), Rome, Beirut, Madrid, London, Tokyo, Sydney, and Seoul.

William H. Read is a Research Fellow at the Harvard University Center for International Affairs. Reprinted with permission from *Foreign Policy, XVIII,* Spring 1975. Copyright by National Affairs, Inc.

That distributor, Viacom International, Inc., while not nearly so large as Exxon or ITT, is no less a multinational corporation than either. In fact, TV program distributors are the inheritors of an early multinational enterprise—the American film industry. The development pattern of the movie business—national saturation followed by exporting and internationalization—is a course print and electronic media unwittingly may be following. The foreign policy implications of internationalization—a process by which an organization becomes *controlled* by parties of more than one nationality—are probably the same for the mass media as for a manufacturing firm. Such an organization is expected to be less inclined to faithfully support Washington's policies. The days when Henry Luce spoke of "our policy," reflecting the outlook of both *Time* and the Department of State, have faded not only with Luce's passing, but also as it acquired a 1.3 million international circulation.

Whether the mass media support government policies (as *Time* did, for example, by selecting General Westmoreland as "man of the year") or oppose them (as *The New York Times* did by publishing the "Pentagon Papers") is essentially an internal matter. But there are foreign public opinion implications. The more direct foreign policy considerations stem from the unhappiness of other governments, which feel their countries are victimized by powerful American media mercantilists. The issue can be described in terms of free flow of information versus what may be called the right of information privacy. For years, this was mainly an East-West dispute with the Communist jamming of our short-wave broadcasts as the focal point. Then a North-South dimension emerged. And now, in the case of direct satellite broadcasting (DBS), it's everybody against us, with the United States opposed to any restrictions on DBS, while all others prefer some controls.

The controversy over the transnational outpouring of information from the United States, of which DBS is only the tip of the iceberg, can no longer be analyzed in Cold War terms, as not much useful mileage can be gained by driving that ideological vehicle today. Furthermore, some of our best friends are crying the loudest. A good example is Canada. In one battle, a popular Canadian author, Richard Rohmer, attacked *Time* for "shoving the American point of view at all its readers in Canada" (where the magazine's circulation figures, as a percentage of population, are higher than in the United States). Rohmer had a specific complaint about *Time Canada*. One of his books was then first on *The Toronto Star's* best-seller list, but was not included among *Time Canada's* list of best-selling books (in the United States). There is also controversy in broadcasting, where the Canadian Broadcasting Corporation has established "Canadian content" goals which limit foreign (read American) imports.

About a year ago, a symposium on the international flow of TV programs was held at the University of Tampere, Finland, During the meeting, the attitude of those critical of what has been termed "information (or cultural) imperialism" was summarized by Finnish President Urho Kekkonen. He said that he had "read a calculation that two-thirds of the communications disseminated throughout the world originate in one way or another in the United States." He felt that this constituted an unacceptable, one-way, unbalanced flow that did not possess the depth and range which the principles of freedom of speech require.

Such a harsh conclusion seems prematurely unjustified, given the paucity of data so far collected about transnational media. But the concern is genuine. What is the cultural impact of our news agencies, magazines, and television programs abroad? How do they affect public opinion in other countries? What does this mean for foreign policies? These important questions have not yet been given adequate examination.

The Information Elite

Some preliminary work by researchers of the U.S. Information Agency concludes that a so-called "international information elite" is growing. This group, an Agency document says, is "linked by many factors transcending national, cultural, or regional differences. These factors have mainly to do with increasing similarities in their education, in their exposure to contemporary ideas, and *through increasing use of international media*." (The emphasis is mine.)

A typical member of the international information elite could be described as "a 37-year-old non-American, who has attended either a university or technical school, probably is now a business executive earning $13,386 a year, which enables him to own a car, buy life insurance, and occasionally travel to foreign countires." That happens to be a composite profile of a person who either subscribes to *Time* or buys a copy at a newsstand each week outside the U.S.

Not so many years ago when this country was deeply engaged in ideological warfare, the international spread of our mass media would have been a welcome development. It still can be, and should be. For our ability to influence foreign events rests partly on "presence," and the international dissemination of our mass media is a highly visible sign of U.S. overseas involvement and is, on balance, a credible American representative. But this has not been, nor will it be, a trouble-free development.

TV-Watching Abroad

Anyone who has traveled abroad knows that American TV programs are as popular abroad as Coca Cola. Foreign sales in virtually every country of the world account for nearly a fifth of the producers' revenue. The biggest buyers in dollar terms are Canada, Japan, Australia, and the United Kingdom. But in terms of broadcast hours—it is estimated that between 100,000 and 200,000 hours of programming are exported annually from the United States—the distribution is approximately equal in Latin America, Asia, and Europe.

The United States has a dominant position in the international TV program marketplace; a domination achieved in the now classic operating methods of many multinational enterprises. Television, a highly technical field, developed rapidly in the United States, and saturated the domestic market in a few years. Initial random sales of popular programs to stations abroad sparked interest and created overseas markets, before there was significant competition.

A boom in overseas sales during the last decade appears to have peaked, partly due to growing foreign competition. Still, American firms have a lion's share of the profitable international TV market. The following table, taken from [a 1973] study, illuminates two striking facts about world television commerce:

1. There is considerable empirical evidence supporting the charge that the flow of information is essentially one-way. There were only three stations which imported as little as 1 per cent of their programs: the American commerical stations (which certainly must be the world's most prolific television broadcasters), the Japanese educational station, and the Chinese station in Shanghai. Small and less-developed countries, on the other hand, often imported a majority of their programs.

2. The flow of TV programs is far from unrestricted, although only a few countries—such as Canada and Britain—actually have established quotas. Other apparently potent limiting factors are political considerations and cultural barriers: witness the comparatively low percentage of programs imported by France—9 per cent, the Soviet Union—5 per cent, China—1 per cent, Japan's commerical station—10 per cent. Even when percentages are higher, these factors still can come into play. For example, during the Allende administration in Chile, where 55 per cent of TV programs were imported, an episode of "Mission Impossible," which dramatized the fall of a Castro-like regime, was cancelled. And in Saudi Arabia, where 31 per cent of programs shown were imported, the intitial selections were "Wild Kingdom" and "Victory at Sea," neither of which showed unveiled women.

An unanticipated sensitive area encountered by some American television merchants, and one which, as most domestic station owners know, can be very profitable, was the area of operations. American expertise and capital flowed abundantly to TV stations around the world during the early and mid-1960's. NBC, for example, had financial interests in TV stations in Australia, Venezuela, Mexico, Jamaica, Barbados, and Hong Kong and management and technical assistance contracts in Saudi Arabia, South Vietnam, West Germany, Wales, Mexico, Lebanon, Sweden, Peru, the Philippines, Argentina, Yugoslavia, Jamaica, Kenya, Nigeria, and Sierra Leone. In recent years, however, NBC's international business dwindled, partly because, an NBC official says, "foreign television systems became more and more self-sustaining."

Moreover, some seemingly promising ventures, such as Time-Life's broadcasting activities in Latin America, came a cropper for deeper reasons. "To make money you've got to control an operation and no government is going to let outsiders control its television," says Barry Zorthian, former head of the now defunct Time-Life Broadcasting, which once was deeply involved in Venezuela, Argentina, and Brazil.

Today the question increasingly being faced by U.S. program exporters is whether foreign stations, most of which are government operated, will continue to import large quantities of American shows. It may be premature, but it is not unreasonable to conjecture that the U.S. television production industry will internationalize as did its Hollywood film-making predecessors. There have already been some coproductions of television programs in foreign countries which by-pass quotas and assure access to at least one important foreign market. Last summer, for instance, U.S. public television screened "The Impeachment of Andrew Johnson," a coproduction between Washington's National Center for Television and the British Broadcasting Corporation.

Television Programming
1970-1971
(in percentages)

Country/Television Station	Imported	Domestic
Canada/CBC*	34	66
Canada/RC*	46	54
United States/16 commercial*	1	99
United States/18 noncommercial*	2	98
Argentina/Canal 9	10	90
Argentina/Canal 11	30	70
Chile*	55	45
Columbia	34	66
Dominican Republic/Canal 3/9	50	50
Guatemala*	84	16
Mexico/Telesistema	39	61
Uruguay*	62	38
West Germany/ARD	23	77
West Germany/ZDF	30	70
Finland	40	60
France	9	91
Iceland	67	33
Ireland	54	46
Italy	13	87
Netherlands	23	77
Norway	39	61
Portugal	35	65
Sweden	33	67
Switzerland/Deutsch*	24	76
United Kingdom/BBC	12	88
United Kingdom/TV*	13	87
Bulgaria	45	55
German Democratic Republic	32	68
Hungary	40	60
Poland	17	83
Rumania	27	73
Soviet Union/Cent. 1st*	5	95

Soviet Union/Estonia	12	88
Yugoslavia/Beograd	18	82
Australia	57	43
People's Republic of China/Shanghai*	1	99
Republic of China/Enterprise	22	78
Hong Kong/RTV & HK-TVB (English)*	40	60
Hong Kong/RTV & HK-TVB Guiness*	31	69
Japan/NHK General	4	96
Japan/NHK Educational	1	99
Japan/Commercial Stations	10	90
Republic of Korea/Tong-yang	31	69
Malaysia	71	29
New Zealand*	75	25
Pakistan	35	65
Philippines/ABC, CBV	29	71
Singapore*	78	22
Thailand/Army TV*	18	82
Dubai	72	28
Iraq	52	48
Israel	55	45
Kuwait	56	44
Lebanon/Telibor	40	60
Saudi Arabia/Riyadh TV*	31	69
Saudi Arabia/Aramco TV*	100	0
United Arab Republic	41	59
Yemen*	57	43
Ghana*	27	73
Uganda*	19	81
Zambia*	64	36

* This data is based on sample week(s); all other figures are based on the full year 1970-1971. Repeats are included.

If the TV industry takes this route, two results may be anticipated: (1) the television production industry should become less controversial and, at the same time, (2) cross-national cooperation will mean diminution of any participating nation's ability to control the cultural and social content of its TV programming. The explanation is simple—joint ventures undercut cries of imperialism, and they also require production of programs suitable for (''salable to'' is perhaps more apt) at least two countries.

The Print Media

The transnational dissemination of American print media, unlike TV, is not comparatively new nor does it reach the vast foreign audiences that television does. Its expansion into the world market has occurred under various circumstances.

Reader's Digest, with a foreign readership of 100 million, in 13 language editions, brought out its first foreign language edition—Spanish—in 1940, in an attempt by its patriotic publisher, DeWitt Wallace, to counter Axis influence in Latin America. Thirty-three years later, *Newsweek* launched what it proclaimed to be "the world's first *truly* international newsweekly" intended to inform "corporate decision-makers and government leaders around the world."

With less ballyhoo, American news agencies grew to the point that UPI has subscribers in 113 foreign countries and territories and says that its dispatches are translated into 48 languages. News agency logos have been joined abroad by those of the U.S. supplemental news services and the unique *International Herald Tribune* (in which *The New York Times* and *The Washington Post* are part owners) which is available at newsstands in over 70 countries. When the Bamboo curtain lifted a bit, AP and UPI quickly signed exchange agreements with Hsinhua, the Chinese news agency. Our print media have not cornered the international market, of course. But the fact is that Agence France Presse and *The Economist* are not really dangerous competitors for UPI and *Time*.

Like TV, U.S. print media frequently are controversial, although foreign leaders tend to view the putative dangers of print more in political than cultural terms. Virtually every week, either *Time* or *Newsweek* (or both) is censored, banned, or confiscated by a government somewhere. News agencies are usually more immune, because their copy passes first through the hands of local editors.

All this is taken as a fact of life in international business by the print merchants, most of whom are deeply committed to (i.e., financially dependent upon) continued successful foreign operations. To insure success, these communicators have adapted their organizations to not merely exporting an American product, but to tailoring their information wares for foreign consumption.

There are differing opinions, however, on the extent to which editorial content should be modified and the way in which it should be marketed to foreign audiences. *Time*, influenced by the success of its Canadian edition, convinced that a strong American identity remains crucial, and mindful that it must offer something more than its many national imitators, is thinking regional. *Time* launched a European edition in March 1973, modeled on its Canadian format, adding a short, usually four to six page section of European news to an otherwise U.S. magazine. *Time Asia* may follow. *Newsweek*, with a global strategy in mind, began publishing an international edition. Its editorial content is about 50 per cent different from its U.S. edition.

Before American publishers began adapting editorial content for non-American readers, they already had adopted geographic advertising editions, enabling advertisers to reach audiences in specified areas such as the Atlantic region, Common Market countries, or the British Isles.

Even though these and other adaptive processes have occurred there is still the question of socio-political influence. That question can be debated from either a push or a pull viewpoint. Is *Time Europe* helping to lead the continent to greater cohesion or merely following a trend? Is *Newsweek International* championing global interdependence or just reflecting it? Either way, both have made commitments, and these commitments, it should be emphasized, have an American perspective.

A Question of Influence

American mass media certainly have a dominant position in the international marketplace, but seldom do they overwhelm a single national market. (Notable exceptions are *Time* and *Reader's Digest* in Canada, where these two American publications account for more than 50 per cent of all magazine advertising in the country.) [*Time* and *Reader's Digest* have shared a unique status in Canada. They were specifically exempted from a tax law making advertising in foreign magazines nondeductible. In other works, a Canadian company advertising in *Time* deducted the cost from its taxable income, but could not do so for ads placed in *Newsweek*.] Declassified U.S. Information Agency media habit surveys reveal that U.S. mass media products are usually part of an informational mix, and the U.S. position varies from country to country.

There are, however, some commonly discernible influences. Standards are set by the American mass media, as evidenced, for example, by the numerous imitations of the *Time* and *Life* formats or the duplication of scheduling of television programs. Also, much information gets disseminated simply because of the economics of mass distribution. (I recall, for example, that newspapers in Southeast Asia printed the same news agency accounts of the Vietnam war as did the U.S. press, instead of more relevant stories about social, political, and economic issues in their neighboring country).

This exposure to U.S. values has prompted consideration as to whether there is a causal relationship between U.S. mass media and certain desired or undesired (depending on your viewpoint) attitudes and actions in foreign countries. Opinions vary. U.S. diplomats argue that our media generate an aura of credibility and stability for the United States—net pluses in the conduct of foreign policy. Foreign leaders, especially those average politicians who seek to divine the national will and then champion its causes, can get caught between competing demands. On the one hand, there may be apprehensions about cultural and informational encroachments, perhaps prompted by and/or coupled with protectionist demands by indigenous mass media producers. On the other hand, there may be popular appetites for consuming U.S. exports, the supposed benefits of favorable international publicity, or sought-after local investment. Finally, there are a few social scientists (most have ignored international media) who share Professor Herbert I. Schiller's worry about the possible emergence of "knowledge conglomerates."

How did such U.S. influence come about? In reality, the pervasiveness of American electronic and print media abroad grows not out of some conceptual design, but out of the same interacting phenomenon that enabled the widespread growth of our multinational corporations. The media reaped the benefits of our large capitalist system, the development of technology at home, the post-war economic and political positions of the United States, and the increasingly international use of English. Its penetration of foreign markets, however, goes beyond economic impact. It is a profound challenge to cultural integrity as well.

John Kenneth Galbraith, the Canadian-born Harvard economist, has said that while his former countrymen "talk about economic autonomy" they might well be advised to be "much more concerned about maintaining the cultural integrity of the broadcasting system and with making sure that Canada has an active, independent theatre, book publishing industry, newspapers, magazines, and schools of poets and painters." These, in Galbraith's opinion, "are the things that count." Few intellectuals would disagree, but popular appetites remain hungry for American magazines, TV dramas, and the rest. The middleman is the official who sits in Ottawa while the masses happily watch "All in the Family," and while a small elite group screams that he should pull the plug on the value-loaded, American world of Archie Bunker.

Nations which have been politically and economically dependent on the United States have, perhaps unwittingly, become culturally dependent too. And we know even less about the impact of multinational mass media than we do about multinational businesses.

Putting aside the closed-door stance of Communist countries, what might be a reasonable policy on this issue of foreign governments to follow? I suppose the ideal goal would be to attempt a balance which would preserve native culture while remaining open to the Americanized world culture. Such a two-tiered approach may be put to the test shortly, as new technology, such as satellites, has offered American mass media mercantilists new means to turn their present international communications flow into a torrent. Hours of as yet inconclusive United Nations debate have taken place about direct broadcasting by satellite.

Will the answer be found calmly in the open international marketplace? Or, if there is an outcry, will it be muted, even stilled, by reciting the U.N. Declaration on Human Rights' freedom of information passage? Perhaps. But not for much longer, I suspect. And if I'm right, then we may soon be facing an international cultural crisis just as we have had to face an international economic crisis. "Cultural protectionism" may be on its way.

Bibliography

This listing supplements both the Read and Schiller articles. An excellent overview of the development of national and international systems of broadcasting is Walter B. Emery's study of the same name, sub-titled *Their History, Operation and Control*, Michigan State University Press, 1969. Another book that provides a certain kind of overview, primarily directed toward issues, is Heinz-Dietrich Fischer and John C. Merrill, eds., *International Communications: Media, Channels, Functions*, Hastings House, 1970. Supplementary sources are: Andrew R. Horowitz, "The Global Bonanza of American TV," (*More*) (May 1975), pp. 6-8 ff.; Tapio Varis, "Global Traffic in Television," *Journal of Communication* (Winter 1974), part of a special issue on international communication, or see the larger report from which his article is drawn: Kaarle Nordenstreng and Tapio Varis, *Television Traffic–A One-Way Street? A Survey and Analysis of the International Flow of Television Programme Material*, Paper No. 70, in the Reports and Papers on Mass Communication Series, Unesco, 1974; and Alan Wells, *Picture-Tube Imperialism: The Impact of U.S. Television on Latin America,* Orbis Books, 1972. For a closely related problem on the use and control of satellite communication, see especially Olof Hultén, "The Intelsat System: Some Notes on Television Utilization of Satellite Technology," *Gazette* (1973),pp. 29-37, and the special issue of *Society* (September/October 1975) on "Communications vs. Powers." All of the latter articles are important, but be sure to consult Ithiel de Sola Pool, "Direct-Broadcast Satellites and Cultural Integrity," pp. 47-56. An article dealing with the political development of Intelsat is Steven A. Levy, "INTELSAT: Technology, Politics and the Transformation of a Regime," *International Organization* (Summer 1975), pp. 656-680.

The Electronic Invaders
By Herbert I. Schiller

For twenty-five years, the "free flow of information" between nations has been a widely sought objective of the United States, generally supported in the international community. Enunciated and promoted by the United Nations Educational, Scientific, and Cultural Organization (UNESCO), with more than a little U.S. prodding, there was general, if not unanimous, agreement that an unimpeded communications traffic was a good thing and that people everywhere benefited when it occurred. If the concept was not always respected in practice, at least it was never frontally attacked as a principle.

A dramatic reversal of this outlook is now underway. It is becoming apparent to many nations that the free flow of information, much like free trade in an earlier time, strengthens the strong and submerges the weak. In the case of information, the powerful communicator states overwhelm the less developed countries with their information and cultural messages.

Though information that moves internationally flows through many channels—movies, books, periodicals, television programs, radio broadcasts, tourists, merchandise exports, cultural exchanges—the medium which has brought the issue into focus is the new technology of communications satellites, broadcasting from space. Communications satellites which will soon bring television programs *directly* into individual living rooms across the globe (an informed guess puts direct satellite broadcasting less than ten years away) is forcing a long hard look at just what imagery already is flowing across national boundaries through more conventional means.

Currently, television is either imported on film or tape and used locally; moves across contiguous national frontiers (most Canadians, for example, can and do watch U.S. programs from stations across the border); or is picked up from communications satellites by ground receiving stations, under *national* control, and distributed to local audiences through national networks. Broadcasting directly into home receivers from sky-borne satellites which respect no national frontiers will be accomplished with more powerful satellites and modified receivers, both of which are already technologically feasible but not yet operable.

Two decades of exposure to U.S. television exports (*I Spy, Mission Impossible, Laugh In*) make the possibility of direct, unmediated television transmission from the United States to *any* home in *any* nation a cause for traumatic anxiety in international communications-cultural circles.

After all, television is a global phenomenon. In 1970 more than 250 million television sets were in use around the world in 130 countries. The United States had 84 million, Western Europe had 75 million, the Soviet Union 30 million, and Japan 23 million. China had only 200,000 sets, Indonesia had 90,000 and India a mere 20,000. Yet other developing nations had considerable numbers of receivers. Brazil, for example, had 6.5 million sets; Argentina, 3.5 million; Venezuela, 720,000; the Philippines, 400,000; South Korea, 418,000; Nigeria 75,000; and Egypt 475,000.

Herbert I. Schiller is professor of communications at the University of California, San Diego. He wrote *Mass Communications and American Empire;* his most recent book is *The Mind Managers,* Beacon Press, 1973. Reprinted with permission from *The Progressive* (August 1973). Copyright 1973 by The Progressive Publishing Co.

The President of the United Nations General Assembly, Poland's Stanislaw Trepczynski, expressed anxiety over unrestricted transmissions at the opening of the 27th General Assembly [1972]: "In an age of unprecedented development of information media, of tremendous flow of ideas and of artistic achievements, concern for preserving the characteristics peculiar to the different cultures becomes a serious problem for mankind."

UNESCO itself, the acknowledged guardian if not parent of the free flow of information concept, has had some second thoughts recently about its hitherto favored principle. In October, 1972, it adopted a declaration of "Guiding Principles on the Use of Satellite Broadcasting for the Free Flow of Information." Article IX of the draft read: " . . .it is necessary that States, taking into account the principle of freedom of information, *reach or promote prior agreements* concerning direct satellite broadcasting to the population of countries other than the country of origin of transmission." (Emphasis added.)

The U.N. General Assembly passed a similar resolution in November by a vote of 102 to 1—the United States was the single dissenting voice.

A sample of national views, expressed in the United Nations' Political Committee before the vote, is illuminating for what it reveals about the widespread feelings and fears over cultural matters of which we hear or see little in our own mass media. For example, the French delegate asserted that "each state has the right to protect its culture." The delegate from Colombia expressed fear of "an ideological occupation of the world by the superpowers and their advertising mentality." Zaire's delegate said his country had been subject to subversion by private radios and was therefore aware of the possible danger of direct television broadcasting by satellites. His country, he added, wanted to be able to have control over information from outside. The Minister for Home Affairs of India said direct television broadcasting could be used to generate mistrust and conflict or for undesirable or harmful propaganda, and such use "would certainly constitute interference in the internal affairs of States." The delegate from Chile said that if new space techniques were not subjected to international rules, Latin America would be subjected to the political, economic, and cultural contagion of the large imperialist monopolies of North America. He added that the people of Latin America were rebelling against imperialism which was trying to impose on them a culture contrary to their well-being.

Aware of the extent and depth of these national sentiments, in both UNESCO and the U.N. General Assembly, that cut across ideological lines, the official U.S. position has tried to deflect the argument into a discussion of technological feasibility. Former Ambassador George Bush in the United Nations and chief U.S. delegate William Jones in UNESCO minimized the dangers of cultural invasion and insisted that direct broadcasting was many years away and therefore no cause for immediate concern or organizational effort to regulate it.

Ironically but predictably, the U.S. diplomatic effort, formulated to sidestep an issue which unites most of the world against America as the foremost source of global communications pollution, incurred the wrath of the media moguls in the United States. Unwilling to accept a tactical retreat, insistent on their right to dominate world information flows, and indifferent to the needs and opinions of weaker states no matter how numerous, the no-nonsense American media managers reacted sharply.

Frank Stanton, then CBS president, member of the Presidentially appointed U.S. Advisory Commission on Information, and longtime chairman of the Radio Free Europe organization, wrote a lengthy article, "Will They Stop Our Satellites?" published in *The New York Times* October 22, 1972. In it he claimed that "the rights of Americans to speak to whomever they please, when they please, are [being] bartered away." His chief objection to the UNESCO draft of Guiding Principles on the Use of Satellite Broadcasting is that censorship is being imposed by provisions which permit each nation to reach prior agreement with transmitting nations concerning the character of the broadcasts.

Stanton finds the right of nations to control the character of the messages transmitted into their territories both dangerous and a gross violation of the U.S. Constitution's provision for freedom of speech: "The rights which form the framework of our Consitution, the principles asserted in the Universal Declaration of Human Rights, the basic principle of the free movement of ideas, are thus ignored."

Stanton apparently believes that the U.S. Constitution, fine document that it is, should be the binding law for the international community, whether it wishes it or not. Yet as long ago as 1946 the Hutchins Commission on Freedom of the Press rejected the easy assumption that the espousal of free speech in the U.S. Constitution was the basis for insisting on an unrestricted international free flow of communication.

"The surest antidote for ignorance and deceit," the Commission noted, "is widest possible exchange of objectively realistic information—*True* information, not merely *more* information; *true* information, not merely, as those who would have us simply write the First Amendment into international law seem to suggest, the *unhindered flow* of information! There is evidence that a mere quantitative increase in the flow of words and images across national borders may replace ignorance with prejudice and distortion rather than with understanding." (Emphasis in text.)

Moreover, is the freedom of speech that the U.S. Constitution guarantees to the individual applicable to multi-national communications corporations, of which Stanton is so powerful an advocate? Are CBS, ABC, and RCA "individuals" in the sense that most people understand the term? And, if a nation does not have the right to regulate and control the information flowing into and past its borders, who does? CBS? ITT? Stanton?

Stanton's view assumes an identity between the profit-making interests of a handful of giant communications conglomerates and the informational needs of the American people. The error is compounded when the same corporate interests are placed above the needs of all nations for cultural sovereignty. The great majority of Americans have absolutely no capability, financial or technological, of speaking "to whomever they please, when they please," outside their own country (or inside, for that matter). The voices and images which are now, and will be, transmitted overseas are those produced by our familiar communications combines, scarcely grassroots organizations.

Stanton, in the best prose of the Cold War decades, argues that "leaders of too many countries have a deadly fear of information which could lead their people to topple the regimes in power.'' Possibly. More likely, many leaders have a ''deadly fear'' of the cultural effects of the programming the major U.S. commercial networks would be pumping into their countrymen's television sets. Some leaders are aware that many Americans are troubled with the character of the material that floods their homes. They know that there is an increasing number of parents who are outraged with the daily television shows that assault their children's minds (and from which, incidentally, CBS in 1970 derived $16.5 million in profits).

Perhaps those who are concerned with national cultural development in other countries do not want to wait the twenty-five years it took before Americans began to question the effects of exposure of their children and themselves to cartoons, commercials, and the likes of *Dragnet, Mod Squad, I Spy*, and other well known commercial offerings.

Arthur Goodfriend, a former State Department consultant, recently wrote in *The Annals*, ''In an era of electronic communication...what is imperialism? Is it simply a policy of territorial extension? Or does it embrace the invasion of human minds?''

Should the international community be criticized for also asking this question? International regulation of direct satellite broadcasting is not an example of censorship that strikes at ''the fundamental principle of free speech.'' It is a necessary measure to enable all societies to have a role in determining their cultural destinies.

Stanton and his friends—*The New York Times* supported his position editorially and complained about ''censorship of the global air waves''—have it wrong. Liberty is not threatened. CBS profits could be. Freedom of thought is not challenged. RCA's markets may be.

The UNESCO declaration of ''Guiding Principles'' and the U.N. General Assembly's resolution regulating space broadcasting will not eliminate the cultural domination by a few that already exists in the world. They do signify, however, that the brief era of American global/cultural hegemony, established under the seemingly innocuous principle of ''the free flow of information,'' is coming to an end.

There will be difficulties in the transitional period ahead. Some arbitrary national actions are inevitable. But the worldwide homogenization of culture is too high a price to pay for the maintenance of an arrangement which produces benefits for only a tiny cluster of U.S. communications conglomerates.

Bibliography

The bibliography that follows the Read article also is useful here. For a further exposition of Schiller's views, see his book *Mass Communication and American Empire*, Augustus M. Kelley, 1969 and Schiller's ''Freedom From the 'Free Flow,''' *Journal of Communication* (Winter 1974), pp. 110-117. Also concerned about the effects of American television upon other cultures is Carroll V. Newsom, ''Communication Satellites: A New Hazard for World Culture,'' *Educational Broadcasting Review* (April 1973), pp. 77-85. The best single source of information on national and international mass communication is *World Communications: A 200-Country Survey of Press, Radio, Television and Film*. Unesco Press, 1975. This publication brings together relevant facts and figures from around the world as well as offering special chapters on problem areas, such as communication via satellites and training facilities in mass media.

July 4 ~ the King's View

GR

By his EXCELLENCY

WILLIAM TRYON, Esquire,

Captain General, and Governor in Chief in and over the Province of *New-York*, and the Territories depending thereon in *America*, Chancellor and Vice Admiral of the fame.

A PROCLAMATION.

BY THE KING,

A Proclamation,

For fuppreffing REBELLION and SEDITION.

GEORGE R.

WHEREAS many of our Subjects in divers Parts of our Colonies and Plantations in *North-America*, misled by dangerous and ill defigning Men, and forgetting the Allegiance which they owe to the Power that has protected and fuftained them...

In Obedience therefore to his Majefty's Commands to me given, I do hereby publish and make known his Majefty's moft gracious Proclamation above recited; earneftly exhorting and requiring all his Majefty's loyal and faithful Subjects within this Province, as they value their Allegiance due to the beft of Sovereigns, their Dependance on and Protection from their Parent State, and the Bleffings of a mild, free, and happy Conftitution; and as they would fhun the final Calamities which are the inevitable Confequences of Sedition and Rebellion, to pay all due Obedience to the Laws of their Country, ferioufly to attend to his Majefty's faid Proclamation, and govern themfelves accordingly.

WM. TRYON.

GOD SAVE the KING.

July 4 ~ the Patriots' View

IN CONGRESS, JULY 4, 1776.

A DECLARATION

By THE REPRESENTATIVES OF THE

UNITED STATES OF AMERICA,

IN GENERAL CONGRESS ASSEMBLED.

WHEN in the Course of human Events, it becomes necessary for one People to dissolve the Political Bands which have connected them with another, and to assume among the Powers of the Earth, the separate and equal Station to which the Laws of Nature and of Nature's God entitle them, a decent Respect to the Opinions of Mankind requires that they should declare the causes which impel them to the Separation.

We hold these Truths to be self-evident, that all Men are created equal, that they are endowed by their Creator with certain unalienable Rights, that among these are Life, Liberty, and the Pursuit of Happiness...

Signed by ORDER and in BEHALF of the CONGRESS,

JOHN HANCOCK, PRESIDENT.

ATTEST,
CHARLES THOMSON, SECRETARY.

PHILADELPHIA: PRINTED BY JOHN DUNLAP.

Multiplying Media Debates

The phrase is on everyone's lips. The Media. Did *Time* and *Newsweek* glorify violence by putting photos of women who were accused of trying to assassinate President Ford on their covers? Did The Media "get" Nixon? Will The Media prove Lee H. Oswald was part of a conspiracy? Why didn't The Media do a better job in describing the nation's financial crisis? What about all of the violence in The Media? Do Media people have ethical standards? Are Media people all liberals?

However, the general level of public understanding about The Media is quite low, despite the attention given news coverage, television commericals, new movies, best selling books and the world of public relations and advertising.

One thing should be kept in focus during these debates about media performance and responsibility. There are in this nation many persons who do not respect the First Amendment. This became clear during the Nixon years when high government officials attempted to manipulate the public against the press and used illegal means to intimidate those who were reporting events crucial to the survival of this country.

If those who wish to pass repressive laws against reporters get their way (whether on the national, state or local level), the erosion of freedoms will include those of speech, assembly and political action. The key to all of these is the press freedom guarantee. So while it is admirable that all forms of media action are analyzed by media critics, citizens groups and even in some cases government agencies (Federal Communications Commission, Federal Trade Commission), it is First Amendment language which makes healthy criticism possible.

Following the resignation of President Nixon the news media gained in general popularity. While there was a deep sense of dissatisfaction across the land, caused mainly by a disheartening economic crisis, many persons seemed to at least tolerate the "bad news" which came from the television screen or headline. Yet the national mood was vague and it appeared possible that another Spiro Agnew could turn the people against "the messengers" if deep political splits developed such as those caused by Vietnam and Nixon's policies.

While the credibility of newspersons gained slightly because of Watergate and other scandals, other areas in the media world were opened to heavy criticism. Television networks battled critics of commercials, hiring practices and specialized programming such as documentaries. Liberals and conservatives alike bombarded network headquarters with suggestions and complaints. In the middle of much of this was the Fairness Doctrine, called a violation of the First Amendment by some and labeled the last hope of the oppressed minority by others.

In the television news field the opponents of "happy talk" news seemed to be in the majority, but there was a continued frenzy of activity at ratings time and outside consultants were utilized more than ever by stations trying to keep pace. Elaborate studio sets, an increased number of "pretty faces" and an unfortunate trend toward the "top 40" approach were part of the general formula.

Concerns about values being disseminated by all forms of media caused a spate of discussions about sex and violence. Some of these debates concerned the alleged sophistication of the general audience and how commonly used words could be put into print or onto the air without embarrassment. Others were about the number of murders (11,000 or 18,000?) an average child would witness on television and in the movie theatre before age 18. Still others dealt with the theory that sex should be discussed more—in a healthy way—and that the real obscenities are unlawful acts, such as those portrayed on violent television police shows and often committed by the actor policemen themselves. Some were worried that the censors in society would continue to allow great amounts of violent material to be displayed—attempting to impose their moral standards mainly in the area of sexually explicit books and movies—and would stop political comments which they deemed ''unpatriotic'' or ''harmful to the public.''

While all of this was going on, there was concern that the ethical standards of many media persons—news, entertainment, public relations, advertising, management—were no higher than those of persons in other areas. Out of this comes the realization that while the media institutions sometimes set standards and dictate taste, for the most part they cater to popular demand and reflect current standards and attitudes.

This means the private citizen must constantly demand superior performance of those who bring us the news or make those commercials, while simultaneously protecting the basic rights of those media persons. By logic that includes not only the Walter Cronkites and the editors of the well-known newspapers but also the editors of the local underground newspaper, the off-beat radio station announcer and those who sometimes irritate us with their overplay of news, creation of disgusting movies or publication of cheap magazines or books.

The laws of sedition, libel and obscenity offer protection against dangerous or grossly offensive media acts, while the avalanche of media criticism found in print and on the air today seems to insure constant discussion of media behavior which some would like to improve.

10 Government and the Media

THE
FIRST
AMENDMENT

Our Fragile First Amendment

By Michael Emery

American journalists were being thrown into jail before the Bill of Rights was 10 years old, despite the First Amendment's underscoring of the concept of press freedom and the "people's right to know."

Since those early days of the republic, events have demonstrated that the First Amendment guarantee of freedom of the press is a fragile thing, its potency largely dependent upon the administration in power, the makeup of the courts, and the support of the people.

This delicate balance was reflected in Richard Nixon's battles with the Senate committee investigating Watergate and later with Judge John J. Sirica and Special Prosecutor Leon Jaworski, before an astonished and confused public.

That was followed by a rash of "gag orders" by judges, arguments over the need for a national shield law to protect reporters' sources and great anxiety over the ominous nature of Senate Bill 1, called by leading reporters a repressive bill against the flow of information. The future of the First Amendment was not clear and it probably never will be perfectly protected.

Nearly 200 years ago similar uncertainty and controversy marked the birth of the Bill of Rights.

The 55 founding fathers who drew up the Constitution in 1787 seemed more concerned with the mechanics of setting up a new government than in protecting the people against repression by that government.

James Madison's journal of the secret proceedings, published 53 years later, showed only one reference to press freedom—a motion by delegates from Massachusetts and South Carolina "that the liberty of the press should be inviolably observed."

But most delegates agreed with the argument that "it is unnecessary. The power of Congress does not extend to the press." The motion died, seven states to four.

So it went with proposals to insure other freedoms. Delegates argued that there was no need to mention rights which either were assumed to exist automatically or were under the jurisdiction of state constitutions (religion, assembly, trial by jury, speech, press).

Thus the framers of the Constitution finished their remarkable document that summer in Philadelphia with no Bill of Rights.

State conventions, however, as they met to ratify the Constitution, called for restrictive amendments to prevent misconstrual or abuse of power.

Sharpening the debate was the growing struggle between Federalists like Alexander Hamilton who favored strong centralized government, and anti-Federalists like Thomas Jefferson who believed the new nation should be a union of states, each keeping strong local control.

Proposals to amend the Consitution were part of a scheme by states-rights advocates to weaken and discredit it, the Federalists asserted.

Michael Emery, co-editor of this readings book, is on the journalism faculty at California State University-Northridge. He also is co-editor of *America's Front Page News, 1690-1970.* This updated overview of press freedom battles originally was prepared for the *Los Angeles Times.*

The Stamp Act—1976

Nevertheless, drawing upon Virginia's Declaration of Rights, among other sources, 12 amendments were proposed, and 10 eventually were submitted to the states for ratification as the Bill of Rights.

The press freedom clause went through various forms, some of which would have applied to the states, or to all branches of government, not just Congress. As eventually worked out by Madison and others in a House-Senate conference committee and submitted to the states in 1789, the First Amendment provided:

"Congress shall make no law respecting an establishment of religion, or prohibiting the free exercise thereof; or abridging the freedom of speech, or of the press, or the right of the people peaceably to assemble, and to petition the government for a redress of grievance."

The strength of the press guarantee was soon to be tested, when Congress, controlled by the Federalists, suddenly drew the issue of national power vs. individual rights by passing the Alien and Sedition Acts during the estrangement with France in 1798.

The sedition law made it a federal offense to "write, utter or publish . . .any false, scandalous or malicious writing . . .against the government of the United States, or either house of Congress . . .or the president" or to stir up opposition to any lawful act of Congress or of the president.

Opponents of the restrictive laws, led by Madison and Jefferson, relied on the inherent power of the states to defend the rights of the individual, while also dramatizing the government's political persecution to gain public support.

The sedition law died in 1801, not to be revived until World War I. But its repressions—11 federal sedition trials including eight involving newspapers, plus prosecutions at the state level—awakened many persons to the freedom issues involved.

Theorists already had before them the 1793 book on liberty and press freedoms by Robert Hall, an Englishman, which had drawn the distinction between sentiment and opinion on one hand, and conduct or behavior on the other. Only overt acts should be considered sedition, he wrote.

The Alien and Sedition Acts were only one of the many crises for the American press. Mob action, wartime censorship, court orders and government secrecy continued to hamper newsmen.

Mob action swirled around abolitionist editors in the 1830s as dissension grew over slavery. In 1837, Elijah Lovejoy, editor of the *St. Louis Observer*, was killed when he refused to renounce his right to condemn slavery.

In 1835, a Southern-dominated Congress passed a gag law which prohibited abolitionist literature from entering Southern states. By 1859, it was a crime in some states to subscribe to a newspaper opposed to slavery.

During the Civil War, Secretary of War Edwin Stanton caused telegraphed news reports to be checked first by his office, then sometimes delayed or stopped.

Government and press clashed in 1908 when President Theodore Roosevelt, angered by allegations that an American syndicate had corruptly gained millions of dollars during building of the Panama Canal, sued Joseph Pulitzer's *New York World* and the *Indianapolis News* for criminal libel. The government lost the case.

But far worse was to come were the Espionage and Sedition Acts in the closing years of World War I. There were 900 convictions in 1917-18, amid widespread abuses of personal freedoms by government and the courts. Congress also allowed the government to ban from the mails about 100 newspapers, mainly unpopular radical and pro-German papers, reviving memories of the abuses under the Alien and Sedition Acts of 1798-1800.

Fear of communism also has brought heavy pressures on the press.

In the so-called "Red Scare" of 1919-20, brought on by the Bolshevik takeover in Russia and the Industrial Workers of the World (IWW) movement in America, Atty. Gen. A. Mitchell Palmer instigated the arrests of socialists, labor union advocates and alleged radicals by the thousands.

Sen. Joseph R. McCarthy of Wisconsin touched off another "Red Scare" in the early 1950s, capitalizing on fears stemming from the success of Communists in China, and America's confrontation with Communist forces in Korea. Newsmen who punctured McCarthy's allegations of Communists in the State Department were accused of being "soft" on communism or "pink."

The Vietnam war brought similar pressures on journalists to accept the administration's view of the conflict.

These culminated in the Pentagon Papers case of 1971, in which for the first time in history the government got the courts to impose prior restraint—to stop four newspapers from publishing articles on the Pentagon Papers. The restraining order later was lifted.

Moves against television reporters have been at least as strong.

CBS President Frank Stanton was threatened with contempt of Congress because he refused to release unbroadcast materials and notes used in making the devastating documentary, "The Selling of the Pentagon," stimulating a struggle over whether these "outtakes" of unbroadcast film can be demanded by investigators.

Apprehension among broadcast journalists was heightened by the Nixon administration proposal that renewal of local station licenses hinge upon the local manager's handling of network news, which he does not initiate.

These moves were accompanied by vigorous attacks from former Vice President Agnew on the fairness of the press and finally from President Nixon himself—notably in a televised news conference on Oct. 26, 1973—as the Watergate scandal swept away the final bits of the President's credibility.

Within hours of the President's charges that he had been the victim of "outrageous, vicious, distorted reporting," his aide, Patrick Buchanan, was pressing for legislative and legal action to "break up the power" of the three major television networks. Singled out as a target for bitter criticism was CBS news correspondent Walter Cronkite, the acknowledged dean of broadcasters.

Taking note of moves and threats against the media, the International Press Institute of Geneva in its 1973 report warned that the Nixon adminsitration was bent on "chipping away at press freedom through the courts and by the threat of court action."

But the words "Congress shall make no law . . .abridging the freedom . . .of

The first time a printer affirmed the right to publish without prior authority of a government official was in 1721 when James Franklin published his New England Courant, a copy of which is shown here with brother Ben's pseudonym "Silence Dogood" appearing on the right side.

the press'' do not cover all threats to press freedom, even if the courts gave them their strongest interpretation.

And the Supreme Court, despite some encouraging interpretations of press law, has never approached an absolutist position.

Historically, the press' record has been mixed.

On the one hand, it has lived up to its highest ideals with the powerful antislavery editorials of Horace Greeley in the last century and support of integration in this century, with exposure of corruption in business and government, with denunciations of abuses of immigrants, poor housing, exploitation of children and women, and discrimination at all levels; and with facts and opinions on foreign ventures ranging from the War of 1812 to the bombing of Hanoi.

On the other hand, the press has had many failings over the years. Much of the press was slow to push for progress in race relations, education, and health and ecology matters. Handling of technical subjects has not always been adequate. Most papers were unable or unwilling to recognize the significance of Watergate and the secret Laotian and Cambodian bombings.

It should not go unnoticed that many newspaper and broadcast executives who advocate strong press freedom laws are the same persons who work hand-in-glove with government and law enforcement officials. Treating their papers and stations mainly as business operations, they often support the candidacies of narrow-minded, partisan politicians who end up being negative influences in society.

The need for a continued fight against legislative and judicial tyranny is obvious. The *Los Angeles Times* lamented in late 1975: ''For the first time in the history of the country, the courts, the chief defender of the Constitution and in utter distain of that Constitution, have claimed the power of wide censorship over the American people, a censorship that strikes at the heart of democratic government.''

The paper, commenting on a decision by Justice Harry A. Blackmun which temporarily upheld a controversial Nebraska ''gag order'', left this argument for its readers: ''The courts, no less than legislatures and executives, are accountable to the people, and must function in the spotlight of public exposure and scrutiny.''

This heightened concern over judicial abuses came at a time of disclosures of CIA and FBI crimes against persons and property and widespread corporate corruption—shocking, disgusting stories which demonstrated the absolute need for fearless reporting and the leaking to newspersons of documents which reveal misuse of power and money. The First Amendment guarantees such journalism and must not be blue-penciled by the timid or the vindictive.

Bibliography

The colorful story of American press freedom battles is contained in Edwin Emery's *The Press and America* (Prentice-Hall, Inc., 3rd edition, 1972; 4th edition pending), the interpretative history of newspapers and broadcasting. Two excellent surveys are Leonard W. Levy's *Freedom of the Press from Zenger to Jefferson* and Harold L. Nelson's *Freedom of the Press from Hamilton to the Warren Court* (Bobbs-Merrill, 1966). The Reporters Committee for Freedom of the Press (Room 1112, 1750 Pennsylvania Avenue, N.W., Washington, D.C. 20006), the Society of Professional Journalists, Sigma Delta Chi (35 E. Wacker Drive, Chicago, Ill. 60601) and the Freedom of Information Center (University of

Missouri) issue frequent reports on cases and yearly analyses, all of which are available upon request. Journalism reviews also should be checked when studying press freedom incidents, along with the editorial pages of leading papers and the commentaries/editorials of broadcast stations. Other background sources: William L. Rivers, *The Adversaries: Politics and the Press* (Beacon Press, 1970); Walter B. Emery, *Broadcasting and Government: Responsibilities and Regulation* (Michigan State University Press, 1971); Donald L. Gillmor and Jerome A. Barron, *Cases and Comments on Mass Communication Law* (West, 1969, revised, 1974); Harold L. Nelson and Dwight L. Teeter, Jr., *Freedom and Control of Print and Broadcast Media* (Foundation Press, 1969, revised 1973); Kenneth S. Devol, *Mass Media and The Supreme Court: The Legacy of the Warren Court* (Hastings House, 1971, revised 1976); William A. Hachten, *The Supreme Court on Freedom of the Press* (Iowa State University Press, 1968). Also see the bibliographies in Chapter Four of this book.

The President and the Press

By David Wise

President Richard Nixon was in a good mood.

He had left Bucharest that afternoon; now his plane touched down at Mildenhall Air Force Base, England, the last stop on what had been a successful journey around the world. The crowds cheered the President along the way. Only two weeks earlier, on July 20, 1969, the United States had become the first nation to land men on the moon.

Prime Minister Harold Wilson had gone to the Air Force base, eighty-five miles north of London, to greet the President. As he chatted informally with Wilson at a reception at the officers' club, Nixon said he planned to send moon rocks to every chief of state. At the time, there was a good deal of concern, later discounted, that germs might exist on the moon to which earthlings had no immunity. Because of these fears of real-life Andromeda Strain, the Apollo 11 astronauts had been sealed up in a capsule and quarantined upon their return from outer space. Well aware of this, Nixon told Harold Wilson that he also had another gift in mind. He might find a few "contaminated" pieces of the moon, he said, and give them to the press.

Nixon was, of course, joking, but the story revealed with clarity his attitude toward, and relations with, the news media. Nixon's bitterness toward the press is legendary, perhaps best symbolized by his now classic remark after his defeat in the 1962 gubernatorial race in California: ("You won't have Nixon to kick around any more. . . .") On the other hand some of the men who went to work for Nixon after he became President have often left the impression that they would very much enjoy kicking around the press.

On election night, 1968, fifteen minutes after Richard Nixon issued his victory statement, about twenty GOP advance men gathered in the empty ballroom of the Waldorf-Astoria in New York to accept congratualtions from John Ehrlichman,

David Wise, Washington bureau chief of the New York *Herald Tribune* before its demise, is the author of *The Politics of Lying; Government Deception, Secrecy and Power.* Copyright © 1973 by David Wise. Reprinted by permission of Random House, Inc. An expanded version of this article appears in THE POLITICS OF LYING, by David Wise.

"WHEN THIS ELECTION'S
OVER, DICK NIXON
WON'T HAVE THE PRESS
TO KICK HIM
AROUND ANYMORE!"

1972, The Register
and Tribune Syndicate

their chief. The happy, elated Nixon workers next heard from J. Roy Goodearle, a
tall, beefy Southerner who was Spiro Agnew's chief advance man (and later the
Vice-President's principal political liason with Republican Party leaders).

"Why don't we all get a member of the press and beat him up?" he asked.
"I'm tired of being nice to them."

Unbeknownst to Goodearle, Ehrlichman, or the other advance men, Joseph
Albright, then Washington bureau chief for Long Island's *Newsday*, was standing
in the room and wrote down the remark. Goodearle does not deny it; Agnew's
former press secretary, Victor Gold, speaking for Goodearle, insisted to me that "it
was a joke." "Perhaps so," says Albright, "but nobody laughed."

In the spring of 1972, columnist Nicholas Thimmesch of *Newsday* was invited
by Jack Valenti to a private advance screening of *The Godfather* at the Washington

headquarters of the Motion Picture Association of America. Seated in the small theater, Thimmesch suddenly felt someone grab his hair from behind and yank his head back sharply against the seat.

When Thimmesch was able to turn around he saw that the hair-puller was the President's chief of staff, Bob Haldeman, about whom Thimmesch had recently written a somewhat critical profile. (The article termed Haldeman's manner ''brusque'' and ''clinical,'' and quoted Haldeman as saying: ''I guess the term 'sonofabitch' fits me.'' Haldeman's crew cut, the profile added, ''hasn't changed since the beginning of the cold war.'' Despite this column, Thimmesch was held in exceptionally high regard by the Nixon Administration.) Apparently Haldeman did not approve of the length of Thimmesch's hair.

''Oh, pardon me,'' said Haldeman, ''I thought it was a girl sitting there.''

It was the newspapers that broke the story of the ''Nixon Fund'' during the 1952 presidential campaign—the $18,235 collected from wealthy contributors to help pay for his political expenses, or as Nixon put it, ''to enable me to continue my active battle against Communism and corruption.'' As pressure mounted over the fund, General Eisenhower threatened to force Nixon to resign as the Republican nominee for Vice-President. Nixon prepared to deliver his famous televised ''Checkers'' speech.

''My only hope to win,'' he wrote in his book *Six Crises*, ''rested with millions of people I would never meet, sitting in groups of two or three or four in their livingrooms, watching and listening to me on television. I determined as the plane took me to Los Angeles that I must do nothing which might reduce the size of that audience. And so I made up my mind that until after this broadcast, my only releases to the press would be for the purpose of building up the audience which would be tuning in. Under no circumstances, therefore, could I tell the press in advance what I was going to say or what my decision would be. . . . This time I was determined to tell my story directly to the people rather than to funnel it to them through a press account.''

And so Nixon went before the television cameras. He invoked Pat's Republican cloth coat, his little girl, Tricia, and his little black and white cocker spaniel dog (''regardless of what they say about it, we are going to keep it''). The public response was overwhelmingly favorable; Nixon flew to Wheeling, West Virginia, to meet Eisenhower, wept on Senator William Knowland's shoulder, and stayed on the ticket.

But the lesson of all this was not lost on Nixon: the newspapers had threatened his political career; television had saved it. The words in *Six Crises* remained a manifesto and guideline to his dealings with the press. The way to deal with newspapers was to tell them very little, build up suspense, and then go over their heads to the people via television.

Nixon can keep track of what the networks and news media are saying about him through the ''President's Daily News Briefing,'' the highly detailed private digest prepared for him by his speechwriting staff. Copies are not meant for public consumption, of course, but when the President was in China in February, 1972, a reporter got hold of one, and it showed that, even in Peking, Nixon could read what was being written and said about him in fantastic detail.

Television reports, for example, had obviously been clocked with a stopwatch, since the precise number of minutes and seconds of each network story was given, for example: "NBC led with 5:20 from the banquet...1:30 of RN toast and 1:20 by Chou." This meant Nixon could tell by a glance at the summary that American viewers watching NBC-TV got ten seconds more of Nixon than of Chinese Premier Chou En-lai. The log, which covered February 25, went on to say that NBC's Herb Kaplow had done a two-minute report from the Forbidden City. "Both better film and audio of RN than was the case in live coverage." For the "2nd night in a row," the summary noted somewhat sourly, "CBS led with busing story."

In discussing coverage by CBS—which has not been the Nixon Administration's favorite network—the digest said: "Still frustrated in getting news was Cronkite...as he said reporters were again turning to sightseeing." White House correspondent Dan Rather, the log said, did a report on acupuncture. "We saw a fellow under lung surgery—no pain. Then Dr. Dan in his operating room outfit concluded if it was all as it had been demonstrated, and he gave no reason to cause one to think it was otherwise, the operations witnessed were 'amazing.' " The sardonic reference to Rather as "Dr. Dan" implicitly questioned his ability to make medical judgments; and the tone of the President's news summary suggested that Rather had clearly been taken in by acupuncture and those clever Chinese. The log concluded with several single-spaced pages of reports on newspaper coverage of the trip, quoting headlines and going into great detail about treatment of the news, photographs, cartoons, and editorials.

One can only speculate about the cost, the tremendous effort, and the man-hours it must take to monitor the television networks and dozens of newspapers in such minute detail every day, then boil it down into written form, assemble it, and—when the President is out of Washington—transmit it to him.

The Administration sees political advantage in attacking the press, says Hugh Sidey of *Time*, "but don't discount their general hostility toward the press. It bubbles to the surface all the time. I once asked JFK what ever possessed him to call the steel men SOB's. He said, 'Because it felt so good'. Some of that is here in the attacks on the press. Under Truman, Eisenhower, Kennedy, and Johnson, the staff guys would bitch and moan about us, but there was always a sense of public trust, that they were awed by the responsibility given to them, and they understood this and would talk about what they were doing. They would talk about things. You could talk, write about, or disagree with them, but at the end of the day you could have a drink with them. There is no sense of that with these people.

"This crowd came in like an occupying army. They took over the White House like a stockade, and the Watergate, and screw everybody else. They have no sense that the government doesn't belong to them, that it's something they're holding in trust for the people."

"We feel the general pressure," says Tom Wicker, associate editor and columnist of the New York *Times*. "No administration in history has turned loose as high an official as the Vice-President to level a constant fusillade of criticism at the press. The Pentagon Papers case was pressure of the most immense kind. You have the Earl Caldwell case. If they indict Neil Sheehan, it will be pressure. In a sense, even the Ellsberg indictment is a form of pressure.

"There is a constant pattern of pressure intended to inhibit us. What the lawyers call a chilling effect. To make us unconsciously pull in our horns." In December, 1971, Wicker said, he had received a telephone call from James Reston: "Scotty called me from Washington. I was in New York, and something had come up about the Sheehan case. I said, 'I don't think we ought to talk about this on the phone'. I don't know if they were listening. But if they can make us feel that way, hell, they've won the game already."

One comes away from an interview with presidential press secretary Ronald Ziegler with the feeling of having sunk slowly, hopelessly, into a quagmire of marshmallows. But unless a newsman is out of favor, Ziegler is at least accessible to the press. To an unprecedented degree in the modern presidency, President Nixon is not.

Ziegler says that there has been no intent to intimidate the press. "Unless the press can point to efforts on the part of the government to restrain them, they shouldn't care. I suppose if we were in a debate, someone would point to the Pentagon Papers. I feel the government had to take that view, do what they did." Ziegler paused. "And after all," he said, "the Pentagon Papers were published."

The executive suite on the thirty-fifth floor of the Columbia Broadcasting System skyscraper in Manhattan is a tasteful blend of dark wood paneling, expensive abstract paintings, thick carpets, and pleasing colors. It has the quiet look of power.

Over breakfast in the small private dining room of the executive suite, Frank Stanton, the president of CBS for twenty-five years, talked candidly about the relationship between government and the television industry. I was interested, I explained, in pressure by government on the TV networks. I particularly wanted to know about telephone calls from Presidents; I recognized that this was a delicate subject, but I assumed that as head of CBS he had received some. He had, as it turned out, from several Presidents.

"I had a curious call from LBJ," he said. "It was one night back in 1968, at the time of the Democratic platform committee hearings in Washington." Johnson called on a Tuesday, Stanton said; it was August 20, and Dean Rusk was scheduled to testify at an evening session of the committee. As Stanton recalled the conversation, it went as follows:

LBJ: Are you going to cover Dean Rusk tonight?
Stanton: Yes. We're covering the whole thing.
LBJ: No, I mean are you going to cover it *live*?
Stanton: Why?
LBJ: Rusk has an important statement.
Stanton: If you're saying Rusk is going to have an important statement, we'll cover it live. But he has to be there on time.
LBJ: OK, just tell me the time—I'll have him there.

Stanton: Well, 9:00 P.M. But you really have to get him there on time. We'll be cutting into the Steve Allen show, and people are going to be furious if there is nothing going on.

Stanton knew that the Steve Allen show (which on that night starred Jayne Meadows and the Rumanian National Dance Company) began at 8:30 P.M. and ran for one hour; viewers would naturally be disappointed, he reasoned, if time were preempted for a political broadcast and the screen showed an announcer doing "fill." The CBS president had visions of the Secretary of State arriving late and the television audience getting nothing: no Steve Allen, no Jayne Meadows, no Rumanian dancers, not even Dean Rusk.

The conversation with President Johnson continued:

Stanton: How long will Rusk speak?
LBJ: Not long—why?
Stanton: We've got a special on blacks coming on at 9:30 P.M. and I don't want Rusk to collide with that.

The President assured Stanton there was no need to worry; the Secretary of State would be there on time, and he would be off before the special.

Johnson was true to his word. Precisely at 9:00 P.M. CBS correspondent Roger Mudd began introducing the broadcast from a booth in the hall. "Suddenly," Stanton said, "you could see Mudd look up, startled. Rusk was starting in right at 9:00 P.M., straight up."

The President of the United States had called the president of CBS and sweet-talked Steve Allen off the air and the Secretary of State on the air, in prime time, for a specific political reason, which he did not share with Stanton. That afternoon Democratic liberals had circulated a draft plank for the party platform calling for a halt to the bombing of North Vietnam. Lyndon Johnson wanted Dean Rusk on nationwide television, at an hour when he would have maximum exposure, to head off the inclusion of any such plank in the platform.

Rusk followed his marching orders. "We hear a good deal about stopping the bombing," he said. "...If we mean: Let them get as far as Dupont Circle but don't hit them while they are at Chevy Chase Circle, that would be too rude, let us say so." The party platform, Rusk said, should "state objectives" but not outline "tactics or strategy." In other words, no antibombing plank.

Rusk, in fact, made no important announcement; but presumably Johnson had to tell Stanton *something* to justify handing over the network to the President at 9:00 P.M. As it turned out, however, viewers were treated to a drama that was entirely unexpected, even by the President. Just as Rusk was finishing his twenty-five-minute statement, he was seen being given a piece of wire copy announcing the Soviet invasion of Czechoslovakia.

In plain view of the television audience, Rusk huddled with platform committee chairman Hale Boggs for a moment, and then announced: "I think I should go see what this is all about." And he hurried away.

Stanton, of course, had been watching CBS, waiting for that important statement. About twenty minutes later he got a call from the President. Did Rusk show up on time? Johnson wanted to know. Yes, said Stanton, hadn't the President been watching?

"No. Dobrynin came in to tell me what happened [in Czechoslovakia], and I've been tied up. I've just convened the National Security Council."

"Can I use that?"

"Yes."

"Excuse me, I want to tell our people this."

Stanton hung up and passed on his scoop to CBS News.

It eventually became known that a summit meeting between Johnson and the leaders of the Soviet Union was to have been announced at the White House the next morning, August 21. But the Czech invasion killed the projected meeting, to Johnson's bitter disappointment, and there was never any White House announcement that it had even been contemplated. In retrospect, Stanton harbored some suspicion that Rusk had planned to announce the summit meeting that night on CBS. Now Stanton was a very old and close friend of Lyndon Johnson's, and he was understandably reluctant to think that the President might have been fibbing to him about Rusk having an "important statement."

When the President of the United States wants network time, he calls up and gets it. Or he has one of his assistants call. Not only Lyndon Jounson, but *all* the Presidents have had a consuming interest in television. The medium has a fascination for Presidents, an interest that is easily understood, since so much of their political success depends on the skill with which they use it.

A telephone call from a President to the publisher of the New York *Times*, for example, is not an unknown event, but one cannot, somehow, picture Lyndon Johnson calling up Arthur Ochs Sulzberger and saying: "Punch, Dean Rusk is going to have an important announcement tonight, and I want you to give it page-one treatment, eight-column head with full text and pictures. What time does your Late City close?"

But when a President calls the head of CBS, or NBC, or ABC, it is not easy, or even advisable, to brush him off. In the fall of 1971, Julian Goodman, the president of NBC, went to Rome for a staff meeting of NBC correspondents in Europe. One of the reporters at the private meeting complained that Nixon was "using" the television networks to speak to the American people whenever he pleased, for free; he had done so something like fourteen times up to that date.

Goodman agreed. But the correspondent persisted. "Julian, what is your attitude toward President Nixon's requests for television time?"

"Our attitude," said Goodman evenly, "is the same as our attitude toward previous Presidents; he can have any goddamn thing he wants." [Ed. Note: The networks tightened these policies during the Ford administration.]

Sometimes a presidential aide or appointee manages to act as a buffer between the White House and the networks. Newton Minow, the Chicago attorney whom President John Kennedy made chairman of the Federal Communications Commission, recalls that Kennedy once expressed dissatisfaction with NBC News.

One night in April, 1962, Minow said, in the midst of Kennedy's fight with the steel companies, the Huntley-Brinkley show on NBC included "a long speech by somebody who took the President apart. I happened to have watched it. We were having a small dinner party at home and I was getting dressed when my wife said, 'The President is on the phone.' " As Minow recalled the conversation, it went this way:

JFK: Did you see that goddamn thing on Huntley-Brinkely?
Minow: Yes.
JFK: I thought they were supposed to be our friends. I want you to do something about that. You do something about that.

Minow said that the President did not, as the story later got around in the television industry, ask that the FCC chairman take Huntley-Brinkley off the air. But, said Minow, the President "was mad."

Minow added: "Some nutty FCC chairman would have called the network. Instead I called Kenny O'Donnell [Kennedy's appointments secretary] in the morning and I said to him, 'Just tell the President he's lucky he has an FCC chairman who doesn't do what the President tells him.' "

When a President desires to make a television broadcast, there are standing arrangements to handle his request, procedures worked out between the White House and the Washington bureaus of the major networks. At the time Lyndon Johnson was President, the networks told the White House they needed six hours to make the technical arrangements for a White House broadcast; they could do it in three, they said, but could not guarantee a good picture, or any picture. Despite this, Johnson often demanded instant access to the networks and got on the air within one hour.

Johnson used TV so frequently that finally he asked for—and the networks agreed to provide—"hot cameras," manned throughout the day in the White House theater, with crews continually at the ready. Johnson could then walk into the theater and go on the air live, immediately. During the Dominican crisis he went on television on such short notice that he burst into the regular network programming with almost no introduction, startling millions of viewers.

"Once Johnson went on the air so fast," an NBC executive recalled, "that we couldn't put up the presidential seal. When a network technician said we need a second to put up the seal, Johnson said, 'Son, I'm the leader of the free world, and I'll go on the air when I want to.' "

There is a seeming paradox in Richard Nixon's view of television. On the one hand, television saved his political career in 1952, and he has often had kind words for the medium. Note, for example, that in his 1962 false exit ("You won't have Nixon to kick around any more"), he states: "Thank God for television and radio for keeping the newspapers a little more honest." As President, he told Cyrus Sulzberger in 1971: "I must say that without television it might have been difficult for me to get people to understand a thing."

On the other hand, as President, Nixon criticized the networks. It was with Nixon's blessing that Spiro Agnew launched his celebrated attack on network news analysts. Nixon's Administration has made systematic efforts to cow the networks and destroy the credibility of the press, including television news.

There is no inconsistency, however, if one understands that in Nixon's view television ideally should serve *only* as a carrier, a mechanical means of electronically transmitting his picture and words directly to the voters. It is this concept of television-as-conduit that has won Nixon's praise, not television as a form of electronic journalism. The moment that television analyses his words, qualifies his remarks, or renders news judgments, it becomes part of the ''press,'' and a political target.

In discussing Nixon and television, therefore, one must distinguish between television as a mechanical means of communication and television as an intellectual instrument. ''Pure'' television is OK, television news is not. As President, Nixon's use of television flows logically from these basic premises. Thus at every opportunity Nixon solemnly addresses the nation, but he has usually avoided the give-and-take of the televised news conference. Only in the first setting does Nixon have total

Lights!
Camera!
Obfuscation!

control—except for the analyses afterwards by network newsmen, which Spiro Agnew's attacks were specifically designed to discourage. In short, to Richard Nixon, television ideally is the mirror, mirror on the wall.

In April of 1971, John Ehrlichman, the President's chief assistant for domestic affairs, complained in person to Richard S. Salant, the president of CBS News, about Dan Rather, the network's White House correspondent. Ehrlichman was in New York to appear on the CBS Morning News with correspondent John Hart. Afterwards Hart and Ehrlichman adjourned for breakfast at the Edwardian Room of the Plaza, where they were joined by Salant. The President's assistant brought up the subject of CBS's White House reporter.

"Rather has been jobbing us," Ehrlichman said. Salant, seeking to inject a lighter note into the conversation, told how Rather had been hired by CBS in 1962 after he had saved the life of a horse, an act of heroism that resulted in considerable publicity and brought him to the attention of the network. It was then that Rather went to work for CBS News as chief of its Southwest bureau in Dallas. When President Kennedy was assassinated in that city, Rather went on the air for the network, and his cool, poised coverage of the tragedy gained him national recognition. After Dallas, Salant explained to Ehrlichman, CBS brought Rather to Washington, in part because the new President, Lyndon Johnson, was a fellow Texan.

"Aren't you going to open a bureau in Austin where Dan could have a job?" Ehrlichman asked Salant. He then accused Rather of never coming to see him in the White House, and he suggested it might be beneficial if Rather took a year's vacation.

That evening, following a presidential press conference at the White House, Ziegler told Rather crypically that President Nixon's obvious failure to recognize him at that conference had "no connection" with something that "you are about to hear."

Rather heard the next morning. Salant telephoned William Small, head of the CBS Washington Bureau. Small called Rather in and told him about the breakfast at the Plaza; he assured Rather that his standing with CBS was not affected. He said he was mentioning the episode simply because sooner or later Rather was bound to learn about it. Rather told Small it was true he had not seen much of Ehrlichman at the White House—because Ehrlichman would not see him.

Now, however, Ziegler urged Rather to see Ehrlichman and talk the situation over. When Rather walked into Ehrlichman's office, he found Haldeman waiting there as well. The conversation, with just the three men present, was blunt on both sides. As Rather reconstructed it, the dialogue proceeded as follows:

> *Ehrlichman*: I wanted to tell you to your face I wasn't in New York for this purpose. . . . I didn't know there was going to be a breakfast. When the conversation went in the direction it did, I told them what I thought, which is I think you're slanted. I don't know whether it's just sloppiness or you're letting your true feelings come through, but the net effect is that you're negative. You have negative leads on bad stories.
> *Rather*: What's a bad story?
> *Ehrlichman*: A story that's dead-assed wrong. You're wrong 90 percent of the time.
> *Rather*: Then you have nothing to worry about; any reporter who's wrong 90 percent of the time can't last.

Haldeman (breaking in): What concerns me is that you are sometimes wrong, but your style is very positive. You sound like you know what you're talking about, people believe you.

Ehrlichman: Yeah, people believe you, and they shouldn't.

Rather: I hope they do, and maybe now we are getting down to the root of it. You have trouble getting people to believe you.

Erhlichman: I didn't say that.

At one point Ehrlichman complained that "only the President, Bob, and sometimes myself" knew what was going on, and "you're out there on the White House lawn talking as though you know what's going on."

At the Plaza breakfast with Richard Salant, Ehrlichman had also singled out CBS correspondent Daniel Schorr for criticism. Schorr, said Ehrlichman, reported what the critics said about Nixon's domestic programs, but not the Administration's side. A few months later Schorr was under investigation by the FBI. Early on the morning of August 20, 1971, Ellen McCloy, Salant's secretary, received a telephone call at CBS News headquarters on West Fifty-seventh Street in Manhattan. The call was from one Tom Harrington, "He's the CBS FBI man," Miss McCloy explained. "He always opens up his conversations by saying 'Tom Harrington FBI.' "

He did so on this occasion, explaining to Miss McCloy that she would be getting a call from another FBI man "who is checking on Dan Schorr." Salant was not in yet, so his secretary called him at home to alert him to the fact that the FBI was on the trail of a CBS correspondent. When the second agent called Miss McCloy, she gave him Salant's listed number in New Canaan, Connecticut. "He was in a big rush," Miss McCloy recalled. "He gave the impression he had to have the information right away." The FBI man then called the CBS News president at his home, asking for the names of people who knew Dan Schorr. In the meantime Miss McCloy called Bill Small in Washington, Schorr's boss, to let him know what was happening.

The FBI agent called Miss McCloy back twice. With Salant's permission, she provided the names of other officials for him to talk to at CBS. Salant confirmed that the FBI agent who telephoned him presented the matter as "very urgent." The sort of questions he was asked about Schorr, Salant said, were: "Was he loyal? Did he go around with disreputable people?"

Schorr, a gray-haired, bespectacled family man of fifty-five, and a veteran of twenty years at CBS, definitely did not have the reputation of hanging around with disreputable people. A serious, hard-working newsman, he specialized in covering health, education, welfare, the environment, and economics.

As Schorr recalls the sequence of events, it began on Tuesday, August 17, when Nixon, in a speech to the Knights of Columbus, promised that "you can count on my support" to help parochial schools. The producer of the CBS Evening News—the Walter Cronkite show—called Schorr and asked for a follow-up story. Schorr went to see a source, a Catholic priest active in the field of education, who told him the Administration was doing nothing to aid Catholic schools.

On Wednesday night Cronkite ran a film clip of Nixon's speech promising to aid parochial schools, then cut to Schorr saying there was "absolutely nothing in the

works'' to help these schools. On Thursday, Alvin Snyder, the Administration's deputy communications director for television, telephoned Schorr, asking him to come to the White House because ''Peter Flanigan and others thought I didn't have the facts.'' Late in the day Schorr met at the White House with Pat Buchanan, Terry T. Bell, deputy commissioner of education, and Henry C. Cashen II, an assistant to Charles Colson, who was then special counsel to the President. ''They began reading figures off very rapidly,'' Schorr said. He suggested that they put their main points down on paper and said he would try to get it on the air.

On Thursday, the same day that Schorr was summoned to the White House, a member of the White House staff requested the FBI to investigate the CBS correspondent.

On Friday morning Schorr reported to the CBS studios in Washington. An

FBI agent was already there questioning Small, who declined to answer until he knew the reason. "I don't know except it has to do with government employment," the FBI man said. Not having learned much from Small, the agent then wandered over to Schorr's desk and started asking routine questions—age? family? occupation?

Without thinking, Schorr began answering, then suddenly stopped and said he would not say anymore until the agent specified what employment he was talking about. Since the agent would not or could not, Schorr refused to answer any further questions.

"Is that what you want me to report?"

"Yes."

"Do you mind if I ask other people about you?"

"Yes."

Schorr explained to the agent that he was in a "highly visible" occupation; it would soon get around that he was being investigated and it might seem as though he was looking for a job. And that, Schorr explained, could be harmful to his reputation and position at CBS.

"All the rest of the day," Schorr said, "calls came in from all over from people who said they had been approached by the FBI. Fred Friendly [the former president of CBS News] called from his vacation home in New Hampshire. They had telephoned him and asked to see him, but he said he would not talk to them without checking with me. They called Bill Leonard and Gordon Manning, both vice-presidents of CBS News. They called Ernie Leiser, the executive producer of CBS specials. Sam Donaldson of ABC was called. Irv Levine of NBC, who was with me in Moscow, was called; they wanted to know how I carried on as a correspondent in Moscow." When some of those questioned asked why the FBI was making these inquiries, they were told that Dan Schorr was being considered for a high government post, a position of trust.

Then Schorr discovered that "the FBI had talked to my neighbors, including Marjorie Hunter of the New York *Times*." One neighbor reported that Schorr's home had apparently been under surveillance. By now Schorr was determined to know more. "There were two theories at CBS: first, that it was a real employment investigation, and second, that it was an adverse investigation as a result of my stories on Catholic school aid. But if there was a job involved, where the hell was it?"

On November 11, the Washington *Post* published a detailed front-page story about the FBI investigation. The story said the probe had been initiated by the office of Frederic V. Malek. As personnel man in the White House, Malek earned a reputation as "the Cool Hand Luke" of the Nixon Administration.

The storm broke over Ron Ziegler at the White House morning press briefing. Schorr, Zielger told newsmen, was being checked for a job in "the area of the environment." Malek, Zielger added, was in charge of searching "across the nation" for "qualified people." Claiming "I am trying to be forthright with you," Ziegler nevertheless repeatedly ducked the simple, direct question of who had

The inauguration of
Jimmy Carter was a gala
event and every minute
was captured by televi-
sion cameras, print
reporters and photog-
raphers. The American
people shared in the
spectacle as they do
every major happening,
good or bad.

ordered the FBI investigation. He kept saying that "...it was part of the Malek process." But the transcript of the briefing does include this exchange:

Q: Is it your understanding Mr. Malek was aware that an FBI check was under way?
Ziegler: Yes.

In an interview published the next day, Malek seemed to imply that there had been a full field FBI probe. Malek said someone on his staff—again unidentified—had asked the FBI to investigate Schorr but "the message somehow got bungled. Somehow something went wrong. Either I wasn't clear on what I wanted or the staff wasn't clear or the FBI. A breakdown occurred."

Something indeed had gone wrong, and Senator Sam J. Ervin, Democrat of North Carolina, a Southern defender of constitutional liberties, announced a Senate investigation of the episode.

"Job or no job," Schorr told the Ervin committee, "the launching of such an investigation without consent demonstrates an insensitivity to personal rights. An FBI investigation is not a neutral matter. It has an impact on one's life, on relations with employers, neighbors, and friends."

Considering the Administration's protestations of innocence, it was surprising how little cooperation Ervin received. The President declined to let any staff member testify—Malek, Herbert Klein, and Colson all refused invitations—but the White House sent a letter to Ervin, saying that Schorr "was being considered for a post that 'is presently filled.' " The letter was signed by John W. Dean III, counsel to the President. Nixon, the letter added, had decided that such job investigations in the future would not be initiated "without prior notification to the person being investigated." On the same day the letter was published, the Washington *Post* quoted an unnamed White House official as saying that the job for which Schorr had been investigated was that of assistant to Russell E. Train, the chairman of the Council on Environmental Quality. The story indicated that the Administration thought Schorr might produce a series of television programs on the environment.

The leak was not entirely convincing, since Train had no assistant producing TV shows, and the White House letter to Ervin distinctly said the job was "presently filled." In fact, the council had no one with the title or duties of assistant to the chairman; no such job existed.

Much of the pressure by government on the networks takes place out of public view. The telephone calls from White House assistants and the visits to network executives by presidential aides are seldom publicized. For the most part, however, it is CBS that feels the greatest pressure under the Nixon Administration. The official who bears the brunt of that pressure is Richard Salant, the president of CBS News.

Salant, a lawyer turned news executive, occupies a high-pressure job; he wears glasses, has a receding hairline, and chain-smokes. Unlike some network executives, he is unusually outspoken. Salant reeled off a list of pressures from and contacts with CBS emanating from the Administration.

In February of 1971, he said, CBS did a segment on Agnew on the program *60 Minutes*. Narrator Mike Wallace reported that Agnew's grades at Forest Park High School "were mediocre at best." CBS asked to see the grades, Wallace added, "but school principal Charles Michael told us Agnew's record was pulled from the file when he became Vice-President." The program, tracing Agnew's early career, also noted that he once served as personnel director at a supermarket and, like other employees, "Agnew often wore a smock with the words 'No Tipping Please' on it."

After the broadcast, Salant said, the President's director of communications, Herbert Klein, telephoned him. "Klein called and said he wanted to see me. He came to New York and came to my office and made small talk. Then he got around to the point; he said the Vice-President didn't see *60 Minutes*, he never looks at those things. *But Mrs. Agnew saw it and didn't like it.*"

Salant told Klein that *60 Minutes* had broadcast letters from viewers who did not like the Agnew program; CBS would be happy to receive a letter from Mrs. Agnew.

Once Klein telephoned Reuven Frank, then president of NBC News, to protest a broadcast by David Brinkley. Frank became so furious that he stormed next door into the office of Richard C. Wald, then vice-president of NBC (later Frank's successor), to let off steam.

"Relax," said Wald, "he gets *paid* to call you."

A few days later on a Saturday morning, the White House telephoned Frank at home. Frank was annoyed since he was kept waiting on the line, it was his day off, and he hadn't had his breakfast yet. He started to do a slow burn again. Finally Klein came on. He was calling, he announced cheerily, to say he had seen something he *liked* on NBC; he just wanted Frank to know.

It may be that no single example of government power directed at television news means very much—Dan Rather survived John Ehrlichman's bemoanings, Salant's sympathy for Judy Agnew was limited, and so on—but taken together, such incidents constitute a pattern of pressure that has dangerous implications. It is by means of such contacts that political leaders attempt to influence the presentation of the news so as to put the government in the most favorable light.

The First Amendment clearly protects the printed press. But the Founding Fathers, after all, did not foresee the advent of television, and the degree to which broadcasting is protected by the First Amendment has been subject to shifting interpretation. Technology has outpaced the Constitution, and the result is a major paradox: television news, which has the greatest impact on the public, is the most vulnerable and the least protected news medium.

Only economics limits the number of newspapers and magazines that may be published. But the number of radio frequencies and television channels is finite; the rationale for government regulation is that stations would otherwise overlap and interfere with each other. Cable television may one day erode the technological argument for government regulation by opening up an unlimited number of channels, but for the moment the networks remain under government supervision and the Dean Rusks will continue, when they want to, to replace the Steve Allens and the Rumanian dancers on short notice.

The government's ultimate power over the networks is its ability to take away a license at renewal time and give it to someone else. Public television, dependent on Congress for funds, is even more susceptible to government intervention than the networks; the Nixon Administration has made no secret of its discontent with public television.

Walter Cronkite believes the Nixon administration attacked the news media "to raise the credibility of the Administration. It's like a first-year physics experiment with two tubes of water—you put pressure on one side and it makes the other side go up or down." He added: "I have charged that this is a 'conspiracy'. I don't regret my use of that word."

By applying constant pressure, in ways seen and unseen, the leaders of the government have attempted to shape the news to resemble the images seen through the prism of their own power. The Administration's attacks, Richard Salant acknowledged, have "made us all edgy. We've thought about things we shouldn't think about."

Bibliography

Wise's article gives the necessary background for current discussions about the abuse of executive power and attempts to intimidate newspersons. Testimony at Congressional hearings in 1975 indicated that the privacy of newspersons was invaded by government officials, through the FBI, as far back as 1940, and that the electronic surveillances increased in the early 1960s. A thorough analysis of the Nixon administration's battles with the networks—which relates directly to the Wise article—is found in *The New Yorker* of March 17, 1975, written by Thomas Whiteside. CBS News Correspondent Dan Rather's book, *The Palace Guard* (with Gary Paul Gates, Harper & Row, 1974), offers a close look at the Nixon White House and attitudes held toward the news media by high officials. When updating this information and studying the Ford administration, students might check the *Columbia Journalism Review* and the *Alfred I. Dupont-Columbia University Survey of Broadcast Journalism*, an annual summary of various developments in broadcasting which includes government attempts to hinder the flow of information.

What's Fair on the Air?

By Fred W. Friendly

At 1:12 P.M. on the afternoon of Nov. 25, 1964, Bob Barry, the announcer on duty at radio station WGCB, Red Lion, Pa., threaded a tape made in the Tulsa, Okla., studio of the Christian Crusade. At 1:14, he began reading a commercial for Mailman's Department Store. Sixty seconds later, he gave station identification, pushed the "start" button on Tape Recorder 1 and raised the level of the audio pot just in time for the opening fanfare of "The Battle Hymn of the Republic." The Rev. Billy James Hargis was on the air in Red Lion, York, Spry and Dallastown.

The Rev. Mr. Hargis, in a stinging personal attack, lashed out at Fred J. Cook, an investigative reporter who in his own crusades had taken aim on a wide range of targets, from Richard M. Nixon to J. Edgar Hoover, from the C.I.A. to the F.B.I. His most recent book had been a highly critical biography of Barry Goldwater, published during the conservative Senator's unsuccessful race for the Presidency.

Fred W. Friendly is Edward R. Murrow Professor of Journalism at the Columbia Graduate School of Journalism and an adviser at the Ford Foundation. This article, which appeared in *The New York Times Magazine* (March 30, 1975), is adapted from this book, *The Good Guys, The Bad Guys and The First Amendment,* © 1975, 1976 by Fred Friendly, and is used with the permission of Random House.

In 1964, Hargis had believed that the election of Barry Goldwater was essential "to the survival of a free America" and he was outraged by Cook for writing the book "Barry Goldwater: Extremist of the Right" as well as an article, "Hate Clubs of the Air," which appeared in *The Nation* and classified Hargis as a bigot. Hargis attacked Fred Cook as "a professional mudslinger," accused him of dishonesty, of falsifying stories and of defending Alger Hiss. The Hargis attack lasted less than two minutes, and the air time it filled cost $7.50.

The voice of Billy James Hargis was familiar to the people who listened to WGCB, which offered a rich diet of conservative, anti-Communist opinion derived from the evangelical vision of "the infallible word of God." There are hundreds of stations like it throughout America, many of them clustered in the Bible belts of Pennsylvania, Texas and Oklahoma.

If that day's Hargis broadcast seemed routine, however, it also turned out to be an element in a larger story of politics and communications law. For it would generate a key legal dispute over the fairness doctrine—the idea that the Government has the right to order a broadcaster to grant reply time to a person or group that claims to have suffered from a broadcast over the public airwaves.

This article began with research for a textbook on the history of the fairness doctrine, and the Hargis broadcast was a logical point of focus. For Mr. Hargis's attack upon Fred Cook would cause Cook to demand reply time of WGCB, and the resulting legal case would end in a Supreme Court decision directing the Red Lion station to grant Cook's request. The decision would stand as a commanding precedent fortifying the Government's position in subsequent fairness doctrine cases, and the name "Red Lion" would come to stand for the power of Government to intervene directly in the content of broadcast programing on fairness grounds.

Before long, however, the historical research turned into an exercise in investigative reporting. For it became clear that the basically well intentioned concept of the fairness doctrine has on occasion been perverted—used for political purposes. Fred Cook, it turns out, did not bring his action against WGCB simply as an offended private citizen; instead, his actions grew out of a politically motivated campaign to use the fairness doctrine to harass stations airing right-wing commentary, an effort inspired and managed by the White House and the Democratic National Committee and financed in large measure with political contributions.

The facts of that effort are startling enough in themselves after the Watergate story, with its generally accepted assumption that dirty tricks in the Nixon White House were unique. But the story of the fairness doctrine effort during the 1964 campaign also illuminates—with striking irony—the subtle and fascinating interplay of power politics and regulatory policy. In the Red Lion case, for example, many of the agency bureaucrats, Government lawyers and judges tended to dismiss the broadcasters' claim that freedom of expression might be "chilled" by court decisions extending Federal regulatory control over the content of radio and television programs—little realizing that at the time, they were granting implicit legal sanction to an unsavory project of political censorship by the Democrats.

Furthermore, this sanction, unwittingly ratified by the highest court in the land, would later embolden the Nixon Administration in its attempts to lean on broadcasters unfriendly to the President. The Red Lion precedent has been cited most recently in a case brought by a Nixon-Agnew era broadcasting watchdog group in response to a 1972 NBC documentary about corporate pension plans. That case was decided in favor of the network only this month in the Court of Appeals for the District of Columbia, but an appeal to the Supreme Court is planned. It focuses the First Amendment aspects of fairness doctrine policy even more sharply than did the Red Lion case. For in Red Lion the issue was relatively limited—the right of an individual to gain Government-ordered reply time if he has been attacked by an irresponsible commentator. But in the pensions case, the issue is broad—the right of an interest group to gain Government-ordered satisfaction if it doesn't agree with the editing and interpretation of the facts by professional journalists.

As a general concept, the fairness doctrine arose from the fact that more people wished to broadcast over the airwaves—a public resource—than the electromagnetic spectrum could accommodate. Its outlines were formalized in a 1949 F.C.C. report, which directed broadcast licensees to operate in the public interest (1) by devoting a reasonable amount of time to the coverage of controversial issues of public importance, and (2) to do so fairly by affording a reasonable opportunity for contrasting viewpoints to be voiced on these issues.

So stated, the doctrine seems innocuous, yet the second provision, the part usually enforced, mandates that the Government should have some power to influence the content of broadcasting. A station's fairness record has come to be considered a factor in the F.C.C.'s decision to renew its license, although only once, in the case of the flagrantly racist WLBT in Jackson, Miss., did a television station lose its license to operate on fairness doctrine grounds. Even in that case the F.C.C. acted reluctantly only after Judge Warren Burger and his colleagues on the Court of Appeals ordered it not to renew WLBT's license. More common was the application of the personal-attack provision, under which a person who felt his character had been maligned over the air could apply to the offending station for free time to respond. (It is important not to confuse the fairness doctrine, which applies to news and public affairs programing and has to do with content, with the concept of equal time, a mathematical formula for apportioning air time among candidates during political campaigns.)

It was in 1963 that the doctrine began to change from a vague public-interest policy to an instrument of politics and inhibition. That year, President Kennedy worried that one of the noblest goals of his Administration—the nuclear test-ban treaty with the Soviet Union—was being jeopardized by right-wing commentators who denounced the treaty and argued against its ratification. His political strategists monitored stations broadcasting such commentary and then prompted test-ban treaty advocates to demand time to state their side of the issue, citing the fairness doctrine in their letters to the stations involved. The campaign resulted in a dramatic number of broadcasts favoring the treaty in areas of the country where such views might not otherwise have been heard. The White House believed this political use of the fairness doctrine had made an important contribution to the eventual Senate vote to ratify.

In 1963, Kennedy and the Democratic National Committee believed that the Republicans might nominate Goldwater and that the right-wing radio commentators who supported him could damage the President's chances for re-election; they decided to see if the fairness doctrine could again be used, this time for partisan political purposes. (It is important to remember, in light of the following, how ominous the thunder on the right seemed in those days. During this period I was an executive of CBS News; we did some aggressive reporting about the influence of right-wing extremists and incurred the wrath of many, and of Senator Goldwater, who for a period during the 1964 campaign refused to appear on CBS news programs.) The result was a campaign that continued under Lyndon Johnson through the 1964 election year; in the process, events were set in motion that would lead to the Supreme Court's decision in the Red Lion case.

On Oct. 12, 1963, one of President Kennedy's chief political assistants, Kenneth O'Donnell, invited Wayne Phillips, a skilled publicist who had helped run several Administration conferences on urban problems, to the White House. Phillips, a former New York Times reporter and part-time faculty member of the Columbia School of Journalism, was then an assistant to the director of the Housing and Home Finance Agency. At a meeting in the Fish Room, O'Donnell instructed Phillips to see if the fairness doctrine "could be used to provide support for the President's programs." Phillips in turn hired Wesley McCune, who made a business of keeping an eye on right-wing groups, to monitor the radio right. Since now there was no focused debate, as there had been over the test-ban treaty, the idea was simply to harass the radio stations by getting officials and organizations that had been attacked by extremist radio commentators to request reply time, citing the fairness doctrine. All told, Phillips recalls, this effort resulted in over 500 radio replies.

In the midsummer of 1964, with Goldwater the Republican nominee, the Democrats decided to expand the fairness doctrine effort. Phillips, now an executive of the Democratic National Committee, retained the public relations firm of Ruder & Finn, which set about organizing a bipartisan front organization, The National Council for Civic Responsibility. Arthur Larson, a prominent liberal Eisenhower Republican and once head of the United States Information Agency, was recruited to lead the blue-ribbon panel whose members shared serious concern over the growth of the John Birch Society and other elements of right-wing extremism.

Larson would deny in public that the organization of the group had anything to do with the Presidential campaign, and funds for the council were solicited through newspaper advertisements signed by a wide range of the most respected moderate and liberal intellectuals in the country. Yet more than half of the money Larson set as his fund-raising goal came from major Democratic party contributors at the direction of the Democratic National Committee. Furthermore, the Democrats sought to encourage—and to camouflage—these big party contributions by linking the council to the Public Affairs Institute, a tax-exempt "citizen's lobby" group that had been funded in 1948 by several unions, but had existed in name only for many years.

James H. Rowe, a Washington lawyer and adviser to Presidents from Roosevelt to Johnson, called his old friend Dewey Anderson, executive director of the moribund institute, and learned that its tax-exempt status was still in effect. Anderson, then 67, recalls being escorted by Rowe through a side door of the Democratic National Committee offices to meet National Chairman John Bailey and Treasurer Dick Maguire. Anderson remembers being told by Rowe and Bailey, "We got the money and you got the tax exemption and we need you to fight these right-wing radio extremists." Anderson, happy to be summoned from retirement, agreed to join the campaign. So the National Committee for Civic Responsibility became the National Committee for Civic Responsibility of the Public Affairs Institute with initial funding of $25,000, directly from the Democratic National Committee.

The committee used the money raised—estimated at $200,000—to amplify the effort begun by Phillips and McCune. It produced and sponsored broadcasts to counter right-wing extremism, and it printed and distributed literature exposing the John Birch Society and other extremist groups. The radio shows, as shrill as those they were designed to counter, were called "Spotlight" and were narrated by commentator William Dennis, the madeup name for an actor employed by Ruder & Finn.

After the election, Phillips wrote in an evaluation report that the monitoring campaign had "resulted in over 1,700 free radio broadcasts," and that "even more important than the free radio time, however, was the effectiveness of this operation in inhibiting the political activity of these right-wing broadcasts."

Most of those who were involved in this combined White House-Democratic National Committee-Ruder & Finn effort and who will talk about it today are not proud to recall their participation. "Our massive strategy was to use the fairness doctrine to challenge and harass the right-wing broadcasters and hope that the challenges would be so costly to them that they would be inhibited, and decide it was too expensive to continue," says Bill Ruder, who had been an Assistant Secretary of Commerce in the Kennedy years. A former Ruder & Finn executive who handled the account has little doubt that "if we did in 1974 what we did in 1964, we'd be answering questions before some Congressional committee."

Larson, who had long been a target of the radical right, recalls his role with a sense of embarrassment. "The whole thing was not my idea," he says, "but let's face it, we decided to use radio and the fairness doctrine to harass the extreme right. In the light of Watergate, it was wrong. We felt the ends justified the means. They never do." And then he adds sadly, "I guess I was like a babe in the woods."

No major news organization reported these "sleazy and seamy activities" as Dewey Anderson characterized them recently, although four months after the election another man named Anderson reported in the "Washington Merry-Go-Round" column the covert use of Democratic party funds to finance the Committee for Civic Responsibility front. But Jack Anderson could not possibly have known about the far-reaching fairness doctrine implications of these irregularities, for at that time the Red Lion case was just getting under way.

Wayne Phillips and the Ruder & Finn organizers of the fairness doctrine effort, had hired freelance writer and reporter Fred Cook to help out with research and writing. He freely acknowledges that he was paid $1,500 by Ruder & Finn to produce material to be used in pamphlets, the ''Spotlight'' broadcasts and other projects to combat the right. Cook also undertook other tasks as a result of his association with Phillips and McCune. His book on Goldwater, it turns out, was encouraged and would not have been published without the subsidization of the Democratic National Committee. The technique, similar to Laurance Rockefeller's financing of the Victor Lasky book critical of former Supreme Court Justice Arthur Goldberg, was simple enough. The Democratic National Committee offered in advance to buy 50,000 copies of the book. The offer virtually guaranteed the cost of printing and Cook's advance of $1,000. Correspondence indicates it was the key element in the decision of Grove Press to publish the book.

In the meantime, Phillips, in May of 1964, began conversations with Carey McWilliams, editor of the *Nation,* as well as with Cook, about an article exposing right-wing radio activities. Cook acknowledges the close working relationship he had with the Democratic National Commitee at this time and says, ''It was only natural that while I was working on the Goldwater book, Phillips would suggest the 'Hate Groups of the Air' piece.'' The *Nation* agreed to run the article and pay the author a modest fee. Phillips and McCune provided Cook with much of the research material and a master tape of the most virulent far-right broadcasts.

Billy James Hargis was one of those who had figured prominently in the *Nation* article, and there are some indications he had an inkling that there was more to the growing anti-extremism movement than met the eye. In any case, he decided that November to attack Fred Cook in one of his broadcasts. He mentioned Cook's anti-Goldwater book and then made a number of assertions intended to discredit its author, among them that ''Cook was fired from The *New York World Telegram* after he made a false charge publicly on television against an unnamed official of the New York City government. . . .''

It is true that Cook was discharged from The *World Telegram & Sun* in 1959 under clouded circumstances. He and another *Telegram* reporter, Eugene Gleason, had prepared a report on slum clearance mismanagement. During the preparation of the article, Gleason told Cook that he had been offered a bribe by a city official, and Cook repeated the story in a television interview. The next day, Gleason admitted to the District Attorney that he had fabricated most of the bribe story, and both men were fired from The *Telegram*. Cook always claimed that he was a victim of Gleason's bravado and eventually obtained a letter from Manhattan District Attorney Frank Hogan exonerating him of any responsibility for the false accusations made on the television program.

The imprecision of Billy James Hargis's statements about Cook made him a choice target for the fairness doctrine effort, which continued even though election day had passed. Phillips and Democratic National Committee lawyers helped Cook to draft and mimeograph a letter demanding time to answer Hargis' ''scandalous and libelous attack,'' and they provided him with a detailed list of the stations that normally broadcast Hargis. Cook sent out 200 letters; about 50 of the stations agreed to air a reply. The response of WGCB in Red Lion, Pa., however, was uncompromising. It said flatly, ''Our rate card is enclosed. Your prompt reply will enable us to arrange for the time you may wish to purchase.''

The rest of the Red Lion drama was played out in the courts. Fred Cook turned to the F.C.C. for redress, and the agency directed WGCB to give him free reply time. The station's owner, the 82-year-old Rev. John M. Norris, declaring that ''the devil was loose in the F.C.C. corridors,'' decided to sue in the Court of Appeals in Washington, D.C., and lost. The court upheld the commission's right to order WGCB to provide Cook with free reply time. The F.C.C., emboldened by this favorable ruling, published a new set of rules ''to clarify and make more precise the obligations of broadcast licensees where they have aired personal attacks and editorials regarding political candidates.'' They specified that stations and networks must notify within a week all persons attacked during the discussion of an issue and offer them reply time. Failure to provide notification could result in the forfeiture of $1,000.

Then the case took a portentous turn. The larger community of broadcasters had been watching the Red Lion events with increasing anxiety, and they were hardly reassured by Mr. Norris's plans to take his case to the Supreme Court. They feared the curmudgeon from the hills of Pennsylvania would be routed in the Supreme Court, and that the resulting precedent could give the F.C.C. new legal muscle to implement the fairness doctrine.

The self-appointed champion of the industry's cause was W. Theodore Pierson, the *pro bono* legal counsel for the Radio-Television News Directors Association, an unincorporated group of some 1,000 news managers and editors of radio and television stations. He decided to mount an attack on the fairness doctrine that would be purposely separated from the embarrassing Red Lion case and designed to steal the spotlight from it. His plan was to fight the F.C.C.'s proposed personal-attack rules, an effort in which he was eventually joined by CBS and NBC.

Pierson brought a suit challenging the proposed rules in the Seventh Circuit Court of Appeals in Chicago, a court that, he believed, did not share the pro-F.C.C. leanings of the D.C. bench. He also retained Harvard law professor and former Solicitor General Archibald Cox to represent the broadcasters.

Pierson's strategy worked. In a unanimous opinion, the Chicago court struck down the F.C.C.'s rules on right of reply to personal attack as ''colliding with free-speech and free-press guarantees contained in the First Amendment. . . .'' The Washington and Chicago court tests had resulted in two diametrically opposed decisions on the constitutionality of the fairness doctrine. This conflict in the circuits insured that the Supreme Court would accept the appeal. The News Directors Association case was consolidated with the Red Lion case for a date in the highest court in the land.

In the Supreme Court, Red Lion's lawyer was Roger Robb, selected by Norris because he wanted ''a true believer, not one of those fancy-pants Eastern liberals.'' Robb relied heavily on First Amendment rhetoric. ''We submit,'' he argued, '' that the command of the First Amendment is that ''thou shalt not abridge [free speech]. And it is not 'You may abridge, but please try to keep it reasonable.'' For the industry, Archibald Cox argued that the personal-attack rules could have a chilling effect even if they were never applied, a position that Solicitor General Erwin Griswold, representing the Government, quickly attacked as hypothetical.

In questioning the three lawyers, the Justices made it clear that their main concern was the matter of access—whether the First Amendment should mean that broadcasters can use their own right of free expression in order to limit the free expression of others. Justice White asked if the Government that gave franchises to radio stations ought not "to be able to require that they let somebody else into the facility now and then when there is good reason to do so." And Justice Black asked if "there would be no relief that the man could get from the radio station that permitted him to be personally attacked."

Cox attempted to answer that the vision of "the insulated listener that the commission hypothesizes" had been proved unrealistic. Broadcasting, he argued, with its multitude of outlets and its complementary relationship to other news media, has given the public greater means to communicate, not less.

But the seven participating Justices (William O. Douglas was ill, and before the decision, Abe Fortas, in the midst of his own troubles, recused himself) sided with the Government. In a unanimous ruling in June of 1969 they upheld the right of the F.C.C. to order Red Lion to grant Fred Cook reply time, and they reversed the Chicago Seventh Circuit Court opinion that the personal-attack rules were in violation of the First Amendment. The Court did acknowledge that the First Amendment was not irrelevant to broadcasting and noted that "Congress . . .forbids F.C.C. interference with the right of free speech by means of radio communication." But the opinion proclaimed "that it is the right of the viewers and listeners, not the right of the broadcaster, which is paramount."

Justice Byron White, writing for the unanimous Court, stated: "There is nothing in the First Amendment which prevents the Government from requiring a licensee to share his frequency with others and to conduct himself as a proxy or fiduciary with obligations to present those views and voices which are representative of his community and which would otherwise, by necessity, be barred from the airwaves."

Mr. Norris and the broadcasting community were finally undone. Norris sent Fred Cook a letter offering him 15 minutes of air time at no cost. Cook responded by thanking Norris for the offer but declined to accept it. "I cannot see much point at this date in raking up and rehashing the entire episode. . . ." Cook says he did not know the case had gone to the Supreme Court until a local newspaper notified him of the decision.

The Red Lion decision was hailed at the F.C.C as a "cardinal teaching," solidifying the fairness doctrine into law. At last the vague policy based on the fuzzy notion that the Government ought to have some power beyond the traditional libel laws to keep broadcasters from behaving irresponsibly had received the sanction of the highest court in the land. And what was more, the Court had used its understanding of the doctrine to intervene directly in one station's programing—it did not simply tell the Red Lion station that it must be fair to Fred Cook; it ordered it to grant him free time to broadcast on its station. The fallout from the decision did

*The fairness doctrine, the Court decided in another historic case, could not be applied to such broadcasts. That case involved a suit by Business Executives Move for Peace, an antiwar group that had been denied the right to purchase one-minute spots on WTOP, Washing-

not take long to appear. Shortly after the opinion was handed down, the F.C.C decided for the first time to take away a radio station's license for its "failure to comply with the fairness doctrine . . ." as well as its failure to inform the commission of its program plans. The station was WXUR in Media, Pa., owned by the ultraright Rev. Carl McIntire. (In a dissent to the Court of Appeals decision upholding the F.C.C. ruling, Judge David Bazelon protested that the license removal was like "going after gnats with a sledgehammer.")

But there was also a more subtle and more important result: The Red Lion decision had been read as definitely affirming that the First Amendment could not be considered an absolute guarantee of free speech as far as broadcasters were concerned; the broadcasters' rights under the First Amendment were to be balanced by the rights of viewers and listeners.

This was no small matter, for in this pre-Watergate, Vietnam-racked period, the Nixon White House was seeking systematically to politicize broadcasting. A Supreme Court decision that could be construed as the opening wedge for Government involvement in decisions of content on a broadcast-by-broadcast basis meshed with the aspirations of the Nixon Administration.

There is evidence, furthermore, that major broadcasters were in fact inhibited by the Government during this period. They granted Richard Nixon more free air time than any President had ever sought before to announce and explain his programs. And with few exceptions, they acquiesced in the demand of the White House that views too critical of the President and his policies be kept off the air—when, for example, the Democratic National Committee sought to purchase reply time to the President.

This reaction, of course, was more a matter of politics than of written law, and with the Watergate scandals, the politics would shift in such a way that broadcasters, along with journalists, would find themselves less on the defensive. But before that happened another case entered the courts, this time at the insistence of a group with a rightist orientation. The case threatened to tighten by another notch the Government's potential fairness doctrine power over broadcasters.

The broadcast involved was a far more substantial item than a $7.50 episode of the Christian Crusade. Entitled "Pensions: The Broken Promise," it was a major network documentary on corporate pension plans and how they often fail to keep faith with the workers they are supposed to benefit. It was broadcast on Sept. 12, 1972, over 175 stations of the NBC network.

In one of the strange coincidences of fairness doctrine history, NBC's interest in the idea that workers were not receiving their due from pension plans had been stimulated in part by an article in The *New York Times Magazine,* which happened to be written by freelance writer Fred J. Cook.

The pensions broadcast captured the poignancy of aging workers who described, often in moving, graphic detail, first-hand experiences of pension plan abuse. It also included a number of interviews with U.S. Senators and authorities involved with pension-plan reform. There were some fleeting interviews with defenders of pension plans, including an executive representing the National Association of Manufacturers. Strictly on professional grounds, the documentary might be

ton. In a strange coalition of Justices as diverse as Burger and Douglas, the Supreme Court agreed that "editing is for editors" and broadcasters could not be ordered to sell time to political activists. For different reasons, the Nixon Administration and the networks rejoiced in the decision.

The F.C.C. has also ruled on the fairness questions raised by paid commercials. In 1966, acting on a complaint of a 23-year-old Columbia Law School graduate, John F. Banzhaf III, the commission ruled that radio and television stations were required to provide some response time to cigarette advertising. By 1969, antismoking commercials had proved themselves effective, and Congress, in an act of pragmatic statesmanship, passed the Public Health Act of 1969, which ordered all cigarette advertising off the air.

In 1970, Friends of the Earth, an environmental group, complained that the NBC station in New York was airing automobile commercials that promoted the sale of cars using high-octane gasoline. After prodding from the court, NBC and Friends of the Earth entered into a "secret" agreement that provided for some 120 antipollution commercials to be aired. Since then, the F.C.C. has ruled that the fairness doctrine is not applicable to the ordinary commercial that simply promotes the sale of a product.

faulted for not having included a brief example of a pension plan that worked. Such a portrayal would have heightened the contrast with those with fail. However, the narrator of the program, Edwin Newman, purposely prefaced his final summary with a disclaimer: "... we don't want to give the impression that there are no good private pension plans. There are many good ones, and there are many people for whom the promise has become a reality."

But there was no attempt by NBC to create a stopwatch balance. Producer David Schmerler and his executive producer, Eliot Frankel, had been aroused and offended by the pension abuses uncovered by their research and that of a Senate labor committee. Schmerler says: "What we were doing was building an emotional program out of people who felt they had been terribly wronged." And although "Pensions: The Broken Promise" received an American Bar Association gavel and the George Foster Peabody Award, among others, it also was credited with stimulating the sweeping remedial action that Congress applied to the problem in a 1974 pension reform law.

The praise was not universal, however. A Los Angeles actuary, Richard Solomon, felt the program had unfairly represented his profession and helped persuade a group called Accuracy In Media, Inc. (AIM) to file a formal complaint with the F.C.C. demanding reply time for the pension-plan industry. AIM's membership includes many names generally associated with the right-wing view of the press (Abraham H. Kalish, Marine Corps Gen. Lewis W. Walt, Eugene Lyons and Morris L. Ernst) though its founders and original directors included some moderates (Dean Acheson, Dr. Harry Gideonse and Edgar Ansel Mowrer). The identities of all of AIM's financial backers are not revealed, although knowledgeable sources will confirm that one wealthy individual who made a major contribution to the group was Shelby Cullom Davis, a major contributor to Nixon's campaigns who eventually was appointed Ambassador to Switzerland by the former President. AIM's largest contributor, a wealthy Connecticut industrialist, refuses to be identified.

AIM charged that the documentary presented a "grotesquely distorted picture of the private pension system in the United States...giving the impression that failure and fraud are the rule." It accused NBC of presenting "a one-sided, uninformative, emotion-evoking pitch." The intent of the action was to get the F.C.C. to order the network to schedule additional coverage of the pensions question to correct the "deliberately distorted" presentation.

The F.C.C. rejected AIM's allegation of distortion, but did hold that NBC had violated the fairness doctrine. And, mindful, no doubt, that the Supreme Court in its Red Lion decision, had recognized that the Government could use the fairness doctrine to justify a specific order relating to program content, the agency ordered the network to broadcast balancing material. For years the F.C.C. had refused demands by irate groups to second-guess the fairness of such documentaries as "Biography of a Bookie Joint," "City of Newburgh," "Harvest of Shame" and "The Selling of the Pentagon," and Chairman Burch had previously pledged that the agency would continue to do so. This, then, was the first time the F.C.C. had found a network television documentary in violation of the fairness doctrine. NBC, which might have complied with the commission's order by scheduling a follow-up report on the Today Show or the NBC Nightly News, refused, and instead entered an appeal with the Court of Appeals for the District of Columbia.

NBC's defense, argued in court on Feb. 21, 1974, by Floyd Abrams, the 37-year-old attorney who had worked with Alexander Bickel representing The *New York Times* in the Pentagon Papers case, was that the fairness doctrine had been misapplied. The network's position was that the commission's decision constituted an impermissible intrusion into matters of news discretion. The documentary, the network contended, did not fall under the purview of the fairness doctrine because its topic, abuses in pension plans, was not in itself a controversial issue of public importance. Had the program been about the overall performance of pension plans, good and bad, the network said, then the fairness doctrine would have applied: in that case the question would have been, does America's pension system work successfully? And it would have framed a truly controversial issue. But the existence of abuses in pension plans is a matter of fact, and the network argued, not controversial. NBC reinforced this point by asserting that the documentary recommended no remedial course of conduct other than to suggest that individuals check their own plans to see if they are being treated well; had the program endorsed specific measures to reform pension practices, it would have become controversial.

In response, the F.C.C. conceded that the program did treat the subject of some abuses, but argued that NBC was unreasonable in denying that it had not also presented viewpoints on the issue raised by AIM—the over-all performance of the private pension system considered as a whole. In sum, the F.C.C's position seemed to be that while a network's journalistic judgment should be given the widest possible latitude, it could be challenged under the fairness doctrine in cases where editing seemed unbalanced to an unreasonable degree. In effect, the agency held that the Government could serve as a super editor of last resort.

John Pettit, general counsel of the F.C.C., suggested that NBC may not have fully understood what the F.C.C. and the Supreme Court required in the seeking out of reasonable opportunity for opposing views, and recalled the Red Lion language stating the licensee's responsibility to "conduct himself as a proxy or fiduciary with obligations to present those views and voices which are representative of his community and which would otherwise, by necessity, be barred from the airwaves."

Because of the urgency of the case, the court had dispensed with formal briefs, therefore, the oral arguments were decisive far beyond their usual impact. In his quiet way, Floyd Abrams had hit hard at what he called the F.C.C.'s misuse of the fairness doctrine and wasted little time on the customary First Amendment rhetoric. When the court handed down its decision, in the fall of 1974, two of the three judges identified themselves with the NBC argument about the misapplication of the fairness doctrine, and "Since we reverse on [that] ground, we have no occasion to consider [First Amendment] arguments," which had been the central core of Red Lion and most other fairness-doctrine appeals.

Six months later, on March 18, the full court issued a ruling upholding its three-man panel and though AIM said it planned to take the case to the Supreme

Court, it appeared that NBC and Floyd Abrams had won a decisive round. Among broadcasters, there was a sense of relief. For if the decision had gone the other way, the court would have legitimized the idea that the Government could in effect substitute its judgment for that of the network as to what issue was involved in a broadcast documentary and order that more air time be given to elements that the journalist never thought central to the story. This, the broadcasters feel, would genuinely restrict their efforts at investigative reporting. It would mean that every assertion of wrongdoing by persons or groups would have to be balanced with an equal statement of their claims to innocence—however unbelievable they might be. The result would be confusion and, more often than not, outright misinformation. In addition, the broadcasters feared, a decision for the Government would make it difficult to air any program that took a point of view.

These fears have been allayed for the time being, however, and we are left to ponder the larger implications of these cases. The first is simply that high-minded principles of regulation are tricky, even dangerous, to administer in a society of powerful competing interests, and all of the parties involved—the executive, the broadcasters, the courts and the public—need to understand the process more completely than they do now.

As we have seen, the Supreme Court decision in the Red Lion case was based on questions of personal attack and access, on the idea that a broadcast licensee has "obligations to present those views and voices which are representative of his community and which would otherwise, by necessity be barred from the airwaves." Thus, Red Lion was, above all else, the enabling act of the fairness doctrine. The decision transformed an ethic of fairness into a rigid law proposed by the F.C.C. and enacted by the judiciary. This decision became a major prop for the Government's position in the pensions case.

And yet the assumption that the problem in the Red Lion case was access for Fred Cook's views is, in light of what we know today, demonstrably false. Fred Cook with his *Nation* magazine attack on Hargis and other "Hate Clubs of the Air," and his subsidized book against Goldwater, was hardly a classical case of a man in need of access. And though the Court did not know it when it heard the case, his motivation for taking action against the Red Lion station was not just to gain access to the public air waves in order to defend himself against an attack so much as it was the product of a carefully orchestrated program initiated by politicians to inhibit views they believed to be harmful to the country, as well as to their own political fortunes.

In the pensions case, which grew out of another era of high-level Government hostility to broadcasters, the Red Lion precedent served to bolster the Government's position that it had a right to broad influence (over) broadcast content, a claim that may or may not have been laid to rest by the Court of Appeals for the District of Columbia. Indeed, after the court's most recent ruling, an official of the F.C.C. was quoted as saying, "The fairness doctrine is alive and well," and it remained clear that the basic dispute is far from settled. The crucial test will apparently have to wait until another television or radio case works its circuitous course from the newsroom through the regulatory agency to the high court.

In light of all this, it is tempting to say that the fairness doctrine should be abolished—any regulatory principal so susceptible to political abuse is clearly a threat to free speech. And in fact, some powerful broadcasters want the Government totally out of broadcast journalism, and they cite the 1974 landmark First Amendment case that applies to newspapers—*Tornillo v. The Miami Herald*, in which the Supreme Court decided "it has yet to be demonstrated how Government regulation in this crucial [editing] process can be exercised consistent with First Amendment guarantees of a free press." During the arguments Justice Harry Blackmun made an observation that was as relevant to *Red Lion* as it was to *Tornillo*. "In this country, for better or worse, we have opted for a free press, not fair debate."

And yet, many serious observers of the broadcast industry are apprehensive about the removal of all requirements for responsibility on the part of broadcasters. Most agree that in the case of WLBT in Jackson, Miss., the decision of the F.C.C to withdraw the station's license was justified—over a long period of time, the station had shown itself to be grossly unfair to the black people in its community. Furthermore, the power of the major broadcasters is so awesome, that the thought of their exerting it totally unchecked is hard to accept. One need only ponder the fact that not too long ago the International Telephone & Telegraph Corporation was seriously interested in purchasing one of the major networks to understand the possible danger of unregulated broadcasting.

The real lesson to be learned from studying these cases is that the Government seems to have lost its sense of priorities in applying the fairness doctrine. It is the second requirement of the doctrine that broadcasters should "afford reasonable opportunities for opposing viewpoints." The first requirement is "to devote a reasonable amount of broadcasting time to the discussion of controversial issues." It is the breach of that first obligation that should be considered decisive; concern for opposing views should not be emphasized to the extent that coherent discussion of controversial subjects becomes inhibited.

The basic issue is whether the Government will encourage or discourage broadcasters from the probing, hard-hitting journalism that their financial interests resist but the public interest demands. In this sense, the proper definition of the fairness doctrine will influence the essential quality of broadcast programing.

In the resolution of the contradictions between the fairness doctrine and the First Amendment, between *Red Lion* and *Tornillo*, rests the base of the American system of broadcast journalism so vital—now more than ever—to the proper functioning of our democratic process.

Bibliography

Some broadcasters believe the Fairness Doctrine is unconstitutional; others want it repealed because they don't want to be bothered with the demands of community groups desiring more access. Other persons, although believing the rules don't work as intended, fight repeal because they fear the corporate power of the networks will only increase over the years. The debate is endless and Friendly's article gives it the neccessary background. See other articles in this book which deal with the access problem and *Issues in Broadcasting* (Mayfield, 1975), co-edited by Ted Curtis Smythe and George A. Mastroianni, which contains several pieces, including Tracy A. Westen's *"Fair Play on the Air,"* originally published in (MORE), January, 1972. Also valuable are Harry S. Ashmore's *Fear in the Air: Broadcasting and the First Amendment–the Anatomy of a Constitutional Crisis*, (Norton, 1973) and *The Center Magazine* issue of May/June, 1973. The legal citation for the Supreme Court decision which upheld the Fairness Doctrine is *Red Lion Broadcasting Co. vs. FCC,* 395 U.S. 367, 89 S. Ct., 1794 (1969).

Journalism in Government

By Joseph P. Lyford

Joseph P. Lyford teaches in the Graduate School of Journalism at the University of California, Berkeley. His article originally appeared in *The Center Magazine,* the publication of the Center for the Study of Democratic Institutions, Santa Barbara, Calif. (July/August, 1974) and is used with the Center's permission.

In Harry Truman's free-wheeling recollections, as recorded by Merle Miller in *Plain Speaking*, one recurring theme was his old-fashioned and rather appealing distrust of designated experts. He was the last President, it seems, who was always on guard against the generals, officials, and bright young men in whom his successors were to place such unqualified trust. But it was experts as a caste he suspected rather than expertise. When, through trial and error, he discovered men with a special wisdom, like George Marshall and Dean Acheson, he exploited them unmercifully.

On the reverse side of Truman's skepticism of titled authorities was a belief in the mental and moral competence of the people—that is, provided they were dealt with honestly by their leaders. He shared Lincoln's "patient confidence in the ultimate justice of the people." Like Lincoln, he spoke in simple unequivocal language, as if he were addressing his neighbors down the street in Independence, Missouri.

If Truman's approach seems a trifle archaic now, when public attitudes are thought to be nothing more than the by-product of media campaigns, it paid off at a time when politicians and television scarcely knew each other, and when McCarthyism had only just begun to pollute the public discourse. The people not only elected Truman to a second term in the White House, they also displayed a great reluctance to abandon their personal trust in him after his Administration came under attack for alleged corruption and softness on Communism. And, cynics to the contrary, Truman's confidence in the people's common sense was not misplaced. As George Gallup observed in the Center's American Character interview series a few years later: "We have accumulated a mountain of evidence by now on how the American people actually felt about all the major issues of the last twenty years. . . . Looking back . . . it is possible to say that the judgment of the people has often been wiser than the judgment of Congress, or even of the experts."

Truman distrusted the expert caste because he had little confidence in the quality of the information on which they depended. As an elite, the caste also displayed what Truman considered a "Hahvud" disdain for the sort of personal dialogue with the public with meant so much to him. Because of his low regard for the news sources of the designated experts, in or out of government, he decided to set up his own reporting "bureau" in 1948 when all the Washington insiders were predicting that Tom Dewey would beat him. In this case, the bureau was his friend Leslie Biffle, sergeant-at-arms of the Senate. Disguised as a chicken peddler, Biffle toured the hinterlands in a pickup truck, talked to everyone, and returned to tell the President he had nothing to worry about in the 1948 campaign. Biffle was right, and it simply confirmed what the President had felt all along: that if a man hung out his shingle as an expert, there was a good chance he didn't know what he was talking about.

It is unfortunate that Truman's biographers never questioned him closely on his reasons for distrusting the traditional sources of eastern wisdom, or on his ideas about journalism. For, in a sense, his experience qualified him as a muckraker of sorts who very early in the political game learned the difference between official and unofficial truths, and realized the danger of taking the assurances of even his political allies at face value. He had the instincts of a good reporter, unwilling in critical situations to put all his faith in intermediaries, seeking, rather, to put himself in personal touch with people and events. These were habits he cultivated first as an inquisitive county judge and then later as chairman of a Senate Committee to Investigate National Defense. With that background he might have provided us with a perceptive, prophetic critique of parochial, in-house government-information systems and the people who run them. But although Truman was aware of these deficiencies he did little to correct or expose them, and this made it easier for later Presidents to build up the illusion of an omniscient executive branch deriving its knowledge from a network of secret and infallible informants.

Much is now being written about how administrations after Truman misrepresented important issues, how they lied and concealed information almost as a matter of course. What is not being stressed is that not all the deception was deliberate. While Presidents were misleading the public, they and their designated experts were being systematically misinformed by their own intelligence and information-gathering apparatus. Once the apparatus had been enlisted by the executive branch to support its public propaganda activities, it took on a life of its own and victimized its inventors. Because of his Army-inspired reverence for the staff system and official channels, President Eisenhower was an especially easy target for an information and intelligence setup which had been conditioned to provide facts to fit policies already adopted at the top. This dependence on doctored information and in-house expertise, protected from cross-examination by representatives of the public, continued in the Kennedy, Johnson, and Nixon Administrations; and it was accompanied by an intensified arrogance toward Congress and the press. Any differences of opinion within the house of the Chief Executive were muffled because dissenters were reluctant to reveal their views. The appearance of a united front of experts on Vietnam policy in the Kennedy Administration, for instance, was made possible because George Ball kept his opposition to the policy within the White House family.

In this situation, the public began to be convinced, at least partly, that, since everything that was important was either secret or terribly complicated or both, it was in no position to review or question Presidential proposals or actions. The theory of the public's incompetence was the assumption underlying George Kennan's attack on the feasibility of democratic control of foreign policy. It was this assumption that later accounted for the supercilious attitude of Presidential science advisers toward public protest against continued atmospheric tests of nuclear bombs, even though the protesters included distinguished scientists outside the government. The clandestine commitment of Eisenhower and Kennedy to an invasion of the Bay of Pigs illustrates how far our national leadership, secure in its own superior wisdom, had gone in denying the public any participation in decisions about Cuban policy.

Once the ideal of the dialogue between the governors and the governed had gone out of style, it seemed perfectly logical for the executive branch to try to eliminate criticism from outside amateurs by classifying more and more information, and by injecting heavier doses of ''supernews'' into the news media. This process was accompanied internally by an accelerating decay of the government's information systems. Pressure was increased on the systems to provide data to support ''company policy.'' A good example of the results were the optimistic tales about the success of the pacification program which intelligence experts relayed from Saigon. The most spectacular instance of false intelligence being concocted on order was the account of the Gulf of Tonkin incident fabricated by the Defense Department and relayed to the President and the press, an account used to secure the unwitting approval of the Senate for President Johnson's personal declaration of war against North Vietnam.

Johnson was one of a long line of Chief Executives who was hoodwinked by his experts and intelligence operatives. Lincoln had his own reasons for distrusting the whole lot. During the darkest days of the Civil War he not only had to contend with the imperfect counsels of General McClellan, he was also afflicted with Allan Pinkerton, detective, (yes, the original) who, as the Union's master spy, consistently overestimated Confederate troop strength by two or three hundred per cent. President Kennedy also suffered, not always in silence. After the Bay of Pigs fiasco, planned on the basis of faulty intelligence on popular attitudes about Castro in Cuba, he remarked to a newspaperman that, if only the press had fully exposed the invasion plan beforehand, adverse public reaction might have forced its cancellation. Perhaps this was a roundabout way of saying that an informed public might have saved him from his own advisers.

In the wake of Vietnam and Watergate, with the myth of the omniscient Presidency in decline, the question arises as to how we get out of a situation in which we are constantly being confronted by unforeseen crises about which we possess so little vital information. How can government better educate itself and speak more openly and informally to the people? Some obvious steps toward the goal would include drastic limitations on what information can be classified and the dismantling of much of the government's propaganda apparatus. But these changes by themselves would not amount to much without a thorough-going reform of the procedures by which the executive branch collects, evaluates, and disseminates information intended for internal use and on which—under more open administrations—the President and his Cabinet base their conversations with the press.

A key part of such a reform could be the establishment of a corps of highly qualified professional journalists inside the executive branch, who would be responsible for providing federal agencies with objective and sophisticated reporting from the field. The information gathered by these journalists-in-government ought to be made available also to the press as long as it does not fall within the area of national security, narrowly defined. To attract the best journalists, the government should offer salaries competitive with the private media and guarantee them protection from political meddling from any direction, possibly by giving them civil-service status. Eventually this group of journalists-in-government could constitute a continuous reporting service that would displace many of the present poorly trained information-gathering personnel. At the very least, the journalists could provide an alternative to existing systems within the government.

What are these existing information-gathering systems? If they can be categorized at all, they seem to fall into three types: publicity and propaganda ("public information"); field reporting for internal use; and intelligence.

Public information includes the whole range of government contacts with the mass media, nongovernmental institutions, inquisitive citizens, and their elected representatives. Officially the multi-multimillion-dollar public-information program is supposed to educate the public, provide a public account of the government's behavior, and supply data on problems with which the agencies deal. However, the public information system has served mainly as a device for withholding information, protecting officials, and obscuring the origin of bureaucratic decisions. The system also standardizes governmental responses to the news media at all levels of the bureaucracy. The Nixon Administration has augmented its policy of news suppression by placing severe restraints on contacts between lower echelon officials and the press, the idea being that there is less chance of embarrassing disclosures if the initiation of all press contacts is controlled by the White House. The President has also sought to inhibit conversations between government and the press by placing wiretaps on reporters and on bureaucrats suspected of unauthorized disclosures, and by introducing a bill in the Senate which would impose heavy fines and jail sentences on reporters and officials involved in the transmission and publication of classified government material, no matter how innocuous that material may be.

A second category of information activity in the executive branch is the field-reporting systems which supply political, economic, and social data to professional staff in the middle and upper levels of the bureaucracy. However, many agencies—in the regulatory field, for instance—have no field-reporting service of their own; consequently they depend heavily on information supplied by the private interests whom they are supposed to regulate. One obvious example of such an agency is the Federal Communications Commission, which leans on the broadcasting industry for its guidance. In evaluating the public service record of a TV or radio licensee, the F.C.C. ought to have some pretty good information on how the people in a community feel about the licensee's operations; but it has no independent reporting service. So in most cases the F.C.C. has no idea what the public thinks, and even when a license renewal is being contested, the hearings are usually monopolized by special-interest groups competing for the license. Likewise, when a major debate on communications policy is underway, the protagonists are commercial competitors. Rarely are the views of the unorganized, unfinanced, and nebulous public heard in such controversies.

The government also tends to rely on secondary, prejudiced sources when it appoints commissions of private citizens to do its reporting for it. Despite the appearance of public participation, the interests of the institutions under investigation often dominate and subvert the inquiries. When, for example, the Surgeon General's Advisory Committee looked into the effects of televised violence on child behavior in 1969, the broadcasting industry was able to veto several possible nominees for the Committee, and it secured several places on that body for its own people. As a result, the Committee's report in 1972 watered down the findings of laboratory studies conducted by the National Institute of Mental Health.

The bulk of the output of the government's field reporting activity appears to move laterally in the lower reaches of the bureaucracy, like water moving along a rock ledge. Only infrequently does it rise to the top. Political appointees who head federal agencies do not like to be bothered with the "news" that comes in over these bureaucratic wires, especially if the signals do not harmonize with administration policy. This division of federal agencies into separate, noncommunicating lobes has its parallel in some large private corporations. In most of the timber and paper industries, for instance, company policy is set in boardrooms hundreds of miles, mentally and physically, from their field operations, often with results that are not only unhealthy for the company but disastrous for the localities affected. An exception is the Weyerhaeuser Company, headquartered in Tacoma, in the midst of its operations. Weyerhaeuser's policies are described by forestry experts as the most enlightened in the industry.

Among the witnesses to this fact of bureaucratic life—i.e., the discrepancy between what is presumed to be true at the top and what is perceived as actually true at the bottom—are journalists who have studied the action in the streets and ghettos, in welfare agencies and municipal hospitals, on battlefields and in Asian hamlets, in farm communities and Indian reservations, etc. They know that contradictions between what is presumed and what is perceived are inevitable when the information going to the authorities is filtered through subordinates whose jobs depend on the rosiest estimates of the programs they are appointed to administer.

The third type of government information activity is the discovery and interpretation of information of a "sensitive" nature, the collection of intelligence. The distinction between sensitive and nonsensitive material is vague because much of the information gathered by military intelligence—such as data on political repression in South Vietnam—does not involve national security, even though it is collected by a defense agency. Further complicating the matter is the fact that there is a considerable body of information which the government can justifiably classify, if temporarily, even though it does not relate to defense, diplomatic negotiations in progress, or law enforcement. An example of such information might be the results of incomplete tests of a new drug being conducted by the Food and Drug Administration.

In view of the wide variety of subjects with which intelligence agencies deal today, it is unfortunate that they are dominated by people who still believe that secret agents are going to save the world. Effective intelligence operations ought to involve more than the swiping of enemy secrets. What is needed are good journalists who can see the political or social aspects of a military, law enforcement, or diplomatic problem; and fewer house detectives who can't. And far more information gathered by intelligence agencies ought to be unclassified; it should be available to Congress and the public.

These three categories of government information activity are only approximations. A specific agency's information setup is determined by its history, mission, leadership, and personnel. No two agencies are alike, either in how they instruct themselves or in how they relate to the public. Also, because of the uncommunicative nature of most career bureaucrats, there has to be some guesswork about how they get and use information. But I have discussed these descriptions of the present system with several dozen federal administrators, and they have acknowledged that they are realistic. Their reaction is, what can be done about it? Several have expressed interest and some skepticism in the idea of putting journalists to work in their agencies. Then comes the question: What kind of journalists are you talking about? How would such journalists survive as professionals inside the system?

Any attempt to persuade federal bureaucrats or media people of the value of journalists in government runs into one big roadblock right at the start: their assumption that it is impossible for a journalist to go into government without being automatically transformed into a public-relations man. The record so far sustains that assumption, but the record can be changed. Other professional people— lawyers, doctors, scientists, engineers—can work in politically sensitive government positions without compromising their professional standards. There is no reason why journalists cannot perform, *as journalists*, if given the opportunity. They would be far removed from the "supernews" business. In order to bring their agencies into touch with more of the facts of life, the journalists would work in the field; check theories, pronouncements, and documents against what they could observe at first hand; and relay back to their agencies the comprehensive, accurate reports on which sensible policies could be based. The loyalty of these journalists would be to the best standards of their profession, not to some officious bureaucrat.

If a reporter is tough and skillful enough to do his or her job on a daily newspaper without being browbeaten by a publisher, he or she can work without being pushed around by a government agency head. The government journalist ought to have the same qualities that a managing editor looks for in a correspondent: energy, initiative, ingenuity, a quizzical temperament, and an ability to write in clear, direct language. He should be an investigator, not a recorder, and be familiar with the methods of other reporting professions such as the law and the social sciences. He should know when and how to use the knowledge of specialists, to spot the genuine article, and to know when a specialist is sticking to his subject and when he is simply voicing his own political opinions. He ought to have developed a sensitivity to what might happen, as well as what is going on at the moment; a feeling for trends and situations not signaled by a specified event. He should be as interested in discovering questions as in finding the answers.

Some of the journalists would need special education in such matters as the environment, housing, race, agriculture, urban redevelopment, defense, foreign affairs, land use. But it would be better if most of them were generalists, able to handle varied assignments when given the time to prepare themselves. They should be able to analyze the significance of community controversies, to conduct attitude surveys ("precision journalism," Philip Meyer calls it), and gain the confidence of the people they interview, no matter what their ethnic or social background.

If these seem like stiff requirements, there are journalists who can meet them, and more would be available if openings in government journalism were in prospect for the many gifted students who now go into law, teaching, and the social sciences because of the scarcity or unattractiveness of jobs in the commerical news media.

It will be argued that the task of reporting and interpreting complicated highly technical subjects should not be left to generalists. And of course they shouldn't, not entirely. But the generalist is badly needed today in a government teeming with specialists. Like the general practitioner in medicine, he has access to technicians and specialists when he needs them. What is important is that the journalist be wise enough to understand the implications of what he observes and to recognize his own limitations—and this is where the specialist is often weak. The narrow field of vision of so many experts in the State and Defense Departments is one reason why their reporting over the past decade has had so many blank spots and has sometimes been inferior to that of our better press correspondents. The Department of Justice is another agency that is handicapped by poor eyesight. It would have better understood the conditions on our campuses and in our ghettos in the nineteen-sixties if it had used "storefront reporters" (journalists who spend a lot of their time in the neighborhoods and on the streets before, during, and after turning in their stories) instead of F.B.I. agents as information sources. Even in crime situations good journalism has often shown its superiority to police work, cases in point being the press exposure of false accusations in the Wylie-Hoffert murders in New York, and the work of local reporters in the Patty Hearst kidnaping case in San Francisco. (At least one reporter, Tim Findley of the San Francisco *Chronicle*, had information on the case well ahead of the F.B.I., although his newspaper sat on the material for weeks, according to Findley, who has since quit the *Chronicle*.)

In my own exchanges with federal officials I have frequently been told that government journalists operating alongside traditional government intelligence and information systems would create severe tensions and rivalries. The journalists would be quickly looked upon as "Inspector Generals," in other words, intra-agency tattletales. This apprehension is based on a misconception. In this case the government journalists would be reporting from the field, outside the bureaucratic structure. As long as the bureaucrats refrained from meddling in the reporter's work there is no reason why they should not be able to get along with each other. Of course the presence of the journalists could create some tension, if, as seems likely, their reporting were used as a yardstick against which information from other government sources would be measured. However, tension growing out of that kind of competition is not undesirable.

Objections to the idea of government journalists will also come from publishers and editors who will see such a proposal as the forerunner of a government press. Curiously enough, this charge is likely to come from the same media people who have accommodated themselves rather comfortably to the present situation in which the news media are manipulated, if not at times co-opted, by the "super-news" factories. The fact is that we already have a government press. And why not? The First Amendment does not grant the private media exclusive rights to gather and publish information. The difficulty is that the government press now puts out agitprop instead of information; as a result, both government officials who want to provide accurate data to the media and the media themselves suffer. Journalists functioning *as journalists* in government, by improving the quality and reliability of information circulated within agencies, could raise the credibility of what the agencies offer the media.

Admittedly this is hard to sell to anyone who regards as Holy Writ the proposition that objective journalism is the private preserve of newspapers and TV networks and that any reporter who accepts government employment is joining the prostitutes' union. Such people believe that the privately owned media are by nature honest and that the government is always lying. But even a cursory inspection of the history of American newspapers reveals that the government has never had a corner on flawed reporting or self-serving propaganda. Nor is it necessarily true that government cannot tolerate a truth-teller in its midst. A great deal of good literature and film about America, including James Agee's *Let Us Now Praise Famous Men* and Pare Lorentz's *The River*, has been produced with government support. More recent evidence that muckrakers and critics can survive, if uncomfortably, in government can be found in the work of such diverse persons as Rachel Carson, Janet Till (the F.D.A. doctor who exposed the thalidomide scandal), and Admiral Hyman Rickover. And, across the Atlantic, Great Britain has a state-supported broadcasting system that, even with the handicap of the Official Secrets Act under which the British media operate, does about as good a job in informing the public as our commercial networks.

In *The Artillery of the Press*, James Reston wrote that "it may be that news and the analysis of news in a democracy are too important to be left to newspapermen." He suggested that there are people in government, as well as in the universities, business, and the professions, whose insights ought to be given more regular attention by the news media. In using the word "newspapermen" rather than "journalists," Reston seemed to imply, whether he intended to or not, that it is the newspaper as an institution rather than the journalist as a professional that is unequal to the tasks of public enlightenment. Certainly the journalist, free from the limitations of an unenterprising newspaper, has continually used the resources Reston mentions and has provided the extradimensional *New Yorker* type of reporting-in-depth which is rarely found in newspapers other than *The New York Times*, the *Wall Street Journal*, the *Los Angeles Times*, and the *Washington Post*.

If news and its analysis are too important to be left to newsmen, one might also say that the gathering and analysis of news inside our government is too important to be left to civil servants and bureaucrats. If government is supposed to inform itself and explain itself, it is already in the reporting business, whether we like it or not. Therefore, it needs the professional journalist inside as well as outside the structure of government.

The question we must face is not whether government should have the power to educate, but how it uses that power and whether it can heal itself. It has not been ordained that the ineptitude and arrogance that have corroded the government's educational power must always be with us. The framers of the Constitution can hardly have envisioned the state as an enemy of the people. If we truly believe in the civilization of the dialogue, we cannot be resigned to the interruption of honest conversation between the governor and the governed.

Bibliography

Professor Lyford acknowledges in his article the arguments against his proposal. Yet he opens discussion about the miscommunication within official institutions which hinders effective government. Could Lyford's plan work on a local level? A student project might involve interviews with newspersons and government officials to gain their attitudes. For background see James E. Pollard, *The Presidents and the Press: Truman to Johnson* (Public Affairs Press, 1964), James B. Reston, *The Artillery of the Press* (Harper & Row, 1967) and David Halberstam, *The Best and the Brightest* (Random House, 1972), a classic story of miscommunication and misconceptions.

The Regular Use of Classified Information

By Max Frankel

Max Frankel, a *New York Times* editor, was chief of the paper's Washington bureau during the Pentagon Papers case of 1971 when he submitted an affidavit in U.S. District Court, excerpts from which explain the unique relationship of government documents and the flow of information.

The government's unprecedented challenge to the *Times* in the case of the Pentagon papers, I am convinced, cannot be understood, or decided, without an appreciation of the manner in which a small and specialized corps of reporters and a few hundred American officials regularly make use of so-called classified, secret and top-secret information and documentation. It is a cooperative, competitive, antagonistic and arcane relationship.

Without the use of "secrets" that I shall attempt to explain in this affidavit, there could be no adequate diplomatic, military and political reporting of the kind our people take for granted, either abroad or in Washington, and there could be no mature system of communication between the government and the people. That is one reason why the sudden complaint by one party to these regular dealings strikes us as monstrous and hypocritical—unless it is essentially perfunctory, for the purpose of retaining some discipline over the federal bureaucracy.

Presidents make "secret" decisions only to reveal them for the purposes of frightening an adversary nation, wooing a friendly electorate, protecting their reputations. The military services conduct "secret" research in weaponry only to reveal it for the purpose of enhancing their budgets, appearing superior or inferior to a foreign army, gaining the vote of a congressman or the favor of a contractor. High officials of the government reveal secrets in the search for support of their policies, or to help sabotage the plans and policies of rival departments. Middle-rank officials of government reveal secrets so as to attract the attention of their superiors or to lobby against the orders of those superiors. Though not the only vehicle for this traffic in secrets—the Congress is always eager to provide a forum—the press is probably the most important.

In the field of foreign affairs, only rarely does our government give full public information to the press for the direct purpose of simply informing the people. For the most part, the press obtains significant information bearing on foreign policy only because it has managed to make itself a party to confidential materials, and of value in transmitting these materials from government to other branches and offices of government as well as to the public at large. This is why the press has been wisely and correctly called the Fourth Branch of Government.

I turn now in an attempt to explain, from a reporter's point of view, the several ways in which "classified" information figures in our relations with government. The government's complaint against the *Times* in the present case comes with ill-grace because government itself has regularly and consistently, over the decades, violated the conditions it suddenly seeks to impose upon us—in three distinct ways:

First, it is our regular partner in the informal but customary traffic in secret information, without even the pretense of legal or formal "declassification." Presumably, many of the "secrets" I cited above, and all the "secret" documents and pieces of information that form the basis of the many newspaper stories that are attached hereto, remain "secret" in their official designation.

Second, the government and its officials regularly and customarily engage in a kind of *ad hoc, de facto* "declassification" that normally has no bearing whatever on considerations of the national interest. To promote a political, personal, bureaucratic or even commercial interest, incumbent officials and officials who return to civilian life are constantly revealing the secrets entrusted to them. They use them to barter with the Congress or the press, to curry favor with foreign governments and officials from whom they seek information in return. They use them freely, and with a startling record of impunity, in their memoirs and other writings.

Third, the government and its officials regularly and routinely misuse and abuse the "classification" of information, either by imposing secrecy where none is justified or by retaining it long after the justification has become invalid, for simple reasons of political or bureaucratic convenience. To hide mistakes of judgment, to protect reputations of individuals, to cover up the loss and waste of funds, almost

The Supreme Court upheld the right of newspapers to publish government documents detailing how the U.S. got into the Vietnam War, after a classic battle between lawyers for the papers and the government.

everything in government is kept secret for a time and, in the foreign policy field, classified as "secret" and "sensitive" beyond any rule of law or reason. Every minor official can testify to this fact.

Obviously, there is need for some secrecy in foreign and military affairs. Considerations of security and tactical flexibility require it, though usually for only brief periods of time.

But for the vast majority of "secrets," there has developed between the government and the press (and Congress) a rather simple rule of thumb. The government hides what it can, pleading necessity as long as it can, and the press pries out what it can, pleading a need and right to know.

Some of the best examples of the regular traffic I describe may be found in the Pentagon papers that the government asks us not to publish. The uses of top secret information by our government in deliberate leaks to the press for the purposes of influencing public opinion are recorded, cited and commented upon in several places of the study. Also cited and analyzed are numerous examples of how the government tried to control the release of such secret information so as to have it appear at a desired time, or in a desired publication, or in a deliberately loud or soft manner for maximum or minimum impact, as desired.

Bibliography

For the complete story of the Pentagon Papers case see Sanford J. Ungar's *The Papers and The Papers* (Dutton, 1972). Related to the discussion of reporters' use of information are shield laws and the Freedom of Information Act. See the index of the University of Missouri's *Freedom of Information Center Reports* for specific references.

11 The Problems of Television News

The Selection of Reality—

Lessons of a Living Room War—

Murrow—a Model for Broadcast Journalists—

The Selection of Reality

By Edward Jay Epstein

Each weekday evening, the three major television networks—the American Broadcasting Company, the Columbia Broadcasting System, and the National Broadcasting Company—feed filmed news stories over lines leased from the American Telephone & Telegraph Co. to the more than six hundred local stations affiliated with them, which, in turn, broadcast the stories over the public airwaves to a nationwide audience. The C.B.S. Evening News, which is broadcast by two hundred local stations, reaches some nineteen million viewers; the N.B.C. Nightly News, broadcast by two hundred and nine stations, some eighteen million viewers; and the A.B.C. Evening News, broadcast by a hundred and ninety-one stations, some fourteen million. News stories from these programs are recorded on videotape by most affiliates and used again, usually in truncated form, on local news programs late in the evening. Except for the news on the few unaffiliated stations and on the noncommercial stations, virtually all the filmed reports of national and world news seen on television are the product of the three network news organizations.

The process by which news is gathered, edited, and presented to the public is more or less similar at the three networks. A limited number of subjects—usually somewhere between twenty and thirty—are selected each day as possible film stories by news executives, producers, anchor men, and assignment editors, who base their choices principally on wire-service and newspaper reports. Camera crews are dispatched to capture these events on 16-mm. color film. The filming is supervised by either a field producer or a correspondent—or, in some cases, the cameraman himself. The film is then shipped to the network's headquarters in New York or to one of its major news bureaus—in Chicago, Los Angeles, or Washington—or, if time is an important consideration, processed and edited at the nearest available facilities and transmitted electronically to New York. Through editing and rearranging of the filmed scenes, a small fraction of the exposed film—usually less than ten per cent—is reconstructed into a story whose form is to some extent predetermined. Reuven Frank, until two months ago the president of N.B.C. News, has written:

> Every news story should, without any sacrifice of probity or responsibility, display the attributes of fiction, of drama. It should have structure and conflict, problem and denouement, rising action and falling action, a beginning, a middle and an end.

After the addition of a sound track, recorded at the event, the story is explained and pulled together by a narration, written by the correspondent who covered the event or by a writer in the network news offices. Finally, the story is integrated into the news program by the anchor man.

Network news organizations select not only the events that will be shown as national and world news on television but the way in which those events will be depicted. This necessarily involves choosing symbols that will have general meaning for a national audience. "The pucture is not a fact but a symbol," Reuven Frank once wrote. "The real child and its real crying become symbols of all children." In

Edward J. Epstein, a political scientist, is the media critic who earned his credentials with the much discussed book, *News From Nowhere: Television and the News.* His *Between Fact and Fiction: The Problem of Journalism* contains 10 of his essays. From *News From Nowhere,* by Edward Jay Epstein. Copyright © 1973 by Edward Jay Epstein. Reprinted by permission of Random House, Inc. Most of the material in this book originally appeared in *The New Yorker.*

the same way, a particular black may be used to symbolize the aspirations of his race, a particular student may be used to symbolize the claims of his generation, and a particular policeman may be used to symbolize the concept of authority. Whether the black chosen is a Black Panther or an integrationist, whether the student is a militant activist or a Young Republican, whether the policeman is engaged in a brutal or a benevolent act obviously affects the impression of the event received by the audience. When the same symbols are consistently used on television to depict the behavior and aspirations of groups, they become stable images—what Walter Lippmann, in his classic study ''Public Opinion,'' has called a ''repertory of sterotypes.'' These images obviously have great power; public-opinion polls show that television is the most believed source of news for most of the population. The director of C.B.S. News in Washington, William Small, has written about television news:

> When television covered its ''first war'' in Vietnam, it showed a terrible truth of war in a manner new to mass audiences. A case can be made, and certainly should be examined, that this was cardinal to the disillusionment of Americans with this war, the cynicism of many young people toward America, and the destruction of Lyndon Johnson's tenure of office. . . . When television examined a different kind of revolution, it was singularly effective in helping bring about the Black revolution.

And it would be difficult to dispute the claim of Reuven Frank that ''there are events which exist in the American mind and recollection primarily because they were reported on regular television news programs.''

How were those events selected to be shown on television, and who or what determined the way in which they were depicted? Vice-President Spiro Agnew believes the answer is that network news is shaped ''by a handful of men responsible only to their corporate employers,'' who have broad ''powers of choice'' and ''wield a free hand in selecting, presenting, and interpreting the great issues in our nation.'' Television executives and newsmen, on the other hand, often argue that television news is shaped not by men but by events—that news is news. Both of these analyses overlook the economic realities of network television, the effects of government regulation on broadcasting, and the organizational requirements of the network news operations, whose established routines and procedures tend to impose certain forms on television news stories.

David Brinkley, in an N.B.C. News special entitled ''From Here to the Seventies,'' reiterated a description of television news that is frequently offered by television newsmen:

> What television did in the sixties was to show the American people to the American people. . . . It did show the people, places and things they had not seen before. Some they liked, and some they did not. It was not that television produced or created any of it.

In this view, television news does no more than mirror reality. Thus, Leonard Goldenson, the chairman of the board of A.B.C., testified before the National Commission on the Causes and Prevention of Violence that complaints of news distortion were brought about by the fact that ''Americans are reluctant to accept the images reflected by the mirror we have held up to our society.'' Robert D. Kasmire, a vice-president of N.B.C., told the commission, ''There is no doubt that television is, to a large degree, a mirror of our society. It is also a mirror of public attitudes and preferences.'' The president of N.B.C., Julian Goodman, told the commission, ''In short, the medium is blamed for the message.'' Dr. Frank Stanton, vice-chairman and former president of C.B.S., testifying before a House committee, said, ''What the media do is to hold a mirror up to society and try to report it as faithfully as possible.'' Elmer Lower, the president of A.B.C. News, has described television news as ''the television mirror that reflects . . .across oceans and mountains,'' and added, ''Let us open the doors of the parliaments everywhere to the electronic mirrors.'' The imagery has been picked up by critics of television, too. Jack Gould, formerly of the *Times*, wrote of television's coverage of racial riots, ''Congress, one would hope, would not conduct an examination of a mirror because of the disquieting images that it beholds.''

The mirror analogy has considerable descriptive power, but it also leads to a number of serious misconceptions about the medium. The notion of a ''mirror of society'' implies that everything of significance that happens will be reflected on television news. Network news organizations, however, far from being ubiquitous and all-seeing, are limited newsgathering operations, which depend on camera crews based in only a few major cities for most of their national stories. Some network executives have advanced the idea that network news is the product of coverage by hundreds of affiliated stations, but the affiliates' contribution to the network news programs actually is very small. Most network news stories are assigned in advance to network news crews and correspondents, and in many cases whether or not an event is covered depends on where it occurs and the availability of network crews.

The mirror analogy also suggests immediacy: events are reflected instantaneously, as in a mirror. This notion of immediate reporting is reinforced by the way people in television news depict the process to the public. News executives sometimes say that, given the immediacy of television, the network organization has little opportunity to intervene in news decisions. Reuven Frank once declared, on a television program about television, ''News coverage generally happens too fast for anything like that to take place.'' But does it? Though it is true that elements of certain events, such as space exploration and political conventions, are broadcast live, virtually all of the regular newscasts, except for the commentator's ''lead-ins'' and ''tags'' to the news stories, are prerecorded on videotape or else on film, which must be transported, processed, edited, and projected before it can be seen. Some film stories are delayed from one day to two weeks, because of certain organizational needs and policies. Reuven Frank more or less outlined these policies on ''prepared,'' or delayed, news in a memorandum he wrote when he was executive producer of N.B.C.'s Nightly News program. ''Except for those rare days when other material becomes available,'' he wrote, ''the gap will be filled by planned and prepared film stories, and we are assuming the availability of two each night.'' These ''longer pieces,'' he continued, were to be ''planned, executed over a longer period of time than spot news, usable and relevant any time within, say, two weeks rather than that day, receptive to the more sophisticated techniques of production and editing, but journalism withal.'' The reason for delaying filmed stories, a network vice-president has explained, is that ''it gives the producer more control

David Brinkley (top, talking to student editors) worked with Chet Huntley for 14 years on NBC. Following Huntley's retirement Brinkley served as a "roaming commentator" and later joined John Chancellor (middle left) in the anchor position. Edwin Newman (middle right) continued as a leading correspondent. At ABC, Howard K. Smith, news analyst, and Harry Reasoner, anchorperson, (bottom left) were joined by Barbara Walters. The popular Frank Reynolds (bottom right) provided on-the-spot coverage.

Walter Cronkite, considered the "dean" of television newscasters, thought of himself as a "managing editor" and disputed the contention that television had a "star system." But like it or not "Uncle Walter" was the star of CBS, shown here preparing copy at his busy desk. Cronkite teamed for years with another "dean," commentator Eric Sevareid (middle) and correspondents like Dan Rather, Morley Safer and Mike Wallace of the "60 Minutes" show.

over his program." First, it gives the producer control of the budget, since shipping the film by plane, though it might mean a delay of a day or two, is considerably less expensive than transmitting the film electronically by satellite or A.T. & T. lines. Second, and perhaps more important, it gives the producer control over the content of the individual stories, since it affords him an opportunity to screen the film and, if necessary, reedit it. Eliminating the delay, the same vice-president suggested, could have the effect of reducing network news to a mere "chronicler of events" and forcing it "out of the business of making meaningful comment." Moreover, the delay provides a reserve of stories that can be used to give the program "variety" and "pacing."

In filming delayed stories, newsmen are expected to eliminate any elements of the unexpected, so as not to destroy the illusion of immediacy. This becomes especially important when it is likely that the unusual developments will be reported in other media and thus date the story. A case in point is an N.B.C. News story about the inauguration of a high-speed train service between Montreal and Toronto. While the N.B.C. crew was filming the turbotrain during its inaugural run to Toronto, it collided with—and "sliced in half," as one newspaper put it—a meat trailer-truck, and then suffered a complete mechanical breakdown on the return trip. Persistent "performance flaws" and subsequent breakdowns eventually led to a temporary suspension of the service. None of these accidents and aberrations were included in the filmed story broadcast two weeks later on the N.B.C. evening news. David Brinkley, keeping to the original story, written before the event, introduced the film by saying, "The only high-speed train now running in North America has just begun in Canada." Four and a half minutes of shots of the streamlined train followed, and the narration suggested that this foreshadowed the future of transportation, since Canada's "new turbo just might shake [American] lethargy" in developing such trains. (The announcement of the suspension of the service, almost two weeks later, was not carried on the program.) This practice of "preparing" stories also has affected the coverage of more serious subjects—for instance, many of the filmed stories about the Vietnam war were delayed for several days. It was possible to transmit war films to the United States in one day by using the satellite relay, but the cost was considerable at the height of the war—more than three thousand dollars for a ten-minute transmission, as opposed to twenty or thirty dollars for shipping the same film by plane. And, with the exception of momentous battles, such as the Tet offensive, virtually all of the network film was sent by plane. To avoid the possibility of having the delayed footage dated by newspaper accounts, network correspondents were instructed to report on the routine and continuous aspects of the war rather than unexpected developments, according to a former N.B.C. Saigon bureau manager.

The mirror analogy, in addition, obscures the component of "will"—of initiative in producing feature stories and of decisions made in advance to cover or not to cover certain types of events. A mirror makes no decisions; it simply reflects what takes place in front of it. . . .

The search for news requires a reliable flow of information not only about events in the immediate past but about those scheduled for the near future. Advance information, though necessary to any news operation, is of critical importance to the networks. For, unlike newspapers and radio stations, which can put a news story together within minutes by means of telephone interviews or wire-service dispatches, a television network usually needs hours, if not days, of "lead time" to shoot, process, and edit a film story of even a minute's duration. The types of news stories best suited for television coverage are those specially planned, or induced, for the convenience of the news media—press conferences, briefings, interviews, and the like—which the historian Daniel J. Boorstin has called "pseudo-events," and which by definition are scheduled well in advance and are certain to be, if only in a self-fulfilling sense, "newsworthy." There are also other news events, such as congressional hearings, trials, and speeches, that, although they may not be induced for the sole purpose of creating news, can still be predicted far in advance. The networks have various procedures for gathering, screening, and evaluating information about future events, and these procedures to some degree systematically *influence* their coverage of news.

Most network news stories, rather than resulting from the initiative of reporters in the field, are located and assigned by an assignment editor in New York (or an editor under his supervision in Washington, Chicago, or Los Angeles). The assignment desk provides material not only for the evening news program but for documentaries, morning and afternoon programs, and a syndicated service for local stations. Instead of maintaining—as newspapers do—regular "beats," where reporters have contact with the same set of newsmakers over an extended period of time, network news organizations rely on ad-hoc coverage. In this system, correspondents are shunted from one story to another—on the basis of availability, logistical convenience, and producers' preferences—after the assignment editor has selected the events to be covered. A correspondent may easily be assigned to three subjects in three different cities in a single week, each assignment lasting only as long as it takes to film the story. To be sure, there are a number of conventional beats in Washington, such as the White House, but these are the exception rather than the rule. Most of the correspondents are "generalists," expected to cover all subjects with equal facility. And even in fields for which networks do employ specialist correspondents, such as sports or space exploration, better-known correspondents who are not experts in those fields may be called on to report major stories. The generalist is expected not to be a Jack-of-all-trades but simply to be capable of applying rules of fair inquiry to any subject. One reason network executives tend to prefer generalists is that they are less likely to "become involved in a story to the point of advocacy," as one network vice-president has put it. It is feared that specialists, through their intimate knowledge of a situation, would be prone to champion what they believed was the correct side of a controversy. But perhaps the chief reason that generalists are preferred to specialists is that, being able to cover whatever story develops, they lend themselves to an efficient use of manpower. The use of ad-hoc coverage leads to the constant appearance "on camera" of a relatively small number of correspondents. One network assignment editor has suggested that it is "more for reasons of audience identification than economy" that a few correspondents are relied on for most of the stories. The result, he continued, is a "star system,'' in which producers request that certain leading correspondents cover major stories, whatever the subject might be. Another consequence of having small, generalist reporting staffs is that the networks are able to do relatively little investigative reporting. . . .

What is seen on network news is not, except in rare instances, the event itself, unfolding live before the camera, or even a filmed record of the event in its entirety, but a story about the event which has been constructed on film from selected fragments of it. Presenting news events exactly as they occur does not meet the requirements of network news. For one thing, the camera often is not in a postition to capture events while they are happening. Some news events are completely unexpected and occur before a camera crew can be dispatched to the scene. Others cannot be filmed either because of unfavorable weather or lighting conditions (especially if artificial lighting is unavailable or restricted) or because news crews are not permitted access to them. And when institutions, such as political conventions, do permit television to record their formal proceedings, the significant decisions may still take place outside the purview of the camera. But even if coverage presents no insurmountable problems, it is not sufficient in most cases simply to record events in their natural sequence, with all the digressions, confusions, and inconsistencies that are an inescapable part of any reality, for a network news story is required to have a definite order, time span, and logic.

In producing most news stories, the first necessity is generating sufficient film about an event, so that the editor and the writer can be assured of finding the material they need for the final story. Perhaps the most commonly used device for producing this flow of film is the interview. The interview serves several important purposes for television news. First, it enables a news crew to obtain film footage about an event that it did not attend or was not permitted to film. By finding and interviewing people who either participated in the event or have at least an apparent connection with it, the correspondent can re-create it through their eyes.

Second, the interview assures that the subject will be filmed under favorable circumstances—an important technical consideration. In a memorandum to his news staff, Reuven Frank once gave this advice about interviewing:

> By definition, an interview is at least somewhat controllable. It must be arranged; it must be agreed to. . . . Try not to interview in harsh sunlight. Try not to interview in so noisy a setting that words cannot be heard. Let subjects be lit. If lights bother your subject, talk to him, discuss the weather, gentle him, involve his interest and his emotions so that he forgets or ignores the lights. It takes longer, but speed is poor justification for a piece of scrapped film.

To make the subjects appear even more dignified and articulate, it is the customary practice to repeat the same question a number of times, allowing the respondent to ''sharpen his answer,'' as one correspondent has put it. At times, the person interviewed is permitted to compose his own questions for the interviewer or, at least, to rephrase them. Rehearsals are also quite common.

Third, interviews provide an easy means of presenting an abstract or difficult-to-film concept in human terms, as Reuven Frank has explained:

> The best interviews are of people reacting—or people expounding. . . . No important story is without them. They can be recorded and transmitted tastefully . . . nuclear disarmament, unemployment, flood, automation, name me a recent major story without its human involvement.

Although the networks have instituted strict policies against misleading "reenactments" and "staging," film footage is sometimes generated by having someone demonstrate or enact aspects of a story for the camera. Bruce Cohn, a producer for A.B.C. News at the time, explained the practice last year to the House Special Subcommittee on Investigations during hearings on "news staging." Describing the difference between hard news and feature stories, Cohn said, "Generally speaking, a feature story is only brought to the public's attention because the journalist who conceived of doing such a report thinks it would be of interest or of importance. Therefore, a feature story must be 'set up' by a journalist if it is to be transformed into usable information. There is no reason why this 'setting up' cannot be done in an honest and responsible manner . . . people involved in feature stories are often asked to demonstrate how they do something . . . in fact, by its very nature, a feature story may be nothing but what the subcommittee negatively refers to as 'staging. . . .' "

Since network television is in the business of attracting and maintaining large audiences, the news operation, which is, after all, part of the networks' programing schedule, is also expected to maintain, if not attract, as large as audience as possible. But a network news program, unlike other news media, apparently can't depend entirely on its content to attract and maintain an audience. To a great extent, the size of its audience is determined by three outside factors. The first is affiliate acceptance. If a progam is not carried, or "cleared," by the affiliates, then it simply is not available to the public. (A.B.C. has significantly increased the audience for its evening news program since 1969 by increasing the number of stations that clear it from a hundred and twenty to a hundred and ninety-one.) The second is scheduling. A program that is broadcast at 7 P.M., say, stands a good chance of drawing a larger audience than it would at six-thirty, since more people are usually watching television at the later hour. (The television audience increases all day and reaches a peak at about 9 P.M.) The third factor is what is called "audience flow." Network executives and advertisers believe that a significant portion of the audience for any program is inherited, as they put it, from the preceding program. According to the theory of audience flow, an audience is like a river that continues in the same direction until it is somehow diverted. "The viewing habits of a large portion of the audience—at least, the audience that Nielsen measures—are governed more by the laws of inertia than by free choice," a network vice-president responsible for audience studies has remarked. "Unless they have a very definite reason to switch, like a ballgame, they continue to watch the programs on the channel they are tuned in to."

Many network executives believe that network news is even more dependent on audience flow than are entertainment programs, or even local newscasts featuring reports on local sports and weather conditions. Richard Salant, the president of

C.B.S. News, has said that "you'll find a general correlation between the ratings of the network news broadcast and the local news broadcast—and probably the local news is the decisive thing." But what of the selective viewer, who changes channels for network news? Network executives, relying on both audience studies and personal intuition, assume, first, that there is not a significant number of such viewers, and, second, that most of them choose particular news programs on the basis of the personalities of the commentators rather than the extent of the news coverage. Acting on these assumptions about audience behavior, the networks attempt to improve the ratings of their news shows by hiring "star" commentators and by investing in the programs that precede the network news. For example, in a memo to the president of N.B.C. several years ago, a vice-president responsible for audience analysis made this suggestion for increasing the ratings in Los Angeles of the network's evening news program:

> It seems to me the only surefire way to increase our audience at 3:30 P.M. (and actually win the time period) is with Mike Douglas [a syndicated talk show, which N.B.C. would have had to buy from Group W Productions, a subsidiary of the Westinghouse Broadcasting Company]. At 5-6 P.M. our news then should get at least what KABC is getting (let's say a 7 rating).
> Coming out of this increased lead-in—and a *news* lead-in, at that—I believe that [the evening news] at 6 P.M. will get a couple of rating points more....

Similarly, a network can invest in the local news programs that precede or follow the network news on the five stations it owns. N.B.C. concluded from a detailed study that it commissioned of the Chicago audience that local news programs, unlike network news, which builds its audience through coverage of special events, can increase their ratings through improved coverage of weather, sports, and local events. The study recommended, for example, that the network-owned station in Chicago hire a more popular local weather-caster, since "almost as many viewers look forward to seeing the weather as the news itself." The networks also assist the affiliated stations with their local news programs, by providing a news syndication service. This supplies subscribing stations with sports and news stories through a half-hour feed, from which the stations can record stories for use on their own news programs.

Implicit in this approach to seeking higher ratings for network news programs is the idea that it doesn't make economic sense to spend large amounts on improving the editorial product. Hiring additional camera crews, reporters, and researchers presumably would not increase a news program's audience, and it definitely would be expensive. For instance, not only does each camera crew cost about a hundred thousand dollars a year to maintain, in equipment, salaries, and overtime, but it generates a prodigious amount of film—about twenty times as much as is used in the final stories—which has to be transported, processed, and edited. N.B.C. accountants use a rule-of-thumb gauge of more than twenty dollars in service cost for every foot of film in the final story, which comes to more than seven hundred and twenty dollars a minute. And it is the number of camera crews a network maintains that defines, in some ways, the scope of its newsgathering operation. "The news you present is actually the news you cover," a network news vice-president has said. "The question is: How wide do you fling your net?"

In 1968, when I had access to staff meetings and assignment sheets at the three networks, N.B.C. covered the nation each day with an average of ten camera crews, in New York, Chicago, Los Angeles, Washington, and Cleveland, plus two staff crews in Texas [L.B.J. was President] and one staff cameraman (who could assemble camera crews) in Boston. (In comparison, C.B.S.'s local news operation in Los Angeles, according to its news director, uses nine camera crews to cover the news of that one city.) Today, N.B.C. says it has fifty domestic camera crews, but this figure includes sports, special events, and documentary crews, as well as local crews at the network's five stations. C.B.S. says it has twenty full-time network news crews, in New York, Chicago, Los Angeles, Atlanta, and Washington, and A.B.C. says it has sixteen, in New York, Chicago, Los Angeles, Washington, Atlanta, and Miami. Each of the networks also has camera crews in nine cities overseas. To be sure, when there is a momentus news event the networks can quickly mobilize additional crews—those regularly assigned to news documentaries, sports, and local news at network stations, or those of affiliated stations—but the net that is cast for national news on a day-to-day basis is essentially defined by the crews that are routinely available for network assignment, and their number is set by the economic logic of network television.

Another element in the economics of networks news is the fact that it costs a good deal more to transmit stories from some places than it does from other places. The lines that connect the networks with their affiliates across the country can normally be used to transmit programs in only one direction—from the network's headquarters in New York to the affiliates. Therefore, to transmit news reports electronically from any "remote" location—that is, anywhere except network facilities in a few cities—to the network for rebroadcast, a news program must order special "long lines" between the two points from the American Telephone & Telegraph Co. The charges for the "long line" are now fifty-five cents a mile for up to an hour's use and seven hundred and fifty dollars for a "loop," which is the package of electronic equipment that connects the transmission point (usually an affiliated station) with the telephone company's "long lines." It is even more expensive to order stories sent electronically by means of the satellite-relay system—eighteen hundred and fifty dollars for the first ten minutes of a story from London to New York and about twenty-four hundred dollars for the first ten minutes of a story from Tokyo to New York—and these costs are charged against the program's budget. The weekly budget for the N.B.C. Nightly News is in excess of two hundred thousand dollars, and that of the C.B.S. Evening News is almost a hundred thousand dollars, but more than half of each is committed in advance for the salaries and expenses of the producers, editors, writers, and other members of the "unit," and for the studio and other overhead costs that are automatically charged against the program's budget. (Differences in the billing of these charges account for most of the difference in the budgets of the N.B.C. and C.B.S. programs.) At C.B.S., about forty-nine thousand dollars a week, or eight thousand dollars a program, is left for "remotes." Since a news program needs from six to eight film stories a night, and some satellite charges can be as high as three thousand dollars apiece, the budget, in effect, limits the number of "remote" stories that can be transmitted in an average week.

Because of differences in transmission costs, producers have a strong incentive to take news stories from some areas rather than others, especially when their budgets are strained. The fact that networks base most of their camera crews and correspondents in New York, Washington, Chicago, and Los Angeles reinforces the advantage of using news stories from these areas, since they involve less overtime and travel expense. It is not surprising, then, that so many of the film stories shown on the national news programs originate in these areas. Although the geographical distribution of film stories varies greatly from day to day, over any sustained period it is skewed in the direction of these few large cities. It is economically more efficient to consign news of small-town America and of remote cities to timeless features such as Charles Kuralt's "On the Road" segments of the C.B.S. Evening News. This suggests that if network news programs tend to focus on problems of a few large urban centers, it is less because, as former Vice-President Agnew argued, an "enclosed fraternity" of "commentators and producers live and work in the geographical and intellectual confines of Washington, D.C., or New York City . . .[and] draw their political and social views from the same sources" than because the networks' basic economic structure compels producers, willy-nilly, to select a large share of their filmed stories from a few locations.

The Fairness Doctrine requires broadcasters to provide a reasonable opportunity for the presentation of "contrasting viewpoints on controversial issues of public importance" in the course of their news and public-affairs programming. Unlike the "equal time" provisions of Section 315 of the Communications Act—which applies only to candidates running for a public office and requires that if a station grants time to one candidate it must grant equal time to other candidates, except on news programs—the Fairness Doctrine does not require that opposing arguments be given an equal number of minutes, be presented on the same program, or be presented within any specific period. It is left up to the licensee to decide what constitutes a "controversial issue of public importance," a "fair" reply, and a "reasonable time" in which the reply should be made. Moreover, broadcasters are apparently not expected to be equally "fair" on all issues of public importance; for example the Commission states in its "Fairness Primer" that it is not "the Commission's intention to make time available to Communists or to the Communist view-points."

Although no television station has ever lost its license because of a violation of the Fairness Doctrine, the doctrine has affected the form and content of network news in a number of ways. Most notably, the Fairness Doctrine puts an obligation on affiliates to "balance" any network program that advances only one side of an issue by themselves providing, in the course of their own programming, the other side, and the affiliates, rather than risk having to fulfill such an obligation, which could be both costly and bothersome, insist, virtually as a condition of taking network news, that the networks incorporate the obligatory "contrasting viewpoints" in their own news reports. The networks, in turn, make it a policy to present opposing views on any issue that could conceivably be construed as controversial.

This pro-and-con reporting is perfectly consistent with the usual notion of objectivity, if objectivity is defined, as it is by many correspondents, as "telling both sides of a story." It can, however, seriously conflict with the value that journalists place on what is now called investigative reporting, or simply any reporting the purpose of which is "getting to the bottom" of an issue, or "finding the truth," as correspondents often put it. A correspondent is required to present "contrasting points of view" even if he finds the views of one side to be valid and those of the other side to be false and misleading (in the Fairness Doctrine, truth is no defense), and therefore any attempt to resolve a controversial issue and "find the truth" is likely to be self-defeating. . . .

A frequent criticism of television news is that it is superficial—that it affords only scant coverage of news events, lacks depth or sufficient analysis of events, and engages in only a minimum of investigative reporting. The assumption of such criticism is that television newsmen lack journalistic credentials, that producers and executives are lax or indifferent toward their responsibilities, and that changing or educating the broadcasters would improve the news product. But the level of journalism in network news is more or less fixed by the time, money, and manpower that can be allocated to it, and these are determined by the structure of network television. Any substantial improvement in the level of network journalism, such as expanding coverage of events to a truly nationwide scale, would therefore require a structural change in network television that would effectively reorder its economic and political incentives, rather than merely a change of personnel.

Another common criticism is, again, that network news is politically biased in favor of liberal or left-wing causes and leaders, because a small clique of newsmen in New York and Washington shape the news to fit their own political beliefs. In this critique, network news is presumed to be highly politicized by the men who select and report it, and the remedy most often suggested is to employ conservative newsmen to balance the liberal viewpoints. Since, for economic reasons, much of the domestic news on the network programs does in fact come from a few big cities, and since in recent years many of the efforts to change the distribution of political values and services have been concentrated in the big cities, the networks perhaps have reported a disproportionately large share of these activities. The requirement that network news be "nationalized" further adds to the impression that the networks are advancing radical causes, for in elevating local disputes to national proportions newscasters appear to be granting them uncalled-for-importance.

Left-wing critics complain that network news neglects the inherent contradictions in the American system. Their critique runs as follows: Network news focuses not on substantive problems but on symbolic protests. By overstating the importance of protest actions, television news invites the audience to judge the conduct of the protesters rather than the content of the problem. This creates false issues. Popular support is generated against causes that, on television appear to rely on violent protests, while underlying economic and social problems are systematically masked or ignored. Broadcasters can be expected to help perpetuate "the system," because they are an important part of it. Thus, one critic writes, "The media owners will do anything to maintain these myths . . . They will do anything to keep the public from realizing that the Establishment dominates society through its direct and indirect control of the nation's communication system.'' In fact, however, the tendency to depict symbolic protests rather than substantive problems is closely related to the problem of audience maintenance. Protests can be universally comprehended, it is presumed, if they are presented in purely symbolic terms: one group, standing for one cause, challenging another group and cause. The sort of detail that would be necessary to clarify economic and social issues is not easily translated into visual terms, whereas the sort of dramatic images that can be found in violent protests have an immediate impact on an audience. Newsmen therefore avoid liberal or radical arguments not because they are politically committed to supporting ''the system'' but because such arguments do not satisfy the requisites of network news.

Finally, in what might best be called the social-science critique, network news is faulted for presenting a picture of society that does not accurately correspond to the empirical data. Spokesmen selected by television to represent groups in society tend to be statistically atypical of the groups for which they are supposedly speaking; for example, militant students may have appeared to be in the majority on college campuses in America during the nineteen-sixties because of the frequency with which they were selected to represent student views, when in fact data collected by social scientists showed that they constituted a small minority. It is generally argued that such discrepancies stem from a lack of readily usable data rather than any intent on the part of journalists to misrepresent situations. The implication in this critique is that if network news organizations had the techniques of social scientists, or employed social scientists as consultants, they would produce a more realistic version of the claims and aspirations of different segments of society. However, the selection of spokesmen to appear on television is determined less by a lack of data than by the organizational needs of network news. In order to hold the attention of viewers to whom the subject of the controversy may be of no interest, television newsmen select spokesmen who are articulate, easily identifiable, and dramatic, and the ''average'' person in a group cannot be depended on to manifest these qualities. More over, the nationalization of news requires that spokesmen represent the major themes in society rather than what is statistically typical. Given the organizational necd to illustrate news stories with spokesmen who are both dramatic and thematic, network news cannot be expected to present a picture that conforms to the views of social scientists, no matter how much data or how many technical skills the social scientists might supply.

As long as the requisites remain essentially the same, network news can be expected to define American society by the problems of a few urban areas rather than of the entire nation, by action rather than ideas, by dramatic protests rather than substantive contradictions, by ''newsmakers'' rather than economic and social structures, by atypical rather than typical views, and by synthetic national themes rather than disparate local events.

Bibliography

There are dozens of books and articles important to this subject. Robert Mulholland's article in Chap. 5 updates some of the technical facts. For additional views, consult Paul H. Weaver's "Is Television News Biased?" *The Public Interest* (Winter, 1972); Edith Efron's *The News Twisters* (Nash, 1971); William Small's *To Kill a Messenger: Television News and the Real World* (Hastings House, 1970); Fred Friendly's *Due to Circumstances Beyond Our Control* (Random House, 1967); Daniel St. Albin Greene's "Making a Television News Show," *Seminar Quarterly*, March, 1970; and Spiro T. Agnew, Nov. 13, 1969 speech to Iowa Republicans. Useful background information can be found in: Ben Bagdikian's *The Information Machine* (Harper & Row, 1971); Columbia University's annual *Survey of Broadcast Journalism,* Robert McNeil's *The People and the News* (Pacific Books, 1968). Also see regularly: *Journal of Broadcasting, Television Quarterly* and other periodicals. In his 1975 work *Television: The Most Popular Art*, Horace Newcomb compares the drama and ritual found in entertainment programs to the action in television news and offers some thought-provoking comments.

Lessons of a Living Room War

By Leonard Zeidenberg

From the offices of network news executives in New York to those points halfway around the world in Hong Kong, Bangkok, Tokyo, and the Philippines where the broadcast journalists who covered the Indochina story have scattered, there is a drawing of breath, a feeling of exhilaration and wonder subsiding, a great unwinding.

America's Indochina war, television's first war—what the *New Yorker's* Michael Arlen has called America's living room war—is over. The satellite feeds of color-film coverage of the war, shown on the networks within a day of the event, are no more; the last special on the war has been done. The news now flowing out of the region is about the victorious North Vietnamese and Viet Cong and Khmer Rouge; peace and all of its complications are now the subject on which the media must develop experts.

Indochina had been a major effort. From the early 1960's, when reporters and cameramen and soundmen began trickling into South Vietnam to cover the guerrilla war, until the last couple of months, when the South Vietnam military suddenly unraveled and the networks hurriedly dispatched correspondents and camera crews to bureaus that had been reduced in strength following the departure of the last American troops in 1973. ABC, CBS and NBC put more than 600 personnel into the region (although the figure includes network news executives gone to demonstrate to the men and women on the scene their efforts were appreciated and to get some first-hand idea of the story and who remained only a few days, as well as local Vietnamese and third-country nationals). And at the height of America's military

Leonard Zeidenberg, a senior Washington correspondent, prepared this analysis for *Broadcasting's* May 19, 1975 issue. It is reprinted with the permission of the publication.

involvement, in the late 1960's, each of the networks maintained a bureau of more than 40 staffers and employes that transmitted upwards of 80 filmed reports a month (two or three a day, seven days a week) and eight or 10 radio pieces each day. (Actually, ABC, with its four radio networks, gobbled up audio tape at a more furious pace. Its five or six correspondents were expected to file at least three brief cuts on each story, for a total of up to 30 a day.)

Nor was that the full product of American radio and television coverage of the war: A number of stations and broadcast groups sent reporters and cameramen to search out and report on the activities of troops from home.

It was a rare day that a correspondent carrying a camera or accompanied by a cameraman did not approach a body of American troops somewhere in Vietnam and cry out, ''Anyone here from Des Moines?'' or ''Albuquerque?'' or ''Atlanta?'' Westinghouse Broadcasting Corp. was the largest independent broadcasting organization providing on-scene coverage of South Vietnam and Cambodia; the bureau it established in Saigon in 1965 offered a steady stream of reports until its last two correspondents—Leonard Pratt and Jim Browning, normally Group W's Bonn bureau chief—were evacuated on the morning of April 29, 1975.

All this cost, in dollars and cents, is hidden behind corporate reluctance to divulge such information and the difficulty in apportioning costs. However, there is one estimate that all three networks combined spent about $40 million, and NBC News's president, Richard Wald, says the network probably spent ''something more than $10 million since 1963.'' When group and individual station efforts are added, the estimates crowd $50 million.

But the financial cost, whatever it is, and the effort of the men and women in the field to produce and file the enormous volume of material that poured through the television screen and the radio receiver over the years are meaningless in themselves. What do they add up to? That remains a subject of controversy. For television probably made a long and painful war longer and more painful; it projected into the American home night after night not only pictures of American troops dead and dying and killing, but of the terrible destruction American might was wreaking on a peasant society. It was a new and disturbing image of America that Americans were given.

The more fundamental question of which the matter of image is only a part—of how well television performed its role as journalist—is one that will concern historians for years. But some judgments are already in. Michael Arlen, in the May 5 *New Yorker*, says that ''television news was crucial—in its commissions and omissions—to the American public's comprehension.'' But, he also says, ''I think it is evasive and disingenuous to suppose that, in its unwillingness over a space of 10 years to assign a true information-gathering function to its news operations in Washington and Vietnam, American network news did much beyond contributing to the unreality, and the dysfunction, of American life.'' The *New York Times*'s James Reston takes another view: ''Maybe the historians will agree that the reporters and the cameras were decisive in the end. They brought the issue of the war to the people . . .and forced the withdrawal of American power from Vietnam.'' And although the reporters of press, radio and television are being blamed for the defeat

of American policy and power in Indochina, Mr. Reston writes, it should be remembered that "in the long tragic history of the war, the reporters have been more honest with the American people than the officials . . ."

There are other commentators, too. An analysis of CBS News' reporting on national defense matters in 1972 and 1973, prepared for the conservatively oriented Institute for American Strategy, concludes that the network operated from a generally antidefense-establishment bias, and that in its handling of the Vietnam war specifically, CBS News stressed that the South Vietnamese government was "corrupt, repressive or unpopular and that the South Vietnamese troops were doing poorly." (Mr. Arlen in his May 5 *New Yorker* article made the contrary point that reporters of all three networks generally avoided such criticisms even though they were aware of their validity.)

For those government officials whose Vietnam policy collapsed in ruin on April 30, the time has not yet arrived for an assessment of the impact of the media on the conduct of the war. But one assessment is likely to emerge in a book that Dean

CBS' Morley Safer reported this story of Marines burning huts in 1965 and was subjected to intense pressure because he tried to show the brutal nature of some U.S. actions.

Rusk, secretary of state in the Kennedy and Johnson administrations, is writing. Mr. Rusk teaches constitutional law at the University of Georgia, in Athens, and the book will reflect his background—the constitutional system as seen from the secretary of state's office. It will also include some chapters on the news media.

For the present, Mr. Rusk prefers to withhold comment on the media's performance; as a private citizen he wants the privilege of choosing his times to be "controversial." But he offered this observation last week: "If the President and Congress ever find themselves in a situation where they have to deal with this kind of thing again, God forbid, they will have to deal with the question of censorship."

The press was not censored in South Vietnam—primarily, Mr. Rusk suggested, for legal and practical reasons (censorship was not authorized by Congress; besides, there was no unity of command between the U.S. and South Vietnamese, not even among U.S. forces)—rather than for any particular concern for press freedom. As a result, the war, with all its "horrors," was fought in everyone's living room, with the effect, Mr. Rusk feels, of eroding the public support for the war. Whether the U.S. should permit Vietnam-type coverage in the future while an opponent does not "is a big question," he says. [Ed. Note: the war was not officially authorized by Congress either, making official censorship difficult.]

Whatever the judgment of history, it seems fair to say that journalists—print as well as electronic, for that matter—generally pursued the story one day at a time, or at the most one issue at a time; they did not attempt to arrive at fundamental truths about the war. NBC's Wald acknowledges that television did not put the story together as well as it might have. But, he says, the "disparate items" that make up the Vietnam story were the subjects of NBC reports—in the news programs, *Today Show* byliners and news specials. "We gave a picture, but it was a mosaic, not a daily cartoon strip of what was happening . . .We were doing a daily report, and we were criticized for not doing an annual survey." Richard Salant, CBS News president, and Nick Archer, ABC's vice president of Television News Services, make the same point: Examine the over-all product; it was all there.

One is more likely to hear expressions of dissatisfaction about the coverage from the men who had been in the field rather than from the executives and editors. ABC's Ted Koppel feels that television did only "a good surface job," given the medium's limitations—principally the three-minute snippet of time normally allowed a piece on an evening news show. And CBS's Morley Safer, whose coverage of the war established him as a major broadcast journalist, feels that television was too concerned with the "bang-bang" aspect of the war—the battle—and too little interested in the "why" of a story.

But Mr. Safer is impatient, too, with Arlen-type critics: "They are looking for that one special, that one documentary, that will end the war the next morning, that will cause the soldiers to lay down their arms and the politicians to hang themselves from the lampposts in Washington. It doesn't work that way; it's a matter of accretion; of building stories here and there, persuading by the weight of evidence, at least as perceived by the reporters."

Although the executives in New York may not have ordered their Saigon bureaus to, as Mr. Salant says, "shoot bloody," there is no question that television did concentrate on American troops in battle. Some news executives say, with a touch of impatience, that it was a war, after all, one in which 55,000 Americans died. It was true, too, that television technology and economics in large measure helped shape the coverage. Because they worked in a visual medium, camera crews were forced to move out into the field; they could not rely on the handouts and briefings in Saigon. They needed pictures. And the pressure for the action scene was great; besides the inherent drama that producers of nightly news shows appeared to find irresistible, a fire-fight could be shown more easily in the brief time available in a half-hour news show than could a standupper on, say, the political and social upheaval caused by the pacification program on a village.

And as the war progressed, the improvements in the technology increased the pressure for on-the-scene reports. Cameras and related gear became increasingly portable; where cameramen and soundmen once were burdened under more than some 35 pounds of equipment, they were in the final stages of the war carrying less than half that amount of weight and in a more convenient configuration; sound amplifiers had been reduced from four pounds to one pound in weight and made part of the camera, and wireless microphones were in use. More important, the availability of satellite ground stations in Hong Knog and Bangkok in 1970 finally made possible the airing of filmed reports on virtually a same-day basis; previously film was flown either to Tokyo for satellite transmission or, more likely, to Los Angeles or San Francisco, where it was fed into the network lines, sometimes two days behind the event.

But there were other reasons—personal, professional and tactical—for the combat coverage. Battle stories were, correspondents agree, easy to do. There was, for the first time in an American war, no censorship. The military—whatever other faults the press corps saw in it—was cooperative in providing radio and television crews with the jeep, helicopter or fixed-wing aircraft needed to reach the scene. And courage was the main resource required, not the background or knowledge political or social stories demanded. What's more, as NBC's Ron Steinman, who ran the network's Saigon bureau in the late 1960's, says, "There were times when combat was a consuming moment... Some reporters liked combat better than anything else. They were 'war lovers,' guys who wanted to be in that 'up' situation. The adrenalin starts pumping, and they go."

Some of the correspondents who were there admit to the emotional attraction of battle. ABC's Koppel, who went to Vietnam on his first major assignment in 1967, spent that year in the country and then shuttled in and out as Hong Kong bureau chief from 1969 to 1971, and who is now ABC's diplomatic correspondent is one. He talks of the "tremendous excitement" of covering a battle. "The excitement becomes like a drug, a shot of adrenalin, when you have been in a dangerous situation and then you have been flown out—to Danang, say. The freedom and release can't be duplicated in any other situation. You felt entitled to enjoy that night before you went out again."

But the war took its toll of those who covered it. NBC's Welles Hangen, Roger Colne, a French soundman, and Yoshihiko Waku, a Japanese cameraman, have been listed as missing since they were captured in Cambodia on May 31, 1970. Another NBC cameraman, Dieter Bellendorf, a German, was captured in

Cambodia in April 1970 and is still listed as missing. CBS lost five killed—George Syvertsen, a correspondent; Gerald Miller, a producer; Duong Van Ri, a South Vietnamese, and Ramnik Lekhi, an Indian, both cameramen, and Yeng Sam Leng, a driver. All died at the hands of Cambodian rebels in 1970. Three other CBS employes disappeared that year in Cambodia—Tomoharu Ishii, a Japanese cameraman; Kojiro Waku, a Japanese sound technician, and freelance cameraman Dana Stone, an American. And ABC lost two Singaporean cameramen killed in action in 1972—Terry Khoo and Sam Kai Faye. (The loss of Mr. Khoo was a particularly painful one to a generation of ABC staffers who had known him in South Vietnam. Steve Bell, in an ABC radio special, *Scenes from a War* on May 2, recalled him as a brave, highly skilled professional cameraman who had probably saved Mr. Bell's life on at least one occasion and had undoubtedly steered him onto a number of good stories. Besides eulogizing Mr. Khoo, who after 10 years in Vietnam was killed in Quang Tri on what was to have been his last day on assignment, the brief account afforded the public a glimpse of the non-Americans who provided a kind of continuity to the story being told by Americans who visited Indochina in waves.)

But if battles overshadowed other stories, the correspondents did cover the "soft" stuff, too—the political and economic stories, the progress of the campaign to win the hearts and minds of the people, the effort to Vietnamize the war. ABC's Bill Brannigan developed a speciality in South Vietnamese politics. CBS did stories on Saigon's black market. NBC's Robert Hager recalls that when he arrived in Saigon in 1969, his editors were looking for something other than battle footage. "By 1969, people had seen a lot of the war; now the important thing was to tell a story—Is Vietnamization working? Is the war winding down? It wasn't enough to get a firefight. But if a firefight story broke, we covered it."

What's more, throughout the war, the networks did a number of specials and documentaries. CBS presented more than 100, including 116 segments of the occasional *Vietnam Perspective* series in the 1960's, that date back to a special on May 7, 1954, on John Foster Dulles and the Geneva Conference that ended the first Indochina war. NBC did 54 specials between 1965 to the present, besides two weekly series—*Vietnam Weekly Review*, which ran from April 17, 1966, to May 14, 1967, and *Vietnam: The War This Week*, which was broadcast from March 17, 1966, to July 7, 1968. ABC covered the war from a variety of points of view in the 99 half-hour segments that constituted the series, *Scope: The War in Vietnam,* which began on Feb. 10, 1965, as well as in 15 specials dating back to 1964.

It cannot be assumed the specials and documentaries were always successful in illuminating the Vietnam experience. One correspondent who recalls CBS's Feb. 14, 1967, *Vietnam Perspective: Air War in the North*, which CBS described as "an assessment of the scope and the effectiveness of U.S. bombings of North Vietnam and the growing controversy in the country over the air attacks," said the other day, "What the hell did it mean?"

As was true of the country as a whole, the war had a maturing experience on those who covered it. NBC's Wald concedes that "everyone's perception of the war changed; we didn't think the war that important at the time.'' And CBS News President Richard Salant says that, initially at least, the war was covered as if it were an extension of World War II. That was a war in which right and wrong were easily distinguished and in which the American cause was clearly and automatically the virtuous one.

That attitude seemed reflected in a CBS piece on a bombing mission in 1965, one in which Walter Cronkite rode piggy back in a Canberra jet that divebombed Viet Cong in the jungle above Danang. (In later years, after some of the lessons of the war were learned, a correspondent probably would have referred to ''suspected Viet Cong.'') Could the American public have identified with anyone but Walter Cronkite at that point?

But even then television was raising questions. The late Frank McGee, concluded an NBC special on the war on Dec. 20, 1965, with the comment that the government had not yet made a ''compelling argument'' as to why an independent South Vietnam ''is so vital to American national interests that it transcends doubts about the legality and morality'' of American involvement in the war. And if that argument cannot be made, he added, the U.S. should withdraw.

There were, in addition, snapshots issuing from the daily routine indicating the networks were not afraid to look the strange war in the eye. In the same year that Walter Cronkite went along on a bombing mission, CBS's Safer joined a Marine unit on what started as a routine mission to the village of Cam Nhe, and filmed the Marines setting the huts afire—150 destroyed in response to a burst of gunfire, even though the Viet Cong had clearly left the area.

The piece was a landmark. David Halberstam, who won a Pulitzer prize for his coverage of the war for the *New York Times*, recalled the Cam Nhe incident in an article for the May 16 *New Times*: ''The Zippo day. It was a total reversal of the American myth: The American legend of the West has the Americans in the white hats protecting women and children; the Indians are the savages who brutalize the innocents. It was a moment that touches the soul, and it would often be repeated.''

He was right. In 1967, NBC broadcast film of the chief of the South Vietnamese national police firing a bullet into the head of a bound Viet Cong. And three years later, the network's Phil Brady broadcast allegations that President Thieu and Vice President Ky were profiting from the drug traffic in South Vietnam.

All three networks did remarkable work in covering the Communists' massive Tet offensive of 1968, which swept over all the country's major cities. Coming after official U.S. estimates that the Communists could no longer mount a major offensive, Tet helped persuade the Johnson administration the war could not be won, and the uncompromising look the cameras presented to the American public of the fighting—including the bloody attack on the U.S. embassy in Saigon—is regarded by those who were in the American mission at the time as having played a major part in shaping the public's attitude toward the war.

ABC's Dick Rosenbaum spent most of his time as Saigon bureau chief from 1966 to 1969 in his office. But Tet brought the war to him: ''I sat watching the flares, seeing them blow up the embassy. I looked at the presidential palace, and saw tracers and explosions. I looked out another window, and saw fighting at the dock. It was an unbelievable experience." And that was the experience conveyed to the American people.

Walter Cronkite visited South Vietnam for a special on the offensive. And the experience left him sufficiently moved to conclude the program with an uncharacteristically editorial comment. "To say that we are mired in stalemate seems the only realistic, yet unsatisfactory conclusion." The "only rational way out . . . will be to negotiate (and) not as victors."

Two years after that, Paul Harvey, who has never been confused with Walter Cronkite, told his ABC Radio audience the U.S. should leave Indochina—that it should not persist "in fighting protracted, debilitating wars far from home."

The reports raising questions about America's involvement generated pressures. After his Cam Nhe report was broadcast, CBS's Safer was advised by a Marine colonel that he might receive a bullet in the back. NBC's Brady found himself barred from re-entering South Vietnam when he attempted to return from a vacation after his report on alleged corruption in the Saigon government. Secretary of State Dean Rusk suggested that reporters get on "the team" (in response to what he said was a "loaded question" from John Scali, then with ABC and now the United States Ambassador to the United Nations, Secretary Rusk said, "Whose team are you on?") and the military seemed to favor those reporters who did. Presidents Johnson and Nixon railed against critics in the media; indeed, it was critical analyses by network correspondents of a speech by President Nixon outlining his Vietnam policy in November 1969 that touched off the attack, unprecedented in the depth of its fury, that then-Vice President Agnew undertook against the media, particularly network television.

(The government was not the only source of pressure the networks—CBS, at any rate—encountered. "The affiliates were at us constantly," Mr. Salant said the other day. "There was a great deal of complaint about how negative our stories were. A special delegation came in once—in the early 70's—and advanced the notion that a group of them visit Vietnam to talk to our correspondents." Mr. Salant said the idea was dropped.)

The government pressures appeared to be counterproductive. The reporters in South Vietnam grew increasingly skeptical of official information; briefings at the "5 o'clock follies," were often rancorous affairs, with reporters challenging the civilian and military briefers repeatedly. "The story was always different from what you were told," says Robert Toombs, who managed NBC's Saigon bureau in the late 1960's and now operates out of New York as a field producer.

What was probably more disturbing was that members of the U.S. establishment were not being honest with each other. Morley Safer recalls a trip to a town in the delta with William Colby, now the director of the Central Intelligence Agency but then deputy ambassador to Saigon. Mr. Colby was briefed by the team of American specialists aiding the South Vietnamese on the progress the South Vietnamese were making in asserting control over the region. Mr. Safer says that the reports were uniformly encouraging; "it seemed like a revivalist meeting." But that night, over drinks, the members of the team sought Mr. Safer out privately, and said the glowing reports they had given were a "lot of bullshit" designed to please their boss, a tough Army colonel. "It's our ass if we tell the truth," one official said. The correspondent had been taken along on the understanding that whatever he learned was off the record, so he never reported what he had heard. But the intelligence did nothing to shrink the degree of skepticism with which he received official information.

The criticism the media heap on the government information specialists is not being repaid in kind. Barry Zorthian today is Time Inc.'s Washington vice president for government affairs. But his memories of Saigon when he served as chief spokesman for the U.S. mission between 1964 and 1968, are still green, though he does not recall his relations with the media as "hostile." He says that, "as a general statement, the press did a first-rate job." Of course, not every correspondent or story was "great," and there are stories he would like to have seen handled differently. "But ultimately, the judgment of the public on the war comes through, and most would say it was a correct judgment." Major General Winant Sidle, who is now stationed at the Pentagon but who as a brigadier general was chief of information for the Military Assistance Command, Vietnam, is somewhat less generous; "I don't agree with those who say the coverage was all bad."

But both sounded a theme heard also from some Saigon bureau chiefs and network news executives—the lack of experience on the part of many of the correspondents who were dispatched to South Vietnam. The networks were served by a number of veterans, but for the most part, it was the younger men, eager to advance careers, who volunteered; and then the tours were relatively short—six months to a year, 18 months in some cases. [Ed. Note: This was in contrast to time spent by veteran press association reporters who provided a sort of continuity.]

"We had trouble getting good people to stay longer periods of time," says ABC's Archer. "It makes it tough on political stories, which require experience. The young correspondents were great on guts in covering firefights, in getting to where the action was . . . It takes more experience to develop contacts, and know how to report."

Like the other networks, ABC attempted to prepare the men it sent out, exposing them to returned personnel, plying them with books, and sending them to Washington for briefings at the State and Defense Departments. But not all personnel received that much preparation. Mr. Zorthian recalls one man a network plucked out of a regional bureau and shipped to Saigon on two days notice. As General Sidle says, a number of correspondents "got on-the-job training in Vietnam." What's more, inexperienced reporters were not the only problem, in the U.S. mission's view. The editors and news executives in New York were another. Mr. Zorthian recalls an occasion when the Department of Defense sent Saigon a sampling of television clips that had been shown on the networks, and they were played back for the correspondents: "Some of the people were embarrassed at what had been done to the copy and film."

Perhaps. But, over-all, the network news executives and correspondents who covered the war are not embarrassed. The network executives are probably right in insisting that in the torrent of information broadcast journalism produced, the whole story was presented. And there seems little question that television shaped the popular conception of the war, as Dean Rusk and James Reston suggest. But talk of television's impact on society may be obscuring another point, one probably as valid and at least as important—the effect of the war in shaping broadcast journalism. Some reporters may never have learned how to use a military telephone and some television documentaries may have been meaningless or plain wrong. But over the last 12 years as Vietnam grew from a minor disturbance to a national obsession, as reporters scattered through the country, looking not only for the story but its meaning, the war became for the correspondents and news executives involved, a training ground in the journalistic imperatives of skepticism and independence and responsibility.

Bibliography

There are dozens of books and hundreds of articles dealing with the Vietnam War which these broadcasters were trying to cover. The 1962-64 media coverage is best described in David Halberstam's prophetic *The Making of a Quagmire*. (Random House, 1965). Particularly interesting for its analysis of press-government relations is Dale Minor's *The Information War* (Hawthorn, 1970). Highly acclaimed among the general descriptive books is Frances Fitzgerald's *Fire in the Lake* (Little, Brown & Co., 1972). Related directly to this summary analysis by *Broadcasting* is Michael Arlen's *Living Room War* (Viking, 1969).

Murrow—A Model for Broadcast Journalists
By Edward Bliss, Jr.

Only 10 years have passed since Ed Murrow died. It seems longer than that. It seems an age since we heard his broadcasts defending individual liberty and his nightly analyses of foreign and domestic events. Ten years later, as one who set standards for his profession, he is in no way forgotten. Fred Friendly, his longtime collaborator, compares Murrow to the North Star, saying, "Today in broadcast journalism, it is still the Murrow bearing against which the profession measures itself and occasionally corrects its course." Recently, Edwin Diamond, the media critic, said that reading Murrow's broadcasts now is "a sad reminder of what broadcast journalism can be, and is not."

Edward Bliss, Jr. was a news editor with CBS for many years and is now head of the Broadcast Journalism Program at The American University in Washington, D.C. His article, which appeared in the May 31, 1975 issue of *Saturday Review,* is used with his permission.

I first met Murrow in 1946, after he had left London, which he loved, to become a CBS vice-president in New York. He commanded the network's news operations, and I was one of several persons called into his presence to explain why a certain "feed" from overseas had failed. He looked very young and handsome in his Savile Row clothes, seated behind a large desk. He listened politely to the conflicting testimony of various technical and editorial types, but it struck me that he cared little about assessing blame. I suspect he was going through the motions expected of a vice-president. Murrow had no appetite for rehashing past mistakes. It was always the next broadcast he had his mind on; he assumed that everyone around him was doing his best.

In the whole history of journalism, perhaps no other reporter has become famous quite so fast. This was due not only to the quality of Ed Murrow's reporting but also to the medium itself. Radio, burgeoning in the news field, produced a mass audience that no newspaper or magazine could match. Radio was faster, more pervasive, more personal than print, so that Murrow was transformed in the public mind, as by magic, from being one of many reporters covering the Battle of Britain

to *the* reporter covering that battle. His trademark, ''This is London,'' became a notice to American listeners that what had happened in the bloody, sweaty, tearful struggle that day was about to be told.

Archibald MacLeish addressed himself to this phenomenon on December 2, 1941, at a New York dinner held in Murrow's honor. He told Murrow, who was in the audience, ''You have accomplished one of the great miracles of the world . . . . You destroyed in the minds of many men and women in this country the superstition that what is done beyond 3,000 miles of water is not really done at all; the ignorant superstition that violence and lies and murder on another continent are not violence and lies and murder here; the cowardly and brutal superstition that the enslavement of mankind in a country where the sun rises at midnight by our clocks is not enslavement by the time we live by; the black and stifling superstition that what we cannot see and hear and touch can have no meaning for us.''

When Murrow spoke at this same dinner, he said that America must decide— and soon—how far and how fast it would go in order for democracy to survive. He said, ''Come as I do from the creeping blackout of liberty all over Europe, I am grateful that our decision will be taken in the full light of free and better-informed debate than exists anywhere else in the world, for such is our heritage and may it always be our habit.''

Free speech, free debate. It would be the recurring theme in his broadcasts for the next 19 years. He would say over and over, as in the case of the congressman who was denied a passport because of suspected leftist leanings, ''It's surely a matter worth arguing about.'' Friendly tells how, when CBS resumed its regular programming after President Johnson's crucial Gulf of Tonkin speech, Murrow, fatally ill, telephoned the network, protesting that. Such a declaration by the President cried out for instant analysis—for discussion and debate.

Murrow believed in news. He did not doubt what he was trying to do or the public's need to know. But as Eric Sevareid said the day Murrow died, ''Himself he doubted.'' He was forever asking himself, ''Is this good enough?'' That is what troubled him—not who would be upset by what he said, but whether it was right. And if it was right, was he communicating? Could the language be improved? How could the issues, so complicated, be made plain? He had standards—unexcelled today—that he was trying to meet.

I worked with Murrow in the production of his nightly broadcasts on CBS Radio and am the person who told him Joe McCarthy was dead. ''Let me see what comes in,'' he said. He gave no sign of satisfaction in the death of this man who represented what, in this country, he detested most.

That night Murrow led with the McCarthy story—name, age, survivors, cause of death. No review of the senator's career, only the essential details, completely straightforward. Looking back, I can see that from Murrow's standpoint this approach was exactly right. In 1957 everyone knew the background; it was recent history. Murrow believed that if he had gone into that history, so filled with controversy, his words might have been misinterpreted. He might have appeared to some listeners to be dancing on McCarthy's grave.

His fears were well founded. Richard Rovere in his book, *Senator Joe McCarthy*, quotes Murrow as saying, "I think I have never been more objective in reporting anything. Yet in the morning I found myself upbraided by hundreds for callousness, gloating, and fraudulent compassion."

I have no idea of the exact date—it was early in 1959—but what happened, if you saw it, was unforgettable. Murrow, script in hand, had gone from his office to Studio 9. It was three or four minutes before the radio broadcast was to start. His face was unusually pale. He held the script with both hands, which rested on the table; still the script trembled. I watched apprehensively through the glass panel and saw him say something to George Bryan, his announcer.

Suddenly, Murrow got up and came into the corridor where I was standing. In a small cubicle across from the studio, Blair Clark was preparing his program, "The World Tonight." Murrow stood in the doorway. "Blair," he said, "can you read for me?"

It was an emergency. Only seconds remained before Murrow was due on the air. Clark took Murrow's script and went into the studio. Bryan read the amended introduction, "And now, substituting for Edward R. Murrow, here is Blair Clark." I looked to see how Murrow was. He was walking, a bowed figure toward his office. Some green filing cabinets, holding old scripts, stood against the wall outside what was called "the Murrow area." There he stopped. I did not realize until then that he was crying. He folded his arms over the top of one of the cabinets and put his head down on them. He was sobbing like a child.

At that time, he had been broadcasting for 21 years. It was the first assignment that he had missed.

Murrow had not been well for some time. It was something all of us who worked with him knew. He coughed too much—smoked too much—and it seemed that some of the joy in his work was gone. Part of this was due to his continuing battle with the corporate brass; much of it was that he was not well. One thing about Murrow was that the door to his office was always open. A time came when it was closed for a while every afternoon. His doctor had ordered him to lie down on his couch to rest in the middle of the afternoon. The closed door was an ominous sign.

I didn't know on January 20, 1961, that his broadcast that day was to be his last. A week before the Kennedy inauguration, he had asked me to put together a batch of background material. I have that material, double-spaced for easy reading, before me as I write. I see that among the odds and ends of information which Murrow had marked as potentially usable was a reference in an old issue of *Puck* to "that fine political pastry, the Presidential turnover." It was the kind of mischievous language Murrow found irresistible.

As was usual for the inauguration, the networks were assigned working space in the basement of the Capitol. Entering the CBS quarters, which were filled with typewriters and electronic gear, I saw Bob Skedgell, who had charge of news coverage for CBS Radio. He looked pleased. He told me, "Ed says he will do a piece for us from the radio booth. We've scheduled it for right after his television spot.'' Skedgell was pleased because Murrow had remained loyal to radio. Television was king, but on this Inauguration Day radio would not be shortchanged.

Murrow and I had a separate work area, a small, temporary room smelling strongly of sawed pine. There were three monitors—one for each network—and two typewriters on a makeshift desk. In mid-morning Murrow appeared, looking tired. I knew he had been suffering cruelly from insomnia. He put paper in his typewriter and began writing a commentary; it was to run two minutes and was based on the advance of Kennedy's address, which was distributed in the midst of the historic snowstorm that had struck Washington the night before.

He wrote slowly, thoughtfully. Once a word was down on paper, it was there to stay. He filled the page—18 lines, triple-spaced—and not a word was crossed out. His last line was: ''He appeared to recognise thruout [sic] his brief inaugural—only 1,200 words—that difficulty is the excuse history never accepts.''

On the monitors we saw the oath-taking and watched Robert Frost wrestle with his poetry reading and John Kennedy give his inaugural address. After Kennedy had finished speaking, Murrow went back to the typewriter and wrote a new lead: ''It was a speech full of confidence, without arrogance.'' He wrote it above his earlier lead so that no room was left at the top of the page. Then he took another sheet of paper and filled out the two-minute spot. ''The oath,'' he wrote, ''was of course the heart of the matter, the most solemn moment in our national drama. . . .'' It was what he had felt, watching what took place.

I am not sure how much of this he used, finally, on nationwide television. I do know that when he came back from the TV studio to put on his overcoat, he looked so beaten that it was hard for me to remind him of the radio spot.

''Do I have to do it?'' he asked.

''You said you would.''

He did not want to go up to the radio booth. He did not want to do another broadcast. But he did. The radio booth was outdoors, raised on stilts so that it stood 20 feet above the ground, and it had a high window, facing the inauguration platform, allowing a clear view. The broadcaster reached this improvised studio by climbing a wooden ladder, straight up. It was like a ladder coming out of a swimming pool, except that it was two stories high. The sky was clear after the storm. The ceremonies had taken place in bright sunshine and sub-freezing cold. Murrow climbed the ladder and broadcast the radio piece he had promised.

Today, 10 years after this faithful man's death, I think of the diligence with which he reported every threat to freedom, whether it was the inability of the American Civil Liberties Union to hire a hall in Indianapolis or a political smear on the record of an unimportant Navy lieutenant or Joe McCarthy or restrictions on freedom of the press. Murrow seemed to take every assault on freedom as an assualt on himself. He reacted with anger. The anger and indignation were deep.

I thought I knew why. I believed it was because, as a matter of principle, he resented any infringement on freedom. But I did not really understand until his widow, Janet Murrow, said the reason was that Murrow, who had done obits on democratic governments in Europe, appreciated the mortality of democracy and was genuinely, and perpetually, fearful the same might happen here. That was why every symptom of tyranny alarmed him and forced him to speak.

Murrow was not intimidated by McCarthy and spoke so that millions could hear. What would he have said about the scandals of the Nixon administration? I like the way Fred Friendly once answered that question. "Ed," he said, "would have reacted with a sense of outrage—and a sense of history." I myself believe Murrow would have recognized in those scandals the symptoms of tyranny. Surely he would have been alarmed; surely he would have spoken. And I believe he would have said that it would be villainous for the press to play down the story. For he would see democracy endangered.

In a speech that he made after he became director of the United States Information Agency, Ed Murrow warned of the danger of taking freedom too much for granted. He said that if a confused public finally loses faith in America—in those who govern and those who inform—"then distrust, dissatisfaction, fear, and laziness can combine to turn them in desperation to that 'strong man' who can take them only to destruction."

At another time he said, "We were born free." He was filial toward this legacy of freedom. It was almost a kind of ancestor worship. He said of Englishmen under the blitz, "They were worthy of their ancestors." In his McCarthy broadcast he said, "We will not walk in fear, one of another. We will not be driven by fear into an age of unreason if we dig deep in our history and our doctrine and remember that we are not descended from fearful men."

Murrow would not be enthusiastic about the state of public-affairs programming today. He would admire many of the new generation of reporters and envy some of them. But for local station and network managers he would remain a hair shirt, pressing for coverage of more subjects in more depth in more prime time.

This man who was against any interruption of news by even a single commercial might ask how it is today that the network evening news is interrupted four times by commercials, while popular entertainment programs like "All in the Family" and "Sanford and Son" are interrupted only twice. He would decry the "happy talk" format in news and the threatening epidemic of news specializing in crime and sex. Addressing an annual meeting of the Radio-Television News Directors Association in Chicago, he said, "If radio news is to be regarded as a commodity, only acceptable when salable, then I don't care what you call it—I say it isn't news." That was Murrow speaking about radio news in 1958. He might well say the same about some television news in 1975. Salable is what "tabloid" and "happy talk" are all about.

Being human, Murrow made mistakes. But as he promised in the first broadcast of the radio series that began in 1947 and ran for 12 years, he endeavored to be the first to correct them. Repeatedly, in later on-air reports, he corrected errors of fact that had been presented in newscasts. But perhaps his most publicized mistake—a monumental error of judgment—was made after he had left CBS. That was when, as director of the USIA, he tried unsuccessfully to keep the BBC from showing the CBS documentary "Harvet of Shame." It was highly ironic, because Murrow himself had helped produce this film dealing with the plight of America's migrant workers and because he had so dauntlessly championed freedom of information throughout his career. Later, he publicly acknowledged his bad judgment. It was what might be called Murrow's own "Bay of Pigs."

The day Murrow died Eric Sevareid said, ''He was a shooting star. We shall live in his afterglow a very long time.'' Sevareid also said, ''We shall not see his like again.'' In a sense that observation is true. There will be only one Ed Murrow. For there to be another would require an identical meeting of man and event. He was a ''first''—the first reporter of renown in his medium. But who can say that another broadcast reporter of his fiber will not—cannot—appear?

Bibliography

The life and times of Edward R. Murrow can be studied by reading Alexander Kendrick's fascinating book *Prime Time* (Little, Brown and Company, 1969). Also available is *In Search of Light: The Broadcasts of E.R.M.* (Avon Books, 1972).

Times have changed since the days of Edward R. Murrow. Ratings are king and dictate the building of elaborate sets such as this one at NBC's Los Angeles station. KNBC offers two 60 minute news shows and the NBC Nightly News each weekday evening from 5-7:30 P.M. Here anchorman Jess Marlow (center) reads the news while three specialists (consumer affairs, sports, special report) wait their turn.

Summaries of Radio, Television and Cable Television—1976

Facilities. Radio stations—8,010 radio stations in operation: 4,459 commercial AM; 2,752 commercial FM, and 799 noncommercial FM. *Television stations*— 961 television stations in operation: 513 commercial VHF's; 196 commercial UHF's; 97 noncommercial VHF's, and 155 noncommercial UHF's. *Cable television stations*—3,350 operating cable systems serving 7,300 communities.

Homes served. Radio—An estimated 98.6 percent of all homes have radio receivers. Approximately 290 million sets are in homes; 110 million sets are out of homes (automobiles, etc.). *Television*—An estimated 97 percent of all homes have television receivers. There are approximately 112 million television sets in the U.S.; 48.6 million of these are color sets. Approximately 44 percent of all U.S. homes have two or more television receivers. An estimated 86 percent of all homes can receive UHF signals. *Cable television*—An estimated 10.0 million subscribers are linked to cable television systems, about 15 percent of all U.S. television households.

Listening and viewing. The average American home listens to radio for approximately three hours each day, according to Arbitron Radio Service. The average American home watches TV for six hours and 49 minutes per day, according to A. C. Nielsen statistics. A study by R. H. Bruskin Associates shows the average adult viewer watches just under three hours of television daily. Television viewers who are hooked up to cable television systems "view 11.5 percent more television" than do non-CATV viewers, according to a 1974 Arbitron study.

Advertising revenue. In 1974, the last year for which the FCC has issued figures, radio had $1.6 billion revenue and $84 million profit. Television had almost $3.8 billion revenue and $737 million profit. Radio's profits were down 23.6 percent from 1973; most of the decrease was among AM stations. Television's profits were up 12.9 percent from 1973. Cable television, which gets most of its revenue from subscriptions and installation charges, had only about $3.5 million revenue from advertising which appeared on "origination" channels. Total income for cable was approximately $500 million with no profit figures available.

Sources: Federal Communications Commission reports, *Variety, Broadcasting, The Official Associated Press Almanac, 1976, The Statistical Abstract of the U.S., 1975;* Arbitron Press Releases, *Nielsen Newsletter.*

12 Obscenity, Violence and Drugs

Dirty Business in Court—

Scenario for Violence—

The Impact of Photographs—

That Word—

The Censorship of Song Lyrics—

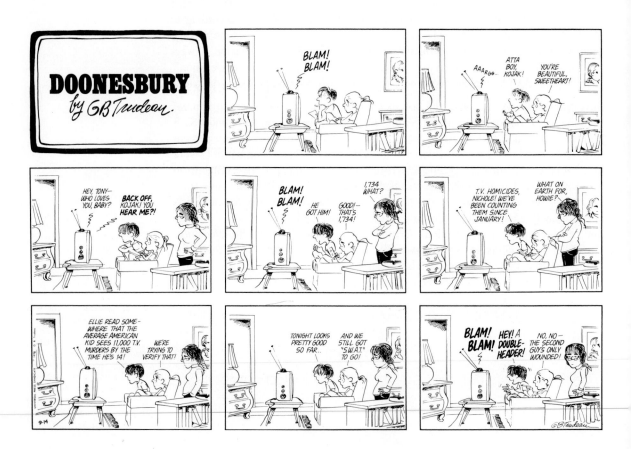

Dirty Business in Court

By Harriet F. Pilpel
and Marjorie T. Parsons

> No government has ever succeeded in finding a balanced policy of combatting unhealthy sexual propaganda without injuring legitimate freedom or provoking other or equally grave disorders.
>
> —Jacques Leclerq, Catholic University of Louvain

It is one of the odder paradoxes of the Victorian era that while motherhood was enshrined, sex, which must have had something to do with that hallowed state, developed a bad name and came increasingly to be equated with obscenity. In the early years of this republic, laws reflected concern with such social warts as blasphemy and public drunkenness, but obscenity was not viewed as a major problem. By 1873, however, obscenity was perceived as a full-fledged issue in the United States, and the federal Comstock Act was passed to cope with it, followed by a train of "little Comstock Acts" in the states. Nonetheless, as time went on, the courts and various administrative agencies tended to recognize that the sweeping sexual prohibitions of the Comstock laws violated constitutional guarantees. By 1957 the United States Supreme Court in *Roth v. U.S.* and other cases appeared to permit a wide latitude of expression. Then, on June 21, 1973, by a narrow 5 to 4 majority, the Court handed down a series of rulings with grave implications for First Amendment freedoms.

While some commentators expressed cautious optimism that the new holdings might not prove too damaging, it soon became apparent that Justice Brennan, in his dissenting opinion, had all too accurately diagnosed them as "nothing less than a rejection of First Amendment premises . . . and an invitation to widespread suppression." As the effects of the rulings became evident, the optimists reasoned that the manifest confusion might generate its own remedy: the Court would amend or clarify or reverse itself in its decisions on pending cases.

The long-awaited decisions last June in the *Carnal Knowledge (Jenkins v. Georgia)* and *Hamling v. U.S.* cases did little to encourage that hope.

What is the background of the 1973-1974 Supreme Court obscenity decisions? What follows from them? How should they be approached? Most significantly, what can be done about them?

The First Amendment to the U.S. Constitution prohibits government from passing any law abridging freedom of speech and press. For many years, two Supreme Court Justices, William O. Douglas and Hugo Black, steadfastly maintained that the Constitution means exactly what it says: no abridgement of expression. Nevertheless, for decades the majority of the Court has held that "obscenity is not protected by the First Amendment," though a precise definition of what it is has eluded the court and led to a tangle of confusing rulings. Justice Potter Stewart said at one point: "I may not be able to define it, but I certainly know it when I see it." So, it seems, does everyone else. But what is "known" to be obscene varies erratically with the viewer. A Girl Scout pamphlet is "obscene" in the state of

Harriet Pilpel is an author-lawyer, who specializes in First Amendment freedoms and sex and the law. She also chaired the ACLU Communications Media Committee. Marjorie Parsons is coordinator for the National Ad Hoc Committee Against Censorship. She was for many years executive story editor for MGM; in recent years she has been a free-lance writer and editor. This piece appeared in *The Civil Liberties Review*, Vol. 1, No. 4 (Fall 1974) © 1974 American Civil Liberties Union and is used with permission of that publication.

Washington; *The Dictionary of American Slang* in Florida; *Soul on Ice* in Connecticut; *Spoon River Anthology* in Illinois; *Slaughterhouse-Five* in North Dakota; *Catcher in the Rye* in half the states of the union.

The 1966 *Memoirs v. Massachusetts* decision attempted to pin down the eely concept of obscenity. For a work to be judged obscene, it had to pass all three parts of the Court's new test: 1) the "dominant theme" of the material "taken as a whole" had to appeal to "prurient interest in sex" and 2) it had to be "patently offensive to the average person, applying contemporary community standards" and 3) it had to be "utterly without redeeming social value." In the earlier *Roth* decision, the Court had carefully noted that "sex and obscenity are not synonymous. . . . Sex, a great and mysterious motive force in human life, has indisputably been a subject of absorbing interest to mankind through the ages; it is one of the vital problems of human interest and public concern."

Certain refinements of the general test evolved at various times in response to specific situations. For example, the Court made it clear that if material was beamed directly at children, a somewhat different test would apply. Moreover, the question of whether particular material is obscene could be affected by the context of its presentation. The Court took a dim view of "thrusting" explicitly sexual material on unwilling adults in public places, and of "pandering" or promoting material in an offensive manner. Two federal postal statutes were passed, one requiring the sender of "sexually oriented material" to identify it as such on the wrapper. The other provided that people not wishing to receive material they regard as obscene need only register at the post office their refusal to accept mail from a named sender and such mail would not be delivered to them.

On the surface the obscenity issue appeared to be taking on more rational dimensions. Obscenity actions were still being brought (sometimes aimed more at politically or socially dissident ideas than at over-explicitness about sex), but on the whole they did not succeed. Beneath the surface, however, a well organized anti-obscenity ferment was working. The "traffic in obscenity and pornography" was found to be of such "national concern" that Congress funded a commission in 1967 to study "the causal relationships between such materials and anti-social behavior" and to recommend appropriate means to deal with the problem. The president appointed nineteen distinguished members (one, Kenneth Keating, subsequently resigned to become Ambassador to India) to the Commission on Obscenity and Pornography, and they embarked on an intensive two-year study of the subject. Since there were little or no hard data to support a causal connection between pronography and crime, 70-odd carefully designed scientific studies were undertaken to determine what, if any, the connection might be.

The conclusion, the commission reported in 1970, was that none existed. On the contrary, empirical evidence clearly indicated that pornography appeared to act as a safety valve to ease tensions that might otherwise erupt into criminal activity. Offenders imprisoned for sex-related crimes, for example, reported they had a more restrictive upbringing and significantly less early exposure to pornography than their peers who did not become entangled with the law. The profile of the typical

In a cover article surveying contemporary American attitudes toward and laws on pornography, *Time's* editors expressed concern about the relationship between print and film pornography and prostitution, massage parlors and criminal elements.

user of pornography revealed a middle-aged male, white, middle class, married, very likely to have gone to college and with a 25% chance of having attended graduate school.

Almost every adult American is exposed to some pornography at some time, but it is estimated that only about 2% become more-or-less steady consumers of it. In one study married couples volunteered to view explicitly sexual films over a considerable period of time. They showed little change in their sexual behavior patterns beyond increased ease between husband and wife in talking about sex; they did, however, develop growing and finally overpowering boredom with the films. Yet 56% of Americans apparently feel that pornography causes "moral breakdown," although only 1% thought they personally could be in any way affected by it. It is noteworthy that their concern is not for themselves but for others who, they fear, are more vulnerable.

As a result of these and other studies, two-thirds of the commission recommended repeal of all laws restricting the access of consenting adults to any material of their choice. President Nixon ridiculed and the Congress disowned the report. On the other side, concerned groups formed an Ad Hoc Committee to urge that the report be given a fair hearing and judged on its merits.

Then in June 1973, a Supreme Court majority consisting of Nixon's four appointees (Chief Justice Warren Burger and Justices William Rehnquist, Harry Blackmun, and Lewis Powell), joined by Justice Byron White, handed down a number of decisions that the dissenting justices and many others regarded as a major threat to First Amendment freedoms. One immediate result was that more than 150 anti-pornography bills were introduced in 38 of the 44 state legislatures in regular session during 1973-1974. New laws, by no means all of them bad and many much less restrictive than the Court said was permissible, were passed in fourteen states; action may still be taken in others. Much of the trouble deriving from the 1973 holdings has originated in the rash of city, county, and other local ordinances, some so restrictive they would ban the portrayal of an infant's bare bottom. (What, asked one plaintive librarian, was she to do about *Your New Baby*, a popular illustrated book on the care of newborns.)

Many specific problems stemmed from the 1973 holdings. Thus, while to many it had seemed clear that the "community standards" part of the tripartite obscenity test established by the Court in 1966 referred to national standards, the majority opinions in 1973 declared that national standards were not intended, and observed that the standards of Maine and Mississippi (states) and those of New York and Las Vegas (cities) need not necessarily be the same. It is not surprising, therefore, that a hodge-podge of laws was adopted, defining the community as the state, "the county or lesser subdivision" (Florida), the "local community" (Iowa and Virginia), or "the community from which a jury is drawn" (Alabama). Whether material is considered obscene could depend, in border towns, on which side of the street it is distributed.

Under the June 1973 decisions the "social value" part of the test changed; the question was no longer whether a work was "utterly without redeeming social value"but whether it lacked "serious literary, artisitc, political, or scientific value." Apparently if religious, educational, and just plain entertainment values count at all, they have to be smuggled in under one of the four approved categories. In *Miller V. California* the Court said that to determine whether a work is obscene, the "trier of fact," that is, usually a jury made up of "average persons," applying "contemporary community standards," would have only to "find that the work, taken as a whole, appeals to prurient interest." This might make some sense if a 1969 nationwide Gallup poll had not found that 58% of the adult sample, presumably made up of average persons, had never read a book from cover to cover. In any event, the 1973 holdings have led a number of communities to deny their citizens the right to enjoy a wide range of obviously non-obscene works: *The Grapes of Wrath* by John Steinbeck, *Go Ask Alice*, Anonymous (Christopher Award 1972, Maxi Award 1973), *In the Night Kitchen* by Maurice Sendak (winner of six "Best Children's Book of 1970" awards including the Hans Christian Andersen Medal), *The Learning Tree* by Gordon Parks (Spingarn Medal 1973), *Playboy* magazine, and the 1973 Motion Picture Academy Award nominee, *Carnal Knowledge*.

Jenkins v. Georgia, one of the two cases on which the Supreme Court ruled on June 24, 1974, involved *Carnal Knowledge*; the Court unanimously decided that the film was not obscene. It had been hoped, in the face of the legislative and judicial chaos that followed the 1973 holdings, that perhaps one or more of the majority justices would be moved to join Justice Douglas in his minority opinion that all expression is protected by the First Amendment; or with the Brennan-Marshall-Stewart position that the government has no right to dictate to consenting adults what they may choose to look at or listen to in private. Instead, the same five-justice majority that produced the 1973 opinions reaffirmed its earlier stance with some emendations that rendered the whole obscenity problem even more obscure.

On the positive side, *Jenkins* does seem to narrow the range of what may be judged obscene. The Court reiterated the *Miller* rule that what is intended to be prohibited is "representations or descriptions of ultimate sexual acts, normal or perverted, actual or simulated," and "representations or descriptions of masturbation, excretory functions, and the lewd exhibition of the genitals." But it observed that "Nudity alone does not render material obscene." The fact that the Court unanimously regarded *Carnal Knowledge* as not obscene would be more reassuring if on the same day the Court had not also decreed that defendants in obscenity cases have no right to introduce as a defense "comparable materials" that have been judged non-obscene.

However, the Court pointed out in the 1974 decisions that "juries do not have unbridled discretion in determining what is 'patently offensive.' " Normally a jury's decision on the *facts* of a case are not subject to judicial review; only errors of procedure of convictions based on laws thought to be in violation of the Constitution are. The Supreme Court stated in 1973 that obscenity is a matter of fact to be determined by a jury; the Georgia Supreme Court, in upholding the lower Georgia court's decision, had gone along with this view. Once again enmeshed in the nettlesome question of what obscenity is, the Supreme Court in 1974 decided it is not so much a matter of simple, or even complex, fact as a "legal term of art" (*Hamling*). "Obscenity," then, concerns an evaluation so basically unreliable that jury verdicts on it must be subject to judicial review to ensure that they square with what the Court had in mind in *Miller* and related cases. "It would be wholly at odds with *Miller*," the Court stated, "to uphold an obscenity conviction based on a defendant's depiction of a woman with a bare midriff, even though a properly charged jury unanimously agreed on the verdict.''

This may legitimate bikinis and perhaps *Your New Baby*; but it does not, in the minority opinion of Justices Brennan, Stewart, Marshall, and Douglas, ''extricate the Court from the mire of case-by-case determinations of obscenity.'' Nor does it ''diminish the chill on protected expression that derives from the uncertainty of the underlying standard.'' As long as the *Miller* formula prevails, ''one cannot say with certainty that material is obscene until at least five members of this Court, applying inevitably obscure standards, have pronounced it so.''

As for community standards, the Court not only failed to rescue them from the limbo of *Miller*, but drew community boundaries even more amorphously. Jurors need not rely on the standards of a ''hypothetical statewide community,'' much less a national community, but may be guided by their understanding of the standards of ''the community from which they come.'' And it is even ''proper to ask them to apply community standards without specifying what 'community' ''!

Hamling v. U.S., decided the same day as the *Carnal Knowledge* case, was, like the 1973 majority opinions a 5 to 4 determination. Again the majority addressed itself to ''community standards.'' The parties appealing the lower courts' rulings were convicted of mailing sexually explicit material to advertise their illustrated edition of *The Report of The Commission on Obscenity and Pornography*. The jury was unable to reach agreement on whether or not the book was obscene, but it did decide that the advertising brochure, also illustrated, was. Much of the argument in the case (tried prior to *Miller*) concerned the admissibility of evidence indicating that by the standards of southern California, where the case was heard, the material was not obscene. A university student, under the direction of her journalism professor, had polled a random sample of 718 residents of San Diego County, a substantial majority of whom expressed the view that ''the material should be generally available to the public.'' The presiding judge refused to admit the poll in evidence, solely on the ground that it reflected local standards rather than the standards of ''the nation as a whole,'' which he understood earlier Supreme Court decisions to mandate.

The Supreme Court majority in *Hamling*, though it stated that the publishers should have whatever benefits *Miller* afforded them on this score, declared that the failure to admit local standards, and the judge's instruction that the jury must consider only the sensibilities of the nation as a whole, would not have ''materially affected the deliberations of the jury.'' The minority opinion differed rather vehemently: '' . . .in addition to the palpable absurdity of the Court's surmises that the introduction of the San Diego study could not have affected the jury's deliberations . . .the Court's assertions that the jury could not have ruled differently if instructed to apply local, not national, standards evinces a claim to omniscience hardly mortal.'' The minority opinion recalled that the *Miller* rationale for supporting local rather than national standards was precisely that it *would* permit a local community to apply a more permissive test to materials it found accpetable, regardless of what the rest of the nation thought.

If the "local standards" of *Miller* provided cold comfort for those in the case found guilty of promoting an obscene publication, the *Hamling* gloss offered no greater solace. They argued that since the postal statute under which they were convicted was a federal law, yet subject to widely varying local interpretation, the law should be declared void because it is too vague. The majority opinion dismissed this argument summarily, seeing no inconsistency or constitutional impediment. Not so the minority: "Under today's 'local' standards construction . . .the guilt or innocence of distributors of identical materials mailed from the same locale can now turn on the dicey course of transit or place of delivery of the materials. . . . National distributors choosing to send their products in interstate travels will be forced to cope with community standards of every hamlet through which their goods may wander. Because these variegated standards are impossible to discern, national distributors, fearful of risking the expense and difficulty of defending against prosecution in any one of several remote communities, must inevitably be led to debilitating self-censorship that abridges First Amendment rights of the people.

Another disappointing aspect of the 1974 decisions concerns the question of the need for prior civil proceedings to determine whether a work is legally obscene before criminal actions may legitimately be brought against those who purvey or present that work. Without this safeguard, the situation is analogous to a road where the speed limit varies capriciously from five to 55 miles an hour, with no speeds posted, though drivers on the highway are held criminally liable if they violate limits they have no way of knowing until they are arrested. The 1973 Supreme Court majority opinion in *Paris Adult Theater I v. Slayton* seemed to bear in the direction of prior civil proceedings; it was hoped that in the *Hamling* and *Jenkins* decisions, the Court would advance further in that direction. Instead it by-passed the issue, merely echoing the 1959 ruling in *Smith V. California* which held: "It is constitutionally sufficient that the prosecution show that a defendant had knowledge of the contents of the materials he distributes, and that he knew the character and nature of the materials." In effect, where even the sophisticated intellects of the Supreme Court justices cannot reach agreement, a teacher, bookseller, or librarian who looks at a work must decide in advance whether or not it is obscene, risking criminal prosecution if the guess is held to be wrong.

On balance, it would seem that *Jenkins* and *Hamling* leave the First Amendment in greater disarray in 1974 than even *Miller* portended in 1973. The Supreme Court has made it clear that a woman's bare midriff is not obscene, but we can be sure of very little else. What may be judged obscene is apparently subject to the standards of communities which have no ascertainable boundaries and in fact need not even be *any* specific community. Criminal actions may constitutionally be pursued against librarians, booksellers, film exhibitors, museums and gallery staffs, and many others without any prior notice that what they are presenting may be considered offensive under whatever "community standards" turn out to be. A producer of materials distributed nationally may be liable to prosecution at any or all points en route as well as at the points of origin and destination. Everyone engaged in the transmission of ideas is charged with the responsibility of not merely outguessing the Supreme Court, but of correctly divining what thousands of communities, by their own idiosyncratic lights, may decide is obscene.

The picture, however, is not wholly discouraging. The Court's rulings caused many legislatures to reexamine their obscenity laws, and several of them decided to remove some of the more restrictive facets despite the Court's decisions. South Dakota, West Virginia, and Iowa repealed their adult obscenity statutes and substituted laws regulating only materials for minors. Vermont, which only had a minors statute, added a mandatory prior civil proceedings provision. North Carolina retained the pre-1973 *Memoirs* test and added mandatory prior civil proceedings. A highly threatening bill was defeated in Pennsylvania and another was significantly diluted in New York. On the negative side, Nebraska passed a most repressive bill. In Oregon, which had a perfectly workable minors-only and public display statute, a "bad" bill was pressured through the legislature, but determined opponents managed to gather enough signatures to force a referendum. The voters will decide in November (after this article goes to press) whether to retain the old law or adopt the new one. In many other states, legislatures have been marking time to see how the Court's 1974 decisions might affect proposed legislation, much of it very repressive. Legislative action may now, of course, be expected.

At no time in recent years has the right to read, see, and hear been under more serious challenge than it is today, not only for young people but for their elders. The real target in many "anti-obscenity" actions is not obscenity at all, but unpopular, dissident, irreverent, or satirical expression unsettling to current complacencies. The crux of the problem, as Justice Douglas has observed, is that censorship "casts too wide a net," suppressing ideas that clearly deserve protection, and often destroying innocent people in the process.

Trying to legislate morality can prove a tricky business; our earlier noble experiment, Prohibition, should alert us to some of the traps into which we may be stumbling. At best it is an exercise in futility, since it is doubtful that any culture has ever succeeded in wiping out pornography. At worst it imperils the very basis of the society it purports to protect, the freedom of expression that Justice Cardozo called "the matrix, the indispensable condition of nearly all our other freedoms."

Bibliography

For a better understanding of the issues raised here, besides checking basic texts used in mass communication law classes, the student might consult Victor B. Cline, editor, *Where Do You Draw the Line? An Exploration into Media Violence, Pornography and Censorship*, Brigham Young University Press, 1974, several articles debating the issue of complete freedom and regulated freedom in some areas. Also see Ray C. Rist, ed., *The Pornography Controversy,* Transaction Books, 1975. Contains 14 articles on pornography, tending toward the pro-freedom view.

Also important is a piece by Paul Bender, "The Supreme Court's Decision on Obscenity", which appeared in the previous edition of this reader and originally was published in the *Los Angeles Times*. Bender was general counsel for the national Commission on Obscenity and Pornography (1968-70) and is a professor of law at the Pennsylvania Law School. A special issue of *Public Interest* (Winter, 1971) offered four responses to Walter Bernes' "Pornography vs. Democracy: The Case for Censorship." Other journals, and law reviews, have carried similar articles. One of interest was Leonard Berkowitz'

"Sex and Violence: We Can't Have It Both Ways," found in *Psychology Today* (Dec. 1971). Regarding the content of films, excellent background could be gained by reading the *Wisconsin Law Review* (1970) article "Self-Censorship of the Movie Industry: An Historical Perspective on Law and Social Change"—a 47-page treatment discussing movie ratings and the response of the film industry to law and public policy.

Scenario for Violence

By George Gerbner

The debate over violence on television has settled in for a long run. It promises to outlast both "Kojak" and "Hawaii Five-O." While the partisans haven't yet come to blows, neither have they settled much. It may be they've been arguing over the wrong issues.

Television culture has three seasons: starters, replacements and summer reruns. This fall, however, is the beginning of more than some 27 network programs. The industry's much-touted "family hours" plan is getting off to its shaky start, and along with it the perennial brouhaha about TV violence and sex (sex on *television*?) has been moved from its customary place in summer reruns time to the starter season. With two Congressional committees getting into the act, and with our Violence Profile of the last starter season indicating an upswing in video mayhem, network promises are in for a thorough going-over. Or is it all a charade for public consumption? What are the issues behind the hearings, the reports and the research?

The way a culture depicts sex and violence is symptomatic of its definition of humanity and is indicative of the structure of its power. The conflict over that depiction goes beyond fads and fashions and becomes part of the general contest over who should define that which safely entertains (in both senses of the world) and that which threatens the established social order.

In our time, that contest revolves mainly around television. The symbolic representation of violence and sex in the mainstream of American culture has become a battleground in the larger struggle over the control of that mainstream.

Perhaps there is no more significant battleground than the depiction of vital human acts. But the battledust of clichés and oversimplifications clouds the issues and confuses experts and laypersons alike. Everyone is supposed to know what sex and violence mean; the debate is about how to deal with them. But they mean very different things in "real life" and on television. Real life violence maims and kills; television violence demonstrates, which is the essence of its symbolic functions. The question of what it demonstrates (the communication question) must be tackled before we turn to the question of how to deal with it.

Even many communication researchers set out to investigate only what they assumed or feared stories of violence might cause instead of first studying what they

George Gerbner is Professor of Communications and Dean of the Annenberg School of Communications, University of Pennsylvania. He is co-editor of *Communications Technology and Social Policy; Understanding the New "Cultural Revolution";* and editor of the quarterly *Journal of Communication.* This article, from the Oct. 1975 *Human Behavior* is used with Dr. Gerbner's permission.

might mean. By limiting their focus to preconceived effects such as aggression, they have ignored the full range and diversity of symbolic functions (including fear of victimization and the cultivation of a hierarchically structured sense of risk and power) and thus may have actually obscured the real significance of the rise of a mass-produced common symbolic environment largely ruled by violence. Politicians and bureaucrats have been simplistic for more understandable reasons. Sex and violence make "good issues" because they exploit fears about moral breakdown and the erosion of public safety and order. But behind the gestures and the jockeying is the unarticulated struggle for influence over television as the central cultural arm of the industrial order.

The contest revolves mainly around television. The symbolic representation of violence and sex in the mainstream of our culture has become a battleground in the larger struggle for control of that mainstream.

From the vantage point of a communications researcher involved in the study of television violence for various commissions, I would like to sketch the progress of that struggle and then focus on what our research seems to say about the meaning of violence and how that should affect the issue of control.

"ANTIVIOLENCE BOMB UNDER MEDIA", cried *Variety*'s front-page banner headline on January 29 of [1975]. Since then the industry's bomb-disposal squad, the National Association of Broadcasters (NAB), dampened the sputtering device by declaring a two-hour *cordon sanitaire* of evening "family programming." We are now witnessing the first round of that experiment. Even the Motion Picture Association of America—under its new code and rating administrator, communications professor Richard D. Heffner, who was pressed by complaints from some communities and especially from distributors abroad—gave its first X rating on grounds of violence alone—if one can call "violence alone" the offending scene in a Japanese martial arts movie entitled *The Street Fighter* in which the hero vividly castrates a 300-lb. black rapist.

It is too early to tell whether the new NAB code will stick and just how it will work. Independence may circumvent it, authorized exceptions may defeat it, time zones may confuse it, the kiddies may stay up later (more than 20 million of them already watch beyond 9 p.m.; 3 million still hang on at midnight!), the "adult" fare may become even more exploitive and the lack of definition may confound the whole effort. But, in any case, the "family hours" will not stem the tide of congressional and public concern.

The "antiviolence bomb" is not a passing phenomenon. It is, according to *Variety* analyst Morry Roth, a growing national mood and movement. Some cities (Chicago, for example) are drafting antiviolence statutes that will certainly wind up in the courts, and these are also affected by the new movement. "Unlike the antiporno laws," writes Roth, "the antiviolence movement would have a large portion of the liberal intelligentsia on its side, a not inconsiderable factor. So, too, the blue-collar class that worried about porno undoing its daughters is increasingly beginning to believe that the media is [sic] creating the growing violence in the streets. A coalition between Archie Bunker and The Professor is not too wild a dream."

That coalition is no longer a dream. Conflicting pressures converge on TV as the most universally visible common scenario and symptom of an increasingly troubled society. In less than a quarter century, video has come to symbolize all that pagan rites, priestly mumbo jumbo, Machiavelli, the robber barons, Wall Street and Madison Avenue meant to former generations of crusaders and critics.

Violence, like pornography or crime, is largely a matter of definition. Most societies, including ours, define it one way for rulers and another way for the ruled. We are not as likely to decry as violent the force used in maintaining the established order as that used in transgressing or threatening it. Historically, concern about symbolic sex or violence arises when the "wrong" people are exposed to it. Obscenity became a legal concept when cheap printing made it available to the lower classes. The great 19th-century debates about pulp literature and the penny press set the stage for the controversy (and research) on the effects of movies and led to the adoption of the motion picture and broadcast codes of industry self-regulation.

Senator Estes Kefauver, whose crime investigations spread the "myth" of the Mafia and marked national television's coming of age (and his own rise to national visibility), chaired the first Senate Subcommittee on Juvenile Delinquency to inquire into the industry's inside workings. The next chairperson, Senator Thomas J. Dodd, made political hay of video lawlessness (before he himself was censured for real corruption) and added volumes to the archives on TV violence and children. Senator John O. Pastore took up the cudgels a few years ago and, as chairperson of the Senate Subcommittee on Communications, has wielded them longer and more skillfully than has anyone before him.

Televised hearings demonstrated what the medium could do for (and to) politicians and started the politicos thinking about what they could do with the medium. In the wake of a presidential assassination and the civil rights and antiwar turmoil, two months after the student takeover of Columbia University, a month after the uprising in France and five days after the shooting of Robert F. Kennedy, President Lyndon B. Johnson established the National Commission on the Causes and Prevention of Violence and named Milton S. Eisenhower to head it. When the commission completed its work and released its findings, including *Violence and the Media*, the reports were buried and the recommendations quickly swept under the rug. That was not unusual; it happened to the Kerner Commission, the Pornography Commission, the Scranton "campus unrest" Commission. The creation of a presidential commission serves as a symbolic act that usually calms the populace and scares the target industry. The practical results are generally achieved within six months. The Eisenhower Commission, for example, was set up in June 1968. What effect its media investigations were to have was achieved by December of that year when network presidents were called on the carpet to tell the commission what they had done or intended to do. By the time the volumes of findings (including our own research report) came out, the political situation had changed, and another committee was already at work on the same problem.

That this other effort did not follow the pattern of presidential commissions was largely due to the skill and timing of Sen. Pastore. Using as leverage the anxiety that gave rise to the Eisenhower Commission plus the turbulent televised images of the Chicago Democratic Convention and a new "law-and-order" administration, Sen. Pastore set in motion a government process that would be capable of follow-up and would provide fixed targets for future demands for action. He recalled how the smoking-cancer "link" had been established as a basis for official policy. So in March 1969 he wrote a letter to the new secretary of Health, Education and Welfare (HEW) requesting that he direct the U.S. surgeon general to appoint a Scientific Advisory Committee to conduct a study to determine if there was a link between TV violence and antisocial behavior such as might constitute a public health hazard.

The request was quickly accepted. However, following the precedent set by the surgeon general's Advisory Committee on Smoking and Health, the industry (in this case television) was given the opportunity to blackball seven from a list of 40 social scientists on grounds that they had already taken an affirmative position on the issue. No scientific groups were similarly invited to exclude proindustry representatives; after all, it was the cooperation of the industry, and not of the scientists, that was to be sought. Of the 12 committee members finally chosen, two were network staff researchers, two were consultants to the networks and one was a former TV industry employee. The flap over stacking the deck in this way threatened the credibility of the work for a while but actually turned out to stiffen the backs and strengthen the hands of the drafters of an objective report. Two years, $1 million, one extensive independent research program and five volumes of findings later, for the first time in the history of any media research, an industry-approved committee of scientists unanimously agreed that there "was some preliminary indication of a causal relationship" between exposure to television violence and violent behavior. The first press accounts misread the report, but, called to elaborate before Sen. Pastore's subcommittee, the surgeon general bared the teeth in it:

"After a review of the committee's report and the five volumes of original research undertaken at your request, as well as a review of previous literature on the subject, my professional response today is that the broadcasters should be put on notice. The overwhelming consensus and the unanimous Scientific Advisory Committee's report indicates that televised violence indeed does have an adverse effect on certain members of our society."

"While the committee's report is carefully phrased and qualified in language acceptable to social scientists, it is clear to me that the casual relationship between televised violence and antisocial behavior is sufficient to warrant appropriate and immediate remedial action. The data on social phenomena such as television violence and/or aggressive behavior will never be clear enough for all social scientists to agree on a formulation of a succinct statement of causality. But there comes a time when the data are sufficient to justify action. That time has come."

At the end of the March 1972 hearings, Sen. Pastore declared that "what has taken place in the past few days is nothing less than a scientific and cultural breakthrough. For we know there is a causal relation between televised violence and antisocial behavior which is sufficient to warrant immediate remedial action. It is this certainty which has eluded men of good will so long."

I am not so sure that the "break-through" was as much scientific and cultural (previous reports contained similar evidence) as it was political. Pastore succeeded in using his position as chairperson of the committee that must pass on legislation affecting broadcasting licensing and other industry matters to vest responsibility for "his issue" in government agencies that could be prodded whenever the situation demanded it. In his breakthrough statement, Pastore immediately called upon the HEW secretary, the surgeon general and the FCC to establish a "violence index" that would yield annual reports "measuring the amount of televised violence entering American homes."

That was when the "antiviolence bomb" began to tick. Pastore knew there already *was* a violence index because I had developed it for the surgeon general's Scientific Advisory Committee and because it had been introduced into the record of the same hearing by Rep. John M. Murphy of New York. So he could just sit back and wait—but not too long.

The secretary designated the National Institute of Mental Health (NIMH) as the HEW agency carrying on after the Scientific Advisory Committee discharged its duties. NIMH convened a conference of research consultants in June 1972 to discuss what to do about the senator's request. They recommended broadening the scope of the research and constructing a profile that would take account of the social relationships portrayed in the violence and their effects on viewers. Our research team, now including coinvestigator Larry Gross and other associates, received a NIMH grant for a broadgauge project on television content and effects, called Cultural Indicators, including the development of the violence profile. Pastore was told that everything was under control and results would be forthcoming in two to four years.

Two years later, Pastore held further hearings. NIMH director Bertram S. Brown pleaded for another two to four years and advised the senator that a social science research council committee was reviewing research options and directions. I presented our newly developed violence profile. Network presidents also testified and Pastore congratulated them but warned that "we will keep your feet to the fire."

At year's end FCC chairperson Richard E. Wiley, prodded by Pastore and pressured by the Appropriations Committee, met with network presidents in a series of private sessions. Out of these sessions came the NAB plan. In February, the FCC issued a report announcing what the networks already promised and praised them for their promises. Pre-occupied with energy hearings and FCC nominations, Pastore called the plan "a wonderful idea," said he'd call hearings this fall and, at least temporarily, passed the cudgels to House Communications Subcommittee chairperson Torbert MacDonald. With his freshly streamlined, staffed and budgeted subcommittee geared up and ready to take its turn in the limelight, MacDonald blasted the FCC announcement as "like writing a letter to Santa Claus." He announced his intention to hold hearings of his own and gave clear notice that the "family hour" plan will not defuse the "antiviolence bomb."

TV Guide (February 8, 1975) carried a column by Kevin Phillips that revealed a deeper concern. "Demographics suggest that television violence has its greatest effect in low-income ghetto areas," wrote Phillips. "I hasten to say that the network impetus is not one of social disruption but private profit." He concluded that "as winter turns to spring and summer, unemployment is almost certain to rise to levels not seen since the 1930s . . . Violent crime could reach unprecedented levels . . . If a clear nexus can be found, measures must be taken to suspend or prohibit certain types of programming."

The "antiviolence bomb" plot seems to include mounting pressure on the networks as somehow responsible for exacerbating if not actually causing social unrest under worsening conditions. The scenario is well calculated to keep the networks' "feet to the fire." But is it not strange to claim that the modern corrupters of youth and inciters of the dispossessed are not some errant philosophers or reformist prophets or radical pamphleteers but the cautious cultural organs of corporate America? Would the business establishment incite costly social disruption just for the sake of profits derived from TV violence? I believe that it is both more parsimonious and more plausible to suggest that the social control functions of symbolic violence may—from the point of view of "law and order," if not mental health—outweigh the disruptive consequences.

Historically, symbolic violence in storytelling from tribal rites to fairy tales, pulps, news, movies and television served to instill awe of authority and to demonstrate preferred notions of how power works in the family, community, nation and universe. The individual mayhem such exhibitions inspire may be the price we pay, appalling as that is to increasingly more people, for the collective cultivation of a sense of danger and fear and ultimate acquiescence in a hierarchy of social controls. Those controls work when most people voluntarily submit to them most of the time.

Assisting that process by symbolic means are the ritualistic demonstrations of power and authority through dramatic violence. Television raised that ritual to the assembly-line efficiency of more than seven acts of violence per prime-time hour and (our children obviously need more education) double that number per cartoon-time hour.

Our research shows that violence is central to the symbolic world of television drama. It shows who can get away with what and how. It teaches that the risks of victimization are high and unequal.

The rate of violence per dramatic program or cartoon play has been remarkably stable all through years of agitation, investigations and debates. Our research, now in its eighth year, shows that violence is central to the symbolic world of television drama. It shows who can get away with what and how. It teaches that the risks of victimization are high and unequal. TV's kill ratio (the number of victims divided by the number of violents in each group) defines the pecking order (but not crime statistics) or society. On top of the heap are mature white males; on the bottom lie the bodies of children, the old, the poor, the nonwhite and young or single women. Our research also shows that both children and adults who spend much of their lives in the "world" of television learn some assumptions of that world and project them onto social reality.

The chief social function of symbolic violence is in what it teaches about types of people and power. As we reported to the surgeon general in *Television and Social Behavior,* "Symbolic hurt to symbolic people and causes can show real people how they might use—or avoid—force to stay alive and to advance their causes. The ritual of dramatic violence demonstrates the relative power of people, ideas and values in a clash of personalized forces.... The distribution of roles related to violence, with their different risks and fates, performs the symbolic functions of violence and conveys its basic message about people."

That message is one of social typing: different types of people possess different degrees of human violability. It is the message to which every *homo sapiens* must be subjected for a long time and in large doses before the notion of social violence—cool, calm, uniformed efficiency with which people are killed simply because they belong to a type called *enemy*—becomes conceivable, let alone practicable. Slight fluctuations in the massive release of that message into the common symbolic environment would make little difference so long as the inequity of the pattern remained, or even sharpened. (Some muting of violent characterizations that the networks offered Pastore and the public were accompanied by increases in the margin of victimization suffered by the already deprived groups in the world of TV drama.)

Symbolic violence can thus achieve some of the repressive aims of real violence and do it much more profitably and, of course, entertainingly. Fearful people want—demand—protection and will accept, if not actually welcome, oppression in the name of safety. Our research shows that heavy viewing of television cultivates a sense of risk and danger in real life. Fear invites aggression that provokes still more fear and repression. The pattern of violence on TV may thus bolster a structure of social controls even as it appears to threaten it.

We need a new approach to the social function not only of symbolic violence but also of television itself. Television is the universal curriculum of young and old, the common symbolic environment in which we all live. Its true predecessor is not any other medium but religion—the organic pattern of explanatory symbolism that once animated total communities' sense of reality and value, and whose relationship to the state is also governed by the First Amendment.

Which brings us to the question of controls. The problem cannot be avoided because television has never been without an imposed system of content controls. The question is what should be the proper purpose of controls and how could that purpose be best achieved?

The first requirement for transforming the power struggle into a more informed and responsible debate is the recognition of the repressive (rather than only incitive) social functions of symbolic violence, and of television itself as someting like a corporate religion relating to the state as only the church did in the past.

The second requirement is the recognition that broadcasters' responsibility for long-run social goals and consequences depends more on a structure of supports and rewards than on the mechanics of controls. The exclusive dependence of commercial broadcasters on advertising budgets limits their scope and thwarts their exercise of broader responsibility. The formula that governs broadcasting is not social need, popularity or even audience wants. It is "cost per thousand viewers"—what enough people will buy at the least cost to the sponsor. Assembly-line violence that fits the conventional pattern of power is a dramatic commodity of only moderate acceptability but even lower cost. That is why it is a profitable as well as socially functional ritual of the TV religion.

There is not much to be gained from debating the controls without also considering where the supports and rewards will come from if television is to serve social purposes broader than those that now sustain its prejudicial patterns of victimization. Ultimately, the job can only be done by TV's artists and professionals under arrangements that support rather than distort their own best judgments. Both Senate and House subcommittees announced public hearings for this fall. The challenging task of institutional remodeling needs the discussion of alternatives, and time for development. The new round of hearings on sex, violence and other vital functions could do no better than to begin that task.

Bibliography

There is widespread concern about violence on television and in the movies. An important source is the *Surgeon General's Report by the Scientific Advisory Committee on Television and Social Behavior* (U.S. Govt. Printing Office, 1972). That committee also issued *Television and Growing Up: the Impact* of *Televised Violence*. (U.S. Govt. Printing Office, 1972). Also see: *Mass Media and Violence: A Staff Report to the National Commission on the Causes and Prevention of Violence*, the section ''The Effects of Media Violence on Social Learning'' (U.S. Govt. Printing Office, 1969); T.F. Baldwin and C. Lewis, ''Violence in Television: The Industry Looks at Itself'' found in *Television and Social Behavior, Vol. 1, Content and Control* (U.S. Govt. Printing Office, 1972); the other volumes of the *Television and Social Behavior* series edited by E. A. Rubenstein, G. A. Comstock and J. P. Murray and other reports issued by the Govt. Printing Office; reports of the Annenberg School of Communication in Philadelphia, including *The Violence Profile No. 5* (1973), edited by the author of this article, G. Gerbner, and L. Gross. Other sources include: the *Report of the National Advisory Commission on Civil Disorders* (Kerner Report), 1968, Chap. 15, ''The News Media and Disorders'' and *Rights in Conflict*, the Walker Report to the National Commission on the Causes and Prevention of Violence, 1968, pages 287-327, ''The Police and the Press'' (Chicago Democratic Convention violence). Students at the Lemburg Center for the Study of Violence, Brandeis University, have made contributions. One of these was Terry Ann Knopf's ''Media Myths on Violence'' published in the 1972 edition of this book and in the Spring, 1970 *Columbia Journalism Review*. Also see Otto N. Larsen's collection *Violence and the Mass Media* (Harper & Row, 1968). For one historical viewpoint there is Simon M. Bessie's *Jazz Journalism: The Story of Tabloid Newspapers* (Dutton, 1938).

The Impact of Photographs

By Nancy Stevens

The photographs made by Boston Herald American staff photographer, Stanley Forman, of a firefighter's attempt to rescue a young woman and a two-year-old child, the subsequent collapse of the fire escape and the young woman's plunge to her death, have raised many troubling questions and aroused angry responses from newspaper readers. Forman's photographs, of what he had expected to be an ordinary rescue scene, were picked up by AP and UPI wire services. Within hours, they appeared on front pages of newspapers from the Herald American's competitor, the Boston Globe, to the morning editions in Tokyo. According to Boston Herald American managing editor, Sam Bornstein, his office has received about 250 tear sheets from foreign and domestic papers.

The actual pictures have been heralded as a photojournalist's once-in-a-lifetime achievement.

But for most people who viewed the photographs in their local newspaper, the experience evoked feelings more often associated with a nightmare.

Reader reaction was violent and outspoken against the publication of Forman's photos. Hal Buell, AP executive Newsphoto Editor, conducted a survey of national reader reaction and editorial response. Those readers who agreed that pictures should have been published cited considerations of public safety, need for reform, and the need to be realistic. One reader of the Costa Mesa (California) Daily Pilot, wrote in favor of editor Tom Keevil's decision to pick up the AP photos. ''Everyman lives and dies. Maybe we will all have better social awareness.''

Nora Ephron, in her media column in the November issue of *Esquire* magazine, responded to the taboo of publishing photographs depicting death. ''Death happens to be one of life's main events,'' declared Ephron. ''And it is

Nancy Stevens is a New York based freelancer who writes for the *French Photo,* the *Village Voice* and *Camera 35*. Her article is used with the permission of *News Photographer,* the official publication of the National Press Photographers Association Inc. It appeared in the October, 1975 issue. Photographs by Stanley Forman are used with permission of the *Boston Herald American.*

Exclusive Photos

Rescue at Hand and Then a Fall

Dramatic Rescue Attempt Begins.

Victims Wait As Firefighter Reaches for Ladder.

Exclusive Photo Sequence by Stanley Forman
Copyright 1975 by The Boston Herald American

Photographer's Story of Pictures

"I made all kinds of pictures because I thought it would be a good rescue shot over the ladder . . . never dreamed it would be anything else."

Photographer Stanley Forman was talking about taking today's dramatic pictures of a fire escape collapse.

"I kept having to move around because of the light situation. The sky was bright and they were in deep shadow. I wouldn't have had any detail."

"I was making pictures with a motor drive and he, the fire-fighter, was reaching up and, I don't know, everything started falling.

"I followed the girl down taking pictures . . . I made three or four frames.

FORMAN

"I realized what was going on and I completely turned around, because I didn't want to see her hit.

"I just knew in my mind, it wasn't going to add to anything. She fell behind a picket fence. I wouldn't have seen it anyway."

Forman, a native of Revere, will complete his ninth year on the staff of The Hearst Newspapers in Boston in November.

Fire Escape Collapses Under Victims

Woman and Child Plunge as Firefighter Dangles.

They Plummet to Ground.

453

The Hartford Times

Hartford, Connecticut

...elopment bill gets a new life

Egypt will le...
U.N. force s...
3 more mor...

Ford read...
new oil p...

Ford feels
he'd beat
Kennedy

San Francisco Ch...

Seconds From Death

Rescue Near—
Fire Escape
Collapses

THE CHRONICLE-TELEG...

Where is the $320,000

Marsico is freed on $50,000 bond in theft of auto li...

Seconds to safety ...

'Outright lies,' says
Dickerson of charges

Regrets of era
Stafford predicts new space age

THE EVENING SUN 5 STAR

BALTIMORE, WEDNESDAY, JULY 23, 1975

Guard Killed In Shootout
With Store Robbers He...

...raelis
...nting
...rrorists

Both Sides
Stalemated
On Energy

Astronaut Regrets
End Of This Era

With Rescue An Arm's Length Away,
Woman Falls Five Stories To Death

...BEE

Egypt OKs 90-Day UN Extension

Sheer Terror...

Life, Then Death

LOS ANGELES EVENING AND SUNDAY
HERALD with EXAMINER 8 STAR

Dockmen

NO
FOR...

East Coast
Men Won't
Load Wheat

BEE-R...
STUN...

Boston Herald America...

...use Keeps Oil Price Co...

Safety So Near...Then A Death Fall

Metro
Edition   The Birmingham News

Serving A Progressive South

Agents stage giant lotter...

17 loc...
Metro

The weather

Top of THE NEWS

Able hand
back in fight
—Page 11

City pensions,
other benefits
—Page 2

Local and state

irresponsible—and more than that, inaccurate—for newspapers to fail to show it . . ."

Voices raised against publication were strident in their condemnation of their local editors' judgement. Newspapers were criticized for "cheap journalism," voyeurism, irresponsibility, poor taste, and invasion of privacy. One irate reader of the *Seattle Times* cancelled his subscription. Another wrote, "You're giving our kids a nightmare."

For many editors the most important question was one of censorship. Marshall L. Stone, the managing editor of the *Bangor (Maine) News,* wrote "If it were a mistake to run them, it would likewise have been a mistake not to run them. Those are the horns of the editor's dilemma."

Lenora Williamson, in a column in *Editor and Publisher* (August 30) quoted Buel as he explained an editorial decision to publish the photographs. "You're cursed if you do, and cursed for manipulating the news if you don't."

However, there is another side to the impact of the photographs on the public. In the Boston area, there were signs of immediate reforms instigated by the fire photos. Two weeks after the fire, the *Boston Herald American* ran an article about the city's new safety drive. Mayor Kevin H. White announced the addition of 100 building, fire and housing inspectors. Previously, seven city employees had routinely inspected emergency escape exits. Furthermore, Housing and Building Commissioner Francis W. Gens announced a new regulation requiring periodic private certification for all apartment and mercantile buildings, lodging houses and places of public assembly.

A fire in Boston is not news in California, but the photographs will serve a purpose. Forman has received requests from fire departments across the country for copies of his photos for study purposes to improve fire fighting techniques. Copies have also been requested to call attention to the ongoing campaign to improve safety conditions.

"The only newsworthy thing about the pictures," concluded Nora Ephron in *Esquire,* "is that they were taken. They deserve to be printed because they are great pictures, breathtaking pictures of something that happened. That they disturb readers is exactly as it should be: that's why photojournalism is often more powerful than written journalism."

That Word

By John McMillan

John McMillan is executive editor of the Huntingon (W. Va.) *Advertiser & Herald Dispatch* and a member of the editorial board of *The Bulletin of the American Society of Newspaper Editors* (ASNE), where this article appeared in its May/ June, 1975 edition. It is used with permission of *The Bulletin.*

Dan Mahoney is president of Dayton Newspapers, Inc., which owns the *Dayton Journal Health* and is, in turn, a subsidiary of Cox Newspapers, Inc.

Charlie Alexander was until [recently] the editor and publisher of the *Journal Herald*.

The issue was the use twice of the word "fucking" in a page one text.

Publication of the text was, says Alexander, an attempt to describe "how what seems like a stupid killing can happen."

Publication of the text without editing, says Mahoney, made the *Journal Herald* seem like *Screw* magazine.

The text—one federal agent's description of how he shot and killed another agent—was published above the flag of the *Journal Herald* on March 19. Page one of the *Journal Herald* on March 25 reported below the fold: "Alexander Resigns as Editor of The JH."

Alexander's statement said, "The ownership of the Dayton Newspapers, Inc., has termed indefensible my failure to delete two obscenities from a page one story. . . . Since I am the person responsible and since the ownership could hardly be expected to have continuing confidence in an editor who manages one of their properties in a manner they consider indefensible, I thought it only proper to offer my resignation. Needless to say, it was accepted."

Whatever one thinks of Alexander's printing the unexpurgated text of the agent's statement—which also included "son of a bitch" and "God damn it"— Alexander clearly is not a vulgar sensationalist.

His ex-boss, Mahoney, says Alexander is "a very able guy, I am very fond of Charlie. I admire his integrity."

Alexander's colleagues in ASNE—who with three exceptions offered no immediate expression of sympathy or understanding—had thought enough of him to nominate him for the board this year. He had twice served as chairman of the ASNE Education for Journalism Committee and presently is News Research Committee chairman.

To understand the Alexander affair—if understanding is possible—requires background on both the Dayton newspapers and the killing of the federal agent.

Dayton Newspapers, Inc., owns not only the *Journal Herald* but also the *Daily News*. But Dayton is not a typical two-newspaper monopoly.

The late Gov. James M. Cox, the Democratic foe of Warren Harding in 1920, hailed from Dayton. The *Daily News* was his newspaper. Col. Frank Knox, the Republican who served as Franklin Roosevelt's Navy secretary in World War II, owned the *Journal* and the *Herald*.

When Cox rescued the faltering *Journal* and *Herald* in late 1948, after Knox's death, he combined the two. But he promised Dayton he would preserve the city's Republican voice in the *Journal Herald*.

The Dayton newspapers are published from the same building. But because of the Cox promise, their news and editorial departments are totally independent— even to the extent of having two newsrooms, two libraries, two photo departments and two sets of video display terminals. All hands agree the two Dayton newspapers compete vigorously.

Alexander made all news and editorial decisions for the *Journal Herald,* Thanks to the Cox commitment he had far more independence than most other U.S. editors.

Even when the theoretically Republican *Journal Herald* called for President Nixon's impeachment after the Saturday Night Massacre and endorsed the Democratic candidiate for governor of Ohio, Alexander was left alone by the management of Dayton Newspapers, Inc.

This is not to say, of course, that Alexander and Mahoney never talked. Financial and production matters obviously required communication. And the news was a topic, too.

The *Journal Herald* twice published the obscenities in 1971, and Mahoney then noted his distaste for the word.

And Alexander asked Mahoney whether the *Journal Herald*'s news and editorial content had any connection with the newspaper's circulation loss. The Sept. 30, 1972 ABC audit showed sales of 113,870. Circulation now is said by Dayton Newspapers to be about 102,000.

Alexander says he was assured his circulation problems lay elsewhere. "No one ever said anything to me that led to any feeling of critical disenchantment," he adds.

Until, of course, the text.

Casper C. Gibson and Jerry D. Johnston were agents in Dayton for the Alcohol, Tobacco and Firearms Division of the U.S. Treasury. In their office on Sept. 23, 1974, they argued. They started screaming. Johnston pulled a gun. Gibson grabbed it, the gun went off and Johnston died. A grand jury failed to indict.

The government, upset by a killing involving two of its own law-enforcement officers in a federal office, attempted to withhold details of the shooting.

An investigative reporter for the *Journal Herald* talked to grand jurors and dug out many of the facts.

Apparently stung by its competitor's reporting, the *Daily News* applied to the Treasury under the Freedom of Information Act for the documents in the Johnston killing. They eventually were forthcoming.

Even now it is not entirely clear how the *Journal Herald* obtained Gibson's statement before the *Daily News*.

To non-Dayton readers, the Gibson statement may not seem especially remarkable. UPI and AP staffers in Columbus, for example, could not remember three weeks after the event whether they had used much or any of it after it was published in Dayton.

But it was a big story in Dayton. Arnold Rosenfeld, the managing editor of the *Daily News,* remains irritated that the *Journal Herald* got it first.

In fact, the Gibson statement—minus the obscenity and together with other material on the case that the *Journal Herald* did not have—received major attention in the *Daily News,* too.

Can the shooting be described effectively without the obscenities?

Rosenfeld says, "Each editor must make his own judgment."

He ordered the obscenities deleted. His reasons:

● The Daily News has a long-term policy against using such words;

● He thought use of the words would become an issue, obscuring the shooting itself;

● His own sense and feeling for Dayton told him the words would not be acceptable to most readers.

Rosenfeld and Mahoney agree that the management of Dayton Newspapers, Inc., did not discuss with the *Daily News* newsroom how the case should be reported.

Alexander did not easily allow the obscenities to be printed in the *Journal Herald*.

He had required for several years that any copy including profanity or obscenity going beyond the work "hell" appear in print only after being initialed by himself or Ralph Langer, the managing editor. The *Journal Herald* did not print the obscenities of the Nixon tapes. Alexander estimates that he ordered unacceptable words removed from stories five to 10 times a year.

"The public does not want us to be salacious," he says. "You can so outrage the readership that the decision (to print obscenities) overshadows the effect of what's being reported."

In the case of the Gibson text, the decision to print was Alexander's. He pondered it during an afternoon. When he saw Langer, Alexander ruled that the text be printed without editing. He asked for no one else's opinion.

Why leave in the obscenities?

Alexander attempted to explain, in a column that appeared on the editorial page the same day his resignation was announced on page one.

"What the account of Gibson tells us with a vividness that I would hope none of us or our children would forget is that killing in most cases is the final, but not the crucial act. The crux comes when the common love and respect we ought to have for each other dissolves into hate, and we turn the corner from passionate verbal combat or quarreling to mortal combat. . . .

"There comes the moment of truth when we must decide whether we are men and women or animals of the jungle. Gibson's account is the story of two men who made the turn. . . .

"To me, the telling of that message from an incident of real life, including in one instance the raw vulgarity used by a man blind with rage, is a lesson that every man, woman and child should perceive in all its dimensions. It is shocking—it surely should be. . . .

"To view the story as a mere verbal account is to miss its deeper significance. In an era when homicide is on an alarming rise . . .we wonder why the admonition that 'thou shalt not kill' is having so little impact? Is it because of vulgar language? Or might it be because we are so preoccupied with the superficialities of life—the trappings—that we ponder only casually, if at all, the real meaning of the drama that goes on within those trappings."

After he resigned, a minister told Alexander that he saw no sense in objections to obscene words when almost no one seemed to object to obscene acts.

But objections to the words there were.

Forty-two letters to the editor were received in protest. The circulation department estimated that 100 to 150 subscribers cancelled.

Langer said the telephone protests to him fell into one or more of three categories:

- "I don't want to read that word."
- "You're contributing to the downfall of society."
- Children might read the word.

Alexander, at this writing, is unemployed at age 46. He admits to welcoming the time to read and think. "But it's the uncertainty (about the future) that keeps you from enjoying (the leisure)."

He is heartened by a letter of commendation from his Presbyterian Church Session, by a sympathetic Carl Rowan column and by letters to the editor in his support that the *Journal Herald* has printed since he resigned.

"Before Mr. Alexander's resignation," said one, "the *Journal Herald* was a better paper. . . . Its pages contained vital and important news unflinchingly reported. . . . How shocking is the newly revealed willingness of Dayton Newspaper management to mess in the news."

"It is incomprehensible to me," said another, "that any reader could have read the Gibson article without understanding the message of intemperate language leading to intemperate behavior."

But some applauded. "On the March 24 newscast on Channel 7 I was greatly relieved to learn that the person responsible for the gutter language printed in your paper has resigned," a reader wrote.

While disturbed about loss of his job and gratified by support from his friends and some strangers in Dayton, Alexander is also "puzzled."

How did he lose his job over the publication of two words? As another Dayton newsman said, "You didn't get divorced because you come home with lipstick on your shirt."

"We were very upset, and he wouldn't back down," says Mahoney.

Alexander did not learn of Mahoney's displeasure until 36 hours after publication. The message came from Charles E. Grover, executive vice president of Dayton Newspapers.

Grover said in a conference with Alexander that use of the words was "indefensible."

If Alexander had indicated then that he might have been wrong, Mahoney says, he still would be editor of the *Journal Herald*. "We would not have fired Mr. Alexander on this issue." Mahoney adds.

But Alexander—who does not think he was wrong—says he wasn't given the opportunity for discussion either of the issues or the reasons for his judgment.

Alexander remains convinced the unexpurgated Gibson statement was important for his newspaper to publish.

"It's a matter of truth," says Alexander.

"We're the people who have to sell this newspaper," says Mahoney.

The story as published.

EDITOR'S NOTE: It was Monday, "just like any other Monday," said Casper Carroll Gibson in his statement to the assistant U.S. attorney. Except that this particular Monday (Sept. 23, 1974) became a living horror to Gibson, who during a quarrel, shot and killed his friend and colleague, Jerry D. Johnston. Both were agents of the Alcohol, Tobacco and Firearms division of the Treasury Dept. The argument began simply enough, over the issue of transfers. Both men wanted out of Dayton. Johnston had a special reason—his mother was dying of cancer in Texas. But when Gibson told Johnston he, too, wanted a transfer, Johnston became enraged, afraid that if Gibson were transferred, it would ruin his chances for one. Johnston was so angry, Gibson says, that he swore, ''sort of mean, or nasty like.'' Gibson made this reply, a reply that led to a horrible nightmare:

I sort of got mad, too, and I said, ''Well, I can't worry about you, I've got to do what I think is best for me.'' I said, ''I want out of here, too.'' And he yelled at me something about: you know, ''rotten son of a bitch,'' or something, and we exchanged a couple of words like that. And then, like I say, I was mad, and then I said something that I wish before God I could bring back, if I could bring the words back, if the words could come back to my lips before I said it. I was sorry after they were out.

But I said, ''Jerry, if the Western Region (of the agency) knew about the bonds, and the Spencer case, you wouldn't be going anywhere.'' And he said ''You're just about the kind of a son of a bitch to tell them.'' And I said, ''Yes, I am,'' or, ''Yes, by God, I am,'' or something to that effect.

And then we just sort of fell quiet for a few minutes—not a few minutes. I mean this whole thing was seconds, microseconds, And we fell quiet for just seconds, and I got up and I was going to leave the room, because I knew things were hot, and a lot of water passed over the dam. And I got up and I was going to leave, I was going to get a drink of water, or go down that hallway, I don't know, I was just going to get out of the room for a few minutes, because I knew we needed it, both of us. . . .

I got up to leave, and I got about almost to the door . . .and he yelled for me—called me back, something, ''Gibson, come back here a minute,'' or something to that effect. So I turned around and walked back. . . .

And he started screaming at me. I mean, his teeth were—his lips were drawn back across his teeth, and he was screaming at me. And he screamed something to the effect, ''Gibson, God damn it, you are fucking with my family. You are fucking with my future. I am not going to let you do it. I'll kill you first.'' And when he was saying this the gun was coming up, and right in my face, and the whole hand, the gun and all, was doing like this (illustrating), the gun was moving and everything. And when he said that I just grabbed the damn gun and pushed it, the gun and his hand, and I just grabbed with both hands and pushed it, and there was a terrible roar, the damn gun went off. . . .

Bibliography

Certainly there is a trend in the use of most explicit language by songwriters, movie and television script writers, book and magazine article authors and even newspaper reporters. In many print publications the days of ''—— of a ——'' or ''———— you'' are gone. Others strongly disagree and say that films and publications meant for family viewing or reading should be edited so as to avoid embarrassment. A few years ago Lee H. Smith, a former *Newsweek* editor, asked in the *Columbia Journalism Review* ''Is Anything Unprintable?'' (Spring 1968). There have been various articles about the new ethnic humor as articulated by the casts of All in the Family, the Jeffersons, Sanford and Son and other popular television shows. There follows in this book an article about the lyrics of songs. This is all part of a debate which may never be resolved; taste is an individual judgment and each case must be taken on its merits, to see if the particular words were in context or used for shock value or showed prejudice against a particular person or group. Articles in (*More*), *Columbia Journalism Review, Quill,* local journalism reviews, the *Bulletin of the ASNE* and other journals have dealt with these questions of language. For a specific reference to the use of sex to sell records, see David DeVoss, ''Aural Sex: The Rise of Porn Rock,'' *Human Behavior* (July 1976), pp. 64-68.

The Censorship of Song Lyrics

By Nicholas Johnson

The Federal Communications Commission issued the following public notice March 5, 1971 on the subject of lyrics. The dissent of Nicholas Johnson relates not only to the issue presented then but to the question continually faced by the recording and broadcast industries: How to allow the free expression of "creativity."

A number of complaints received by the Commission concerning the lyrics of records played on broadcasting stations relate to the subject of current and pressing concern: the use of language tending to promote or glorify the use of illegal drugs as marijuana, LSD, "speed", etc. This Notice points up the licensee's long-established responsibilities in this area.

Whether a particular record depicts the dangers of drug abuse, or, to the contrary, promotes such illegal drug usage is a question for the judgment of the licensee. The thrust of this Notice is simply that the licensee must make that judgment and cannot properly follow a policy of playing such records without someone in a responsible position (i.e., a management level executive at the station) knowing the content of the lyrics. Such a pattern of operation is clearly a violation of the basic principle of the licensee's responsibility for, and duty to exercise adequate control over, the broadcast material presented over his station. It raises serious questions as to whether continued operation of the station is in the public interest, just as in the case of a failure to exercise adequate control over foreign-language programs.

In short, we expect broadcast licensees to ascertain, before broadcast, the words or lyrics of recorded musical or spoken selections played on their stations. Just as in the case of the foreign-language broadcasts, this may also entail reasonable efforts to ascertain the meaning of words or phrases used in the lyrics. While this duty may be delegated by licensees to responsible employees, the licensee remains fully responsible for its fulfillment.

Thus, here as in so many other areas, it is a question of responsible, good faith action by the public trustee to whom the frequency has been licensed. No more, but certainly no less, is called for.

Dissenting Opinion of Commissioner Nicholas Johnson

This public notice is an unsuccessfully-disguised effort by the Federal Communications Commission to censor song lyrics that the majority disapproves of; it is an attempt by a group of establishmentarians to determine what youth can say and hear; it is an unconstitutional action by a Federal agency aimed clearly at controlling the content of speech.

Nicholas Johnson, former FCC commissioner and author of the popular *How to Talk Back to Your Television Set,* is editor of *access,* a publication devoted to criticism of the broadcasting industry. See his article earlier in this book.

Under the guise of assuring the licensees know what lyrics are being aired on their stations, the FCC today gives a loud and clear message: get those "drug lyrics" off the air (and no telling what other subject matter the Commission majority may find offensive), or you may have trouble at license renewal time. The majority today approves a public notice which (1) singles out as "a subject of current and pressing concern: the use of language tending to promote or glorify the illegal use of drugs such as marijuana, LSD, 'speed,' etc.;" (2) emphasizes the importance of "someone in a responsible position...knowing the content of the lyrics;" and (3) raises the specter of loss of license unless the "pattern of operation" is such that a "responsible" employee knows the content of song lyrics played on broadcasting stations.

The contrived nature of this offensive against modern music is demonstrated by the fact that, the majority itself concedes, "the licensee's responsibility for, and duty to exercise adequate control over, the material presented over his station," is "a basic principle" of FCC regulation; it is so basic that today's action is completely unnecessary. Licensees (that is, owners of stations) simply *can't* listen to *everything* broadcast over their stations; they have to delegate responsibility for knowledge of content to their employees; and we can assume under existing regulations that those employees *do* know what is being played. We can also assume that licensees are well aware of the Commission's power to prohibit material that falls within statutory prohibitions and beyond constitutional protection. Why, then, this focus on "language strongly suggestive of, or tending to glorify, the illegal use of drugs . . ."—whatever that means—unless the intention is in fact to censor by threat what cannot be constitutionally prohibited?

Moreover, there is a serious question as to whether the majority is in fact really as concerned about drug abuse as it is in striking out blindly at a form of music which is symbolic of a culture which the majority apparently fears—in part because it totally fails to comprehend it. If the majority were in fact concerned about drug abuse, they surely would not choose to ignore song lyrics "strongly suggestive of, and tending to glorify" the use of alcohol, which is the number one drug abuse problem in this country.

It is common knowledge that drunken drivers kill *each year* nearly as many Americans as have been killed during the entire history of the war in Southeast Asia. There are more alcoholics in San Francisco alone than there are narcotics addicts in the entire country. Kenneth Eaton, Deputy Director of the Division of Alcohol Abuse and Alcoholism at the National Institute of Mental Health, recently declared: "In relative terms, the physical consequences of heavy drinking are far larger and more serious than those of heroin use"; he added that the likelihood of death in withdrawal from chronic alcoholism is much greater than in withdrawal from heroin addiction. Dr. Robert L. Dupont, Director of the Washington, D.C. Narcotics Treatment Agency, agrees "absolutely" with Eaton:

It's non-controversial.

~~Heroin as a drug is really quite benign compared to alcohol, which is a poison.~~

We have two really serious drug problems in Washington, heroin and alcohol.

I do not think it's the business of the FCC to be discouraging or banning *any* song lyrics. But if the commission majority is *really* interested in doing something about the drug problems in this country, and is not just striking out at the youth culture, why does it ignore songs like "Day Drinking"...or "California Grapevine"...or countless other similar lyrics?

And why has the Commission chosen to focus on record lyrics and yet ignore commercials which use language "tending to glorify the use of drugs generally"? In asking Congress for a study of the effects on the nation's youth of nearly $300 million worth of annual drug advertising on television, Senator Frank Moss of Utah has said:

> The drug culture finds its fullest flowering in the portrait of American society which can be pieced together out of hundreds of thousands of advertisements and commercials. It is advertising which mounts so graphically the message that pills turn rain to sunshine, gloom to joy, depression to euphoria, solve problems, dispel doubt.
>
> Not just pills; cigarette and cigar ads; solf drink, coffee, tea and beer ads—all portray the key to happiness as things to swallow, inhale, chew, drink and eat.

Commissioners Rex Lee and Thomas Houser have expressed similar concerns in this very proceeding. How can anyone possibly justify the FCC's failure to examine the impact of commercials such as the following on television:

> (Music) ANNOUNCER: Leave your feeling of tension behind and step into a quiet world. You'll feel calmer, more relaxed with Quiet World. The new modern calmative. Each tablet contains a special calming ingredient plus a tension reliever to let you feel relaxed. More peaceful. So leave your feeling of tension behind with Quiet World. The new modern calmative.

This commercial was broadcast over WCBS-TV in New York at 3:25 p.m. to an audience made up primarily of mothers and children. Why do the majority choose to ignore these gray flannel pushers?

The answer to these questions is simple: the exclusive concern with song lyrics is in reality an effort to harass the youth culture, a crude attempt to suppress the anti-establishment music of the counter-culture and the "movement."

It is a thinly veiled political move. This Administration has, for reasons best known to the President, chosen to divert the American people's attention to "the drug menace," and away from problems like: the growing Southeast Asian war, racial prejudice, inflation, unemployment, hunger poverty, education, growing urban blight, and so forth. When the broadcasters support this effort they are taking a political stance. Especially is this so when they, simultaneously, keep *off* the air contrary political views. When we encourage this trend, we are taking equally political action.

The majority's interest in the whole song lyrics issue was substantially increased by the Defense Department's Drug Briefing, which was originally prepared for a briefing of radio and record executives under the President's auspices at the White House. *It is not surprising that the Nixon Administration and the Defense Department, two primary targets of the youth culture, should try to strike back.* But it is revealing and somewhat frightening that many of the song lyrics singled out as objectionably pro-drug-use by the White House and Defense Department turn out, in fact, to have nothing whatsoever to do with drugs. *They relate instead to social commentary.* Thus, the Defense Department spokesmen singled out a song by the Doors which says: ''War is out—peace is the new thing.'' The White House finds alarming another which says:

> Itemize the things you covet
> As you squander through your life
> Bigger cars, bigger houses,
> Term insurance for your wife. . . .

Is anything that attacks the values of corporate America or the military-industrial-complex now to be interpreted by the FCC and broadcasters as an incitement to drugs?

Beyond the hypocrisy of this blind attack on the youth culture, this action is legally objectionable because it ignores the Supreme Court's ruling that the First Amendment protects speech which has any socially redeeming importance. People differ as to how they feel about the reasonableness of the drug life as a way out of the often absurd qualities of life in a corporate state. I happen to believe in getting high on life—the perpetual high without drugs. But no one can argue that the use of drugs—by rich and poor, middle-aged and young—is not a controversial issue of public importance today. How can the FCC possibly outlaw the subject as suitable for artistic comment? How can it possibly repeal the applicability of the fairness doctrine to this subject?

The courts have frequently invalidated licensing schemes which give the licensing agency such unbridled discretion, or which are so broad, that a licensee is deterred from engaging in activity protected by the First Amendment. Thus, in *Weiman v. Updegraff*, 344 U.S. 183, 195 (1952), a case involving loyalty oaths demanded of prospective teachers, the Supreme Court condemned the provision, saying: ''it has an unmistakable tendency to chill that free play of spirit which all teachers ought especially to cultivate and practice; it makes for caution and timidity in their associations by potential teachers.''

As Mr. Justice Black has written:

> [A] statute broad enough to support infringement of speech . . .necessarily leaves all persons to guess just what the law really means to cover, and fear of a wrong guess inevitably leads people to forego the very rights the Constitution sought to protect above all others.

Barenblatt v. United States, 360 U.S. 109, 137 (1959) (dissenting opinion). This danger, inherent in the overbroad and necessarily vague action which the Commission takes today, is compounded when it involves the natural sensitivity of those whose very existence depends on the licensing power of the censoring agency.

Simply by announcing its concern with the content of song lyrics as they relate to drugs, the Commission is effectively censoring protected speech. The breadth of the regulation is aggravated by the vagueness of the standard used—''tending to glorify.'' *What does that mean?* It could include ''Up, Up and Away'' sung by the Mormon Tabernacle Choir. Some so-called ''drug lyrics'' are clearly *dis*couraging the use of drugs. Others, while less clear, can most reasonably be read to opposing drug usage. Many informed people argue that even the programs and public service spots designed to *discourage* drug usage are often as likely to have the opposite effect. How is the poor licensee to know which lyrics are "tending to glorify"? Will he risk his license over such an interpretation?

In *Burstyn v. Wilson*, 343 U.S. 495 (1952), a statute which authorized denial of a license if the licensor concluded that the film reviewed was "sacrilegious" was held by the Supreme Court to be an unconstitutionally overbroad delegation of discretion. The Commission's action today is bound to be interpreted as a threat that the playing of certain song lyrics could threaten license renewals.

Justice Brennan summarized the Supreme Court's concern with actions which have a "chilling effect" on the exercising of rights protected by the First Amendment:

To give these freedoms the necessary "breathing space to survive," . . .[we] have molded both substantive rights and procedural remedies in the face of varied conflicting interest to conform to *our overriding duty to insulate all individuals from the "chilling effect" upon exercise of First Amendment freedoms* generated by vagueness, overbreadth and unbridled discretion to limit their exercise."

Walker v. City of Birmingham, 388 U.S. 307, 344-45 (1967) (dissenting opinion) (emphasis added). This is a classic case of Federal Agency action which is bound to have a "chilling effect" on the exercise of First Amendment rights.

The Commission's action today will have a chilling effect on the free spirit of our songwriters, because of the caution and timidity which today's action will produce among licensees. It will have a similar effect on the record industry, because of the relationship between the radio play of a record and its economic success. And where, after all, do we get authority to regulate *that* industry by putting pressure on the move to require the printing of lyrics on dust jackets?

We are more dependent upon the creative people in our society than we have ever fully comprehended. "Legalize Freedom" says the latest bumper sticker. Full human flowering requires the opportunity to know, and express creativity, one's most honest-as-possible self. Governments are instituted among men—according to our Declaration of Independence—to promote "life, liberty, and the pursuit of happiness." We seem to have drifted quite a way from that goal. Not only do we need creative freedom to promote individual growth, we also need creative artists to divert social disaster. *The artists are our country's outriders. They are out ahead of our caravan, finding the mountain passes and the rivers. They pick up the new vibrations a decade or more before the rest of us, and try to tell us what's about to happen to us as a people—in the form of painting, theater, novels, and in music. In order to function at all, they have to function free.* When we start the process of Kafkaesque institutional interference with that freedom—whether by Big Business or Big Government—we are encouraging, rather than preventing, the decline and fall of the American Empire: its view of the future, and the fulfillment of its people.

I hope the recording and broadcasting industries will have the courage and commitment to respond to this brazen attack upon them with all the enthusiasm it calls for. Given the power of this Commission, I am afraid they may not.

For all these reasons, I dissent.

Bibliography

The 1968-69 edition of the *Survey of Broadcast Journalism* published by Columbia University dealt with the advertising which Johnson objects to in this article. His articles ''Public Channels and Private Censors'' *(Nation,* March 12, 1970) and ''The Wasteland Revisited'' *Playboy,* (Dec. 1970) and his book *How To Talk Back to Your Television Set* (1970) relate to this FCC dissent. Of course for a detailed study the student should refer to the FCC proceedings and to court rulings such as those mentioned here. As for the lyrics, only an actual check of books sold by various music companies would allow a judgment as to whether some popular songs contain ''excessive language'' as defined by the individual critic.

Index

Credits

Chapter 1

5, Cover reprinted with permission from *access*, 1028 Connecticut Avenue, N.W. Washington, D.C. 20036. *36*, Ad reprinted courtesy of WMT. *42*, Ad used with permission of Bonneville International Corporation.

Chapter 2

54, Cover photograph by Humphrey Sutton. Copyright © 1976 by Harper's Magazine. All rights reserved. Reprinted from the January 1977 issue by special permission. *76-77*, Cover of TV Guide by George Giusti. Reprinted with permission from TV Guide Magazine (R) Copyright © 1976 by Triangle Publications, Inc., Radnor, Pennsylvania. Cover of Quill from The Quill, published by the Society of Professional Journalists, Sigma Delta Chi. November 1975 issue. Cover by Murray Olderman. New Yorker cover drawing by Saxon; © 1972 The New Yorker Magazine, Inc. Rolling Stone cover used with permission of Rolling Stone. Time cover reprinted by permission from TIME, The Weekly News Magazine; copyright © Time, Inc., 1974. San Francisco Bay Guardian cover reprinted with the permission of the San Francisco Bay Guardian. More cover reprinted with permission of More. Newsweek cover courtesy of Newsweek.

Chapter 3

92, Rolling Stone cover used with permission of Rolling Stone. *95*, Front page reprinted with permission of the Washington Post. Copyright 1973. *99*, Cartoon copyright the Los Angeles Times. Reprinted with permission. *103*, Cover reprinted with permission of the Saturday Review; November 1975 issue. *107*, Cover by Arky and Barett. Used with permission. *113*, Cover courtesy of Newsweek. *137*, Back page of the CJR reprinted with permission of the Columbia Journalism Review.

Chapter 4

138, Cartoon copyright 1975, Los Angeles Times. Reprinted by permission. *143*, Front page reprinted by permission of the Village Voice. Copyright © the Village Voice, Inc., 1976. *145*, Cartoon copyright Los Angeles Times. Reprinted with permission.

Chapter 5

158, Photograph courtesy of CBS News. *162*, Photographs courtesy of UPI. *163*, Top photo by Charles M. Rafshoon. Bottom photos courtesy of UPI.

Chapter 6

182, Cover—Steve Schapiro for PEOPLE WEEKLY Magazine; © 1976, Time Inc., All rights reserved. *190*, Top cover courtesy of Newsweek. Bottom cover reprinted by permission from TIME, The Weekly News Magazine; copyright © Time, Inc., 1974. *198*, Cartoon copyright Los Angeles Times. Reprinted with permission. *201*, Front page reprinted by permission of The NATIONAL ENQUIRER. *206*, Top front page courtesy of the Telegraph Herald. Bottom front page copyright 1977, Los

Angeles Times. Reprinted by Permission. *207*, Top front page reprinted courtesy of the Chicago Tribune. Bottom front page © 1977 by The New York Times Company. Reprinted by permission. *222*, Cartoon copyright Los Angeles Times. Reprinted with permission. *228-236*, Book ads reprinted from the February 17, 1975 issue of *Publishers Weekly*, published by R.R. Bowker Company, a Xerox company. Copyright © 1975 by Xerox Corporation. *267*, Ad © Copyright CBS, Inc., 1976. All rights reserved.

Chapter 7

268, Cover reprinted with permission of Ebony. *273*, Cover of Jet reprinted with permission of Jet. Cover of Black Stars reprinted with permission of Black Stars. Cover of Now reprinted with permission of Now. *282*, Ads by permission of SIN TV Network. *289*, Cover used with permission of El Popo.

Chapter 8

306, Ad used with permission of United Airlines.

Chapter 9

338, Cover courtesy of Atlas World Press Review, 230 Park Avenue, New York, N.Y. 10017. *352*, Illustrations courtesy of Northridge Journal. *354*, Cartoon copyright Los Angeles Times. Reprinted with permission.

Chapter 10

356, Cover from The Quill, published by the Society of Professional Journalists, Sigma Delta Chi. September 1976 issue. Cover by Kenneth Stark. *358*, Cartoon copyright Los Angeles Times. Reprinted with permission. *362*, Cartoon copyright Los Angeles Times. Reprinted with permission. *369*, Cartoon copyright Los Angeles Times. Reprinted with permission. *372*, Cartoon copyright Los Angeles Times. Reprinted with permission. *374*, Photographs courtesy of UPI. *400*, Photo used with permission Wide World Photos Inc.

Chapter 11

402, Photo reprinted with permission of ABC, *406*, Top photo and middle left photo courtesy of NBC. Middle right photo courtesy of UPI. Bottom left photo courtesy of ABC. Bottom right photo courtesy of ABC and NBC. *407*, Photos courtesy of CBS. *419*, Photo used with permission of Broadcasting. *427*, Photo courtesy of UPI. *432*, Photo used with permission of KNBC.

Chapter 12

434, Cartoon copyright, 1975, G.B. Trudeau/Distributed by Universal Press Syndicate. *437*, Cover reprinted by permission from TIME, The Weekly News Magazine, copyright © Time, Inc., 1976. *444*, Cover copyright © 1975 by *Human Behavior* Magazine. Reprinted by permission. *449*, Cartoon copyright Los Angeles Times. Reprinted with permission. *453-454*, Photographs by Stanley Forman and reprinted with permission of the Boston Herald American, copyright 1975. All rights reserved.